Newspaper Design For The Times

Louis Silverstein

*Former Assistant Managing Editor of The New York Times
and Corporate Art Director of The New York Times Company*

VNR

VAN NOSTRAND REINHOLD
New York

Copyright © 1990 by Van Nostrand Reinhold

Library of Congress Catalog Card Number 89-16433
ISBN 0-442-28321-0

Printed in the United States of America

Van Nostrand Reinhold
115 Fifth Avenue
New York, New York 10003

Van Nostrand Reinhold International Company Limited
11 New Fetter Lane
London EC4P 4EE, England

Van Nostrand Reinhold
480 La Trobe Street
Melbourne, Victoria 3000, Australia

Nelson Canada
1120 Birchmount Road
Scarborough, Ontario M1K 5G4, Canada

16 15 14 13 12 11 10 9 8 7 6 5 4 3 2 1

Library of Congress Cataloging-in-Publication Data

Silverstein, Louis.
   Newspaper design for the times/Louis Silverstein.
     p. cm.
   Includes index.
   ISBN 0-442-28321-0
   1. Newspaper layout and typography. I. Title.
Z253.5.S53 1990
070.5'722—dc20   89-16433
                                                   CIP

To Helen

For Anne and Dan

Contents

Acknowledgments

For most of the projects in this book, and for most of my years at *The Times,* my assistant and colleague was Robert Pelletier. He contributed in every possible way, from format development, to production liaison, to keeping designs on track in the difficult first days of conversion. That projects were successfully implemented was due in large measure to his efforts.

I express appreciation here to members of the large art staff of *The New York Times:* the art directors who took over after the initiation of new formats; the artists who helped in art production; the map and chart department under the management of Andy Sabbatini; the photo studio under Ed Gross; and two successive managing art directors, the late George Cowan and Ron Couture. These are people who never said "no" if "yes" was even a remote possibility. In particular, the work of the art directors, who continue to breathe vitality into the formats, must be acknowledged. Individual *Times* pages designed by art directors other than myself are credited accordingly.

At *The New York Times,* form and content became so interrelated that a design separate from editorial considerations was unthinkable. It was good fortune that cast me into working intimacy with powerhouse creative editors: in A. M. Rosenthal's executive editor's office, with Rosenthal, Arthur Gelb, and Seymour Topping in developing *Times* sections and in daily design solutions; with Harrison Salisbury and Herbert Mitgang in starting up the Op-Ed page; and with John Oakes and Max Frankel on the editorial pages.

Implementing the designs were newsroom "desks" with whom the art directors worked. Desks included the editor in charge, a deputy, copy editors, and make-up editors. Collective acknowledgment is due all contributors in the often difficult efforts to change the old ways of doing things and put out new sections and designs.

An extraordinary joining together of forces at *The New York Times* marked the years of innovation and change in the projects described here. Ivan Veit, who had created an elite promotion department with sophisticated standards in copy as well as design, went on to become executive vice president of the company and a leading proponent of modernizing the design of the newspaper itself. Mr. Veit paved the way for my crossing the border that separated news and business. I am grateful to him for making my role in the changes possible.

Arthur Ochs ("Punch") Sulzberger led the way from the beginning of his tenure as publisher of *The Times,* marshaling talents from all departments. Hardly a day went by, I believe, that my associates in the newsroom and I did not benefit from his confidence and support in kicking off projects and his critical judgment when ideas were presented.

During most of the years covered in this book, design efforts received critical support from the top executives on the production and business sides of the paper: Walter Mattson, production manager, general manager, and, finally, president of The New York Times Company, and John D. Pomfret, who has since retired as executive vice president. John Pomfret, in a succession of management jobs, was a creative collaborator for the news department in general, and for me in particular. His flinty-hearted budgeting helped keep the art operation (as well as others) respectable in times of financial belt-tightening; there was no belt-tightening of aggressive, creative ideas.

In the team spirit, acknowledgment must also be made to members of the composing room, to foremen like Walter Rogers and Stanley Brothers, who simply helped get things done. Particularly in the hot-metal days, when the suburban sections, the Op-Ed page, and the theme sections were first kicked off (as well as many projects not represented in this book), men like these were truly comrades-in-arms.

On the regional newspaper redesigns at Sarasota and Lakeland, Florida and at Florence, Alabama, Mary Holdt, now senior designer of *The Times'* regional newspaper group, stepped in to provide expert design help in the critical first days of new formats, particularly in the demanding lifestyle pages. Along with those of Bob Pelletier, her efforts helped give many new designs successful starts.

It would make a list too long for these pages to include all whose contributions led to successful redesigns of the regional papers, but I must express appreciation at least to the leaders: at Sarasota, to publisher Elven Grubbs, executive editor Bill McIlwain, assistant managing editor Diane McFarlin, news editor Kyle Rote, graphics editor Peter Trigge, and chief artist Joe Escourido. What a team that was! (Except for the absence of McFarlin and Trigge, who went on to other things, it still is.)

At Santa Rosa, California, publisher Jim Weeks, editor Mike Parman, and graphics editor Randy White helped make the redesign project more of a pleasure than many such projects turn out to be.

At Lakeland, I remember with appreciation Elven Grubbs, publisher before going to Sarasota, and Tim McGuire, editor, for their forceful and creative collaboration, which was continued by executive editor Louis "Skip" Perez and managing editor Mark Mathes (before he went on to bigger things in the company).

Jack Harrison, president of the regional newspaper group from my early involvement to the present, and later Seymour Topping, director of editorial development for the group, supplied support, ideas, and personnel in various proportions that helped make the designing easy.

I express appreciation to my greatest collaborator—my wife Helen, who shared with me every serious problem, from design problems to human relations problems. There were plenty of both. She never failed to provide insights that balanced tough perception, design judgment, and the necessary pinch of sympathy. Our collaboration continued in her encouragement and help with this book.

I want to thank William McBride, a gifted editor with a feeling for editorial and design integration, and Leonard Harris, former director of corporate communications of The New York Times Company, for their help in reading the manuscript and their knowledgeable advice on general approach as well as specific detail. I also thank Nancy Pelkus for helping in some of the research, typing, and nailing down of loose ends.

I want to express appreciation also to Lilly Kaufman, my editor at Van Nostrand Reinhold, and to Conni Carmody and Liz Geller, production editors on the project. They were calm, confident, and solicitous, and kept the project moving in mysterious ways that I learned to count on and trust.

Preface

This book describes some of my work in designing newspapers for The New York Times Company. I hope it will be interesting and helpful to newspaper designers and art directors, to designers who may be considering a career in the expanding world of newspaper design, and to editors and newspaper executives who want to produce better and better-looking newspapers. In describing these design solutions, I attempt to show procedures, alternative arrangements, and in some cases, false starts that may provide additional insight into the published solution.

Design solutions are set against relevant backgrounds, including competitive marketing situations, the personalities involved, and historical factors. Not always apparent, these are some of the factors that are inevitably and properly reflected in a design. Comments range from technical and analytical to anecdotal. The common thread is the attempt to show "why" as well as "how."

The book focuses on elements from five papers: *The New York Times; The Ledger* of Lakeland, Florida; the *Times Daily,* published in Florence, Alabama; the *Sarasota Herald-Tribune* of Florida; and *The Press Democrat* of Santa Rosa, California.

These papers are part of The New York Times Company group of newspapers, which now numbers 35, including the parent paper. I worked on these projects in my capacity as assisting managing editor of *The New York Times* and corporate art director of The New York Times Company, in effect the company's chief designer. The five papers range from a big city, New York, to a small rural-industrial area, Florence, Alabama. I've selected elements from these papers where each had an especially interesting design problem and a successful design solution. Many problems are common to most newspapers, of course. I've attempted to avoid duplication by accenting different aspects of the design problems in each chapter.

The pace of design and technological change in newspaper design and production techniques in the United States has accelerated extraordinarily in recent years. I have tried to choose examples that remain relevant or reflect aspects of journalistic design that remain constant, whatever the technology.

The New York Times

Without ever announcing a "redesign," *The New York Times* is generally credited with having transformed itself from an excellent paper without any pretensions of special visual interest to one generally considered a leader in visual interest. In 1984, in a national survey of editors and designers sponsored by the Society of Newspaper Design, *The New York Times* was designated the best designed paper in the United States. And in 1989 the American Institute of Graphic Arts awarded *The Times* its gold medal for design leadership. This book illustrates and describes some of the ingredients that went into that transformation, focusing particularly on the Op-Ed page, regional sections, The Home Section and other daily themed sections, the Travel Section, Metropolitan News, and an approach to "journalistic graphics."

The Ledger

The redesign of *The Ledger,* in Lakeland, Florida in 1979, seemed to me at the time to be a "textbook" example of a successful newspaper redesign project. With allowances for technological improvements, I think this is still true. Everything went smoothly, from the development of a step-by-step procedure, to the working relationship between the people at the paper and myself as format designer, to the design ideas. Add to this the synchronization of the redesign with a change from afternoon to morning publication, accompanied with a wholehearted promotional effort and the modernization of the physical plant, and you have a good example of how a redesign project can provide a platform for constructive change across the board for all departments of the paper. At the time of redesign in 1979, circulation was 43,000 daily and 60,000 on Sunday. Daily circulation rose to 50,000 within a year, and now, ten years later, stands at 90,000, with Sunday circulation at about 100,000. At the time of this writing, we are producing a comprehensive update of the design of *The Ledger*, reflecting the growth in circulation and market, and continuing the general character and many of the features of the basic design.

Times Daily

The *Times Daily* of Florence, Alabama is the smallest of the papers, about 28,000 in circulation at the time of the redesign in 1982. The redesign is particularly interesting because so much of the typography derives directly from editorial ideas, and because the personality of the publisher was an important factor.

The mood here was different from New York and Sarasota, more similar to Lakeland. The publisher's mandate was a challenge: He wanted simply the best, the snappiest paper he could get; he wanted it quickly, and the word "tradition" was not nearly as much in the vocabulary of redesign as it was in Sarasota or New York. Guy Hankins was a Western publisher. He was large, with a scraggly beard and a broad belt around an ample waist. He was extremely enthusiastic and forceful. I like to think he got the kind of design he deserved.

Sarasota Herald-Tribune

The *Sarasota Herald-Tribune* at the time of redesign in late 1983 had a circulation of about 100,000 daily and about 130,000 on Sundays. It saw itself as a small big-city newspaper, the quality, full-range newspaper of the area, an important part of the community establishment. It had a conservative demeanor, based in part on a Bodoni resemblance to its namesakes, the old *Herald Tribune* of New York and the *International Herald Tribune* published in Paris.

The paper had a market penetration at the time of over 70 percent and a dedicated readership said to be even more proprietary about the paper than that number indicates. There was, therefore, more than the usual concern on the part of the publisher and The New York Times

1975: Eight columns, two parts.

1990: Six columns, four sections.

Company executives that we not endanger this loyal support with changes that would appear to readers as too revolutionary.

Yet, in Florida's tough, competitive market, the paper clearly needed improvement journalistically and modernization visually if it was to flourish. This redesign was a balancing act, juggling the pragmatic need to change with fear of changing too much.

The Press Democrat

In Santa Rosa, the mood of redesign was California-style ebullience. The new publisher, Jim Weeks, the new executive editor, Mike Parman, and the new graphics editor, Randy Wright, were all eager for a "new" Press Democrat. Surveys showed that readers respected the paper but would welcome a more modern product.

At the time of redesign the paper was reasonably healthy in circulation with about 85,000 daily and about 100,000 on Sunday but faced a classic circulation problem in the outlying communities around the home base of Santa Rosa.

Particularly to the south in Marin County, in the communities that lay between San Francisco and Santa Rosa, there was need to hold off the growing influence of the *San Francisco Chronicle* as it spread north with the growth of suburban San Francisco.

Weeks emphasized the need to attract single-copy sales and to incorporate strong competitive color in the design, seen against a background of California's prominent line-up of papers in which color and design are extremely important.

The design in Santa Rosa marked a transition typical, I believe, of change taking place in many U.S newspapers, from a design that depended for graphic appeal almost exclusively on a large photo as the centerpiece of each page to one dependent on the full range of design tools —typography, photo, art, and graphics. Reflected also was a change in graphic roles. In the old paper, a capable, energetic photo editor was the dominant graphic figure. The new design ushered in a graphics editor, part journalist, part designer, as the dominant graphics figure. The photo editor moved to a larger role that included color and quality control as well as photography.

Introduction

Common denominators

Certain design problems and concerns are common to most newspapers. Common denominators apparent in each of the newspapers in this book include: the visualization of the paper as a whole rather than parts; a greater emphasis on configuration, the architecture of a publication; the emphasis on not only format design but also creative day-to-day design implementation; greater integration of the designer into newsroom thinking and procedure; emphasis on the use of graphics—especially considering the vast capabilities of the computer—on graphics used in a journalistic context; increased color capability; and emphasis on excellent typesetting as the basic building block.

Configuration

Probably the most basic of the common denominators is the attempt to deal with the *total* aspect of a paper or section, and not with fragmented pieces. The parts are seen in their relation to the whole, including in particular the creative distribution of advertising and editorial spaces, the "configuration." It is the architectural structure of the paper, where the design begins.

It is true that certain aspects of the hard news presentation of *The New York Times* have resisted this approach. The national news report, for example, starting in one section and jumping to another, can hardly be called architecturally rational. However, compelling reasons for this exist, stemming from press determinants that dictate that the number of pages in certain sections must be equal to the number in other sections. Nevertheless, where a new design has been introduced in *The Times*, it has grown out of a comprehensive approach to configuration.

Format and implementation

The format is the beginning, not the end, of what readers see. The format design is basically management's responsibility. The object is to put a plan and specific graphic tools into the hands of the day-by-day editors defining the desired character and visual thrust, making it easy for non-designers to consistently put out a good-looking paper. At the same time, the format must allow and encourage some variety and creative discretion.

The day-by-day implementation by editors and staff provides the daily creative product the reader sees. Without creative implementation, any newspaper format will soon appear flat. But the daily design must never lose sight of the cumulatively positive effect of adherence to the general style and character as expressed in the agreed-upon format.

Recognition of these two broad design functions—format and implementation—can help in analyzing a paper's problems. In a critique, one may find so many areas in implementation that are poor that one is forced to conclude that the problems are not in the implementation at all but in the format.

On the other hand, one might find that the basic elements are good: typefaces are well chosen, the newspaper is well organized, and so on. However, pictures may be used in a pedestrian fashion, stories may be inadequately edited, and page layouts may be monotonous. More text may appear where there should be a graphic visual aid or a service box. The paper may lack warmth or wit. Clearly these problems stem from unimaginative implementation. A new format might shake things up for a while, but a shake-up of staff might be necessary to keep it going. The format design is the price of admission to the dance floor. Once in, we can dance, or just sit around. That's the implementation.

The designer in newspapers

The earliest of the redesigns in this book took place at *The New York Times* around 1966, when the paper was made up in metal type, each page assembled in a heavy steel frame (the chase) in a factory room dominated by steel counters and low-hanging fluorescent lights against the background clatter of linotype machines. When a page was ready, two men, who had been standing by patiently, rolled up a steel table on wheels, cranked it up to counter height, and slid the chase off the counter to go to the next step in the heavy-duty production process of the hot metal days.

The area around the Page One chase, where compositors and editors worked in quiet tension under overhead lights, resembled a hospital operating room. An art director's presence in the composing room was then virtually unknown. Responsibility for carrying out layouts rested with make-up editors who enjoyed a latitude in what they could do to make all those pieces of metal fit together on deadline. On the following day the art director would look at the page he had designed the night before, with special interest in seeing to what degree the printed page resembled his layout.

The art director didn't carry much more weight in his own area of operation. Editors, working closely with picture editors, were the visual initiators, going to the Art Department when they felt the need for some special visual treatment—particularly in the Sunday feature sections.

As corporate art director of The New York Times Company and before that as promotion art director, I had on rare occasions visited the editorial art department. I remember likening it to a pit—the Black Hole of Calcutta came to mind. The room was very large, perhaps 125 feet long, poorly lighted, with forbidding waist-high, foot-thick oak dividers separating the place into aisles. An editor, with a picture editor trailing, would come in, look into the pit, select a body, and say: "Here, do a layout. This picture on top, this one on the bottom. Crop them like this. I need it in thirty minutes because so-and-so is catching an early train."

An art director's incursions into the composing room were acts of courage. Insisting on involvement in the page make-up in metal as a natural extension of my efforts at the drawing board came very close to precipitating more than one wild-cat strike by the compositors. It was not unknown for the entire composing room, numbering at any one time perhaps 100 people, to lay down their pica rulers and type slugs and walk off the floor in protest of what they considered an infraction of the union-management agreement. From the managers' viewpoint, my assistant, Bob Pelletier, and I were also an unwelcome presence, tolerated because our mission had the blessing of higher-ups in the organization. Even John Pom-

fret, at the time general manager of the paper and one of the chief architects of creative change at *The Times*, would stand by menacingly at closing time on the eve of a new section. More than once he took me out to dinner to get me off the composing room floor.

In this atmosphere, prevalent even in the newspaper with the biggest art staff in the country, one can easily extrapolate the state of art in newspapers in general. It is not surprising that with this grudging acceptance, let alone the poor quality of newsprint reproduction, few graphic designers were attracted to work in newspaper offices.

A major goal for change was to establish a climate where good designers enjoyed reasonable status and where they could do work to be proud of. Only by demonstrating in the paper every day that we were serious about upgrading the design could this be accomplished. So the earlier design efforts were important not only for themselves but also for the salutory effect they had on our ability to attract talented people.

A measure of change can be seen in the make-up of the Art Department at *The New York Times*. While the numbers remained about the same for many years, the complexion of the department changed enormously: the number of retouchers shrank from 9 to 2, while the number of art directors jumped from 2 to between 14 and 18—the number growing with the years and projects. These and other changes moved the Art Department from a production-oriented service to a creative arm, culminating in 1969 with the wholly logical move of integrating the department into the News Department soon after the News and Sunday departments were themselves integrated under executive editor A. M. Rosenthal.

The designer's role

A measure of a paper's commitment to effective design and graphic excellence can often be seen in the degree to which a designer is integrated into the workings of the newsroom. In a large paper an officially designated art director and perhaps a graphics editor will oversee the design. In a smaller paper a talented desk editor with special interest in design is either designated or takes the role of graphic and design leader.

The close working relationship of the art person and the desk editors and executive and managing editors—those who initiate and approve ideas—will benefit readers with richer presentations. At best the art director or designer participates in news meetings and planning sessions, has a base—a desk or office—in the newsroom, and has clear lines of responsibility in relation to other people in the newsroom, particularly the news editor, who might be responsible for the front page and other key pages; the photo editor, who previously might have carried sole responsibility in visual matters; and to various section heads.

It has taken a very long time for newspapers to make a place for designers to work as colleagues in the creative process rather than to serve as specialists invited in for a limited role when needed. If we consider other important media—magazines, television, posters, books, and advertising down to the imaginative communications we see on T-shirts—we know that no one in these fields would do without the aid of a professional designer. In newspapers the opposite had been true until 15 or 20 years ago.

The Society of Newspaper Design, which started in 1978 with a handful of members, boasted over 1200 in 1989, including a large percentage of editors. Yet even now when so much has been accomplished recently in newspaper design, there is still a long way to go before the design position is institutionalized as is, for example, the news editor's.

If the news editor leaves, everyone knows the position must be filled as soon as possible by the best qualified person. In the design area, however, especially in medium to smaller papers, a person might be tapped from anywhere to provide design talent, with lines of authority unclear. Usually this person is in a service position. He or she is called upon by those editors who need him or her and more or less ignored by others except for specific and limited tasks. Understandably, the feature sections (softer news) are associated with the designer, and the hard news, the heart of the paper, goes its own way.

To meaningfully fit a design person into the daily operation is often difficult and painful. In a big paper, for example, the relationship between the picture editor and his deputies and the foreign, national, and particularly city editors may be strained, with wrangling over the use of pictures not at all uncommon. How does the designer fit into this? Who's in charge?

Papers attack this dilemma in different ways. Too often, too much is left to the designer's assertive abilities in defining his or her role.

Some papers have dealt with the problem more directly. At the *Providence Journal,* Dave Gray is in charge of photos, graphics, and design. The photo desk works harmoniously within larger news and design objectives.

At the *Sarasota Herald-Tribune* (Chapter 9), the paper after redesign employed three artists in its art department, but their role has been essentially to provide illustrations, graphics, and layout help when needed. Otherwise, interested editors do the designing. Only recently did the paper designate a graphics editor, Peter Gentile, whose contributions are already clear in the growing paper.

At Santa Rosa's *The Press Democrat* (Chapter 10) the hiring of a talented graphics editor was made a prerequisite before embarking on the redesign project, to ensure that a competent "point man" would be on staff in California to implement the new format. Seymour Topping, director of editorial development for affiliated papers of The New York Times Company since 1986, has described one of his functions as making certain the right people are in place to be able to sustain the journalistic ambitions represented by the format changes, now a part of his overall responsibility.

The Press Democrat was able to hire Randy Wright, whose background included editing, education in art, and a deep-rooted interest in design. As graphics editor at Santa Rosa he not only performed the essential role of project leader in the redesign but was given clear responsibility to oversee the design of the front page.

Many publishers and editors are not always clear about what they expect from an art person. They hire an artist who does illustrations and wonder why more charts aren't getting into the paper. Or, they hire someone expert at the Macintosh but are disappointed that no marked improvement in the appearance of the section fronts is apparent.

Even if all the visual talents required by a good newspaper could be found in one person (very often a young person not paid a great deal), the working day is too short for one person to do it all. Therefore, priorities have to be set.

To help executives in The New York Times Company who approve the new hires, I drew up the following analysis at the time of the Sarasota redesign.

ART PEOPLE

Format designer. An expert in design and typography who is experienced in the design of publications. He or she may be on the staff of a large newspaper, but is more likely to be an outside consultant who can deal with the design in its broad implications of editorial focus and marketing requirements.

Art director/designer/layout person. A staff member talented in typography, design, and general artistic judgment who is responsible on a day-to-day basis for monitoring the visual aspects of the paper's presentation and works with editors in conceiving and executing effective news and feature presentations on a daily basis.

Illustrator. A person whose essential talent is geared to creating drawings for the paper. These can range from small black and white spot drawings that may take 20 minutes to full-color half-page illustrations that may take days. Such a person can also be responsible for doing "graphics" (defined in this case as maps and charts), but it is good to remember that a talented illustrator is not likely to consider the drafting of maps and charts alone to be fulfilling work or full use of his or her talents.

Graphics person. This can be a "graphic artist" or a "graphics editor" depending on importance assigned to the job and if the position involves overseeing a staff. Today, proficiency in producing maps, charts, diagrams, and other graphics cannot be separated from proficiency in using computers; but the graphics person ideally is journalistically well-informed, artistically sensitive, and tuned in to editorial thinking and processes, not merely a technician at the terminal.

With the enormous and still growing commitment to computer graphics in newsrooms all over the United States, emphasis has moved from manual design and illustration to computer-produced and -transmitted graphics. Considering this, it may be more important than ever to have a clear understanding of what one can and cannot expect from the different art functions that make a good newspaper.

Redesign procedure

The steps in a redesign project can be summed up generally as follows, with variations, of course, in each newspaper.

1. The newspaper assembles a design committee. It is extremely important that someone with authority in the newsroom be designated staff leader of the project. He or she will be the "point man" who gets the formatting done, schedules work, monitors results, and serves as a liaison with the outside design consultant.

2. The consulting designer visits the paper for a couple of days for meetings, tours, and briefings to learn about the community and the paper. The subjects covered range from demographics and marketing surveys to typographical history. Central, of course, are meetings on content ideas and business goals and opportunities. These discussions lead to a rudimentary storyboard that visually outlines configuration ideas. Examining microfilm or bound copies of the paper from its start can be helpful to gain a sense of tradition and continuity, which every paper likes to foster even as it changes. At *The New York Times*, for example, in a year of deep concern about the radical change from eight to six columns, it was helpful to discover that in the 1870s the paper was published in six columns. And at *The Dispatch* in Lexington, North Carolina, a proposed new logo was discovered to be in the same generic type family as a logo used way back in the paper's hundred-year history; consequently the new lettering was promoted as the *re*establishment of a tradition rather than a departure.

3. The actual designing begins. Rough layouts of pages are paralleled by logo sketches and experimental type settings. A thumbnail storyboard for configuration from front to back is prepared. Not until then are individual pages considered. It is difficult, I believe, to work intelligently on a cover design or the design of a significant inside page without this visual sense of how the page relates to the pages around it.

Factored into the selection of typefaces, in addition to the personal likes and dislikes of editors and designers, are more pragmatic considerations, such as the degree of conservatism in the community, the last date of major change, and the appearance of competing newspapers.

4. It's a good idea to present ideas before things get too buttoned down, or before they even *seem* to be buttoned down. It's obviously important to get reactions at the paper and work them into the design thinking. Also important is the participation of the design

committee and others in the *process*, making it easy for members to express themselves, rather than difficult with too slick and finished a presentation.

A first presentation is likely to include sketches in dummy form of key pages in the main news section and sketches of other section covers. Not worrying about consistency at this point is helpful. Some dummy pages set in type are included, with possible alternate approaches.

The storyboard is also included in the first presentation. This is the first visualization the committee and the designer share on space and content aspects of the design, issues that up to this point were considered only verbally. The storyboard helps to focus on the larger issues of space arrangement and potential costs in terms of extra newsprint, if that proves necessary.

When the general design approach is approved by executives and the committee, the agenda then includes work with department heads to deal with aspects of their sections that need special attention and to flesh out their pages in terms of new content. During this stage of the redesign, separate meetings with the advertising and production heads are included.

5. Next the design procedure moves on two tracks: The newspaper begins the preparations for its production, paralleling the designer's work in fleshing out aspects of the design.

Having settled on typefaces, the newspaper must usually order some new fonts and insert them into its system.

Committee members are usually eager to start making up their own sample pages, but it is wise to contain this until the important display typography is formatted correctly and adequate style sheets are prepared. This takes between one and two weeks and is a vital step. It is not difficult to get the fonts from the supplier, but it can be troublesome to get the typesetting equipment to deliver precisely the proper letter, word, and line spacing, not to mention special kerning and contraction or expansion of letters, easily within the capability of contemporary equipment. Headline style sheets, usually from 12 to 72 points of each of the basic display faces, are prepared.

There may be one or more rounds of

telephone or fax communication on this—also performed directly on the computer if designer and newspaper are hooked up—to perfect the basic typographical building blocks. If the committee goes ahead with sample pages before the typesetting is just right, critiquing the pages becomes a wasteful and confusing chore, since people may be setting type differently and poor typesetting may have a discouraging effect on the look of the pages. If the typesetting is good, it's gratifying how easily the pieces of the new design start clicking into place. At a critical point in the process, the newspaper staff starts realizing some good results.

Meanwhile, final elements of the design are being completed. Reproduction copies for all the important standing heads are produced. After the start-up, a newspaper should have the capability of easily producing any kind of heading out of its own computer formats. But for "opening day," to ensure that the headings are as perfect as possible, veloxes are sometimes made, to use directly and/or print into pads.

6. The newspaper desks make up an agreed-upon number of sample pages, usually between 20 and 24, for key parts of the paper. There should be several different pages for the front page and the other section covers.

Critiques follow. Usually the first round of pages is about 80 to 85 percent on target. A week or 10 days of turn-around time is allowed for remakes. This is a good time for a series of upbeat meetings which begin to focus on creative implementation of the format rather than the format itself. The designer might sit down with members of the news desk and draw up with them several ways of handling that day's news in the new format style.

7. A "dodger"—a sample press run of the approximately 24 pages or more that have been developed up to this time—is printed. The dodger serves two important purposes: In the newsroom the pages will constitute the best possible guide for style. For the publisher and the Promotion Department, the dodger is essential in presentations to civic leaders and the advertising community and to all the other aspects of promotion.

The dodger also has a third, less tangible benefit: the psychological lift to all concerned of being able to hold in their hands a sample of the new paper, well-printed and with good color. The project suddenly feels worthwhile and "real" at a critical time when everyone has been working very hard and longs to see the results of all the effort.

8. Special additional parts of the paper, not previously dealt with, are designed. This could include a big effort for the Sunday paper or for special sections of the paper such as an entertainment tabloid or a week-end magazine.

9. Dry runs are conducted. Up to now, pages have been produced with emphasis on the result, not on production efficiency. Now it is important to schedule a series of dry runs—sometimes two are enough—to test the staff's ability to produce the new paper on deadline.

10. Start-up. Extra design help is made available in the days preceding and following going "live" with the new design. The first day is difficult, but the days immediately following may be even more so. Getting a jump on designed pages the first week can give the paper a flying start that keeps quality high for months ahead.

In summary, the process can be seen as follows: In the first stage the redesign is on the designer's desk, with the newspaper staff helping in the design. Gradually, the project is moved from the designer's desk to the editors' desks, as they assume responsibility and the designer now helps them.

Color

With the exception of *The New York Times*, a common concern in the projects represented in this book is the use of color. (At *The Times*, in early 1980, some of the tabloid sections were printed in color at outside presses; and plans to print some of the regular Sunday sections in color began to be considered.) The earlier designs, in smaller papers with limited capabilities, tended to emphasize spot color. The later designs, at bigger papers with new facilities, were more ambitious with full color projected for most section fronts. The weather report usually gravitated toward a back page of one of the sections, a color position.

Attitudes toward color express the yearning to pack in the competitive color used in *USA Today*, coupled with the desire not to look like it. A neat trick, but usually frustrating. This approach is misguided because it fails to recognize that the color in virtually every nook and cranny of *USA Today*'s front page is a harmonious and natural part of a totally different approach to the whole news operation, from the way it reports the news in an intricate mosaic of short bursts to the organization of its news department. It is fallacious to try to separate the use of color from the design itself, as if they were separate and unrelated problems.

As described in Chapter 3, *The Ledger*, it seems the best color pages are simply the best designed pages with color. Occasionally, no doubt, an exceptionally large color photo will provide exceptional interest and carry a page. But as a rule, the page design should enjoy a certain amount of intricacy in content and design using as much as possible the full graphic palette, including color.

Another often-expressed attitude is, "Oh, I'm all for color, but a color picture should be used only when the color is important in the picture, or when the color is exceptionally good." This attitude, which is probably rooted in the transitional days of terrible reproduction, seems increasingly irrelevant since it segregates color from the mainline of the operation, when, in fact, technology makes the use of color more practical. A healthier attitude would be to make a commitment to everyday use of color display and to choose pictures for their overall effectiveness in the newspaper, without overemphasizing the technical excellence of color reproduction.

One of the problems in stressing only "good" color is the question of what makes a "good" color photograph. Many editors and production people are so concerned about reproduction quality that the selected photos, predictably, tend to be bright, simple, and sharp-edged. Unfortunately they are also often static, posed, and predictable—qualities usually at odds with the reporting of news.

Newspaper Design
For The Times

Suburban Weeklies

THE NEW YORK TIMES

Turbulent times

Background for change

The design of the four new suburban sections of *The Times* in 1976 occurred against a background of many years of turbulence and change. First, unsettling relations existed with the 10 unions that represented most of the employees. Negotiations were ongoing almost all the time, often in varying degrees of crisis, and disastrous strikes resulted. Second, around 1965, a period of depressed earnings entered a critical phase. Annual report figures showed that *The Times* earned more from its minority ownership in Canadian newsprint plants than from the efforts of its almost 5000 highly skilled and, in many cases, famous employees.

A third background factor involved efforts by The New York Times Company to improve its financial situation. As did other companies during those years, *The Times* started to diversify in 1971, purchasing a group of 13 newspapers, several magazines, and a TV station from Cowles Communications. Diversification gave the company a broader base of profit and strengthened its hand in negotiations with its unions.

At roughly the same time, The New York Times Company went public on the American Stock Exchange, thereby broadening its capital base. Also, changes were made in areas of management leadership, putting the Advertising and Marketing Departments in new hands and beginning a series of changes in the newsroom that culminated in the consolidation of the Sunday Department and the News Department, which up to then were two quite separate fiefdoms. The new consolidated department was under the direction of A. M. Rosenthal as executive editor and a new team, of which I became a member. I previously had been corporate art director, reporting to the publisher. The Art Department had not been part of the News Department but was a service group under separate direction. The new scheme of things consolidated Art, Sunday, and News into one department with one management. Consolidation occurred formally after the suburban sections were started, but movement toward this end began earlier.

A fourth background factor was a series of

Easy access
Circulation Department map shows the location of the Carlstadt plant in relation to the metropolitan area and four suburban regions reached by the new weeklies.

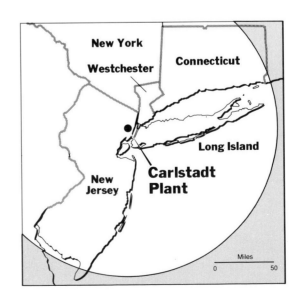

research efforts and department-by-department self-analysis sessions in which the editors and some writers were asked to explore, with the widest latitude and in the greatest depth, every aspect of improving the newspaper.

The research projects were conducted by various outside consulting firms and explored almost every conceivable aspect of *The Times* operation. Most significantly, the research concentrated on locating potential readers and deciding what needed to be done to convert them to actual readers. Consultants analyzed the management structure and policy at *The Times*, including everything from personnel policies and promotion opportunities, to salary structure and ways to attract and keep bright, aggressive, new managers.

My own promotion in 1969, from art director of the Promotion Department to corporate art director, followed my involvement in various projects, including changing the text face of the paper; cleaning up the Sunday section headings; redesigning the Book Review and The Week in Review; and designing the Op-Ed page, as well as others. These projects were outside the bailiwick of the News Department, but my gradual acceptance by the editors—or at least the top editors—in the newsroom was a factor that led to the dramatic departure from the existing *Times* style in the suburban sections.

The key to success

People at *The Times* may differ on which design project was the beginning of what probably would be generally acknowledged as a revolution in content and design.

Without a doubt, the Op-Ed page was one watershed. The everyday appearance of large, ambitious, and sometimes "far out" illustrations and unusual layouts in the newspaper certainly could not fail to be noted by the editors in the newsroom, who for the most part preferred traditional make-up practices, as did their peers in most other newspapers.

Many significant steps, including the Op-Ed page, preceded the design of the new suburban sections. Their design, however, was the first major project in which staff from the news, business, and production sides of the paper collaborated with the designer from scratch.

I believe this creative teamwork was one of the keys to the successful genesis of the Long Island, New Jersey, Connecticut, and Westchester Weeklies. In the past, the pattern at *The Times* (and probably at most other newspapers) was, at best, polite cooperation from adversarial positions. Requirements from each side for page configuration—the distribution of news and advertising spaces—were laid out in position "white papers," like legal briefs. The visual matter of page-by-page division of space was spelled out in almost legal language to ensure no loopholes existed to invite transgression.

A place of my own

The publisher, Arthur Ochs Sulzberger, and the top executives of the company led the way to an integrated effort on the new sections. Mr. Sulzberger presided at meetings that initiated the project and then personally approved designs and concepts at steps along the way.

A work space was carved out of the crowded building in abandoned office space on the 10th floor that was scheduled to be overhauled but would be available for a few months. This work space carried a certain significance, with some trappings of influence. In the recent past, *The Times* had engaged in major projects, such as the publishing of the *Pentagon Papers* or the planning of a New York City afternoon paper (produced in prototype but never actually published) and had set aside special work areas for the task forces, cordoned off with ostentatious security measures to ensure secrecy. Needless to say, a considerable cachet was attached to the chosen people who worked day and night on these momentous and secret projects.

To design the new suburban sections, a work area was again set aside. A warehouselike room with cast-off desks became the regular work space for myself and my assistant, Bob Pelletier. Here Arthur Gelb, then assistant managing editor, worked on content and configuration for the new sections. John Pomfret, then assistant general manager of the paper, sometimes met with us to ensure that the new design would reflect advertising and marketing desires. I believe design was the catalyst that brought the news and advertising points of view together harmoniously and profitably for everyone, including the reader.

A presence in the suburbs

The suburban sections were created to bolster our efforts to reach suburban readers in the face of increasingly tough local competition. At the time, the Sunday *Times* had a circulation of about 1,100,000. About one-third of these readers lived in the suburbs. On Long Island, *Long Island Newsday* had become strongly entrenched. It was, and remains, a thick, chockfull tabloid with page after page of advertising servicing its widespread community of homeowners with all kinds of shopping information, as well as well-targeted news content. In New Jersey, *The Bergen Record* had already zoned itself with marked success on its way to becoming *The Record*. In Westchester, the Rockland County papers were growing in quality and readership, and in Connecticut, local papers also were more aggressive.

The Times enjoyed substantial readership in all these communities, particularly on Sunday. A series of surveys backed by detailed figures confirmed what was plain for anyone to see: The basic *Times* reader was no longer the businessperson on Wall Street. A whole group of new readers existed out there in the suburbs, including young men and women growing up with their post-World War II children, with new and wider ranges of interests.

Troubled union relations were a continually inhibiting problem that put *The Times* at a disadvantage in this competitive situation. The smaller papers in the suburbs had been helped enormously by new developments in technology. When our Sunday suburban sections were introduced, some of the suburban newspapers were already enjoying the fruits of photocomposition; many of them were already in offset production. At *The Times* we were still in metal, producing an eight-column paper, with the columns getting narrower and narrower, on narrower sheets of paper that reflected sharply rising newsprint costs. We were printing letterpress, with reproduction, particularly of photographs, comparing badly to the smaller papers around us who were

Before
First page of Sunday suburban news before the redesign is shown. The pages were zoned parts of the regular news report. The effort to make a separate section with a real front page was yet to come. Originally, only New Jersey and Long Island were zoned.

4

printing in offset. Yet the inability to agree with one or more of the 10 unions involved at any one time kept us from realizing some of the benefits the smaller papers in the suburbs were already enjoying.

But there was also plenty of positive movement. Negotiations with the unions culminated in 1974 in an agreement that finally allowed across-the-board modernization. A momentous step was taken in developing a new printing plant across the Hudson River in Carlstadt, New Jersey, a "state-of-the-art" wonderland the size of six football fields under one roof, with eight press units occupying one little corner of the vast space, with Harris circular inserting machines, and the latest in track delivery and loading systems for the trucks. The new Carlstadt plant was the production linchpin for the new suburban sections. The sections would be edited, designed, and made up in New York but printed for the most part in New Jersey. The new arrangement would not only ease the burden on the presses on 43rd Street but would also simplify problems of distribution posed by printing in Manhattan and trying to get the papers out to the suburbs through New York's traffic jams. Along with other advance sections printed in Carlstadt, the paper could be distributed to Long Island, New Jersey, Westchester, and Connecticut with efficiency and reliability.

Earlier efforts

Earlier attempts had been made in the News Department to deal with suburban news. These attempts had been designed within the limiting confines of the existing make-up style in the newsroom. Headings were in the generally modest news style, and only slight additions in editorial space had been allotted. Earlier ambitions and investments had obviously not paid off in reader interest or advertiser enthusiasm.

Capital investment
The vast interior of the Carlstadt, New Jersey plant, operational in 1976. The eight Goss presses, 30 by 1988, the new Harris rotary insertion equipment (right), and the strategic location of the plant helped make possible the production and distribution of the four suburban weeklies.

Front page

Magazine approach

The central idea for the new suburban sections was to develop a newspaper section with some of the attributes of a magazine, to make it stand out from the rest of the Sunday paper.

It had been established that because of production and distribution schedules and the impracticality of attempting to cover local news in the many communities represented, most of the content would be relatively soft news, though by no means exclusively so.

I began with the idea of a very big picture dominating the top half of the page, giving the appearance of a magazine cover on newsprint. Any reasonably good photo, for example, imaginatively cropped and well reproduced, would be arresting on the basis of size alone. The essential point was that the photo had to be overly big, breaking the mold of the standard newspaper page and suggesting something completely different. It couldn't be only bigger than usual in the same visual context as before. The reader had to perceive it as a new *kind* of section.

The first layout showed a horizontal photograph across the full width of the page. Following this, alternate layouts were made that varied the shape of the picture but adhered to the original idea of dominant size.

Another visual idea designed to set the section off as something special was the banner angled at the top of the page, borrowed from magazines. An element on an angle like this is ordinarily difficult to incorporate into the rigorously vertical and horizontal newspaper makeup. Here the banner carries the section title, complementing the logo of the newspaper. This is set in the center of the page as it is in all the other sections of the Sunday paper, reflecting the feeling of the front page. The formal centering seems appropriate for the traditional Old English logo.

To make the slash look as if it has been *superimposed* on the page, it overlaps and partially covers the logo, adding some sense of dimension. (It's hard to believe in 1989 the stir this provoked in 1975.)

The heavy gray bars, together with one-point rules, make an exaggerated kind of Scotch rule without appearing as fussy as standard

The four suburban weeklies
Right: New Jersey and Long Island were kicked off in 1976, Westchester and Connecticut a year later. Big pictures on Page One emphasized the new visual approach.

Title banner
Facing page: First issue of the Long Island Weekly featured the headline on an angle, creating a graphic unit with the title banner. Editors had to shift from hard news style to a new magazine/newspaper style in words as well as design.

In Search of The Great Gatsby

The author gazing across Manhasset Bay as Fitzgerald might have seen it

The New York Times/Fred R. Conrad

Watching Stanley Run

By DEE WEDEMEYER

IN THE belief that there are no world leaders of the stature of Adenauer, Churchill or Roosevelt in these troubled times, Stanley Arnold of East Hampton is offering himself as a candidate for President of the United States.

"We need a President who combines judgment and daring," explained Mr. Arnold in an interview in the parking lot of Newick's restaurant in Dover, N. H., where his campaign van was becalmed briefly. "I think I could be another Roosevelt and that's what is really needed in this country today is another Roosevelt."

When New Hampshire voters cast their ballots. Tuesday, they will have a choice of two Long Islanders, Ellen McCormack, a Merrick housewife, who is running on an antiabortion platform and Stanley Arnold, a compelling and curious figure in the election who is urging voters, among other things, to vote alphabetically.

Mr. Arnold, 60, is the founder, with his father, of the Pick 'n' Pay supermarket chain in Cleveland, which was sold before he moved to New York where he has become widely regarded in the business world as a genius in marketing and sales promotion. In 1972 he ran for Vice President and had 87 pledged delegates at the Democratic National Convention. This year he declared for the Presidency and put his name on the ballot in New Hampshire, Oregon and Wisconsin.

He has been energetically introducing himself to voters up and down New Hampshire in recent weeks, campaigning in subfreezing temperatures and reaching into a brown paper bag full of buttons with his picture surrounded by the words "I'm not a politician."

If New Hampshire voters could vote with a contest blank in 25 words or less, Stanley Arnold might win in a landslide. As founder of Stanley Arnold & Assoc., a 41-person concern with offices in the Seagram Building on Park Avenue and earlier as head of the sales promotion division for Young and Rubicam, the advertising agency, Mr. Arnold was responsible for creating contests that had millions of entries.

Among his credits: Win a mattress full of money for Simmons; win your height in dollar bills for Rinso; win a bathtub full of cash with Dove soap; win a treasure island for Piel's beer and win the Life of Riley on the Riviera for Gulf Oil.

He once painted a horse blue to demonstrate to a client that his idea was a horse of a different color. He once hired the world's tallest man to show that one of his ideas was heads above all the others and he once changed his middle name, Norman, to Macy's to show his enthusiasm for the department store. (He's gone back to Norman now.)

Considering the promotional talents Mr. Arnold could bring to bear in a campaign, his New Hamp-

Continued on Page 22

Retracing Fitzgerald's Footsteps

By HERBERT MITGANG

"THE scene is the Long Island that hangs precariously on the edges of the New York City ash dumps—the Long Island of gaudy villas and bawdy house parties," wrote H. L. Mencken of Scott Fitzgerald's "The Great Gatsby" when it came out in the mid-twenties.

Well not quite, old sport.

The valley of ashes? Changed, something like Robert Moses' reputation, into a park in Flushing, hard by a potholed boulevard celebrating the fast-food franchised way of life: the Colonel's chicken delight, towers of pizza, fish-and-chipperies, big macs and burger kings in Queens. The overbred lady golfer in the novel who

cheated to win? Possibly—in one of the towns up the North Shore around Republican Oyster Bay, where the family heirlooms include white-and-brown spectator pumps inherited along with the choker of pearls.

And Doctor T. J. Eckleburg's yellow spectacles staring down godlike on an advertising billboard? Definitely—at last count, there were a half-dozen competing optometrists along the main drag in West Egg, which nonliterary maps show as Great Neck.

The tantalizing Fitzgerald quest today involves places rather than people. Surprisingly, one well-known biographer misplaced the "Gatsby" house and, predictably, real-estate agents sell it often. I determined to see if I could find where Scott and Zelda had lived

Continued on Page 17

Lottie Blair Parker home in Great Neck in the 1920's. It was the inspiration for the Gatsby house.

A Dramatic Awakening

By CLIVE BARNES

A COMMUNITY defines itself in many ways—and many one of them is geographical. What is Long Island? It is partly Nassau County and partly Suffolk County, all on a narrow spit of an island full of beaches, country clubs and suburban living. A land of commuters, martinis and golf. But recently there has been, it seems, at least to an alien from Manhattan, some new sense of community identification.

It was put to me the other day by an Oyster Bay resident, who said: "Increasingly people, living on Long Island are thinking of themselves as Long Islanders." He cited a number of indications of this, including the gradual development of a kind of indigenous Long Island theater.

For communities just outside Manhattan, whether they are in the other four boroughs (the Brooklyn Academy of Music with its associate the Chelsea Theater, is the exception that proves the rule), New Jersey, or Long Island, all suffer in their own efforts to provide home-grown performing arts from their proximity to the Big Apple. For miles around Times Square when people think of theater, they usually think of Manhattan.

But things are changing. Oh Long Island, for example, there are a number of dinner theaters and community theaters. Dinner theaters, a new vogue, are much the

same in suburban societies all across the country. They really got going some five or six years ago in the Chicago area, and they have spread like crabgrass. For very sound economic reasons. To go to a musical on Broadway costs fares, gas, parking, meals, tickets, drinks and baby-sitters. It can build up to a big bundle for a night out—indeed there are times when one can imagine the wife saying to the husband: "Shall we go to the theater next Thursday or to the Bahamas for the weekend?"

The dinner theater cuts down on all this—provides a package. A typical Long Island dinner theater is the Fox Hollow Inn in Woodbury. It offers a show (at present through April 25 it is "I Do! I Do!" with Bob Carroll and Estella Munson) with what it describes at a "gourmet dinner," and parking facilities, all for $12.95 Sunday through Thursday, $14.95 on Friday and $15.95 on Saturday. Add the cost of a few drinks, and, if you like, a slight additional surcharge for a special "gourmet entree," and you still have an economically manageable package. The meals at such establishments will not match up to those at Lutece or La Caravelle, and the show may not be the Best of Broadway, but the price will be right.

Long Island also abounds

Continued on Page 6

Clive Barnes, The Times drama critic, is an occasional viewer of theater on the Island

Scotch rules. Though bendays in metal printed quite poorly (these were still hot metal days), we used the finest screen our letterpress process would take. The benday would act as "color," giving some unexpected bulk to the heading but not overwhelming other typographical elements that attempted to stay within the dignified guidelines of the paper as a whole.

Bookman and Stymie Black

Even early on, it seemed clear to me that Bookman should be the basic headline face for *The Times* sections. The Sunday Business section, The Week in Review, and the Book Review, all produced by the Sunday Department, then independent of the News Department, had already been redesigned around Bookman heads (having abandoned various forms of Cheltenham, News Gothic, and Lydian).[1]

But the Bookman family did not include a bold face. (Today, when Bookman Bolds do exist among the infinite varieties of cold type, the wisdom of the original designer in limiting the weights is affirmed by the bulbous appearance of most Bookman Bolds.) A contrasting or complementary bold face had to be found.

In the earlier redesign of *The New York Times Magazine* I had replaced a rather weak slab-serif face, Karnak Black, with the firmer, blacker Stymie Black, whose letters, even in metal, fit together tightly and made a strong graphic presence. The slab-serif character complemented the blunt look of Bookman, becoming the contrasting bold accent that broadened the typographical palette in the suburban sections and eventually in the daily themed C sections.

Oversize type in the bold teasers designed for the bottom of the page offered a good opportunity to use the contrasting black type. Also feature-style initials set in the text of the cover stories provided another area for accent.

In the earliest issues, headings for the lead story ran on an angle parallel to the section title, making a unified typographical unit in a rather unusual treatment. The device gave the sections a special look that took them out of the realm of straight up, down, and sideways newspaper make-up, but in following issues, the device was abandoned.

[1] The first Bookman as the primary headline in the modern cycle of redesign occurred quietly in the Sunday News of the Week in Review in the middle 1960s, when Lester Markel was Sunday editor and redesign was a word not even thought about, let alone uttered.

Generally credited with having changed the Sunday *Times* from a newspaper to a journalistic byword, Markel had presided over the creation of the News of the Week in Review and had personally mixed the ingredients including the typographical elements that made up the unique section. Markel reigned like the Sun King. I worked safely away from the epicenter of his court, five stories removed in the Promotion Department, but I was aware of the awe that surrounded him.

Into this unfamiliar territory—the Sunday department on the eighth floor—I was dispatched by Ivan Veit, then executive vice president of the company and by the publisher, Arthur Ochs Sulzberger, to consult with Lester Markel about improving the typography of his section.

Markel's office was about 40 feet long with his desk at the far end protecting still another private room. The visitor grew faint before making it to the desk. When I finally sat down, Dan Schwarz, the assistant Sunday editor, was called in. Markel opened the discussion with a few shorthand remarks in his guttural voice that were totally unintelligible to me and then to my astonishment closed the discussion. I looked to Schwarz for help, but none came. I realized that if I left, I would have no sense of what to do. I stayed seated and asked questions which drew some grudging answers but established, at least, some common ground.

At the time, the News of the Week in Review was set in a mixture of typefaces that included Cheltenham Condensed capitals, Bookman subheads, and a bit of Cheltenham Bold. It was dignified and unique, but the typography looked old. I came back with a proposal to print all heads and subheads in Bookman upper and lower case. The proposal, supported by Mr. Sulzberger, was put into effect. About a year later when I was asked to "modernize" the Book Review, the Bookman look (actually, the faces were Bookman and Antique, which looks like a slightly heavier Bookman) seemed the right way to go.

Ingredients

Typographical ingredients of a format. The Stymie
Black is used as a black accent for the Bookman.
Broad benday bars with 1-point rules create a heavy
Scotch rule effect, giving the sections "color" and a
distinctive character.

Flexibility

Three front pages show different design approaches. Left: 1976 cover is strongly conceptual and graphic. Center: A 1977 page makes the most of routine photos, with attention to dramatic *scale* differential. Considered a daring departure at the time, art breaking into the masthead area adds dimensional interest. Right: An early page combines unusual treatment of a chart with witty lifesize scale of the birds. Designers, left to right: George Cowan, Gary Cosimini (Connecticut Weekly), George Cowan (Long Island Weekly).

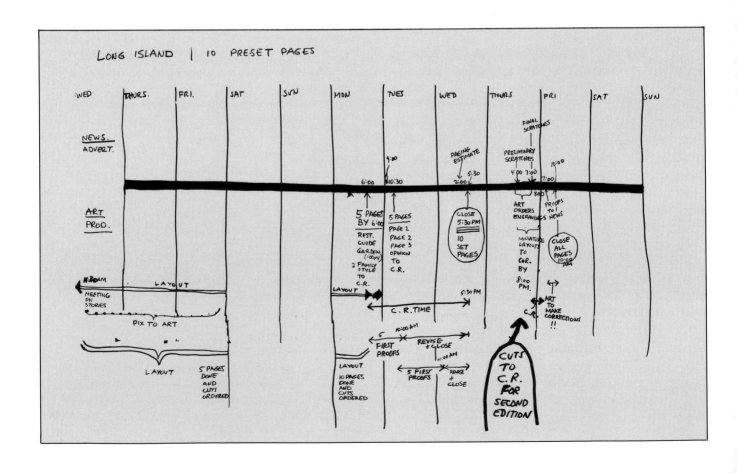

A place for news

Initial rough layouts featured two additions that at the time were new at *The Times*. The first was the use of the prominent "teaser" box. The second innovation was the optional use of a dominant front page picture with a "reefer" (a teaser, or promotional reference) line to its story on the inside. In other words, the editors and designers were freed from the necessity of running a picture with the lead story. Thus if a good image was not available to accompany the front page story, the option existed to find a good image from a lesser story on the inside of the section.

After the suburban weeklies had been running for a few years, shifts in staffing put a new group of editors and designers in place. Out of touch with the original concept, they were having trouble handling late-developing stories on Page One. They said that the design preplanning that had been built into the process frequently forced them to firm up the page before they had their most news-oriented story.

It became necessary to meet to reaffirm the concept of the page. Some of the original layouts were reexamined, and it was pointed out that the preplanning design could concentrate on a news feature that provided the visual center of the page, while a broad right-hand column (the traditional lead position column in the lexicon of *The Times*) could be filled in at the very last minute with the news lead.

In many newspapers, sections of this kind, originally conceived with big picture impact, seem to lose their magazine quality. Some seem to straddle, a bit uneasily, the original idea of a strongly dominant centerpiece and the more conventional idea of a news page that demands a certain number of stories and inches of text on the page. (This kind of straddling, of course, is generally the undoing of a design idea. Any design represents a commitment, a crossing of the street. To straddle means you start crossing but can't bring yourself to get the rear foot off the sidewalk.)

After a new design gets going, a reexamination of the design becomes necessary to either reaffirm it or define new guidelines. Sometimes a new editor or designer will be the catalyst for reexamination, bringing new opinions and prejudices to the job and wanting design changes to conform to his or her views. Sometimes the format design itself is at fault, becoming limiting or tiresome.

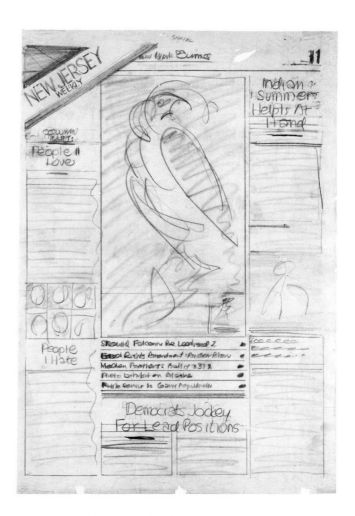

Something for everybody

An early rough sketch spells out main aspects of the format, use of an inside photo as on a magazine cover, the prominent index, and the slash logo. The sketch also demonstrates a hard news story on the right and an important position for a column on the left.

Basic ingredients

Facing page: *Format, people,* and *procedure* are the three basic ingredients that go into a redesign project. The time chart attempts to deal with the problem of daily newsroom procedure shifting to take full advantage of a weekly cycle.

Configuration
The accordian principle

Continuity front to back

Since the suburban weeklies were totally new sections, it was possible to design a configuration of the pages from the ground up. We were not inheriting a file of advertiser preferences around which we had to build, but we did need to create a publication with continuity from front to back that made the most of the content material on inside pages, at the same time satisfying advertising realities as much as possible. We wanted to avoid the look of a section that was all front page with only squirts of editorial material among the ads on the inside pages. The news-to-advertising ratio was not very high—around 40 to 60 percent. (Each of these suburban sections was only part run, of course, and ads in it were relatively inexpensive.)

After the strong front page, we wanted a reasonably strong news presence on Pages 2 and 3 to get the reader into the section. Then smaller news holes would follow as ads became more prominent. Roughly in the center I tried to carve out a "centerpiece" area for some main features to be presented in a strong graphic way. Smaller spaces followed, allowing for self-contained departments as well as jumps and short pieces. On the inside back cover or the facing page, an opinion page rounded out the content. The opinion page, featuring guest articles, letters, and prominent illustrations, gave each suburban section a more local and self-contained feeling.

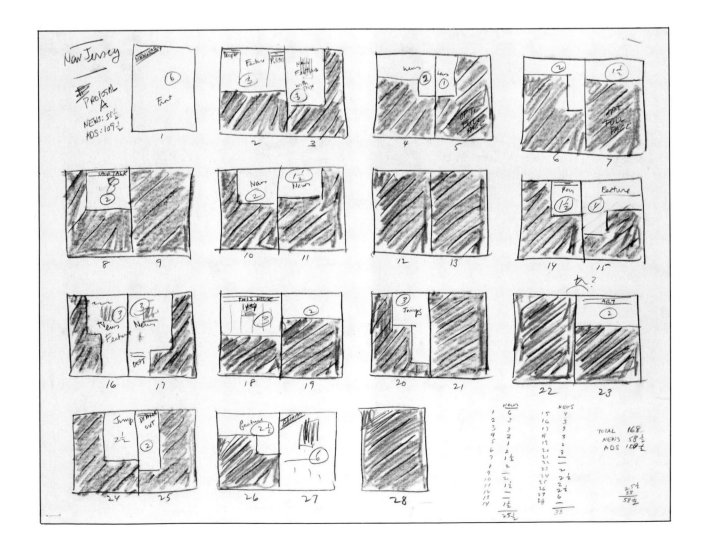

Opening spread

Above: Pages 2 and 3 open the section with a major news feature on Page 3 and three varied items on Page 2. This was the first issue of the new section. Close attention is paid to detail: typographical detail, use of illustrations as in the Fletcher Knebel piece, use of dot separators in the columns, and the balancing placement of the readout on Page 3. Right: a variation of Page 2.

Anatomy of a tight issue

Left: A storyboard drawn on a 19″ x 24″ tissue, with advertising spaces indicated by diagonal lines, lays out the section for easy visual comprehension.

13

For the first time in a section in *The Times,* the ads were moved to the outside margins of the pages, making inverted wells for editorial material around the gutter. (In the past, ads had been stacked to the right of each page.)

Especially in tight publications, the ads-to-the-outside arrangement gives the editorial material a stronger presence than do those that allow the ads to interrupt the editorial flow. The partial spaces around the gutter buttress each other, giving greater importance to the editorial material as the focal center of the double spread. This is even more apparent where small spaces—one or one-and-a-half columns—are involved. We even went so far as to allow stories to jump over the gutter. It seems to me that this is a better solution to the problem of small spaces than using two stories and jumping both of them. A pervasive problem stems from the fact that many inside pages come from the advertising make-up person late in the production cycle. Editors are frequently confounded by the small editorial spaces that are sprung on them, forcing them to truncate good stories, hold them over, or leave out pictures they would like to run. Putting the small spaces together around the gutter allows a longer story to retain some importance in display, and sometimes even allows a picture to be used that otherwise would be lost.

Proposed first in the suburban sections, the ads-to-the-outside make-up became standard thereafter for all the new and redesigned sections of *The Times.* Exceptions exist in specific situations, but generally the principle works. It has been applied also in the redesign of affiliated New York Times Company papers.

For design purposes, one's perception of the paper in general overrides the problem of ad placement. Traditionally, because of the necessity to parcel out units of work under tight deadlines, editors tend to think of a paper in terms of page units. By and large, they do not think of the pages the way the reader sees them, as double spreads. On many pages the resulting design is much the same, because of style discipline and the serendipitous nature of most news pages. But in planning the format of a paper, and particularly in dealing with set pieces, I think it makes sense to visualize the paper in terms of spreads.

The basic configuration of the suburban sections provides a strong beginning, center, and ending (the opinion page). As volume of advertising increases or decreases, these three areas continue to be focal points. Increased advertising volume simply spreads out the focal areas; decreased volume brings them closer together. John Pomfret called this "the accordion principle." Of course in magazine publishing, this approach would be only one of many variations on the distribution of space. But at *The Times* this comprehensive approach was a new idea, reflecting a determination to give readers a publication fleshed out with material of interest from beginning to end. For the advertising sales representative, the advantage of the approach is clear: Editorial high points of interest, planned from cover to cover, provide a menu of desirable locations for advertising.

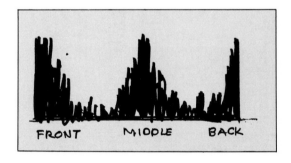

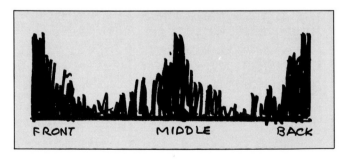

Accordion
Black indicates concentrations of news from cover to back cover. As ad volume increases, the publication expands with flow of editorial interest maintained in the same pattern.

14

The storyboard

The storyboard, miniature pages showing the entire sequence at a glance, became a basic tool for preparing configurations. Although indispensable in books, magazines, and television, the storyboard was an unfamiliar tool to most newsrooms. In traditional newspaper routine, the basic unit is the page. Editors and ad people lay out pages one at a time, usually on preprinted, quarter-size sheets, indicating the placement of news and ads. To plan a 24-page section, for example, the editor or ad person in all probability would draw 24 separate make-up sheets, which are then clipped together.

In advertising, magazines, and television, such an approach would be considered primitive. In these worlds every visual device available is used to help creators see things as the consumer will ultimately see them—as a fluid, ongoing, interrelated whole. That's what a storyboard does. By drawing thumbnail-sized spreads, in se-

Around the gutter

Interior double spread from center portion of the section demonstrates the ads-to-the-outside configuration providing maximum editorial impact around the gutter. Ads also benefit from the organized, forceful presentation. Design: George Cowan.

quence, all on *one piece of paper,* all parts of the entire publication can be viewed simultaneously. The storyboard makes it easy to visualize what happens when you move an ad or an editorial element from one place to another. It's a tool that provides greater comprehension, mastery, and flexibility in designing a publication.

Most publications that use a storyboard have the rectangles preprinted. I like to draw them on a 19″ x 24″ tissue pad. (Drawing the rectangles may seem labor-intensive perhaps, but it actually takes no more than about 40 seconds and provides the feeling of actually *drawing* a publication from the ground up.) It's something like roughing out a figure in a life class before you start working on the details.

Working on a storyboard with an editor or advertising person can be creatively fulfilling, as you move elements around and congratulate yourselves on how well things are working out. The storyboard is then a kind of visual playpen. Or the storyboard can become a nasty battleground where traditional adversaries fight their battles. In either case, the storyboard makes it easier to identify and confront configuration issues.

Departments, columns, service

The new sections would give readers lots of new service material. Departments and columns were planned on such subjects as food, art, dining out, and home repairs. Prominent among the new features was a new half-page entertainment guide edited for each of the four regions. To accommodate the more important of the features, the agreed-upon configuration provided for fixed spaces—across the full page to a depth of at least one third, for example, for the "This Week" entertainment guide. Rather than depend on visually unexciting halftones handed out by public relations firms, the format dictated a collage-like grouping of several pictorial elements in a prominent box, with the type incorporated into it to make a designed graphic treatment. In the hands of a good designer, these little collages can be exciting. In the hands of someone untalented visually, they are hardly ·worth the trouble. The collages ran for many years, and in fact provided good design training for younger people on the staff. Eventually, however, they were dropped in favor of straight halftones, with captions positioned below them.

Above, Around the gutter
(Facing page, top): Small spaces benefit from around-the-gutter treatment. With two separate small newsholes the use of a picture, readout, and story of this length would be unlikely. The headline jumps across the gutter.

(Facing page, bottom): An example of another small space treatment around the gutter with the headline contained on one page. Designing across the gutter can present an opportunity rather than a handicap.

'Ghost Village,' Once an Arsenal, Is a Bicentennial Magnet

By RICHARD PHALON

"We don't want a Williamsburg here. Our philosophy is a very low-key interpretation of life."

Batsto: Oasis in the Pine Barrens

Cont'd on Following Page

Older Men Entering Priesthood

By JAMES ANANIA

Rev. Eugene Koch: Serene optimism

Cont'd on Following Page

HOME CLINIC

Protecting Roof's 1st Line of Defense

By JOHN WARDE

ROOF gutters aren't just trim. They provide a first line of defense against many serious and expensive problems resulting from poor drainage. Consequently, it's important to inspect gutters regularly and to perform maintenance promptly.

Fall and spring are the best times for rejuvenating gutters. Warm, dry, sunny days during Indian summer are especially suitable.

Begin by cleaning the gutter troughs along the edges of the roof. Choose a dry day after a period of good weather, so the gutters and debris in them will not be wet. Work from an extension ladder; be sure to prop it at a safe angle (its distance away from the house at the bottom should equal one-quarter its extension) and project it at least 12 inches above the roof edge. Don't lean a ladder against a broken or loose gutter. Wear rubber-soled shoes and heavy work gloves.

First, plug the downspout opening at the end of the gutter with a rag. Cut a piece of plastic or light metal (such as scrap aluminum siding) to fit the inside of the trough, then use it to scrape the contents of the gutter into a pile. Trowel the debris into a bucket, which you can then carry down the ladder ... empty.

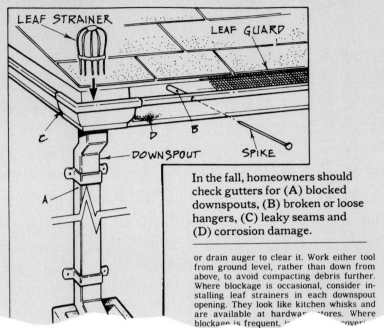

LEAF STRAINER   LEAF GUARD

DOWNSPOUT   SPIKE

C   D   B   A

In the fall, homeowners should check gutters for (A) blocked downspouts, (B) broken or loose hangers, (C) leaky seams and (D) corrosion damage.

... a whisk ...

or drain auger to clear it. Work either tool from ground level, rather than down from above, to avoid compacting debris further. Where blockage is occasional, consider installing leaf strainers in each downspout opening. They look like kitchen whisks and are available at hardware ... stores. Where blockage is frequent, ...

shape. Renail loose spikes. Broken hangers must be replaced.

Seams that leak where gutter or downspout sections join can be sealed with silicone caulk. It's best to disassemble the joint first, apply the caulk to both surfaces, then reassemble the sections. However, certain joints in vinyl gutters are not meant to be sealed, so don't seal them accidentally. These are expansion joints, and their purpose is to allow the vinyl to shrink and swell as temperatures fluctuate.

Expansion joints are found primarily where the downspout joins the gutter, but sometimes also where long sections of gutter lengths are linked together. If it is impossible or impractical to disassemble leaking gutter joints to seal them, clean the surfaces as best you can, then apply a generous amount of caulk on the inside of the gutter. Try to work it into the joint from above, smooth the caulking so it doesn't create ridges, which may trap and funnel water into the leaky area.

Galvanized gutters sometimes corrode. Likewise, wooden gutters decay in spots. To repair such damage, one method is to clean the area thoroughly with a wire brush or coarse sandpaper, coat it thickly with asphalt roofing cement, then press a thickness of heavy-duty aluminum foil into the cement over the damaged area. Apply another layer of cement and another sheet of foil. Finish with a third layer of cement, and smooth it carefully so the patch won't affect the flow of water. For minor pinholes, a dab or two of roofing cement without the foil may be ...

FOOD

By FLORENCE FABRICANT

For Clams, a Simple Sauce and Pasta

ONE of the simplest and quickest yet most pleasing ways to prepare clams is in a simple sauce to put over pasta. Combined with fresh tomatoes or herbs, the dish has a decidedly summertime cast.

The clams to use for dishes such as the ones that follow are the smallest available — littlenecks. These clams are steamed open with various seasonings and served in their shells on the bed of pasta. They are not chopped, as they might be for an old-fashioned red or white clam sauce, so they must be small enough to be tender when eaten whole.

If your fish dealer is willing to cooperate, ask for the smallest possible littlenecks to be selected for you. Before cooking the clams, scrub them well with a brush to remove any grit or sand that might cling to the shells.

The best pasta to use for these dishes is linguine, either plain or green, but not an egg pasta. A medium-sized macaroni such as penne would also be good.

Nancy Duniger

tomatoes or mushrooms). Bring to a simmer, cover the pan and steam the clams until they open.

While the clams are cooking, you should also be cooking the pasta. In fact, it is a good idea to bring the water for the pasta to a boil before adding the clams to the saucepan.

When the clam sauce is finished, the clams will have added their juices. Do not add any ad...

3 tablespoons extra-virgin olive oil
3 cloves garlic, chopped
¼ cup chopped onion
36 littleneck clams, scrubbed
1 cup chopped fresh plum tomatoes
½ cup dry white wine
1 pound linguine
Generous pin...

four warm plates.

4. Season the clams with the hot peppers. Taste the sauce to be sure it is not too salty. If necessary, add a little water to cut the saltiness. Spoon the clams in their shells along with the sauce in the pan over each serving of the linguine. Sprinkle each serving with parsley and basil and serve at once.

1 pound spinach linguine
Freshly ground black pepper
2 tablespoons finely minced chives.

1. Melt the butter in a heavy saucepan. Add the shallots and sauté over low heat until tender. Stir in the mushrooms and sauté until they begin to give off their juices. Stir in the clams.

Departments

There were numerous departments in addition to those illustrated above, including Theater, Art, People, Politics, Letters, and more. The four-line Stymie Black initial signals a departmental feature and provides a dark accent. The scale and excellent graphic quality of the clam illustration is especially effective. Design: Marivi Pulido.

'Psychic Phenomena' lecture in Madison

Bach Family Concert at Ramapo College

Allegra Kent with Edward Villella and New Jersey Ballet Company

Bessie Smith in Black Film Festival at Newark Museum

'Yankee Doodle Fought Here' at Smithville Theater

A Most Baroque Concert in Montclair

Viveca Lindfors in Toms River

New Jersey Puppet Theater in Paramus

Collage

This Week feature occupies a third to a half page, always at the top across the full width of the page. A highlights box was designed to be a collage that was fun to design and would add some sparkle and individual character to the listing. After many years the treatment became more straightforward. Boxes designed by Mary Sillman.

A separate opinion page

Light-hearted Op-Ed

The inside back cover, conceived as an "Opinion" page, ran originally with a half-page, feature-type article facing it. These were later transposed, with the full Opinion page on the left and the half-page on the right. The heading for the page, for example, "New Jersey Opinion" provided an opportunity to repeat the graphic trademark of the diagonal slash on Page One. The sections ran 36 or more pages, and the repetition of the trademark at the end of the section was a reminder of its special identity. Photographs tended to be large and a little more "arty" than elsewhere in the section. Also the page made a good showcase for large illustrations, in a generally lighthearted version of an "Op-Ed" style.

The diagonal slash makes layout at the top a bit tricky. Tucking the slash into the corner of a large photo is the easiest way to make it work. Sometimes awkward white spaces are produced if care is not given to proper placement of the elements around the slash. Like most Op-Ed formats, a bit of audacity each week is needed to keep the page alive and preserve its ability to surprise.

Inside back

Above: The Opinion spread originally placed the full page on the right of the inside back cover spread. This was reversed later to give the ads right-hand page display, but the layouts remained essentially the same.

The slash

Facing page: The design works with the angled banner, an unconventional element encouraging unusual arrangements. The page, top to bottom, is designed as a single harmonious unit. The centered "Educating the Senate" headline avoids the monotony that often dulls such a horizontal treatment. Designed by George Cowan.

NEW JERSEY OPINION

The Infernal Tower

By FRANK TERRANELLA

ASIDE from its use as New York's bedroom, New Jersey also serves as the nesting ground for the transmitters of a number of New York radio stations.

To the casual observer, this fact may mean little outside of the fine radio reception afforded New Jersey residents. However, if you are one of the unfortunates who live in their shadow, the towers become a frustration of Jersey living.

Gazing out of a car window on the New Jersey Turnpike on any evening, you can see their flashing red lights, creatures of the meadowlands. They seem harmless enough with no sign of homes nearby, except for the one being built for the Giants. However, there are many other transmitters in Northern New Jersey that are not quite so remote.

The one I know best is on the outskirts of the town of Lodi. Throwing out 50,000 watts of "top 40" rock 24 hours a day, this giant among transmitters is situated in the midst of one of the most densely populated areas of Bergen County. True, the area was not more serene when the tower was erected. But the eager builders who sold the many houses within feet of the transmitter appear to have given no thought to any inconveniences this was to cause. And so today there are people who pick up their telephones and hear WABC loud and clear.

Transmitters are fickle creatures. Their power outputs vary with direction. Thus, a home 500 yards away may escape the tentacles while another, situated on a strong direction line, may be enveloped a mile away.

I was among the latter. Living about a half-mile from the towering intruder on Route 17 in Lodi, I was an unwilling listener of WABC for three years. What this means is that any transistor radio brought to my home knew only one AM station. My television set never simply flashed "please stand by" when there were interruptions in service. Instead, I had musical interludes by the Jackson Five.

My biggest mistake was buying a $400 stereo. For three years, I never played a record without accompaniment from Big Brother. Picture listening to a soft passage of Debussy, only to have the mood broken by a loud station ID and a gong!

But by far the most annoying prank of the ever-present radio waves was their intrusion in my telephone. Every time I picked up the phone I was greeted with my misplaced Musak even before I got a dial tone. I have friends who to this day think I lived at a radio station for three years.

But that is all in the past now. I've moved to Ridgefield Park, out of the domain of the mighty 770. From time to time I still hear the sounds of my old unwelcome visitor, but always on somebody else's radio.

To the many Jerseyites who continue to suffer so that New York might have radio, I offer my sincere sympathy. For myself, I dream of a pirate AM radio station parked on the front lawn of the president of ABC. ∎

Mr. Terranella, who lives Ridgefield Park, is an editor with the Ossining Citizen Register in Ossining, N.Y.

"HELP, HELP"

Educating the Senate

By JOSEPH W. HUEMER

THE Senate of the State of New Jersey has done it again. Nothing! Nothing in the interests of the people it is supposed to represent; nothing to help the school children who are defenseless against vested money interests. The majority of the Senate voted to defeat the income-tax bill.

Further procrastination on an income tax will wreak incredible havoc in our schools and create chaos beyond repair for years to come.

I have just completed three years supervising student teachers in the schools of Morris, Union, Somerset, Warren, Essex and Sussex Counties for Fairleigh Dickinson University. It was a rewarding experience. I watched many dedicated, efficient and humane teachers in our elementary and high schools work hard to educate our young people. The mediocre or disinterested teacher seemed to be the exception rather than the rule.

It continues to amaze me that public education in this state is as fine as it is, considering the relatively poor support education has had through the first three-quarters of this century. Only now are the most important professionals in our way of life getting a fairly decent living wage—that is, if they will be working next year in New Jersey.

Far more important than all the vicious and deteriorating forces in our society that the teacher must counteract—violence, pornography, alcoholism, drugs, inflated recreational pursuits, greed—is the joy of seeing a child develop. That is the soul-satisfying reward of teaching. The young people are our most precious heritage and our only real ultimate hope.

This should be the time, the Bicentennial year of 1976, to redouble efforts in education. Once again, we have a huge reservoir of talented, eager beginning teachers with no jobs to go to.

This is the time for us to cut our classes in half, to provide more for the academically talented child and for the slower, or somehow handicapped child.

The rewards will far outweigh the minuscule cost. Instead of putting pennies into the education pot and billions into the destruction of all mankind, we should end the nightmare of financially troubled schools.

Senators who have delayed the funding of public education should go. They do not live in the true concept of the Bicentennial New Jersey—which had the finest schools in the country, in the 1920's, 30's, 40's and 50's—should have the best now.

The sooner we awaken to the fact that American education has been the bulwark of our way of life, the sooner we will recharge the destiny of and justify the role of our wonderful America. ∎

Joseph W. Huemer is a Professor of Education at Fairleigh Dickinson University and the author of "The United States in a World of Neighbors." He is also a consultant on the Gifted Child for Morris County.

The "Walkaway" Mental Patients

By PAUL MOGIN AND ROBERT LACK

THE mentally ill have long been society's lepers. Recent events in New Jersey suggest that when mental illness is coupled with criminality — either alleged or proven—public attitudes are likely to be not only apprehensive but almost hysterical.

Several encounters between "walkaway" mental patients and the public—some violent—have triggered a statewide controversy over security at state mental hospitals. In the furor of accusation and denial, charge and countercharge, the danger actually posed by such patients has been vastly exaggerated.

Following the assault on a patrolman outside Marlboro State Psychiatric Hospital in February, police and politicians joined in demanding tighter security, especially for patients charged with or convicted of crimes. On May 3, the State Assembly unanimously approved a bill introduced by a Freehold Democrat, Walter J. Kozloski, that would permit such security for patients on criminal detainers. The Kozloski bill would amend New Jersey's "Mental Patient's Bill of Rights," which stipulates that a patient cannot be placed under tighter security merely because of his criminal record.

It is a sad comment on the lower house of the State Legislature that not one member rose to challenge the Kozloski amendment. The "Bill of Rights'" requirement that security fit the patient's clinical condition makes far more sense than the Kozloski amendment's presumption that criminality implies dangerousness, a presumption several sociological studies contradict.

Singling out detainer patients is a strange response to the walkaway problem, for such patients constitute only a small fraction of the total number of walkaways. At Marlboro, for example, only 15 percent of all walkaways in 1975 were on detainer, and the alleged assailant in the February incident was not a detainer patient at all. Nor are detainer patients a homogenous group: Some have been convicted of crimes, others merely charged; the crimes involved range from murder to traffic violations.

When a policeman gets beaten up, things happen, but in the brouhaha at Marlboro few remembered that this assault was only the third serious walkaway incident in two years of housing almost 900 patients and surviving hundreds of walkaways. It was also forgotten that tightened security would not be without its costs. An environment resembling a prison can hardly be conducive to therapy, and therapy, after all, is the chief purpose of a mental institution.

This does not mean that nothing can be done to prevent walkaways. Much can be achieved by improving diagnoses both at municipal and county jails and at mental hospitals' admissions wards. At present, prisoners know that if they feign a suicide or a psychotic episode they will be sent to one of the low-security mental hospitals.

The answer lies not in turning the mental hospitals into jails, but in keeping these manipulators from reaching the mental hospitals in the first place.

Although better screening can reduce the walkaway problem, there is little reason to believe it can eliminate it altogether. As long as mental hospitals are not prisons, there will always be the occasional incident, the incident that some will find reason to exaggerate. Others may perhaps accept such a risk as a tolerable price to pay for a just and humane society. ∎

Paul Mogin and Robert Lack are students in the research program in criminal justice at Princeton University's Woodrow Wilson School of Public and International Affairs.

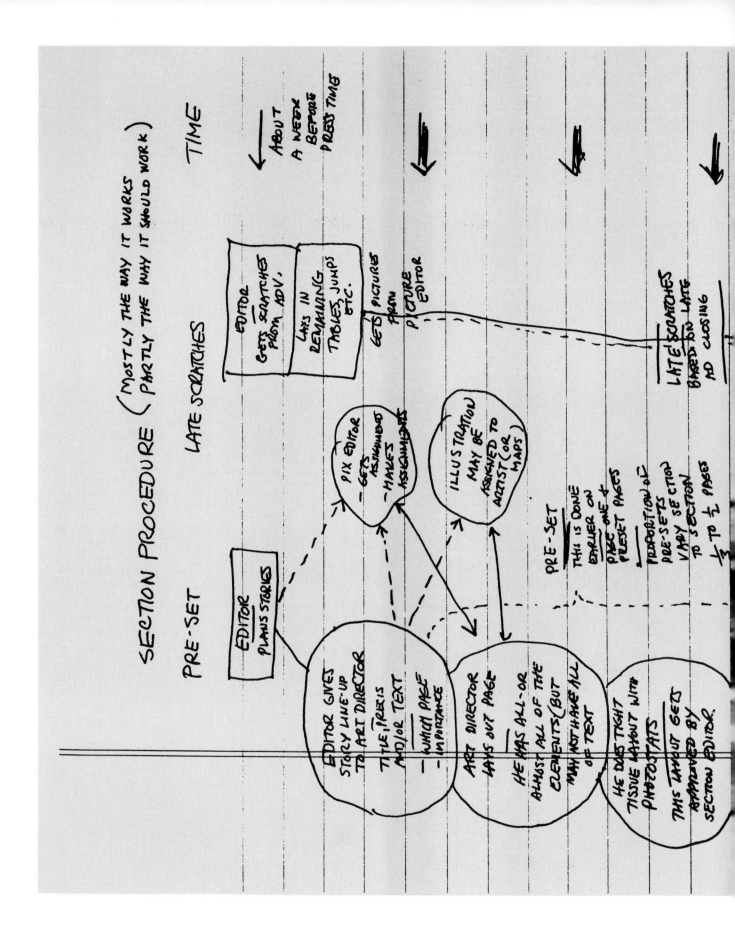

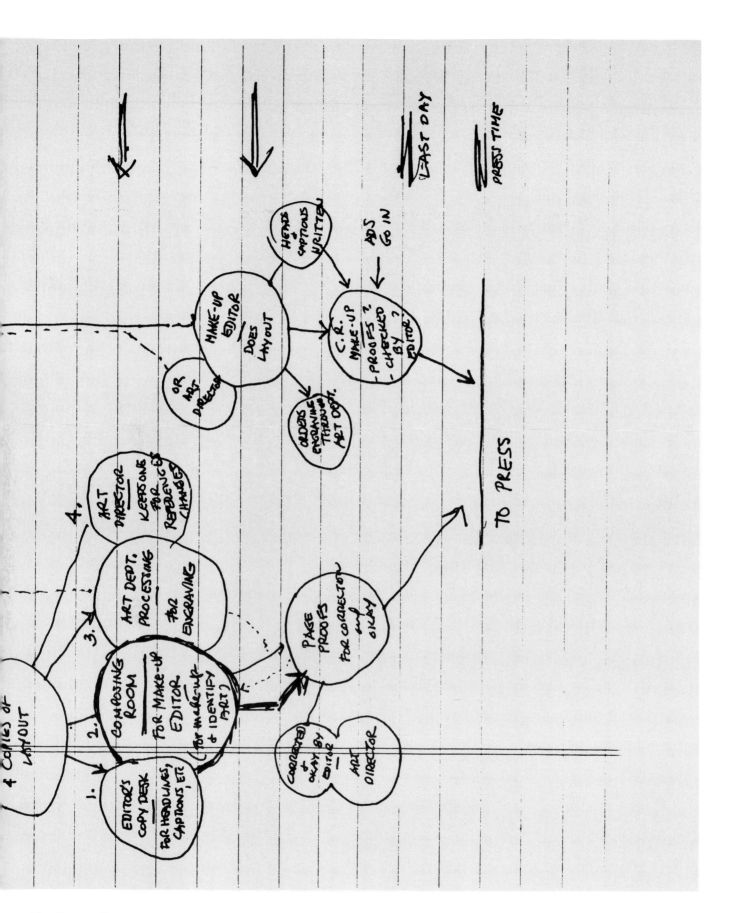

Design and procedure

In kicking off the new weeklies, I attempted in this drawing to visualize the weekly creative and production procedures. It was necessary to understand the working relationships between the News, Production, and Business Departments and to design new procedures to accommodate the needs of the art director, a new and essential cog in the machine. Designing procedures were part of the design process.

23

Ralph STEAD

By William E. Co

The C.I.A. and the Public

in deducing how we must have learned of it and shutting us off from it.

I might add that we do not censor

Congress has provided for itself a way of resolving the dilemma between the need for secrecy in intelligence

ican principles and that it must more open and responsive to our pi lic than the intelligence activities

The idea of Op-Ed

Background

The idea of a new "Opinion" page was formally kicked off at *The Times* at a meeting in 1967 in the publisher's conference room. (I had never heard the expression "Op-Ed" before; as far as I know, the expression was born with the page.) Arthur Ochs Sulzberger presided over the meeting, which included the top executives in the News, Sunday, Editorial, and Business Departments. The purpose of the meeting was to discuss the idea and feasibility of this new page in the daily paper.

At the time, I was promotion art director of *The Times*. I had been promoted to the job after the departure of my predecessor, George Krikorian. I had worked hard over some dozen years to continue the high standards he had set. The chief executives of the company increasingly consulted me on various design projects for the newspaper itself. These assignments usually came from Mr. Sulzberger or from Ivan Veit, who at the time of the initial Op-Ed meeting was executive vice president of the company. Mr. Veit was promotion director when I joined *The Times'* promotion department; with his expanded role in the company came expanded and interesting assignments for me.

One assignment had been the conversion of the paper's text face to a larger, more legible design. Another assignment was modernizing the Sunday section nameplates. At that time, the section headings featured boxes in the two "ears" right and left of the title, with the section numeral repeated on each side. Among other changes, the redesign eliminated this duplication and placed the number in the right-hand corner only. This was hardly revolutionary, but it provoked one elderly reader to complain that as a long-time reader in Connecticut he walked every Sunday to

Before
In the years before the Op-Ed page, obituaries and miscellaneous news items ran on the page facing the editorial page.

his local vendor and flipped through the sections, from the *left* side, to make sure all the sections were there. His complaint: The number was now on the wrong side!

At that first Op-Ed meeting, James Reston, then executive editor, spoke eloquently of the need for a new forum in *The Times,* where what he termed "the frontier of ideas" could be given due coverage. Other editors expressed the need to publish points of view different from those expressed by our editorials or staff columnists.

Over many months I worked with different editors on the project, but the basic design remained essentially the same—a structured page, with Bookman headings, all the same size, in non-news style. The first dummy layout featured a drawing by the West German artist Hans-Georg Rauch.

A question arose initially about whether there should be an ad on the page. Eventually a design accommodating an optional quarter-page ad was selected. It seemed to us to occasionally run an ad on the page would be an asset. The ad would relate this forum of ideas to the real world and to the rest of the newspaper. As a premium ad especially designed by advertisers for the page, it would help pay for the expanded space and the planned, high quality illustrations.

The page finally got the go-ahead under the direction of Harrison Salisbury, with Herbert Mitgang as deputy editor. Agreeing from the start that we must seek different graphic solutions than those offered by political cartoons, we made field trips to libraries and art galleries. We also wished to avoid using artists who were already associated with any other publication.

We agreed from the start also that we would not run a drawing in a size that made it look too small. To attract the best artists we had to ensure that their work would be effectively displayed. I drew up a scale of payments that was considerably more than newspapers were accustomed to paying but considerably less than some of the artists we anticipated using could expect from magazines or advertising clients. At first this was hinged on the degree of creative contribution. A mere "illustration" of a written piece was worth one price, but a "conceptual" drawing in which the artist added some unique idea was worth more. This became laughably unmanageable, and I settled on a more mundane approach—a unit of payment for each column width.

With the new Op-Ed page on the right side of the spread, it was necessary to fine-tune the editorial page on the left to make the pages compatible with each other.

We started the page with the part-time help of a picture editor, Sally Forbes, and an art director, Bob Melson. David Schneiderman soon joined as assistant editor. J. C. Suarez, who had a wide acquaintance with European artists, joined the staff as my assistant and then as art director of the page. Under his direction and then under successive art directors—George Delmerico, Steve Heller, Pam Vassil, and Jerelle Kraus, who worked on the page for eight years—the flow of good art became a flood. Artists from Europe, South America, India, and Pakistan brought exotic spice to *The Times'* corridors.

I have no doubt that, appearing as it did in the daily newspaper, in the heart of what was then considered the "good gray *Times,*" the Op-Ed page helped set the climate for design changes that followed, for the creation of new sections, and for the direct involvement of designers and art directors in the editorial process.

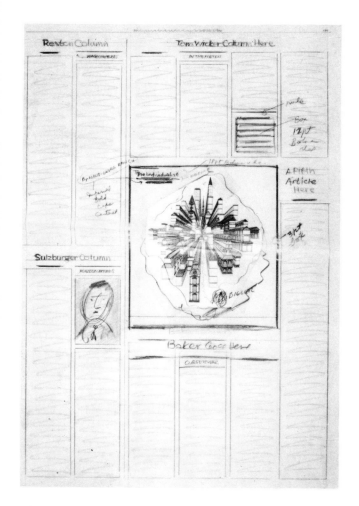

First rough

The first sketch for an Op-Ed page is shown. Basics were all-the-same-size Bookman headlines departing from a "newsy" feeling; the kind of conceptual drawing done by West German artist, Hans-Georg Rauch; and a wider-than-normal six-column measure.

27

A time of anger
Bad for the country, good for Op-Ed

Eugene Mihaesco

In the early 1970s, in the first years of the Op-Ed page, the country was going through a time of anger, conflict, and frustration over such divisive issues as the war in Vietnam, the struggle for civil rights, Watergate, the near-impeachment of Richard Nixon, concern about the environment, the use of nuclear power, and emerging roles of Third World countries. Underlying was a current of doubt about basic American values, seen in the articles on these issues and phenomena like the "generation gap" and student unrest. As if to counter these concerns, a minor undercurrent of nostalgia for a real or fancied more satisfactory American past also found expression in articles that were paeans to such subjects as old New York, the month of February, middle age, and the double decker bus.

It was a bad time for the country but a good time to start the Op-Ed page. Overnight appeared this prominent new forum where politicians, experts, and ordinary citizens could make themselves heard in a way that went far beyond a "Letter to the Editor." Today, when virtually every newspaper, big or small, includes an Op-Ed page in its basic content, it seems remarkable that before 1969 the concept barely existed, and the appellation "Op-Ed" did not exist at all.

Op-Ed art

The kind of art that appeared on the page and set the tone for what is now often referred to as "Op-Ed art" stemmed from two sources. First was the desire to use illustrations on the page that were not political cartoons. Political cartoonists have had and enjoy today an unquestionably important place in newspaper journalism. Since cartoons in newspapers, particularly on editorial pages, were prevalent it seemed imperative that we use different graphic techniques if we were to project a sense of something new.

Fortunately, the desire for something graphically new coincided with a longstanding policy of *The Times* to avoid running its own political cartoons on the editorial page or anywhere else. This firm policy stands as a tribute to the perceived power of the visual image or at least to the power

of political cartoonists. Over its long history, *The Times* has been more than willing to engage in the editorial give-and-take that the divergent points of view of writers and columnists inevitably project in words. But it has never wished, nor seen the necessity, to give to an individual cartoonist the kind of dominant voice a political cartoon would carry on its editorial page.

This traditional attitude undoubtedly played a part in the acceptance of the new Op-Ed art among editors at the paper, since the art usually conveyed a general, often cosmic view. An article might deal with the torture of political prisoners

Mihaesco on Nixon
Above: Eugene Mihaesco rendered with wit and precision President Richard Nixon's precarious position in one of the legal disputes following Watergate disclosures. Mihaesco was one of the early contributors to the Op-Ed page.

One of the shapers
Facing page: Brad Holland's broad statements ideally suited the Op-Ed page and helped shape its image. Conceptual and graphic daring and draftmanship go hand in hand in the flow of tears and the mysterious flying wisp above the head.

HOLLAND

Brad Holland

The Meaning of Grief

By Peter Marris

CAMBRIDGE, MASS.
a severe personal loss,
the purposes attached
em to have become un-
re at first numbed and
ng, angry, guilty, sleep-
eek release from their

conflicting impulses —
o escape into a future
orgotten and new pur-
ningful again.
e other: The comfort of
recalls the anguish of
is to deny all that the
rouses anxieties of be-

these conflicted emo-
lly and painfully begin
ntinuity in their lives,
oss, yet rescues the es-
ose of the past, so that
deepest attachments

re a crisis of meaning.
f an exhausting effort
emotional as practical.
s to work itself out in
ts our familiar expecta-
— divorce, retirement,
metimes even when we
bewildered by its con-

provoked by personal
a disintegration of our
rld in which we seek to

nay be so gradual that
ere it began, nor when
wledge it. But we then
eavement, which will
s to grief, both in our
d as a social drama.
instance, I read in my
is the worst since the
partmental meeting, the
of permanent positions
se news, perhaps, next
ermarket, I cannot be-
gs of routine groceries.
former director of the
cy admits that he de-

es reinforces a nagging
of the familiar assump-
life — that my money
it it seems to promise,
s earn me a living, that
stem under democratic

d is a deeper anxiety
nds on a careless ex-
esources, which is al-
to starvation. As such
nulate, the mood grows
uncertainty about our
trol events, which de-

deny this loss of meaning. For if our assumptions collapse, none of the skills by which we have learned to manage our lives are any longer trustworthy. We cling to the hope that a new President, more adroit economic management, luck and technological resourcefulness will set the problems to rights in predictable ways.

But the more events undermine the complacency of this underlying conservatism, the more it shades into a grief reaction — a retreat into a past we cannot recover, whose nostalgic security only makes the reality of the present more unbearable.

At the same time, radical movements that seek a total reconstruction of society broaden their appeal, for they offer an escape into a coherent future, to which our present confused and cor-rupted purposes are irrelevant.

it cannot resolve them, and so becomes abortive and destructive, like a morbid grief. It displaces the conflict into a political struggle, which no longer recognizes the personal search for meaning in a confused social context.

We cannot work out our ambivalence by alternating between these ideological refuges as the bereaved alternate, because each has externalized and made an enemy of the impulse it cannot contain, and demands an unwavering loyalty. Hence we need to find social expressions of the ambivalence of loss, which neither deny it nor displace it, but articulate a common search for meaning.

Tribal institutions have evolved in contemporary Africa, for instance, which both reassert the traditional ideals of tribal society and yet or-

work of p
which peop
amid the co
without sel
tural inheri

In much
States have
tural roots
more meani
contradicts
to their exp
ized about
ance by soc

Hence th
and trouble
ments and
uals of mo
pressions of
mately rec

The wom
responding
grief at the
that seems
tween none
uality, and
altogether
terms.

This exc
tradictory
conventiona
of any mov
perience of
alent, it mu
they can be
us is searc
lives, we ca
experiences
own.

Those wh
resolutions
stand in th
may seem.
gration of a
without ma
gration.

The insti
solutions w
tutions and
pressive of
which at
Hence grie
overwhelm
obtuse gest

If we can
text of life
a sense of
stand and
their grief.
grief in oth
the reality
natives tha
for, we will
ess of reint
tive for eve

Peter Marr

by a Central American dictator. The illustration might show creatures in a jungle or nails piercing a wall. At its best an Op-Ed illustration looked more *important* than a cartoon and provoked viewer participation in a way associated with the appreciation of fine art. Sometimes, however, an

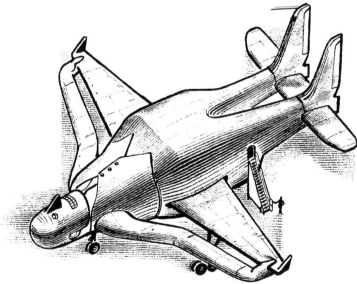

von Woerkom and Suter

Top: An illustration by Fons von Woerkom, a Dutch artist who came to New York via *The Toronto Star*, for a piece by Senator Patrick Moynihan on a United States caste system. Bottom: David Suter's double images seem to speak simultaneously in the artist's and analyst's voices. The illustration accompanied a piece by Senator William Proxmire on the deficit.

illustration would be mystifying. When this happened, comments ranged from good-natured acceptance of an errant attempt at brilliance to the hostile fury sometimes seen in viewers of Ad Reinhardt's virtually all-black canvas called "Black on Black" at the Hirschorn Museum in Washington.

The second factor in the development of the Op-Ed style was the prevailing mood of frustration and anger that found expression on the page, a natural environment for illustrations that in some ways went beyond even the best satire of the political cartoon. The climate led to artists who dealt often in broad themes and whose techniques, though widely varied, tended to be slower, denser, and often more intricate than newspaper readers were accustomed to in cartoons.

Op-Ed art drawings tend to be conceptual, serious, "artistic," more dark than light in mood. Many of the drawings borrow from surrealism in juxtaposing apparently unrelated elements. Techniques vary greatly and imaginatively; they can be traced at least as much to the world of fine art as to the world of commercial illustration.

In general, the techniques feature cross-hatch, fine, and elaborate linework that suggests wood engraving, and painstaking draftsmanship, of a quality seen more in galleries or quality magazines than in newspapers. Artists who appeared in the early months and contributed to the ongoing character of the page include: Ralph Steadman, from England; Fons von Woerkom, from Holland; Brad Holland, Anita Siegel, and Marshall Arisman, from the United States; Eugene Mihaesco, from Romania; Hans-Georg Rauch, from West Germany; and Topor and Colos, from France. There were many, many others. The first drawing to appear in the section was by Ralph Steadman. It was a cheerless view of depraved-looking victims of urban living groping blindly down a somewhat abstract street of vertical lines. I had come across the drawing at a party in Steadman's apartment in London and had brought it back, anticipating that it would not be long before the new Op-Ed page ran an article on urban decay.

Photographers, too, contributed to the Op-Ed character. In particular, the surrealist photos of Jerry Uelsmann and the dreamlike sequences of Duane Michaels appeared.

But it was not all heavy going. There was room for an occasional A. O. Blechman airy drawing, a collage, or a whimsical treatment of old engravings.

The dark side

Top: Ralph Steadman's drawing, accompanying a piece on the dark side of city life, ran the second day of the new page. Left: Anita Siegel's intricately designed collage illustrations contributed to a resurgence of the technique in magazines and newspapers. With Siegel, and other Op-Ed artists, initial distrust of *The Times* as an "establishment" bastion had to be overcome.

Editorial page

Tombstone to horizontal

Over a period of about 20 years starting in the 1960s, printed rules in newspapers went from generally vertical to generally horizontal, following the pattern of the page make-up itself.

The Times' editorial page had been strictly vertical in days of hot metal, as were the pages in most papers. The editorials ran all the way down one column, then jumped up to the top of the second column. The columnists and letters "tombstoned" down the page from the headings lined up at the top. The column headings were set in Bodoni, which, with the other typefaces on the page, made an odd but not atypical combination, for that era. The columns of type were set close together in the style of the newspapers of the day, separated by vertical column rules.

Between the earlier period of vertical rules and the present one emphasizing horizontal rules, a brief period existed when newspapers used very few rules. This occurred in the early days of cold type, when papers were trying to cope with the new paste-up techniques. It is no coincidence, I believe, that publishers began to see the esthetic merit of "white space" and a more open page at the same time it began to cost more to print rules. In the days of hot metal production, the compositor had to separate the columns of type with a strip of metal, whether or not the metal printed. The printing of the rule was free, so to speak. But in cold type production, to print a rule involved the positioning of an adhesive strip of tape, an extra operation. Furthermore, in

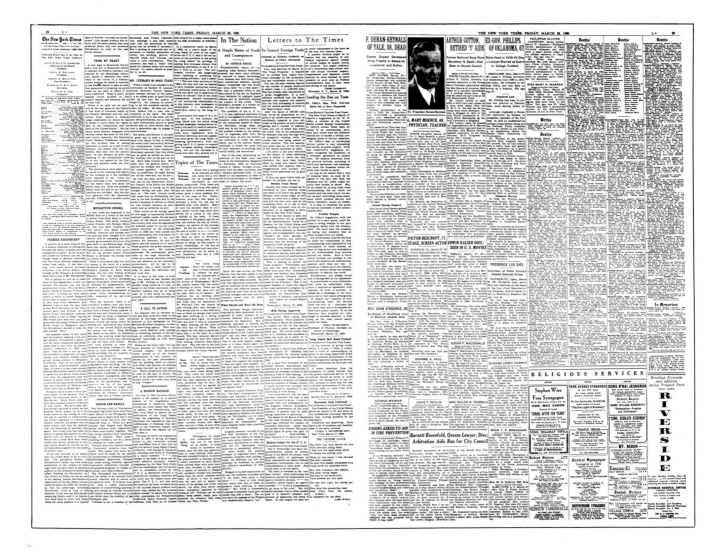

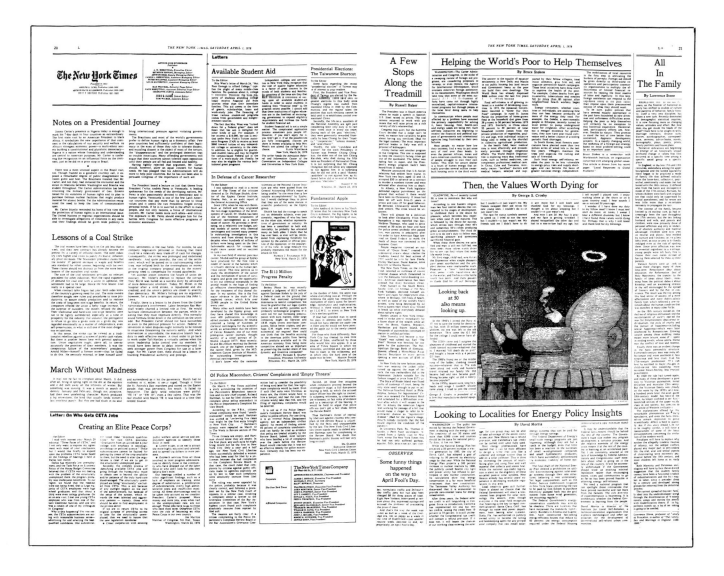

the first somewhat chaotic, fumbling days of cold type, these delicate, flexible tapes which needed to be placed by well-trained eyes and hands were likely to be crooked, or wobbly, or pasted in the wrong place. Therefore, rules in general went out of fashion for a while.

When the Op-Ed page was created, an important by-product was more space for letters on the editorial page, which could now occupy a full vertical half of the page. With so many letters, it was desirable to revive use of horizontal rules positioned directly above and below the type of the letter headings. The rules helped to structure and organize the mass of unequal texts and foster a feeling of alignment.

The use of horizontal rules above and below a headline derived from contemporary magazine usage. Magazines, in turn, had found inspiration in earlier newspapers, when cut-off rules, graduated rules, and typographical dingbats were commonly used. In contemporary usage the horizontal rules fill the full measure of the column, which helps to define the column measure

Evolution

Facing page (1958 vertical): Editorial page spread before redesign and the facing page use extreme vertical make-up, with "tombstone" headings typical at the time. Above (1978 horizontal): After Op-Ed, the editorial page shows sharply strengthened typography, horizontal make-up combined with a vertical feeling, and use of horizontal rules. Note the separation of masthead names into top and bottom boxes to keep from overwhelming the top.

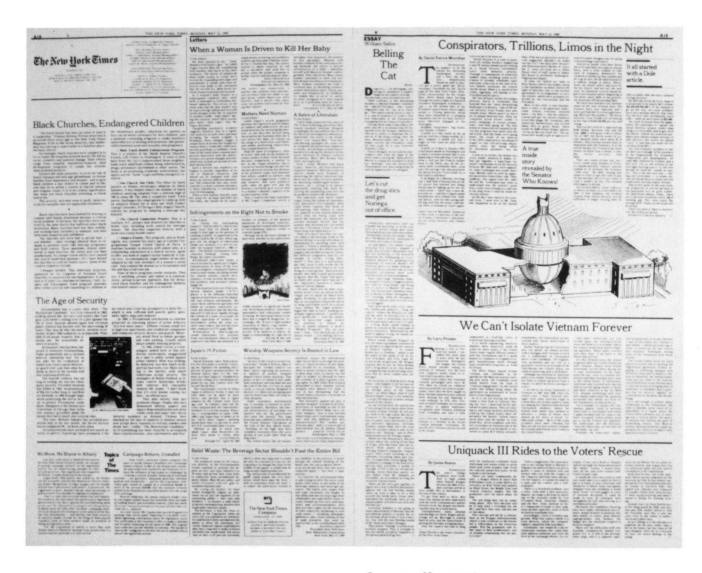

Sans serif accent

1988 spread shows further changes in use of Franklin Gothic as a sans serif accent on the editorial page and more flexibility, with pictures, in the editorial columns.

and imparts a trim and aligned appearance that helps make up for the absence of the old vertical rules.

Editorials

The editorial page was designed on a vertical axis first, down the center, to allow subway readers to fold the paper vertically and not go crazy trying to read across the fold. Then the page was divided into horizontal units to give the reader less formidable stretches of type to read and a quicker grasp of the elements on the page. Also the horizontal units built headline accents, and this provided restful spaces into the middle parts of the page.

Editorial headlines were increased in size to accompany the increased horizontal measure of the text to give them appropriate importance in the editorial and Op-Ed spread when seen as a whole.

A traditional element on the editorial page had been "Topics of The Times," a column of comment on miscellaneous matters, which did not carry the weight of editorial opinion. It ran a couple of times a week and was moved to the bottom of the newly widened editorial columns.

A variety of voices

Other elements were invented by the editors to provide a variety of voices in addition to the full-fledged stentorian voice of the editorials themselves. "The Editorial Notebook," a signed comment on a local issue, and "Worms and Apples," a forum where good and bad developments in the life of the city could be recognized or condemned, were examples.

Not only did these elements give the editorial page editors ways to deal with different degrees of opinion, they also gave the make-up of the editorial columns a welcome flexibility. No longer did the editorials arbitrarily have to fill up the same amount of space every day. For the reader, the varied elements provide more inviting typography as well as a welcome range of content from formal to informal.

Keeping up with Op-Ed

Modest typographical changes and the use of small illustrations were considered in making a harmonious two-page spread with the Op-Ed page. The editorial page is appropriately quieter than the Op-Ed page but is in the same typographical mode.

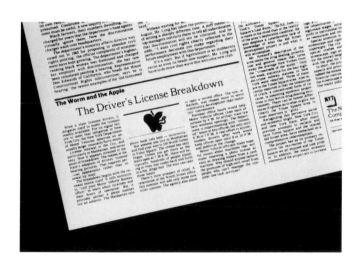

Different voices
Shown are two of the features that give the editorial page editor a variety of voices. Running at the bottom of the editorial columns, they relieve the editorials of the necessity of occupying exactly the same space every day.

Breaking the mold

Surprise, accents, scale

At its best, the Op-Ed page exploited possibilities for flexibility and variety in layout that could delight and surprise as much as the art itself. But inevitably its appearance in the same place every day with its built-in limitations placed a heavy burden on the ability of the designer to always provide a surprising look. With such frequent exposure even the most unusual kind of art unfortunately began to appear less exceptional. Like television, the page became a voracious consumer of talent.

Certain built-in factors do inhibit free-wheeling design. These include the daily existence of one or more columns that are always the same predetermined length; the quarter-page advertisement that runs in the lower right-hand corner; and the format rules that dictate short, usually one-line, feature-style headings of a prescribed size.

But selection of unexpected content material, surprise in the treatment of illustration, and wit in the use of type was encouraged. The latter, for example, often led to long, amusing, multiline headlines and off-beat use of large initials.

Change of pace

Above left: Models constructed by Roger Law and Peter Fluck were photographed in *The Times* studio. Unexpectedly exaggerated indentation accents the vertical panel and provides a change of pace. Design: Steve Heller.

Poem

Left: The generous space allotted to the poem, balancing the white space in the blurb on the right side of the page, and oversize initials offer the reader a surprisingly different look. Illustration by Brad Holland; Design: Steve Heller.

Unifying illustration

Facing page: Two articles on drugs are tied together in this illustration by Brad Holland. Design: Steve Heller.

Lisbon's Shrinking Nest Egg

By C. L. Sulzberger

LISBON — Portugal's revolution, whose ultimate course remains unclear, was historically both prompted and financed by the right-wing, army-supported dictatorship created by Antonio de Oliveira Salazar. The revolution has so far succeeded only in creating a left-wing military dictatorship.

A violent change had been prompted by the fact that Salazar left this country West Europe's poorest, least healthy and most illiterate, stuck with an untenable empire. Yet revolution was backed by an emergency nest egg of almost $5 billion in hard currency hoarded by the stingy strongman.

It was inevitable that the house of cards bequeathed by Salazar should tumble down and that the pretentious, costly imperial claims in Guinea, Mozambique and Angola should dissolve in violence and discouragement that finally focused here at home.

The professional officers, who had fought uselessly against the world's decolonialist tide, brought back Marxist ideas nourished by their own bitter disappointment and mustered behind the temporary figurehead of General Spinola to turn a new page.

As revolutions go, this one came in a bear market. The international recession hasn't made things in the least bit easy for the group of officers now running the show to the counterpoint of a confusion of argument among politicians—mostly in various Marxist shades (politicians including several returned from exile).

Portugal is losing foreign exchange at the rate of about $1.5 billion a year. This means that unless the flow can be staunched, Salazar's nest egg won't last beyond 1978. Some aid and credits have been negotiated (including from the United States) but the ruling Armed Forces Movement (A.F.M.) finds itself forced to spend capital before any final decision has been taken on where the revolution is headed.

Because of endemic unemployment (near 10 per cent) about a million Portuguese have temporarily emigrated to West Europe in search of jobs. Remittances they send, which used to total about $700 million—Portugal's largest source of foreign currency—have already shrunk more than 25 per cent and are steadily declining as the workers are squeezed back home. The number two source of hard money, tourism, once $400 million annually, has fallen perhaps 80 per cent.

Economically the country is hard hit. Although wages have been doubled, they still average little more than $40 weekly because this is an underdeveloped land. Assorted labor troubles have caused shutdowns; production has suffered; some foreign plants have closed; and the A.F.M. decrees that workers shall not be discharged.

As a result, factories produce goods they cannot sell; inventories have climbed to an unhealthy degree; and firms threatened with bankruptcy are

FOREIGN AFFAIRS

bailed out by nationalizations. Workers are still on payrolls but the Government is acquiring ownership of uneconomic properties as long-term disaster shapes up.

Added to this is the problem of returning refugees from former colonies. Day after day planes arrive loaded with families and their bundles, without funds or the promise of jobs. Ultimately they are likely to add extra social, economic and even security burdens (above all disgruntled ex-soldiers).

Last year, following the initial phase of the "flower revolution" behind the facade of General Spinola, the A.F.M. issued a program stressing the three D's—decolonization, democratization, development. Decolonization has succeeded and basically the people are pleased. But democratization is a dead letter, caught up in party repressions and factional divisions within the A.F.M. itself. Development hasn't even begun.

Since March 11, when Spinola fled the country after an unsuccessful coup attempt to get back the power he had lost, the A.F.M. has taken some genuine revolutionary steps. It nationalized banks and insurance companies which loomed large on the dictatorship's horizon because of Salazar's financial bias.

This move was well received; most people correctly blamed giant private institutions for Portugal's over-all backwardness. The A.F.M. also began land reforms.

But few important other social or economic moves have been made and freedom is vanishing. There are increased mutterings asking what the revolution is about. These are by no means answered by the plethora of exhortatory posters and slogans covering city walls. And in the north, which contains two-thirds of Portugal's nine million population, a reactionary Church—lagging behind contemporary Spain's in secular outlook—dominates a very considerable body of opposition.

Because of these factors the revolution marks time as the A.F.M. seemingly consolidates military dictatorship while talking about austerity, wage restraints and the production battle. Economic chickens are coming home to roost. Before you can say Antonio de Oliveira Salazar they will be pecking away at the late dictator's reactionary nest egg.

Brad Holland

The Poppy Whose Sap Is Anti-Life

By Charles B. Rangel

WASHINGTON — The deadly red opium poppies of Turkey are again in full bloom—legally.

When the Turkish Government announced its unilateral decision to lift the ban on opium-poppy cultivation, in violation of executive agreements, it gave repeated assurances that it would act to prevent illegal diversion of opium gum, the raw material for heroin. But now the poppies are being harvested without any evidence that adequate controls have been imposed.

Pious promises are not sufficient to block the flow of Turkey's drugs into the United States.

There have been some arrests of Turkish farmers for planting more than their quota of poppies, but the "cautious optimism" of many Turkish and American officials over successful policing of the crop is still unwarranted. As one spokesman for the Drug Enforcement Administration realistically noted, "Their record on controlling the farmers has not been good in the past."

Since the planting of the new crop last fall, United States Federal and state law-enforcement agencies report that heroin stockpiled during the ban is being released for sale. The dealers anticipate additional supplies from the 1975 crop.

The Drug Enforcement Administration has admitted that it cannot effectively stem the flood of drugs into our country. The truth of that confession is already evident on the streets of New York. Higher quality heroin from the stockpiles is now available in greater quantity. In fact, the Drug Enforcement Administration has told me that the latest Turkish crop will hit New York's streets in late August and early September.

While the 1975 crop is estimated to be 50 per cent larger than earlier crops, the Administration has adopted a "don't step on anyone's toes" attitude. Our representatives at the State Department and at the United Nations are content to dance in diplomatic circles and ignore Turkey's failure to act. Apparently they have also forgotten that the United States paid Turkish farmers over $35 million not to grow opium poppies. Initial White House opposition to the lifting of the ban has melted into politely expressed concern over possible diversion without insistence on workable controls.

In addition, the United States is giving another $3 million in technical aid to Turkey to help enforce the new regulations.

Secretary of State Kissinger traveled to Turkey in May to discuss the Cyprus situation. President Ford is now pushing Congress to resume arms sales to Turkey.

Despite the vote of the House International Affairs Committee to lift the arms embargo, many members of Congress feel that no satisfactory agreement can be reached on either Cyprus or military aid without strong Turkish action to prevent drug traffic.

Turkey asks America to trust her good faith. In light of how little we have learned about how Turkey intends to insure that her crop is used only for pharmaceutical purposes, that is a naive request while heroin addiction continues at a tragic rate.

While newsmen have been given access to the poppy fields as part of a Turkish public-relations offensive, experts from the Drug Enforcement Administration and the United Nations have been denied full opportunity to supervise the policing effort.

The Ford Administration cannot sit silently while a bumper crop of poppies is harvested and the incidence of heroin abuse in New York City rises to the epidemic levels of the late nineteen-sixties. The President should promptly convene the National Security Council to devise a strategy for combating the smuggling of narcotics into the United States.

When President Ford speaks of maintaining American strength in world affairs, he should keep in mind the lives of hundreds of thousands of our own youth, not simply the seizure of a merchant ship.

Charles B. Rangel, Democrat, represents New York's 19th District in Congress, and is chairman of the Congressional Black Caucus.

Drugs Whose Flowers Are Life

By Stephen L. DeFelice

To all our other troubles, add one more—a crisis in the discovery of valuable and needed new drugs.

Drugs are by far the most effective weapons in the treatment of patients. Imagine life today without polio vaccine, penicillin, digitalis, insulin, diuretics, anesthetics, tranquilizers and all the other drugs that keep us alive and free of pain.

Today, few valuable new drugs are being discovered in the United States. Little or no experimentation is being done to discover them. Our system of drug discovery offers little hope of a cure for our four million diabetic patients, our 23 million hypertensive patients, or the millions who suffer from such devastating diseases as multiple sclerosis, schizophrenia, rheumatoid arthritis or heart disease.

The principal blame for this lies with Congress, which has evidently accepted consumerism's false ideal of a completely no-risk existence and has forced upon the Food and Drug Administration such restrictive regulations as to discourage drug investigation and thus effectively cut down new drug discovery.

This country has the brain power, the technology and the money to restore us to world leadership in drug discovery. What we lack is an environment conducive to and supportive of a more productive discovery system.

There are two phases in drug discovery. One is preclinical—pharmacology, chemistry, toxicology and other types of nonhuman research. The other, however, the clinical phase, is the critical one. Every hypothesis or observation made preclinically must be tested in humans before a potential discovery becomes a reality.

This is where our hang-up is. The consumerists will not let us forget the horror of thalidomide or the immorality of the untreated syphilitic patients at Tuskegee, although the lessons of both have been long since absorbed.

"Our ethic in this country," a former F.D.A. commissioner has observed, "does not permit — at least not in present-day context—a needless surrender of one life."

But we know this to be false. Everything we do in living our lives today involves some risk, and most of us add to that from time to time.

The fact is that human experimentation under controlled conditions carries with it no risk greater than we take every day in our travels, our work, our athletic pursuits.

Surgical procedure labors under no such restrictions as do drugs. In the last decade, surgery has achieved miracles. Drug discovery, on the other hand, has fallen precipitously. Yet surgery affects far fewer people than does drug therapy.

It is obvious that we need a new system of drug discovery and a movement is being organized to educate the public and the Congress in this need and its solution.

There are five positive actions that should be taken. We should:

- Reduce Federal control over innovative clinical drug research and return responsibility for supervision to the experts, the academic community.
- Return the role of the F.D.A. to its proper competence—supervision of drugs already on the market or scheduled to go there. Most adverse effects come from old but indispensable drugs, like digitalis and insulin, because their use is not closely monitored as are new drugs under clinical study.
- Provide insurance—probably Government insurance — against damage suits to institutions, drug research committees and clinical investigators.
- Initiate a new specialty in medical schools, the clinical drug developer —a generalist able to guide new drugs through the complexity of scientific judgments and social barriers.
- Make a national effort to assemble groups of volunteers from among all parts of the population—the healthy, the sick, the rich, the poor—who would be available to help evaluate new drug ideas.

The amount of physical and mental suffering that exists today, despite all our modern therapy, is vast. In scientific, social and moral terms, it is certainly acceptable and even desirable for some of us to take small risks, even big ones, to diminish this vastness.

Stephen L. DeFelice, M.D., a drug expert and former chief of clinical pharmacology at Walter Reed Army Institute of Research, is the author of "Drug Discovery: The Pending Crisis."

Separating American Messages

By Frank Stanton

The Commission on the Organization of the Government for the Conduct of Foreign Policy, appointed by the Congress and the President, issued its report on July 1. Among its many recommendations, a section on the American overseas informational and cultural programs endorses the findings of an independent nongovernment panel.

Our panel of experts, which I had the privilege of heading, was constituted because over the last few years those in and out of Congress concerned with the oversight of these programs have questioned their effectiveness and organizational arrangements in today's interdependent world.

We learned that what is usually called the information and cultural program or public diplomacy is really composed of two quite separate functions: the articulation of day-to-day American policies, and the cultural communications programs supporting longer-range policy objectives.

Since all of these efforts are intended for overseas audiences, there are clear differences in the way these audiences accept our *political* messages and our *cultural* messages. They know that the former flow from the Government, while the latter come from the American scene as a whole. They accept the political messages as Government controlled; they welcome the cultural messages precisely because they consider them not to be governmentally controlled.

As George Kennan recently stated: "The Government does not make culture and should not try to use it as a means of political expression and propaganda. The cultural community, on the other hand, does not make policy and should not seek or bear the responsibility for stating it."

There should be a separation between the conduct of *political*-information operations and *cultural*-information operations. Other countries recognize this separation. While I do not want to suggest this course because of the practice of others, it is neither novel nor untried.

■

Having decided conceptually to separate the direct support of foreign policy—the articulation and advocacy role—from the indirect support of foreign policy—the cultural communications role—and having further decided that both are necessary and mutually supportive elements of a dynamic foreign policy, we concluded that they must be organized separately to be effective.

The articulation and advocacy of current foreign policy requires the closest kind of operational integration with the State Department's policy process and hence should be located in the department. The cultural communications operation, however, should be a step removed organizationally from this process. It should concentrate on programs designed to create and reinforce favorable attitudes about this country without being harassed by day-to-day foreign policy issues. The long-range strategic objectives should be pursued without the pressure of tactical policy requirements.

The longer-range cultural operations have been, on the whole, more effective. This cultural-information operation should be in a separate agency, not in the State Department but with its director reporting to the Secretary of State, since his operations are conducted in support of foreign policy.

■

What of the Voice of America? It has three functions: to broadcast accurate, effective, and comprehensive news; to portray the variety and uniqueness of American society; to present the foreign policy of the United States.

The Voice is a tactical tool for policy articulation and, at the same time, a strategic tool for cultural communications. In addition, and most importantly, it is a broadcaster of news. The structural conclusion is evident: Since it is impractical to divide the Voice or to have it located in three places at once, the problem is obviously to choose the functional location which does least violence to the performance of the other two functions. Placing it in either the State Department or in the new agency would severely compromise its independence as a source of news. A location outside either of these bodies would avoid this and other problems.

The Voice should be set up as a Federal agency under a board of directors, five in number, reflecting its functions. The Secretary of State would be represented on the board to see that the policy articulation function is adequately fulfilled. The director of the new agency would be on the board to advise on the portrayal of American society, and three members from the private sector, having broad experience in public diplomacy and appointed by the President with the approval of the Senate, would round out the board. This arrangement would permit the Voice to function as a credible medium serving the interests of the United States.

Frank Stanton served as chairman of the Panel on International Information, Education and Cultural Relations, Center for Strategic and International Studies, Georgetown University. He was formerly president of CBS, Inc.

Education of Derek Bok

By ANTHONY LEWIS

CAMBRIDGE, Mass., March 26—Some undergraduates invited Harvard's president-elect to tea the other day, and he went. That may not sound like news. At this university, after thirty years of presidential remoteness from students, it is.

Derek Bok, preparing to take over from Nathan Pusey in July, has quietly begun to make a new presence felt at Harvard. He decided not to move into the president's official res-

AT HOME ABROAD

idence, in the College Yard, because he and his wife thought it an inappropriate place to bring up their children. Instead they will live a short distance away in a neighborhood on the other side of Harvard Square.

In a hideaway at the Law School, of which he was dean, Bok is trying to think about the problems of the great private university before they overwhelm him. And he is accepting student invitations: tea with eight or ten in a Harvard house, dinner at Radcliffe, just talk.

"They've heard I'm accessible," he says, "and they're testing me out."

What he is learning in those conversations may give an insight into student attitudes of interest to others than college presidents. For while the excesses of emotion and irrationality have dropped off here, as elsewhere at American universities, the concern remains—concern about education and about this country.

The war, for example.

"I don't know about other places," Bok says, "but Vietnam is still the dominant public issue here. I do not think the concern has gone away to any extent. There is just bewilderment about what to do, and frustration.

"The students feel no response from the Government in terms of human life. They hear about military considerations and withdrawal rates, not about the number of people being killed in Indochina. They get back from Washington an insensitivity to the human cost of what we are doing."

One question students bring up is to what extent a university president can and should take positions on public matters. Bok says "They want to be part of an institution whose officers speak out on grave moral issues."

That is not exactly a self-executing formula, and some people in Cambridge suspect it will be the hardest test for Derek Bok. He is inevitably, doubtless unfairly, compared with his friend Kingman Brewster of Yale, who has spoken out so strongly on Vietnam and other issues. The indications are that Bok is by nature a much less committed person.

But the students talk more with him about educational policy than politics. One thing of which Bok is already convinced is that Harvard will more and more have to carry the burden of justifying teaching methods and content to students: "It won't work anymore, teaching students in ways whose significance they cannot see."

Assumptions are going to have to be examined. One of them, Bok thinks, is the whole pattern of American education in terms of time—12 years of school, then four of college and more of graduate school.

Bok sees all kinds of questions in that area: Should young people take time off to work before or during college, to reduce the risk of boredom from continuous schooling and give them a clearer notion of why

> *'I don't know about other places . . . but Vietnam is still the dominant public issue here. I do not think the concern has gone away to any extent. There is just bewilderment about what to do, and frustration. The students feel no response from the Government in terms of human life.'*

they are at college? Should you shorten the period of education at one stage in people's lives and then bring them back later, when their minds would welcome refreshment? Should undergraduate and graduate years be somewhat compressed together?

He is convinced from experience that law students, at least, tend to be bored and unsatisfied as they near the end of their 19 years of education. But Bok thinks the problem is hard to answer within the universities because part of it lies outside.

"One reason they remain students," he says, "is that they don't see what there is of real value to do afterward. They hold out against a life of routine work or meaningless money-making.

"The law student, for instance, does not want to be just a gun for hire. Half the law students, if you asked them what they want to do, say they want to practice poverty law or consumer law or something like that, but there simply are not that many opportunities. It is up to society to provide a way for students to go on expressing their idealism in life."

A Poem by Buckminster Fuller

Sent as a Telegram to
Senator Edmund S. Muskie of Maine

There is dawning world-around
comprehension
Of the existence of a significant
plurality
Of alternative energy source
options
Available for all Earthians' vital
support,
Which now intuitively fortifies
Maine's far-sighted citizens' and friends'
Spontaneous expression of abhorrence
For any petroleum refineries or storage
Anywhere along its complexedly meandering
Deep-tide coastline.
Because humanity is born
Helpless, ignorant and naked
Nature must anticipatorily provide,
Protect and nurture humanity's regeneration
By spontaneously assimilatible
Environmental resource availabilities
Under omni-favorable conditions.

But originally permitted ignorance
No longer may be, self-excusingly, pleaded
As justification for failure to employ
The now known to exist
Omni-self-supporting technical capabilities
To produce unprecedentedly advanced
Standards of living
And freedoms of thought and actions
For all humanity,
Without any individual
Being advantaged
At the expense of another,
All of which feasibilities
Are inanimately powerable
Well within our daily energy income
From extraterrestrial sources
And all accomplishable without pollution.

By tapping the billion years' long
Safe-depositing of fossil fuel energies,—
As petroleum and coal, within the planetary crust
Humanity was self-startered
Into inauguration of world-around
Electromagnetic energy resources integration,
Accomplished exclusively
By industrialization's ever-evolving knowledge
Regarding ultimate feasibility
On non-biologically harvested
Metabolic support of all humanity.

Humanity had to be self-startered
Into bounteously underwritten
Trial and error gropings
From whence gradually emerged
Mind-discovered comprehension
Of some of the eternal principles
Governing the availability and feasible
employment
Of cosmically-constant, astronomical quantities
Of inherently inexhaustible energies
Of self-regenerative Universe.

Because humanity now has learned
How to gear directly into the inexhaustible
energy
Of the main engines of Universe
It is no longer justified in attempting
To accommodate its ever-expanding,
Knowledgeable functioning in Universe
By ignorantly keeping its foot on the self-starter
To obtain its evolutionary propulsion
Only from the swiftly exhaustible
Fossil-fuel storage battery energies
Or from its perishable, one-season crops.

Realistic accounting
Of the time and foot pounds
Of energy-work, invested by nature,
In the land-born agriculture's—
And seaborn algae's
Impoundment of Sun energy,—
Exclusively by photosynthesis,—
And its progressive conservation
As dead organic residues progressively covered
By wind and waterborne dustings
Siftings and siltings buried and sunken
To critical, gravitationally actuated,
Pressure depths and temperatures
Within which unique conditions
The hydrocarbon residues are chemically
converted
Into coal and petroleum,
Discloses an overall time and pressure
Energy accounting cost
Of one million dollars per gallon of petroleum
(Or its energy equivalents in coal)
As calculated at the present
Lowest commercial rates
At which kilowatt hours of energy
May be purchased from public utility systems.

Failure thus to reckon
The fundamental metabolic costs,
Is to be economically reckless.
Further reckless expenditures
Of our fossil fuel energy savings account
To which future generations
Needs must have emergency access
As a self-re-startering recourse,
Is equivalent to drilling a hole
From the sidewalk into a bank vault
Pumping out money
And calling it free-enterprise discovery
Of an energy wealth bonanza.
Physical energy convergent as matter
Or divergent as radiation,
Compounded by weightless metaphysical
know-how,
Have altogether provided the means
For Earthians' progressively greater participation
In Universe's inexorable evolutionary
transformings,
The participation being accomplished exclusively
By Human-intellect directed ingenuities,
In progressive rearranging
Of the physical furnishings
Of our spherical, space-boat home,
In such a way as progressively to support
Ever-more lives in ever-more ways
With ever-increasing health.

Naught gets *spent* but human time
As cosmically inexhaustible energy
Is tapped exclusively
By intellect-discovered and employed
Cosmic principles
Which to qualify as principles
Must be eternal.

Real wealth
Is Universally self-generative energy
Harnessed by mind to regenerate
Human lives around our Planet,—
Increasing wealth means
More regeneratively self-supporting days ahead
For more lives
Ranging first within Earth's biosphere
And subsequently by ever-increasing exploration
Within Earth's extra-terrestrial
Cosmic neighborhoods.

Such ever-evolving greater know-how wealth
Provides the means
With which specifically to augment
The ever-expanding, anti-entropic
Intellectual responsibilities of humanity
As local Universe's local problem solver
Which problem solving is human intellect's
exclusive,
Complementary and essential functioning,
In support of total, scenario-Universe's
Self-regenerative integrity.

Physics shows
That universal energy is undiminishable.
Experience teaches
That every time humanity initiates
Intelligibly logical experiments
Human intellect always learns more.
Intellect cannot learn less
Intellect is growthfully irreversible.
Both the physical and metaphysical advantage
gains
Of intelligently harvested know-how,—
Reinvested as competent energy-transforming,—
Always produces
Inherently irreversible wealth growth.

This is contrary to yesterday's
Now scientifically and technically obsolete
Concept of a self-exhausting,
Ergo, progressively expendable—
And ultimately spent Universe,
With assumedly progressive failure phases
And their negative economic accountings
Whose bankruptcies are as yet employed
By all political economies,
Together with their depletion tax evasions
Covering only physical property depletions
With no capitalization, nor depreciation
allowances
Of the metaphysical competence of humanity's
mind
Without which there would be
Neither human life self-awareness
Nor its wealth
Of capable conceptioning.

Modern physics renders it
incontrovertible
That celestial energy is
nonexhaustible
Only the fossil fuel savings
account
And perishable human muscles
And the self-startering, but limited,
Hydro-carbon impounded energies
Are terrestrially exhaustible.
Humanity's economics are as yet ignorantly
geared
Exclusively to the annual energy harvesting
cycles
And bankruptcy accounting
Of ignorance permeated yesteryear's
Human brain reflexing
As conditioned, by floods, fires, droughts and
pestilence,—
And frequently ruined crops,
Whereby millions of humans perished.

Brilliant and potentially effective
Managerial capabilities and leadership potentials
Are as yet diminishingly extruded
Through minuscule accounting and customs
apertures,
Which force those capabilities
To concentrate exclusively and myopically
Only upon *this* year's production
This year's election and
This year's profit
While blindly overlooking
The infinitely reliable cyclic frequencies
Governing the 99 per cent of reality
Lying outside human sense apprehending
And lying outside this year's considerability
Which vast, invisible reality
Is the great electromagnetic spectrum
And its astrophysical event recurrency rates,
Which range from split-second atomic
frequencies
To multi-billion year astro-physical lags
All of which cyclic event reoccurrences
Are guaranteed to humanity as absolutely
reliable
By the exclusively science-discovered
Cosmic behaviors' integrity.

Despite the industrial revolution's
Momentary fumbling and mess—
As occasioned uniquely by the myopia
Generated by 'this year's accounting' limitations—
It now is discernible scientifically—
That unwitting Earthians
Gradually are being shifted
Over an epochal threshold,
Successful crossing of which,—
If not totally frustrated by reflexive inertias,—
Will witness the successful gearing of all
humanity
Into the eternally inexhaustible, energy system
Of omni-self-regenerative celestial mechanics.

Humanity is as yet acquiring
Its many human support increasing
Techniques and practices
For all the growing reasons.
We only expand wealth production
Under mass-fear mandates of war.
We could acquire, peacefully and directly
A total humanity supporting productivity
And comprehensive enjoyment of our whole
planet
By simply deciding to do so.
Whatever we need to do
And know how to do
We can afford to do!
This is the cosmic law
Now in clear scientific evidence,
And the more love,
The more satisfactory the wealth augmentations.
Whether history entrusts you or others
With progressively greater responsibilities
At this crucial-to-Earthian's-survival moment
Depends upon whether you, they, or both of you
Comprehend these epochal transitional events.

The State of Maine's Bay-of-Fundy's
Twice-a-day, fifty-foot tides
Are pulsated by Sun-compensated, Moon-
pulls,
Those tides will be pulsated twice daily
As long as the Moon and Earth co-orbit the Sun,
Fundy provides more economically harvestable,
Foot-pounds of energy daily
Than ever will be needed by all humanity
While attaining and sustaining ever-higher
Standards of living,
Greater and more healthful longevity
Than heretofore ever experienced.

It is economic ignorance of the lowest order
To persist in further surfacing and expenditure
Of the Earth's fossil fuels—
It is even more ignorant and irresponsible
To surface and transport oils
Of Arabia, Venezuela, Africa and East Indies
To refineries and storages on the coast of Maine
Thus putting into ecological jeopardy
One of the world's
As yet most humanly cherished
Multi-islanded, sea coast wildernesses.
In view of Fundy's tidal energy wealth
Such blindness is more preposterous
Than "carrying coals to Newcastle."
It is accelerated human suicide.

On the other hand we must recall
That Passamaquoddy's semi-completed
Tidal generating system
Was abandoned on the officially stated,
Ignorant, political-economics assumption
That electricity could not be transmitted
Beyond 350 miles
And therefore could not reach
Any important industrial centers.
It is known in political actuality
That Passamaquoddy was discontinued
Through the combined lobbying efforts
Of Maine's paper pulping and electric power
industries
Whose political policy logic was persuasive
Despite that those two industries
Have together succeeded
In polluting Maine's prime rivers
To kill all but a pittance
Of the Maine coast's once vast fishing wealth.

Space-effort harvested
Scientific know-how and the
computer capability
Have together made possible
The present inauguration
Of one million volt transmissions
And a 1,500 mile delivery range
Of underground, electric power network systems.
Many Passamaquoddies could be plugged
Into the invisible underground,
Transcontinental, time-zone spanning,
Electrical energy network integration
And thence relayed to Alaska
While picking up Canadian Rockies water power
Along the way.
The integrated North American network
Could not only be trans-linked
Through Mexico and Central America
Into an Amazon-to-be-powered
South American network
But also across the Bering Straits
From Alaska to Russia
To join with their now completed
Eastern extension of Western Russia's network
Powered by northward flowing, into-the-Arctic
Siberian river systems.
This now feasible, intercontinental network
Would integrate America, Asia and Europe
And integrate the night-and-day, spherically
cycling
Shadow-and-light zones of Planet Earth
And this would occasion the 24-hour use
Of the now only fifty per cent of the time used
World around standby generator capacity
Whose fifty per cent unused capacities
Heretofore were mandatorily required
Only for peakload servicing of local non-
interconnected energy users.
Such intercontinental network integration
Would overnight double the already-installed
and in-use,
Electric power generating capacity of our Planet.

And lying well within
The progressive 1,500 mile hookup reachability
From an American-Russian power integration
Are the intercontinental networks of China,
India and Africa.

It is everywhere around the world
Incontrovertibly documented
That as the local kilowatt hours
Of distributed electrical energy increase
The local birth rate
Is commensurably diminished and longevity
increases.
In respect to any of its specific geographical
areas,
The birth rate of that area
Trends in inverse proportion
To electrical energy generation and distribution,
The sudden world population bulge
Which has occasioned
Dire population increase predictions
Was occasioned first by the failure to die
Of those who used to die
And secondly by the continued new birth
acceleration
Only within the world's
As yet non-industrialized countries.
As world industrialization will be completed
By twentieth-century's end
The ever-diminishing birth rate
Of the industrial countries
Will bring about world population stabilization
By 2000 A.D.

Universe has no pollution
All the chemistries of the Universe
are essential
To its comprehensive self-
regeneration.
The ninety-two regenerative
chemical elements
Associate, disassociate and intertransform
In a wide range of time-lag rates.
All the dumped chemistries
Spoken of ignorantly as "pollution" or "waste"
Are always needed *elsewhere*
In the intelligent integration
Of World-around energy regenerating
economics.
All the sulphur emitted annually
From the world's industrial chimneys
Exactly equal to the amount of sulphur
Being taken annually to keep industry going.

And while the byproduct chemistries
Are in high concentration
Before going out the stacks or nozzles
They can be economically distributed
To their elsewhere-needed functioning.
After leaving the stacks or nozzles
The byproduct chemicals are so diffuse
As to be economically unrecoverable
In their diffuse state the byproducts
Often become toxic
To various biological species,
The ultimate overall costs of which to humanity
May easily be the cessation of terrestrial life.

Yesterday's preoccupation with major energy
harnessing
Primarily for the killing of humans by humans
Now can be comprehensively redirected
To intelligent and responsible production
Of a total-humanity sustaining system.
Swift realization of all the foregoingly
considered
Epochal transition of human affairs
From a "might" to a "right"
Accounted and inspired
World economics
Is now scheduled for swift realization
By inexorable evolutionary events
To be accompanied by maximum social stresses
With only one alternative outcome
To its total human advantaging—
The alternative is human extinction
Aboard our Planet.

All thinking humanity young or old
Not only will condone
Reversal of public position taking
When it is predicated upon
Better and more inclusive information
Than was at first available
In fact it will think even more favorably
Of the integrity
Of those who admit error for humanity's sake
At the risk of losing previous political support.
So well informed is the young society
Which now is taking the world initiative
That only such integrity of long distance thinking
And unselfish preoccupation
Can win its support.

I pray you will make your stand
Swiftly and unambiguously clear
As being against any further incursions
Of petroleum into Maine
Or of pipelines in Alaska.
I pray that you will concurrently
Initiate resumption of Passamaquoddy
Together with initiation of a plurality
Of such Fundy tidal energy convertors
With combined capacities
Sufficient for celestial-energy support
Of all human life aboard our Planet
To be maintained successfully
Until Earth-based humanity
Has successfully migrated
Into larger cosmic neighborhood functioning.

Buckminster Fuller is an inventor, philosopher and poet.

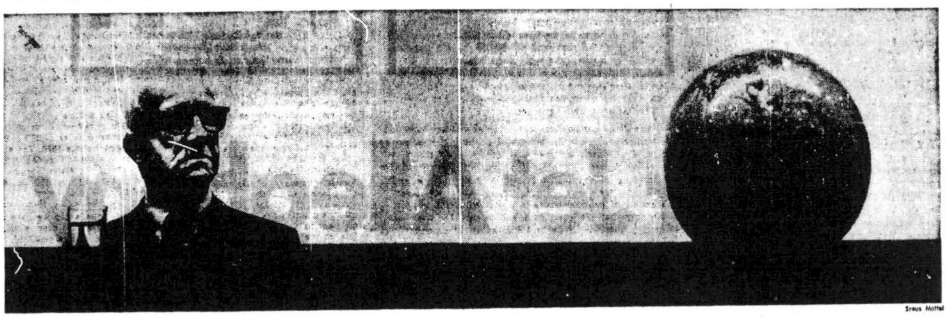

Syeus Mottel

There was never any question of the need for an art director on this new page—a position that five years earlier might have been considered appropriate for a picture editor. But here, the need to *design* the page as well as to find appropriate illustrations was recognized. Variety of visual treatment, silhouettes, collage, montage, photosequences, multiple small images rather than one big one, a page rich with unusual typography, illustrations as initials, and so on, are precisely the possibilities a professional designer is trained to explore. In designing the Op-Ed page for *The Times,* and then in planning for its daily implementation, the full range of graphic possibilities were explored. We did not wish to settle for layouts as predictable as an inside news page.

In other words, filling square holes with good art was not enough. We wanted the art to be used cleverly, synthesized with the type and layout. We wanted readers to say, "Aren't those *Times* editors clever!" and not merely, "Ah, those *Times* editors! They can afford to buy the best art."

Breaking the mold

On the Op-Ed page, as everywhere else in a newspaper, the projection of surprise, variety, and wit most likely begins in the mind of an editor. Wonderful art may sometimes carry the page, but the true vitality of the page starts, of course, with the subject matter and viewpoints the editor chooses to print.

Less obvious is the importance of variety in the kinds and lengths of texts published. The day-after-day presentation of the same number of pieces, with the same number of words, approximately 750, is a design burden for any editor or designer. The reader cannot help but feel, subliminally or otherwise, that he or she is getting a prepackaged product. Memorable Op-Ed pages are often the ones that broke the mold: a

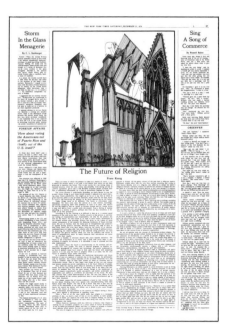

Free-wheeling
Facing page: In the first few days of the new Op-Ed page, this almost full page devoted to a single poem signaled to readers the broad spectrum of material and the free-wheeling approach to be expected from the new page.

Breaking the mold
Three pages break the mold. The first with a step layout that creates an unusual shape in the center of the page; the second with the almost forbidding mass of type that says, "I may be difficult . . . but I'm important"; and the third, with the playful, yet oddly disturbing design that echoes this surprising open letter from a prominent fugitive. Left: Illustration by M. Prechtl, design by George Delmerico and Louis Silverstein. Center: Illustration by Hans-Georg Rauch, design by Delmerico. Right: Illustrations by Victor Juhasz, design by Steve Heller.

poem by Buckminster Fuller that ran five-sixths of the whole page; "A Note from the Underground" by Abbie Hoffman, punctuated by provocative drawings playing around the initials; a large box with a drawing about nuclear idiocy by Brad Holland, accompanied by related quotations; a lengthy piece on capitalism that ran in three installments; a nearly full page of fragmentary letters and notes from children in concentration camps. Apart from the arresting subject matter, each provided a welcome variety of *texture* to the page.

Op-Ed, updated

In 1983, after the Op-Ed page had been running for 13 years, Max Frankel, then editorial page editor, asked me to suggest ways to revitalize the page. Since its inception, the page itself had gone through the stewardship of three editors, several art directors, and some minor changes in headline treatment. The page had seemed to be going flat—perhaps because events and issues of the period themselves seemed anticlimactic after the turbulent early 1970s; or perhaps because ed-

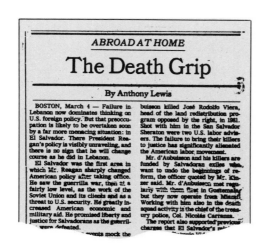

Less bookish

The treatment of columns was given a typographical lift in 1984. Franklin Gothic in the overline titles and three-line initials made a sharper, less bookish appearance. Truncated Scotch rules provide a crisp accent. Because the rules stop suddenly at different lengths, visual tension and unexpected white space is created that give readouts some extra sparkle. The size of the type in the readout is about as large as it can go, acting virtually as a subhead. It becomes more important than ever that the words be succinct and to the point.

Update

Dummy paste-up for updated Op-Ed page shows 1) bolder horizontal rules; 2) option of larger headline, 54 points at top of page; 3) use of subheads; 4) option of strong typographical break-ups of long texts; 5) use of analytical drawing; and 6) strengthened treatment of a regular staff column.

Rough sketch

Facing page: Major pieces are tied together with larger headline size and use of subheads, with very large Bookman initials. Staff columns use three-line Franklin Gothic initial regularly; major guest articles can use Bookman in a variety of ways to contrast with the columns. Although larger headline sizes are now prescribed, discretion is still necessary to avoid imbalance with the rest of the paper.

Shoreham: Stop It Now

OBSERVER
Russell Baker

Failures
Of
Friendship

M

NEW YORK
Sydney H Schanberg

Equal
Ter for
All

E

S

Shoreham: Let's Get On With It

E

It was no
surprise to find
Ed Meese
on my
doorstep

41

itors and designers had fallen victim to the day-after-day routine; or perhaps because the page had by this time become graphically outflanked by new sections and redesigns introduced elsewhere in the paper. Good art—in many cases by artists who had earlier been associated with the Op-Ed page—was now appearing all over the paper. Typography and design had grown more adventurous elsewhere in the paper. In the more recently designed sections, we had been able to exploit strains of courage and invention that were only faint glimmers when the Op-Ed page was started. It was time to apply some of the newly acquired energy to an Op-Ed page that seemed to have grown middle-aged.

New layouts

For important pieces, proposed new layouts reemphasized the occasional use of a special centerpiece treatment that would dominate the page, with a corresponding upscaling of the headline size. This could be particularly effective on those days when an open page allowed a vertical design with a large panel down the center. Also suggested was the grouping together of stories with prominent subhead treatment, tied together with a single large heading. This would give a long, important mass to the topic and add the typographical variety of the subheads.

The new layouts suggested the increased use of large Bookman set-in initials, particularly in the important articles or groupings. These would contrast with the more modest initials designed for the regular columnists.

Mr. Frankel wanted a clearer graphic distinction between our regular columnists and the one-time guest writers. The Bookman designations, set between modest rules, that eight years earlier had seemed quite bold were now redesigned to run in blacker Franklin Gothic caps under a stronger rule, above the title of the piece. This was accompanied by a three-line Franklin Gothic initial set in the text.

Blurbs that were used to fill out space or to break up masses of type were redesigned with more strength and sparkle. The sparkle came from a heavy rule that ran partway across a half-point rule—a truncated Scotch rule. The rule made an accent above and below the blurb type, but by stopping short, allowed the eye to slip down or up to the text that was interrupted by the blurb.

These changes gave the whole page more typographical bite than it had before but retained a basically conservative approach that did not violate the character of the news section in which the page appeared, or departed too much from the character of the facing editorial page.

Free-form

A 1988 page shows new typographical elements in a free-form design that sets off the illustration from interesting white spaces. The same artist, Horatio Fidel Cardo, provides a small drawing for a second article on the page. Illustrations by the same artist in two different pieces on the same page is often a neat touch to unify a design, but care must be taken to avoid confusion about disparate articles being related. Design: Jerelle Kraus.

Graphic option

Facing page: Adding the option of a photograph, map, or some other kind of illustration, small and used only occasionally, nevertheless adds a graphic tool to the editorial page editor's limited repertoire.

Big bang, small space

The new editorial page design that accompanied the Op-Ed page allowed more letters to be printed in a more prominent way. Around the time of the inauguration of the Op-Ed page, letters to the editor numbered about 30,000 a year, increasing every year to the present 75,000.

As part of the effort to give the editorial page a visual lift that would keep it compatible with the Op-Ed page, the daily use of at least one small drawing or an occasional photo was proposed for the "Letters" section. These drawings were to be considered more important than the average one-column "spot" used to break up columns of type. Importance was due to their position in one of the most influential, prominent places in the paper and their enormous potential for graphic impact in the otherwise gray editorial page wall of text.

It was emphasized that the drawings be visualized and drawn specifically for the one-column measure and not be just any drawings reduced to one-column size. A close-up kind of cropping and a bare-bones wit in the use of images was necessary. In short, these little illustrations could pack the wallop of a poster. The potential was enhanced further if two or more drawings could be made to relate to each other graphically or in subject matter. Examples would be a close-up of an eye as the central image in one spot and an ear in another; or hands in some significant gestures; or two or three architectural details. Such treatments could give an extremely powerful voice to the artist working in relatively small spaces.

An even more dramatic use of small space for an occasional, carefully selected picture was possible in editorials. Here, an occasional small map, photo, or chart could run to add to the clarity of an editorial viewpoint.

Of course, to find or assign such pictures and images on a daily schedule implies effort and manpower beyond the capabilities of smaller papers. But finding and using picture resources can be made easier with determined preplanning. Morgues of visual material can be built up; free-lance photographers and illustrators can be interviewed and lined up for occasional use in the same way that news stringers are developed; libraries of readily available books of contemporary prints, drawings, old engravings, typographical dingbats, and many other kinds of illustrative material can be assembled to make available art of high quality. These books should not be confused with books or computer files of "clip art" featuring drawings which are often patently commercial, bland, or poorly drawn.

How to View the Statue

The Statue of Liberty, 305 feet of stone and steel and copper, is the most monumental of monuments. Yet what she symbolizes best is movement.

Liberty shimmers under the overlay of one symbol after another. She was nominally intended, a century ago, to bespeak French-American friendship. But what the sponsors really had in mind was a colossal political statement, to shore up fragile republican sentiments in France.

Other images protrude as sharply as the rays of her tiara, representing the sun, or the seven seas, or the seven continents. The torch conveys enlightenment, or haven, or vigilance. With her broken chains, one immigrant said, she was Saint Freedom.

The Statue did not become the "Mother of Exiles" until Emma Lazarus wrote her famous sonnet for a fundraising drive; the poet's words were not added to the base until 1903 — 17 years after completion.

best place is "from a ship moving to port across her gaze." For as the ship moves, so does the Statue.

At first, "Liberty appears to be striding powerfully forwards, the lines and contours of her form (especially the drapery folds) sweeping together upwards in a forceful movement to the torch.... But as the ship passes in front of the statue ... the dynamic image retreats and a second figure emerges standing still and rigidly erect."

There, finally, is the strongest symbolism of all: motion. Energetic thrust verges rapidly into monumental stability.

The very abundance of symbols is one reason Liberty grips our imagination so firmly, generation after generation. She leaves each era free to discern its own imagery. But motion has become the enduring symbol, literal for all who sailed to port across her gaze and figurative for those whose Golden Door was actually the Golden Gate or

43

Toward Better Legal

Florian

To the Editor:
The recent strike by Legal Aid Society lawyers underscored the need

---

|Afro-Americans, as they achieve greater parity of political and social

...eums Exhibit

There's no end to art's lessons.
If the Mayor wants to threaten the museums into providing the public with more classes and lectures, so be it. After all, they help, and sometimes

Bob Gale

help enormously. But to my mind, information about an object is to the side of the experience of it, and museums can be wordlessly educational.
But the Mayor's object is revenue. I can think of no surer way to lower the quality of life still further in this town than to push museums into poverty by

---

may be broader, i.e., oil, coal or gas.
An analysis based on information obtained directly from utilities and on

ZIP Supreme

To the Editor:
So the Postal Service is planning to switch to a nine-digit ZIP code to allow for a great improvement in efficiency. The fact of the matter is that the day of the computer has truly arrived.
Nine digits are all we have on our Social Security cards; the first three are a code for the region of first registration, which closely corresponds to the first three digits of current ZIP codes.

Subway System'

SUTER

cleaner and quieter, the stations more attractive to the eye — and nose. But they carry only a fraction of the daily passenger load and don't begin to measure the 725 miles of track that bring the subterranean serpentine network within easy walking distance of every resident of this city.
We've got nothing to compare to the art-gallery stations of the Paris Métro, the rubber-cushioned ride of Toronto or the punctuality of Mos-

---

...sed Is Not Pres...

tive detention prior to trial violates the presumption of innocence. The person arrested is not presumed innocent by the criminal justice system. To the contrary, there has already

Nurit

been a finding that there is probable cause to believe that person is guilty.
Certainly, it would have been appropriate to give no weight to the presumption of innocence in the setting

---

Land of Good Sports

To the Editor:
I wish to commend you on the continuing relevance, timelessness and importance of the editorials in The New York Times.
In your Jan. 2 editorial "Blow the Whistle on Hockey Violence," in the midst of the Soviet slaughter of the people of Afghanistan and Soviet belligerent movement elsewhere, you ad-

---

Is it worth it?

Designers are urged to pay great attention to the small one-column illustrations planned for Letters every day. They were not to look like bigger illustrations reduced to one column, but they must look designed for the space: small in size, but big in graphic interest, succinct, and simple. Possibilities for graphic and conceptual wit must also be made the most of, to echo and support the individualistic and often idiosyncratic nature of the letters. This takes time and effort on a daily basis. Is it worth it? That's what editors have to decide. Made part of a daily planned procedure, it may be easier than it seems.

The Ledge

Background: across-the-board changes

No-frills: Page One

Inside Section A: "People" and beyond

Local/State: simple headings

Other sections: no-frills continued

Visual aids: in the composing room

Background
Across-the-board changes

The redesign of *The Ledger* in Lakeland, Florida, in 1979 set a pattern in The New York Times Company for handling later projects, in establishing the design as part of a broad comprehensive approach to improving every aspect of the paper and its marketing. In a sense, the design becomes a platform for change.

At Lakeland big changes occurred in almost every area of the paper's operation. The New York Times Company drew on its full range of talent and resources to help in this broad, synchronized effort. The changes included:

1. Conversion from afternoon to morning publication.

2. State-of-the-art production improvements in second-generation typesetting (photo, not yet digital), and new presses with increased color capacity.

3. Expansion and modernization of the physical plant.

4. Consideration of the paper in wholly new terms of editorial sections rather than in units dictated by press capacity alone.

5. Ambition for growth that involved greater competition with strong neighboring papers.

6. Zoning considerations that needed to be built into the design.

In addition, a fleet of new trucks and new coin-operated boxes were ordered and an expensive promotion and marketing effort was made.

Also, a new publisher and a new editor were in place, each with an obvious stake in the paper of the future, who were not carrying any of the emotional baggage of the paper of the past.

This was not my first redesign of an affiliated newspaper for The New York Times Company, but it was the most comprehensive; and a step-by-step redesign procedure evolved from the effort.

The design itself is interesting, I believe, because to a greater degree than usual, a simple, single, typographical idea was able to be imposed on the whole paper.

Before
Right: Before redesign in 1979. *The Ledger* had been redesigned a few years earlier. Typical for the period were horizontal make-up, "promo" boxes at the top, no column rules, a single type family, and rudimentary use of color.

New design
Facing page: The "modern" new *Ledger* reached out to the reader more forcefully in every aspect, from logo and picture usage to color and a stronger, extremely modern typeface. Yet it bridges the past, building on many old characteristics—the wide column, the sans serif type, and the logo. Emphasis on horizontal make-up changed in favor of both a vertical *and* horizontal make-up. Page layout by the news desk.

AT A GLANCE

City buses get tower of power. 1B

U.S. hockey player Al Iafrate is checked at the wall by Czech player Jiri Lala.

Czechs knock out U.S. 1D

Local

Joseph Walter Long, a well-respected and devoted Polk County educator whose career spanned four decades, died Thursday morning. He was 51. 1B

Three proposed Polk County manufacturing plants that plan to hire 185 workers got approval Thursday to issue a total of $4.2 million in industrial revenue bonds. 2B

Summary

The Senate voted 85-18 Thursday to stop a filibuster by opponents of the death penalty, indicating a bill to restore capital punishment for some federal crimes has a good chance of passage. 6A

David, the 12-year-old "bubble boy" forced by illness from the sterile chamber which protected him from infection since birth, was doing "much better" Thursday after treatment for vomiting, diarrhea and fever, doctors said. 8A

Democratic presidential front runner Walter F. Mondale likened John Glenn's tax plan Thursday to "voting for Reaganomics twice," and said it would cost the average family nearly $900 year in higher taxes. 11A

A white patrolman said he shot a black county worker when the man turned suddenly, but he wasn't sure whether the victim was reaching for a concealed handgun because "it all happened so fast," a police detective testified Thursday. 3B

Today

Friday, February 10, 1984 — Today is the 41st day of the year with 325 days remaining... In 1893, comedian Johnny Durante was born in New York City... In 1964, the House of Representatives passed the Civil Rights Act... And in 1967, a fire at the Las Vegas Hilton Hotel killed eight people and injured about 200... Ten years ago Chairman Peter Rodino said the House Judiciary Committee would be shirking its responsibility if it didn't call President Richard Nixon to answer any questions it had about his conduct in office... Five years ago, Rival factions of the Iranian military fought in Tehran, as thousands of armed civilians roamed the streets of the Iranian capital calling for the ouster of Prime Minister Shahpour Bakhtiar... Actress Judith Anderson is 85 years old, Opera singer Leontyne Price is 57, Singer Roberta Flack is 44. And Olympic swimmer Mark Spitz is 34... Quote for Today: "To speak kindly does not hurt the tongue." — French proverb

Weather

Mostly fair today and Friday with highs in the low to mid 70s. Details. 2A

Tip of the day

Use a recipe box for addresses rather than a book. It'll easier to replace a card with a new address than scratch out an old address.

Action Line	5C	Entertainment	4C, 5C
Astrology	6D	Legals	7C
Business	4B	Life/Style	1C
Classified	7C	Local	1B
Comics	7D, 8D	Obituaries	2B, 7C
Conversation	6C	Sports	1D
Crossword	7D	Television	13A
Editorial	14A		

The Ledger

25¢

Friday, February 10, 1984, Lakeland, Florida, Vol. 78, No. 111

Officials dispute shelling

Shelling may have hit Syrian command. 12A
Will McGrory column. 14A

By W. Dale Nelson
The Associated Press

WASHINGTON — Administration officials Thursday offered differing justifications for the American shelling of Beirut and the nation's two top Pentagon leaders publicly disputed the White House account of when President Reagan decided to redeploy U.S. Marines in Lebanon.

Meanwhile, one administration official reportedly said the phased withdrawal of the Marines from the Beirut airport area could take as long as "early summer."

Speakes

The shelling is solely to defend the multinational force in Lebanon and not to prop up the country's tottering government, said White House spokesman Larry Speakes. He said the agreement with Congress authorizes shelling only for this purpose.

But Defense Secretary Caspar Weinberger said defense of the Lebanese government was in fact one reason for the firing.

Weinberger

Speakes had said Reagan approved the redeployment plan "in principle" Feb. 1, but in an appearance before Congress, Gen. John Vessey, chairman of the Joint Chiefs of Staff, turned to Weinberger and said:

"If the decision was made on the first of February, you and I spent an awful lot of time in meetings in the last week to no avail."

In another development, congressional sources said Gen. P.X. Kelley, Marine commandant, was apparently unaware of Reagan's decision to order a phased withdrawal of the Marines
See Officials on Page 12A

Naval guns blaze again

Syrians warn U.S. 9A

By Farouk Nassar
The Associated Press

BEIRUT, Lebanon — The U.S. 6th Fleet bombarded the rebel-held ridges outside Beirut for a second day Thursday, after government and rebel gunners traded deadly artillery barrages around the divided and devastated city.

Lebanese and Syrian reports claimed U.S. Navy jets also went into action over the mountain area Thursday but a U.S. military spokesman denied it.

About 50 more U.S. Embassy employees and dependents were airlifted out by helicopter Thursday to 6th Fleet ships offshore, U.S. Marine spokesman Maj. Dennis Brooks reported. That brought to about 140 the number of American civilians pulled out thus far, for transfer to the safety of Cyprus.

Lebanon's embattled Christian president, the U.S.-supported Amin Gemayel, remained out of sight Thursday.

Gemayel, whose Moslem-Christian Cabinet resigned last weekend, is trying to patch together a new "national"
See Navy on Page 12A

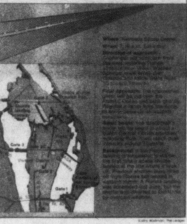

Planned Florida landing of Space Shuttle Challenger

Cathy Robinson, The Ledger

One more time

Mission Specialist Bruce McCandless has a unique view of the Earth as he flies his jet-powered backpack around the tail of the Space Shuttle Challenger Thursday morning. It was the second free flight for McCandless and fellow Mission Specialist Robert Stewart. Unlike Tuesday's operation however, this one had some disappointments. In a happier note, NASA officials say the weather may yet cooperate and allow Challenger to land at Kennedy Space Center Saturday morning as planned. Story. 10A

Heart stopped 400 times, but patient didn't

By Marcia Dunn
The Associated Press

PITTSBURGH — A retired clerk whose failing heart stopped more than 400 times within five days is leading an almost normal life after a rare operation, and said Thursday he feels "wonderful."

"I look at myself now and I feel more like I did before the problem were required," George Derrick, 58, said in an interview after his daily 30-minute workout at his Pittsburgh home.

To say I'm a medical miracle ... it's the experience of other people who have had my life. It's only begun to sink in," said Derrick.

His heart had been producing abnormal electrical impulses resulting in rapid heartbeat, a disorder known as ventricular tachycardia. Doctors blamed the problem on a heart attack in 1982 which produced a tissue scar that disrupted the organ's electrical system.

In an unusual operation last October, surgeons pinpointed the trouble with an electrical monitor and removed scar tissue.

Doctors said Derrick's heart mapped an "extraordinarily abnormal" number of times, but they are confident he can lead a long, normal life.

"I think this is a beautiful example
See Ticker on Page 12A

Deadly avalanche

Rescue workers search for victims amid cars piled up in an avalanche in the Ardennes near Innsbruck, Austria, Thursday. According to unofficial reports, at least five people died in the avalanche. Severe weather problems have hit most parts of Europe the last few days. Story. 6A

Bartow upset by possible DOT move

By Stephanie Tripp
The Ledger

BARTOW — Local officials are upset about a proposal that could take the District 1 headquarters for the Florida Department of Transportation away from Bartow — and 600 jobs along with it.

Rose Thornburg, president of the Bartow Chamber, sent a letter to Gov. Bob Graham last week saying the business community opposes the move from Bartow to Tampa.

"To me, it's a slap in the face to Polk County because we have just as much to offer in Polk County as they do in Tampa," Mrs. Thornburg said. The office has a payroll of $9 million a year, she said, and much of the money is spent in Bartow.

The recommendation to change the structure of the DOT is one of two alternate proposals suggested by the Governor's Management Advisory Committee, which is composed of eight people with private sector management experience.

"We agree with previous reports and statements which have questioned the policy of locating district headquarters in rural areas rather than in urban centers," the committee stated in its final report last October.

But Bill Hula, a spokesman for state
See State on Page 12A

The second round

The Ledger was one of the many papers that had already gone through a first round of modernization. An earlier redesign under the direction of Edmund Arnold helped bring the paper out of hot metal composition into the contemporary era of cold type (photocomposition).

Characteristic of the Arnold design was a wide column of briefs down the left side of the page (referred to in The New York Times Regional Newspaper Group as a "W column"), generous use of white space, and a single display typeface, a medium-bold version of Techno in the Futura style. The nameplate logo and section heads were set in Trump italic. At the time of the early redesign, the use of straightforward type for a logo had been a big step into contemporary design. By the time The New York Times Company acquired *The Ledger* in 1971, as part of a package deal with Cowles Communications that included other publications, the new management thought the paper needed an overhaul. With a new publisher in place and after appropriate market studies, The New York Times Company decided on profound changes, with a major commitment of money, expertise, and resources by the parent company. It was decided to go from afternoon to morning; to renovate the offices and the entire plant with major construction of new press and mailroom facilities; to look for better regional news coverage and distribution; and to redesign the paper.

Open house
Visitors wait in line for the tour and open-house party that celebrated the modernized plant and new design.

The chief news executive at the time of the redesign was the managing editor, Tim McGuire. Tim did not fit my impression of a top editor. His scraggly beard matched a puckish casualness, all of which, however, masked his enthusiastic attention to every detail of content and design. Despite his genial good fellowship, he had developed such a firm command of things he wanted to do in the paper that his first memo on the subject gave me pause. "This guy is going to box me in with his pre-set ideas, and I haven't even got started," was my reaction. Today the idea of the designer becoming involved with content from the ground up is fairly well accepted, but in 1979 it was not. (Here again, tribute needs to be made to Edmund Arnold, who for many years talked about design as a function of good journalism, not merely as attractive embroidery.) My fears proved to be groundless. Tim saw that as designer I would need to be involved a great deal more than just to decide on flush left or centered headlines, and I appreciated that his detailed grasp of content by no means precluded genuine enthusiasm for modernization. Publisher Elven Grubbs helped strike a good working balance between the roles of publisher and editor. Jack Harrison, president of The New York Times Regional Newspaper Group, also kept in close touch with the project.

In any design project, the character of the client and the kind of mandate given the designer are inevitably reflected in the result. Sydney Gruson was the executive vice president of The New York Times Company in charge of affiliated operations. People knew Gruson to be not only an unusually creative executive but also an equally sound newspaperman. When I talked to Gruson about the upcoming Lakeland project and asked what he wanted to achieve with the redesign, he answered "Just make it the best-looking newspaper in Florida."

A first rough

Before getting into the requirements of typesetting, paste-up, and computer formatting, a thick soft china-marking crayon is the designer's useful tool to help visualize the page as a whole and develop a structure and typographic idea.

Dummy page

A type dummy firms up the headline treatment ultimately used, but uses a horizontal reefer treatment later dropped in favor of placement down the side.

No-frills

At the time of *The Ledger* redesign, the idea of using a single typeface for the main display throughout a newspaper was already dominant in many papers as they went into redesign for cold type. Esthetically, after centuries of crowded pages with all kinds of typefaces jammed together, the neatness and orderliness of a single headline style seemed refreshingly modern.

More pragmatically, as newspapers and equipment manufacturers wrestled with new technologies and production procedures, a single typeface made production much simpler. In fact, in the early years of photocomposition, relatively few typefaces were available. (And most of those that did exist looked as if they had been carved out of soap.)

Unfortunately, as papers simplified their typography, most of them seemed to acquire a blandness at odds with the serendipity and vitality commonly associated with a daily newspaper. When smaller papers made changes without professional typographical help, they emerged in their new type dress devoid of design focus with a lackluster use of type badly set on the new machines.

The single type family was settled on by many papers simply because it was cheaper and easier. It was used in its available varieties—upper and lower case, capitals, italic, bold, light, and condensed—and it often emerged as a weak and uncertain version of the previous paper.

Headline display

The Ledger's typography represented an effort to work with a single family of type as others were doing, but with a graphic focus, strict logic, and a minimal use of typographic "furniture"—peripheral or decorative typographical elements—that would have avoided the pitfalls of blandness and uncertainty. The format for the most part attempted to extract the maximum eloquence from a strongly designed typeface, Avant Garde, without resorting to such familiar helpful devices as boxes, Scotch rules, cut-off rules, and reverse (white type on black, gray, or color) panels. The design hinged simply on distinct variations in size and weight of the type, on the unusually forceful design of the letter characters, and on a strictly functional use of rules.

Lakeland Mayor Dies

OLD: TEMPO BOLD

Miamians turn down tax cut

NEW: AVANT GARDE BOLD

More modern cut

New Avant Garde display type family projects the same image as the old Techno. The new style features a modern, big x-height and the new, more conversational *down style* in capitals with only the first word capitalized.

The simple approach

Facing page: All the display is Avant Garde, top to bottom, in two weights with no italic, including bylines and captions. A minimum use of rules gives the type more play. The heavy bars around the overline reefer give it genuine importance formerly associated with "skylines" of hot metal days. The delicate forms of the logo's Trump letters contrast with the severe blackness of the headline, but the rather large size and intricacy of the logo helps it hold its own.

AT A GLANCE...

Fast action avoids gas inferno. 1B

Motorized vehicle in the wrong place.
Ray Weiss/The Ledger

Guard kept things under control. 17A

Local

Students of the three Auburndale schools hit by Tuesday's tornado won't go back to school until Monday — then, it will be double sessions for two of the schools. 1B.

The amount of uninsured property damaged by Tuesday's tornado that struck in and around Auburndale is the key in whether Polk County will get federal aid. 1B.

Residents sorted through the rubble. National Guard jeeps rolled down littered roads. Ambulances and medics stood by if needed. Sun Acres subdivision had the look of a war-torn village Wednesday. 2B.

Volunteers are returning to the American Red Cross shelter in K-Ville for the second time, asking for more bologna sandwiches, cookies and Kool-Aid. They've already taken 30 sandwiches out to the Sun Acres site. They've come for 70 more. 2B.

Summary

Virtually all Contac Nasal Mist and Sine-Off Once-A-Day Sinus Spray on store shelves throughout the country are being recalled because of possible bacterial contamination, the Food and Drug Administration announced Wednesday. 6A.

Two strong supporters of Sen. Herman Talmadge emphatically contradicted on Wednesday sworn testimony given by the senator's chief accuser about the delivery of funds which Talmadge is accused of converting to his personal use. 7A.

A prominent Iranian Jew and seven Moslems, including a wealthy industrialist, were cut down by revolutionary firing squads Wednesday. 8A.

Today

May 10, 1979 — Today is the 130th day of the year, with 235 days remaining . . . The Albany Tulip Festival will begin today . . . Today is Confederate Memorial Day, observed in North and South Carolina . . . The Union Pacific and Central Pacific Railways merged, forming the first transcontinental railway on this date in 1869. To celebrate its completion, a golden spike valued at about $400 was driven by Leland Stanford, president of Central Pacific. It's said that he missed the first stroke . . . Quote for today: "A tourist is a fellow who drives thousands of miles so he can be photographed standing in front of his car." — Emile Ganest.

Weather

Rains may continue with a 50 percent chance of afternoon or evening thundershowers. For details, see Page 2A.

Tip of the day

To wash feather pillows place them in the bath and rub with shampoo and water. Then jog on them. Result: clean pillows and good exercise.

Disaster aid depends on damage. 1B

The Ledger

SUNRISE EDITION

15°
S

Thursday, May 10, 1979, Lakeland, Florida, Vol. 73, No. 199

SALT II accord reached

Terry Morse/ Joe Escourido/The Ledger

Vance, Dobrynin negotiate terms

WASHINGTON (AP) — Winding up nearly seven years of hard bargaining, the United States announced agreement Wednesday with the Soviet Union on a treaty to slow the nuclear arms race.

President Carter said he and Soviet President Leonid I. Brezhnev will sign the treaty at a summit meeting as soon as it can be arranged.

"The American people have no more deeply felt wish than to enhance our nation's security and to reduce the risk of nuclear war," Carter said in a speech prepared for delivery to a Democratic Party congressional campaign fund-raising dinner.

There was no simultaneous announce-ment from the Soviet Union. A senior White House official said he expected the Russian people would be informed through the Soviet press.

When a decision is reached on the time and place for the Carter-Brezhnev summit meeting there probably will be simultaneous announcements in Washington and Moscow, said the official, who asked not to be identified.

Secretary of State Cyrus R. Vance, who negotiated the settlement on key provisions with Soviet Ambassador Anatoly F. Dobrynin, made the formal U.S. declaration that — except for a "few remaining secondary items" — the treaty was finally wrapped up.

U.S. officials said there were no hitches. They said the remaining details were technical and could be handled by the U.S. and Soviet delegations in Geneva who will prepare the treaty text over the next two or three weeks.

Defense Secretary Harold Brown, speaking for the Pentagon, gave assurances that "SALT will contribute significantly to our security."

Brown said that even with the treaty, the United States will have to expand its defense efforts, and particularly its strategic nuclear forces.

Vance emphasized the hope the pact carries for "a safer America and a safer
continued on 17A

Pact to face tough struggle in Senate

By Hedrick Smith
The New York Times

WASHINGTON — Probably not since the Senate rejected Woodrow Wilson's bid to join the League of Nations in 1919 has a

Analysis

president confronted so precarious a struggle in Congress on foreign policy as Jimmy Carter faces over the strategic
continued on 17A

Auburndale mood calm

By Bob Boyle
Ledger staff writer

AUBURNDALE — The mood was calm here Wednesday in the wake of the previous day's killer tornado.

"I'll bet we have a lot to be thankful for," Jack Truitt said, and pointed to the middle school across the street. "There could have been a lot of kids killed in that building. It's really a miracle."

The middle school was the first of the three schools to be hit and suffered the worst damage. Officials said they doubted the building would ever be reopened.

While more than 40 inmates of Polk Correctional Institution collected debris and loaded trucks donated by businesses for the clean up, teachers at the schools were busy saving anything that might help them begin classes on Monday.

"Our main concern has been to save the audio-visual equipment and other electric things like typewriters, plus school books and paper," seventh-grade teacher David Sutherland said. "We are still worried about the weather," he added. "If we get more bad weather the entire structure might fall."
continued on 17A

Woman, girl swept away despite efforts

ST. PETERSBURG (AP) — With a raging whirlpool of floodwater swirling about him, Bert Collom snatched his 14-year-old daughter to safety. But his wife and other teen-age daughter were swept to their deaths in a storm sewer.

The terror of death still showed on the face of Collom's wife, Judith, 37, when they pulled her body from a drainage ditch, rescuers said Wednesday.
continued on 17A

The view from the top of the wall at Auburndale Middle School.
Mary Jones/The Ledger

Polk tornado 'most devastating'

By John Druckenmiller
Ledger staff writer

SUN ACRES — The Rev. S.T. McGinnis has lived through three tornadoes, but he said Tuesday's twister was "the most devastating."

"This is the most damage for a populated area I've ever seen," said the pastor of The Peoples Church of Winter Haven on Spirit Lake Road. "It's unbelievable."

Thursday, McGinnis joined members of his flock in sorting through the remains of their trailers in the Sun Acres area south-west of Auburndale, which was the area hardest hit by the 1:20 p.m. tornado that skipped across the Auburndale area.

McGinnis joined John and Barbara Dunn and Bill and Marlene Burch as the couples sorted through the twisted metal of their late mother's trailer on King Avenue.

Mrs. Dunn and Mrs. Burch said they were glad their mother didn't live to see the devastation.

Meanwhile, their neighbors poked through the crumbled structures they once called home.

One man, Jerry Fears, lifted pieces of debris that sent his wife to the hospital. Family and friends helped Fears collect items from the trailer he rented from his brother Howard.

The trailer that was shattered — with his wife Linda inside — when the tornado swept across the trailer park in a southwest-to-northeast path.

Mrs. Fears was listed in serious condition in the intensive care unit of Lakeland General Hospital Wednesday night.
continued on 17A

Avant Garde seemed well suited to the design idea. It is available in a good variety of weights and is very much a "modern" typeface, having been designed and introduced by Herb Lubalin around 1954. Avant Garde had achieved considerable popularity in advertising and to some degree in magazines, but to my knowledge it had not yet been used in newspaper editorial display. The roundness of the characters and the way the vertical strokes pack together give a slightly eccentric pace to the flow of the letters, as well as a tight look hardly ever seen in the days of hot metal. The roundness of the letters with their unexpectedly open interior spaces, and the degree of weight of the Avant Garde Bold, which is quite authoritative but not too black, seemed a refreshing change from the frequently used black Univers type that seemed to dominate many of the papers in Florida.

The choice of Avant Garde was important, too, because of its similarity to the old display typeface, Techno. Avant Garde, in the same Futura family as Techno, is a modern extension of it, with very short ascenders and descenders, a correspondingly exaggerated x-height, and an extremely tight-fitting letterspace displacement. The general family resemblance to Techno was desirable because the paper had only recently been redesigned.

Two of the four basic weights of Avant Garde type were chosen—Bold and Light. The Extra Light is used only in certain prescribed ways, not in the headline schedule at all, and the Extra Black is not used in any way. Avant Garde has no italic, an important aspect of the original design format. I eschewed developing and using an italic Avant Garde for the same reason I believe Lubalin left italic out of his original design —the resolute roundness of some characters combined with the unusual vertical feeling of others do not lend themselves to slanting. On the newspaper page, the steady beat of the type, in whatever sizes or weights, would be a cohesive force.

Logo—sticking with Trump

The logo had been running for about a decade in Trump italic. It seemed at best rather weak, and particularly so alongside the Avant Garde. As with the headline typeface, it seemed desirable to find a way to retain as much of the character of the existing logo as possible, since it had only recently been changed, but to give it greater strength and authority. A roman version of Trump was the answer, considerably larger than its previous size with concurrent added weight. The flush left style was in keeping with the no-nonsense, contemporary typographical approach the Avant Garde seemed to demand, and also accented the single typographical structural scheme from top to bottom of the page.

A decorative touch

Since a key aspect of the new marketing strategy was conversion of *The Ledger* from an afternoon to a morning publication, an oversized "AM" was designed to provide a promotional signal to the reader. Drawn by hand in the general style of Avant Garde, it provided a decorative splash, in color, at the top of the page.

Reefers

Perhaps the most original idea for its time in the design of the front page was the placement of the reefers in the upper corner of the wide column running down the left side of the page. Even as early as 1979, the much used reefers (called "box-cars" or "promos") running across the top of Page One in an increasing number of papers seemed to be largely ineffectual. The type was usually weak, the art poor, and the color raw or faded.

The design of *The Ledger* featured, instead, unexpectedly large type positioned not in boxes, but as a bulletin list down the side. I suggested that the large-size type in the rather tight space would encourage a succinct, snappy style of writing. It was hoped that the reefers would reach off the page and engage the reader, rather than sit placidly in fussy little boxes across the top of the page. Strong, but not necessarily big, picture images would of course also be used. Cropping, silhouetting, and witty selection of images would be important.

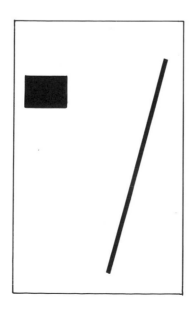

1984 page

This layout features an unusual configuration that makes an angular thrust from right to left down the page. The page does not depend on overlarge display type, dominant pictures, or a flooding of color to exude vitality and movement. Page layout: Mark Mathes.

Sears to sell Tower. 4B

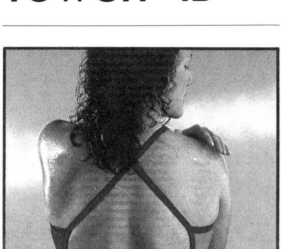

Uniack

Pain, pain, go away. 1C

Local

The board of directors of Sooner Defense met Monday with representatives of the Virginia company that hopes to use Sooner as its entry into the defense contracting business. 1B.

Lakeland residents will decide on Nov. 8 whether to approve proposals that would add 1,235 acres to the city and increase the population by almost 10 percent. 2B.

Summary

California education officials have uncovered incidents dating to 1985 in which school personnel in 45 public elementary schools changed answers on standardized state tests that measure a school's progress in reading, writing and mathematics. Officials said more schools might be guilty of cheating. 4A.

Israelis vote today in an election tied to 11 months of violence that has cost the lives of more than 300 Palestinians and 10 Jews, including a rabbi's daughter and her three children killed in a weekend attack. 4A.

The Supreme Court on Monday stepped into

Mulberry delivers deadline. 1B

Female gridder Monica Novak   Evelio Gonzalez/The Ledger

Girl tries her hand at football.1D

This new way of handling reefers met the requirement that they be prominent in the coin-operated honor boxes, which account for a significant part of *The Ledger's* sales (as they do for most newspapers in the South). Nevertheless, the Circulation Department wanted the option of another reefer, at the top of the page in a more conventional fashion. This was accommodated by putting the extra reefer between heavy color rules at the top of the page in skyline fashion. This reefer should not run every day but be used to signal something special to the reader. In general this still seems to be a good idea. Many papers fail to apply strict judgment when it comes to selection of top-of-the-page reefers, lessening the reefer's effectiveness. After a while, readers may not actually read the reefers—they *see* them, but they don't *read* them.

Color

Increased use of color was one of the chief considerations in the redesign. While the first months of transition to the new design and new presses produced improved color in the half-tones, only a modest increase in the overall amount of color was achieved because of technical problems and the need to master new procedures. Like most newspapers—with the well-known exception of *USA Today* and a few others—*The Ledger* remains conceptually black and white, with color pictures and elements appearing more frequently, but without being truly integrated. However, in the early months and increasing recently, the limited use of color combined with the design helped make the page effective. The intricacies of the black and white typography, the color bars, panels, and half-tones and, of course, the choice of a good color photograph work together to make the whole page come colorfully alive. Newspapers are coming to realize that the arbitrary application of color to every corner of a page is not the most effective, tasteful way to use it.

USA Today might be considered the exception to this generality. *USA Today* floods every corner of the page with color. I believe that *USA Today* is not an exception, however, but rather proof of the design-color relationship. The use of color in *USA Today* is part of an original and encompassing philosophy touching all aspects of the operation—the journalistic approach, the writing, quality control and, of course, the design. The apparent effectiveness of color in *USA Today* is due as much to its integration into the overall design approach as to its high quality and lavish distribution. In attempting to draw on color or some other isolated aspect of *USA Today's* design, disregard for an integrated overall format is why so many newspapers fail.

Down-the-side reefers
Facing page: Reproduced here at actual size, the "promo" corner is virtually a small poster. The picture is much more than a "spot," contributing a real display element to the page, offering a good opportunity for imaginative cropping.

Inside Section A

"People" and beyond

Page 2A, called "People Page," attempts to present familiar kinds of material in interesting new ways. The format builds variety into the page in the treatment of different items.

For example, the feature, "Faces," was created to institutionalize a daily picture treatment. Creative cropping and an occasional silhouette was encouraged. The extra-large, one-word lead-ins provided a place for catchy words and an eye-catching shift in type scale.

Weather

The weather package, cleaned up and expanded, featured a satellite photo, relatively new at the time, but which now falls far short of the kind of emphasis currently placed on weather. As part of a 1990 redesign, the weather package at *The Ledger* was given a new fixed position, more space, and a large local map.

FACES

Bucky is the burial place for 101,757 persons. Bianca Jagger and escort John Beaus Lyon head for the dance floor at Studio 54 in New York Friday. Bianca, who is divorcing rock star husband Mick Jagger said "I'm in love again" while talking about Lyon.

Beauty burial place for 101,757 persons. Bianca Jagger and escort John Beaus Lyon head for the dance floor at Studio 54 in New York Friday. Bianca, who is divorcing rock star husband Mick Jagger said "I'm in love again" while talking ...... City Cemetery is the burial place for 101,757 persons. Bianca Jagger and escort John Beaus Lyon head for the dance floor at Studio

Nightly the burial place for 101,757 persons. Bianca Jagger and escort John Beaus Lyon head for the dance floor at Studio 54 in New York Friday. Bianca, who is divorcing rock star husband Mick Jagger said "I'm in love again" while talking persons. Bianca Jagger and escort John Beaus Lyon head for the dance floor at Studio 54 in New York Friday. Bianca, who is divorcing rock star husband Mick Jagger said "I'm in love again" while talking about Lyon.

Faces

The dummy layout for this part of the People Page shows how variety in scale in cropping helps vitalize even a simple arrangement of photos. The sense of unusual scale is enhanced by the large 32-point terse lead-ins.

A lot of people

Facing page: The design, as this actual Page 2A shows, allows for a picture spread of the day. The extra large lead-ins help keep the center of the page lively.

People page

Farah Fawcett, Ryan O'Neal plan to tie the knot in near future

VENICE, Italy (AP) — Actress Farah Fawcett and actor Ryan O'Neal announced Tuesday they will marry in Venice "soon."

"I am very happy and let me tell you Venice is the most beautiful city in the world," said Miss Fawcett, who was previously married to actor Lee Majors.

Miss Fawcett and O'Neal are here as guests of Italian fashion designer Roberta di Camerino for a brief vacation.

"It's so beautiful. I will never forget this trip," Miss Fawcett said.

Cher may draw fine for noise

LAS VEGAS, Nev. (AP) — Responding to complaints from musicians that they are "going deaf," a state agency wants to fine entertainer Cher and Caesars Palace $180 for a performance she gave that was allegedly too loud.

The Nevada Department of Occupational Safety and Health said Tuesday the hotel had contested the citation, issued after the department wired three musicians in the hotel's orchestra with sensitive sound monitoring equipment. A committee will decide if the citation was justified.

Caesars officials and Cher were not available for comment.

The sound level during the July 3 show reportedly reached 115 decibels.

The sound check came as the result of a complaint lodged by Musicians Local 369, which has mounted a campaign to have the volume cut at some performances.

Sex legend remains hospitalized

LOS ANGELES (AP) — Actress Mae West remained in Good Samaritan Hospital in satisfactory condition Tuesday, following a stroke three weeks ago that has left her unable to speak, a hospital source said.

Hospital administrators have refused to confirm officially that Miss West, 88, was at their facility, but a reliable hospital source who asked not to be identified told The Associated Press that she was there and would remain in the hospital indefinitely.

Her agent, Jerry Martin, has refused to confirm or deny the report.

The hospital source said Miss West was in a tightly guarded celebrity suite and that strict orders had been given to keep her presence secret.

Prostitute organizer leads drive to close nude-model theater

SAN FRANCISCO (AP) — Prostitute organizer Margo St. James, a leading advocate of the right to sell sex, is heading a petition drive to try to lift the license of a nude-model theater near her home. The theater's attorney said her attempt would be resisted.

Margo St. James

"To walk by there and see this, it's just disgusting to see," said Ms. St. James, organizer of the pro-hooker group COYOTE, or Call Off Your Old Tired Ethics, which promotes the legalization of prostitution.

The object of Ms. St. James' ire is the Erotic Theater in the heart of the city's North Beach neighborhood. The theater features looks at nude models, and is located on a street that had been relatively free of sex trade.

"It's not contradictory. I would fight long and hard to keep a real sex parlor open somewhere else," she said. "I don't want it on that block."

Ms. St. James, who said she hasn't been a prostitute for a number of years and is now a licensed private detective, said Monday she gathered 400 signatures in three days to support her request to the city permit appeal board to repeal the Erotic's license.

Symphony conductor resigns

DETROIT (AP) — Conductor Antal Dorati, who led the Detroit Symphony Orchestra to world-class status in three years, has resigned the musical directorship because he says recent budget cuts threaten its future.

Dorati, who came to Detroit in 1977 after eight years as musical director of the Washington, D.C. National Symphony, told the Detroit orchestra's board chairman Robert Semple he would be willing to conduct the new season and pledged a campaign to generate funds for the symphony.

Alf turns 93

AP photo

The grand old man of the Grand Old Party, Alf Landon, celebrated his 93rd birthday Tuesday talking to friends and relatives by telephone. Landon missed his daily ride on his 26-year-old horse, Red, but planned to make his regular luncheon with friends. A birthday dinner with his family is planned.

Philippe Junot ready to tell all; Sly getting $10 mil for 'Rocky III'

Is Princess Caroline's estranged husband, Philippe Junot, getting ready to throw the book at his lovely young ex-wife-to-be? Sources close to the international playboy report friends of Junot have approached at least two major New York publishing houses regarding his writing a tell-all tome about his ups and downs with the Grimaldis of Monaco. Junot reportedly got the idea when representatives of two Italian magazines approached him about spilling the beans in print for a royal fee. The price tag attached to Junot's book full of memories? At least $1 million!

United Artists confirms that the rumors Sylvester Stallone will receive a total of $10 million to appear in "Rocky III" are indeed true. On completion of the film, Sly will receive a check for $5 million. Then, for the next five years (regardless of the box-office take), Sly will receive a million each year. That's in addition to a percentage of the gross. Filming is scheduled to begin next March in this, the third in the already profitabe series about heart-of-gold fighter Rocky Balboa.

Don't believe the rumors linking "Xanadu" stars Olivia Newton-John and Michael Beck — it's merely wishful thinking on Universal's part to spark a little interest in that God-awful piece of tripe. Olivia's real love is a dancer (who appears briefly, by the way, in "Xanadu") named Matt Lattanzi. As for Beck, whom you may remember for his gruff performance as the leader of "The Warriors," his heart really belongs to singer-song-writer Cari Kappel. Matter of fact, they are engaged.

"Airplane" star Robert Hays is very serious about his high-school sweetheart, recording engineer Terry Becker.

Sources close to Candice Bergen swear the actress

TIPOFF

Philippe Junot    Sylvester Stallone    Candice Bergen

will marry "Pretty Baby" director Louis Malle soon but the lady herself says it just isn't so. True, she's "very close" to the distinguished French director, but, according to Candy, everything's dandy for now sans marriage.

Harrison Ford, who plays Han Solo in "The Empie Strikes Back" and the original "Star Wars," is solo-ing with a beautiful screenwriter by the name of Melissa Mathison.

Two recently completed films are in need of repair work. Joseph E. Levine's "Tattoo" mystery starring Bruce Dern and Maud Adams wrapped months ago, but Dern recently flew to Japan to lens one more scene to help clarify the action. You'll recall the Los Angeles-based group, Women Against Violence Against Women has already lodged protests with producer Levine over what they consider an initial advertising campaign "abusive to women."

FACES

AP photo

Face of the '80s

Jennifer J. Laumen, 21, of Orlando, reacts as she is named 'Face of the '80s' Monday night at the Pierre Hotel in New York. The young woman won a competition sponsored by Merle Norman Cosmetics and Ford Models Inc., for 'beauty and fashion face of the '80s.'

AP photo

Heavy step

Singer-actress Barbra Streisand, looking a bit hefty, and her companion Jon Peters arrive at New York's Winter Garden Theater to attend a performance of the new Broadway musical '42nd Street' Monday evening.

AP photo

Captain's helper

Bill Cosby, left, draws a laugh from Bob 'Captain Kangaroo' Keeshan Monday on the set of the CBS-TV children's program. The occasion was a party on the set marking the addition of Cosby as host of 'Picturepages,' a daily feature for preschool children on the Captain's show.

Weather: Slight chance of afternoon and evening showers

Forecast

Today

Partly cloudy through Thursday. A slight chance of mainly afternoon and evening thunderstorms. Evening lows in the 70s and afternoon highs around 90. Rain probability 20 percent in the afternoon and evening hours.

Extended

Friday through Sunday: Partly cloudy with scattered, mainly afternoon and evening thundershowers. Afternoon highs in the upper-80s and evening lows in mid-70s.

Tides

At Tampa Bay: High at 3:36 p.m. Lows at 9:29 a.m. and 10:24 p.m. Sebastian Inlet: Highs at 9:14 a.m. and 9:29 p.m. Low at 3:14 a.m.

Sunrise today	7:11 a.m.	Moonrise today	8:00 a.m.
Sunset today	7:39 p.m.	Moonset today	8:40 p.m.

Zone

1.3 — Partly cloudy days, mostly fair nights through Thursday. Widely scattered thundershowers, mainly during the afternoon. Lows tonight in the 70s.

2.4 — Partly cloudy days, mostly fair nights through Thursday. Widely scattered thundershowers, mainly during the afternoons. Low tonight mid-70s. Highs today and Thursday low-90s coast to mid-90s inland.

5.6.7.8 — Partly cloudy through Thursday. Only a slight chance of afternoon and evening thunderstorms. Lows from the mid-60s to around 70. Highs near-90.

15.17 — Partly cloudy through Thursday. A slight chance of showers and a few thundershowers. Lows in the 70s. Highs near-90. Rain probability 30 percent today and tonight.

10.11.12.14.15.16.18.19.21 — Partly cloudy through Thursday. A slight chance of mainly afternoon and evening thunderstorms. Lows in the upper-70s. Highs around 90. Rain probability 20 percent during the afternoon and evening hours.

20.22 — Partly cloudy through

Thursday. A chance of showers and a few thundershowers. Lows in the 70s. Highs in the upper-80s. Rain probability 40 percent today and tonight.

23 — Partly cloudy through Thursday. Lows mostly in the upper-70s. Highs mostly in the mid-80s. Rain probability 30 percent today and tonight.

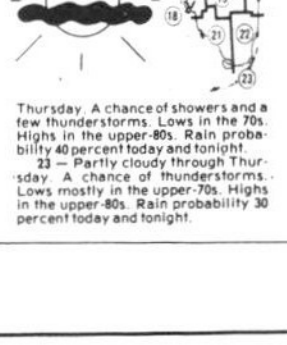

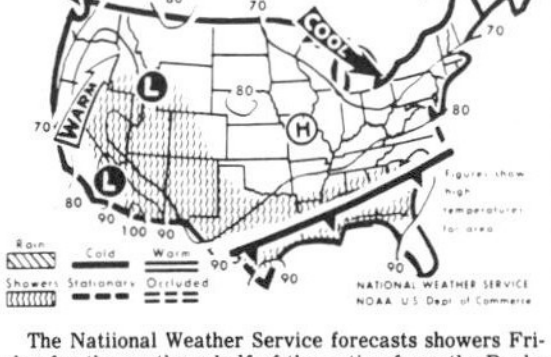

The National Weather Service forecasts showers Friday for the southern half of the nation from the Rocky Mountains east to Georgia, including the Gulf Coast states.

Farm

All Areas
Precipitation — A 20 to 30 percent chance of mainly afternoon and evening thundershowers through today with a few night and morning showers along the middle and lower east coast. Rainfall amounts will be generally less than one half inch in showers, with only isolated amounts possible up to one inch.

Dew — Moderate tonight wetting vegetation to 10 hours and drying off by 10 a.m.

Temperatures — Highs today mid-90s inland areas to around 90 near the coast. Lows tonight near 70 panhandle and north with low to mid-70s central and south.

Winds — Variable at 10 mph or less panhandle and north and mostly easterly at 10 mph or less central and south, except for afternoon onshore breezes near coastal areas. Winds mostly calm at night. Brief gusty conditions in and near thundershowers.

Marine

St. Augustine to Jupiter Inlet out 50 miles — Winds east to northeast around 10 knots through tonight. Seas 3 feet or less. Winds and seas higher near few thunderstorms.

Jupiter Inlet to Key Largo out to Bahama Bank; Key Largo to Dry Tortugas including the Florida Straits and Florida Bay — Winds northeast 10 to occasionally 15 knots through tonight. Seas 2 to 4 feet. A light chop on Florida Bay. Winds and seas higher near scattered thunderstorms mainly tonight.

Cape Sable to Tarpon Springs 50 miles — Winds variable mostly east and northeast around 10 knots through tonight. Seas 3 feet or less. Winds and seas higher near a few thunderstorms.

Tarpon Springs to Apalachicola out 50 miles — Winds variable around 10 knots through tonight. Seas 3 feet or less. Winds and seas higher near a few thunderstorms.

Temperatures

Florida

	H	L	Prc.
Apalachicola	87	73	
Daytona Bch	87	71	1.15
Fort Myers	93	78	
Gainesville	90	68	.16
Homestead	90	71	
Jacksonville	88	72	.10
Key West	89	79	.10
Miami	88	73	.10
Orlando	90	70	.38
Pensacola	90	74	
Sarasota	88	72	.01
Tallahassee	93	67	
Tampa	90	73	
W Palm Bch	88	73	.28

National

	Hi	LO	Prc
Albany	76	39	
Albuque	64	62	1.06
Amarillo	79	58	.80
Anchorage	57	44	
Asheville	89	56	
Atlanta	94	72	

Atlantic City	75	64	
Baltimore	90	59	
Birmingham	100	67	
Bismarck	87	60	
Boise	84	56	.01
Boston	75	53	
Brownsville	98	76	
Buffalo	78	57	.12
Charlstn, SC	84	72	.16
Charlstn, WV	87	61	
Cheyenne	58	45	.01
Chicago	74	66	.68
Cincinnati	90	62	.05
Cleveland	78	59	.16
Columbus	85	63	.46
Dal-Ft Wth	92	69	.03
Denver	56	50	.49
Des Moines	72	61	.04
Detroit	78	60	.78
Duluth	74	47	.63
Fairbanks	61	35	
Hartford	78	40	
Helena	74	42	
Honolulu	87	75	
Houston	90	78	
Indnaplis	88	68	
Jacksnville	90	70	
Juneau	58	47	.33
Kans City	79	69	
Las Vegas	83	69	.13
Little Rock	90	71	
Los Angeles	76	63	
Louisville	93	68	.26
Memphis	101	77	
Miami	85	76	
Milwaukee	71	64	.41
Mpls St P	70	53	
Nashville	98	70	
New Orleans	98	76	
New York	88	61	
Norfolk	86	61	
Okla City	93	66	
Omaha	71	59	.01
Orlando	90	74	
Philad'phia	85	67	
Phoenix	99	80	
Pittsburgh	80	61	.31
Ptland, Me	69	42	
Ptland, Ore	93	52	
Rapid City	70	44	
Reno	80	48	
Richmond	88	60	
St. Louis	93	77	
St.P-Tampa	90	73	
Salt Lake	72	56	.12
San Diego	75	63	
San Fran	80	55	
Seattle	78	50	
Spokane	79	48	
St Ste Marie	61	55	.49
Tulsa	95	75	
Washington	95	71	

Canada

Temperatures were not available from the National Weather Service at press time.

World

	Hi	Lo
Amsterdam	64	50
Athens	85	60
Bangkok	91	82
Beirut	73	59
Belgrade	73	59
Berlin	63	50
Bogota	66	45
Brussels	64	53
B Aires	64	53
Cairo	84	71
Copenhagen	68	61
Dublin	63	52
Frankfurt	57	57
Geneva	68	59
Helsinki	68	57

Hong Kong	88	81
Jerusalem	90	64
Jo'burg	68	45
Kiev	79	55
Lima	64	59
Lisbon	73	64
London	68	54
Madrid	86	70
Manila	88	72
Mexico City	75	54
Montreal	68	45
Moscow	66	48
New Delhi	89	74
Nicosia	95	68
Oslo	61	46
Paris	75	55
Rio	m	m
Rome	84	57
San Juan	90	77
Seoul	77	61
Sao Paulo	m	m
Singapore	88	77
Stockholm	68	61
Sydney	64	50
Taipei	88	79
Tel Aviv	84	61
Tokyo	77	68
Toronto	73	63
Vancouver	75	52
Vienna	64	53

Summary

Local

Tuesday was partly cloudy and warm.

	Tue. High	Tue. Low	Record High	Record Low
Temperatures:	91	74	95	69

	Tue. to date	Sept. Normal to date	Year Normal year
Rainfall to date: *	—	Sept. 1.21 1.98	37.93 39.10

* rainfall is from 6 p.m. Monday to 6 p.m. Tuesday.

National

Up to eight inches of rain drenched parts of southwestern Texas on Tuesday and flash flood watches and warnings were issued for parts of the state during the day. Thunderstorms continued from the western side of the lower Mississippi Valley across the southern Plains and Kansas. Showers and thunderstorms also were scattered from southern Iowa and northern Missouri, across the northern Ohio Valley, into western New York and Pennsylvania. Storms also were scattered along the southern Atlantic coast and Florida.

Tuesday's satellite cloud picture recorded at 1 p.m. shows high clouds and thundershowers along a frontal band from the Great Lakes to New Mexico and thunderstorms throughout the southern Rockies and central Plateau as well as in western Texas. Broken middle clouds cover eastern Texas and Louisiana.

Continuous weather information is available over VHF radio 162.55 MHz.

Moon phases

First Quarter   Full Moon   Last Quarter   New Moon
Sept. 17   Sept. 24   Sept. 30   Oct. 8

Nation

Compiled from Ledger wire services

Nuke-test cave-in injures 12

LAS VEGAS, Nev. — An underground nuclear test blast triggered a tunnel cave-in Wednesday, injuring at least 12 atomic scientists and engineers, one of them critically. Officials said no radiation escaped.

The injured workers were in trailers on the desert surface, checking instruments that recorded the blast, when the ground fell "a dozen or so feet," said U.S. Department of Energy spokesman Jim Boyer. "A collapse in this hard-rock area is very unusual," he added.

The accident occurred shortly after noon — three hours after a nuclear test code-named Midas Myth-Milagro was detonated 1,168 feet underground.

"There was no escape of radiation when the earth subsided," Boyer said, adding that the workers were "bounced around" as the ground gave way beneath trailers.

Boyer declined to give details of the test at Rainier Mesa, about 90 miles northwest of Las Vegas, except to say that it was "less than 20 kilotons."

Upset about new braces, Texas teen commits suicide

PLANO, Texas — Apparently upset after getting new braces on his teeth, a 14-year-old "computer whiz" shot and killed himself, becoming the seventh teen-ager in this Dallas suburb to commit suicide in the past 12 months.

Plano police Sgt. J.C. Randall said David Eugene Harris shot himself with a .357-Magnum pistol about 8:30 p.m. Monday. Randall said the youth pulled the weapon from the nightstand in his parents' bedroom.

His parents, Mr. and Mrs. Gene Harris, said their son did not leave a note, but they told police he had been in good spirits until he came back from the dentist's office with a mouthful of braces.

"His _____ said that's the only reason they could _____ himself," Randall said.

AP photo

A fence shadow casts patterns at the snowbound Roxy drive-in theater near Elmira, N.Y.

Blizzard blows 'full bore' out of the Rockies

The Associat

Signals
Inside Section A the words "Nation" and "World" act as headings for briefs and flags signaling subsections. The large bold initial contrasting with the light type makes a designed-looking graphic unit.

World

Compiled from Ledger wire services

Soviet Union expels two Britons trying to bring in Zionist books

MOSCOW — Two British tourists were expelled from the Soviet Union for trying to bring "Zionist books" into the country, the official news agency Tass reported Wednesday.

The two were identified as Maurice Schneider, a 47-year-old electrical engineer, and his wife Susanne, a 39-year-old teacher.

Tass said they were kicked out of the coun _____ attempted smuggling of literature, _____ tent bodie _____

Editorial spread

Above: Dummy layouts create an optimum space for Op-Ed with a minimum of two Op-Ed pieces. The configuration, however, is flexible, allowing a third piece to go down the gutter. The pages are designed as a spread. Bold and light type is again used functionally, setting off the editorials from the columns. A photo on Op-Ed in the dummy suggests possible variations from syndicated cartoons, one of which already is anchored on the editorial page.

Mark-up

Left: Layouts were marked up to act as initial style guides until the paper could format elements and make its own working style sheets or style book.

The Ledger

LAKELAND, FLORIDA SINCE 1924

John R. Harrison, President
Elven Grubbs, Publisher
Louis Michael Perez, Editor
Will F. Corbin, Managing Editor
James Fuller, Production Director
Jim Johnson, Circulation Director
E. Walter Garris, Controller
Don Whitworth, Advertising Manager

NYT A NEW YORK TIMES COMPANY

EDITORIAL

Benjamin Hudson drowning

Why residents of the Lakeland urban area should continue to be exceedingly uneasy about the quality of service provided by Herndon Ambulance...

On Memorial Day, May 26, rescue teams were dispatched to Lake Parker. Witnesses reported seeing 11-year-old Benjamin Hudson Jr. disappear in the water.

A fire department rescue team quickly responded, as did a Herndon emergency vehicle. Young Benjamin's body was found after about 15 minutes. And according to one report, rescuers felt a slight pulse when he was pulled from the water.

But when he arrived at the Lakeland General Hospital emergency room only a few minutes away, he was dead.

The refreshing elements of this story are the fast response of the fire department and Herndon rescue units, as well as the quick recovery of the boy's body from the water.

The disturbing elements, however, overwhelm all else. They indicate, once again, that Herndon is not providing the best emergency service available. They indicate, once again, that the City Commission — which licenses the service — is lackadaisical when it comes to monitoring Herndon's performance.

Herndon's performance was less-than-adequate in the Benjamin Hudson drowning in several respects.

The ambulance unit which was used in this emergency was not an Advanced Life Support (ALS) unit, but rather a Basic Life Support (BLS) unit. The difference can be critical. Herndon has no state-certified ALS vehicles, according to state emergency medical services records. And that means that — under state laws and regulations — Herndon is not permitted to perform the more sophisticated ALS functions such as administering intravenous (IV) fluids at accident scenes and inserting endotracheal tubes in drowning victims.

In the case of Benjamin Hudson, no life-sustaining IV fluids — such as adrenalin and sodium bicarbonate — were administered. Nor was an endotracheal (ET) tube used. An oxygen mask was. But we have been told by one emergency room doctor that an ET tube is preferred in treating drowning victims because it gets oxygen to the lungs, while it guards against the victim choking on his own vomit. Moreover, an adult-size oxygen mask on a child's face frequently results in the loss of valuable air.

Another cause for concern is that neither of the two Herndon personnel who worked the Hudson drowning was a state-certified paramedic. That may explain, in part, why they did not administer IV fluids or use an ET tube; state regulations preclude them from performing those procedures. Furthermore, the lack of a state-certified paramedic on this emergency run shatters the credibility of Herndon President Idus Willis. In early April, Willis promised that by the end of the month he would require a state-certified paramedic on every Herndon emergency call here.

The response of Lakeland General Hospital emergency room officials is, at best, puzzling. In March, we were told that no LGH emergency room doctor would authorize IV at accident scenes unless the individual performing the procedure was a state-certified paramedic. Now we are told doctors may authorize someone to administer IV even though that individual is not a state-certified paramedic.

The doctors who take it upon themselves to authorize someone who is not a state-certified paramedic to administer an IV had best be mindful of one fact: They are defying state regulations adopted under Florida Statute 401, and thus opening themselves to undefined liability.

But back to the drowning death of Benjamin Hudson. Doubtless, the Herndon technicians who worked the case are capable, dedicated individuals. Doubtless, they did everything within their power to revive the young man. But, in too many respects, their hands were tied.

Would the immediate administration of IV fluids have kept Benjamin Hudson alive that day? Would the use of an ET tube by a qualified state-certified paramedic have made the difference?

The tragedy is that no one will ever know the answer to those questions.

The lesson of Venice

James Reston

VENICE — The leaders of the industrial world have come here in a vaguely pessimistic mood, but in a way this fabulous city is a symbol of their hope.

Few cities in the world seem more beautiful or more fragile. Yet not one has endured so many broken dreams and alliances and still survived to welcome the latest temporary politicians of the world.

Are Carter, Giscard d'Estaing, Schmidt and Thatcher worried about inflation, old narrow quarrels, and new warrior nations from the East? Venice has seen it all before. For centuries, the scientists have been sure that this watery paradise would be undermined by the restless tides, and even the poets have been predicting "the death of Venice" for centuries. Here is Lord Byron's lament:

> "Oh Venice! Venice!
> When thy marble walls
> Are level with the waters, there shall be
> A cry of nations o'er thy sunken halls,
> A loud lament along the sweeping sea!

Well, it wasn't quite like that when Carter and his colleagues arrived. Venice was full of sunshine and the voices of the hawker and the laughter of children.

Some things clearly have changed in Venice. The quiet slip of the gondolas, with flowers on their prows, has been overwhelmed by the hum — sometimes the roar — of the sleek new motorboats, but there are no "sunken halls." Moss thickens at the waterline of the old houses, and fresh new green plants spring out of the crevasses in the ancient walls, but somehow they stand, defying gravity and the gathering pollution.

President Carter came to Venice, fresh from a visit to the pope, warning his colleagues to beware the invaders of Afghanistan. They had a full agenda: what to do about the common defense of a civilized world — an old question — what to do about the future of Judea and Samaria, of Islam and Jerusalem, and what to do about oil, the new god of the Middle East and of the industrial world.

Nobody is expecting much from this meeting. The contemporary leaders are divided about the Middle East, and even about the defense of the West. They have come here to define long-range economic and political policies, without knowing who among them will be around to carry out their plans after the coming elections in the United States, Germany and France.

Yet this place and time are a rebuke to the pessimistic mood of this conference. It is just 40 years this month since the Nazi military conquest of France. The restoration of Europe since then and the liberation of the colonial peoples are among the greatest achievements of human history. Carter and company are not dealing in Venice with the problems of defeat, but with the dilemmas of success.

Forty years ago, after the Nazi occupation of Paris and the long struggle of the American armies up the spine of Italy, nobody would have imagined that Europe would be enjoying in 1980 the highest standard of living in its history.

Or that Western Europe, despite many differences, disputes and disappointments, could have made such progress in reconciling the ancient enmities of France and Germany and have made such progress toward a Common Market, if not yet toward a common mind.

Even a generation ago, it would have been hard to believe that the defeated nations of the Second World War would in 1980 be challenging the United States for supremacy in the export markets of the world, and that the president of the United States, after having maintained an army of over a quarter of a million Americans for over 30 years in Europe, would be meeting with the leaders of Europe, Japan and Canada in Venice to appeal for cooperation in defense of world peace.

There are obvious differences between Carter and his allies here about how to deal with the Middle East, Afghanistan, and the menace of Soviet missiles targeted on Western Europe, but never in the history of the free nations have their leaders met to discuss their common problems as frankly and on terms of such equality as they are doing here this weekend.

Venice must be enjoying and even being amused by its latest influx of spectacular visitors, by their proclamations and their protective guards — and by their multitudes of reporters, who have very little indeed to report.

Long since, Venice has heard prophecies of its own destruction, of natural forces that would sink it into the sea, of all the other beautiful names that have vanished into the abyss of history.

But here Venice is, beaming in the sunshine, a Coney Island in a cathedral, no longer believing in the religious tradition that produced its monuments, but still alive with the clamor of life and the wondering eyes of a new generation.

New York Times columnist James Reston began his career with The Times in 1939, and was once chief of its Washington bureau.

Eggs

From Scientific America

The intact shell surrounding a raw egg is remarkably strong. Many people know that if you clasp your hands with an egg between them, each end touching the center of a palm, it is almost impossible to break the egg by squeezing. What is not so well know is the difficulty of smashing a raw egg by tossing it high into the air and letting it fall onto grass.

The May 18, 1970, issue of "Time" described a flurry of such experiments that took place in Richmond in England after the headmaster of a school did it for his students. A local fireman dropped raw eggs onto grass from the top of a 70-foot ladder. Seven out of 10 survived. An officer in the Royal Air Force arranged for a helicopter to drop eggs from 150 feet onto the school's lawn. Only three out of 18 broke.

"The Daily Express" hired a Piper Aztec to dive-bomb an airfield with five dozen eggs at 150 miles per hour. Three dozen of them were unharmed. When eggs were dropped into the Thames from Richmond Bridge, three-fourths of them shattered. That proved, said the school's science teacher, "that water is harder than grass but less hard than concrete."

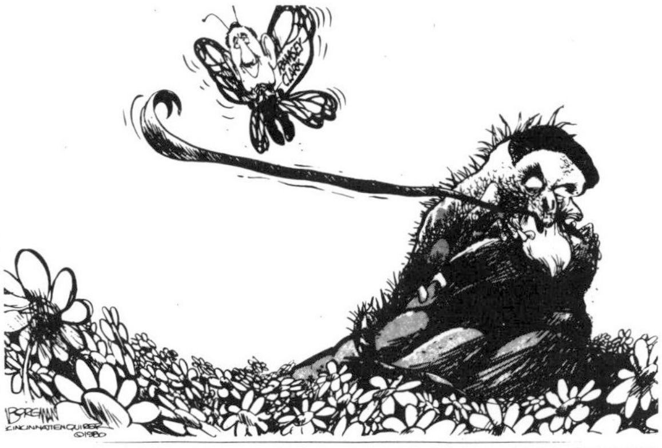

Jim Borgman — Cincinnati Enquirer

Readers write on Ramsey Clark

Voice of the People

Letters are welcome

The Ledger welcomes letters to the editor for publication in the Voice of the People column. Letters should bear the writer's true name, address and phone number. Upon request, names may be withheld from publication. But all unsigned letters will be rejected. Generally, letters must not exceed 400 words, and all letters are subject to editing. Please address letters to:

Voice of the People
P.O. Box 408
Lakeland, Fla. 33802.

EDITOR:

Your editorial, "Ramsey Clark's bad trip," (June 12) states "By shooting off his lip in Iran, Ramsey Clark did favors for nobody, just nobody." As I see it, by shooting off your lip denouncing his integrity and education by cute and clever insinuations, you did favors for nobody, just nobody.

Why this attack on Ramsey Clark? Dozens have uttered similar opinions about American/Iranian relationships, among them the Rev. William Sloane Coffin, Riverside Church, New York City; United Methodist Bishop C. Dale White of Princeton, N.J.; the Rev. William Howard, president of the National Council of Churches, all of whom have been in Iran recently . . . and the list goes on.

Ramsey Clark may not be an "anguished parent waiting outside the embassy gate for a brief visit with a son" but he is an American humanitarian who, with many, is anguished that few newspapers are trying to enlighten the American public as to the reasons for such strong anti-American feelings among Iranians.

The American Friends Service Committee "urged President Carter to help Americans become aware of the role of the CIA in overthrowing a popular nationalist leader in 1953 and installing the Shah, in aiding SAVAK, the Shah's dreaded secret police, and in militarizing Iran through military aid and sales." (The Churchman, St. Petersburg, January 1980).

I have complimented The Ledger when I felt it presented viewpoints that increase knowledge and tolerance. The fair columns on Ramsey Clark by Mary McGrory and James Weighart, appearing in The Ledger one day before your comment, are in that category. In my opinion, yours is not.

RAINY KISSLING
Lakeland

Jail, not support, needed

EDITOR:

Would anyone care to answer a few questions that occur to me:

1. Why does your paper publish anything to promote Ramsey Clark, when he was guilty of treason in Vietnam and only because we are not at war with Iran, is not guilty there? Do I have the same right to be heard?

2. Why, in your opinion, is Ted Kennedy still running for president? Does he hope Carter will goof so badly before the Democratic convention, get shot before the same, or, perhaps, feel anyone as unpopular as he, needs the protection of the Secret Service he gets as a candidate?

3. Why is Anderson still going, since he too should know that no one wants him for president? Does he hope to get another $100,000 to run as an Independent?

These all seem a bit hard for me to understand. As a veteran (WWII), retired from Civil Service Fire Dept. and a taxpayer, it would seem anyone who disobeys the law, defames the country he lives in, and gives aid and sympathy to known enemies of ours, should be in jail, not supported by the news media.

A. RAY HORNE
Fort Meade

Clark should pay penalty

EDITOR:

The following telegram has been delivered to President Carter:

"The 66,000 members of the American Legion, State of Florida, demand the prosecution of Ramsey Clark.

"Federal law bans unauthorized travel to Iran by American citizens and provides a possible $30,000 fine and a 10-year prison sentence for the violation thereof.

"Ramsey Clark has not only deliberately violated this prohibition, his statements give aid and comfort to the radicals who hold hostage the 53 American citizens. If we were officially at war with them, he would also be guilty of treason.

"Therefore, he should suffer the full penalty of the law."

We strongly urge all concerned citizens to take similar action. We must draw the line. We must halt those who would go to the enemy camp and hide behind the guise of "freedom of speech" to give aid and comfort to those who would destroy our country.

RAY MATTOX
Commander
The American Legion
State of Florida

Why condemn Clark?

EDITOR:

I am a Southern American and proud of it. I wish all we Americans would stand up and say so.

Why is Mr. Carter so heated up about Ramsey Clark going to Iran? I know Mr. Carter put a ban on going to Iran. But did he have the right to do this? I think Mr. Clark did what he thought he had to. Maybe he did as much good as all the other people who have gone over there. Maybe he heard more over there than Mr. Carter or his men want anyone to hear. He didn't apologize as did the mother of one of the hostages.

So why condemn Mr. Clark? Could it be Mr. Carter wants us to take our mind off the Cuban mess we taxpayers have here in Florida?

Did Mr. Carter have the right to open his arms and heart to people from other countries? I have not seen on TV or in the papers where any of them have gone to Plains, Ga., or to Washington, D.C.

EVA BRATTON
Polk City

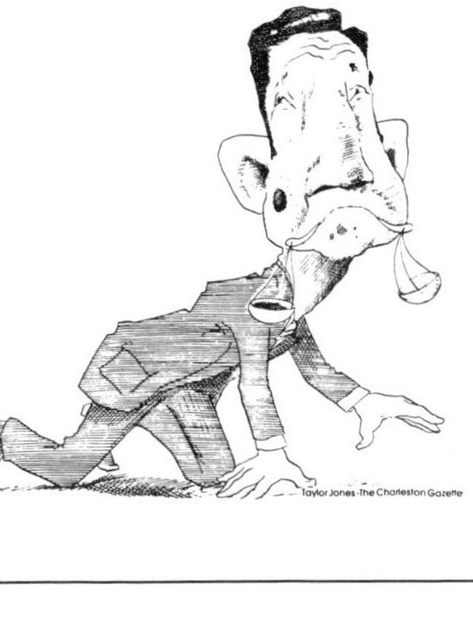

Taylor Jones - The Charleston Gazette

Citizens can foil crime

EDITOR:

The criminal justice system and its elements in Polk County worked hard to hold the line against crime and criminal. Last year, we sustained one of the very smallest percent increases in major crimes in any county in Florida.

The support, involvement and assistance of the citizenry, business, civic and church leaders is needed.

Lakeland citizens interested in forming Neighborhood Watch Groups for crime prevention can call Mr. Dick Kirchen, Anchor Insurance, at 682-3151, the Lakeland Police or the Sheriff's Department. Advice and assistance will be given. Interested citizens may also call me at 533-0411 ext 214.

It is said that "All that is needed for evil to prevail is a few good men and women . . . doing nothing." So it is with crime and crime prevention.

Later in the year, the Lakeland Chamber of Commerce Crime Prevention Action Group is sponsoring Mr. Fred Storaska, nationally known lecturer on the prevention of rape. Every woman in Polk County will want to consider attending this special crime prevention event.

H.E. DANIELS
Criminal Justice
Task Force
Coordinator
Bartow

A gig or garland?

EDITOR:

I used to love The Ledger. Especially "Conversation Pieces." I read my paper in the same sequence every morning.

First, the local news, which I find very informative. Second, I whiz through the front section to make sure no national disasters have occurred as I slept (such as Ted Kennedy opening a driver training course for young Americans).

"Conversation Pieces" is kind of my "dessert reading" and I really enjoyed it until recently. My main complaint is Bonnie Cleaver's "Confessions of a Housewife." I find her about as interesting as a string of dead catfish. That applies also to her parakeet, her macho fireman-husband, her four kids and her new swimming pool. BORING!!!!!!

I love Erma Bombeck and despise Art Buchwald. You choose to alternate the two columnists when it looks like you could either make room for both or poll your readers to see which one they prefer.

I read "Dear Abby" faithfully. Sunday is my very best paper-reading morning, as I have more time. Alas, no "Dear Abby" appears in the thickest paper of the week!

Finally, come on Will Corbin! We were proud for you when you announced the birth of your daughter. However, I found subsequent articles concerning your daughter's first steps, first words, etc., a little like the bumper sticker that reads, "Let me tell you about my grandchildren."

I would be very interested to know if other readers feel as I do on these issues. Do I get a gig or a garland?

J.H.
Winter Haven

Flexible make-up

The top half of the Op-Ed page is the minimum space agreed upon for editorial matter, but the ad placement sometimes allows for more. Small pieces that can be made into boxes, like the Work and Family box, help break up gray type masses and attract the browsing eye. "The other hand" label of the dummy was dropped in favor of, first, Opinion II and then Opinion.

Sunday editorial

Facing page: On Sunday, the columnists move over to an expanded Op-Ed page and Letters grows on the editorial page.

Local/State

Simple headings

An early rough tissue and dummy paste-up (see accompanying illustrations) carried out variations in size and weight of the one typeface from top to bottom, including the section heading titles. A no-frills design, I hoped, would not only achieve a recognizable character, but would also have a good deal of lasting power.

The section headings couldn't be simpler; with a band across the top, they make the most of the forceful design of Lubalin's letter forms. The customary bold rule separating the heading from the page below was dropped in favor of the bold rule at the very top of the page, making the heading title an active part of the page itself. Subsidiary headings—"Briefs" and "Polk Pulse"—were treated in the same way.

Patching

A first step to provide zoned editions to different communities was to create treatments at the bottom of Page 1B to highlight the name of a community. This designated area allows quick, efficient replating for different readerships.

In some of the later redesigns on other newspapers, the ability to replate for zoned editions became even more important than at *The Ledger*. This treatment at the bottom of the page was then expanded and sometimes accompanied by changes in the "Briefs" column and in the title of the section. (See chapters on the *Times Daily*, Florence and *The Press Democrat*, Santa Rosa.)

Two "patches"
The first rough shows the bottom of the page designed as an easily changed separate unit for zoning the content of the page, with a community label set in above the photograph. The dummy page above, marked up for spacing style, shows a modified treatment with the patch designation set more quietly between two rules.

Patching flexibility
Facing page: The patch sometimes goes across the bottom, emphasizing its flexibility in the format. It moves up frequently to become a more integral part of the section front.

In brief

Non-residents to pay more for burial

FROSTPROOF — City officials here welcome visitors as long as they are alive. But visitors who die in this town will have to pay extra if they want to stay in the city's Silver Hills Cemetery.

In hopes of "extending the life of the cemetery," the City Council Monday set two sections aside for burial of crematory urns and infants. City Manager Dan Ruhl said the move will save space in the cemetery, because five urns can be buried in a normal sized burial plot and three infants can be buried in the same space.

The council approved a rate structure for the two categories, similar to the sliding scale paid for regular plots. The council agreed to charge city residents $35 for urn plots, residents living within five miles of the city $45 and those from further away $55.

Infant plots will cost $45 for residents, $65 for those within five miles and $100 for others.

Ruhl said the reason non-residents are charged more is simply because "we don't want them filling up our cemetery." Since rates for residents here are far less than they are in other area cemeteries, Ruhl said the cemetery could soon reach its capacity if it were opened to everyone at the city rate.

Strickland studies motion for inmate transfer

BARTOW — Circuit Judge Tim Strickland spent most of Tuesday studying a motion to transfer a Polk County Jail inmate because of poor jail conditions, but will not release a decision on the case until today.

The motion, filed by Assistant Public Defender Rex Dimmig on behalf of Daniel Charles Reilly, said the jail violated constitutional rights.

Strickland is still studying written arguments filed Monday by Dimmig. The state filed no arguments in rebuttal.

Claimant in sex discrimination, city officials meet with EEOC

DAVENPORT — Harriet Rust, who filed a complaint of sex discrimination against Davenport in April, met with city officials at an Equal Employment Opportunity Commission fact-finding conference Tuesday, but Town Attorney Dale Willingham said no offers of settlement were made.

Mrs. Rust filed a complaint with the EEOC after a hiring committee bypassed her application for a job as recreation director and hired Robert Lane. Mrs. Rust contends she was turned down for the job because of her sex and that Councilman Kenneth McNabb was responsible for Lane's hiring.

She said McNabb indicated she couldn't do the manual labor involved.

Mayor Robert Bradbury, McNabb, Mrs. Rust and Willingham attended the conference.

"I don't want to comment on it," Willingham said, "We were placed under oath, and no court reporters were there. We really did not accomplish anything."

Mrs. Rust said she learned at the meeting that her case would be turned over the the Miami EEOC office — which is the next level. She said she was told an investigator would be assigned to her case.

Monday night football gets approval of Frostproof council

FROSTPROOF — Chalk one up for Howard Cosell and the other broadcasters on Monday night football telecasts.

Unpaid City Council members here have voted to change their meeting nights in order to avoid conflicts with ABC's Monday night football broadcasts and give the city clerk more time to assemble city bills before the monthly meeting. The council Monday voted to change its meeting night from the second Monday of the month to the third Tuesday.

City Manager Dan Ruhl said the change was necessary because not all bills to the city arrive before the second Monday when that day falls earlier than the tenth of the month. Since the council must approve payment of all bills, this has meant a one month delay in payment at times, Ruhl said.

A change to the third Monday was originally proposed, but the council rejected that proposal and voted 5-2 to make Tuesday's the meeting night so that football broadcasts would not be missed.

Polk County Grand Jury deliberates

BARTOW — The Polk County Grand Jury met for several hours Tuesday, but issued no indictments.

State Attorney Quillian Yancey said the grand jury did not finish their inquiries and would meet again next week.

Possible subjects of indictments were not revealed.

Sheriff's Department to auction bikes

BARTOW — Sixty bicycles will be on the auction block Saturday as the Polk County Sheriff's Department tries to get rid of the recovered stolen bicycles it has accumulated this year.

The auction will start at 9 a.m. at Building No. 232 at Bartow Air Base, sheriff's spokesman Steve Hulsey said. Each bike will go to the highest bidder, he said.

Polk pulse

DIAL 68-PULSE (687-8573)

Today's question: Should more Green Swamp land be taken off of the state's environmental protection list?

Tuesday's question: Two massage parlors raided Thursday evening by the Sheriff's Department were back in business Friday night. Should the department continue to act against the establishments?

YES: 50%
NO: 50%

No, I don't think they should continue raiding them, but Sheriff Mims will do just what the church says . . . No, I don't think the raids by the sheriff's department should continue because they serve no purpose at all unless one of the sheriff's friends is trying to get elected agian this year, in which case it would make sense . . . Yes, continue to crack down also on illegal gambling . . . Yes, I think the department should continue, that's an excellent job . . . Yes, they should be closed for good . . . I think the people in Polk County elected a sheriff not a minister to take care of the moral issues . . . Yes, but too much news about it could help advertise the places . . . Yes, but only if drugs are involved.

State exempts land from Green Swamp

By Ron Cunningham
Ledger capital bureau

TALLAHASSEE — Gov. Bob Graham and the Florida Cabinet Tuesday exempted more than 27,000 acres of land from the area of critical state concern encompassing the Green Swamp.

The unanimous vote came over the protests of environmentalists, who said the action presented potential dangers to flood plain and possible water recharge areas near Polk City.

The exemptions — almost 20,000 acres along the southern boundary of Lake Juliana and Polk City, and nearly 8,000 acres south of the city of Clermont — represent about about 8.5 percent of the 322,690 acres under rigid state developmental controls for several years.

The Cabinet action came as a result of a new law, passed in a special legislative session, that replaced the critical state concern designation over the Green Swamp following a court challenge to the old law. The new law also required the

See State on Page 2B

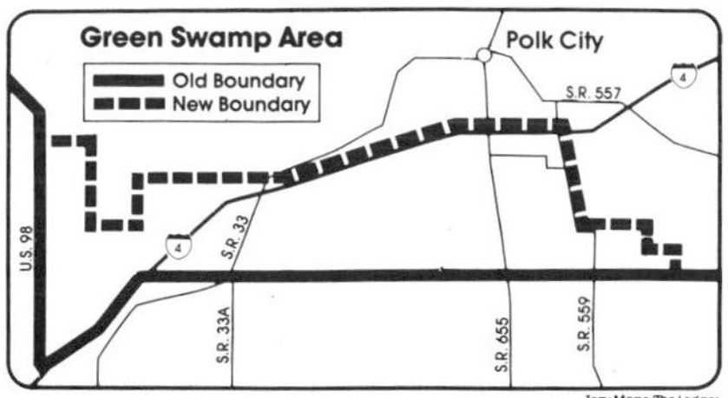
Green Swamp Area
Old Boundary
New Boundary
Polk City
S.R. 557
4
U.S. 98
S.R. 33
4
S.R. 33A
S.R. 655
S.R. 559

Terry Morse/The Ledger

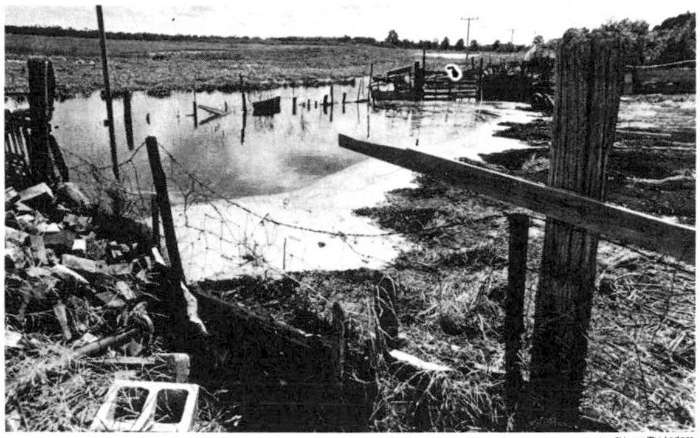

Joe Skipper/The Ledger

Wet and wild

Cora Owens, owner of this property bordering the west side of the Bartow Air base, said she had to evacuate eight pigs to higher ground when flood waters rose about three weeks ago. She is also concerned about the safety of three small children who live on the property. She said an alligator somehow got through the chain link fence that surrounds the airbase and it tries to catch feeding birds in her yard.

First Assembly OKs purchase of Carpenters Home

By Cheryl Nordby
Ledger staff writer

LAKELAND — The First Assembly of God congregation approved Monday night the purchase of 470 acres of the Carpenters Home property north of Lakeland bordered by Lake Gibson, Interstate-4 and U.S. Highway 98, church officials said.

"The only sure thing is if all the contingencies of the contract are met a worship center will at least be built there," said church attorney John Anderson.

Anderson said there are a lot of different ideas on how to use the old Carpenters Home building, including a school and retirement home.

Rev. Karl Strader, the church's pastor, is in Phoenix, Ariz., looking at churches to get an idea of what will accomodate the congregation's needs, Anderson said.

The contract has been signed, he added, but the purchase was contingent on four items:

• Approval of the congregation. Ninety percent (about 350 church members) at Monday's business session approved, he said.

• Zoning. The land is zoned as a planned unit development, so final plans will probably have to be approved by the county's zoning board, Anderson said.

The third contingent is soil boring. Engineers will be testing the soil to see what kind of construction is suitable there, he said.

See First on Page 2B

IN SOUTH POLK

Stavely suing Mulberry for 'wrongful arrest

By Barbara Donaghey
Ledger staff writer

MULBERRY — City Commissioner Dick Stavely announced Tuesday night that he's suing the city for $25,000, citing his "wrongful arrest" earlier this year on charges he was eventually acquitted of.

In addition to Stavely's suit, his co-defendents Jimmy Bradshaw and Randall Mills also are asking for $25,000 each, Stavely said.

A letter to the City Commission from attorney Wallace Story, representing the three men, said the $75,000 is for "damages sustained on account of the wrongful arrests" of the men.

Stavely and Bradshaw were arrested and charged with obstruction of justice when police said they interfered with the arrest of Randall Mills, outside the Mulberry Restaurant, March 19.

Mills was charged with battery of an officer, resisting arrest and driving while intoxicated. When he was pulled over he refused to sign a traffic citation and and began to physically resist arrest, police reports said.

Stavely and Bradshaw came to his aid and were charged with obstruction of justice, reports said. The charge of disorderly intoxication was added later.

Charges against Bradshaw were later dropped for lack of evidence and Stavely was acquitted by a jury in July.

Mills was given two years probation by Circuit Judge William Love on the resisting arrest charge and acquitted on the DWI charge.

At the commission meeting, board members voted unanimously to reject the charge and to forward the matter to City Attorney Denis Fontaine.

Stavely abstained from voting.

After the meeting, Stavely referred questions to his attorney, but said, "Hell, I deserve more than $25,000. I think I deserve $100,000. They gave $95,000 to that nigger lawyer." He was referring to a municipal services discrimination suit filed against the city by civil rights attorney David Lipman on behalf of several black residents.

That suit, settled out of court earlier this year, called for the city to pay Lipman $52,550 in fees and to spend about $280,000 to upgrade services in black neighborhoods.

Stavely said he wasn't mad at the police department.

"I'm not mad at anybody," he said. "I just don't feel I was treated right and that's what laws are for."

Stavely said he had been contemplating a suit for several months.

"I started thinking about it the day they put the charges on me," he said.

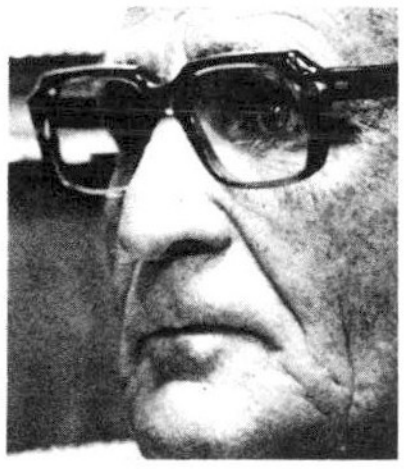

Dick Stavely is seeking $25,000.

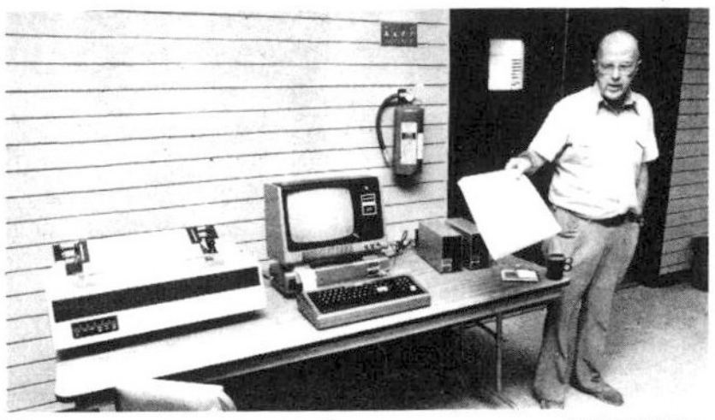

Joe Skipper/The Ledger

Demo computer

This computer which has never before been used by small cities was demonstrated to city commissioners Tuesday afternoon by Mulberry City Manager Joe Mitchell, who has asked the commission to approve the purchase of the $6,500 unit because it will allow the city to do the water and sewer billing itself. In the past, the city has contracted with a Clearwater firm to do its billing for $8,000 a year. Mitchell said the machine will pay for itself in the first year, and will be pure profit after that.

Stewart drops proposal to eliminate utility tax cap

By Barbara Donaghey
Ledger staff writer

MULBERRY — Commissioner Bill Stewart gave up his fight to do away with the city's utility cap Tuesday night after it was evident he lacked support for the measure.

After complaints from Mayor Carl Ellis that his proposal should have been on the agenda and Commissioners Maxo Evans and Dick Stavely, who said they wouldn't support Stewart's recommendation, Stewart said, "I'm going to drop it right here."

Stewart's proposal was to do away with a 10 percent utility cap, and use the $20,000 in revenue that would be taken in to handle water and sewer rate hikes.

"The users of electricity are being taxed 10 percent of the electricity they use. Up to $200," Stewart said.

"A person can have a $200 bill and he pays $20. Another one used $3,000 in electricity and he pays $20 because there's a cap on it," Stewart said.

Approximately 19 businesses would be affected, since they have the biggest utility bills, Stewart said.

"We're becoming insensitive to the needs of low-income families," Stewart said. "I think we owe it to the people living on $300, $400 or $500 a month.

"If we take the entire cap off we would be ahead and wouldn't need to raise the rates one red cent."

Evans and Stavely said they wouldn't support the proposal because it would affect the businesses, which support the city.

"Corporations and businesses help the city," Evans said. "They're the biggest taxpayers."

Evans pointed out W.S. Badcock Corp. donated a swimming pool to the city, which cost more than the money the city would make from the proposal in one year.

"And others do more than that," Evans said.

"We've got to give a break to enhance businesses," Evans said. "I don't believe $1.50 a month (in rate hikes) will hurt a person."

Ellis asked City Attorney Denis Fontaine whether such an action could be considered discriminatory towards businesses.

"It could be looked at as discriminatory," Fontaine said. "They could file a suit and not pay it. It could ripen into litigation if we pick out certain people."

Stewart argued the companies could recover the cost from the extra tax by raising prices "a few cents."

Bartow city employees' union approves new contract

By Barbara Donaghey
Ledger staff writer

BARTOW — Members of the city employees' union gave their approval on a two-year contract with the city Tuesday night.

The contract, which includes a 6 percent raise for the city's 75 employees was passed by a 70 percent margin.

Curtis Smith, chairman of the Industrial and Public Union Local 1998, said, "The 30 percent wanted more money. Money was what they were really upset about.

"We're still not happy about getting only 6 percent this year," Smith said.

The city's final offer included a 6 percent raise for 1980 and 7 percent raise in 1981.

At a final meeting between the union and city negotiators last week, the union was still requesting changes in the contract. But any further negotiations would have to have gone to a special arbitrator, City Labor Attorney Jake Dyal said.

Included in the requests were a 15 percent raise the second year, the right to picket non-job related incidents and an extra holiday.

Other sections

No-frills continued

The no-frills approach continued from Section A and B into the Sports, Style, Business, Food, and Sunday sections. Every newspaper design project challenges the designer to find different ways to represent themes such as "Local," "Sports," "Business," and "Style." Modest variations are sometimes achieved ("SportsMonday" and "Sports Pages" in *The New York Times,* for example). At *The Ledger* the addition of AM provided a touch of individuality as well as emphasizing the paper's conversion from afternoon to morning publication.

The familiar two rules traditionally confining most newspaper datelines were abandoned in favor of the dateline type hanging off a single rule, separated from the headlines below by a designated space. With less separation, the heading and the rest of the page act cohesively. A secondary heading referring to inside elements or sections such as the Classified pages can also be presented in this space.

Sports

The Sports/AM front page picks up the wide left-hand column of Pages 1A and 1B and highlights results and reefers in an echo of the front page. However, here Avant Garde Bold is used, rather than the lighter weight used on Page 1A, partly to avoid the dullness of repetition (a strictly subjective consideration) and partly to unify the page and give the reader a perception of more headlines. Strong emphasis is placed on photos on the Sports front and not on story count. The strong reefer treatment compensates for this.

Life/Style

In the Life/Style section the wide column on the left was dropped to allow big feature treatments across the full width of the page. Provision for a feature columnist was made at the bottom of the page.

Compared to later redesigns on other papers, the Life/Style section was fairly elemental. Later redesigns, even on small papers, have gone into themed daily sections, first introduced in *The New York Times,* and emphasize service material such as tips, boxes, "how to," and consumer information to a far greater degree. Perhaps more in this section than in the others, the strict adherence to the basic Avant Garde typography in forceful sizes gave the section a compelling look. The format decreed an end to the ad hoc innovations in headlines (such as twiggy typography for a story on log cabins and other abominations) found so frequently in the sadly neglected "Women's Pages" of most newspapers at that time.

Business

Because of press requirements Business would run only occasionally as a true section front. Two headings were designed, one in the same style as the other sections when the section enjoyed an outside front page, and a quieter heading for use on an inside front page. In the latter design, as on any other inside page, a regular dateline was employed. The wide column on the left is repeated from Page 1A under a heading for briefs called "High Interest."

Sports section
Facing page: Color in the mid-1980s was still limited, but effective make-up keeps the page lively. The daily question at the bottom of the column is a typographical and informational punctuation mark. The Preps column moves up into the middle of the page to allow for the unusual vertical thrust of the color panel at the bottom. Layout: Dave Reeves.

D

Sports/AM

The Ledger

Thursday, February 16, 1984

Grenelefe tennis tourney opens, 6D/ Freshwater fishing report, 6D

L

Moc women play Florida. 6D

Dreadnaughts victorious. 6D

Cosmos rip Rowdies. 7D

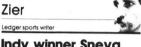

Patrick Zier

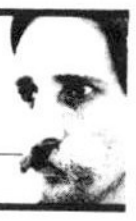

Ledger sports writer

Indy winner Sneva has no Daytona ride

DAYTONA BEACH — Once upon a time, Tom Sneva taught math and driver education at a high school in Sprague, Wash.

It's a good thing he didn't teach logic, because if he had, and if he tried to apply it to his situation now, he might be ready for the funny farm.

Logic dictates that if you win the Indianapolis 500, one of the most prestigious races in the world, you should have people clamoring after you to drive their cars. You should have your pick.

But racing is not logical, and so it is that Sneva is the one doing the begging. As of Wednesday, last year's Indy 500 winner did not have a ride for this year's race.

Further, he is running here in a car which, although it was reasonably strong on the NASCAR circuit last season, may not be good enough to make the Daytona 500 field.

That's because its new owner, Robert Harrington, is in much the same position as Sneva. He hasn't got a sponsor, and without big bucks, you don't make a big splash.

The Sneva-Harrington connection is a one-race deal because Harrington couldn't find a sponsor for his regular driver, Morgan Shepherd, and Sneva got Simoniz to kick in some cash for this race.

As for Indy, Sneva blames his predicament on "bad timing," which also did in Harrington.

"I thought I was set with Texaco," Sneva said. "I had a chance to take several deals last fall, but I turned them down because I thought Texaco was going to back me, and a lot of people didn't even contact me because they knew my situation with Texaco.

"Because of that," Sneva continued, "I passed up a lot of things.

"Then on Jan. 2, Texaco made a 180-degree change. They said they were getting out of racing entirely, and by that time, everybody was set. There just wasn't anything available."

Much the same thing happened to Harrington, who expected to be bankrolled once again by J.D. Stacy.

Harrington had been team manager for Stacy and crew chief on his car, and then Stacy suddenly told him he was getting out of racing.

"I had been proceding on the assumption he would be backing us, and I bought a lot of parts and pieces that I haven't paid for," Harrington said.

"When he got out, I tried to work something else out with Morgan as our driver. As late as last Tuesday, I was still trying to work something out, and Tom knew that if I could get something together, Morgan was going to drive and Morgan knew that if I couldn't, Tom would have the car."

Last Wednesday, Harrington firmed up the commitment with Sneva because, he said, "it gave us enough money to get down here and back and run the race, and it will pay some of the bills."

Sneva, meanwhile, is still trying to land an Indy ride, and is talking with Ted Mayer, formerly with Team McClaren, about driving his car.

"I've always been realistic about racing," Sneva said. "Seven or eight years ago, winning the Indy 500 almost automatically guaranteed you something, but not anymore.

"Look at Johnny Rutherford. He hasn't got a ride either, and he's won Indy three times."

Financial considerations, Sneva said, now take precedent over almost everything else at Indy. What you've done on the track can help you, but it isn't money in the bank.

"I really didn't think winning Indy was that big," Sneva said. "I had finished second there three times, and I only moved up one position.

"But America is a win-oriented society, and finishing second is losing in people's minds.

"After you've been at Indy 10 years, it isn't as big as it seems the first time, but there is a difference — people talk about it all year. I've had more requests to make public appearances. People want you because you won Indy, not because you're Tom Sneva."

But that was last year. In 1984, at Daytona, the 1983 Indy winner is in a car that will probably have its doors blown off, if it makes the race at all.

And as embarrassing as that is, he may still be better off here than in his own back yard, where he might not even be able to play.

Question

Is it true that Joe DiMaggio once hit safely in more than 56 straight games while in the minor leagues?

Answer: Yes. DiMaggio hit in 61 consecutive games while playing for San Francisco of the Pacific Coast League in 1933, his first full season of organized baseball. He was 18-years-old at the time. DiMaggio holds the major league record of 56 consecutive games, set in 1941 with the New York Yankees.

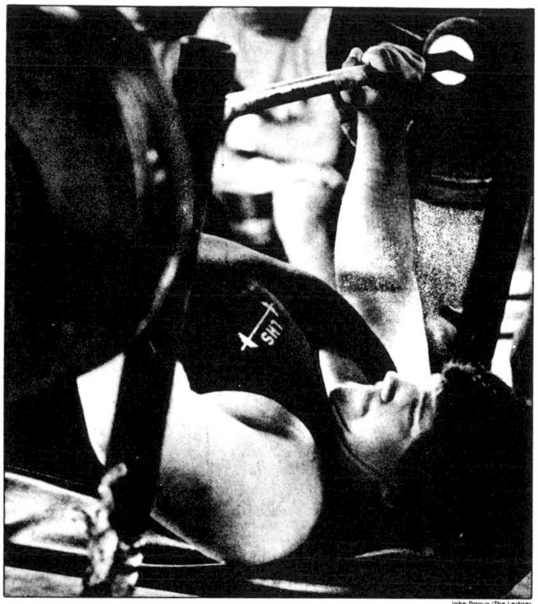

John Raoux/The Ledger

Sets state record

Lakeland High School's David Williams set a new state record of 420 pounds in the bench press Tuesday in the city high school weightlifting meet at Lakeland High School. Williams also set a heavyweight state record for overall weight lifted. For more on the meet, see Page 6D.

Tie drops U.S. team out of sight

Today's Olympic TV schedule, 8D
Olympic results, 8D

By D. Byron Yake
The Associated Press

SARAJEVO, Yugoslavia — America was not watching. The seats were not filled. The goalie was not draped in red, white and blue. The U.S. hockey team played Finland Wednesday at the Winter Olympics, and there wasn't even a winner. They tied 3-3.

Four years ago, the two teams met and it meant something. Enraptured Americans were riveted to their television sets on a Sunday morning, watching a miracle on ice develop before their eyes. A 4-2 victory gave the U.S. team a gold medal.

Goalie Jim Craig, flag over his shoulder, peered into the crowd of thousands, looking for his father. America had won.

Overall, the U.S. Olympic team won 12 medals in 1980. This Olympics has produced a sparse crop of three. The U.S. could be facing its worst performance since it won only six at the 1964 Games.

Prospects for getting more than 12 in the 1984 Games diminished even further when two promising women figure skaters had poor performances in the compulsories. That left chances for an American medal in that event to a sole contender.

The only drama in the U.S.-Finland hockey game Wednesday lasted for only 37 seconds, when the U.S. team took the lead on a late short-handed goal, then lost it with 15 seconds left when Finland tied. The tie made it certain the U.S. would finish no better than seventh in the 12-team field, its worst Olympic hockey showing ever.

"It has not been our year," Coach Lou Vairo said.

"It's been difficult to put aside what everyone expected of us," defenseman Bob Brooke said. "We were intent to do it but it proved to be really, really difficult. There was the buildup for six months (of exhibition games) and what the 1980 team did. It all added up."

There was drama in men's downhill, and of a brighter shade for Americans.

Bill Johnson of Van Nuys, Calif., clocked the fastest

See Johnson on Page 8D

Fulse is filling it up at Fort Meade

Preps

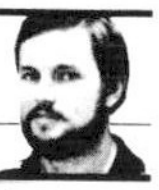

By Del Milligan

FORT MEADE — Lance Fulse has more trouble getting his hands on the basketball than he does putting it through the hoop. That's because once he gets it, chances are it's going to be two, as in points.

Fulse, Fort Meade's 6-foot-6, 245-pound center, is the leading scorer in Polk County with a 28-point average. His 60 percent field goal percentage helps keep him about 10 points better than anyone else.

Fulse, The Ledger's Player of the Year last season when the Miners made it to the state tournament at the Lakeland Civic Center, naturally pulls down a lot of rebounds, considering his height. Sixteen a game to be exact.

And while he is a natural-born scoring machine, Fulse has been criticized on a couple of points. Some say he's not aggressive enough, others that he's not in shape.

For those who believe he's not in shape, take another look. Fulse, who carried a little bulge last season, has trimmed down and converted extra weight into muscle.

And there's two reasons why he's not as aggressive as one might think. "The first game last year, I got thrown out for elbowing a man in the mouth. They told me, 'One more time and you're out for the season,' he said.

"I could play more aggressive, but I hold back," he explained. Coach Archie Gale can't afford to have Fulse on the bench, so he has to play with some degree of caution.

"Sometimes he's criticized for that," agreed Gale. "But if he goes, there goes my inside game. I'm not crazy about him being aggressive."

So you can see there are answers to those detractors. The point is, the man can fill it up. And it's a lot harder to teach somebody how to shoot than it is to light a fire under their Pro Keds and say, "Get it in gear."

Fulse, nicknamed "Big Man," said he's always felt good about his shooting. He used to like to shoot from the deep corner, but since the 10th grade he has moved in and has limited his shots to the paint. Big No. 35 is deadly from the free throw area and has the angles down on the short banks.

Fulse, who also enjoys acting in school plays and is an active member of St. Paul's African Methodist Episcopal Church, is getting more and more attention from college basketball recruiters. He's already visited the University of Tennessee at Chattanooga. And Fulse, with a "3.2 or 3.3" grade-point average, is headed to Texas Tech this weekend. Future trips may include Villanova and Southwestern Louisiana.

Mention of last year's state tournament still hits a sore spot with Fulse. The Miners lost in the semifinal game to Monticello-Jefferson County.

"Gosh, I was mad," he recalled. "We shoulda killed that team. That hurt."

See Milligan on Page 6D

Mocs maul Florida Tech

Florida Southern box score, 2D
Sunshine State Conference standings, 2D

By John Valerino
The Ledger

LAKELAND — Travis Stanley led a balanced Florida Southern scoring attack with 23 points to pace the Mocs to an 82-64 Sunshine State Conference basketball victory over perennial pushover Florida Tech here Wednesday night at Jenkins Fieldhouse.

Stanley hit on 7-of-13 shots from the floor and added a 9-for-10 performance at the line en route to his game-high 23 points as the Mocs improved their league record to 7-5.

Scott Knecht pumped in 16 points for the Mocs, who are now 11-14 overall, while Al Garmon came off the bench to add 14. Paul Woerner, used sparingly this season, got the cobwebs out of his system and contributed 10 points and 10 rebounds in 19 minutes.

Now that we have that out of the way, here's what Wednesday's blowout did for the Mocs. By mauling Florida Tech for the umpteenth straight time, the Mocs remained tied for third place in the SSC with St. Leo College, which defeated Rollins Wednesday, 75-65. Meanwhile in Orlando, league co-leader Central Florida annihilated Villanova of Miami, 75-44. In St. Petersburg, Tampa stayed tied for the SSC lead with Central by outlasting Eckerd, 75-71.

By winning Wednesday, Central Florida and Tampa, both 9-3, clinched berths in the conference's post-season tournament, which will feature the top four teams during the regular season Feb. 24-25 at Jenkins.

By losing Wednesday, Rollins and Villanova both fell to 6-6, one full game behind Southern and St. Leo in the chase for the third and fourth berths in the SSC Tournament.

Now that we've covered that, back to Wednesday's game at Jenkins.

The Mocs struggled in the first half. They shot just 34 percent from the floor and were guilty of some pretty bizarre mistakes, yet they somehow managed to take a 28-26 lead at the intermission.

In the second half, Southern looked like a completely different team. The Mocs finally got their fastbreak in high gear, shot 65 percent from the field and totally

See Mocs on Page 7D

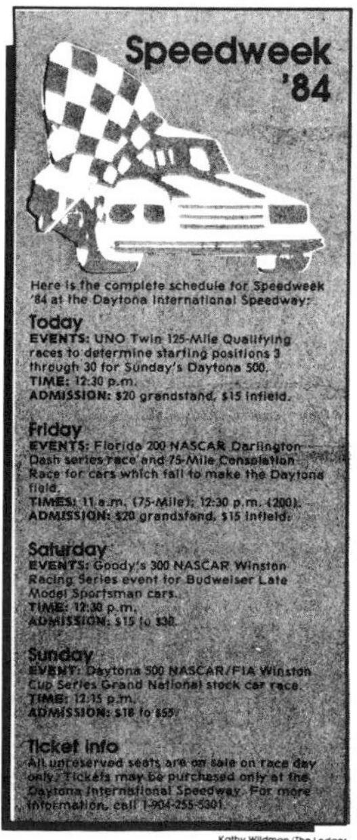

Here is the complete schedule for Speedweek '84 at the Daytona International Speedway:

Today
EVENTS: UNO Twin 125-Mile Qualifying races to determine starting positions 3 through 30 for Sunday's Daytona 500.
TIME: 12:30 p.m.
ADMISSION: $20 grandstand, $15 infield.

Friday
EVENTS: Florida 200 NASCAR Darlington Dash series race and 75-Mile Consolation Race for cars which fail to make the Daytona field.
TIMES: 11 a.m. (75-Mile); 12:30 p.m. (200).
ADMISSION: $20 grandstand, $15 infield.

Saturday
EVENTS: Goody's 300 NASCAR Winston Racing Series event for Budweiser Late Model Sportsman cars.
TIME: 12:30 p.m.
ADMISSION: $15 to $30.

Sunday
EVENT: Daytona 500 NASCAR/FIA Winston Cup Series Grand National stock car race.
TIME: 12:15 p.m.
ADMISSION: $18 to $55.

Ticket info
All unreserved seats are on sale on race day only. Tickets may be purchased only at the Daytona International Speedway. For more information, call 1-904-255-5301.

Kathy Wildman/The Ledger

Marcis has clean hands

By Patrick Zier
The Ledger

DAYTONA BEACH — Dave Marcis is walking around the Daytona International Speedway garage with clean hands these days.

If you don't think that's big news, you don't know Dave Marcis.

Now in his 16th year of Grand National competition, the 43-year-old Marcis has spent most of his time as an independent.

When he wasn't in the car, you could find him under it or bent over it, tinkering with this and fixing that.

An hour after his car was off the truck, while Cale Yarborough, Richard Petty, Bobby Allison and such sat off to the side while others prepared their racers, Marcis was likely to be covered with as much grease as there was in his ride.

While not exactly your buddy-can-you-spare-a-dime independent; his cars ran better than that, Marcis never had a real shot at winning, either.

And every time he got behind the wheel, he knew it.

Once, in the mid-70's, he got into a car owned by Nord Krauskopf, not a real muscle machine but one capable of running up front at times, and he won four races, three in 1976 including victories at Talladega and Atlanta.

The team did not have a major league budget, though, and eventually, it folded and Marcis was scrambling again.

In 1982, he scrambled well enough to win at Richmond in his own car, but generally it was back to the old grind.

Until this year. This year, when the drivers and car owners went into their annual game of musical chairs, Marcis found a place to sit. It was unexpected.

At the end of last year, there was a vacancy in the Rahmoc car (owned by Bob Rahilly and Roy Mock).

Their 1983 driver, Neil Bonnett, was leaving for Junior Johnson's greener pastures.

At first, they thought Ricky Rudd was going to take the ride, but he worked out another deal, and then Rahmoc apparently landed a bigger fish, Richard Petty.

But problems described as "political" by Petty put a

See Marcis on Page 4D

Big display

While the rest of the paper emphasizes typographical structure and tension for page interest, the Life/Style section takes a step toward a more frank visual display. This dummy layout encourages the lead story to go across the full width of the page.

Space for complexity

Large space for display doesn't mean just one oversize picture, which often is simply an easy but superficial way to fill the space. Here a little extra effort provides a variety of images. The contemporary book illustration in the center pleasantly brings the presentation up to date. Layout: Jane Nickerson.

Sunday

A change of pace in the larger Sunday paper usually allows one major feature presentation on the whole page. The one-typeface design for heading and headline gives the page strength and a uniformity it might not otherwise have. Layout: Lynne Croft.

Business on Sunday

An outside front for Business. During the week the Business section is folded inside, with a scaled-down version of the heading (a regular dateline at the top of the page and no logo). The design of all section headings allows the easy placement of small departmental reefers under the flag hairline. Not closed in, these become active parts of the page despite their small size. Layout: Ray Dupuis.

Visual aids

In the composing room

The Ledger composing room
Composing room staff should be as well briefed as the newsroom editors in all aspects of the new design.

Digital typesetting and the third generation of front-end systems were still in the future when *The Ledger* was redesigned. While many elements of the new design could be formatted, many details of the design involving line-up, spacing, and weight of rules depended on skillful, dedicated implementation by the paste-up people in the composing room. Even today, with the ability to format and generate whole parts of a page from an editor's desk, any composing room is a critical place. At *The Ledger*, we paid a great deal of attention to the composing room, recognizing that the effectiveness of a design could be weakened or nullified here.

In our meetings, my assistant, Bob Pelletier, and I made sure that the production people, and particularly the composing room foreman, were present or apprised of what was going on from the first stages of the project. Pelletier made a special point to keep the paste-up staff informed, and we did our best to provide guidance with personal contact and marked-up style sheets.

Earlier experience had shown that on many papers, editors tended to communicate only minimally with composing room staff. In the tense, tight days of actual start-up of a new design, very little leeway was left for the loss of time and emotion spent on the petty bickering and trivial finger-pointing that can occur if every detail is not prepared as carefully for paste-up as it is for the newsroom and the printer.

We found that it paid off to follow through on every detail that could conceivably cause a problem in those first few days. The list of these details for project leaders includes, for example, the following:

1. Throw out veloxes of old-style standing heads.

2. Be sure new veloxes or printed pads are readily accessible, informing the paste-up staff. On start-up night, put new headings in clear view, separated by section, each in an open box marked boldly. Fumbling in drawers should not be necessary. If *everything* is formatted, be sure the formatted heads duplicate perfectly the character and spacing of the designer-produced prototypes.

3. Be sure the editor or designer personally gives the paste-up staff an informative pep talk. Don't depend solely on the production chiefs to adequately communicate the desires of the designer.

4. Be sure style books, style sheets, and sample pages in the new style are distributed in the composing room as well as in the newsroom. But don't expect style books to be much help under deadline. Pelletier and I taped sample pages marked up for style over every paste-up desk in the composing room and made sure others were available for ready reference. If the designer doesn't do this personally, there's a good chance the visual aids will remain unused in an obscure corner, while editors and paste-up staff bicker.

5. Be sure all shifts are informed. No matter how much preparation is done, it's guaranteed that, on start-up night, somebody is going to say "nobody told me about this."

In spite of all efforts, the first days of going over to a new design are bound to be tense and a little frantic. The plus side is the assurance that the new design, if planned adequately, will result in reaffirmed concern for quality throughout the operation. It is likely that the very process of redesign will make procedures as well as the newspaper itself more rational and efficient.

SECTION HEADINGS

CONGRESSIONAL QUARTERLY

HOME IMPROVEMENT

HOUSE DOCTOR

GARDEN TIPS

TRAVEL

DEPARTMENTS

Patrick Zier
Sports Editor

Working Woman
By Niki Scott

COLUMNS

Standing heads

These are the basic building blocks. Most are formatted into the system, but at Lakeland it was necessary to provide veloxes in the early experimental stages of page make-up. Standing heads can be dealt with in a hierarchy of three orders: section, column, and department. Subdivisions and other categories exist, but this analysis can help clarify in a desk editor's mind whether he or she is thinking of, for example, a by-line round-up of items or the more personal opinion piece generally expected from a columnist. Especially in Life/Style, Sports, and Business, ambiguities like this may contribute to a murky, mixed-up report.

More than one way

A popular half-page feature in the old paper, dealing with brief profiles, was retained but with a facelift. Redesign layouts used action headlines instead of name labels; essay style instead of a repetitive résumé style; and Notes added to give some extra content to the large space. The layouts show different ways of handling the same material to keep it lively, starting with action pictures, not mug shots. Below is the feature as it ran in the past, and above and right, are the three proposals for change.

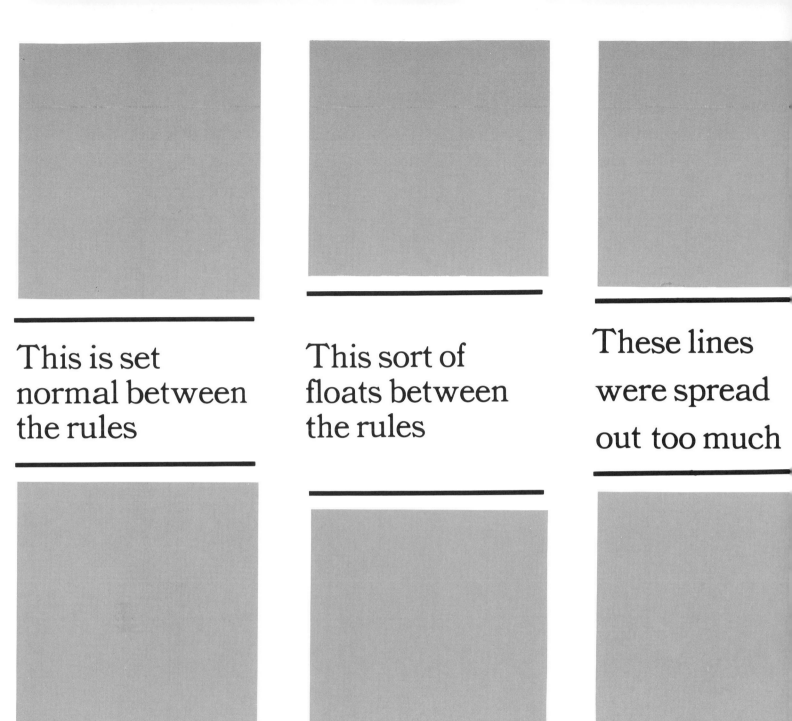

This is set normal between the rules

This sort of floats between the rules

These lines were spread out too much

Visual aids

Many spacing judgments had to be made in the composing room rather than in the first-generation computer system. Visual aids provided to guide newsroom and production staff are useful in style books and for general training purposes.

Times Daily

FLORENCE, ALABAMA

Absorbing the flavor

Enthusiastic people

My first contact with Guy Hankins, publisher of the *Times Daily* in Florence, Alabama, was a telephone call for help that was difficult to refuse. Mr. Hankins was the newly installed publisher of the paper recently acquired by The New York Times Company. I had never met him. His first words on the phone were, "If you don't come down here and redesign this paper, I'm going to have a heart attack." I went. He was obviously going to be a terrific client.

Hankins was overwhelming in his zeal to get things done. The other key people in the redesign effort were Don Browne, executive editor, quieter than Hankins, but just as enthusiastic, and Rusty Starr, managing editor, who had recently come to Florence from the *Wilmington Star-News*, North Carolina, where he had participated in a redesign project. They made a good team. Browne brought to the project his experience on a large metropolitan daily, *The Baltimore Sun*, and Starr proved to be the indispensable point man, who combined newsroom experience and technical knowledge, which he directed to the task of conversion.

My contacts and those of my assistant in New York, Bob Pelletier, were mostly with these three men. When the general approach was approved, our efforts then shifted to the main desks in the newsroom, News, Features, Sports, and Business, as we tried to incorporate specific ideas from

The place
Traffic in downtown Florence. Industrial plants and the bridge leading to other communities across the river are in the background.

each. Circulation at that time of redesign stood at 28,000 daily, 34,000 on Sunday. The news staff numbered 28. It was considered that expanded efforts in a bureau across the river from Florence would necessitate an increase in news staff, but there was no budget for an artist or designer. The paper would have to depend on its existing staff and the occasional use of the one artist employed by the Advertising Department.

When we went "live," it was scheduled that Bob Pelletier would work in Florence with the editors and in the composing room for a week or so to help give the new design a good send-off. In this way the pattern of a "hands-on" approach we followed from the start continued. The time devoted to the redesign of a project—five or six months for a paper of this size—is not only a period of implementing changes but of education for everyone involved.

The two days of my first visit were spent absorbing the flavor and history of the paper and in acquiring some sense of the community. Like a great many smaller papers in the United States at that time, the *Times Daily* had already "modernized" itself in response to the requirements of cold type and other technological changes. The result was the same as in most other papers—a bland paper featuring one headline face, the ubiquitous Bodoni Bold. I looked at old issues on microfilm, going back in the paper's 125 years of existence. I toured the various communities with Don Browne. Florence is located in the Muscle Shoals area on the Tennessee River toward one end of the Tennessee Valley Authority (TVA) system. This is the vast network of dams and waterways created by Franklin D. Roosevelt's New Deal, which reclaimed farmland and brought cheap electricity to a particularly depressed area. TVA was one of the most dramatic and visible projects in FDR's efforts to bring the country out of the Depression.

At the time of the redesign project, the area was suffering through a depressed economy once again. In the early 1980s, setbacks for Detroit's auto-makers in a losing battle with foreign imports caused the closing of a large Ford plant, the area's largest single employer, in Florence. Aluminum plants, fed by the electricity generated at the Muscle Shoals Dam, also slowed down. Unemployment in the area rose to about 18 percent, much higher than the national average. (In 1988, unemployment was down to about 8 percent, still higher than the national average, but representing a slow, steady comeback.)

Despite this economic condition, Jack Harrison, president of The New York Times Regional Newspaper Group, felt the time was ripe to improve the paper and expand its coverage and influence in communities beyond Florence.

The *Times Daily* was an afternoon paper. Looking ahead, executives of the company anticipated the probability of a conversion to morning publication. The strengthening of the "product" was considered a necessary forerunner for significant future expansion.

Identity problem

A new flag

A civic problem was also a newspaper identity problem. The identity problem was reflected in a logo that was too complex, referring to four different towns and an earlier merger. *The Florence Times* had merged some years back with *The Tri-City Daily*. The "tri-cities" were Sheffield, Muscle Shoals, and Tuscumbia, all located directly across the river from Florence.

When I suggested that "Quad Cities" might be a logical designation, the civic problem then emerged. Despite the efforts of some people in the communities, resistance to the idea that these four towns constituted a single community still existed. When driving around, it was difficult to tell when you left one town and entered another. Yet despite their physical relationships, with many areas of homogeneity, the communities insisted firmly on being separate civic entities, with, for example, separate chiefs of police.

Though published in the town of Florence, the paper claimed all four towns as its constituency. It was important to affirm this to forestall any other paper's entry into the market and to establish a solid base for further growth. Instead of an ordinary dateline, therefore, the names of all four towns are prominently displayed, making the paper the property of each community, as well as of the region. The typography gives them equal billing but avoids any suggestion of a formal relationship. Consolidation, of course, would help the paper as well as the communities. The type treatment is a gentle, noncontroversial push in this direction. To improve coverage in the three towns across the river, bureau representation was increased and was accompanied by marketing efforts.

The logo is in the broad general character of the old logo, but the awkward wording, "Florence Times Tri-City Daily" was dropped since the town designations were already in place above the logo. The logo was reduced to the unified *Times Daily*. The type, Times Bold and Times Bold italic, has a somewhat cursive quality suggestive of classic newspaper logos. The weight is strong and the size is rather large, but the thicks and thins of the type allow the logo to relate to and become

Before

Left: The *Times Daily* shown as it appeared before the redesign. The logo retains intact the names of the two papers merged previously. In the early 1980s, the reefer boxes across the top were already a common feature in U.S. newspapers.

Proposal

Facing page: The dummy paste-up of the new design, with the four towns featured at the top, shows more display than ultimately achieved, because edition designations were added. The dummy encouraged a variety of picture treatments and the use of Times Roman subheads to provide an active typographical texture. The "front page within the front page" at the bottom shows the use of different headline styles.

Another caption goes here

Florence/Sheffield/Tuscumbia/Muscle Shoals

Times Daily

The all area team: Special feature — 23

VOLUME 113 - NO. 341   TUESDAY, DECEMBER 7, 1982   25 CENTS

Police kill anti-nuclear activist after 10-hour seige

Bomb threat proves false; acted alone

By Peggy Sanford
Staff Writer

Everyone has read about the excitement of white water floating. You know, a river out west, rubber raft with or without guide, swift current, dips, turns, spills, thrills. But the trouble with riding the rapids is that you can't really appreciate the natural surroundings. To see, try scenic floating, for which no special skills are needed. If you can sit, you can float. It's so safe, even children participate. Indeed, scenic float trips are considered a kind of G-rated family entertainment.

An absolutely stunning river to scenic float is the Snake, in western Wyoming's Grand Teton National Park. Float trips come in various lengths and styles: 5-, 10-, even 20-mile journeys. Some commence at sunrise; some in late afternoon. There are picnic lunch and supper floats. One company, the Triangle X Ranch, offers a unique overnight package that includes a late afternoon float, supper, overnight in a teepee, breakfast, and an early morning float. Such an adventure costs $60 per adult and $35 for children under 16. For the overnight, the client arrives at the ranch at 5 P.M. The drive to the meeting place is in itself an experience, for Triangle X is located in the heart of the scenic Teton Valley known as Jackson Hole. Here a visitor has an unimpeded view of the entire majestic Teton range with its snow-and glacier-capped peaks, as well as miles of sagebrush flats. (The ranch also offers hunting and wilderness trips; it is also a working dude ranch with accommodations, meals, guides and unlimited horse-riding privileges for about $70 a day.)

Shortly after 5 P.M. a van pulling a huge rubber raft on a trailer arrives. Within 15 minutes the pas-

Gray portion of map shows areas to be dredged and filled in the proposed expansion of the Florence port.This grave marker was among 25-30 that were overturned by vandals in the Florence cemetery. Shoals area businesses should be on the lookout for counterfit $100 bills now circulating locally.

Panels eye new canal plans

By Peggy Sanford
Staff Writer

Everyone has read about the excitement of white water floating. You know, a river out west, rubber raft with or without guide, swift current, dips, turns, spills, thrills. But the trouble with riding the rapids is that you can't really appreciate the natural surroundings. To see, try scenic floating, for which no special skills are needed. If you can sit, you can float. It's so safe, even children participate. Indeed, scenic float trips are considered a kind of G-rated family entertainment.

An absolutely stunning river to scenic float is the Snake, in western Wyoming's Grand Teton National Park. Float trips come in various lengths and styles: 5-, 10-, even 20-mile journeys. Some commence at sunrise; some in late afternoon. There are picnic lunch and supper floats. One company, the Triangle X Ranch, offers a unique overnight package that includes a late afternoon float, supper, overnight in a teepee, breakfast, and an early morning float. Such an adventure costs $60 per adult and $35 for children under 16. For the overnight, the client arrives at the ranch at 5 P.M. The drive to the meeting place is in itself an experience, for Triangle X is located in the heart of the scenic Teton Valley known as Jackson Hole. Here a visitor has an unimpeded view of the entire majestic Teton range with its snow-and glacier-capped peaks, as well as miles of sagebrush flats. (The ranch also offers hunting and wilderness trips; it is also a working dude ranch with accommodations, meals, guides and unlimited horse-riding privileges for about $70 a day.)

Shortly after 5 P.M. a van pulling a huge rubber raft on a trailer arrives. Within 15 minutes the passengers are at the launch site, ready to board. Everyone dons a life jacket (park regulations) and sits on the rounded edges, the midsection, or the floor of the 20-foot-long rubber raft.

Weather:
Sunny, warm

For a while there are none. Teton peaks, always visible in the tance, hardly move. The water rushes by the floating raft, guided by the man who stands as he works

Heart attack kills Marty Robbins
Succumbs after 6-day fight for life

By Peggy Sanford Sanford
Staff Writer

Everyone has read about the excitement of white water floating. You know, a river out west, rubber raft with or without guide, swift current, dips, turns, spills, thrills. But the trouble with riding the rapids is that you can't really appreciate the natural surroundings. To see, try scenic floating, for which no special skills are needed. If you can sit, you can float. It's so safe, even children participate. Indeed, scenic float trips are considered a kind of G-rated family entertainment.

An absolutely stunning river to scenic float is the Snake, in western Wyoming's Grand Teton National Park. Float trips come in various lengths and styles:

Marty Robbins

5-, 10-, even 20-mile journeys. Some commence at sunrise; some in late afternoon. There are picnic lunch and supper floats. One company, the Triangle X Ranch, offers a unique overnight package that includes a late afternoon float, supper, overnight in a teepee, breakfast, and an early morning float. Such an adventure costs $60 per adult and $35 for children under 16. For the overnight, the client arrives at the ranch at 5 P.M. The drive to the meeting place is in itself an experience, for Triangle X is located in the heart of the scenic Teton Valley known as Jackson Hole. Here a visitor has an unimpeded view of the entire majestic Teton range with its snow-and glacier-capped peaks, as well as miles of sagebrush flats. (The ranch also offers hunting and wilderness trips; it is also a working dude ranch with accommodations, meals, guides and unlimited horse-riding privileges for about $70 a day.)

Shortly after 5 P.M. a van pulling a huge rubber raft on a trailer arrives. Within 15 minutes the passengers are at the launch site, ready to board. Everyone dons a life jacket (park regulations) and sits on

the rounded edges, the midsection, or the floor of the 20-foot-long rubber raft. Floaters can also hold onto a rope that runs along the edges of the boat, but within minutes the growing feeling of security makes one uncling tight fingers.

The rafts are guided by experienced and intelligent young boatmen, who invariably — according to the brief bios in the brochures the companies offer — have two or three degrees. If you're lucky, for your float you might get Stuart Rugg, a zoologist working for his Ph.D.

As the southbound, downwater ride begins, Stuart, who is the Triangle X Ranch senior boatman with eight years of experience, delivers a virtual nonstop monologue: "The Snake is running quickly this year. Heavy snows and a massive late spring meltoff. Today it's rather fast. That's why I'm working so hard — actually using the oars to slow the boat down, not speed it up — even though it doesn't look as if I'm exerting myself. June and early July — there goes a beaver! — the water is high and quick. Many people hesitated to float.

A short goes here

The rafts are guided by experienced and intelligent young boatmen, who invariably — according to the brief bios in the brochures the companies offer — have two or three degrees. If you're lucky, for your float you might get Stuart Rugg, a zoologist working for his Ph.D.

As the southbound, downwater ride begins, Stuart, who is the Triangle X Ranch senior boatman with eight years of experience, delivers a virtual non-

---

Quad Cities Datelines

Florence:
Two arrested in bar

An absolutely stunning river to scenic float is the Snake, in western Wyoming's Grand Teton National Park. Float trips come in various lengths and styles: 5-, 10-, even 20-mile journeys. Some commence at sunrise; some in late afternoon. There are picnic lunch and supper floats. One company, the Triangle X Ranch, offers a unique overnight package that includes a late afternoon float, supper, overnight in a teepee, breakfast, and an early morning float. Such an adventure costs $60 per adult and $35 for children under 16. For the overnight, the client arrives at the ranch

Sheffield:
Girl wins contest

As the southbound, downwater ride begins, Stuart, who is the Triangle X Ranch senior boatman with eight years of experience, delivers a virtual nonstop monologue: "The Snake is running quickly this year. Heavy snows and a massive late spring meltoff. Today it's rather fast. That's why I'm working so hard — actually using the oars to slow the boat down, not speed it up — even though it doesn't look as if I'm exerting myself. June and early July — there goes a beaver! — the water is high and quick. Many people hesitated to float. In Colorado there were a couple of spills.

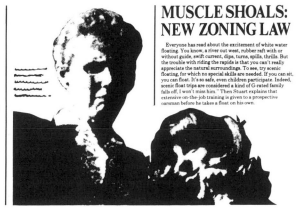

MUSCLE SHOALS: NEW ZONING LAW

Everyone has read about the excitement of white water floating. You know, a river out west, rubber raft with or without guide, swift current, dips, turns, spills, thrills. But the trouble with riding the rapids is that you can't really appreciate the natural surroundings. To see, try scenic floating, for which no special skills are needed. If you can sit, you can float. It's so safe, even children participate. Indeed, scenic float trips are considered a kind of G-rated family falls off, I won't miss him." Then Stuart explains that extensive on-the-job training is given to a prospective oarsman before he takes a float on his own.

Tuscumbia:
Plant reopens with 52 jobs

Shortly after 5 P.M. a van pulling a huge rubber raft on a trailer arrives. Within 15 minutes the passengers are at the launch site, ready to board. Everyone dons a life jacket (park regulations) and sits on the rounded edges, the midsection, or the floor of the 20-foot-long rubber raft. Floaters can also hold onto a rope that runs along the edges of the boat, but within minutes the growing feeling of the National Park, the Ranger Service licenses the oarsmen. Whoop! There's an old raven! They even send an incognito inspector" — Stuart looks at each passenger with mock severity — "to every float company at least once a season to check on service and compliance with

With 52 jobs

For a while there are none. The Teton peaks, always visible in the distance, hardly move. The water rushes by the floating raft, guided by the boatman who stands as he works the oars. An occasional hawk soars overhead. After a bend in the river, the passengers see a moose in the water. Sensing visitors, he dunks his head (moose are uniquely adapted with a nose flap for underwater swimming) and moves away. No one speaks. Plip, plip, come the sounds of the oars dipping the water. The raft floats beneath the dome of a perfectly blue sky.

Experimental logos
Above: Early rough sketches show logos based on the Quad Cities idea, staking out the desired wider constituency for the paper.

Contrasting types
Facing page: Franklin Gothic Extra Condensed caps, packed solidly, contrast in weight and style with the Times Roman Bold headlines. The 1-point horizontal rules define the column measure. A vertical rule is not used, allowing the space to flow freely between the reefers and the news stories, making the reefers more a part of the front page news and providing a bit more graphic tension.

Florence/Sheffield/Tuscumbia/Muscle Shoals LAUDER

TimesDai

VOLUME 115—NO. 66 / TUESDAY, MARCH 6, 1984 / 25 CENTS

Lauderdale County deputies stand near the covered body of a Tennessee man who was killed in gunfight near Zip City

Zip City shootout kills man; 1 hurt

By David Palmer
Staff Writer

ZIP CITY — A shootout Monday evening at a house trailer has left one man dead and another seriously injured with three gunshot wounds.

Grady Ellard Daniel, 62, Route 1, Cypress Inn, Tenn., was dead when Lauderdale County deputies and paramedics from Metro Shoals Ambulance Service arrived, Deputy Coroner Jon Jackson said.

Thomas Williams, 46, Route 3, Rogersville, was undergoing surgery at Eliza Coffee Memorial Hospital Monday night, Sheriff Billy Townsend said.

Townsend said no reason for the shooting has been determined.

"So far we've just classified it as domestic trouble," Townsend said.

Williams was in stable to fair condition at ECM, a hospital spokesman said.

"He was wounded in the right part of the abdomen and once in each shoulder. The doctors said he is going to make it," Townsend said.

Daniel had been shot once in the face and grazed on his left side by bullets from a handgun, Jackson said.

Investigators believe he was shot with a .357 magnum. ... said the bullet that killed Daniel ... for the left eye.

The sheriff's department and the ambulance service were both notified of the shooting at about 5:25 p.m., apparently by Reba Williams, the ex-wife of Thomas Williams.

Mrs. Williams was contacted by the TimesDaily but would not comment about the shooting.

Authorities said the ex-wife and Daniel were apparently inside the trailer, which is located on Lauderdale 8, when the gunfire erupted. The trailer is about 12 miles north of Florence.

There are indications from investigators that the first shots were fired from inside the trailer where Daniel and Mrs. Williams were. The glass of the front door was shattered.

At this stage of the investigation, authorities have speculated that Williams knocked on the door before the shots were fired.

Mrs. Williams, who was identified by Townsend as the occupant of the trailer, is apparently the only witness to the shooting.

Daniel was found crumpled against the outside wall of the trailer wearing house shoes.

"I came in from work this afternoon and did know anything had happened until I got this phone call from a lady wanting to know where the ambulance was going," a neighbor told the TimesDaily.

"A short time later a boy came up to my door told me that two men had been shot," the neighbor said.

part of the headline typography of the page. Generally, the logo needs to be strong to kick the page off with a good graphic start, but not so strong as to disproportionately overwhelm everything else on the page.

A small reefer picture in the right corner serves several purposes: filling up space to give a design rationale for the centered logo; making a counterpoint to the type reefers on the left; and making it possible to add variety every day to the very top of the page. It was clearly stated that the nature of the picture should vary from day to day—for example, a head shot, a close-up, a scene, or a drawing—but in practice, mug shots became the norm.

The type reefers in the upper left corner make a stronger impact in that position than they would in the more customary position in boxes across the top of the page. The black sans serif type, Franklin Gothic Extra Condensed, all capitals, gives the desired bulletin feeling. As originally intended, the reefers would vary in configuration from day to day. Several short three-liners or one or two long ones, with or without pictures, could be used. Together with the weather item, the reefers always fill up the column down to the "Shoals Dateline" cut-off rule.

The sans serif type, packed in the upper left corner, makes a black contrast to the regular headline style, becoming one of the strong identifying graphic trademarks of the whole paper. On inside pages, the type is used differently but with the same graphic intent, to display a quotation (see following pages).

Shoals datelines

At the bottom of the front page, space is allotted for at least four short news items, one for each of the Shoals towns, representing each on a daily basis. The regional edition features "Regional Datelines" with a wider representation of towns. To present an appearance of newsy variety (structured serendipity), the headline styles in this little "newspaper within a newspaper" were varied. But the format decreed precisely the use of four or five headline styles in the Times family for this purpose. The result, then, is that the reader perceives variety, and the editors have an easy-to-follow formula from which to work. The name of the town is always the first word of the headline, followed by a colon in date-line fashion. Picture usage is encouraged to vary considerably day by day.

This is in effect a little front page within the front page. It guarantees the reader in each town a story about his or her town on the front page. A story warranting the lead of the whole paper goes above the line into the main part of the front page, in regular fashion.

Although this idea attracted the editors immediately, it caused concern about the manpower needed to implement it every day. It turned out to be rough going for the first week or so, but the idea soon became an accepted part of daily procedure—an effort that paid off in a more distinctive front page and in reader interest.

With the elements previously described, about half the front page space had been "mortgaged." In the space left for the day's top news, special concern had to be given, therefore, to well-chosen stories and pictures—no fewer than two stories and, if possible, four or even five. Since so much space was already mortgaged, the design of these stories must be varied each day. If this is done, the front page is at least as varied from day to day as any other paper, and often more so.

To summarize, the following is built into the front page format: 7 to 10 stories every day, a high count by today's standards; three to five reefers, with or without pictures; a special reefer in the upper right-hand corner, with a picture; and a guarantee of a good local story, interestingly treated, for each of the four important communities every day.

First week
Facing page: Pictured is a front page in the first week of the new format. The paper's capacity for printing color was limited. The staff-generated map and silhouetted photograph represented considerable increased graphic effort for the staff. Headline count is high, 10 on the page, not including the three bulletin reefers.

Toni Thompson

Weather:
Fair, warm

Shoals weather will be fair again tonight, with a low in the mid-60s. Tuesday will be mostly sunny with a high in the upper 80s.

Florence/Sheffield/Tuscumbia/Muscle Shoals **SHOALS EDITION**

TimesDaily

VOLUME 114—NO. 227 / MONDAY, AUGUST 15, 1983 / 25 CENTS

Tom Rogers Jr. dies after long illness **7A**

Despite deficit, interest rates may go down a bit

United Press International

WASHINGTON — The board chairman of Chemical Bank predicts interest rates, which have gone up recently and stymied the recovery of the economy, will drop slightly by the end of the year.

Major U.S. banks raised their prime lending rate last Monday to 11 percent from the 10.5 percent level that prevailed for more than five months.

"I think the rate will go down by the year's end from the rate where it is now," said Donald Platten, who heads the sixth largest bank in the country.

Speaking on CBS's "Face the Nation" Sunday, Platten blamed the rate increase on Congress' failure to do something to decrease the $200 billion-plus deficit. He said bankers would need "some kind of congressional action regarding income or expenditures" before rates would drop.

Economist Eliot Janeway, writing in Sunday's Washington Post, said runaway international debts are creating a worldwide crisis comparable to the one that preceded the financial collapse of 1929 and the Great Depression.

"The West's bankers and politicians are misleading the public with their assurances that the huge load of short-term international debt constitutes a manageable problem" he wrote.

"The fact is that much of the interest on these loans cannot be paid and most of the principle will not be.

"The situation is spinning out of control and poses a clear and present danger for the entire international financial system comparable to the one preceding 1929."

Platten said Congress is going to have to do something about the United States' deficit because the people are beginning to worry about it. Janeway said only drastic action by Western governments can avert a world financial crisis and save the U.S. economy from a "financial Pearl Harbor."

Although Platten complained about the deficit, he said the economy generally appeared healthy.

"We've dispensed with the word inflation really, it's a non-subject because it is down to 3 or 4 percent as against 13 or 14 percent," he said. "I think what is going on now in the economy is very healthy. I don't think we have to worry about it being too exuberant."

Platten said the recovery would not reach certain industries and high levels of unemployment would persist.

"I think that in certain industries there is going to be no basic recovery in a significant way. I'm afraid that the problem of unemployment is going to continue with us for some time to come and that really is the biggest thing in the country today," he said.

PCB tests to continue

By Laura Simmons
Staff Writer

The Tennessee Valley Authority today issued a summary report of two years of investigative and corrective actions resulting from PCB contamination on the Muscle Shoals reservation.

TVA will continue to monitor drinking water for the reservation and water runoff from the main area of contamination "until we are sure that complete success of the reclamation effort has been achieved," Dr. Mohammed El Ashry, director of TVA's environmental quality, said.

Polychlorinated biphenyls have been linked to cancer and a number of other disorders and are regulated by the Environmental Protection Agency.

The investigation also included fish sampling from Fleet Hollow near Wilson Dam that revealed levels of the toxin above Food and Drug Administration guidelines.

TVA officials said they believe there is no health threat to humans resulting from the fish contamination but they will "defer" to the state health department for final interpretation.

TVA is continuing an investigation into continued allegations by a former employee, Thomas "Bud" Holt, that TVA dumped PCB-containing oil at

Continued on 4A

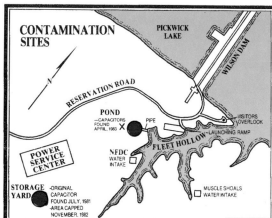

CONTAMINATION SITES — PICKWICK LAKE — WILSON DAM — RESERVATION ROAD — POND — CAPACITORS FOUND APRIL, 1983 — PIPE — VISITORS OVERLOOK — FLEET HOLLOW — LAUNCHING RAMP — POWER SERVICE CENTER — NFDC WATER INTAKE — STORAGE YARD — ORIGINAL CAPACITOR FOUND JULY, 1981 — AREA CAPPED NOVEMBER, 1982 — MUSCLE SHOALS WATER INTAKE — CHERRI HADDOCK-Staff

Man gives arm to get auto back from shop

Credit card not acceptable

United Press International

WEST SPRINGFIELD, Mass. — A man's artificial arm came in handy for collateral to pay for the repairs of his car.

Spartan Muffler Shop manager George Katsoulis said he could not accept payment with a credit card from Donald Vadnais because it was in his mother's name so he swapped the customer's $1,100 artificial arm for the keys

"I didn't want to keep the guy's car," Katsoulis said. "I didn't want to take his arm, either, but he didn't mind."

Vadnais' vacationing mother could not be reached to approve the card's use for a new tailpipe last week so Vadnais gave his right arm.

"At first it was really funny," said Vandais, who lost his right arm 13 months ago in motorcycle crash. "I told my girlfriend over the phone and she couldn't stop laughing."

Vadnais said, however, he found he could not drive with only one arm so a friend had to take the car.

"I didn't realize how much I missed it, you know," he said. "I just felt funny without it. It was the first time I felt handicapped."

Finally his mother was reached and she approved the card's use.

"My mother was shocked," Vadnais said. "She couldn't believe they let me give my arm for the car. She told me to take the card and get it back."

So on Friday the muffler shop accepted the card's use and gave him his arm back.

"It was really a joke," said Katsoulis.

U.S., Mexico key on Central America

United Press International

LA PAZ, Mexico — Despite tough disputes over immigration and economics, the Central America crisis overshadowed the urgent bilateral problems facing Mexican President Miguel de la Madrid and President Reagan in their six-hour summit on Sunday.

Mexico came away with a few concrete benefits, such as the U.S. extension of another $500 million in guaranteed credits for grains and Reagan's offer to increase oil purchases from Mexico for the U.S. strategic petroleum reserve.

The two countries also signed an accord to fight the pollution that is poisoning the air, land and waters along the 1,900-mile common border.

Wide differences remain on illegal immigration and commercial relations — Mexico wants trade barriers lowered — but the starkest contrast came when Mexico argued for non-intervention in Central America.

De la Madrid repeatedly stressed self-determination and non-intervention.

He made a pointed reference in his opening comments to the "shows of force which threaten to touch off a conflagration" directed at U.S. Navy task forces operating off the coast of Central America.

"We want the people of those countries ... to be the masters of their will and their destiny," de la Madrid said.

Mexico maintains that U.S. intervention in the region is as detrimental as the Soviet intervention channeled through Cuba and Nicaragua.

"Because we ourselves have lived through it we can understand this same experience in countries south of our border," de la Madrid said, referring to Mexico's own 1910 revolution, in which about 1 million people died.

While both countries call for non-intervention and self-determination, a senior Mexican diplomatic source has praised leftist-ruled Nicaragua's steps toward establishing electoral policy.

The source also said that the purported supply by the Nicaraguans of arms to leftist Salvadoran guerrillas is a less important arms source than weapons captured from the army itself.

But while Reagan throughout his speeches stressed the enormous cooperation between the two countries, de la Madrid repeatedly underlined the differences.

"The relationship between Mexico and the United States is moment by moment becoming a two-fold priority; we seek to avert our differences and we must resolve those that arise with all due dispatch," de la Madrid said.

SHOALS DATELINES

Tony Shirley helps Randy Bigoney warm up

JON KILLEN/Staff

Russellville: Petition for booze

A petition is being circulated in the Russellville area by citizens and businesses that favor legal sales of alcohol.

Russellville and Franklin County officials said Friday they were not aware of the petition or who was circulating it.

Russellville City Clerk Keith Gladney said the circulators apparently are trying to get enough signatures to call for a referendum so voters can decide if they want legal sales in Franklin.

Gladney said he knew nothing about the petition or where it originated.

Tuscumbia: Liquor to be topic

Colbert County officials have a "long agenda" for Tuesday morning that includes several liquor license applications, according to a spokesman.

The commissioners are scheduled to meet at 10 a.m. at the Colbert County Courthouse in Tuscumbia.

Other business items that are expected to come up include petitions for rights-of-way from the county highway department, the spokesman said.

Florence: Chambers to meet

Members of the Colbert County and Florence Area chambers of commerce Tuesday will be guests of the University of the North Alabama at an "Early Bird Breakfast." The newly renovated cafeteria of the Towers residence hall complex on North Pine Street will be the site of the breakfast, which begins at 7:15.

Grubb, 'Shape up'

Wayne Grubb was not overwhelmed by the physical condition of his players when they reported back to camp Sunday afternoon, but even in his disappointment he says his North Alabama football team has plenty of time to "get everyone heading in the right direction."
See full story, 5B.

Muscle Shoals: Fire guts club

Fire gutted a Muscle Shoals night club Sunday afternoon in the second unexplained blaze in that city within a week.

This morning, Fire Chief Dean Lesley and Fire Marshal Dickie Lesley were still investigating the origin of the fire, which heavily damaged Babe's on Avalon Avenue. A fire department spokesman said the fire began shortly after 1 p.m. in the unoccupied club.

Lesley said today that he had no reason to suspect arson "at this point."

Units from both fire stations responded to the call and had the fire under control within 15 minutes. The spokesman said the fire was beginning to burn through the roof when firefighters arrived around 1:30 p.m.

The club received structural damage and heavy damage inside because of the intense heat and smoke.

Sheffield: Tinga gets recreation bid

Sheffield this morning awarded a contract for landscaping around its recreation center to Tinga Landscaping of Muscle Shoals.

Tinga was low bidder when bids were opened at a special meeting at City Hall. The firm's bid was $13,800.

The city received two other bids, one from Triple B Nursery and Grass Co., Russellville, for $13,958 and one from Murphy Brothers Landscaping, Florence, for $14,930.51.

Tinga will begin work this week.

Opening spread

People

In a relatively tight newspaper, it seemed important to consolidate newsholes as much as possible, to present a strong news presence and avoid dribbling news stories among the ads. We were able to negotiate a very strong opening spread with optional-size ads in the lower right portion of Page 3.

A wide column in bastard measure (17 picas) was built into Page 2 for "People Making News" and for "Datelines" on Page 3. A picture was to run at the top of the column each day. A special style for this was devised with a bold 3 point rule around it, with rounded corners to give the picture a movie-frame suggestion and set it off from the rest of the spread.

The headings for the People items were designated to run in bold, light, and italic, as well as in the regular Times Roman, in the same manner as the "newspaper within a newspaper" on Page One, and for the same reason, to give some visual "bounce" to the items and make them look less like a listing. The one-point rules, top and bottom, relate the items to each other and set them off from the many regular headlines appearing on the two pages.

"Bumping heads" at one point became an issue on pages similar to Page 3, where type quotations lined up at the top with headlines.

Bumping heads was a more relevant issue, I felt, 20 or 30 years ago, when the make-up of newspapers posed a set of completely different problems. Then, newspapers used smaller display type, a wide assortment of faces, headline styles that filled the columns, columns that were squeezed together, and as many as 20 or 30 stories on a page. When all of this was jammed together without any white space relief, two headlines that ran side by side, each tight in its space, were undoubtedly difficult to read, and editors were correct to avoid the situation. But none of these factors are relevant today. With few stories on the page, a flush-left type treatment, clean white gutters separating columns, and more careful make-up in general, "butting heads" need no longer be taboo. Our make-up guidelines provided simple rules to make the arrangement work: 1) play a horizontal, one-line headline against a one-column, multiple-line headline, 2) be sure the horizontal headline stops short of running the full width to allow a minimum of one-half a column width of white space; and 3) make good use of contrasting typefaces.

Labels at the top

Instead of the overworked "Briefs," "Datelines" is used in a reverse panel in Franklin Gothic Extra Condensed caps. The reverse panel lines up exactly with 2 point rules in which "In The Nation" (or "In The World") is set, running across the entire spread not including ads.

The most arresting part of the top of the page treatment was the use of a brief quotation at the top of the Dateline column. The quotation is

PEOPLE
MAKING NEWS

Canadian stunt driver Ken Carter of Montreal died Sunday of injuries sustained when he attempted a midnight jump over a pond in his rocket-powered car in Peterborough, Ont. Carter, 40, had been trying to set a world record by jumping a 300-foot span. His car flipped and landed upside down.

Spelling champion deserved to win

SALEM, Ore. — There may not be a more deserving spelling champion than Blake Hodgetts. He read a dictionary in the car on the way to the state spelling bee and managed to spell tough words like "politicoois" and "omphaloskepsis."

Schoolgirl breaks one of male bastions

LONDON — One of the last bastions of British male chauvinism has crumbled. A schoolgirl was allowed into the men-only pavilion at the Marylebone Cricket Club's famous Lord's cricket ground.

Couple gets rude awakening

WASHINGTON, Pa. — Allan and Mary Jo Stiles had a rather rude awakening during the weekend — a car plowed through the wall of their bedroom, landing an arm's length from their bed.

Nader says OSHA 'demoralized' agency

WASHINGTON — Under the Reagan administration, OSHA has become less of an enforcement agency against industrial hazards and more of an "industry-indoctrinated" bureaucracy, consumer advocate Ralph Nader charges.

Familiar bedfellows make strange politics

HARTSVILLE, Ind. — Familiar bedfellows can make strange politics.

Challenger scores perfect landing

United Press International

EDWARDS AIR FORCE BASE, Calif. — Space shuttle Challenger glided out of the early morning darkness to a perfect night landing on a floodlit ribbon of concrete today, capping a textbook mission that put America's first black in space.

"Shoot that was fun. Let's go do it again."
— Richard Truly

Finale

Fireworks explode over the Nelson-Atkins Museum of Art's building in Kansas City, Mo. Saturday night. The display capped a day of events celebrating the museum's 50th birthday.

Next shuttle carries Spacelab

United Press International

CAPE CANAVERAL, Fla. — Spacelab, a $1 billion research facility designed to let less-astronaut scientists study in space.

Labor Day death toll increasing

United Press International

The Labor Day weekend traffic fatality count topped 270.

Hot holiday predicted

United Press International

Much of the nation suffered through a steamy Labor Day weekend.

WEATHER: PARTLY CLOUDY

Forecasts

Weather summary

Lake Levels

Temperatures

TimesDaily

'We're here so people don't have to be afraid to walk the streets at night.'

Guardian Angel leader Lisa Siwa

Guardian Angels add to problems for Joliet police

JOLIET, Ill. — Police struggling to solve 17 summer slayings now bear an added burden of criticism triggered by the arrival of the Guardian Angels volunteer patrol group.

Chinese stowaway seeking asylum

SAN FRANCISCO — Religious persecution in Communist China drove a 21-year-old Cantonese peasant to swim in Hong Kong, hide on a Mexican freighter and jump ship in the San Francisco Bay Area, seeking asylum in the United States.

Officer who shot boy quits force

STANTON, Calif. — A policeman who mistakenly shot and killed a 5-year-old boy he found clutching a toy gun resigned from the force.

Woman believes twins are good

Guidelines make it harder to get aid

WASHINGTON — New guidelines adopted by the Legal Services Corporation make it more difficult for the poor, the elderly and the handicapped to obtain its services, it was reported.

Citizens Party picks candidate

SAN FRANCISCO — The left-wing Citizens Party has decided to field its own candidate in the 1984 presidential election instead of throwing its support behind civil rights activist Jesse Jackson.

Crimes against people on decline

United Press International

WASHINGTON — A decreasing percentage of young people in the United States may be contributing to the largest drop in the number of Americans victimized by crime in 10 years, the Justice Department reports.

Protesters in Piscataway, N.J., bow their heads in prayer for the 269 persons aboard the Korean plane which was shot down.

Protesters storm Soviet retreat

United Press International

More than 1,000 protesters angry over a shot-down South Korean jet stormed a Soviet diplomatic retreat in Glen Cove, N.Y.

"So far they're very arrogant about the whole thing and they don't seem the least bit contrite."
— Mary Collins

AFL-CIO leaders denounce Reagan's economic policies

United Press International

WASHINGTON — Union leaders prepared for today's Labor Day demonstrations by denouncing President Reagan's economic and social policies that Reagan maintains are bringing "real jobs" to Americans.

"The resurgence of our economy is bringing real jobs — jobs with a future — in the private sector."
— Ronald Reagan

Alaska sends every resident $386.15 check

United Press International

ANCHORAGE, Alaska — In most states people pay income tax and are lucky if they get a refund. In Alaska, the state is mailing out checks for $386.15 to every eligible man, woman and child.

Strong news presence

Pages 2A and 3A start the paper off with a strong news presence. A full-page ad sometimes runs on Page 3A, but 2A is strong enough to carry the reader into the paper. The weather report was expanded in later issues. Illustration shows labels across the tops of the pages, read-outs to break up text, and a stand-alone picture style that builds some white-space relief into the pages.

'My own opinion is that it is very, very dangerous.'

Jack Landau, executive director of the Washington-based Reporters Committee for Freedom of the Press.

Zaccaro pleads guilty to fraud

NEW YORK — John Zaccaro, whose financial dealings haunted the vice presidential campaign of his wife, Geraldine Ferraro, pleaded guilty Monday to a misdemeanor charge of "scheming to defraud" in connection with the sale of five apartment buildings.

Judge George Roberts said that in accordance with an agreement between Zaccaro and the Manhattan district attorney, he would not impose a jail sentence unless Zaccaro committed another offense before sentencing on Feb. 20.

Zaccaro was released without bail.

apparently tried to rob the Pacific Bell Telephone Co. building barracaded themselves inside Monday after customers and employees left the building, police said.

Sailing trip unforgettable

DUNNELL, Minn. — A menacing boat in the pirate-ridden South China Sea, a typhoon near Japan, and serious illness in the Maldives greeted Roger Swanson and his crew during a 27-month sailing trip around the world.

"It was an experience I will treasure the rest of my life," Swanson, 53, said last week after returning to his southern Minnesota home

The idea for th

"They could get a clue of what companies they should make a target for espionage.'

Councilman Bob Reeder talking about Fremont, Calif., officials being concerned with Soviet wiretaps.

Workers gear up r shuttle launch

'The Israelis are growing impatient.'

An unidentified source close to the Lebanese-Israeli troop withdrawal negotiations commenting on the close of the latest talks which ended without an agreement being reached.

Shcharansky appeals to U.S. for husband

GENEVA, Switzerland — The wife of imprisoned Soviet dissident Anatoly Shcharansky said Monday she has

set in rather large, 38 point Franklin Gothic Extra Condensed, making a sans serif black accent in contrast to the Times Roman that dominates the page.

The quotation was designated to be brief and could be selected from any of the stories on the page but preferably from one closely adjacent. In any event, the attribution was to link the quotation to the appropriate story. Used in this manner, the quotation was designed to do two things: First, offer a provocative "hook" on which to focus the reader's attention. I thought this was preferable to the usual "Briefs" label repeated every day. Second, the quotation made a visual punctuation mark on the page, a typographical focus. It was not designed necessarily to run at the beginning of the Nation or World News pages, because in a small paper that could pose make-up problems. It was designed to fit anywhere *within* the area of Nation or World news, to allow flexibility in configuring the paper on a day-by-day basis. Variations in the design allowed the adaptation of different column measures to different page make-ups.

Briefs treatment

Facing page: The Dateline briefs are designed as a wide column down the gutter of the page or, for more make-up flexibility, as two or three columns in regular measure. The attribution should tie up the quote with the appropriate story, which should run adjacent to it.

Breaking through a rule

Right: A stand-alone picture at the top of a page goes right to the top, interrupting the label rules. The vertical thrust provides a full, dynamic look.

Opinion and advice

Editorial page and facing page

The treatment of editorials at the *Times Daily* breaks the vertical pattern found on most editorial pages. They form a horizontal unit going across the full width of the top of the page in four wide columns. The masthead fits comfortably into this block, set off by bold rules, and puts an official-looking stamp on the editorial text around it.

The horizontal make-up is marginally more troublesome to use at first, perhaps, because of the short legs of type. But having the heads break in the right areas is simply a matter of line count, easily mastered the first time around. The prevailing mood on this project, set by the publisher, was not conservative, and this design was welcomed as a refreshing variation on the traditional vertical make-up. The horizontal design also brings the major cartoon into the center of the page and spreads visual interest through the whole page.

The columnist-identifying "sigs" (pictures) are designed on a vertical axis to set comfortably into the wide measures of type. The vertical panels complement the horizontal structure of the page.

I usually look for some small element of strictly local interest to go on an editorial page, for example, a pictorial element, or a question and answer box, or something involving give-and-take between editors and readers. Here, where the *Times Daily* motto was "Serving the Shoals area for 125 years," a feature looking back called "Shoals Past" seemed appropriate. Outside of the interest in the content, such an element gives the editorial a little extra typographical change of pace.

The headline for the first Letter to the Editor is set as a quote in Franklin Gothic Extra Condensed, providing an unexpected accent to the page and tying it stylistically to the surrounding news pages, where the Franklin Gothic is also used as an accent.

Conversation pieces

Ann Landers, Erma Bombeck, other syndicated columnists, and a local column by the editor of the paper, Don Browne, alternate on the page facing the editorial page, to create an Op-Ed feeling, making unnecessary the additional effort created by a more comprehensive Op-Ed page.

Headlines for the columns vary in style—bold, roman, and italic—in the same manner as "People" and the bottom of Page 1A and for the same reasons: to build in a feeling of newsy variety. Packaged together usually without illustrations, the advice columns tend to reflect their "canned" nature. Working in a small (syndicated) cartoon can brighten the package a bit while different headline types add some sparkle.

The names of the columnists and their sigs are designed in boxes to match those on the editorial page. They are designed for different measures, vertical and narrow for inset situations and wider to fit in a full-column measure where the column is too narrow for an inset. (Enlarged to the wider measures, some of the sizes became too deep and had to be trimmed.) The same style is used for columnists throughout the paper.

Question and answer treatment

The paper's resources could not sustain on a regular basis a formal Op-Ed page. Syndicated columnists like Landers and Bombeck, however, are given a somewhat anchored position on the page, with plenty of flexibility for ads built into the planned configuration. Viewpoint is a local point of view by the executive editor. A necessary, but sometimes overlooked, job is designing the handling of the type in such question-and-answer columns as Ann Landers. Here, three bullets in alignment make a visual pause between items.

CONVERSATION PIECES

Memphis rolls out red carpet for Hirt

MENTAL NOTES
Mary Ann Kirby

What do you do with a big, burly trumpet player when he quits the French Quarter and looks for cleaner saloons in which to practice his art?

You offer him Beale Street, birthplace of the blues, immortalized by Florence's favorite son, W.C. Handy.

Jazz great Al Hirt decided New Orleans' famed Vieux Carre was too trashy to attract the kind of crowd he wants to play to. So he shut down his Bourbon Street establishment and looked elsewhere.

That's when Memphis began singing a sweet song of invitation.

Some smart folks up in Elvis' old stomping grounds think they've got just the place for another wandering minstrel.

Just so happens that there's a lot of development going on downtown in the Bluff City.

The Beale Street district has been saved from senseless destruction and is being restored. Clubs are blossoming along Front Street high above the cobblestones lining part of Riverside Drive. It's evident the blues are alive and well in Memphis.

They even took dumpy old Mud Island, once about as inviting as its namesake, and transformed it into a peach of an attraction.

The humming monorails at Mud Island beckon tourists and Memphians alike to walk along a scale model of the Mississippi as the breeze from the real thing makes the summer heat a little easier to take.

The island boasts an outdoor amphitheater that has had its mettle tested with just about everything: the hard rocking of Joe ("Life in the Fast Lane") Walsh; Ricky Skaggs' bluegrass melodies; the smooth sounds of Ella Fitzgerald; the Aussie accents of the Little River Band; the punk-funk of Rick James; and the crescendoes of Ferrante and

and the folks up there want Big Al's trumpet to help keep the tempo alive at a new nightclub planned on Beale Street.

The Shoals knows what a trumpet player can do for a place. We've just finished struttin' our stuff all over Colbert and Lauderdale counties during the W.C. Handy Music Festival.

Because of the Father of the Blues — and the enthusiasm and hospitality of the people who live here — we've relished performances by Dizzy Gillespie, Willie Ruff, the Manhattan Transfer and Roberta Flack, in addition to cherished local talents.

So, we wish Memphis luck on landing Al Hirt. What a boost for the tourist trade that would be — and what a break for the people who call the Bluff City home.

If Memphis succeeds, we'd like to extend an invitation of our own:

Al, if you get a hankering to do a little more traveling, hang a right at Collierville, Tenn., take U.S. 72 southeast through Mississippi into Alabama

Adoption records are best when sealed

ANN LANDERS

Dear Ann Landers: There is a TV show called "Fantasy" that reunites adopted children with their natural mothers. I think it is disgusting. I want to adopt and I would like to see some facts before I go ahead with my plans.

Is it possible for adopted children to get their hands on their original birth records? Can they find their biological mothers? Lord, I hope not. If and when I adopt, I don't want to live in fear that one day I will hear a voice on the other end of the phone or meet face-to-face at my front door a woman who says, "I want to see the child you adopted 15 years ago. She belongs to me."

I can't imagine anything more disruptive to the child or more heartbreaking to the woman who raised the little one than a stranger who demands entry into that young person's life.

Please let me know if you agree. — **Afraid In La.**

• • •

Dear Afraid: The handling of adoption records varies according to the state law. In July the state legislators in Illinois succeeded in passing a bill that will keep adoption records sealed forever. I was behind this effort 100 percent and am delighted it succeeded.

Dear Ann Landers: I'm a social

Rarely discussed is the abuse of young boys by older men. Because I am a friend of two such victims I want all young boys to know that they should never let anyone touch their genitals nor should they follow instructions to touch anyone else's. Just because you are a child does not mean you have to put up with this. Also you should know that being used sexually by another male does not mean you are a homosexual.

If this happens to you, tell an adult immediately — someone you can trust — a parent, a teacher, an aunt or uncle, a school counselor, a minister. You will be telling for your own pro-

---

Landers, Abby, et al.
Left, top and bottom: The advice columnists are grouped under "Conversation Pieces" in various configurations in the Op-Ed position facing the editorial page, providing wide latitude in availability of advertising spaces.

Sigs and bugs
Facing page: Column "sigs" (sometimes called "bugs"), designed in various measures, to notch into a wider-than-normal column or to run at the top of a second column, were made up in all practical sizes, printed into pads, or made up into veloxes. Wide ones sometimes get too deep and should be trimmed at the bottom. On "opening night" it was necessary to make sure all old sigs were gone from the composing room files and new ones were readily available, separated into sections, for the paste-up staff.

UPBEAT
David Palmer

UPBEAT
David Palmer

UPBEAT
David Palmer

HOME-SENSE

HOMESENSE

HOMESENSE

REFLEC-TIONS
Lucille Prince

REFLECTIONS
Lucille Prince

REFLECTIONS
Lucille Prince

Fronts

Outside and inside sections

Score insets

A Sunday Sports front shows a device allowing scores to be set prominently into columns, freeing the headline to tell more of the story without the score.

Story count

Facing page: The sans serif quote is both a graphic accent and a way to humanize the page. At the bottom, a Focus news feature is structured into the design.

The paper publishes four sections in two parts on some days and in four parts on other days, depending on advertising volume. The four section fronts remain constant every day. In a two-part paper, the outside fronts are Main News (1A) and Sports. Local/Region is folded into the A section. The lifestyle section, with the appealingly local title, "Valley Life," is folded into the B section. It is themed every day—Happenings, Food, Trends, Health, and Prime Time (which was launched as a tabloid). Preprinted travel and other sections are added to the Valley Life line-up.

Section headings were designed in Times Roman Bold, the same type used in headlines. With the sans serif Franklin Gothic Extra Condensed already playing a prominent part on the page, typographical variety was achieved without going to yet another typeface. The logo is positioned rather prominently when the page is an outside front. When it runs inside, the logo is dropped.

The visual key to the Local front is the quotation in the upper left that kicks off the column of Briefs below. The quotation is designed to echo the visual theme struck in the main news sections under the heading "Datelines." I felt the repetition of "Datelines" here would be tiresome, especially running alongside the Region/State section heading. The column pushes up to the top of the page to give more action at the top and to avoid the look of superfluous space in the section heading.

For the Briefs running down the left-hand column, the format prescribes that headlines vary from one to three lines, to provide different emphases and to keep the column from looking too much like a listing.

A "Focus" item at the bottom of the local front builds into the page an area for a feature, background, or analysis story.

Valley Life

Formats were designed within the framework of what a two-person lifestyle staff could reasonably be expected to do. Therefore the

90

TimesDaily B

Region/State

'It's a good motion and I'm in favor of it.'

Florence school board member John Landers on high school feasibility study.

Weapon charge against state widow dropped

NEW YORK — A pistol-packing Alabama widow who told police she routed eight muggers with her unloaded pearl-handled revolver was cleared of gun charges and said she knew God would keep her out of jail.

"I'm so happy, I thank the lord," said Roberta Leonard, 67, of Sylacauga, Ala., as she left Criminal Court in Manhattan Tuesday.

A grand jury refused to indict the woman on a charge of illegally carrying a gun and Mrs. Leonard was set free. She could have been sentenced to a year in jail if convicted.

Roberta Leonard

Fire guts Tuscumbia apartment

By David M. Holloway
Bureau Manager

Fire gutted a downtown Tuscumbia apartment building early this morning but for the most part spared two businesses beneath the apartments.

Nine fire departments responded to the 1:15 a.m. blaze at the McNair Apartments at 114½ Fifth St. Firefighters from Tuscumbia, Sheffield, Muscle Shoals, Leighton, Littleville, Barton, Colbert Heights and two other departments fought for two hours to control the blaze.

No one was injured and the apartments were unoccupied at the time of the fire.

Lt. Joe Lyles of the Tuscumbia Fire Department said no cause has been determined. "If I had to guess," Lyles said, "I'd say that it was an electrical fire."

The desk sergeant for the Tuscumbia Police Department first spotted the blaze from the station. Flames were already licking through the roof of the two-story structure.

When firefighters arrived, Lyles said it quickly became evident that help was needed. The other departments answered the call and Muscle Shoals dispatched its new ladder truck.

The fire completely gutted the upstairs portion of the brick building. Large gaping holes were burned through the roof.

Lyles said it was too early to put a dollar amount on the fire, but he said virtually all the contents of the four upstairs apartments were destroyed.

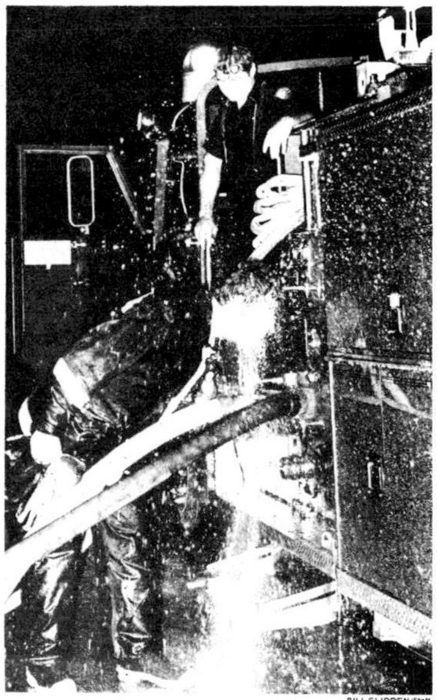

BILL GLIDDEN/Staff

Tuscumbia fireman cools off after battling blaze.

Airport board members dispute recent statements

By Marci Elliott
Staff Writer

Members of the Muscle Shoals Airport Authority board do not agree that the present seven-member board should be wiped out and that a totally new board be appointed, according to board member Howard King.

This is contrary to recent statements in the press and at certain civic meetings, King told members of the Sheffield commission Tuesday night as he spoke for more than 30 minutes following the regular business meeting.

"It's not true that the board members were asked to resign," King said. He said the board members were told the best thing to do was resign and make way for a new nine-member board.

Mayor Edgar Enoch and Commissioner Howard Gamble, who is also mayor-elect, were present while King talked. Commissioner David Johnson was out of town.

King called the local airport one of the finest small airports anywhere "for right now."

But he warned that the four neighboring cities — Sheffield, Muscle Shoals, Tuscumbia and Florence — should take their time and gather as much information as possible before making a commitment to build a new airport.

"Nobody's going to build a new airport for $1 million - you can't build a runway for $1 million," King told the commission.

He also said that before the local airport can get more service, it will have to get more passengers.

Gamble told King after King's presentation that he and others were led to believe at a recent civic organization's meeting that airport board members favored starting over with a new board. Enoch said he also was led to believe this.

"That's not true," King said. He added that although board members do not want to start over with a new board, they favor expanding from seven to nine members to include a representative from each of the four cities.

King said there are many questions surrounding plans for the Airport Authority Board. He indicated that many of them originate with Judge W.B. Duncan of Florence, who King said is spearheading the change.

King again urged the four cities to "get more conclusive answers before they supply any expense money" for the airport.

In other business the commission:

— Hired Delmer Mayfield for the Sheffield Fire Department. Mayfield will fill a vacancy created when Odell Murray replaced retiring fire chief Hunter Hardy.

— Heard city engineer William Paxton's finding concerning property Sheffield owns on River Bluff.

Industry trip success, says Wallace

MONTGOMERY — Gov. George C. Wallace says his hunting trip to Boston last week was success. The target? Industry.

Wallace told the Alabama Governor's Conference on Small Business Tuesday that the trip paid off with a high-technology firm committing itself to put a plant in Huntsville.

He said the company will announce its plans soon to build a factory in Huntsville that will employ at least 400 people.

Florence eyes school feasibility study

By Beth Garfrerick
Staff Writer

Should the city of Florence have one high school or two?

Josephine Redd, newest member of the board, introduced a motion at Tuesday's meeting calling for a feasibility study on the high school issue.

Florence operates Bradshaw and Coffee high schools, each enrolling grades 9-12. Bradshaw's enrollment is around 900, and Coffee has about 1,035 students.

Redd proposed a study by an out-of-town consulting firm which would consider such things as curriculum, school utilization, student population and minority ratio requirements, financial savings, extra-curricular activities and administration.

Her resolution stated that the study should be completed by January 1984 "or as soon thereafter as possible, but no later than June 1984."

Board member John Landers said it would be "conducive" for an independent firm, "not emotionally involved," to take an objective look at the matter. "It's a good motion and I'm in favor of it," he said.

All members voted in favor of the study, with the exception of Claude Flippo, who abstained, claiming insufficient time to examine the issue before voting.

The board then engaged in a lengthy discussion on honoring teachers for meritorious service to the school system. Another Redd proposal called for honoring outstanding teachers, at the recommendation of school principals. This would be done every three months, taking one school at a time, according to her proposal.

The board was undecided on Redd's proposal until Superintendent Dr. Glenn Farmer offered another plan for recognizing teachers.

Farmer suggested a resolution be sent to all school principals calling on them to present the board with names of teachers to be honored, at the best given time for recognition. Teachers would then be honored with resolutions, which would be included in the historical records of the school system.

The board unanimously approved Farmer's recommendation.

State opening satellite office in Shoals area

Through the efforts of four local agencies concerned with economic growth and industrial development, a satellite office of the Alabama Department of Economic and Community Affairs will be located in the Shoals area beginning Oct. 1.

The agencies cooperating in the establishment of this satellite office are the Industrial Research and Extension Center of the University of North Alabama, the Northwest Alabama Council of Local Governments and the Florence Area and Colbert County chambers of commerce.

Dr. Freddie Wood, director of UNA's industrial research center, said the satellite office would have the primary objectives of promoting industrial development, formulating and activating national marketing programs and supporting existing local agencies in industrial development activities.

The Shoals satellite office will be one of five area economic development agencies in Alabama. J.S. (Steve) Thomason Jr. has been named director of this area.

Bill Howard, NACOLG executive director, said he endorses this development.

Residents urged to cut back

GADSDEN — Officials on Lookout Mountain near Gadsden are urging residents to ration their water because the supply is getting low.

It hasn't rained on Lookout Mountain since July 19.

Red Collier, general manager of the Gadsden Water Board, said Tuesday that notices were distributed to 2,300 customers in the Lookout Mountain area urging them to stop watering lawns, washing cars and using water unnecessarily until storage levels return to normal.

Operation Pay-Up brings in delinquent debts

By Peggy Sanford
Staff Writer

Operation Pay-Up is working.

Parents who owe back debt on child support who weren't arrested in Lauderdale County over the weekend have been paying those debts all week to avoid an inside look at the county jail.

Lauderdale court officials launched a roundup Friday of parents delinquent in court-ordered child support. Sheriff's deputies arrested about 50 people Friday night, said county child support supervisor Pat Radel. The debts of those parents arrested that night totalled $3,500, she said.

Radel estimated 200 warrants are outstanding for parents owing child support. The roundup started with 350 warrants. Arrests will continue at least through August, she said.

The arrest campaign is part of Project Pay-Up, which is being conducted statewide this month. August has been proclaimed Child Support Month by Gov. George C. Wallace.

Radel's office and the juvenile court office were flooded Monday with parents coming in to clear their child support debts and have warrants against them recalled.

Since Friday, more than $13,300 in back payments has been collected, above the $3,500 taken in on Friday, Radel said.

Of the $13,300, $7,898 has been sent to the state for welfare payments, the remaining $5,412 is for personal payments, mostly to women out of state, she said.

Release procedures ran somewhat differently during the heat of the roundup. There wasn't room in the county jail to hold all the men and the two women arrested.

"Those who could pay could go home," Radel said. Large arrearages were negotiated, usually allowing release of a person who could pay at least 20 percent of what was owed, she said.

Amounts owed ranged from $45 to $5,000. Radel cited one case of a man $695 behind on a order to pay $5 child support a week. He was released after paying $180 and signing a wage attachment, she said.

College moving

BIRMINGHAM — The 54-year-old Ramsay-McCormick Building in Ensley will be the new home of Alabama Christian College's Birmingham-based extension center, officials said.

Administrator Gene Calhoun said Tuesday that the growing enrollment necessitated making the move, which is scheduled for March 1984.

The school, with an enrollment of 5,500, operates campuses in Huntsville, the Shoals and Mobile. Officials said the move will not affect tuitions, currently $450 per quarter.

Firm reopening

BESSEMER — A firm that closed its doors in Bessemer four years ago will be reopening, and officials said more than 100 people may eventually find work with the plant.

Mayor Ed Porter, who announced the reopening of the R.L. Zeigler Co. Tuesday, said the city gave no special concessions to the company.

Porter said the plant, which opened in Bessemer in 1927, is "like a part of the family coming back to Bessemer."

The company, which produces packaged meats, will initially hire 45 people, said officials.

FOCUS: DWAYNE SANDERS

BILL GLIDDEN/Staff

Dwayne Sanders works out twice weekly.

Disabled engineer self-sufficient

By Laura Simmons
Staff Writer

Five years ago Dwayne Sanders made a slight error in judgment that will leave him in a wheelchair the rest of his life.

While a cheerleader at Georgia Tech, Sanders broke his neck doing a flip off a mini-trampoline at the 1978 Duke vs. Georgia game, the first game of the season.

"I over-rotated forward and my forehead hit the ground," Sanders, 23, said. "I just screwed up."

Paralyzed from the base of his neck down, Sanders has limited use of his arms and almost no use of his hands. The doctors never gave him any hope of walking again.

"They pretty much leave it at that because if they told you any different they might build you up," he said.

Today the handsome native Atlantan is a self-sufficient chemical engineer at the National Fertilizer Development Center in Muscle Shoals. He lives alone in an apartment modified slightly to accommodate his lifestyle.

Sanders spent three months in the hospital, a rapid recovery for his type of injury. He returned to college after missing only two quarters.

"Everything I've done, if you take the rule book it wasn't there," he said.

"Things like that don't change people radically," Sanders said. "If they're determined, that's not going to change. If they're lazy it gives them an excuse to be lazy."

He lived at home a few months and then moved to his fraternity house.

"Moving out, on my own, independent — that was one of those things I wasn't supposed to be able to do," he said.

Back at school, Sanders made better grades than he had as a freshman and became more involved in his fraternity and other campus activities.

"I fit in pretty well," he said. "I had some problems adjusting. It took a while."

His friends had to adjust, too.

"Most of them knew it was better to leave me alone and let me ask for help."

Sanders describes himself as a talker and admits part of the reason is to draw attention away from his wheelchair and to himself.

He has an active social life with friends he's made at the apartment complex. Two days a week, he works out at Ron's Gym, lifting weights.

The wheelchair that serves as his legs has become a central factor in his life. His shower is built to accommodate it; his customized van has a lift for it; the entryway to his apartment has a wooden ramp for it.

It costs $1,200 and has to be replaced every three years. Sanders refuses to install a motor on it, preferring instead to push it himself.

"I think the van has been one of the major vehicles to his being able to adapt," his mother, Betty Sanders, said on a recent visit. "There are not too many places that are not accessible to him.

Curling weights

"He's been a fighter from the very beginning," she said. "He has dealt with it extremely well externally. I often wonder how he deals with it internally."

"You really don't know what you can do until you do it," Sanders said. "It (the injury) could have been a lot worse and I might not have the same attitude if it was a lot worse.

"Ironically, there's been something good come out of it, and that's patience. Patience with yourself. Patience with other people."

Business/Agriculture

'People are much more cautious.'

Bill Cousson on consumer's confidence being shattered by the talk of higher interest rates.

AG-BRIEFS

Senate proposal freezing prices may extend debate

A day-old Senate against an administration-backed bill to freeze target prices for grains and cotton could develop into "quite an extended debate." Senate Democratic leader Robert Byrd said today.

Farm state lawmakers are trying to talk the bill to death. The measure would hold target prices at 1983 levels for another two years.

"It seemed to me there was going to be quite an extended debate." Byrd D-W.Va.. told reporters minutes

Reagan pushing for farmers' aid

The Reagan administration. faced with farm programs that cost more than $21 billion this year. has pushed for a freeze in target prices. which represent the return guaranteed to farmers.

The legislation would save $11 billion over the next five years. said Senate Agriculture Committee Chairman Jesse Helms. R-N.C.

But Sen. Larry Pressler R-S.D. arguing against the legislation. said. "If we do not increase target prices.

Government will subsidize exports

When national average market prices drop below targets. the government makes up the difference between targets and market prices with deficiency payments.

The targets were written into law in the 1981 farm legislation. the administration said. with the

U.S. gasoline prices drop again

WASHINGTON (UPI) — The Treasury Department says government borrowing is about to peak at the end of this year. clearing the way for Federal Reserve Board and administration cooperation to lower interest rates.

The optimistic forecast was given to reporters Wednesday as part of the quarterly estimate of government borrowing. an event closely watched by the money markets.

Treasury Undersecretary Beryl Sprinkel said the government will sell $15.75 billion in securities next week to refund public debt. and raise $9.1 billion in new cash about what traders in government securities had expected.

The latest announcement brought the estimated July-September borrowing to $48 billion. well below the $60.6 billion record set in the same quarter last year.

Sprinkel said a new record for borrowing could be set in the last quarter of this year when an estimated "$60 billion to $65 billion" in borrowing could be necessary.

The government raises most of its operating cash and the funds necessary to finance the deficit by auctioning government securities. Earlier this week the Office of Management and Budget estimated the 1983 federal deficit would be slightly smaller than previously thought. at $209.8 billion.

The amount of government borrowing has a direct effect on how high private businesses must bid to borrow whatever funds are left after the gov-

ernment obtains what it needs. the process by which interest rates are set.

"The revenues have moved up somewhat." Sprinkel said of the government's tax income. because of the economic recovery.

"We are now beginning to see ... the improved trend in economic activity across the country is resulting in more taxes being paid to the treasury. We are hopeful that the fourth quarter will hopefully see the peak ... in our borrowing requirement."

To finance the budget deficit and what is called the "off-budget" deficit the Treasury Department must raise a record total of $226.5 billion during fiscal 1983. which ends Sept. 30.

Sprinkel said $205.1 billion of that would be raised in the marketplace for securities. Another $8.3 billion would be debt-issued to state and local governments and foreign buyers rather than auctioned. The remainder would be cash balances left over from the previous year.

Sprinkel. a frequent critic of the Federal Reserve Board in the past firmly endorsed the Fed's most recently announced monetary targets that would rein in what he said was a "soaring" supply of money in the recent past.

He also said the administration plans to ask Congress to raise the national debt ceiling again by the time borrowing authority runs out sometime in "The revenues have moved up somewhat." Sprinkel said of the gov-

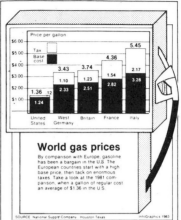

World gas prices
By comparison with Europe, gasoline has been a bargain in the U.S. The European countries start with a high base price, then tack on enormous taxes. Take a look at the 1981 comparison, when a gallon of regular had an average of $1.36 in the U.S.

Price per gallon: $6.00, $5.00, $4.00, $3.00, $2.00, $1.00

United States: Tax .12 / Base cost 1.24 = 1.36
West Germany: 1.10 / 2.33 = 3.43
Britain: 1.23 / 2.51 = 3.74
France: 1.54 / 2.82 = 4.36
Italy: 2.17 / 3.28 = 5.45

SOURCE: National Supply Company, Houston Texas   InfoGraphics 1983

House agrees to kill withholding tax

WASHINGTON (UPI) — The House today overwhelmingly agreed to kill tax withholding on interest and dividends and sent the compromise bill to the Senate for final congressional action.

The House voted 392-18 in favor of the measure. which also calls for tougher taxpayer reporting requirements of interest and dividend income and "backup" withholding for those who fail to report or under report that income.

The bill is expected to be approved

by the Senate and sent to President Reagan for his signature.

A spokesman said House Republican leader Robert Michel of Illinois was assured by the White House today that Reagan would sign the measure because it also includes his Caribbean Basin Initative. a package of tax and trade incentives for 27 friendly nations in the region.

Today's House vote was made possible when House and Senate tax negotiators broke a week-long stalemate Wednesday. Sen. Lloyd Bentsen. D-

Texas. agreed to reverse his position on an unrelated amendment. allowing the conference to drop the addition and finish work on the withholding compromise.

Senate Finance Committee counsel Roderick DeArment. commenting on Bentsen's decision. said: "Our long wait is now over."

Although the members of the joint conference committee tentatively agreed last week to kill the controversial law originally scheduled to take effect July 1. they deadlocked over a

rider to renew authority for state and local governments to issue tax-exempt mortgage subsidy bonds due to expire at the end of the year.

Bentsen said he agreed to reverse his earlier position and promised not to press for the mortgage subsidy bond extension as an amendment to the repealer once Senate Finance Committee Chairman Robert Dole. R-Kan. promised to attach it to the next available vehicle.

"If we failed to break the deadlock and approve this legislation. I'm con-

SELECTED STOCKS

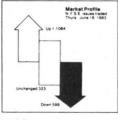

NASDAQ quotations indicate highest bids and lowest offers from market makers in each se curity as of 4 30 a.m. Local OTC quotations (*) indicate inter dealer prices from a market maker in each security as of ap proximately 1 30 a.m. Quota tions do not include retail mark up. mark down or commission

Market Profile
N.Y.S.E. issues traded
Thurs. June 16, 1983

Up 1,1064
Unchanged 323
Down 599

Over-The-Counter Stocks*

	Bid	Asked
American Surgery	11⅝	12⅛
Bruno's	19⅜	20
Ala Tenn	28	29⅛
Central BancShares	24	24⅝
Energy Reserve Group	4¼	4⅜

First Ala. BancShares

	34⅜	35⅛
Banc Independent	35	
First Nat Bk of Flo	44	
Intergraph	42⅝	42⅞
International Remote	8	8¼
Mutual Savings	32	34
Protective Corp	24⅝	25
SouthTrust	21	21¼
Southern United Life	4⅝	4⅞

LISTED STOCKS

A G. Edwards	35⅛		
American Telephone	60⅞	Holiday Inns	43⅜
American Can	41⅛	Humana	33	Sears Roebuck	15⅜
Am South	30⅜	International Minerals	44⅜	Southern Co	17⅞
ARA Services	40	IBM	123⅝	Sterch-Bros	43⅛
Coca Cola	48⅛	J C Penney	62	Tandy	40⅛
Consolidated Foods	48⅛	K mart	35⅛	Tenneco	38⅛
Champion International	25⅜	Kroger	39⅛	Texaco	58⅛
Diamond Shamrock	27⅜	Lowe's	24	Texas Eastern	34⅛
Exxon	36⅛	Merrill Lynch	46⅛	Torch Mark	28⅛
First Mississippi	12	Monsanto	98⅛	Trans American	67⅛
Ford Motor Co	62⅛	National Services	3⅛	Union Carbide	68⅛
General Motors	76	New York Times	82⅛	Vulcan Materials	43
Genesco	8	Norfolk Southern	58⅛	Wal Mart	47
Genuine Parts	44⅛	Reynolds Metals	33⅛	Weyerhaeuser	37⅛
Gordon Jewelers	5⅛	Saunder's Leasing	7⅛	Woolworth	37⅝
				U.S. Steel	25⅛

LIVESTOCK REPORT

Florence Trading Post. Flor ence Tuesday. June 28

By Federal State Livestock Market News

Estimated salable receipts cattle and calves. 200 hogs. 121. Week ago cattle and calves. 265. hogs. 131. Year ago cattle and calves 316 hogs.78

Cattle and Calves. Compared week ago. slaughter cows and bulls mostly steady. too few oth er slaughter classes for trend Feeder classes generally steady. except steer calves 400 500 lbs Firm to 2 00 higher

Slaughter Classes Cows. Utility and low commercial 24 33 00 38 00.. Cutter 17. 32 00 34 00. Canner 28 00 29 75 **Bulls.** Yield grade 1 2. 1500 lbs 43 00 48 00 **Calves** few good and choice 300 500 lbs. 46 50 51 00

Feeder Classes Steers. Med um frame. No 1. one 250 lbs 67 56. few 300 400 lbs. 60 00 63 00. 400 500 lbs. 58 00 62 75. few 64 75. 500 600 lbs. 51 25 58 75. Sel lbs. 59 75. 600 700 lbs. 52 00 55 00 few. 700 800 lbs. 48 00 52 25. Large frame. No 1. few 500 700 lbs. 52 25 55 50. 1 mal frame. No. 1. 300 400 lbs. 52 00 58 00. one 400 00. 400 500 lbs. 49 00 56 00 **Steers** 51 75 Med ium frame. No 2 300 400 lbs. 53 00 55 00. few 500 700 lbs. 46 75 52 75. one. 901. lbs. 44 00 **Heifers.** Medium frame No 1 one 300 lbs. 53 00. 400 500 lbs. 45 50 50 75. couple. 57 00 and 53 75. couple 525 lbs 49 00 low pie 656 lbs. 46 75 and 48 25. few 725 835 lbs. 44 75 45 75 **Cows.** (For Replacement). Medium frame. No 1 and 2. 37 25 40 75 head. few. low and calf pairs. 325 00 385 00

Hogs. Compared week ago

mostly. 71 00 76 50. 400 500 lbs 58 75 65 00. few to 66 50. 500 600 lbs 53 00 61 25 one 61 75. 600 700 lbs 53 00 59 00. one 835 lbs 32 25 **Large frame** No 1 200 300 lbs 68 00 79 50. 300 400 lbs. 63 50 70 00. few 400 500 lbs 58 50 64 25. 500 700 lbs 55 00 59 50 one 800 lbs. 54 00. 1 small frame No 1 200 300 lbs. 55 50 64 00. 300 500 lbs 48 00 57 00. few to 61 00. few 500 700 lbs. 48 00 55 25. Medium frame. No 2 200 400 lbs. 56 00 60 00. 400 500 lbs. 50 00 56 50 arid. Medium and large (mostly medium) frame. No 1. 200 300 lbs 53 50 61 25. 300 400 lbs 51 50 56 00. to 57 00. 400 500 lbs 51 50 54 00. few 500 700 lbs 44 00 50 00. Medium frame. No 2 300 500 lbs. 41 00 47 50. (For Re placement) few medium and small frame. No 1 200 500 lbs Medium frame. No 2 34 00 38 75 small frame 36 00 62 00 Sold by head. few cows 285 00 350 00. cow and calf pairs 350 490. one 550

Hogs Compared week ago slaughter Barrows and Gilts steady. to 1 00 higher. Sows steady to mostly 1 00 lower. Boars 1 50 on

Barrows and Gilts US 1 2 210 250 lbs 45 00 46 25. US 2 210 250 lbs. 44 50 45 50. 250 270 lbs 44 00 46 00. US 1 few 210 240 lbs 38 00 39 00. US 1 few 190 240 lbs 42 00 **Sows** US 1 3 300 500 lbs. 34 00. 150 250 lbs. 25 00 27 00 Feeder classes. steers. med um frame 1 200 300 lbs 61 00 69 00. 300 400 lbs. 57 00 67 00 mostly. 58 00 65 00. 300 470 lbs 55 00 64 75. 500 600 lbs 54 50 63 00. Feeder classes. heifers med um frame 2 200 300 lbs 55 00 62 00. 300 400 lbs 50 00 59 00. and

Estimated salable receipts.

Northwest Alabama Livestock

Auction. Russellville. Monday. July 25

By. Alabama and U S. De partment of Agriculture

Actual salable receipts. cattle and calves 759 hogs. 115. Week ago. cattle and calves 415. Week ago. 131. Year ago cattle and calves. 1102. hogs. 64

Cattle and Calves. Compared week ago. slaughter cows and bulls 1 00 to 2 00 higher. other slaughter classes untested. Feeder steer calves 300 400 lbs. 3 00 to 6 00 higher. 300 400 lbs. 1 00 to 3 00 higher. heifer calves 300 300 lbs. 2 00 to 4 00 high er. few heifers over 500 lbs. Mostly. steady. replacement cows 1 00 to 3 00 higher

Slaughter Classes Cows. few commercial. 2 4.. 39 00 41 25. Utility 2 3. 37 00 47 00. few high yielding 40 00 42 50.. cutter 1 2 31 75 37 25. low to 38 50. Canner and low cutter 1 2. 30 75 32 50. **Bulls.** Yield grade 1 2. 1800 lbs 44 00 48 25.. 750 7 390. lbs 44 00 48 25. **Calves** few good and choice 250 500 lbs. 47 25 52 00 one 54 75

Feeder Classes Steers. Med um frame. No 1. 200 300 lbs. 69 50 80 00. black white face mostly 80 00 89 50. 300 400 lbs 62 00 71 00.. black white face

LIVESTOCK REPORT (cont.)

theme aspect of the section title was played down while the generic title was played up. The themes are treated modestly in 50 percent gray with the "Valley Life" title standing out in black. (In the redesign of some of the bigger papers discussed in later chapters, more elaborate and prominent C section treatments are illustrated.)

Ag and Biz

A notable addition to the paper was a Business/Agriculture page (sometimes two pages) on a schedule of four times a week, which represented a significant increase over previous cover-age. (When the *Times Daily* later converted from afternoon to morning, Business/Agriculture grew to a full-fledged section with financial tables.) "Biz-Briefs" and "Ag-Briefs" were assembled from wire as well as local coverage to get a higher and more serviceable story count. In an unusual arrangement, the "Biz-Briefs" and "Ag-Briefs" occupy respectively the extreme left and right columns of the page, sandwiching the main stories between them (see accompanying illustration). On most days, the two briefs run one over the other, in a single column down the left side, in a more conventional fashion.

Biz-Ag

Facing page: A Business/Agriculture section front highlights Ag-Briefs and Biz-Briefs in the right and left columns. A maximum ad size was prescribed.

Themes

Daily themed sections play up the generic local title, Valley Life. The cancer statistics box provides a hard, useful edge to the kind of feature page that often gets very soft.

"I have the right to take care of Larry Holmes."

Fighter Larry Holmes in discussing upcoming title defense against Scott Frank.

Weaver lists refs as opponents, too

INGLEWOOD, Calif. — Mike Weaver puts referees and judges on his list of opponents.

"I know in my heart I'm still the champion," the former World Boxing Association heavyweight titleholder said after signing to fight Stan Ward on Sept. 14 at the Forum.

Weaver, 25-10-1 with 17 knockouts, lost his title to Michael Dokes in a controversial 63-second bout last December. The fight was stopped by referee Joey Curtis. Dokes and Weaver battled to a 15-round draw in a May 20 rematch with Dokes retaining his crown.

"Dokes held, thumbed me and did everything illegal," Weaver said at a Forum news conference. "I'm the uncrowned champion. I'm going to continue to claim that until someone beats me — not no referee or no judges."

Martin blames

Inside pages provided opportunity for special kinds of content and typographical treatment. As illustrated here (left), SportsWorld was given a special heading, which ran alongside columns of small-type statistics and brightened up the page. A side effect of the new type style was the neat way Weddings and Engagements could be handled, in Times Roman regular, not bold, with 24-point headings giving an effect half way between announcement and news. Every day a small "Shoals Calendar" runs in an average of about 10 inches. But on Sunday "Shoals Calendar" makes a serviceable, full-page presentation. The type for this listing (see illustration) is a 7½-point size of the regular text face. Preferable to using a sans serif agate type as many papers do, running the listing in the regular text face speaks to the reader in the same typographical "voice" as the news columns, suggesting that this information is provided by the editors and not by a research assistant. The agate sans serif speaks in the voice of charts, statistics, and financial tables. Use of text type adds to, rather than merely complements, the editorial presence, a factor particularly important in a tight space situation.

Other efforts to provide extra touches included spot drawings, where appropriate, and special packaging efforts—as on the comics page.

Freedom with headings
Left: Wherever a special treatment seemed appropriate, it was worked into the design, as in the Sports World heading, but the basic typography is kept consistent.

A neat comics page
Facing page: The comics go past the halfway mark, and are generous in size. The miscellaneous elements often thrown together uninvitingly in many papers are brought together neatly. The little extra graphic symbols tie the left side of the page up with the comics on the right but also add some sparkle.

CROSSWORD

Edited by EUGENE T. MALESKA

ACROSS

1 Scene, as of a battle
5 Schussing equipment
9 Scatter
14 Shortly
15 Lease
16 Delete
17 Carrying case
19 "The —— Mutiny"
20 Toughen
21 Presaged
23 Wasteland
25 Requirements
26 Surrounded by
28 Whinnies
32 Doorway curtains
37 Condescend
38 Byron's "before"
39 Ceremonies
41 Dr.'s group
42 Adjust to fit
43 Ship's windows
48 1776 Loyalists
50 Blessing
51 Shoot from cover
54 Mondrian was one
58 Plant of the purslane family
62 Abraham's wife
63 Latticed bower
64 Carrying charge
66 Fence steps
67 Palo ——
68 Newscasters Pappas and Seamans
69 Onagers
70 Adam or Mae
71 French river

DOWN

1 Flavorful
2 —— fell swoop
3 Convex molding
4 Beg
5 Rialto sign
6 Seaweed
7 Skull protuberance
8 Stock up
9 Dissociates formally
10 Passage
11 Commandos' specialty
12 Slave of yore
13 Noxious growth
18 Nobelist in Physics: 1938
22 Knockout count
24 Row
27 Spigot leak
29 Soccer score
30 Residence
31 Health resorts
32 Fuel of a sort
33 Church calendar
34 Kind of admiral
35 W.W. II area
36 Yugoslav
40 Greek promenade
43 Former Spanish gold coin
44 Holding periods
46 A quadruped
47 Locale of Lake Nipigon
49 Part of R.S.V.P.
52 Small, fleshy fruit
53 School for Yvette
55 Mideasterner
56 Wise men
57 The ones here
58 "Qué médico?" ("What's up, doc?")
59 Food morsels
60 Baseball stats.
61 Fine ——
65 Reagan in 1913

Saturday's Puzzle Solved:

(solution grid)

HOROSCOPE

What kind of day will tomorrow be? To find out what the stars say, read the forecast given for your birth sign.

ARIES (Mar. 21-Apr. 19) Meet with agents and advisers about creative projects. Travel invitations come. Be tactful with sensitive types.

TAURUS (Apr. 20-May 20) Extra credit is yours for the asking. Still avoid needless expenditures. Arrange a family get-together. A loved one may be moody.

GEMINI (May 21-June 20) You're lucky in love now and will attract new admirers. Expect some pleasant surprises. Watch extravagance at homebase.

CANCER (June 21-July 22) You're anxious to get things accomplished, but could be brusque with a co-worker. Fortunate job opportunities come your way.

LEO (July 23-Aug. 22) You'll attract romance and adventure. Celebrate, but don't go overboard in spending. Some are lucky at a game of chance.

VIRGO (Aug. 23-Sept. 22) Begin new domestic projects. Avoid disputes over small matters. Support from a family member is forthcoming. Get rid of clutter.

LIBRA (Sept. 23-Oct. 22) Communications with others are accented. Speak up at group functions. Make important calls. Don't reveal secrets entrusted to you.

SCORPIO (Oct. 23-Nov. 21)

Be ready to capitalize on a quick developing career opportunity. Business picks up now and talks with bosses are favored.

SAGITTARIUS (Nov. 22-Dec. 21) You're bursting with enthusiasm, but avoid overfamiliarity with a higher-up. Increased self-confidence leads to overall success.

CAPRICORN (Dec. 22-Jan. 19) Benefits come by being low-key today. You're better off doing things yourself than entrusting them to the less diligent.

AQUARIUS (Jan. 20-Feb. 18) Be sure to accept social invitations. You'll be introduced to someone who will benefit you in the future. Watch credit card spending.

PISCES (Feb. 19-Mar. 20) Extra initiative and luck combine to put you on top careerwise. A loved one, though, may feel somewhat excluded from your activities.

YOU BORN TODAY are intellectual and analytical. You work well with groups, especially in an advisory capacity. You like public life, but at times need periods by yourself to recharge your energies. In love, you do not always reveal your feelings and suffer therefor. You may be especially talented in banking and can also succeed in the entertainment world. Some of the fields which may appeal to you include law, research, statistics, photography and psychology. Birthdate of Eydie Gorme, singer; George Meany, labor leader; and Frank Gifford, sportscaster.

BRIDGE

South dealer;
North-South vulnerable

(bridge hand diagram)

The bidding:

South	West	North	East
1♡	1NT	Dble	5♣
5♡	Pass	6♡	7♣
Pass	Pass	Pass	7♡

Opening lead — two of diamonds.

It is sometimes difficult to arrive at the best contract when your opponents cramp the bidding space with nuisance bids.

However, these tactics occasionally boomerang, which is what occurred in this deal from the 1966 World Pair Championship when Bufill and Doria of Spain crossed swords with Desrousseaux and Theron of France.

Doria opened the bidding with a heart and Desrousseaux overcalled with a notrump! This type of overcall with a long suit and a weak hand is known in France as the comic notrump (le sans atout comique). Bufill doubled to show a very good hand and Theron added spice to the goings-on by leaping to five clubs.

Doria bid five hearts, thus indicating much more than a minimum opening bid, and Bufil raised him to six hearts. Perhaps Theron should have passed — the bidding unquestionably would have died then and there — but he bid seven clubs as a sacrifice against the small slam he felt sure the opponents could make.

This tactic backfired when it gave Doria a chance to make a forcing pass and in that way invite partner to go on to seven hearts with a suitable hand. The pass was very descriptive, for had Doria held a weaker hand he would have doubled in order to stop partner from bidding a grand slam.

Bufill had no real problem, under the circumstances. He realized that his three aces, facing a forcing pass, were exactly the kind of medicine Doria needed for a grand slam. So he bid seven hearts, which was easily made for a score of 2,210 points, and the comic notrump did not prove to be so comic after all.

Tomorrow: Good reasoning helps a lot.

FRANK & ERNEST

THE RHINOCEROS? IT'S A HIPPOPOTAMUS WITH OPTIONS

WIZARD OF ID

GARFIELD

PEANUTS

BLONDIE

TUMBLEWEEDS

HAGAR THE HORRIBLE

HI & LOIS

BEETLE BAILEY

SNUFFY SMITH

Grissom, Patrick marry

Evening vows uniting Donna Sue Grissom and Charles Dwight Patrick in marriage were pledged Aug. 20. The Rev. Tom Whatley performed the ceremony at Woodward Avenue Baptist Church in Muscle Shoals.

Parents of the bride are Mr. and Mrs. Jimmy Grissom of Muscle Shoals. The bridegroom is the son of Pat Elliott of Muscle Shoals, and the late Mr. Charles Monroe Patrick.

Given in marriage by her father, the bride chose a Victorian silhouette of white Old English net and schiffli embroidery. The entire fitted bodice was encircled at the waistline with scalloped schiffli embroidery. Matching embroidery enhanced the V-shaped yoke, attached with a crystal pleated ruffle and high neckline. The long sleeves closed with covered buttons. Covered buttons also closed the back of the gown. Schiffli embroidery adorned the skirt and chapel-length train. Tiers of crystal pleated ruffles adorned the lower front of the skirt. A crystal pleated ruffle encircled the entire hemline.

A headpiece of schiffli embroidery encrusted with pearls held the bride's fingertip veil of imported illusion encircled with schiffli embroidery.

Maid of honor was the bride's sister, Penny Grissom. Bridesmaids were Debbie Grissom, Cindy Gann and Kim Wallace.

York was best man. Ushers were Rodney Gri-

Mrs. Chuck Patrick

som, Greg Grissom, and Mike Moss.

Completing the wedding party were Kim Brown, flower girl, and Frankie Joe Tubbs, ringbearer.

After a reception hosted at the church, the bridal couple left for a wedding trip to Destin, Fla.

The couple will reside in M

Miss Grigsby bethrothed

Karen Lynne Grigsby and Thomas Owen Tucker Jr. have chosen Sept. 24 for their wedding. The forthcoming event is announced by the bride-elect's parents, Mr. and Mrs. Gerald C. Grigsby of Anderson.

Miss Grigsby graduated from Lauderdale County High School and received a bachelor's degree in nursing from the University of North Alabama. She is employed at Baptist Medical Center-Montclair in Birmingham.

Mr. Tucker, son of Mr. and Mrs. Thomas Owen Tucker of Birmingham, is a graduate of Woodlawn High School. He attended Auburn University and is locally employed.

Lynne Grigsby

Vows will be spoken at 2 p.m. at McElwain Baptist Church in Birmingham.

Sherrod, Posey *plan wedding*

Timra Gay Sherrod and Tommy Dennis Posey have announced wedding plans.

The will be married Sept. 10.

The bride-to-be is the daughter of Montez McCoy and Tim Sherrod of Tuscumbia.

Parents of the bridegroom-elect are Thomas and Mary Lou Posey of Leighton.

Miss Sherrod is a graduate of Deshler High School.

Mr. Posey is a graduate of Colbert County High School.

He received an associate degree from Martin College, Pulaski, Tenn.

He is employed with an airline company in Denver, Colo.

Vows will be spoken at Valley Grove Baptist Church in Tuscumbia.

Sherrod, Posey

Former costume designer directs talents to high fashion

By Gay Pauley
UPI Senior Editor

NEW YORK — In the beginning, there was the hat!

Hats were the start of great fashion careers for the likes of designers Schiaparelli, Halston and Adolfo.

Now comes Lloyd Allen, 31, a native of McAllen, Texas. Allen's recareer began with

ropolitan Opera.

"The first opera I did was 'Aida,'" Allen said. "I can build you a helmet out of plastic made to look like lead. I can do 16 helmets in an hour.

"You learn to make a lot of headgear when you're dressing the Met. There may be as many as 300 people in a company."

Working on opera costumes taught Allen, a music

didn't teach him patternmaking, so his first design, a rain poncho, was one big square and circle stuck together. The circle was the neckline opening and was made into a cowl.

Allen used nylon cire, a shiny, lightweight material, for the ponchos and produced them in a rainbow of colors, each packaged in a small, portable pouch.

Vogue magazine wrote about the and to meet the

len's first production line was the sewing machine in his apartment. Eventually, as volume increased, he cut the ponchos and farmed them out to seamstresses from off-Broadway plays.

Today, five years and several thousand ponchos later, Allen has his own firm featuring cotton sports of sweatshirt

---

Jennifer Matteis and Daniel L. Daniels, Lawyers, Are to Be Married in August

Jennifer Ann Matteis, who graduated cum laude from the Harvard Law School in June, and Daniel Lloyd Daniels, a law clerk, plan to marry Aug. 27.

The future bride is a daughter of Mr. and Mrs. Richard J. Matteis of Greenwich, Conn., who have announced her engagement to a son of Mr. and Mrs. C. Ross Daniels Jr. of Pawling, N.Y.

Ms. Matteis graduated summa cum laude from the University of Pennsylvania, where she was elected to Phi Beta Kappa. She expects to join the New York law firm of Shea & Gould in September. Her father is an executive vice president of Manufacturers Hanover Trust in New York.

Her mother, Vilma Matteis, is a real-estate broker for Preferred Properties in Greenwich.

Mr. Daniels, who graduated summa cum laude from Dartmouth College and was elected to Phi Beta Kappa there, received a J.D. degree cum laude last year from the Harvard Law School. He is a clerk to Associate Justice Neil L. Lynch of the Massachusetts Supreme Judicial Court in Boston. Mr. Daniels expects to join the New York law firm of Sullivan & Cromwell as an associate in September. His father owns the Daniels Agency in Pawling and the Settle Agency in Danbury, Conn., both insurance concerns.

Jacqueline Meyer

C. Christopher Semmes
Jennifer Matteis

Dennis Bradbury
Susan Huffman

Jacqueline Meyer, Lawyer, Engaged

Mr. and Mrs. Robert Meyer of Beechhurst, Queens, have announced the engagement of their daughter, Jacqueline Meyer, to Martin I. Gold, a son of Mr. and Mrs. Gerald Gold of Oceanside, L.I. A December wedding is planned.

Ms. Meyer, an associate in the New York law firm of Bondy & Schloss, graduated from the University of Rochester and the Georgetown University Law Center. Her father, who retired as chairman of the accounting department at William Cullen Bryant High School in Long Island City, was in consultant and

Susan Huffman To Marry in Fall

Mrs. John H. Mortimer of Stamford, Conn., and Robert S. Huffman of New York have made known the engagement of their daughter, Susan Parker Huffman, to Jeffrey Hazen Boal, a son of Mr. and Mrs. H. Bruce Boal of Marblehead, Mass., and Woodstock, Vt. An October wedding is planned.

Miss Huffman, a cum laude graduate of Middlebury College, is an associate marketing manager at Home Box Office in New York. Her father is a public affairs consultant. Her mother, Hilda Mortimer, was formerly assistant director South

Announcement type

Above: Wedding and engagement announcements are set in light type, quieter treatment more appropriate for announcement "headlines." Scale and variety in cropping can make the page look more vital.

Three in two

Left: Pictured is a space-saving treatment set into two columns, with the appropriate stories adjacent, from *The New York Times*.

Dozens of spots

Facing page: Sunday brings together a full page of Calendar listings. Dozens of generic spot drawings to break up the type were supplied as part of the design project. The reverse indent is a sometimes neglected device for making listings easy to read.

SHOALS CALENDAR

Items for the Shoals Calendar may be mailed to the Times-Daily, P.O. Box 797, Florence, Ala., 35631, or called in to the newsroom, 766-8405. Items must be in hand by 5 p.m. Wednesday to be in the following Sunday's calendar. Please include a telephone number in case information must be verified.

All items dealing with a fund-raising event sponsored by an organization must include information on how the proceeds will be used. Franchised activities, taught on a professional basis, will not be listed.

TODAY

The Natchez Trace Genealogical Society will meet at 2 p.m. Sunday, Aug. 14, at the Tuscumbia Utilities Building, 202 E. 16th St. Mrs. Pat M. Mahan will present the program, "In search of Richard Bailey."

The Fred Bradford family will hold its annual reunion Sunday, Aug. 14, at railroad shelter in Spring Park, Tuscumbia. A picnic lunch will be served after lunch.

Members of Major Jesse Thomas Counts family will have their 33rd reunion Sunday, Aug. 14, at Spring Park, Tuscumbia. Those attending are asked to take a picnic lunch. Pictures for the photograph book will be made between 11 a.m. and noon.

Sheffield Band Boosters will meet Sunday, Aug. 14, at 3 p.m. at Sheffield High School band room.

MONDAY

The North Alabama System 34, 36 and 38 Users Group will meet Monday, Aug. 15, at 7 p.m. The meeting is open to all people who have access to IBM computer models SYS/34, SYS/36 or SYS/38. For information, call or write Roy Yancy at Reynolds Metals Company, Listerhill Reduction Plant, P.O. Box 191, Sheffield; phone 386-9557.

Bradshaw High School Band Boosters will meet at 7:30 p.m. Monday, Aug. 15, at the school.

The Lauderdale County Red Cross chapter will conduct a free blood pressure screening Monday, Aug. 15, 9-11 a.m., at Magnolia Gardens II.

Past Matrons and Patrons, OES 195, will meet Monday, Aug. 15, at 6 p.m. at the Senior Citizens Center, Fairgrounds Road, Florence.

TUESDAY

The Shoals 99'ers Home Computers Users Group will meet Tuesday, Aug. 16, at 7 p.m. at the Florence-Lauderdale Public Library. If you own a TI99/4A computer or are interested, call 764-5248.

Single adults will have a covered-dish supper Tuesday, Aug. 16, at 6:30 p.m. in the fellowship hall of First United Methodist Church, Montgomery Avenue, Sheffield. The group meets twice monthly. For information, call Judith Atkins, 383-2124.

The Senior Citizens' annual picnic will be Tuesday, Aug. 16, at shelter 1, McFarland Park, Florence. The Latums will entertain with country and western music. Food will be served at 6 p.m.

A Red Cross multimedia standard first aid course will be held Tuesday and Thursday, Aug. 16 and 18, 6-10 p.m., at the Lauderdale County Red Cross chapter, 318 S. Court St., Florence. The basic course prepares individuals to handle most general first aid emergencies. For information or to register, call 764-2911.

THURSDAY

The Muscle Shoals Chapter of the Alabama Conservancy will meet at 7 p.m. Thursday, Aug. 18, at the Florence-Lauderdale Public Library. The topic for the meeting will be "What's in the water we drink?" An audio-tape of the ABC special "Water: A Clear and Present Danger" will be played. The public is invited.

SATURDAY

The Connective Tissue Disease Association will meet at 2 p.m. Saturday, Aug. 20, in the lounge of Trinity Episcopal Church, Pine Street, Florence. For information, call Evelyn Woodworth, 764-5634, or Jayne Chase, 767-1665.

Sheffield Band Boosters will sponsor a back-to-school yard sale Saturday, Aug. 20, at the north end concession stand at Wright Stadium. No sales will be made before 8 a.m. All proceeds will go toward the purchase of new uniforms for the band.

SUNDAY

The Cleveland family reunion will be Sunday, Aug. 21, 11 a.m.-4 p.m., at Wiginton Community Center, between Hackleburg and Hodges. Those attending are asked to take a covered dish.

UNDATED

The YMCA is now taking registration for its after-school fun program, which begins Aug. 26. Children are picked up from school and activities are provided until parents arrive. For information, call the YMCA, 766-4652.

The Lauderdale County Red Cross chapter has available a new slide series on the Red Cross for showing to clubs and community groups. Any group planning its 1983-84 program schedule may call Tom Hull, 764-2911, about the slide series.

The Underwood-Petersville Watch Patrol is in need of volunteers. Those who would like to volunteer some time each month may call 766-0225.

Quad-Cities Squares will sponsor western square dancing classes beginning in September, at Royal Avenue Recreation Center, Florence. The classes will be for married couples and singles with partners. For information, call 766-6763 or 383-6245.

The Florence Park and Recreation Department is now signing up girls 4-13 years old who are interested in becoming cheerleaders for the Quad-Cities Recreation Football League for boys. The girls will cheer for the Florence teams and will travel to Sheffield and Tuscumbia for some of the games. No tryouts are necessary. To register or for information, call 766-4921 or go to the Broadway Recreation Center office.

Officers and enlisted men who served on the U.S.S. Grayson (DD-435), a World War II destroyer, will have their first reunion Oct. 21-23 in Kansas City, Mo. For information on the reunion, write Don Rasmussen, 560 22nd St. N.E., Salem, Ore. 97301.

The 87th Infantry Division of World Wars I and II will have its 34th annual reunion Sept. 22-25 at the Hyatt Regency Hotel in Nashville, Tenn. The Golden Acorn division was activated and trained as a combat infantry division in both world wars. For information on the reunion, contact Gladwin Pascuzzo, 2374 N. Dundee Ct., Highland, Mich. 48031; phone, 1-313-887-9005.

The 397th Bomb Group, with its 596th, 597th, 598th, 599th Bomb Squadrons, will have its sixth reunion Sept. 30-Oct. 2 at the Holiday Inn, Tampa International Airport, Tampa, Fla. Former members of the World War II 9th Air Force B-26 Marauder Group are asked to contact the 397th Bomb Group Association, Nevin F. Price, Secretary, P.O. Box 1796, Rockville, Md. 20850; phone 301-460-4488.

The 82nd Airborne Division Association is forming an all-airborne chapter. Any veteran of the 11th, 13th, 17th, 82nd, 101st, 173rd, 187th, 188th or any special forces units that were either glidermen or paratroopers can join the group. For details, write to Vulcan Chapter, Lloyd Armstrong, Chairman, 200 Briar Grove Drive, Birmingham, Ala. 35210.

The 307th Infantry Veterans Society (77th), along with units of 305 and 306th Infantries, Division Artillery, 706 Tank Battalion, 302nd Engineers and others will have a "now or never" reunion Oct. 14-16 at the Sheraton-Valley Forge Hotel, King of Prussia, Pa. The 307th saw action in Guam, Leyte, Kerama Retto, Ie Shima, Okinawa and the occupation of Japan. For information, write J.J. Hanifin, 31 Moore St., New Hyde Park, N.Y. 11040.

The 97th Heavy Bomb Group will have its third reunion Sept. 16-17 in St. Louis, Mo., and is seeking combat crewmen of the B-17 Flying Fortress and ground crew personnel of the 97th from 1942-1945, while they were based in England, Africa and Italy. For information about the reunion or the association, write Clarence Hammes, President, 97th Bomb Group Reunion Association, 15 Avilla Heights South, Alexander, Ark. 72002.

The U.S.S. Pittsburgh, CA 72, famed cruiser of World War II and Korean War, will have its sixth reunion Sept. 29-Oct. 2 in Nashville, Tenn. For details, former officers and crew may call J.C. Ayers, 404-820-1601 or 820-2360, or write Box 74, Wildwood, Ga. 30757.

The eighth reunion of the crew members of the light cruiser USS Boise CL 47 from World War II will be held Sept. 21-25 at the Fort Worth, Texas, Hilton. For details on the reunion, write Larry Farmer, 1809 Harrington Ave., Fort Worth, Texas 76106.

Public Meetings

The following public meetings are scheduled for this week in the Shoals area:

Eliza Coffee Memorial Hospital Board. 11 a.m. Monday, administrative offices, Marengo Street.

Sheffield Board of Education. 5:30 p.m. Monday, board offices, West Sixth Street.

Colbert County Hospital Board. 7:30 p.m. Monday, board room, Helen Keller Memorial Hospital.

Rogersville Town Council. 6:30 p.m. Monday, Town Hall.

Anderson Town Council. 7 p.m. Monday, Town Hall.

Colbert County Commission. 10 a.m. Tuesday, courthouse, county commission office.

Florence City Commission. 4 p.m. Tuesday, City Hall, municipal auditorium.

Muscle Shoals City Commission. 5 p.m. Tuesday, City Hall, auditorium.

Lauderdale County Board of Education. 5 p.m. Tuesday, board office, Middle Road.

Tuscumbia City Commission. 5:30 p.m. Tuesday, City Hall, auditorium.

Cherokee City Commission. 6 p.m. Tuesday, Town Hall.

Florence Board of Education. 7 p.m. Tuesday, Richards Center.

Sheffield City Commission. 7:30 p.m. Tuesday, City Hall, commission meeting room.

Colbert County Board of Education. 5 p.m. Thursday, board office, courthouse annex building.

Lexington Town Council. 6 p.m. Thursday, Senior Citizens Building.

Waterloo Town Council. 7 p.m. Thursday, Town Hall.

WEEKLY CALENDAR
MONDAY

Quad-Cities Young People's Group, Alcoholics Anonymous, has an open meeting every Monday night at 8 p.m. at Grace Episcopal Church, Sheffield.

The New Beginnings Alateen Group meets Mondays at 8 p.m. at 316½ N. Court St., Florence. The group is for those 16-20 who have a family member with a drinking problem. For information, call 381-0871.

The Ladies Auxiliary to the Underwood-Petersville Volunteer Fire Department meets the first Monday of each month at 7 p.m. at the fire department. All women in the service area are invited to join.

The Toastmasters Club of Florence meets the first and third Monday of each month at 6:30 p.m. at Western Sizzlin, Florence. Visitors are invited.

The Sheffield Jaycees will meet the second and fourth Monday of each month at 7 p.m. at the Cliffhanger Lounge in Sheffield. Jaycees membership is open to all men between 18 and 36. For information, call Kim Blankenship (day), 383-3222, or Tommy Howard (night), 383-5062.

Firefighters of the Underwood-Petersville Volunteer Fire Department meet the second Monday of each month at the fire department.

Cardiovascular rehabilitation therapy is the topic of a free information session held every Monday, 3-4 p.m., at the canteen at Riverbend Center for Mental Health. The session is open to anyone who has cardiovascular problems and also to those who want to know more about the benefits of cardiac rehabilitation. Dr. Ralph Carson, nutritionist and exercise physiologist, conducts the class. Everyone is welcome, no referral or registration is needed. For information, call Vera Schramm at Riverbend, 764-3431.

Members of the Cloverdale Volunteer Fire Department meet each second and fourth Monday at 6:30 p.m. at the fire department.

Overeaters Anonymous meets each Monday, at 7 p.m., at the rehabilitation center in Muscle Shoals. The meeting is open to the public. No dues, fees or weigh-ins.

The Florence Optimist Club meets every Monday at 6:30 a.m. at the Tourway Pancake House. For information, call 766-3301.

Shoals Stamp Society meets the second Monday of every month at Trinity Episcopal Church, Florence, at 7:30 p.m.

Zip City Volunteer Fire Department meets the first Monday of each month at 7:30 p.m. at the fire hall on Chisholm Road.

Colbert Refunders Club meets the first Monday of each month at 7 p.m. at the Muscle Shoals Vocational Center.

AMEND, Aiding a Mother Experiencing Neo-Natal Deaths, meets the second Monday of each month at 7 p.m. at the Education/Nursing Building on the University of North Alabama campus. AMEND is a support group for parents who experience miscarriages, stillbirths or death of an infant in the first year of life. For information on the group, call 766-4100, extension 311, or 381-3535.

The Pilot Club of Florence meets each second and fourth Monday at Howard Johnson's at 6 p.m. The second Monday a business meeting is held and the fourth Monday is a program meeting.

The Greenhill Pounds Off Starting Today club meets every Monday at 6:30 p.m. at the Greenhill Methodist Church fellowship hall.

The Lauderdale County Chapter of the American Red Cross sponsors a weekly bloodmobile every Monday, from 1 to 5 p.m., at the American Legion Building, 318 S. Court St., Florence. Lauderdale County residents between 18 and 65 are encouraged to donate. For information, call 764-2911.

Sweet Adelines, Pride of Shoals Chapter, rehearses each Monday at 7 p.m. at York Terrace First Church of God in Sheffield. For information, call 383-6444.

Florence Alanon meets Mondays at 8 p.m. at Trinity Episcopal Church, 410 Pine St., Florence. Those who have a family member with a drinking problem and who feel they need help and understanding may attend the meeting or call 381-0871.

Florence Alateen Group meets Mondays at 8 p.m. at Trinity Episcopal Church, 410 Pine St., Florence. The group is for those between 12 and 15 who have a family member with a drinking problem and who feel they need help and understanding. They may attend the meeting or call 381-0871.

TOPS Club AL 184 meets at 6:30 p.m. Mondays at Shoals Seventh-day Adventist Church, Cox Creek Parkway and Jackson Road, Florence.

TOPS Club AL 227 meets at 5 p.m. Mondays in the basement of the bank in Lexington.

TOPS Club AL 356 meets at 6 p.m. Mondays at Nitrate City Baptist Church.

TOPS Club AL 324 meets at 6 p.m. Mondays, Southside Baptist Church, Sheffield.

TOPS Club AL 213 meets at 5 p.m. Mondays at the Senior Citizens Center, Fairgrounds Road, Florence.

TOPS Club Waterloo meets at 6 p.m. Mondays at the Neighborhood Center.

TOPS Club AL 208 meets at 9:30 a.m. Mondays at the YMCA.

TOPS Club AL 191 meets at 6 p.m. Mondays at Wilson School, Florence.

TUESDAY

The Shoals 99'ers Home Computers Users Group will meet the third Tuesday of each month at the Florence-Lauderdale Public Library at 7 p.m. If you own a TI99/4A computer or are interested, call 764-5248.

Recovery Inc. meets every Tuesday at 6:30 p.m. in room 9, Riverbend Center for Mental Health, Florence. For information, call the Mental Health Association in the Muscle Shoals Area, 766-4182.

The Registry of Interpreters for the Deaf meets the second Tuesday of each month at 6:30 p.m. in the conference room of Northwest Alabama Rehabilitation Center, 1450 E. Avalon Ave., Muscle Shoals. All those who know sign language are invited to attend.

Shoals Area Citizens for Life meets on the last Tuesday of every month at 7:30 p.m. The organization is dedicated to pro-life causes. All concerned citizens are invited to participate in the group. For information and meeting locations, call 381-3528 after 5 p.m.

Parents of Hyperactive Children meets the second Tuesday of each month at 7 p.m. Parents and professionals interested in hyperactivity are invited. For information, call Nancy Donahoo, 764-4796.

Cherokee TOPS AL 192 meets Tuesdays at 6 p.m. at Cherokee Library. For information, call 359-6407.

The Self-Help Group for Widowed Persons meets the third Tuesday of each month at 7 p.m. at Riverbend Center for Mental Health, Florence. For information, call 766-4182.

Cyrus Chapter 6 of Royal Arch Masons and Florence Council 74 meets the first and third Tuesday of each month at 7 p.m. at the Florence Masonic Hall.

An alcoholism educational film series is open to the general public the first Tuesday of each month, at 6:30 p.m. in the auditorium at Riverbend Center for Mental Health, Florence. Alcoholism counselors are available, and questions, answers and discussion follow each film. For information, call Gray's Landing, 383-1092.

Florence Commandry 39 meets the second and fourth Tuesday at 7 p.m. at the Florence Masonic Hall.

Florence Emblem Club 93 meets the first Tuesday of every month at 7:30 p.m. at Elks Lodge 820, Chisholm Road, Florence.

TOUCH, a self-help group for cancer patients, their family and friends, meets the third Tuesday of each month at 7:30 p.m. at Riverbend Center for Mental Health, Florence. TOUCH is sponsored by the American Cancer Society in cooperation with the Comprehensive Cancer Center, University of Alabama-Birmingham. For information, call Helen Richards, 766-1813, or Lyda Lilly, 764-1009.

The Zip City Volunteer Fire Department teenage girls' auxiliary meets the last Tuesday of every month at 7 p.m. at the fire station, Chisholm Road. For information, call 764-5445.

The Florence daytime Al-Anon group meets every Tuesday and Thursday, 11 a.m.-noon, at 316½ N. Court St., over City Drugs.

Day-By-Day, for parents whose children have died, meets the second Tuesday of each month at Riverbend Center for Mental Health, Room 113, at 7:30 p.m. For information, call Ray and Sue Burch, 383-6913, or Porter and Virginia Russ, 766-0089.

The Underwood-Petersville Community Watch Patrol will the first Tuesday of each month at 7 p.m. at the Underwood School cafeteria.

Families Anonymous, for the families of drug abusers, meets each Tuesday, 7:30 p.m., at Trinity Episcopal Church, corner of Pine and Tuscaloosa streets, Florence.

Colbert County Rescue Squad sponsors a miscellaneous auction every Tuesday, 7:30 p.m., at the rescue squad building, Shop Pike, Sheffield. Proceeds go to the rescue squad.

Narcotics Anonymous meets Tuesday and Saturday nights at 7:30 at Trinity Episcopal Church, Pine and Tuscaloosa, Florence. Meetings are held in a room near the north wing parking area.

The Shoals Chapter of Safe Energy Alliance meets the fourth Tuesday of each month at 7 p.m. at Florence-Lauderdale Public Library.

The Shoals Area Sierra Club meets at 7 p.m. the second Tuesday of each month at the Florence-Lauderdale Public Library, Wood Avenue, Florence. Persons who enjoy hiking, backpacking and canoeing and who are interested in conservation are invited to attend. Call 766-2919 or 247-3554 for information.

Muscle Shoals TOPS Club AL 138 meets at 6:30 p.m. Tuesdays at the Muscle Shoals Rehabilitation Center.

Western-Style Square Dancing Club meets Tuesday, 7-10 p.m. at Royal Avenue Recreation Center, Florence. Visitors are welcome.

WEDNESDAY

The National Organization for Women meets the second Wednesday of every month in the basement of Florence-Lauderdale Public Library at 7 p.m.

The Florence Jaycees meet the second and fourth Wednesday each month at 6:30 p.m. at Western Sizzlin, Florence. Any man between 18 and 35 is invited to attend.

The Refunders' Club, designed to save dollars and cents, meets the third Wednesday of each month, at 9:30 a.m. at the Royal Avenue Recreation Center, Florence.

THURSDAY

Quad-Cities Squares, a western-style square dancing club, meets Thursdays at 7 p.m. at Royal Avenue Recreation Center, Florence. Married and single couples are invited. George Lavender is the caller. For information, call 766-6763 or 383-6245.

The Muscle Shoals Chapter of the American Diabetes Association meets the second Thursday of each month at Colonial Manor Hospital. For information on the meetings, call 386-8757 from 8 a.m. to 4 p.m.

Quad-Cities Young People's Group of Alcoholics Anonymous meets at 8 p.m. Thursdays at Grace Episcopal Church in Sheffield in a closed meeting.

TOPS Club AL 374 meets each Thursday at 6:30 p.m. at Bibb and Tucker Nursery School on Florence Boulevard. TOPS, Take Off Pounds Sensibly, is open to all family members. For information, call Debbie Johnson, 767-7040, or Sheila Bevis, 764-5239.

Florence Business and Professional Women's Club has a dinner meeting the first Thursday each month at 7 p.m. at Executive Inn, Florence. The club has a business meeting the third Thursday each month at 7 p.m. at members' homes.

Colbert-Lauderdale Chapter of the American Association of Medical Assistants meets the first Thursday of each month at 7 p.m. Guest speakers are featured at each meeting. For meeting place, call Gayle Hill at 383-7194.

Muscle Shoals Jaycettes meet the second and fourth Thursdays of the month at Holiday Inn, Sheffield, at 7 p.m. All young women between 18 and 35 are invited to attend.

Cherokee Jaycees meet each first and third Thursday at 7 p.m. at the bank community room at Cherokee.

The Pilot Club of Tuscumbia meets each fourth Thursday of the month at the Tuscumbia Community Center. The executive board meeting is at 6 p.m., followed by dinner at 6:30 and a program at 7.

Sheffield Alanon Group meets Thursday at 8 p.m. above the RC Cola Building, Jackson Highway, Sheffield.

TOPS Club AL 205, Killen, meets each Thursday at 6 p.m. at Brooks Elementary School. For information, call 757-2742 or 757-1603.

TOPS Club AL 173 meets Thursdays at 6 p.m. at the Sheffield Public Library.

FRIDAY

The Colbert County Chapter of the American Red Cross sponsors a weekly bloodmobile every Friday, from 9 a.m. to 1 p.m., at the Colbert County Courthouse Annex, 120 W. Fifth St., Tuscumbia. Colbert County residents between 18 and 65 are encouraged to donate. For information, call 383-3721.

The Lauderdale County Chapter of the American Red Cross provides a free blood pressure screening every Friday from 10 a.m. to 2 p.m. for the general public at the American Legion building, 318 S. Court St., Florence. For information, call 764-2911.

SUNDAY

An Ostomy meeting is held the third Sunday of every month at M. Shoals United Methodist Church, Avalon Avenue, Muscle Shoals, at 2:30 p.m.

UNDATED

Reynolds Aluminum operates an aluminum recycling convenience center Tuesday through Saturday, 9:30 a.m.-5 p.m., at Regency Square Mall, Florence.

AMEND

AMEND is a group that provides aid for women who have suffered neo-natal deaths. The group meets the second Monday of each month on the UNA campus. Ernestine Davis, one of the group's founders, is shown above with her son.

New, all the way
The new logo goes up on the *Times Daily* building, accompanying a widespread promotion and advertising campaign.

Talking to the reader
Facing page: A 16-page tabloid accompanying the newspaper in the first week gave readers a rundown on the changes in the paper and important aspects of the operation, and introduced each member of the News Department. Here publisher Guy Hankins makes the keynote introduction.

WHY CHANGE?

A newspaper changes its look for the same reasons that many of you often do: to keep up with the times and to reflect our approval of new ideas and new thinking.

Our changes in design and content will make us the sharpest, most distinctive newspaper in Alabama. In our language, we'll have greater eye appeal. Plus, we'll be adding many new features about subjects that affect all of us daily.

But the heart of this newspaper isn't changing. Its heart will remain the news, features and pictures about you in the Shoals — the good people we work with and live with every day. Our greatest mandate is to serve you and to be your most valued publication of record. Also, we won't change our commitment to pursue excellence in journalism, to keep tuned to community needs and to remain feisty and persistent on our professional course.

The staff of your Times Daily accepts these commitments to progressive change, to a better news product and to a stronger Shoals.

R. Guy Hankins, Publisher

The Home Section

THE NEW YORK TIMES

THE

SECTION

The Home Section

If it's Thursday

Friday . . . it's Weekend
Monday . . . it's SportsMonday
Tuesday . . . it's Science Times
Wednesday . . . it's The Living Section

*T*he Times had been grappling with the idea of a four-part daily paper for years before April 1976, when the first of the four-part dailies was finally published. It had been a two-part daily for most of its modern history: world and national news, culture, and the editorial spread in the first section; metropolitan news and business/finance in the second; and sports, the lifestyle page, and other features moving around as the make-up of the paper required.

A four-part paper promised advantages for both advertising and news. The News Department would have four front pages every day and would be able to produce a more organized, accessible paper. Behind each front page, reorganization of news space would allow room for more editorial material when expansion was desired; and four front pages would allow for heightened display. For the Advertising Department, a four-part paper would open up new ad spaces, particularly the four rather than two desirable back pages.

Above these specific advantages was the anticipation of having, quite simply, a better product to sell, modernized and made more appealing to readers and therefore more appealing to advertisers.

The chief problem in producing a four-part paper stemmed from the folding limitations of the high-speed, big-volume presses. In a two-part paper, both sections must have an equal number of pages. In a four-part paper, the first and third sections must have an equal number of pages, and the second and fourth section must be equal, and each pair must equal the other. To change from two to four sections would involve changes in where some ads would run, a matter of consequence to most advertisers.

On the News Department side, uncertainty existed regarding what the new section would be. Everybody was certain of Sections A, B, and D, world and national news in A, metropolitan area news in B, and business news in D; but considerable differences existed about Section C. While we concentrated on launching other projects—the new suburban sections, a wider column structure in the whole paper, and others—the four-part paper was kept simmering on the back burner.

Architectural structure
Facing page: One of the first rough sketches for The Home Section spelled out a strictly structured "architectural" design with what amounted to a magazine cover occupying about one third of the page.

102

103

A different "magazine" each day

The idea of producing a different third section, the C section, on a different subject each weekday was born on the Brooklyn-bound 7th Avenue subway. John Pomfret, then assistant general manager of the paper, and I were going home together, as we frequently did. The conversation never strayed far from the changes we were involved in at *The Times*.

On this subway ride, John brought up the "What should the third section be?" question. Entertainment, fashion, lifestyle, sports, and food were strong candidates. I said, "Why not all of them, a different one each day? We would be giving the reader in effect a different magazine with each day's paper."

It sounded like the answer. I don't know what wheels were set in motion, but within a cou-

ple of months, we were all hard at work on the format of the first C section, the entertainment section for Friday.

Weekend

Weekend was kicked off April 7, 1976. The first section of the paper remained mostly national and world news, and the second section remained mostly metropolitan area news, with jumps from national. Weekend was third. The fourth was business and financial news in the same news style as before, with a modest new heading. Business news now had a permanent home on Fridays, the fourth section of the four-part paper.

It was feared that a section dealing with entertainment and cultural activities would blend into Arts and Leisure coverage and take away ad-

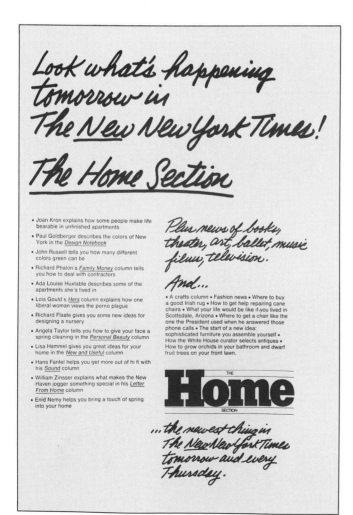

Promotion
Left: An ad for the new section.

Themed sections
Facing page: In addition to The Home Section on Thursday, Weekend, The Living Section, Science Times, and SportsMonday rounded out the weekday line-up. The paper remained two sections on Saturday.

104

vertising from that Sunday section. To counter this fear, Rosenthal and Gelb stressed that Weekend content would be clearly geared to the service concept of what to see, do, and enjoy in the next few days, leaving the broader kind of essays to the Arts and Leisure section.

The service idea was emphasized in the design of the front page by the presence of a "Weekender Guide" that ran across the bottom third of the page. Function followed form. I felt the page needed something distinctive in texture to vary the pattern of blocks of text and provide a distinctive identity. Consequently, a routine guide of events, planned for an inside page, was brought forward to a prominent position on the front page and given a new title, a strong heading, and a new style. This supplemented an unusual top-of-the-page treatment where reefers were lined up like headlines in a bulletin-board style, creating a graphic unit with the actual lead headline.

These are examples of how words, their meaning, and design come together without necessarily following the accepted chronological sequence of first the word and then the design. A design idea is often rejected by an editor (or publisher) as being merely a *design* idea. The designer is told the design doesn't work with the content or is merely decorative.

This argument, sometimes considered the ultimate crusher, is often questionable, it seems to me, or at least it should be questioned. Questioned not because the criticism may be unjustified—a design may be irrelevant or bad for any number of reasons—but because the argument often masks a feeling that a design idea should not be expected to fashion the shape of content to any significant degree. This of course reflects the narrow view that the designer's job is simply to "package" and make look good what he or she is given. Happily, the broader and increasingly more prevalent view is that a designer should be encouraged to contribute a great deal more than just packaging. In the best working relationship, the editor and designer design the paper together.

Weekend was immediately successful. A great deal of promotion was put behind it, including a show-biz party at Sardi's on 44th Street and free copies distributed at Times Square. An increase of 28,000 in circulation was registered that first Friday. This figure settled down to one less sensational, but there was plenty of encouragement, nevertheless, to continue with other C sections.

Other C sections

Six months after Weekend, the Living Section was introduced on Wednesday as part of the second four-part daily. At roughly six-month intervals, Home first appeared on Thursday, followed by SportsMonday.

Tuesday remained open. To round out the four-part week, a section was made up for Tuesday of existing culture and lifestyle material, with a front page that was a mixture of reviews and essays. This mixed bag proved to be unimpressive—in addition to the mishmash of content, there was hardly any space for pictures, a temporary throwback to the "good gray Times."

Within a few months Science Times was introduced instead of the anonymous Tuesday section, and the four-part paper Monday to Friday was complete.

Before Science Times was chosen, interesting discussions took place about the content of this last C section. The Advertising Department wanted a fashion section; a few of us in the News Department wanted to do a science section. I was enthusiastic about a science section, since, as far as I knew, one did not exist on a regular basis in any newspaper; it would be a journalistic first. Also, the nature of the material held the promise of a new visual dimension to the paper, the hard edge of diagrams, charts, and technical illustrations to offset the soft edges of food, lifestyle, and arts pictures. Also, science was an exciting prospect since it would be a natural outgrowth of an important historical aspect of *The New York Times* journalism. *The Times* had gone with Perry to the North Pole, had been present when King Tut's tomb was opened, and had won one of its many Pulitzer Prizes for its exclusive coverage of the explosion of the first atom bomb. More than any other paper in the United States, *The Times* was associated with in-depth coverage of scientific subjects, often arcane, the presence of which on Page One was a source of surprise and delight for many readers. A large staff of science writers was already in place, many of them well known to the general public.

A fashion section seemed to be a tired idea, soft in nature and promising at best to be a poor second to other publications in New York, for example, the Fairchild Company's *W*.

A science section was a natural, at first, in every way but advertising. An immediate hit with readers, surveys showed it to be at least as popular with women as any of the other new sections.

However, for a few years, its success was limited by its apparent inability to attract ads. Then someone in the Advertising Department found the key to new ads in the computer market, business computers and, particularly, personal computers. Classified display ads were put together and became the advertising vehicle of choice for many of the hundreds of new retail computer outlets. With increased advertising the newshole grew, and Science Times achieved respectable proportions.

Character—the same but different

The C sections are designed with the same typefaces and maintain a family resemblance to each other. For accenting display Stymie Black was picked up from the recently designed magazinelike suburban sections. The Stymie, a strong departure from the regular line-up of traditional *Times* typefaces, was the typographical trademark that set the C sections apart from the rest of the paper. The basic headline face, as established in the suburban sections, is Bookman. To make up for relative lightness, the Bookman is used in larger sizes. Other "contemporary" typographical touches were added to these sections that did not apply to the hard news parts of the paper— Bookman in captions, set off with an underlining rule, the by-line set between rules, use of initials, and others.

When talking about any part of *The Times*, from the Book Review to Sports, readers seem to have a comfortable feeling that all the parts of the paper are produced within the guidelines and standards of a single journalistic intelligence. I felt the design of the paper should affect readers the same way and reflect the same unifying philosophy.

Within the overall typographical character, however, each section was designed to project its own image. The logo on each front page, for example, is markedly different, even though all were designed in the same basic Stymie.

As with Weekend's "Weekender Guide," one important element on each front page is featured to set the section apart from the others. For example, SportsMonday has big action pictures across the top fifth of the page, achieving not only high story count, but guaranteeing a panorama of pictorial action on the page. Home featured a prominent reefer box with exceptionally large numerals for page references. The Living Section used small pictures across the top of the page. Weekend had an unusual treatment of reefer headlines grouped with the headline of the lead story, in the same typeface, to provide what was visualized as a "bulletin" effect. Finally, Science Times balanced a horizontal heading at the top with horizontal reefers at the bottom, like slices of bread around a well-filled sandwich.

Later, when a revitalized Business Day was designed out of elements of the traditional Business/Finance section, this front page, too, featured its own special device, a serviceable Business Digest that summed up relevant information, with page references, from the entire newspaper. However, Business Day, Section D of the four-part paper, unlike the C sections, was designed to relate typographically to the hard-news parts of the paper. It did not employ the more flashy use of Stymie Black or the other bolder devices that characterized the C sections.

In addition to the variety built into each format's design, it was understood that the individual nature of each section would itself dictate a different "look."

Arthur Gelb was the editor designated by Rosenthal to oversee the development of the C sections and their week-by-week implementation. We constantly stressed the need to keep each section looking like itself and not some other part of the paper. A photograph of a building in The Home Section, for example, should not suggest Real Estate. Illustrations for the front page of Weekend should suggest the many activities taking place in the New York area, which is the way the stories themselves were conceived; they should not deal with a single theme more characteristic of the Arts and Leisure section.

Beyond all this, Rosenthal and Gelb stressed that lead stories in these "feature" sections must be on the news, not in the sense of reporting a fire across the street but au courant and relevant to what readers would find interesting and useful at that time.

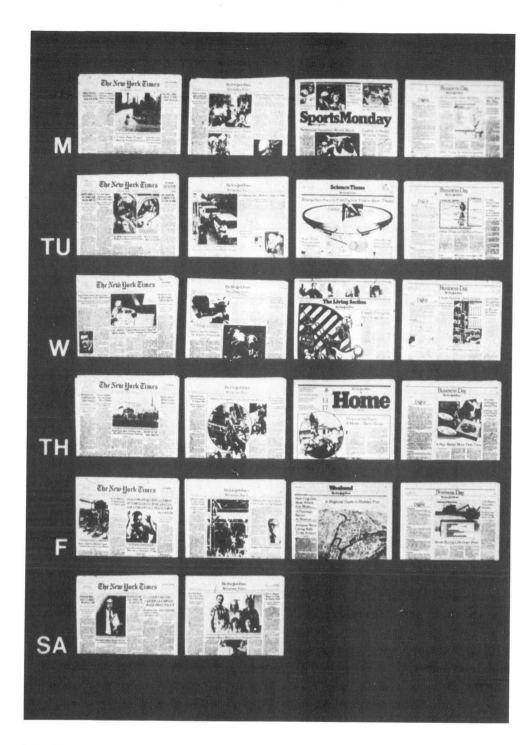

The line-up

This chart shows how the paper appeared Monday through Saturday. The C sections stood out from the rest of the paper each day but still related to the other sections and to each other.

Business Day

Facing page: A promotion broadside announced the forthcoming Business Day section. The new design gave greater prominence to each of the front page stories. The editors said the new design required them to put only high-quality stories on the page. Headline banks were retained to make a bridge to the hard news style of the front page.

Elmhurst to Manhattan— One Classic Style

By ADA LOUISE HUXTABLE

HOME is where you hang your hat and your heart—anywhere in the world except New York. Here, home is the result of Darwinian selection. Life is the survival of the fittest and home is whatever you can find and afford. Mutation of the species is part of the process—in my own case, a natural brownstoner became a reluctant Park Avenue dweller; choice is a delusion even with the luxury of options.

Living well in New York is not so much the realization of a dream as it is a blend of hard economic reality and relentless resolve. The real prizes —the rent-controlled penthouse, the parlor floor with 13-foot ceilings and wood burning fireplaces—go to the swift, the canny, the ruthless and the rich. The rest of us just compromise.

We may be fortunate, favored, smiled on in our careers, achievers by the world's standards, but we still compromise. What many seek and get, and what still eludes the rest of us, is the universal dream that we all carry in our hearts, whether born or migrant New Yorkers, of that special New York life style. It is a magic compounded of Bohemia, the movies and worldly success. It is glass-walled living rooms suffused in sunsets or with a nighttime backdrop of sparkling spires, spacious elegance and just enough of Madison Avenue's treasures to be quietly beautiful but not overreaching or outré, ice tinkling in glasses at twilight to an obligato of erudition and wit, little sitdown dinners for 24 set with Baccarat and vermeil. It is wall-to-wall sophisticated glamour.

This is the dream that brings the young and talented to their hot-plate furnished rooms, that lures the rich and privileged to their penthouse pied-a-terres. It is sometimes achieved on

money, but more often on credit, connections and sheer will. For those of us who never achieve it, the image sustains reality.

There is, in fact, a classic pattern to living in New York, from the initial adventure to arrival in the glossy magazines, and I have reached the point in life where I can reminisce about it with appropriate nostalgia and few regrets.

Mine was a marriage of geographical convenience. World War II had begun, and my husband, an industrial designer, had chosen a one-and-a-half-room bachelor apartment exactly halfway between the two defense plants where he worked in Brooklyn and Long Island. Calculating, probably by slide rule, he found a new apartment house in Elmhurst, Queens. There was a wartime housing shortage, and we moved in.

You have to love a man a lot and not have claustrophobia to spend seven years in one-and-a-half rooms in Queens when you've never been farther than a stone's throw from Central Park. He came equipped, as a proper designer did in those days, with a strong bias toward the Bauhaus and Aalto furniture, and a sense of architectural austerity.

I put ruffles on the Aalto table, added flowered cretonne chairs and tieback curtains to the window with a view of Joe the Tailor across the street. It was a passing phase. He taught me to hate wallpaper. Any color was fine as long as it was white. I retired the ruffles. And with the end of the war we began looking for just the right place.

It took a while, but we found it—the parlor floor of a brownstone on East 76th Street. Those lovely bourgeois-Bohemian quarters were easier to find in those days, before the postwar build-

Continued on Page C12

The New York Times

THE Home SECTION

Instant Furniture Boom: The Latest Look Is Sophisticated, The Assembly Is Easy Page C4

White House Acquisitor

By LAURA FOREMAN

WASHINGTON — When you ask Clement E. Conger, the White House curator, to tell you about himself, the first thing you are apt to find out is that he lives in Alexandria, Va., where his family has held forth for 253 years.

That's two hundred and fifty-three years, mind you. Virginians set a great store in their geneological gloatings. You will also discover that his maternal forebear was none other than William Ramsay, the founder of Alexandria in 1724 and its first and lord mayor under the crown. Furthermore, William Ramsay's wife was George Washington's second cousin, and for her assiduous fund-raising efforts during the American Revolution she was called the most patriotic woman in Virginia by Thomas Jefferson himself.

This sort of thing would be important to any Virginian, but it is particularly vital in Clement Conger's case. Obviously, anybody whose family has hung around Virginia that long has the taste of Petronius, the guile of Odysseus and the ability to talk anybody out of anything. Such virtues come in handy for a White House curator.

The elegant, gray-haired, 64-year-old Virginian, whose gracious manner masks the soul of a born predator, has been White House curator since 1970, and he has begged, borrowed, cajoled, intimidated, wheedled and bought his way into some 500 important acquisitions for the First Residence. He does the same thing for the State Department's magnificent diplomatic reception rooms, but more on that later.

"In seven years, Mr. Conger has lifted the White House collection from a medium level to the front rank of Americana collections of the 19th century," says a biographical sketch put out by his White House office. "He and Mrs. Nixon and Mrs. Ford have refurbished 21 rooms, restoring most of them more authentically than ever before to the elegance they may have had in the first quarter of the 19th century," the sketch continues.

Thus far, Mr. Conger hasn't been overburdened with work by President and Mrs. Carter, who apparently like their new home pretty much the way it is.

Mrs. Carter, according to her press office, has done no redecorating and plans none. Mr. Carter has merely rearranged some furniture and expressed an interest in some new paintings.

"My one meeting with the President so far was about his study, which is next to the Oval Office," Mr. Conger said in a recent interview. "He changed the arrangement of some chairs and settees in the Oval Office, but that's about all.

"He said to me, 'I think maybe I'd like some American Impressionism,' and I said I thought that would be perfect for this room," the curator said. Early this month, three paintings— two John Henry Twachmans and a Dennis Bunker—were delivered to the White House on loan from private collectors and were moved into the Presidential study.

The President was "very pleased, very happy indeed," Mr. Conger said, adding that more American Impression-

Continued on Page C28

How to cope when your apartment's unfinished. Joan Kron on interim decorating. Page C16.

Home front page

Increasing courage

Home was the third C section to be introduced in the daily *Times*. The first two, Weekend and Living, had established the typographical battery, Bookman and Stymie Black, and an increasingly strong graphic look. By the time we got to Home, we had all grown more courageous graphically, so an early rough layout featuring a huge Home logo was readily accepted.

When the first issue of The Home Section appeared, one of the editors in the newsroom exclaimed about the logo, "My God, it's bigger than the 'Men Walk on Moon' headline!" The remark reflects a significant aspect of the new sections of which most readers would not be aware. They were produced by people recruited from various news desks, editors accustomed to thinking in terms of the modest sizes and traditional treatment of *The New York Times'* headlines. In the past at *The Times*, as in most newspapers, sections like these would have been the product of the more free-wheeling Sunday Department or Features Department. The suburban sections, kicked off the year before, also had come from the desks of the newsroom. They had helped set the stage in the News Department for what undoubtedly was a series of visual shocks that if unprecedented might never have been acceptable.

A magazine cover

The original idea was that the logo with the picture under it would create a magazine-size cover unit. The agreement that this big picture could be a teaser to an inside story was a big breakthrough. Running the picture without accompanying text enhanced the magazine cover effect.

I asked my friend Peter Palazzo, the designer of the memorable *Herald-Tribune* format some years earlier, to help kick off the first issue. We got Carl Fischer, well known in advertising and magazine photography, to produce the kind of studio shot envisioned as characteristic of the section. The photo was to be simple and big, with the graphic look of a studio photo, not a square half-tone news photograph.

For the second issue, I used a horizontal picture across six columns to show layout variety for the whole page. (I'm not sure extreme flexibility is always essential. An alternative approach would be to stick to the original design idea, a magazine-size cover unit in the upper right section of the page, but concentrate on creative implementation within the rectangle, which is how most magazine covers are handled.)

First issue

Facing page: The first issue of Home followed the rough layout almost precisely. The silhouetted studio photograph set the pattern for a magazine kind of interest and impact. Using the major illustration as a reefer, without accompanying text, permits greatly increased graphic flexibility.

Later issue

Right: A later issue shows potential for variety in the format that nevertheless retains the general character. The words Arts/Entertainment in the reefer box add front page presence for those subjects running at the back of the section. Design: Tom Bodkin.

Weekend

FRIDAY, APRIL 30, 1976 — L+ 1C

The New York Times

The City Opera Turns to Bellow, O'Horgan. Page 11

Galleries Spring Surprises. Page 14

More Than Jam At the Jazz Clubs. Page 27

Stars Drawing Full Houses in The Suburbs

By JAMES FERON

WHEN Tom Jones strides onstage at the Westchester Premier Theater tonight, the house will be jampacked. Frank Sinatra and Liza Minnelli filled the 3,500-seat center in 10-day runs recenty. And next month, big crowds are expected for Johnny Mathis, Alan King, Bobby Vinton and Paul Anka.

At least 40 of the next 52 weeks at the theater at White Plains Road in Tarrytown are booked solid with big-name singers and comedians, cabaret acts and dance troupes, orchestra concerts and children's plays and a sprinkling of community events, industrial meetings and even high-school graduation exercises.

It is no wonder that groups interested in setting up similar theaters in the suburbs of Boston, Miami and other cities have been visiting the theater and inspecting the techniques of its promoters.

Business is good at the Westchester Premier Theater, a $5.5 million entertainment center that opened little more than a year ago in pursuit of the huge potential audience in the New York City suburbs.

After smoothing out some rough edges in the early months—including acoustical and sightline problems and just plain misjudged bookings—the theater believes it has put together a formula for success in suburbia.

That is apparently trickier than it would seem. Suburban theaters have sprung up throughout the country in recent years in search of America's entertainment dollar, which has been spreading out from the cities along with the middle-class.

But good business has not always been uniform. The now-defunct Nanuet Star Theater, a $3 million theater-in-the-round across the Tappan Zee Bridge in Rockland

Continued on Page 6

Martha Swope

Peter Martins and Suzanne Farrell of the New York City Ballet will perform tonight in George Balanchine's "Jewels" at the State Theater. A booming spring-summer ballet season moves into high gear this weekend and will run well into August studded with special events, galas and superstar performers. Story appears on Page 26.

New Faces Lighting Up The Season On Broadway

By MEL GUSSOW

SEVERAL months ago Keith McDermott might have been the young waiter bringing you spaghetti in a Greenwich Village restaurant.

Iowa-born Marybeth Hurt was acting in everything, everywhere, from Off Off Broadway to Central Park.

Paul Rudd was playing in one of the most highly publicized flops in television history.

Now their time has arrived. Along with a number of other talented newcomers, they are achieving considerable success this season in what is very likely the toughest arena of all—theater in New York. All are on Broadway this weekend, and they are the kind of ascending stars you can expect to be seeing for years to come.

Vivian Reed, in "Bubbling Brown Sugar," and Christine Andreas, in "My Fair Lady," are as close as one can come today to being overnight stars. But most of this season's bright new faces took circuitous routes to the spotlight by polishing their crafts at regional theaters or Off Off Broadway.

•

By any standard, the most acclaimed new face is Paul Rudd, who opened last week in David Rabe's "Streamers" at Lincoln Center. Mr. Rudd made his stage debut in 1968 in Joseph Papp's Central Park productions of "Henry IV, Parts One and Two," playing a messenger, and had one line: "My lord, the King, comes on apace."

This summer Mr. Rudd will play the lord, the King, "Henry V," for Mr. Papp in the park—and his career is really coming on apace. Next fall he will play Romeo at Circle in the Square. At 35, Mr. Rudd now has his pick of the parts.

Despite the actor's long apprenticeship in regional theater, it was television—his role as Brian Mallory, the amiable, opportunistic chauffeur in the ill-fated "Beacon Hill"—that first gave him prominence. It was a character that assumed the natural conformations of the actor. "Brian's bubbly, calculating charm is part of my makeup," Mr. Rudd says.

It is that combination of apparent ingenuousness and covert ambition that has marked many of Mr. Rudd's characterizations to date. In the revival of "The Glass

Continued on Page 20

Some of the promising new performers include, from the top, Paul Rudd, Marybeth Hurt and Keith McDermott.

WEEKENDER GUIDE

Friday

PARKE BERNET PHOTOS

Exhibitions at the Sotheby Parke Bernet auction house are always one-of-a-kind and last-of-a-kind. The displays are set out for public viewing on days before the items are to be auctioned off and visitors can experience the feeling of viewing objects that they would only see in a museum. An extraordinary exhibition of 400 "Important 19th and 20th Century Photographs" may be seen, free, today and tomorrow from 10 to 5. Among the lensclickers represented on sale here are many of the most eminent names in the art: Eduard Steichen, Alfred Stieglitz, Paul Strand, Lewis H. Hine, Walker Evans, Margaret Bourke-White, Man Ray, Robert Capa, Ansel Adams.

The auction house is at 980 Madison Avenue, at 76th Street (472-3400).

HOLLYWOOD IN JERSEY

Movie making is an ancient New Jersey institution, antedating even toll booths. Thomas A. Edison patented the Kinetoscope in 1893 and set up the Black Maria, a movie studio to make films for it, in West Orange. The Newark Museum has opened an exhibition devoted to the days when New Jersey was the movie capital of the world. The show occupies three large galleries on the first floor of the museum. There are photos and posters recalling the Jersey appearances of Mary Pickford, Madge Evans, Lionel Barrymore, Theda Bara. Even livelier are the showings of films made there. In a gallery refitted as an old-fashioned movie house, you will see at 2, 3 and 4 P.M. three 1910 Biograph films: "A Plain Song," "A Lucky Toothache" and "Song of the Wildwood Flute," all made in Westfield.

Admission is free. Open Noon to 5, today and tomorrow, 1 to 5 Sunday. At 49 Washington Street, (201-733-[illegible]).

VARIETY IN WESTBURY

The Westbury Music Fair rang up its first curtain in what was then the wilds of Nassau with "The King and I" in a tent. That was 20 years ago. Ten years later, the Fair raised a hard-top roof with a show starring Jack Benny and Wayne Newton. Now WFM, still in the same place, is observing its 20th anniversary, but it seems much closer to the city than it did then. This weekend, the Music Fair has on deck two performers: Gabriel Kaplan, born in the adjoining county of Kings and star of the TV series "Welcome Back Kotter," and Ben Vereen, who won a Tony for his acting and singing in "Pippin."

Shows are at 8:30 tonight and at 7 and 10:30 P.M. tomorrow. Admission is $8.75 or $7.75. Also Sunday at 7:30; admission, $6.75 and $7.75. Reservations: 516-354-2727, 212-239-7177. On Brush Hollow Road, Exit 34 Northern State Parkway, or Exit 40 Long Island Expressway.

HIGH JINKS IN PRINCETON

The Princeton Triangle Club, for the last 86 years, has gone onstage with a show, usually loud and funny, written and staffed by undergrads, with the help of a few professionals. This year the show is "Mugs Money," which is about gangsters trying to bring back Prohibition. Cast of 60, total company of 100, including orchestra. At the McCarter Theater in Princeton, corner Alexander and College Roads (609-921-8700). Tonight and tomorrow night at 8:30, admission: $3.50 to $5.95. Sunday at 7:30, admission: $3 to $5.50.

LUNCHTIME JAZZ

Long lunch. Good company. Exciting music. That's Jazz at Noon, the Friday perennial that unites jazz buffs every week at Shepheard's in the Drake Hotel, 56th Street and Park Avenue. A week or so ago the bill was Bucky Pizzarelli on guitar, Maxine Sullivan in lovely voice, an obstetrician on flügelhorn, a Montreal psychologist on sax and a man from a shirt company on something else. If you enjoy playing, bring your instrument and see Les Lieber, who will invite you to sit in. There's a $2 admission and you can sit and listen, or have a drink and listen, or eat and listen.

Main lunch courses start at $4 or $5 and no sandwiches are on the menu. The music goes round and round from Noon to 3. Today, the guest name is Sonny Russo, trombone.

BROADWAY TICKETS

You might get lucky and find tickets to a hit show by accident at the box office just before curtain time, but it's a gamble with the odds against you. For those who like to plan ahead, here's a rundown on some of the hard tickets.

"A Chorus Line": Sold out for now. Orchestra seats starting in August. Balcony, June or July.

"My Fair Lady": For Friday and Saturday nights, a couple of weeks away. Usually some tickets for other performances.

"Bubbling Brown Sugar": sometimes, tickets for the Sunday evening 7:30 performance, immediately available. For most other performances, two weeks ahead. Fridays and Saturdays, three weekends ahead.

"Shenandoah": No problems for most performances, but for Wednesday and Saturday matinees, plan six weeks ahead and Saturday nights, four weeks ahead.

Critic's Choice

Swiss Mime

Mummenschanz. This mouthful of a name belongs to a Swiss mime group that is unlike any other. Since it became a surprise hit when I saw the company on its first visit to Alice Tully Hall in 1973, it has left delighted audiences of all ages chortling in their seats and rising to their feet in well-deserved ovations.

Andrès Bossard, Bernie Schürch and Floriana Frassetto, the young artists who make up the troupe, have rejected the traditional mime approach of using illusion to suggest real objects. Instead, they dress up as fantasy figures with human foibles to comment on the human condition. The key element is their use of masks. Mummenschanz, whose name comes down from the Swiss masked players of medieval times, always encases its performers in shapes of stretch jersey or masks.

Mummenschanz will be at Tully Hall at 3 and 8 P.M. tomorrow and at 3 P.M. on Sunday. Tickets are $5.50. ANNA KISSELGOFF

Saturday

JAZZMOBILE STOPS

The Jazzmobile, a summertime wagon on the sidewalks of New York, will park in Town Hall, 123 West 43d Street at 8 P.M., to play tribute to Jimmy Heath, the tenor sax virtuoso. Mr. Heath has written an ambitious musical work, "The Afro-American Suite of Evolution," that will have its premiere at this concert. He will conduct a 35-piece concert orchestra, including chorus, and a dozen special guest artists. On the same program: the Jazzmobile's 20-piece workshop ensemble, top students from the organization's jazz teaching program. Admission: $5, $6, $7. Information: 866-4900.

MUTTONTOWN HIKE

The Long Island Chapter of the Nature Conservancy, a nonprofit, volunteer group that feels about the outdoors much as Thoreau did, is planning a hike. Not an endurance contest, not even a HIKE, just a guided walk through nature for those who show up at the Muttontown Preserve in Nassau at 9:30 A.M. It's free; bring a good lunch with something to drink and wear walking shoes. It's all very informal—you walk as much as you want. The hike is free, and you will see lots of trees, plants, birds and perhaps chipmunks, rabbits, raccoons. Meet at the entrance to the preserve on the west side of Route 106 (a north-south road). Free parking. Nature, rain or shine. Information: 516-367-3225.

HUDSON RIVER MUSEUM

Only 45 minutes from Broadway is the Hudson River Museum in Yonkers which is now mounting one of the largest exhibitions devoted to American theatrical history. "Theatrical Evolution, 1776-1976," displays 600 art works, with three sections devoted to what they call "interpretive media," which means two videotape shows and a slide show depicting 19th-century acting styles. Admission free. On Sunday at 2 P.M., a Circus Day will be staged, with magicians, clowns, acrobats, puppets; admission free. Museum is at 511 Warburton Avenue. Information: 914-963-4550. Open 10 A.M. to 5 daily except Sunday, when hours are 1 to 5.

GAMELAN CONCERT

The gamelan, one of the most ancient of musical instruments, will ring out in most unlikely precincts at 8:30 P.M. "New Music for Gamelan" is the title of the concert at the Kitchen, the upstairs hall that is home

Continued on Page 24

Headline as bulletin

Weekend in this first issue features "bulletin" headlines that act as reefers. It's important that the reefer and headline typefaces and sizes are virtually the same, since the idea is to make the reefers appear more as headlines than as promotional references.

Right up to closing time in the composing room, Arthur Gelb and I were deciding which of two halftones to use, as production people around us gnashed their teeth. It was a real opening night on 43rd Street.

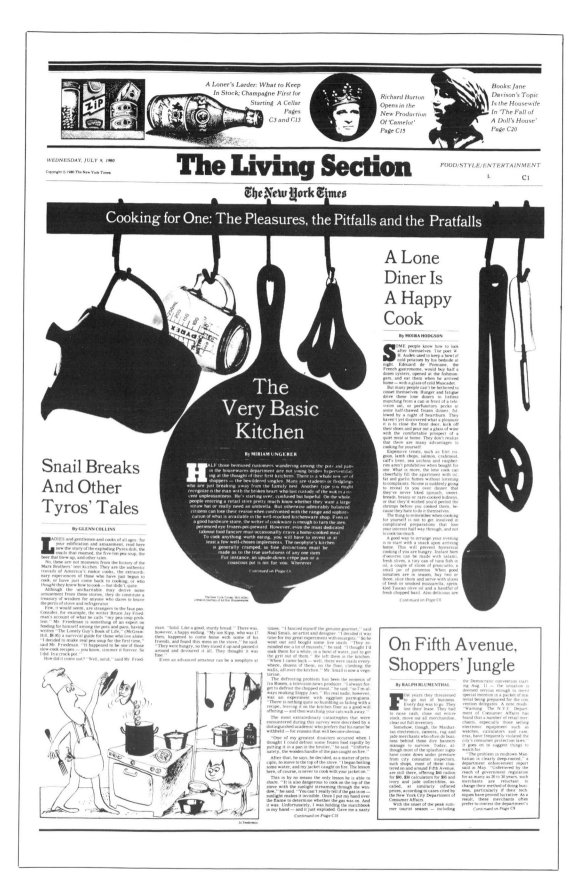

The graphic gamut

Pictured is a strongly graphic treatment of The Living Section after it had been running for a while. Other treatments ran the full graphic gamut from light illustrations to studio photography. Putting the little elements in the reefer strip is a demanding task if the designer wants to avoid the same look week after week. Design: Nancy Kent.

Science Times

The New York Times

Drugs: New Method Proves Effective

Patch Drips Medicine Into Bloodstream

By RICHARD D. LYONS

ONLY hours before Capt. Richard H. Truly flew the space shuttle Columbia to a safe landing on a dry lake bed in California two years ago he was beset by the fear that he was developing motion sickness. Indeed, at least a third of the astronauts who have flown in space have been beset by feelings of dizziness and nausea, and for centuries, many otherwise dauntless travelers, from skippers of ocean going vessels to racing car drivers, have been similarly humbled.

Now, however, a new method for administering drugs, a procedure called transdermal medication, has been developed that uses neither pills nor injections but rather lets the medicine seep through the skin. It is not only helping astronauts and other travelers overcome their occasional bouts of motion sickness, disorientation and malaise. But its apparent success in that area has encouraged at least six pharmaceutical houses to work toward using transdermal medication for cancer chemotherapy, duodenal ulcers, glaucoma, asthma, allergies, hypertension and diabetes, as well as contraception.

In Captain Truly's case, he simply opened the shuttle's medical kit, took out a flexible patch resembling a Band-Aid,

peeled the protective coating off the thumbnail-sized disk, and placed its adhesive side on the skin behind his ear. Each hour the patch was in place it dripped five micrograms of scopolamine, a drug that combats the effects of motion sickness, through his skin into his bloodstream. The Navy astronaut did not become ill, although the drug has apparently not been effective for everyone in space.

Transdermal, a medical term all but unheard of before the 1980's, has suddenly become a buzzword, from the space center at Cape Canaveral, Fla., to the America's Cup races at Newport, R.I., where nearly all the deep-water yachtsmen freely admit to suffering motion sickness on occasion.

Over the centuries physicians have used just about every organ to transmit drugs into the body, but only rarely have they used the largest of all — the skin. The major problem lay not in getting the drugs through the pores and different levels of skin — many drugs are easily absorbed — but in getting just the right amount.

High doses of scopolamine, one of the best drugs available to control motion sickness, may cause a wide variety of side effects up to and including hallucinations. Therefore the pharmacologic problem became one of controlled release, trickling just the right amount of scopolamine through the skin over just the right period of time.

For the last five years a prescription product, Transderm Scop, has been available to ease the symptoms of seasickness

Continued on Page C5

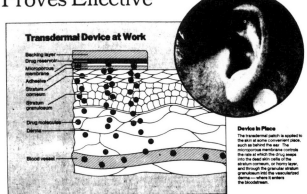

Transdermal Device at Work

Backing layer
Drug reservoir
Microporous membrane
Adhesive
Stratum corneum
Stratum granulosum
Drug molecules
Derma
Blood vessel

Device in Place

The transdermal patch is applied to the skin at some convenient place, such as behind the ear. The microporous membrane controls the rate at which the drug seeps into the dead skin cells of the stratum corneum, or horny layer, and through the granular stratum granulosum into the vascularized derma — where it enters the bloodstream.

Measuring Pallas

Asteroid's shape can be computed from the length of time it blocks a star's light for observers at various points.

3.4 sec.
11.9 sec.
25.2 sec.
34.2 sec.
39.6 sec.
43.2 sec.
44.0 sec.
43.5 sec.
36.4 sec.

Athens, Tex.
Davis Ranch, Ariz.
Gainesville, Fla.
Biloxi, Miss.
Clermont, Fla.
Austin, Tex.
St. Petersburg, Fla.
Venice, Fla.
Hialeah, Fla.

The New York Times / July 19, 1983; source: Marta Marr, David Dunham

George E. D. Alcock, a retired British schoolteacher, has discovered five comets and four novas or exploding stars.

In Astronomy, The Amateur Still Makes His Mark

By WALTER SULLIVAN

ONE night late in May an asteroid named Pallas passed in front of a star. In the grand scheme of things, this was a very small event. But it held the attention of more than 100 astronomers from Baja California to Florida.

Before the night was over these astronomers gathered data that is expected to reveal the most detailed picture to date of the size and shape of any asteroid. They appear to have also chalked up another triumph for amateur astronomy. Most of the observations were, in fact, made by amateurs — and astronomy (along with archeology) is one of the few areas of scientific research where amateurs can make important, even stunning, contributions.

Some astronomical observations require powerful, sophisticated equipment; others do not. Enter the amateurs.

Discovering comets and explosions of distant stars, as well as studying comets and stars that systematically vary in brightness, can be done very well with relatively modest telescopes. Moreover, the chances of making an important discovery are so small that professional astronomers usually turn to more productive pursuits. And even those professionals involved in these studies find it difficult to gain access to powerful telescopes for the long periods of sky-watching usually required to make a discovery.

Amateur astronomy has produced its champions. The Rev. Robert Evans of Maclean, New South Wales, in Australia, has discovered four great star explosions, or supernovas, through many years of comparing old photographs of distant galaxies with what he sees through his telescope.

In Japan, Minoru Honda, who spends his nights watching the heavens and the days tending a kindergarten, has discovered 11 comets and

Continued on Page C7

EDUCATION

Colleges Perplexed By New Draft Law

By EDWARD B. FISKE

ANDRE GINGERICH is a 21-year-old sophomore at Swarthmore College. For the last three years he has been receiving $4,000 a year in Federal grants, loans and work-study funds to help finance his education.

Mr. Gingerich is also a Mennonite who has said he declines to register for a possible draft on the ground that such an act would constitute "participation in preparation for war." Because of this refusal, the native of Harrisonburg, Va., will receive no Federal aid for the coming academic year.

Under a new Federal law that went into effect July 1, colleges are required to deny Federal student assistance to qualified students who fail to

certify that they have registered for the draft.

The law will have obvious effects on an unknown number of students such as Andre Gingerich. It has also led to a complex legal situation in which the Supreme Court of the United States has stayed the injunction of a Federal District Court in Minnesota, while colleges are scurrying to comply with a law the court in Minnesota had declared unconstitutional.

"It's a bureaucratic nightmare," said Catherine Smith, a spokesman for the City University of New York, which must send out 40,000 letters in the next few weeks to recipients of aid to disadvantaged students, the so-called "Pell Grants," who have already filled out their aid applications without the required draft certification.

The new law is the so-called Solo-

Continued on Page C16

Inside The Nautilus
Page C5

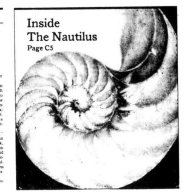

German Is Hailed In Math Advance

By PHILIP M. BOFFEY

Special to The New York Times

WASHINGTON, July 18 — A German has solved a problem that has baffled mathematicians for more than 60 years and has taken a major step toward solving another that has stumped the profession for three centuries.

The German mathematician is Dr. Gerd Faltings, 28 years old, of Wuppertal University, in Wuppertal, West Germany. The problems he has solved lie in the esoteric realms of number theory and algebraic geometry; they relate to the number of solutions that exist for certain kinds of mathematical equations.

A 40-page manuscript by Dr. Faltings is now circulating among American mathematicians and is sparking ripples of excitement.

Serge Lang, professor of mathematics at Yale University, said Dr. Faltings has solved "one of the outstanding problems of the century."

Michael Artin, professor of mathematics at the Massachusetts Institute of Technology, called the paper "extremely important" and said the German's accomplishment was "certainly close" to being "the theorem of the century," at least in the field of number theory.

Barry Mazur, professor of mathematics at Harvard University, called it "a glorious piece of work which will be closely studied by everyone in the field." And Spencer Bloch, a University of Chicago mathema-

Continued on Page C8

ARTS: Season's ticket sales show mixed results, page C11. / **DANCE:** Roland Petit brings 'Proust' to New York, page C11.

BOOKS: 'In Search of Love and Beauty' reviewed, page C14. / **TV:** Cable's Bravo succeeding where others failed, page C15.

A sandwich design

Science Times was the last of the five C sections to be published. The bold rules are used to "sandwich" the front page content. The rules are designed to be away from the top and bottom edge of the paper to enhance the effect. Even more than in the other sections, here the art director must be especially "tuned in" to the subject, since he frequently takes the initiative in planning and executing a diagrammatic treatment. I have vivid memories of conflicts in early issues with writers who failed to see the graphic possibilities in their stories. Design: Gary Cosimini.

Nets defeated, Page 8;
the computer rates
N.B.A. teams, Page 23.

Roger Kahn
Page 3
Red Smith, 4
Peter Maas, 8
Goode's
Matchups
Page 13

Nashville girl, 14, stars
at swim meet, Page 4

Watson wins
Tucson, P. 4

SportsMonday

The New York Times

Copyright © 1978 The New York Times Company   JANUARY 9, 1978

Connors Beats Borg in 3 Sets and Becomes No. 1

Jimmy Connors was his usual aggressive self during his three-set victory over Bjorn Borg yesterday.

The New York Times/Barton Silverman

By PARTON KEESE

In the showdown of world-class tennis for the last year, the world finally got what it was looking for yesterday—a player who could call himself No. 1.

He was Jimmy Connors, who defeated Bjorn Borg, 6-4, 1-6, 6-4, and won the $100,000 first prize in the Grand Prix Masters final at Madison Square Garden. It was a tournament that matched the best eight players of 1977.

But the money, as great as it was, was secondary in this instance. Both Connors and Borg seem to have all that they need and another pile of dollars hardly changes the decimal point in their tax returns. This time, prestige was the uppermost factor.

For now, Connors is the king, beating the man who many claimed was the real No. 1 because of his Wimbledon crown and his defeat of Connors the last two times they met. There won't be any new poll taken today or ballots sent out to experts

Though there will still be debate—because of Borg's previous victories and Guillermo Vilas's conquest of Connors at Forest Hills and in the round-robin section of this Grand Masters—the public has a short memory. Connors's classic triumph yesterday before a tense and volatile packed house should hold the top spot in its mind for a time to come.

The thrilling and beautifully played match proved a much-needed resolution to a tournament that had been derided the last few days because of rules that allowed players to benefit by losing or by not even playing.

Even before Connors and Borg took the stage, another tourney boo-boo cropped up when Brian Gottfried and Raul Ramirez vied in a match that was originally billed as a battle for third place but then changed to an exhibition.

In a change of mind Saturday night, the tournament directors agreed that by letting Vilas have fourth-place money without playing another match, they should also allow Gottfried to have third place without having to play for it.

"We realized our error," said Ray Benton, the tournament chairman, "when Gottfried asked if first and second place might be decided with substitutes if necessary. Since the semis and final are elimination matches, no substitutes should be allowed."

With that explained, Ramirez won the exhibition, 7-6, 7-6, with a "small extra fee" added to his $24,000 fifth-place prize. Gottfried took home

Continued on Page 6, Column 3

Neil Amdur looks at the controversy around the Grand Prix tennis tour. Page 6

Denver's Craig Morton and Cowboys' Roger Staubach

The New York Times/Marilynn K. Yee

The New York Times

Scouts Report On Super Bowl

Football scouting is much like playing chess in that the ability to assess and then exploit strengths and weaknesses can determine the outcome of a game. Scouts are important to a football coach because they provide this crucial information.

The New York Times commissioned scouts to analyze the two Super Bowl teams. Reports were prepared by Jack Faulkner of the Los Angeles Rams and George Young of the Miami Dolphins, with the assistance of William N. Wallace of The Times. Faulkner reports on the Dallas Cowboys, the National Conference champions, and Young reports on the Denver Broncos, the American Conference champions. The teams will meet in New Orleans on Sunday at 6 P.M., New York time.

Scouts usually feel it is unprofessional to try to pick winners; the outcome of the game, they say, is incidental to their analyses. But in this case Faulkner and Young agree Dallas has the better team.

Dallas

Tom Landry does it all. He and his assistants, abetted by computers, leave no stone unturned. He will know everything about the Broncos—the players' college backgrounds, their medical history, when their wives last had babies, how they react under stress, their true speed and measurements. (The figures in the programs are often misleading.)

Landry, who calls all plays, will stick with the stuff that got the Cowboys

into the Super Bowl and will add a few conservative wrinkles.

The Playing Surface

The Superdome's Astroturf is very hard, and it was put down for baseball, not for football, unlike the Tartan Turf

Continued on Page C12

Denver

Red Miller belongs to the new school of coaching that believes in treating athletes like adults and leaving them alone in nonfootball hours. Miller is friendly with his players, and he doesn't beat on them or make practice a drudgery. He certainly has their respect.

Miller, for years an assistant coach for offense, is basically sound in the offensive game, although sometimes he likes to get cute and try to finesse the defenses with misdirection sucker plays. He is not the kind of coach to blow the bugle and yell, "Charge!"

Although he was new at Denver this season, Miller did not change the team much. Joe Collier, who has been on the Bronco staff since 1969, remained in charge of the defense. The offense that, evolved by Max Coley is similar to what Miller taught during his last appointments, at New England and Baltimore.

The Playing Surface

The home field of the Broncos is grass, but they have had a lot of ex-

Continued on Page C12

ARTS/ENTERTAINMENT: Horowitz Returns C26 / What's Happened to 'The Star-Spangled Banner'? C27

When reefers become part of the page

The first issue of SportsMonday. Reefers across the top were designed on a grid system. The black strips at the top make staccato accents, and the label heads make them functional as well. The format designs designated variety within the grid but strict adherence to the typographical scheme. The unusual depth of the reefers make the pictures active parts of the front page report, and the logo an integrated part of the page. This page was planned beforehand, but the live pictures, tennis and the reefers, were put in on deadline. Almost exclusively breaking news, this Sports Section put to the test our ability to change procedures to accommodate an art director.

Big numerals

The logo unit in the upper right defines a vertical third of the page up and down the left side. A reefer unit fits in this channel, with exceptionally large numerals, about an inch high, set in Bookman. The page numbers make an arresting graphic element without being too black. Big numerals used in this way have since become a familiar device, perhaps too familiar, but in The Home Section at the time were fresh and bold. The reefer unit would stay the same in each issue but could slide up and down in the left channel of the page to accommodate a variety of layouts.

Top and bottom

For the front page of The Home Section, as well as the other C sections, the design goal was to have the whole front page work as a unit from top to bottom, like a poster, yet suggest variety and lots of information.

After a year or so, the bottom of the page of some of the C sections seemed to get rather pre-dictable. The inevitable tendency in newspaper procedure to formularize seemed to take effect. Such design predictability usually starts with story count. If a certain number of stories works well one time, providing the desired "mix," it's often a good bet that editors will stick to the same formula the next time. The page is on its way to being cast in concrete.

The problem was considered serious enough to warrant a meeting of all section C designers and editors, during which ways to keep the bottom of the page as unpredictable as the top were discussed. In most parts of the news operation, flexibility and surprise must originate in the mind of the desk editor. If he or she sees the page in terms of pre-set units, a designated story count, a certain number of paragraphs of text necessary before jumping, a certain picture size, and other preconceptions, the designer has little left to do but move the elements around in a superficial manner that most likely will lack freshness. With so many limitations, a good designer is probably not even needed.

A Campus Natural: The 'Veggie Room'

By NAN ROBERTSON

MITCHEL BENSON took to eating peanut butter and lima beans on bagels. Andrea Schwartz sold her dormitory meal tickets to buy sunflower seeds, which she roasted in the microwave oven in the basement of her dormitory. The two, both seniors at the University of Wisconsin and both vegetarians, typify the cunning and ingenuity needed to maintain vegetarian diets on the Wisconsin campus at Madison, where special eaters are discouraged from living in the dorms.

But vegetarianism—for health and philosophical reasons—not only is clearly on the rise on other campuses

For living sensibly—or perilously—as a vegetarian, see **Personal Health, Page C7.**

across the nation but is being catered to by the universities. Paul M. Garvey, director of food services at Smith College in Northampton, Mass., said that vegetarianism was "the most drastic and widespread change in student eating habits" that he could recall. A Northampton native, he has been at

Smith for seven years and in the food business for 20.

A student government questionnaire that the Smithies filled out this month showed that while only slightly more than 3 percent who responded considered themselves vegetarians, 71 percent said they would like to have three or more vegetarian dinners a week. The rest said they would prefer the current one vegetarian dinner a week.

The Smith vegetarians are not purists: Most exclude red meat and pork, few exclude fish, a high protein source; no one excludes dairy products. But, inconsistently, the students voted both butter and bacon off menus two years ago because of their high cholesterol content.

At nearby Amherst, one out of every five students has his meal card stamped so that he can eat vegetarian meals. One out of 10 eats vegetarian meals every day. Food-service managers are discovering that the four-year-old "veggie room," one of the school's five dining halls, is no longer big enough to serve its growing clientele.

Dried fruit, cottage cheese, fresh fruit and yogurt have become so popular that many students who are not au-

Continued on Page C5

The Chocolate Doughnut With a Dial Tone

See Page C10

The New York Times/Gene Massin

DISCOVERIES | Enid Nemy

A Puzzle Through and Through

You have to be a special type to know in advance, and accept, a 500-piece jigsaw puzzle that is still a puzzle when it's finished. Assuming you are such a type, this is to tell you that there is such a puzzle and it's called an Anamorphosis. Assuming you don't know what that is, it's a picture that's been intentionally created to fool the eye, with the earliest known example a drawing by Leonardo da Vinci. The puzzle now available is called "Portrait of a Man standing before a Balustrade" and the picture was painted in 1630 and sent as a gift to King Gustavus Adolphus of Sweden. Harry N. Abrams, Inc., the art book publisher, has come out with the puzzle and for $9, it's yours at Brentano's, Doubleday or the Brooklyn Museum. Oh yes, in case you're wondering—once the puzzle is completed, an enclosed sheet of mirrored plastic is rolled into a cylinder and placed upon a circle at the center. Looked at from the proper angle, the previously distorted image pops into normal perspective and the puzzle is solved.

Be a Good Scout

There's nothing seasonal about the Boy Scouts but somehow new uniforms, sleeping bags and the whole megillah seem to come to the fore with the approach of spring, and the possibility of once again enjoying the great outdoors. The New York Scouting Supply Center carries a complete line of scouting equipment but the cheery news is for families interested in saving money. The Center sometimes has seconds (with mistakes scarcely noticeable) at prices up to 40 percent off. And, from time to time, other items are put on sale, with reductions from 25 to 40 percent. The reduced items are in the basement level and one may telephone (868-4744) to find

Continued on Page C13

Children and Public Violence

By GLENN COLLINS

ONCE again, the instant-replay images of violence have become part of our culture — and once again, parents have been forced to deal with the reactions of their children to a public act of violence. In the days since Monday's attempted assassination of President Reagan, parents have expressed concern about how their children may have been affected by it. Is it advisable to protect children from the knowledge of such incidents? What should parents do if their young children happened to see televised videotapes of

the shooting? And, more generally, how can parents best cope with the pervasiveness of violence in American society?

"In this case, the impression of the event was extraordinarily vivid — the violent action, the people falling, the bloody close-ups," said Dr. John Munder Ross, a clinical psychologist in Manhattan who treats both children and adults. Dr. Ross found television's repetition of the videotapes tasteless and exploitative and believes strongly that children, especially those younger than the age of 6, should not have been exposed to them.

"Certainly the incident had its effect on children," he said, "but the

main thing is that parents should not think that something profound and awful will happen to their children, given their knowledge of the event. Children are both more vulnerable and more resilient than we ordinarily give them credit for."

An incident like Monday's shooting "could be especially hard on children who have lost a parent through death or separation, or for those whose parents are ill," said Dr. Peter B. Dunn, a psychiatrist who treats children and families at the Downstate Medical Center. Such an event can awaken dormant anxieties in children depending upon their ages, he said.

Anger may be a deep concern of children, Dr. Dunn said. "Here they see anger that is so powerful it has overwhelmed the police. They may feel the world is unsafe. Bad people can hurt parents, or hurt me, and policemen can't stop them. And children may fear their own anger, and whether it can overwhelm their own controls, or the controls of their parents. Young children have fantasies of robbers, monsters and burglars that do horrible things, whether there are assassinations or not."

In the inner life of the child, said Dr. Dunn, "Kids love and need heroes, and their heroes are invincible. The central importance of the President as a symbolic figure is deeply embedded in our psyches. Of course, real heroes today — and Presidents — aren't like what they used to be. But Monday's event can raise fears of the loss of the idealized President, who really represents the parent."

How have children been affected? "I'm sure that an awful lot of kids around the country have had nightmares about it, have been talking

Continued on Page C6

Tips on where to garage and park your car in New York — **8**

ARTS/ENTERTAINMENT

Academy Awards presentation: Celebrating in Hollywood and how it looked on TV — **15**

Books: Advice for the President from two former Carter aides — **19**

50's Housing With Lessons for the 80's

See Page C10

An aerial view of Levittown, L.I., in 1950

Making Life Up En Route

By DONALD HALL

IN the best arrangement of life and desire, we never know what we will do next. When I taught at a university, I lived a Tu-Thu schedule with office hours and special appointments. Few hours were fixed; even so, I took leave in order to write full time, and lived as I do now, and developed a taste for it. In 1975 I jettisoned tenure to live the improvised day, rising early each morning without an alarm clock, filling a long day with work, never sure what I will do next.

When I finish writing these sentences I will pick up another pile of papers beside my chair, to work on a project I have in mind; or maybe — and maybe at the last minisecond, I'll decide instead to look at a long poem I am trying to write, or at a different article; or maybe I'll read Stanley Cavell on "The Claim of Reason"; or eat a sandwich; or get some wood from the woodshed.

It pleases me to play each day as if I were making something up on the piano. Shortly after I gave up teaching, I attended my 25th reunion. When I told my classmates what I was up to, they exclaimed over my self-discipline. Well, maybe I live a life of self-discipline; usually it feels more like self-indulgence. All day long, from the moment of waking, I do the forbidden thing: *I do what I want to do.*

Doubtless everything is both itself and its opposite, self and antiself, thesis and antithesis.

Continued on Page C8

Donald Hall improvises his day in the New Hampshire farmhouse his great-grandfather acquired in 1865.

Life at the bottom

Three different treatments project vitality at the bottom of the page, where many pages drift away. On the facing page, the bottom of a Home Section page features a story, a reefer box, and a departmental round-up. The forceful Discoveries heading and the four-line Stymie Black initial are graphic building blocks that help the overall design. Design: George Cowan. Above: Bottom of a Home page shows the reefer index tucked into a text story for extra typographical interest at the bottom of the page. Design: Tom Bodkin. Below: The bottom part of a SportsMonday page shows a carefully designed graphic treatment in a preplanned feature box. Arts/Entertainment reefers, a breaking news story, and a well-cropped vertical halftone provide a rich menu at the bottom of the page. Design: Bob Eisner.

Shortstops Catching a Lot of Attention

By GEORGE VECSEY

WHEN artificial turf was introduced to baseball in the 1960's, it threatened one of the classic plays ever developed at that classic baseball position — shortstop.

Wherever artificial turf spread, like some ominous lawn disease, shortstops could not easily lunge to their right, stab a hot grounder backhanded, and make a long throw to first base. The ball either rocketed past them, or they could not plant their feet on the synthetic surface.

"Going into the hole," a classic shortstop maneuver, was going down the drain.

But shortstops, being a superior breed, are developing new techniques to combat the menace of artificial turf. The latest ploy has been advanced by Dave Concepcion of the Cincinnati Reds, who will sometimes throw the ball on one bounce to first base when he manages to snare it in the hole and cannot risk a direct throw.

This graceful resourcefulness is what makes shortstop one of the premier defensive positions of any sport. The shortstop cannot rely on more strength or tenacity as some other defensive player can, but must have innate smoothness before the first junior-league coach ever points a finger and says, "you — play shortstop."

After more than a decade of coping with cement-like infield

(more on Page C4)

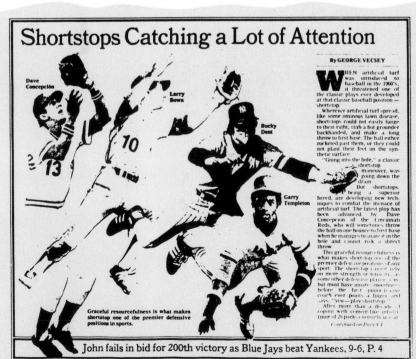

Dave Concepción
Larry Bowa
Bucky Dent
Garry Templeton

Graceful resourcefulness is what makes shortstop one of the premier defensive positions in sports.

John fails in bid for 200th victory as Blue Jays beat Yankees, 9-6, P. 4

Mets Sweep Braves On Swan's Shutout

By JOSEPH DURSO

Craig Swan and Phil Niekro, a pair of $1 million pitchers, staged a solid exhibition of the ancient art of throwing a baseball yesterday in Shea Stadium.

Then, still scoreless in the eighth inning, the New York Mets broke through Niekro's knuckleballs for three runs, a 3-0 victory over an old antagonist and a sweep of their weekend series with the Atlanta Braves.

"We are getting things together," Manager Joe Torre suggested as he headed the Mets toward St. Louis and three games against the Cardinals, who replaced the Mets last week in last place in the National League's East. "It has been difficult, sometimes agonizing. But they are maturing and, best of all, the pitchers are now pitching."

Swan, the No. 1 man on Torre's staff, signed a five-year contract for $1 million in March and has been trying to earn his keep ever since. He responded yesterday with a three-hitter that included only one walk, and he pitched to 32 batters, only five more than the minimum.

Niekro a Match Two Ways

But he was matched all afternoon by the 41-year-old Niekro, a man who had beaten the Mets 21 times in his career. And Niekro also was no slouch in financial matters, having signed a contract that will pay him $4.2 million in large chunks over the next 10 years.

Their duel ended suddenly and controversially with one down in the bottom of the eighth. Frank Taveras singled a double down the left field line for his fourth hit of the game, racing home 24 for 51 during a rampage of nearly two weeks. Then Lee Mazzilli lashed out, and Niekro needed one more out to escape.

But, before he got it, Joan Swan singled a double into right field for the first run of the afternoon. And then Mazzilli also lifted a high pop

Lee Mazzilli after hitting a high pop up yesterday at Shea Stadium.

ARTS/ENTERTAINMENT 'Post-Impressionism' in Capital C11/Books: Psychohistory Indicted C16

Configuration front to back
A matter of give and take

The accompanying illustrations show how the first Home Section on March 7, 1977, was laid out to incorporate space for the numerous new features scheduled by Rosenthal, Gelb, and the newly hired editor of the section, Nancy Newhouse.

In the cooperative process that had happily been established in working on the suburban sections, we in the News Department and the Business Department worked together to distribute the material most favorably throughout the section. Some large spaces would be needed on the inside for large photos and "designed" presentations. In the field of home design, the competition was not so much other newspapers (black and white in New York at the time and limited in their coverage of this kind of material) but magazines such as *House and Garden,* with their advantage of superb reproduction in full color on slick paper. We could compete by using to our advantage the larger-size page for poster impact on Page One and a full range of graphic tools applied throughout, with a good sense of scale (i.e., knowing when to make an element larger or smaller than expected).

The last pages of Home and the other C sections were devoted to cultural news, mostly the same kind of material that had run toward the rear of the front section in the old two-part paper. However, it was necessary to redesign the treatment of this material to conform to the new typographical style of the C sections.

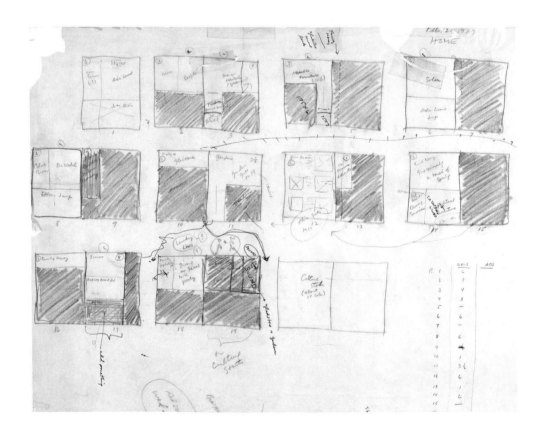

Planning
Storyboard for Home shows tracks of planners
moving spaces around. At the bottom right are
reckonings of news-to-advertising ratio: In 19 pages,
52 columns were news and 62 columns were ads.

118

Page 2
A newly created column and People feature occupy a fixed horizontal half page.

3
At least a half page of space is agreed upon for news features, flexible in format according to ads. New and Useful feature is given accented treatment for variety.

4
With ad spaces pressing, the editorial photo treatment shows use of scale (big chair, little man in inset) for maximum impact. A service sidebar makes a useful package.

5
Around-the-gutter arrangement and bold Scotch rules (bendayed) make the most of a difficult one-column hole.

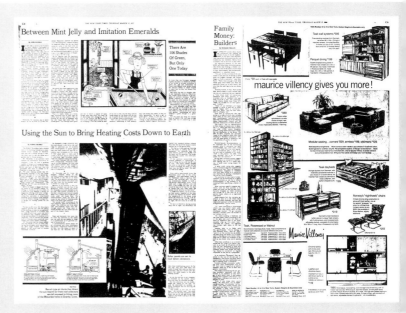

8
Shown is an open page for major editorial display.

Page by page
On this and following pages, Pages 2 through 25 are shown as they appeared in the first issue of The Home Section, fleshing out the configuration outlined in the storyboard.

14
A slip in the first issue: Ads should be on the outside.

15
An important four-column newshole agreed on for the line-up of columnists.

16
Another open page.

22 and 23
Gardening was covered for the first time in the weekday paper.

24
The transition to the regular daily culture report, bringing the section to a 36-page total.

Departments and columns

The first issue of The Home Section ran 36 pages and featured more than 75 columns of editorial content devoted to home and garden material. About another 22 columns of culture news brought up the rear. The original working drawing had been put together on the basis of a 45 to 55 percent news-to-advertising ratio. As in other start-up issues, all the stops were pulled out in allocating news space to ensure a first issue with the best possible display of the new material. Later issues averaged fewer pages, but in general we were able to maintain a generous editorial presence, supported by increased advertising.

At least 10 new departments and regular columnists were developed for Home. For the columnists, rather simple headings were designed with Bookman, the same typeface used in the headlines. Setting the column headings and headlines in the same typeface would give the reader a sense of continuity in the editorial voice. With many columns in the sections, the newsholes would be less fractured. The Ludlow Bookman that we used is a beautiful cut, graceful and generous, with a subtle relationship between thicks and thins. (The section was started in the days of hot metal; the Ludlow design of the letter characters was retained in photocomposition.) The relationship of strong thins and gently swelling thicks, the rounded nature of the letter forms themselves, and the blunted nature of the serifs make this Bookman face a homey, forthright, and trustworthy-looking typeface. However, overall it is rather light. To compensate for the lightness, the column headings were set in a large size, about 54 point, complemented by a rule overhead; the byline was set in Bookman alongside the title, with a vertical slash and some built-in white space.

Department headings were designed to sharply accent the pages. There were fewer departments, so they wouldn't be likely to appear busy or confusing. The departmental title, for example, "Helpful Hardware," was set in Stymie Black capitals, positioned tightly between specially made-up Scotch rules similar to the rules used in the earlier suburban sections (12-point gray benday bars plus 1-point black rules). Used also to set off blurbs, read-outs, and quotes, these rules gave the new sections a special look that was bolder and quite different from anything elsewhere in the newspaper.

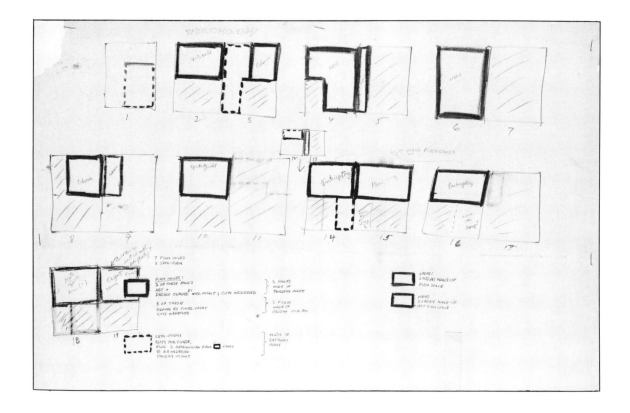

Agreed-upon acreage
This storyboard for SportsMonday attempted to break down the configuration in terms of fixed spaces, shown in solid bold lines, and semifixed spaces, that is agreed-upon "acreage" but flexible in shape (dotted lines).

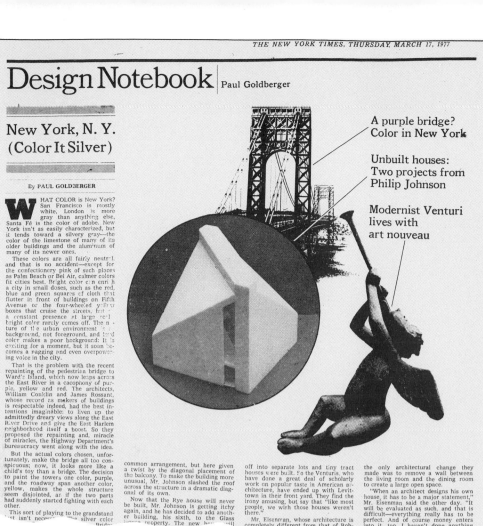

Design Notebook | Paul Goldberger

New York, N. Y. (Color It Silver)

By PAUL GOLDBERGER

WHAT COLOR is New York? San Francisco is mostly white, London is more gray than anything else, Santa Fé is the color of adobe. New York isn't as easily characterized, but it tends toward a silvery gray—the color of the limestone of many of its older buildings and the aluminum of many of its newer ones.

These colors are all fairly neutral, and that is no accident—except for the confectionery pink of such places as Palm Beach or Bel Air, calmer colors fit cities best. Bright color can enrich a city in small doses, such as the red, blue and green squares of cloth that flutter in front of buildings on Fifth Avenue or the four-wheeled yellow boxes that cruise the streets, but a constant presence at large real bright color rarely comes off. The nature of the urban environment is background, not foreground, and loud color makes a poor background: It is exciting for a moment, but it soon becomes a nagging and even overpowering voice in the city.

That is the problem with the recent repainting of the pedestrian bridge to Ward's Island, which now leaps across the East River in a cacophony of purple, yellow and red. The architects, William Conklin and James Rossant, whose record as makers of buildings is respectable indeed, had the best intentions imaginable: to liven up the admittedly dreary views along the East River Drive and give the East Harlem neighborhood itself a boost. So they proposed the repainting and, miracle of miracles, the Highway Department's bureaucracy went along with the idea.

But the actual colors chosen, unfortunately, make the bridge all too conspicuous; now, it looks more like a child's toy than a bridge. The decision to paint the towers one color, purple, and the roadway span another color, yellow, makes the whole structure seem disjointed, as if the two parts had suddenly started fighting with each other.

This sort of playing to the grandstand isn't necessary. The silver color

A purple bridge? Color in New York

Unbuilt houses: Two projects from Philip Johnson

Modernist Venturi lives with art nouveau

common arrangement, but here given a twist by the diagonal placement of the balcony. To make the building more unusual, Mr. Johnson slashed the roof across the structure in a dramatic diagonal of its own.

Now that the Rye house will never be built, Mr. Johnson is getting itchy again, and he has decided to add another building, his sixth, to the Glass house property. The new house will

off into separate lots and tiny tract houses were built. So the Venturis, who have done a great deal of scholarly work on popular taste in American architecture, have ended up with Levittown in their front yard. They find the irony amusing, but say that "like most people, we wish those houses weren't there."

Mr. Eisenman, whose architecture is completely different from that of Rob-

the only architectural change they made was to remove a wall between the living room and the dining room to create a large open space.

"When an architect designs his own house, it has to be a major statement," Mr. Eisenman said the other day. "It will be evaluated as such, and that is difficult—everything really has to be perfect. And of course money enters into it, too. I haven't done anything our apartment

---

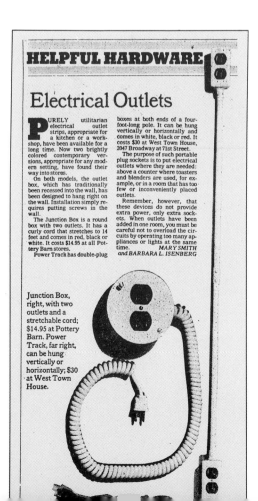

HELPFUL HARDWARE

Electrical Outlets

PURELY utilitarian electrical outlet strips, appropriate for a kitchen or a workshop, have been available for a long time. Now two brightly colored contemporary versions, appropriate for any modern setting, have found their way into stores.

On both models, the outlet box, which has traditionally been recessed into the wall, has been designed to hang right on the wall. Installation simply requires putting screws in the wall.

The Junction Box is a round box with two outlets. It has a curly cord that stretches to 14 feet and comes in red, black or white. It costs $14.95 at all Pottery Barn stores.

Power Track has double-plug

boxes at both ends of a four-foot-long pole. It can be hung vertically or horizontally and comes in white, black or red. It costs $30 at West Town House, 2047 Broadway at 71st Street.

The purpose of such portable plug sockets is to put electrical outlets where they are needed: above a counter where toasters and blenders are used, for example, or in a room that has too few or inconveniently placed outlets.

Remember, however, that these devices do not provide extra power, only extra sockets. When outlets have been added in one room, you must be careful not to overload the circuits by operating too many appliances or lights at the same time. *MARY SMITH and BARBARA L. ISENBERG*

Junction Box, right, with two outlets and a stretchable cord; $14.95 at Pottery Barn. Power Track, far right, can be hung vertically or horizontally; $30 at West Town House.

Home

Design Notebook (above), a new feature kicked off by the architecture critic Paul Goldberger was designed to reflect the structure of the article, which would deal with several different subjects. The graphic mold included a collage, call-outs, and bendayed Scotch rules. Smaller regular features, like Helpful Hardware (left), are given tight, black headings using Stymie Black capitals. The many new columns and departments made it necessary to differentiate between kinds of features.

Broadway | John Corry

Robards, Oscar Notwithstanding, Finds Work

AFTER HE WON the Oscar, Jason Robards said that soon he would be unemployed. Now, however, Mr. Robards has found a job. He will be in Eugene O'Neill's "A Touch of the Poet," which Elliott Martin will produce and José Quintero will direct on Broadway next season. It is to go into rehearsal Aug. 5, open in Toronto Sept. 18, move to the Kennedy Center in Washington on Nov. 7 and come in here just after Christmas. Mr. Robards, Mr. Martin and Mr. Quintero were together in "A Moon for the Misbegotten," and they began talking about doing "A Touch of the Poet" __ __ then. That was in December 1973, when __ __ month con- __ __ ooked

hired some English buskers to march up and down West 45th Street. Then there was the time he laid a rented carpet along West 44th Street from Broadway to Eighth Avenue. Cars wrecked the carpet, and the owner threatened to sue. Mr. Cohen settled out of court.

Thursday, Mr. Cohen is opening "Anna Christie" with Liv Ullmann. He has sent out many elegantly engraved invitations to the opening and to the supper afterward in the Grand Ballroom of the Plaza. Black tie is required. "I think a Broadway opening is an event," Mr. Cohen says. "Jeans and open shirts are terrific for rock concerts, but the theater should maintain dignity."

Mr. Cohen is very serious.

"Besides," he says, "I have five tuxedos myself."

• • •

Probably the hottest Off Broadway producer at the moment, excluding Joseph Papp, who is all around the place, is Craig Anderson. Mr. Anderson runs the Hudson Guild Theater, which this season has done Strindberg's "The Stronger" and "The Creditor," two one acters and "Miss Julie," with Geraldine Page and Rip Torn, and Christopher Hampton's "Savages" with Joseph Maher. "The Stronger" and "The Creditors" has moved to the Public Theater, and Mr. Anderson is now talking about moving "Savages" and Mr. Maher to Broadway next season. Moreover, this summer he will produce "Molly," the new __ __ Gray play, at the S__ __ S.C. Mr. And__ __ backer f__ __

Weekend

The Weekend section featured Broadway (later Stage View), among other columns and departments.

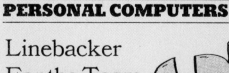

Frontiers: The Oceans

A New Picture Of Earth Emerges

By WALTER SULLIVAN

A REVOLUTIONARY new concept of the earth, which sees its surface as formed of giant plates that collide to thrust up mountains, separate to form mid-ocean ridges and slip side by side along fault lines, has provided the first comprehensive picture of the earth — but it is a picture that is far from complete.

Little is known, for example, about what happens when, as postulated by the theory, a continent splits apart to form a __ __ breaking awa__

Science Times

Above: Frontiers, a new department, was set up. Popular from the start with readers, the section was slow to pick up advertising. Frontiers fell victim to a tighter newshole. Advertising picked up with the advertising of home and small business computers. Right: Personal Computers was introduced to satisfy growing interest in the subject.

PERSONAL COMPUTERS

Linebacker For the Team From Apple

By PETER H. LEWIS

Stuart Goldenberg

APPLE Computer Inc.'s new Macintosh IIcx computer, which was introduced last week, is compact, powerful and versatile

monitor ($1,099) that can show one full 8½-by-11-inch page at a time, and a giant monitor ($2,149) that can show two pages side by side. Both the new monito__ __

124

60-Minute Gourmet

Pierre Franey

COOK a gourmet meal in the time often required to cope with one dish? With inventiveness and a little planning, there is no reason why a working wife, a bachelor or a husband who likes to cook cannot prepare an elegant meal in under an hour. This column will devote itself to main courses and simple accompanying dishes that can be completed within 60 minutes.

Regardless of time, an inventive and qualified chef has two distinct avenues to follow: the classical and traditional or the improvisational. If he's adventurous. he'll indulge in both.

The age-old question is, of course, whether or not an established chef follows recipes when he or she cooks. The answer is no, but in a qualified sense. In strictly traditional matters, most chefs still refer to Escoffier, who has been called the Moses of classic French cookery.

The "quick" recipe with this article has nothing to do with the classics but, rather, is concerned with improvisation: I was challenged by a friend, who likes to serve margaritas before dinner, to concoct a dish with the same ingredients as that potent Mexican libation. My answer to the challenge was shrimp margarita. It has the same ingredients as the drink, with just one exception—the Cointreau or triple sec, either of which is too sweet, has been omitted.

Barbara Bascove

One of the things essential for "compact" cookery, so to speak, is coordination. Plainly cooked rice—and not minute rice, which takes as much time as regular rice and doesn't taste as good—can be cooked according to package directions while the shrimp is cooking. Guava shells are available in cans. Cooking in less than an hour, which most of the people I know do on a Monday-through-Friday basis—takes only a little foresight.

MENU
Shrimp margarita
Rice
............d tomato salad

10 seconds. Add the tequila. Take care, for the tequila may flare up. Add the cream and cook over high heat about

---

Living

Living, like Home, brought a rich new mix to readers. Some of the new material became popular syndicated columns across the country. Jane Brody, for example, was persuaded by Arthur Gelb to forsake science reporting for the Personal Health column (below); and Pierre Franey invented the 60-Minute Gourmet (left). A consumer column (bottom right) was perked up with an illustrated Shopper's Guide; and a Discoveries column (bottom left) uses a boxed collage treatment to highlight items.

Personal Health | Jane E. Brody

Jogging Is Like a Drug: Watch Dosage, Beware the Problems

RECENTLY, A MAN I know in his late 40's suffered a severe heart attack and, within a week, the number of joggers on his block doubled. Spurred by their neighbor's close brush with cardiac death, several men with varying degrees of gray in their hair and fat around their middles joined the ever-growing contingent of both sexes who each morning leap out of bed .... bleach-str....

eventually reveal whether physical conditioning prolongs their lives.)

But enough is currently known about the effects of various forms of exercise on the heart to suggest that activities like jogging offer potentially lifesaving benefits—if they are practiced sensibly according to a personally tailored exercise "prescription" and heeding certain precautions against their hazards.

........rding to Dr. Len.

DISCOVERIES | Angela Taylor

Right: knitted sweater for children, Jenny B. Goode. Below: shell-shaped cakes of soap in a wicker basket, from Soap Scents, 245 East 77th Street.

Below: electric mousetrap, available in the Bailey-Huebner section of Bendel's.

The New York Times / Gene Maggio

Of Sweaters . . .
No child could object to bundling up in a sweater that has the shapes of animals or people knitted into it, both front and back. Suzanne Russell, a Londoner who used to work for Mary Quant, has designed some charming sweaters, made by a cottage industry of British women who knit away as they watch the telly.

the brush, with its fine, rigid tip, was just the thing to achieve a thin line with eye makeup or to outline lips. The brushes are attractively made of bamboo, with a cover to protect the tip. They can be bought for $3 at the Eddie Senz salon in the Drake hotel, 440 Park Avenue (59th Street).

Soaps With Scents

SHOPPER'S GUIDE

Bananas
3 lb. /99¢
A festive dessert.

Eggplant
39¢ /lb.
For party dips.

Question Box | Leonard Koppett

NET HEIGHT BEFORE 1878 — 39

NET HEIGHT NOW — 36

Niculae Asciu

QUESTION: Aside from all the pre-game activity, the Super Bowl itself seemed to go on and on. Was it really much longer than most football games?

It certainly was. The elapsed time was 3 hours 32 minutes, and the average for all National Football League games is 2 hours 54 minutes. The half-time ceremonies lasted longer than the usual 20 minutes, but this did not account entirely for the 38-minute difference. There was in addition a combination of circumstances: the many injuries that required first aid while a player was still on the field, the many penalties and the very deliberate pace of the officials in restarting the clock.

QUESTION: Head coaches in football and basketball have papers in their hands while on the sideline. What is on those papers?

Most of the time, the papers are just something to hold, like a rolled-up program or a copy of the halftime statistics. A few coaches keep notes on plays they want to use. In general, the sideline paperwork, which can be considerable, is handled by assistant coaches, whose proliferation has been a boon to the clipboard industry.

QUESTION: What is "meal money"?

Each player on a professional team receives a daily allowance for meals, tips and other incidentals when the team is on the road. (Hotel and travel expenses are paid by the club.) This per-diem allowance (called "_____ money," although it covers _____

QUESTION: Why is a tennis court 78 feet long—and when did the net get its present height?

The court dimensions—78 feet by 27 feet—were chosen by the All-England Tennis Club in Wimbledon in 1877, when the first comprehensive rules were adopted, and have remained unchanged since. However, the height of the net at the center was lowered from 39 inches to 36 inches in 1878, so this is its centennial year.

QUESTION: Are the bases on a ball diamond equidistant?

Th_____

ly inside their corners, so the actual distance to home is 90 feet minus 27 inches (15, plus 12 for home plate), or 87 feet 9 inches.

Second base is placed with its corner on the spot where the base lines cross, so it extends only 7½ inches toward first and third. That makes the first-to-second and second-to-third distances 90 feet minus 22½ inches, or 88 feet 1½ inches.

QUESTION: What makes a track and field performance an "official" world

pressed in hundredths of a second. In races of more than 400 meters, hand-operated timing devices may be used, and the record is expressed to the nearest tenth of a second.

¶In races of 200 meters or less and in the long and triple jumps, a following wind may not exceed two meters a second (4.473 miles an hour).

QUESTION: Some hockey goaltenders play their position standing up most of the time, and others fall to the ice quickly and often. Is one style better than the other?

Orthodox hockey teachers want the goalie to stay on his feet as much as possible, since this gives him the maximum number of alternatives with which to block a shot. But some successful goalies, such as Gump Worsley and Tony Esposito, became known as "floppers," falling to the ice. The answer is mostly a matter of personal style.

QUESTION: What is the National Hockey League rule on icing?

When a team sends the puck from its side of the center red line past the opposing goal line (the red _____ goes across the _____

SportsMonday

New features and design details, added to the inside of SportsMonday, help set it off from the regular daily sports report and from the Sunday Sports section. Both of these were redesigned at later dates but SportsMonday remained distinctive. The features included Question Box (above) and a Participant Sports spread (below). An arrangement was made for the same artist, Tom Bloom, to do a diagrammatic illustration, not a cartoon, for Question Box every week. Participant Sports, initially given a big play, was cut back later for space-saving reasons and has recently been given more coverage again. Facing page, top: A solution to the characteristic problem on sports pages of grouping short game reports. The smaller heads are 22 points. Together with the 1-point rules and the built-in 10-point space, the heads pop out in newsy fashion, yet the whole unit holds together as a neat package. Circles pep up the agate listings.

76ers Top Celtics, 94-91

PHILADELPHIA, Jan. 8 (AP)—Lloyd Free scored a game-high 20 points today to lead the Philadelphia 76ers to a 94-91 victory over the Boston Celtics in a National Basketball Association game.

The Celtics, who trailed by 15 at halftime, challenged in the fourth period but Free made four baskets and a free throw to move the 76ers from a 76-75 lead to 90-83 with 5:18 to play.

The 76ers twice had leads of 18 points in the second quarter behind the shooting of Free and George McGinnis. McGinnis had four baskets in the period and finished with 16 points.

Blazers on Top

PORTLAND, Ore., Jan. 8 (AP)—Lionel Hollins scored 27 points, 19 in the first half, to lead the Portland Trail Blazers to an easy 122-100 victory over the New Orleans Jazz.

The Blazers, now with a 31-5 record, pulled away with a 9-point scoring streak midway in the first quarter. It was their 39th straight victory at home.

Bill Walton scored 19 points for Portland and Maurice Lucas 17. Walton had 17 of his points in the first half as Portland built a 59-50 lead.

Sonics Win

SEATTLE, Jan. 8 (UPI) — Marvin Webster scored 17 points and grabbed 17 rebounds today and the Seattle SuperSonics held off Golden State in the final minutes for a 99-91 victory over the Warriors.

It was the Sonics' 15th victory in the 18 games since Lenny Wilkens took over as coach on Nov. 30, when the team's record was 5-17.

Nuggets Victors

DENVER, Jan. 8 (AP) — David Thompson ... points and An...

Phil Johnson

performance off the bench to lead the Denver Nuggets to a 109-104 victory over the Chicago Bulls today.

Roberts was given more playing time than usual because Denver's regular forward, Bobby Jones, was sent home before the game with the flu. Roberts responded with 18 points, 16 in the second half.

The victory, Denver's sixth in a row, gave the Nuggets a five-game lead over Chicago in the Midwest Division and extended a Chicago losing streak to five straight.

Bucks Triumph

MILWAUKEE, Jan. 8 (AP)—Brian Winters scored 12 of his 22 points in the third quarter today to lead Milwaukee to a 133-123 victory over Kansas City for the Kings' eighth consecutive loss. It happened only hou... after the dismissal of Coach ...

Kings Oust Johnson

KANSAS CITY, Jan. 8 (UPI)—The Kansas City Kings dismissed Coach Phil Johnson today on the heels of the National Basketball Association team's longest losing streak in two seasons.

When the Kings lost to the New York Knicks, 110-93, last night, it was their seventh straight defeat and 24th loss in 37 games this season.

The 36-year-old Johnson, who had 1½ years left on his contract, was replaced on an interim basis by Larry Staverman.

"It was a corporate decision," said the Kings' president and general manager, Joe Axelson. "If our assessment that we do have good people is correct, we were obviously doing something wrong."

After Winters gave Milwaukee a 77-63 lead, Richard Washington and Bill Robinzine got Kansas City to within 81-73. Then Winters and Junior Bridgeman increased the Bucks lead to 94-79, and Winters soon hit two baskets for a 102-87 lead entering the fourth period.

Lakers Bow

INDIANAPOLIS, Jan. 8 (UPI)—Danny Roundfield made two free throws with 15 seconds to play as the Indiana Pacers defeated the Los Angeles Lakers, 104-103, today.

The Pacers, led by John Williamson's 24 points, never trailed, but Los Angeles three times got within a point.

More basketball news

Nat'l Basketball Ass'n

AT LOUISVILLE
CHICAGO (105)

May 10 7-7 27, Johnson 6 5-6 17, Gilmore 7 7-9 21, Van Lier 1 0-0 2, Holland 7 4-5 18, Armstrong 5 0-0 10, Mengelt 2 0-0 4, Sheppard 0 0-0 0, Poindexter 1 0-0 2, Landsberger 2 0-0 4. Totals 41 23-27 105.

ATLANTA (95)

Drew 9 3-3 21, Brown 5 3-4 13, Hawes 1 0-0 2, Robertson 0 0-0 0, Hill 6 2-2 14, E. Johnson 3 4-4 10, Terry 2 2-2 6, Criss 1 4-4 6, O. Johnson 6 0-0 12, Rollins 4 1-1 9, McMillen 1 0-0 2. Totals 38 19-20 95.

Chicago 28 19 32 26-105
Atlanta 22 18 30 25-95

Fouled out—Brown. Total fouls—Chicago 23, Atlanta 23. Technical—Hill. A—?19.

The Standings

LAST NIGHT'S GAMES
Phoenix 134, Knicks 114.
Chicago 105, Atlanta 95.
Milwaukee 114, Denver 109.
Cleveland 117, Philadelphia 109.

WEDNESDAY NIGHT'S GAMES
Portland 127, Nets 101.
Boston 130, Milwaukee 116.
Detroit 113, Buffalo 100.
Golden State 113, Washington 106.
New Orleans 108, Atlanta 106.
Philadelphia 126, Kansas City 1...
Sa... ... Indi...

New Yorkers, etc. | Charlotte Curtis

ONE woman looked exactly like a goldfish, and the man with the enormous elephant's head attached to his middle won a prize. So did a couple of sad-faced calico clowns and a bearded man in a doublet whose hairdo consisted entirely of straight pins.

"We thought he was either Francis I or Henry VIII," Eleanor Lambert said later. "But he said he was a Third-Century Renaissance American, whatever that is."

Which is what the fashionably gaudy do of a Saturday night in New York, in this instance at a costume ball for the Harkness Ballet Foundation. Miss Lambert, Tammy Grimes, Mary McFadden, Geoffrey Holder and Giorgio Sant' Angelo were the judges. The irrepressible Maxime de la Falaise McKendry was the chairman.

"I'm not going to dress up," Mrs. McKendry said in that determinedly languid way of hers. "It wouldn't be suitable for the chairman."

Mrs. McKendry wore a silver lamé pleated skirt with gold braid piping, a flowered lamé blouse and a silver and black lamé turban. She looked like a gilded Russian peasant. But you could tell it wasn't a costume. It had an Yves St. Laurent label in it.

• • •

George-Paul Rosell, whose press release says "he is rapidly becoming the Party Architect of the East Coast," seems to have organized things. His first party was a Hawaiian luau in Coral Gables, Fla. Last Halloween, he assembled a UNICEF benefit at the Argentine Embassy in Washington. He said his "guests should always be inspired to create their own whimsical fantasy at any of my fetes," whatever that means.

Yet while the gathering was hardly the party of the season, it wasn't a fete worse than death either. Harkness House on East 75th Street is a beautiful old place with a mirrored ballroom, Renaissance mantelpieces, scarlet damask walls and a suitably bronzed staircase. Mr. Rosell enhanced the latter with a continuous rain of gold confetti and rose petals.

Polly Bergen, in a violet Halston chiffon, slipped in, said hello to Margaux Hemingway, who looked vaguely Chinese, but was gone after five minutes. "I was just too tired," Miss Bergen said. Mr. Sant'

A Gaudy Fete, In a Stylish Sort of Way

Leonard Spelor

The white-tied musicians burst into ragtime

Angelo skipped out early, too, saying he had to meet Natty Abascal, the model, and Marina Sciano, the St. Laurent representative.

But by 2 A.M., the party was still going strong,

with lots of dancing, patroness Rebekah Harkness nowhere to be seen, and Betsey Johnson, the designer, hopping around in a sequin maillot with big, bubbly plastic harem pants, an orange and green belt, and a silver mask. Mrs. McKendry said the whole thing was a huge success and that if she had to do it again, she'd be delighted.

"I love the idea of raising money for scholarships," she explained.

• • •

Chamber music enthusiasts had something of a workout at the exquisite old James E. Burden mansion the other night. They waltzed until nearly midnight after huffing and puffing their way up three flights of exceedingly high stairs.

The Burdens' ballrooms, like all really good ballrooms, are on the third floor, near the top of one of the finest circular marble stairways in New York City, and they are 18th-century French rococo with mirrored walls and elaborate wall sconces.

Catherine Devlin-Morgan, the mother superior of L'Ensemble chamber orchestra as well as the party's organizer, had the rooms lighted entirely with candles. And since there were three ballrooms, she set one aside for the champagne and quiche and another as a salon where such elegants as the inimitable Mrs. John Barry Ryan could rest between sets.

For a while, it looked as if Mrs. Ryan might not get there. Something about a quick trip to Guatemala. But she arrived, and plenty of other beautifully dressed people helped her rest. The very notion that Mrs. Ryan cared about L'Ensemble, and she does care, made everybody feel good.

• • •

Two years ago, at L'Ensemble's concert at the old Otto Kahn mansion, Mrs. Ryan was there in all her quick-witted splendor. She is the former Margaret Kahn, and the house was her home. That night's concert, in the room in which she and the late Mr. Ryan were married, brought her back for her first visit in 30 years.

This year's party had its moments, too. Between sets, professionals danced the intricacies of the waltz, and along about 11 o'clock, the proper and very white-tied musicians led by none other than Joshua Rifkin, the world's leading authority on Scott Joplin, let go with a ragtime. When last heard from, everybody was doing the cakewalk.

Private Lives | John Leonard

It happened the first cold Saturday night in his new house. Or, rather, he was new and the house was old, more than 100 years old, a brownstone fixed up inside to look like autumn leaves. And he hadn't known that Saturday was especially cold because, along with the woman of the house and a pair of friends rented for the evening, he had been sitting in front of the fireplace burning money. No real money, of course, but one of those chemical slabs, compounds of sawdust and wax and coloring agents and wrapping paper, for which New Yorkers pay quite a bit of real money in order to pretend for two hours that they are burning a cedar log in a fireplace the size of a qualm.

The children were asleep. The adults, as they would have described themselves, had been discussing whatever New Yorkers discuss at such times—Amy Carter and public schools, Sufi mysticism, petrodollars, the anguish of the Third Dimension—and by midnight it was clear they had reached an adjournment of minds. The friends departed. The woman of the house went to bed. He would gather up the coffee cups and turn off the lights and bar the doors. It was then he discovered that there was no heat: every radiator in the house was cold and silent.

Going to the cellar seemed a sensible idea. Like most cellars, it was full of parts of his life he no longer knew what to do with, cardboard boxes of old emotions. It was also, alas, full of water, a two-inch carpet of water on the cellar floor, and a gurgling, as of blood, in the darkness. Removing shoes and socks, he waded in. The furnace throbbed. By following an overhead pipe from the furnace, he arrived at the source of the water. A valve, cleverly positioned out of his reach, had no apparent purpose other than to gush water on his floor, water that should have gone to the radiators, condensing into steam instead of causing mud.

On a rickety chair, he attacked the valve. It wouldn't budge. Up, again, then, the stairs to what was known, preposterously, as the tool drawer. Like too many New Yorkers, he bought tools one at a time, each for a specific disaster; the drawer was an anthology of these disasters. Nothing availed. The valve, standing by the water, would not be moved.

• • •

... to the Yellow Pages. ... o'clock o...

A Dark Night Of the Soul Springs a Leak

Guy Billout

Nor, when he hit upon emptying the two big green garbage bins ... the front hall ...

steps, barefoot, nipping brandy, waiting for the dawn, a brooder:

"Accustomed as I am to dark nights of the soul, this is the first one that's sprung a leak. Maybe I should turn off the furnace. But I don't know how. Why is it I so seldom know how? Even as a child, I never saw anything in the microscope and my model airplanes looked like birds' nests. Buying a house was a grave error: it doesn't come with a landlord or a super or a handyman, people to blame. To my friends, it may look like autumn leaves. To me, it is a rainbow of debt."

• • •

But he had bought the house to declare his adulthood. His family would no longer be transients, refugees. Mortgages were a form of seriousness. Having sought to expand his protection, had he merely multiplied occasions for incompetence? His children supposed him capable of heroism. What if they found out he couldn't shut a valve, wire a lamp, speak French, read music, solve differential equations, remember to buy flowers, explain seizures of melancholy? What, in fact, could he do?

He could make money, fry bacon, wiggle his ears, get to airports on time, read Latin American novels all the way through, know what happened the previous night in every professional sport, take children seriously, be fair except when it hurt his own feelings, sing tenor and quote Swinburne. Somehow, this didn't add up to much. Where was the manliness? He loathed hunting and fishing, had never been a warrior, didn't dream of sports cars. He resembled a real American father as much as those chemical logs resembled real cedar: a facsimile of wax and sawdust. Would Noah have waited barefoot for a plumber?

Just as he was thinking that adulthood itself is a myth, that we are all of us statistical inferences from credit cards and insurance policies and income tax returns and traffic tickets, there came a voice:

"Dad! What's all the trash doing in the front hall?"

His son—with whom he wanted to discuss the poetry of science, the black hole and the double helix; for whom he would lay down his w... his life; this excellence—w... breakfast.

"Dad," said hi...

Good vertical space

Above: A four-column vertical space displays two of the new columns created for the section. The heavy Scotch rules and the read-outs buttress the small illustrations. The vertical space is a change of pace from the many horizontal spaces used elsewhere in the section.

Scale

Facing page: The figure is shown small and the graphic form of the chair is large, to maintain editorial strength in a confined space.

Off-the-Rack Furniture for the Put-Together Generation

By RITA REIF

IN A HURRY to own a pillow-padded chair, a status steel and glass table or a wall-to-wall, cane-sided sofa?

Well, waiting for such furniture is now a thing of the past for those willing to wield a wrench and put together a chair, table or room full of furniture on their own, at home.

And, in the process, they may save a great deal of money. Assemble-yourself furniture has come of age. And most of the new designs are a marvel of technology—they zip, snap, plug, screw, hook, lace or clip together easily.

That's one reason why, following the lead of mail order concerns and small specialty stores, department and furniture stores are now stocking sophisticated lines of assemble-yourself furniture.

Another reason, according to John Mascheroni, a furniture designer, is that the "put-together generation" of people in their twenties are willing, even eager, to let their fingers do the work if it will save time and money. Since they were born, he said, almost everything they've lived with—cribs, bicycles, stereo systems and shelving—has been assembled by them or their parents.

"Young people today want to buy furniture the way they buy jeans—off the rack," he continued. "Shoppers today are different from yesteryear. They tolerate assembling what they buy if it means savings in money and time. But they balk at waiting six months for delivery."

The idea is not new—most frame beds and redwood picnic tables have traditionally been sold in parts. But now the idea has really taken off on a large scale.

Nobody has quite settled on a name for this furniture. Some call it KD for knock down. Others refer to it as QA for quick assembly. There's also homeworks, assemble-yourself, chair-in-a-bag, room-in-a-box.

"They're used to it," Mr. Mascheroni said of the put-together generation, "and whether they like it or not, KD and QA—whatever you want to call it—is here to stay."

Carl Levine, a Bloomingdale's vice president, agrees. "Today's customers, especially those in the suburbs, are less dependent on services. And when

Zoom chair comes packed flat in a box, assembles in 10 minutes. Overman, $55. At Bloomingdale's.

The New York Times/Gene Maggio

they see a chance to save money, that independence grows."

But despite the moderate prices (savings range as high as one third) and the quick delivery (many are designed to be carried home), there are questions about whether the assembly will be as easy as ABC or will lead to so many mashed thumbs and so much & & ! ! ! that the whole idea will go the way of the antimacassar.

Those who fumble and fail when changing a light bulb may run afoul of disassembled furniture. But the mail order concerns, specialty stores and import firms, which have been reaping brisk sales for more than a decade, have also improved assembly techniques, instruction sheets and the packaging of chairs, tables, sofas and even grandfather clocks.

Mr. Levine recalled that the most efficient techniques for today's assemble-yourself furniture were pioneered by the Scandinavian manufacturers 20 years ago. By 1967, he said, 60 percent of Bloomingdale's modern furniture imports were KD, and those designs were then assembled in the warehouse before they were delivered to customers. Traditional furniture, he said, is shipped from abroad fully assembled.

Today, he reported, 70 percent of the store's modern imports are KD and 25 percent are sold that way—figures that may soon increase.

"By shipping furniture flat," reported Bernard Lavey, regional representative of Fox Manufacturing Company in Rome, Ga., "freight costs are cut by at least one-third." A manufacturer can ship 116 chairs and 116 sofas flat, he said, in the space needed to ship 55 of each fully assembled. That saving, plus economies in warehousing and delivery, he added, might lower the price of a chair in a store from $269 to $199.

Ronald Pass, executive vice president of James David, a furniture manufacturing concern, said that the cost of shipping a chair from St. Louis to Washington dropped from $7.50 to $3 KD; liability rates for KD furniture are much lower than for assembled designs.

At Macy's, where the assemble-yourself collection promises to be one of the most impressive in the store, store executives are the most cautious in discussing the future of this furniture.

"If it's well designed and happens to be KD, we'll sell it that way," vice president Art Reiner observed. He said that the KD aspect of stock in the Innovative Furniture Works department is "incidental."

Mr. Reiner also said that less than 10 percent of Macy's furniture imports come in KD and "KD is not out on the increase."

At W&J Sloane, however, it certainly is. And the reason C. George Scala, president, has increased such offerings both in the summer furniture department of the main store and in the clearance centers, he said, is that they are so much better designed and represent far better values, too.

Where to Find It

The ZOOM chair, disassembled, goes home by subway. The bantamweight wonder (it tips the scale at just under 11 pounds) one of the new KD pieces that have just arrived in town, comes packed in a box measuring 30 inches by 26 inches by 8 inches deep, a carton that has a cutout into which you slide one hand to carry it out of the store.

Once unpacked, the chair is assembled without tools in less than ten minutes. Its foamed polystyrene slab sides are joined by outsized cardboard rolls, the quilted slipcover is pulled over the frame and is then laced like a pair of shoes in place. The design, in beige or brown, by Svante Schoblom for Overman's International, is $55 at Bloomingdale's, 8th floor.

The ZOOM chair, although one of the lightest and easiest to carry, will not be the only furniture that shoppers take home with them. Assemble-yourself furniture in arresting shapes, popular woods and fashionable fabrics—not to mention highly appealing packaging,—has finally arrived. And it's here to stay, experts insist.

Bloomingdale's will also introduce a Danish collection of seating—metal-framed chairs and sofas with puffy, quilted cotton zip-on covers. The armless lounge chair in the group, which will be available in May, will be $139. And, Bloomingdale's "Room-in-a-Box" collection, a sturdy and sparely designed oak group of chests (the three-drawer unit is $100), bookcases and cabinets, will also be available in late May.

The tubular-framed collection that Moreddi, a Simmons Company division, is importing from Sweden, is one of the handsomest to date. Called Innovator, these striking classic designs are also among the easiest to put together.

The Innovator collection includes deep-foam chairs and settees with slipcovers that are secured in place by the tug of a string, and good-quality, cane-sided seating and chairs devised of hinged cushions (they open out to become beds). It will be introduced at Macy's in early April.

Some familiar ideas are being used in some unfamiliar ways in knock-down designs these days. The simple hooks that for decades have joined frame parts of beds secure the four

Tubor-framed chair by Moreddi, $110. April, at Macy's.

corners of chairs, sofas and tables in three collections—all robust and rustic —from the Fox Manufacturing Company at W&J Sloane's clearance center, 163 East 84th Street. The slab-framed modern—the best looking of the three—is of elm, the baluster-framed colonial is oak and the plank-framed casual pine. Prices range from $59 for end tables to $230 for sofas.

Slab-sided designs are in some cases —notably those from the Stratford Company—dressed up with woven rush details. The coffee table in the "Monterey" collection, so embellished, carries a moderate $90 price tag.

James David's collection, dramatically different in styling, has frames of sleek chromed tubes, tables topped with glittering metal-framed glass, and seating padded generously with pillows. Designs range from $35 for a small table to $130 for an étagère. Both groups are available at Abraham & Straus, 5th floor.

Between Mint Jelly and Imitation Emeralds

By JOHN RUSSELL

IF WE ARE to believe that fountain of fancy, Brewer's Dictionary of Phrase and Fable, there are in all 106 different shades of green.

But today, March 17th, only one of them matters. In honor of St. Patrick, an unmistakable shade of green turns up all over the town. Midway in its connotations between mint jelly and imitation emeralds, it is seen to best advantage when mated with a sprig of shamrock. It stands for feasting, dancing, storytelling and a forgiven fondness for strong drink.

It may even, and for this day only, have magical powers: whence the readiness with which Frenchmen and Filipinos, Argentines and Albanians, will sport a green badge as big as a soup plate when they go out this evening. "Honorary Irishman," it reads, and it portends a long night of immunity from inhibition.

This particular green has of course its heroic associations. One of the great folk ballads of the world tells how once upon a time in Ireland "they were hanging men and women there for the wearing of the green." The green in question is everywhere in Ireland, and it comes from a grass like no other: one that starts at every cottage gate and persists even on the campus of Trinity College, Dublin. It is a green to lift the heart, a green to remember in far places, a green to die for.

But it is not, in other contexts, a manageable green. To wear it day in and day out takes more than a very pretty woman: It takes a very pretty redhead with a flawless white skin. As for living with it all around us, not many people have tried. It would be overpowering, like a symphony for 16 cornets and a shotgun. St. Patrick's green is best left to nature, which deals it out quite sparingly.

•

Emeralds, for instance, are in short supply, as far as most of us are concerned. Malachite, likewise: no palace in St. Petersburg was complete without its malachite room, but we can count ourselves lucky if we have even an inkwell or a paperweight made from that most mysterious of minerals. As for the Emerald Hummingbird, we have to go to the high mountains of Hispaniola to see it on the wing.

So St. Patrick and his henchmen started something that we should find it difficult to keep up with every day of the year. There are exceptions, however. If, like Mozart, we reckon the day lost that does not include a game of billiards, then green is integral to our existence. If we habitually go shooting in Austria, green is mandatory as hunting wear. Above all in gastronomy, green is great, all the way. Who among us does not dream of the green-gilled Virginian oyster, the green-fleshed melon, and that gelatinous green turtle meat that was all the rage with the Victorian epicure? Add to such things the sloping green shoulders of a good bottle of Moselle and St. Patrick can come back any time he likes.

•

But green has other associations that are not nearly so pleasant. Green throughout history has had implications of envy, jealousy, revenge, putrescence and vomit. Keen students of the Rev. E. Cobham Brewer and his Dictionary (see above) will remember what he says about green and the Scots: that "men from Caithness look upon it as fatal, because their troops wore green at the battle of Flodden. It is disliked by all who bear the name of Ogilvy and is especially unlucky to the Grahame clan. When an aged man of that name was thrown from his horse he accounted for it by his having a green lash to his riding whip".

That's it, really. Green is a tricky, edgy, mutinous sort of color, and nowhere more so than indoors. Not for nothing do we say of someone who has just heard bad news that "he turned green." Our feelings about green are not so much a matter of taste, though taste may enter into them, as of psychology and physiology. If we live in the country we are likely to have quite enough green outside without bringing it into the house as well. If we live in the city we may nurture house plants by the dozen and yet not go for green on the walls, on the table or in the bed. Green is mischievous.

Who ever got married in green, for instance? Something of folk memory may lurk within this taboo, in that for many generations "to give a girl a green gown" meant to roll her over and over on the grass ("in sport," according to that chivalrous arbiter, the complete Oxford English Dictionary).

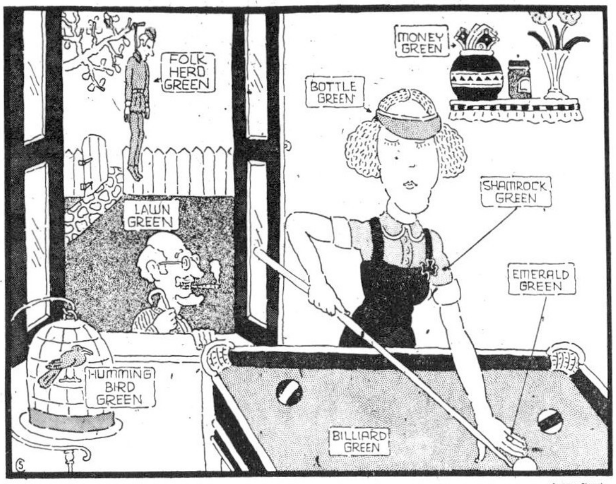

Seymour Chwast

There Are 106 Shades Of Green, But Only One Today

In more than one European language a green old man is a libidinous ancient, to be envied or avoided according to one's sex, age and orientation. In French and Spanish alike, green stands for nature's ability to renew herself in ways that we may not always find convenient.

But green has also its seraphic side: in art, especially. Corot at Ville d'Avray, Caspar David Friedrich in the flatlands of northern Germany, Winslow Homer wherever he cared to set up his easel: All were masters of a green that stands for healing and tranquillity. That is the green that I for one prefer.

Remembering the paintings in question, I also remember what was said 300 years ago by the English poet Andrew Marvell: that nothing in the world was more fun than to sit out in one's own garden, "annihilating all that's made/to a green thought in a green shade."

It's not quite the thing for Central Park on March 17th, this year or any other year, but it's something to plan for.

Using the Sun to Bring Heating Costs Down to Earth

By NORMA SKURKA

The Robert Mocarskys had a double motive for building themselves a solar-heated house outside of Hartford. One was the eventual saving in fuel, the other was to use the house as a guinea pig for future projects.

Mr. Mocarsky is an architect with Galliher & Schoenhardt Architects of Simsbury, Conn. He and a growing number of progressive young architects believe that the design of houses, what they are built of and how they are situated, will have to change in response to rising fuel costs.

The solar heating system that Mr. Mocarsky installed in his new house is only one part of a list of special features intended to cut fuel bills. The architect bought his four-and-a-half acre site in 1973, before the oil embargo, and he was already thinking about solar energy and conservation. "The embargo of 1973 just accelerated my plans," he said.

Before he began to design the house, he boned up on alternate energy, enrolling in courses at the University of Connecticut and reading a variety of magazines dealing with solar energy. He also contacted two Hartford concerns that specialize in solar-heated buildings and eventually hired Douglas Conte of Modern Energy Concepts Inc. to design the heating system for the house.

•

The key to efficiency, Mr. Mocarsky's research assured him, was the ability of the dwelling to keep the sun-gathered heat. Large expanses of windows and air leaks of any kind could cost much in potential heat. Superior insulation, siting and placement of windows were important. And he learned that houses built in Colonial times conserved more energy than many modern dwellings.

Mr. Mocarsky had the house nestled into the hillside so that its north side, facing the strongest wind, was protected. Most large window areas were placed on the south side to receive maximum sunshine.

He designed a large clerestory window and placed it just below the roof ridge for additional sun. All windows were double-glazed to guard against heat loss from conduction, and the insulation was increased—to 3½ inches of fiber glass batts in walls and 6 inches in the roof, plus an exterior skin of inch-thick rigid Styrofoam panels under the clapboard siding and roofing.

Two other features from old houses were incorporated. Vestibules—creating air pockets between the inner and outer doors—protect both entrances. The chimney runs up the middle of the house to allow the bricks to radiate heat to living spaces.

•

Mr. Mocarsky and Mr. Conte, the designer, debated which of the two most common types of solar-heating systems to use, the air or water type. The latter system circulates water in pipes in the rooftop-solar panels and the heat from the sun-warmed water is stored in a large tank.

Because of his location in the Connecticut snowbelt near the foot of the Berkshires, where winters are severe, Mr. Mocarsky eventually decided on the air type. That system circulates air in the solar collectors and that air is piped down into a 40-by-10-by-4-foot bin of rocks under the house floor. The owner-architect chose the latter because he was afraid of freezing problems in the water-type collectors.

The system itself, consisting of the roof collectors, pipes and ductwork, is simple. The collectors are little more than well-insulated boxes with see-through plastic lids. These were inserted between the roof rafters and are part of the house's frame.

•

Pipes and ductwork that carry the air from the collectors to the rooms and the rock bin are similar to those of a conventional oil or gas-fired system of forced hot air.

A one-horsepower blower keeps the air circulating, and three thermostats and several temperature sensors direct its flow, into the rooms or down to the rock bin. Mr. Mocarsky also installed two standard kitchen exhaust fans near the top of the house to move warmer air to the ground level.

"We had no trouble getting financing for the house, or finding any of the equipment," Mr. Mocarsky said. The solar heating system cost $6,000, half for labor, half for materials. The house, excluding the system, will eventually cost $55,000.

If the architect encountered any unusual problems in construction, it was in filling the bin with the 65 tons of rock. "The quarry people dumped the rocks in the driveway and we had to enlist everybody we knew to carry them into the bin by hand," he said. "It took three weeks."

•

Even with a solar-heated house, the Mocarskys aren't free of the utility company. "Any solar-heated house in the Northeast needs a back-up heat source," Mr. Mocarsky said. "It's just not economically feasible to build a 100-percent solar-heated house. You'd need such a large collector area and such a big storage bin that the cost would be way out of line for the dead of winter—the only time when the system would have to run full force."

A 3,000-watt electric coil is his back-up heat source, installed in the main air duct just beyond the blower. When the temperature in the house drops below the thermostat setting of 65 degrees during the day and 55 degrees at night, the coil turns on to heat the air.

To save on electricity during sunless days and at night, the Mocarskys use their Jotul wood-burning stove. So far this year, they have used about two cords of wood from trees on their site. Eventually, they will connect their domestic hot water supply to the solar heating system.

•

As yet the rock bin is not completely insulated, so the system cannot store sun heat for extended periods.

His first electricity bill—for $180—made him "nearly hit the roof," he said. He discovered the problem. A faulty thermostat was not shutting off the electric coil.

"The system is still full of little bugs," the architect said, "but when the costs for the solar equipment come down and as oil and gas prices rise, I believe this house is going to be very economical."

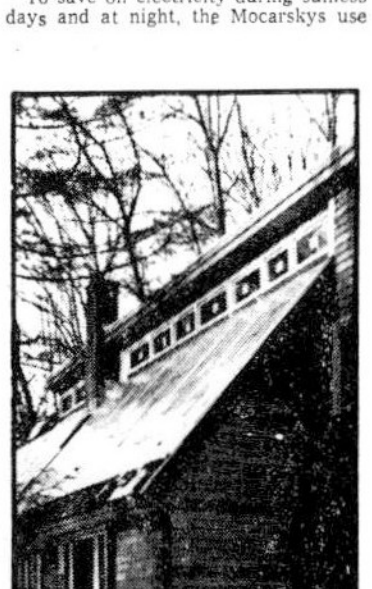

Solar panels are set in roof below clerestory.

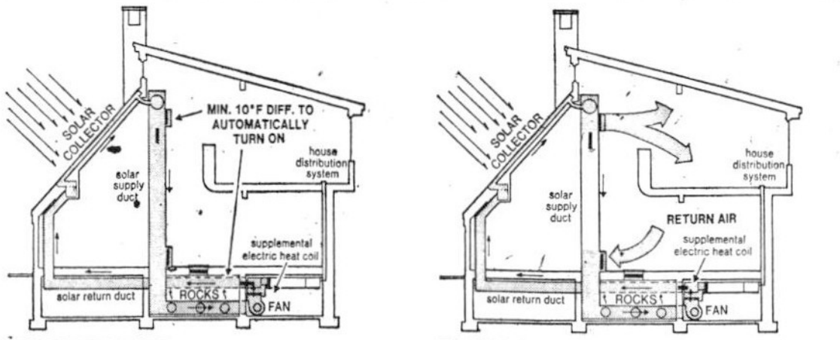

COLLECTING CYCLE
Collecting cycle is a simple closed loop with heated air in the collector forced over the cooler rocks where it loses its heat to the rocks before being blown back up through the collector to be heated again.

DIRECT HEAT CYCLE
Direct cycle operates when house calls for heat during collecting cycle and rocks are not sufficiently heated to meet the demand. System automatically goes back to collecting when house thermostat is satisfied.

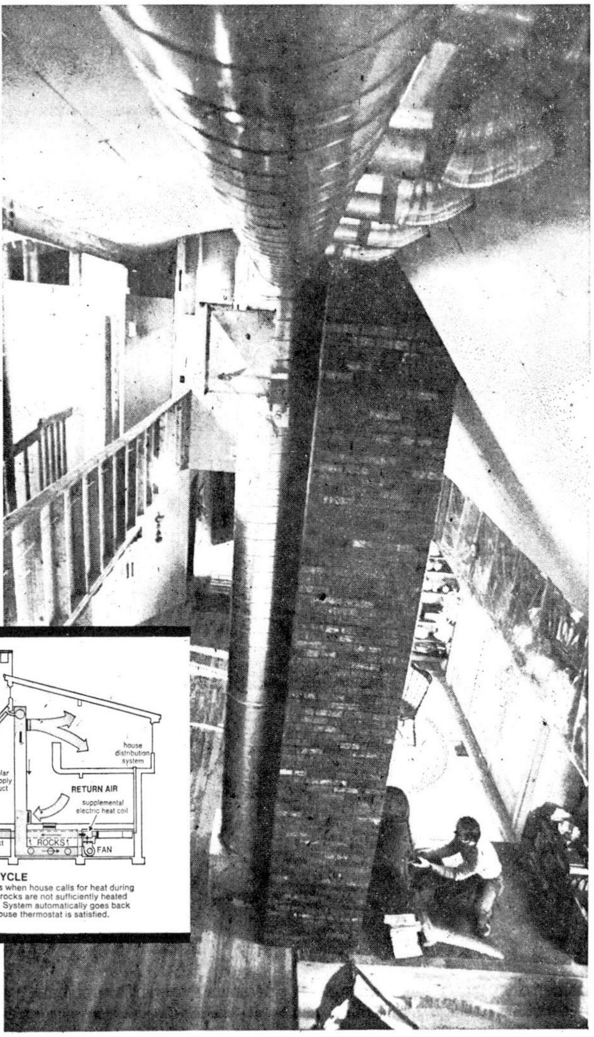

Robert Perron

Barrel-type air ducts that direct the sun-heated air from roof collectors are left exposed in living room of the Mocarsky home in Granby, Conn.

Staff and the hierarchy

Desks of their own

Each of the C sections is organized by its own staff, and each functions much like a separate publication, except for the managing editors who oversee all of the sections. Each staff consists of an editor, a deputy editor, a copy editor or editors, a make-up editor, and staff writers. Each has a budget for free-lance work and illustrations. An art director, assigned from the Art Department, is responsible for the design of the entire publication, as would be the art director of any independent publication.

A question often asked is, "What's the relationship of the art director to the editor?" A lot of concern was caused by this question among editors who may have feared that designers were about to take over the newsroom. The answer is, "The editor is in charge, just as he always has been," but with a difference. In the past, the desk editor had a lot more absolute authority than he has now. He could say about a design, "I just don't like it," and that was the end of it. This climate did nothing to attract or hold a good designer. Today at *The Times* an editor is unlikely to be so arbitrary. Since visual wit and innovation are as much a part of the editor's mandate as the creative assignment of stories, the editor *needs* a good designer to do the job.

The start-up years of the C sections left no doubt in the newsroom of the importance attached to this changeover of *The Times*. Once the sections were in place, the priorities pendulum swung back to hard news, but by then the new sections were firmly established as vital parts of the news operation, with as much stressful attention devoted to them as to any other part of the paper. On closing days in the newsroom, one could see a procession of groups of people, lined up, waiting to show deputy managing editor Arthur Gelb the front page layouts for next week's C sections, while another group might be showing managing editor Seymour Topping the Week in Review and the Sunday Business fronts. The group would include the editor, the deputy, and the art director. The approvals were far from perfunctory. I was frequently called upon to bridge conflicting views, salvage an idea, improve a layout, or help with a headline. After this hurdle, a copy of the approved layout was dropped in Rosenthal's "in" box or, if time were short, Gelb would pop into Rosenthal's office and show it to him. Abe's approval was also far from perfunctory. He said he didn't want to be shown anything for approval if it was too late to make changes if he felt they were necessary.

I think we all knew it was an unwieldly chain of command. But it did convey on a regular basis a message to everyone in the News Department —"We really care about design."

Impact and service

Facing page: An open page provides space for major stories, strong visual presentation, and plenty of service content.

The Travel Section

THE NEW YORK TIMES

Background of a big change

Cooperation between News and Advertising

For years, advertising executives at *The New York Times* wanted to change what was then called the Travel and Resorts section because the section's configuration failed to reflect changing patterns in the travel industry and its advertising. The section had developed in the decades before the explosive growth of air travel and tourism to far places. In the past, travel advertising in *The Times* had represented more modest trips to places closer to home.

To a great extent, the advertising columns in the section consisted of small ads grouped together in classified display fashion under small black headings over each column. For example, a label, such as "New York State," might repeat eight times in 9 point boldface across the page.

New England and Florida were also prominently represented. Although relatively small, the ads were numerous and massed into large blocks.

Alone among the Sunday sections, the Travel section was laid out with the editorial elements in place first, before the advertising units were placed—a reversal of the usual procedure. The ads were then configured around the editorial blocks. Dissatisfaction with the advertising layout developed as more large ads began to come in from airlines, big-time resorts, foreign sources, and large travel agencies. Forced by the traditional configuration of the section to yield the front pages to the old kind of advertising, the new ads occupied newly carved-out spaces in the back of the section.

As it was

Big pictures alone, without an apparent structure or rich typographical palette, are not enough to give the page a graphic lift. The Bodoni headlines used at the time in two sections of the paper were to give way to Bookman as the main display face of the entire paper.

134

In the News Department, advertising dissatisfaction was paralleled by a feeling that the time was ripe to revitalize the section, not merely in design but in tone, content, and quality. By the time the News Department came to this decision in late 1980, we had already made many big changes and innovations in other parts of the paper. In a period of only two-and-a-half years, from early 1976 to late 1978, *The Times* created nine new sections, changed the structure of the paper from eight to six columns for news and nine columns for advertising, and redesigned the Book Review and the Sunday Magazine. Before that, I had designed The Week in Review, formerly called The News of the Week in Review, for the Sunday Department and the Arts and Leisure section, run without a title, but referred to as the Drama section.

The News Department had developed a pattern of working and a confident approach to a redesign project that aimed not for cosmetic tidying up but for substantial change. Work on a redesign project usually started with formal meetings around the conference table in executive editor A. M. Rosenthal's office and often continued in informal sessions at his apartment, where we met for breakfast and more free-wheeling kinds of discussion.

The most exciting and often the most productive meetings were the impromptu free-for-alls that occurred in Rosenthal's office. These working sessions included Abe, Arthur Gelb, myself, and occasionally one or two other editors. The meetings ranged from exhilarating to hilarious, reminding me of small boys planning some adventurous excursion. I doubt that business management experts would approve the procedure, but, without a doubt, the creative level was high. The agenda was always content, hardly ever design. It was a basic principle that a redesign project started with new ideas for content; design would follow.

The first round of memos and meetings produced little more than a rehash of things already in the section. Eventually, however, finding their way into the content proposals were ideas for new regular departments, like Shopper's World, Fare of the Country, Correspondent's Choice, and others. Correspondent's Choice was to draw on the insider's experience of the 25 or more *Times* correspondents deployed around the world. Other ideas for content emerged as the new configuration was designed.

Overriding all of this was Rosenthal's and Gelb's insistence that the new section should aim for more sophistication and excellent writing, feeling that a new, sophisticated section would enable us to attract some of the best writers in the world.

Design approach

The design of this section, even more than other sections, tried to take full advantage of the large scale of the broadsheet newspaper. Size could make up for lack of color. Big pictures, generous maps, and service sidebars would complement each other side-by-side in multimedia fashion.

Two things in particular made the Travel section design significantly different from other section designs. First, the design of the front cover page, eliminating completely all text from Page One, resulted in a graphic page of reefer items, like a super-contents page.

Less obvious was the comprehensive cover-to-cover reshaping of the configuration to give advertisers access to important large display units, rectifying the past imbalanced patterns, while carving out for the News Department substantial spaces for expanded and vitalized content —an original goal. Since the process was so unusually cooperative between the news and the various business departments, dramatic changes were able to be made that might otherwise never have been realized.

In early meetings with the Travel desk editors, it was stressed that we would not be concerned at this point with resources needed to implement a new design—new staffing, budgets for writers, and assignment of artists and designers. These questions were to be deferred until we had an approved dummy in hand and knew what we wanted to do.

This order of priorities may seem obvious, but in many situations concern about money and budget severely inhibits the development of new ideas. Financial and staffing concerns can put the designers and the desk editors out of sync with the designers reaching for new elements to put in the paper, while the editors remain skeptical of management's willingness to pay for them. In these circumstances, a brainstorming session can become more an attempt to shuffle and dress up the same old way of doing things. Therefore, Rosenthal stressed that the job at this point was simply to develop good ideas. He promised that it would be management's job to evaluate the ideas and provide the resources.

Staff considerations

A redesign may indeed require a change or increase in staff. But having the design in hand or in production for a while enables a more realistic assessment to be made of needs. Usually a new format goes more smoothly than originally anticipated. In fact, a newly structured design may very well be *easier* to put together than a less structured old design, once the new guidelines and formatting are learned.

Another consideration is that the new design may be a management initiative that has been imposed on a staff, or at least they may feel that it is being imposed. Therefore, staff may be defensive, consciously or otherwise, about the changes being made to the way they did things in the past. The only way around this attitude seems to be to concentrate solely on the design at hand, let the improvements speak for themselves, and give the staff time to adjust to them and develop their own enthusiasm.

Designing

The meetings finally give way to actual designing. Usually, the process includes making rough layouts on tissues, experimental paste-ups, a final dummy, and then dry runs, with more meetings and approvals along the way. The Travel section, however, progressed a bit more emotionally than usual.

The concept for the Travel front page came effortlessly in the first rough, appearing much as it did when ultimately published. As an overblown contents page—big pictures, some provocative sentences in oversize type that would be part caption, part content listing, and no text—it would be a visual sampler.

The rough layout seemed so exciting that I decided to show it at once to Rosenthal. The reg-ular afternoon news meeting was just concluding. I took the elevator downstairs in a hurry, grabbed Rosenthal's attention as soon as the news meeting broke up, and asked him to come up to look at the layout on the drawing board. Abe's excitement matched mine. He took one look from half-way across the room and said something along the lines of "That's it! Let's do it—just like that!" The project was launched.

Spontaneity and symbiosis

I have wondered what would have happened had I chosen a less spontaneous course, following up the first layout with alternate layouts, working on inside pages, putting together a rough dummy, and pronouncing that I was ready for a presentation at a formal meeting with many people present. Without the executive editor's prior enthusiastic approval, I wonder if the more formal procedure might not have spawned some nervous rationale for a compromise such as: "How about just the lead story starting somewhere on the page?" A reasonable compromise, maybe, but it would have effectively killed a good idea.

On the other hand, Rosenthal could have killed the idea before I had a chance to develop and present it more completely, but that thought never occurred to me. I think this defines as near perfect as imaginable the working relationship between an editor and a designer, a relationship based simply on confidence. I was certain that some scribbles on a pad would mean as much to the editor as they did to me, just as I was usually sure I understood what was in Abe's mind from a single word or phrase. I also benefited from this kind of working relationship with Arthur Gelb and later with Seymour Topping. Gelb described the relationship as "symbiotic."

The New York Times

TRAVEL

Sunday, October 11, 1981

10

Copyright © 1981 The New York Times

As we clickety-clacked across the continent we peered through our picture window at riverfront towns, great...

On Track, Coast t...

country rail trip was to be pure...
landscapes; a nightcap...
promised much less...
four children a...

Starting Sunday, October 11, Travel becomes even more rewarding to readers and advertisers.

...Choice ... 5
...al beauty, the Mauna Kea Beach Hotel
...y unchanged since Laurence S. Rockefeller
...lendid Hawaiian beach. By Robert Lindsey.

What's Doing in . . . Brussels 9
Belgium's capital has richly wooded parks, cobbled
streets, triumphal arches and the Grand Place, the
most striking old square in Europe. By Paul Lewis.

Fare of the Country 11
In Tel Aviv, vegetables stuffed with ground meat and rice,
baked, then served with a hot oriental spice called Zhoug.

Shoppers' World 19
When in Florence, seize the opportunity to buy a handbag, a wallet, a belt. The quality of Florentine leathercraft
is unsurpassed and the prices are lower than back home.

Pritchett's Minorca
A small island in the sun, an eventless
island where the inhabitants have had
more history than
they could con-
sume locally and
have at last drop-
ped out of it. An
essay by the critic
V. S. Pritchett.
Page 7.

Back behind the hills we discovered mysterious monumental sculptures.

Large modern hotels offer every amenity.

---

thus increasing the visibility of the advertising.
- And new full page advertising positions will be established on pages 2, 5, 7, 8 and 11.

Now there's even more reason to schedule a consistent program of advertising in the Sunday Travel section — already an unmatched source of
vacation ideas for the 4,200,000 better-income readers of the Sunday
Times.

But please note that the first issue of the redesigned section will be heavily
promoted in radio c........... .. newsst... ...sters and in-paper ...
C.. kev ...

Promotional announcement
Cover and inside detail of a promotional section
produced by the Advertising Department. One of its
main points is the availability of new full-page
positions in the front part of the redesigned section.

137

Cover

A poster/contents page

This was the first use of Franklin Gothic type in a Sunday section head. Sunday sections hitherto had featured *The New York Times* logo bigger and the section title in relatively small Bookman italic capitals. The "Resorts" in the old "Travel and Resorts" title was dropped. The bolder and simpler title and the small *Times* logo made a stronger, more compact, designed-looking unit, signaling a more graphic approach to the section and providing a bold accent at the top against which the Bookman headlines could play.

In the first dummy, Helvetica Black all capitals was used for the title. The Franklin Gothic, however, seemed more interesting in its subtle variety of bold strokes and more harmonious with the Bookman below, with its own subtle variations in weight of strokes.

The new design meant that this section heading would be different from the other Sunday section headings, which remained in Bookman italic capitals. The new design required a stronger heading. In time, I was sure, other sections would be redesigned and follow the same route.

The front page came out a cross between a poster and an illustrated contents page of a magazine. In a world of slick, full-color magazines and the spectacular color imagery of television,

OLD

NEW

More of a title

The design was the first of the Sunday sections to use Franklin Gothic in the title. The emphasis switched from *The Times* logo to the name of the section itself. The advertising ear on the left was dropped.

The new section

Facing page: An early issue in the new format provides wide sense of scale, from cathedral facades to extreme close-ups of faces to a scenic long view; and typographically, from large Bookman heads and large numerals to small dark Franklin Gothic accents. Identifying the cathedrals in the old engraving was painstaking, but added substance to an otherwise decorative illustration.

Spire to Spire in Wren's London

A Christmastime walking tour of churches designed by England's greatest architect. By R.W. Apple Jr. Pages 10-11.

Correspondent's Choice
6

Fairchild Tropical Gardens, a little-known oasis of quiet near Miami, invites visitors to walk on the grass and smell the flowers. No picnicking and no Frisbees, though — and certainly, no hoopla. By Gregory Jaynes.

Fare of the Country
14

A once neglected South African dish called bobotie — a sort of moussaka whose spiciness reflects its Malay heritage — has emerged from humble kitchens and attained status in Cape Town's fashionable restaurants. By Joseph Lelyveld.

Those Were the Days
23

Notes from a world traveler on voyages by land, sea and air, then and now. Including a lamentation on the final departure of the London-Paris boat train, and why a Queen's Messenger may be a tourist's best friend. By Drew Middleton.

In Rio as New Year's Eve gives way to Carnival, the party never ends. By Warren Hoge. Page 15.

A view of Dalkey Island, crowned with a majestic tower from the Napoleonic Wars.

Hugh Leonard's Dalkey

The author of 'Da,' on a ramble through his hometown, 'a kind of Irish Brigadoon without the mists, the feyness or the tendency to disappear,' where 'a secret is a crime against nature.' Page 9.

even excellent pictures in black and white on the unreliable surface of newsprint were not likely to be sufficiently arresting. But sheer size in the use of pictures would not be adequate. More important than size by itself were two related factors— creating a sense of scale, that is, a relationship of big to small elements to provide a point of reference to gauge relative-size bigness or smallness; and making sure that words and pictures would complement each other so that together they made an impact on the reader greater than either text or picture could achieve by itself. The result would be an equation where a 1 (the words) plus a 1 (the pictures) would add up to a 3 in impact. The right picture with the right words could in this way create visual energy.

To squeeze some text on the page would not only diminish the poster effect but would adversely affect the sense of scale. If we placed text type on the page, 8¾ point, the approximately 30-point type of the captions would look senselessly huge; without the 8¾-point text, the large type would seem appropriate and in proper scale with the page as a whole.

In the past, with traditional photo and text treatment, the front page of the Travel section used big pictures and usually featured two stories on the page. The headlines were set in a handsome cut of Bodoni but, in the context of the page, were rather small. Pictures and type did not interact with each other. The pictures in the Travel and Resort section (and in the Drama section) were like huge boulders emerging from the sea of a quiet cove, with the gray waters of type lapping around them. There was no tension between picture and text. Sometimes a really terrific picture can lift a page by itself. But a format design must work day-in and day-out with average as well as good pictures. The design should seek to use all the graphic tools available in type and in pictures, with as much strength as is consistent with the character of the paper.

Configuration
Proposals and counter proposals

Since one of the objectives of redesigning the Travel section was to improve display opportunities for advertisers, a redesigned configuration was central to the project to an even greater degree than usual. In addition, the unusual cover page and content ideas demanded some special considerations on the inside.

The illustrations in this chapter show three configurations: 1) the way the section was configured before redesign; 2) one of several intermediate proposals, this one from the Advertising Department; and 3) the final, agreed-upon configuration. The first reflects the scattered news approach that was the legacy of standard newspaper make-up. The third shows our efforts to give the section a pace geared to an analysis of the new content—"front-of-the-book" material of smaller items at the beginning; good-sized newsholes for our major stories in the middle; and space at the end for a sign-off. (Originally planned to be Letters, the sign-off at the end became a "surprise" short piece, the signature of the inside back cover.)

The second configuration is the last proposal from the Advertising Department before News and Advertising finally came to an agreement. Notice that spaces for main stories are not as big as finally agreed upon, and few major news spaces appear on right-hand pages. Also, this proposal fails to allow for the concentration of major stories that was desired.

This painstaking give-and-take between the News Department and the Advertising Department demonstrates the importance attached to the configuration. Enormous effort was given to hammering out spaces that satisfied the ambitions of both departments. The new design represented improvement in content and presentation for readers and advantages for the business departments in selling advertising space.

The separation of "Church" and "State" in the form of news and advertising is, of course, deeply rooted in newspaper publishing tradition. The ethical considerations are well known. But in organizing the news and ad spaces in a rational manner, large doses of cooperation are necessary on both sides. In addition, good solutions in this area seem to require extraordinary attention to the nitty-gritty by the top executives, who alone are in a position to re-order basic priorities.

	Cols			Cols
P.1	6		P.15	5
2	—		16	1
3	6		17	
4	1		18	—
5			19	4
6	2½		20	3
7	—		21	3
8	—		22	1
9	6		23	
10	4		24	—
11			25	2½
12	2½		26	—
13	—			19½
14	—			
	28			28
				19½
				47½ TOTAL NEWS

156 TOTAL
− 47½
108½ TOTAL ADVERT.

Ratio
Each suggested configuration was checked to make sure the general news-to-advertising ratio was in the agreed-upon ballpark. The news columns were added up page by page and then subtracted from the total number of columns in the dummy. In this instance, the dummy yielded a ratio of approximately 29 percent news to 71 percent advertising.

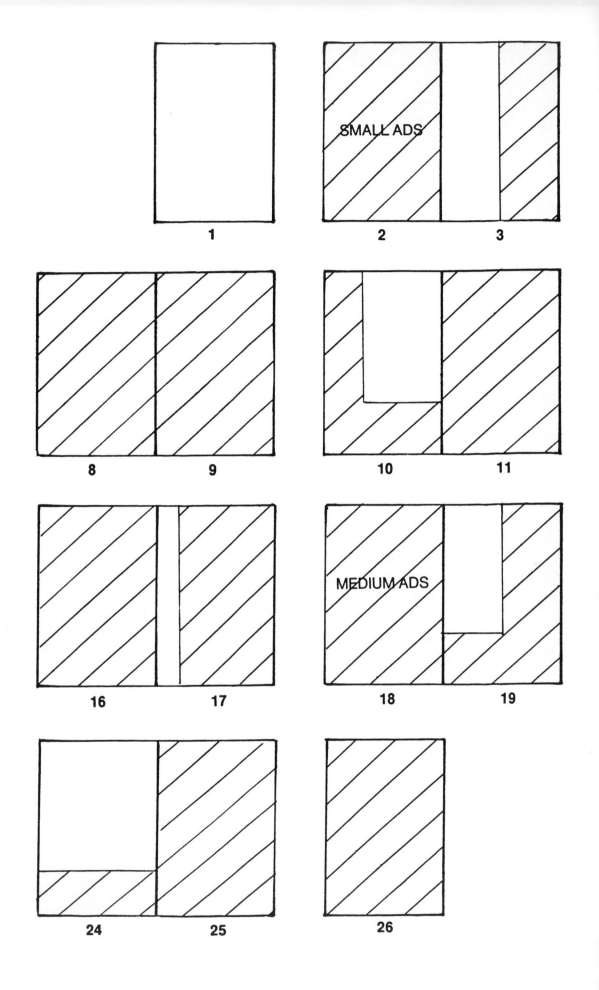

SMALL ADS

1   2   3

8   9   10   11

MEDIUM ADS

16   17   18   19

24   25   26

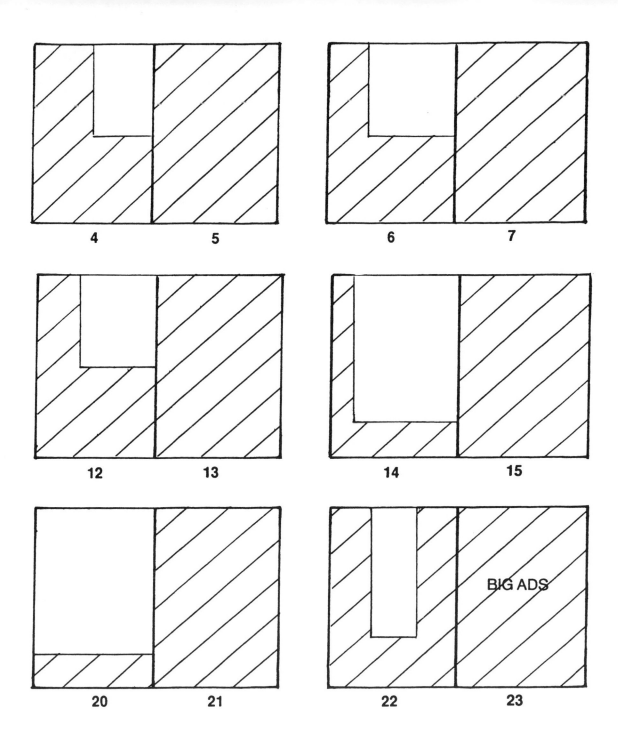

Configuration: Before redesign

Blank areas are news; shaded yellow areas are advertising. A typical issue, compressed for comparison with configurations on following pages, shows ad distribution based on numerous small travel ads that were grouped by area as Classified Display. The configuration is typical in stressing "editorial adjacency" and dominance of advertising on right-hand pages.

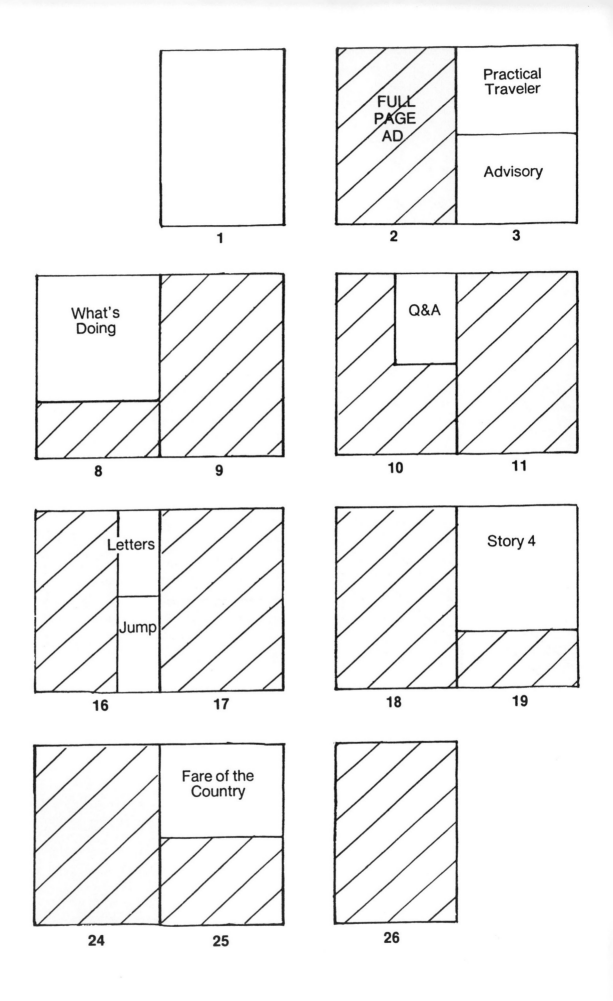

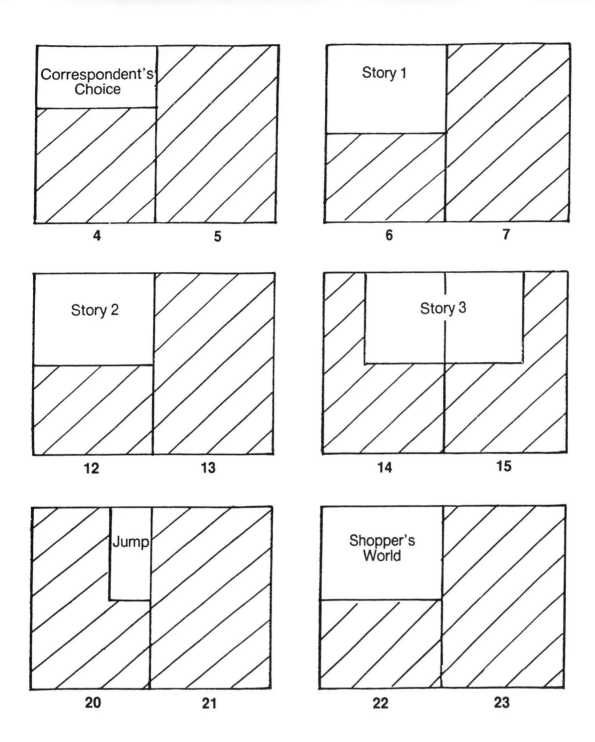

Advertising Department proposal
After much negotiation, this advertising proposal
took into account new content ideas but failed to
provide some dominant editorial spaces, sufficient
right-hand page editorial presence, or sufficient
sense of *flow* from front to back. The elements
already agreed upon included the new Page 3 and
space for four major stories.

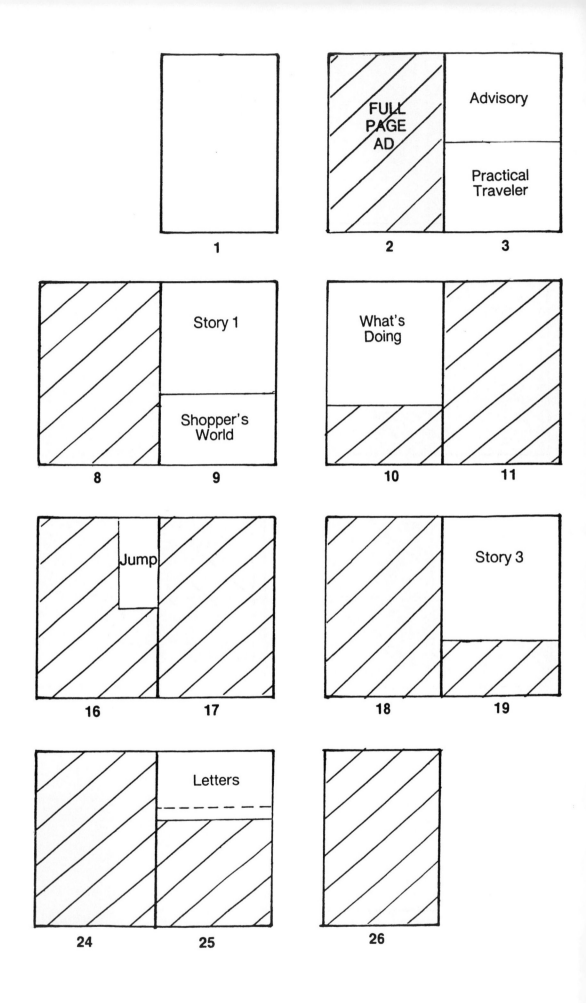

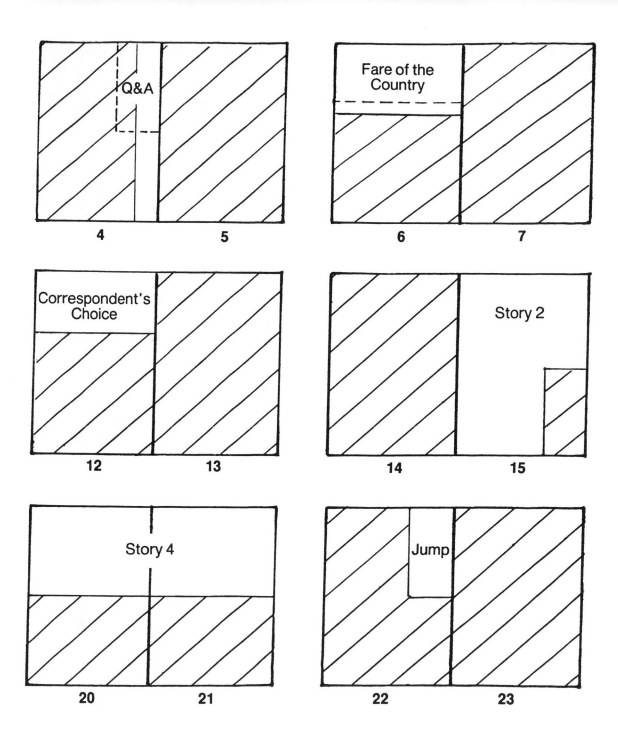

Agreed!

The configuration finally agreed to by both News and Advertising gave right-hand pages to both, with a couple of major spaces allotted for stories. The news presence is considerably enhanced, with advertising spaces still enjoying editorial-adjacent positions. The horizontal half-pages (on 20 and 21) became important in the Travel section's make-up.

"Front-of-the-book" feeling

The elements grow out of the configuration

The Travel Advisory feature almost designed itself as a by-product of the section's configuration. Since the cover was basically a poster, with no actual text, it was desirable to open to a Page 3 that gave the reader a lot of different texts. The multiplicity of small items, plus the service department at the bottom of the page, seemed sure to provide at least one or two subjects the reader would find arresting. Instead, a feature story might have been planned for this page, but this would provide only one subject and headline. Also, a feature page right off would be a rather precipitous plunge into the main articles, using up our quota of feature spaces in the first few pages with the section dribbling away to smaller spaces quickly in the center of the section. It is better to lead up to the big stories in the middle of the section, where big headlines and pictures can reiterate the graphic strength of the cover page.

Page 3, then, could be considered the equivalent of the "front-of-the-book" in magazine make-up, which runs among big ads and leads up to the main *well* of the magazine.

Having already been used in other newly designed Sunday sections, Franklin Gothic was again used as a black typographical counterpoint to the Bookman. Care was taken not to overuse the Franklin Gothic, either in size or frequency. The basic character of the paper remains Bookman; the Franklin Gothic provides accent and broadens the graphic palette.

The headings on Page 3 were devised not only to be identifying labels but also to provide changing overlines that could reach out to the reader with a catchy phrase geared to the day's subject. This is a good example, I believe, of how words and design interrelate. Without the extra descriptive phrases, the department headings alone would make a less interesting design, and the page assumes a more predictable, "canned" look.

Successive Page 3's, on different Sundays after the new design started, show the flexibility of this format to allow creative implementation week after week, without losing its basic character (see accompanying illustrations).

A useful and popular feature, Practical Traveler was a carry-over from the old section. The new design, however, gave it considerably more importance than it previously enjoyed by anchoring it on this newly created opening page.

Editorial concentration

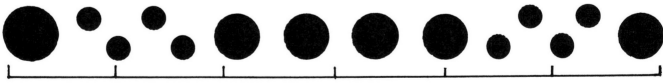

Strong graphic kick-off to the section on Pages One and 3 (Black circles represent degree of editorial presence.)

"Front-of-the-book" editorial elements interspersed among dominant ads.

Main features dominate the center pages, but ad presence continues.

Smaller features break up the strong ad presence.

Agreed-upon horizontal half-page on inside back cover is reserved for a special offbeat editorial feature that winds up the section with a flourish.

Plenty to choose from

Facing page: Dummy layout for Page 3 of the section shows a front-of-the-magazine feeling all on one page. The chock-full informational impression comes on the heels of the graphic front page. Getting a clear Page 3 involved trade-offs with the Advertising Department.

On Montego Bay

What I was seeing began to make sense when the man in the next seat said stolidly: "I hate this flight; it's always jammed full of kids who cry and it's always late."

What flight? The 11 A.M. to Bogotá? Any Avianca flight? A Saturday morning flight?

"What do you mean?" I asked.

"The weekend flight to Colombia in January," he replied. "On the school holidays everyone, including me, endures this five hours of bedlam to go home to see the family. And today is the worst of all, the Feast of the Three Kings."

My husband and I realized that, despite our belief that we had chosen this day at random and despite the tourist cards tucked into our passports, we were just two more lemmings on the seasonal tide that draws families together in Colombia.

In September our son had forsaken the land of ski lifts and longies for a year of study in Colombia, and we were on our way to Bogotá to see him.

When the airborne bedlam had gone on for five hours and we were still in the air, I stood in the aisle for the rest of the flight — about an hour — to salvage myself from permanent folding, spindling and mutilation. When we landed at Eldorado Airport, we got through Customs in an instant — but our son was not there. We were plunged into an anarchy of cabbies. We managed to make some sort of deal and climbed into a car, grappling for our phrase books while speaking a word that required no translation: "Hilton."

The tone of the aerograms from Bogotá had left some doubt that our son would be eager to have us stay at the Hilton; he was ever more concerned about poverty and imperialism. On the other hand, it had been easy to reserve a room at the Hilton while still in New York, and memories of the days when the student was a constant author of steamy bathrooms and soggy towels indicated that a hot shower might be a drawing card after four months.

Soon after we got settled at the hotel, our son arrived, explaining.

Making the China Connection

When the plane for Bogotá was loaded at Kennedy International Airport, there were two passengers for every seat because the adults were draped with babies or toddlers; coloring books, crayons, stuffed animals, blankets and pacifiers dangled over seat backs and from shoulders.

When every crevice was filled, and bottles were rolling around underfoot, the cargo began to go aboard. Far below the window, a conveyor belt carried uphill a stream of chattels that made the zoo inside the plane seem sane: cardboard cartons big enough to hold a folded Super-Bowl linebacker; long parcels belief that we had chosen this day at random and despite the tourist cards tucked into our passports, we were just two more lemmings on the seasonal tide that draws families together in Colombia.

In September our son had forsaken the land

A row of company houses with their original wood siding.

ers and carriages; suitcases swathed in electric cord; map cases six feet long; folded playpens and walkers; stitched-up bundles that he had waited an hour for us at the national arrivals terminal before realizing his error.

While I attempted to adjust to the altitude (8,700 feet), I had time to study the palaces that the Hilton rents for rooms in Bogotá: The faucets on the washbowls are labeled, left to right, "C" and "F." Left to right, they emit hot and cold water, as one expects.

Home Tours And free lunch

The faucets in the shower, however, are labeled, left to right, "C" and "H," and despite this likewise emit, left to right, hot and cold.

I pondered this riddle while gazing out of the hotel window at a huge Christmas decoration on the Cerveza Bavaria building. The problem finally yielded and I prepared a little lecture saying that the dual-control washbowl plumbing must be domestic, and the shower plumbing from the United States. The plumbers, I thought, put the United States handles on backwards because the "C" they recognize as "caliente" for "hot."

Fortunately I did not expend my very scarce breath to explain this ambiguity because the ambiguity walked out of the bathroom in a cloud of steam, lavished in towels monogrammed "H," hair dripping, clutching the imported shampoo. "I am no longer used to being above the second floor," he said.

"You are paying daily what I pay in a month for my apartment. I think I would go crazy in this hotel in a day or two."

on the seasonal tide that draws families together in Colombia.

In September our son had forsaken the land

Restoration In the Bahamas

What I was seeing began to make s when the man in the next seat said stolidl hate this flight; it's always jammed fu kids who cry and it's always late."

What flight? The 11 A.M. to Bogotá? Avianca flight? A Saturday morning fligh

"What do you mean?" I asked.

"The weekend flight to Colombia in J ary," he replied. "On the school holi everyone, including me, endures this hours of bedlam to go home to see the fai And today is the worst of all, the Feast o Three Kings."

My husband and I realized that, despite belief that we had chosen this day at ran and despite the tourist cards tucked into passports, we were just two more lemm on the seasonal tide that draws familie that looked like bales of cotton, duffel l and backpacks — an array to boggle mind. The loading went on for an hour a the cabin had become a 20th-century.

Nothing Like A Cruise

The next day we packed up and left Mother Hilton, and, following a plan that our son had made, took a short flight to Cartagena, on Colombia's Caribbean coast. We had brought from a library a heavy Spanish-language book on the architecture of Cartagena, and something in our brains had failed to register the words our son kept using: "I can hardly wait to get to the coast, I've been dying to go

to the coast." When we got to our hotel in Cartagena, it was 81 degrees outside and the old folk opened the curtains to find that we were overlooking the beach of Boca Grande with five rows of combers sliding up it. A band was playing on the street below and we had a refrigerator already stocked with beer — both local and imported. It was the stuff of a high-school fantasy.

We all emitted pig-like sounds of satisfaction, which indicated that our son was not 100 percent committed to austerity and that his parents were not so far beyond hedonism as they had imagined. We sat on the balcony and drank cerveza while our son, a musician, gave informed comments on the rhythms of the music olson was not 100 percent committed to austerity and that his parents were

Good Time to Rent a 40-Foot Yacht

When the plane for Bogotá was loaded at Kennedy International Airport, there were two passengers for every seat because the adults were draped with babies or toddlers; coloring books, crayons, stuffed animals, blankets and pacifiers dangled over seat backs and from shoulders.

When every crevice was filled, and bottles were rolling around underfoot, the cargo began to go aboard. Far below the window, a conveyor belt carried uphill a stream of chattels that made the zoo inside the plane seem sane: cardboard cartons big enough to hold a folded Super-Bowl linebacker; long parcels that might contain prestressed-concrete columns; string bags full of basketballs; strollers and carriages; suitcases swathed in electric cord; map cases six feet long; folded playpens and walkers; stitched-up bundles that looked like bales of cotton, duffel bags and backpacks — an array to boggle the mind. The loading went on for an hour after the cabin had become a 20th-century

When the airborne bedlam had gone o five hours and we were still in the air, I s in the aisle for the rest of the flight — abo hour — to salvage myself from perma folding, spindling and mutilation. Wher landed at Eldorado Airport, we got thro Customs in an instant — but our son was there. We were plunged into an anarch cabbies. We managed to make some so deal and climbed into a car, grappling for phrase books while speaking a word tha quired no translation: "Hilton."

The tone of the aerograms from Bogotá left some doubt that our son would be eag have us stay at the Hilton; he was ever n concerned about poverty and imperialism the other hand, it had been easy to reser room at the Hilton while still in New Y and memories of the days.

Practical Traveler: On being bumped

hen the plane for Bogotá loaded at Kennedy bnal Airport, there were twgers for every seat because its were draped with babies os; coloring books, crayons, animals, brains had failed to register the words blankets and pacifiers dangled over seat backs and from shoulders.

When every crevice was filled, and bottles were rolling around underfoot, the cargo began to go aboard. Far below the window, a conveyor belt carried uphill a stream of chattels that made the zoo inside the plane seem sane: cardboard cartons big enough to hold a folded Super-Bowl linebacker; long parcels that might contain prestressed-concrete columns; string bags full of basketballs; strollers and carriages; suitcases swathed in electric cord; map cases six feet long; folded playpens and walkers; stitched-up bundles that looked like bales of cotton, duffel bags and backpacks — an array to boggle the mind. The loading went on for an hour after the cabin had become a 20th-century steerage.

What I was seeing began to make sense when the man in the next seat said stolidly: "I hate this flight; it's always jammed full of kids who cry and it's always late."

What flight? The 11 A.M. to Bogotá? Any Avianca flight? A Saturday morning flight?

"What do you mean?" I asked.

"The weekend flight to Colombia in January," he replied. "On the school holidays everyone, including me, endures this five hours of bedlam to go home to see the family. And today is the worst of all the Feast of the Three Kings."

My husband and I realized that, despite our belief that we had chosen this day at random and despite the tourist cards tucked into our passports, we were just two more lemmings on the seasonal tide that draws families together in Colombia.

In September our son had forsaken the land of ski lifts and longies for a our son kept using: "I can hardly wait year of study in Colombia, and we were on our way to Bogotá to see him.

When the airborne bedlam had gone on for five hours and we were still in the air, I stood in the aisle for the rest of the flight — about an hour — to salvage myself from permanent folding, spindling and mutilation. When we landed at Eldorado Airport, we got through Customs in an instant — but our son was not there. We were

Soon after we got settled at the hotel, our son arrived, explaining in embarrassment that he had waited an hour for us at the national arrivals terminal before realizing his error.

While I attempted to adjust to the altitude (8,700 feet), I had time to study the palaces that the Hilton rents for rooms in Bogotá: The faucets on the washbowls are labeled, left to right, "C" and "F." Left to right, they emit hot and cold water, as one expects.

The faucets in the shower, however, are labeled, left to right, "C" and "H," and despite this likewise emit, left to right, hot and cold.

I pondered this riddle while gazing out of the hotel window at a huge Christmas decoration on the Cerveza Bavaria building. The problem finally yielded and I prepared a little lecture saying that the dual-control washbowl plumbing must be domestic, and the shower plumbing from the United

plunged into an anarchy of cabbies. We managed to make some sort of deal and climbed into a car, grappling for our phrase books while speaking a word that required no translation: "Hilton."

The tone of the aerograms from Bogotá had left some doubt that our son would be eager to have us stay at the Hilton; he was ever more concerned about poverty and imperialism. On the other hand, it had been easy to reserve a room at the Hilton while still in New York, and memories of the days when the student was a constant author of steamy bathrooms and soggy towels indicated that a hot shower might be a drawing card after four months.

That evening, as the Feast of the Three Kings was ending, we took a walk to the centro of Bogotá. The student plunged forward into jammed streets — which looked and smelled like Mulberry Street at San Gennaro — buying us pastries, bread, juices. His Spanish was rapid, firm and assertive and our obligatory tourist anxieties about pickpockets and bad water were brushed aside. "On the bus, clutch your handbag as if you love it," he said. "I've been drinking the water since September and I haven't had any trouble." We did as he said and suffered no ill effects. He introduced us to nispero, a fruit, to cheese wrapped in banana leaves, to kumis, a yogurt sort of thing, to the local liquor aguardiente, to foods unrecognizable but delicious, and we suffered no ill results save for the breath-taking effect of the altitude.

The next day we packed up and left Mother Hilton, and, following a plan that our son had made, took a short flight to Cartagena, on Colombia's Caribbean coast. We had brought from a library a heavy Spanish-language book on the architecture of

the United States handles on backwards because the "C" they recognize as "caliente" for "hot."

Fortunately I did not expend my very scarce breath to explain this ambiguity because the ambiguity walked to get to the coast, I've been dying to out of the bathroom in a cloud of steam, lavished in towels monogrammed "H," hair dripping, clutching the imported shampoo. "I am no longer used to being above the second floor," he said. "You are paying daily what I pay in a month for my apartment. I think I would go crazy in this hotel in a day or two."

and drank cerveza while our son, a musician, gave informed comments on the rhythms of the music of Boca Grande.

The faucets in the shower, however, are labeled, left to right, "C" and "H," and despite this likewise emit, left to right, hot and cold.

I pondered this riddle while gazing out of the hotel window at a huge Christmas decoration on the Cerveza Bavaria building. The problem finally yielded and I prepared a little lecture saying that the dual-control washbowl plumbing must be domestic, and the shower plumbing from the United States. The plumbers, I thought, put the United States handles on backwards because the "C" they recognize as "caliente" for "hot."

Fortunately I did not expend my very scarce breath to explain this ambiguity because the ambiguity walked

ove it," he said. "I've been drinking the water since September and I haven't had any trouble." We did as he said and suffered no ill effects. He introduced us to nispero, a fruit, to had imagined. We sat on the balcony

The next day we packed up and left Mother Hilton, and, following a plan that our son had made, took a short flight to Cartagena, on Colombia's Caribbean coast. We had brought from a library a heavy Spanish-language book on the architecture of Cartagena, and something in our brains had failed to register the words our son kept using: "I can hardly wait to get to the coast, I've been dying to go to the coast." When we got to our hotel in Cartagena, it was 81 degrees outside and the old folk opened the curtains to find that we were overlooking the beach of Boca Grande with five rows of combers sliding up it. A band was playing on the street below and we had a refrigerator already stocked with beer — both local and imported. It was the stuff of a high-school fantasy.

We all emitted pig-like sounds of satisfaction, which indicated that our son was not 100 percent committed to austerity and that his parents were not so far beyond hedonism as they had imagined. We sat on the balcony and drank cerveza while our son, a musician, gave informed comments on the rhythms of the music of Boca Grande. ∎

John Smith

Page 3's

Typical pages show variety within the basic design. Later attempts to divide the page vertically proved to be weak and lacking in focus.

Fare of the Country

Facing page: The dummy presentation of this new feature sought to emphasize the different kinds of photographs that could be used, such as this studio shot, and the kind of informational service box that would be used wherever appropriate.

The dummy presentation for the new design was made for a barebones, 28-page issue, but for the most part actual sections run much bigger. In such big sections, extra attention to the design of standing typographical elements can add sparkle and avoid a monotonous, prepackaged look. The Q and A heading, for example, offered such an opportunity for special typographical treatment, remaining, however, in the basic Bookman family.

Fare of the Country

This was one of the several new regular features added to the Travel section. In the photo used on the dummy page (see illustration) the "Scandinavian" model who is about to savor the herring is Robert Pelletier, who helped prepare the dummy. The photo was designed to encourage future designers and editors of the section to reach beyond predictable "newsy"-type photos

that come in from services or routine news photo assignments.

The idea was to encourage more designer-directed photographs, sometimes a difficult accomplishment in the tight schedule of a newsroom picture desk. Even with a large staff on a large newspaper, tight deadlines often make it expeditious to work with available pictures. Only a schedule that allows for planning ahead can make more ambitious efforts possible. A chart at the end of this chapter represents the kind of schedule that was introduced for Travel.

What's Doing

A popular part of the old Travel and Resorts section, the What's Doing In . . . feature, was retained. Readers like to cut it out and keep it on file for future use. To facilitate this, the new design specified a standard size, the top two-thirds of a page, which gives it a more or less anchored

When the plane for Bogotá was loaded at Kennedy International Airport, there were two passengers for every seat because the adults were draped with babies or toddlers; coloring books, crayons, stuffed animals, blankets and pacifiers dangled over seat backs and from shoulders.

Answer:, left to right, "C" and "H," and despite this likewise emit, left to right, hot and cold.

I pondered this riddle while gazing out of the hotel window at a huge Christmas decoration on the Cerveza Bavaria building. The problem finally yielded and I prepared a little lecture saying that the dual-control washbowl plumbing must be domestic, and the shower plumbing from the United States. The plumbers, I thought, put the United States handles on backwards because the "C" they recognize as "caliente" for "hot."

Fortunately I did not expend my very scarce breath to explain this ambiguity because the ambiguity walked out of the bathroom in a

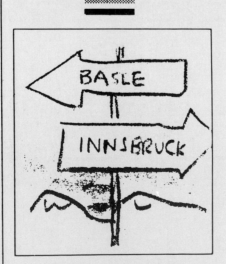

That evening, as the Feast of the Three Kings was ending, we took a walk to the centro of Bogotá. The student plunged forward into jammed streets — which looked and smelled like Mulberry Street at San Gennaro — buying us pastries, bread, juices. His Spanish was rapid, firm

position on a left-hand page among the middle pages of the section, playing against advertisements in the bottom third of the page and on all of the facing right-hand page.

As with Q and A, a special heading was designed. A scattered "spot" illustration treatment was avoided in favor of a focused, collage treatment that would combine pictures and a map to make a forceful central image.

Q and A, dummy layout
Left: One of the new smaller features that ran in small spaces among ads in the front part of the section.

What's doing in Nashville
Facing page: The dummy paste-up showed how this feature would run in a squared-off space, built around a collage center. A serviceable map became a central element.

It's the flip
past Sao
night life,
rival Rue F
a wealth of .
alongside the
glorious bea

Getting Around

When the plane for Bogotá was loaded at Kennedy International Airport, there were two passengers for every seat because the adults were draped with babies or toddlers; coloring books, crayons, stuffed animals, blankets and pacifiers dangled over seat backs and from shoulders.

When every crevice was filled, and bottles were rolling around underfoot, the cargo began to go aboard. Far below the window, a conveyor belt carried uphill a stream of chatféls that made the zoo inside the plane seem sane: cardboard cartons big enough to hold a folded Super-Bowl linebacker; long parcels that might contain prestressed-concrete columns; string bags full of basketballs; strollers and carriages; suitcases swathed in electric cord; map cases six feet long; folded playpens and walkers; stitched-up bundles that looked like bales of cotton, duffel bags and backpacks — an array to boggle the mind. The loading went on for an hour after the cabin had become a 20th-century steerage.

What I was seeing began to make sense when the man in the next seat said stolidly: "I hate this flight; it's always jammed full of kids who cry and it's always late."

What flight? The 11 A.M. to Bogotá? Any Avianca flight? A Saturday morning flight?

"What do you mean?" I asked.

"The weekend flight to Colombia in January," he replied. "On the school holidays everyone, including me, endures this five hours of bedlam to go home to see the family. And today is the worst of all, the Feast of the Three Kings."

My husband and I realized that, despite our belief that we had chosen this day at random and despite the tourist cards tucked into our passports, we were just two more lemmings on the seasonal tide that draws families together in Colombia.

In September our son had forsaken the land of ski lifts

Country Music

Fortunately I did not expend my very scarce breath to explain this ambiguity because the ambiguity walked out of the bathroom in a cloud of steam, lavished in towels monogrammed "H," hair dripping, clutching the imported shampoo. "I am no longer used to being above the second floor," he said. "You are paying daily what I pay in a month for my apart-

What's doing *in*

★ NASHVILLE ★

Tennessee

That evening, as the Feast of the Three Kings was ending, we took a walk to the centro of Bogotá. The student plunged forward into jammed streets — which looked and smelled like Mulberry Street at San Gennaro — buying us pastries, bread, juices. His Spanish was rapid, firm and assertive and our obligatory tourist anxieties about pickpockets and bad water were brushed aside. "On the bus, clutch your handbag as if you love it," he said. "I've been drinking the water since September and I haven't had any trouble." We did as he said and suffered no ill effects. He introduced us to nispero, a fruit, to cheese wrapped in banana leaves, to kumis, a yogurt sort of thing, to the local liquor aguardiente, to foods un-
Kennedy International Airport, the
two passengers for e
adults were draped w
coloring books, cray
blankets and pacifie
backs and from should
When every crevice
were rolling around
began to go aboard. F
conveyor belt carried
tels that made the zoc
sane: cardboard carto
folded Super-Bowl lin
that might contain pr
umns; string bags ful
ers and carriages; sui
tric cord; map cases
playpens and walker:
that looked like bales
and backpacks — ar
mind. The loading we
the cabin had becom
age.
What I was seeing
when the man in the ne
hate this flight; it's a
kids who cry and it's al

What flight? The 11 A.M. to Bogot kumis, a yogurt sort of thing, to the local liquor aguardiente, to foods unrecognizable but delicious, and we suffered no ill results save for the suffered no ill results save for the breath-taking effect of the altitude.

The next day we packed up and left Mother Hilton, and, following a plan that our son had made, took a short flight to Cartagena, on Colombia's Caribbean coast. We had brought from a library a heavy Spanish-language book on the architecture of Cartagena, and something in our brains had failed to register the words our son kept using.

My husband and I realized that, despite our belief that we had chosen

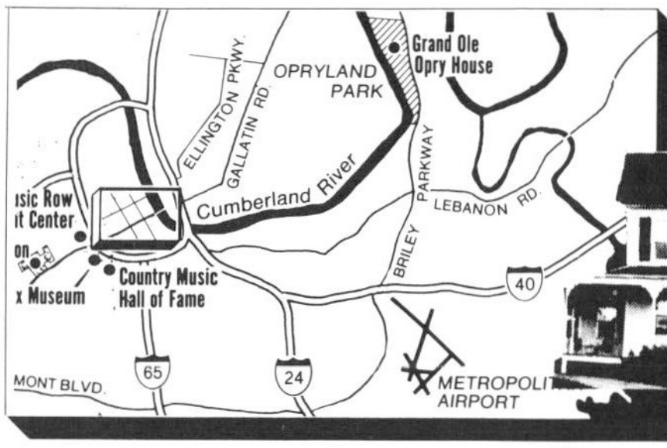

Grand Ole Opry

When the plane for Bogotá was loaded at Kennedy International Airport, there were two passengers for every seat because the adults were draped with babies or toddlers; coloring books, crayons, stuffed animals, blankets and pacifiers dangled over seat backs and from shoulders.

When every crevice was filled, and bottles were rolling around underfoot, the cargo began to go aboard. Far below the window, a conveyor belt carried uphill a stream of chattels that made the zoo inside the plane seem sane: cardboard cartons big

love it," he said. "I've been drinking the water since September and I haven't had any trouble." We did as he said and suffered no ill effects. He introduced us to nispero, a fruit, to contain prestressed-concrete columns; string bags full of basketballs; strollers and carriages; suitcases swathed in electric cord; map cases six feet long; folded playpens and walkers; stitched-up bundles that looked like bales of cotton, duffel bags and backpacks — an array to boggle the mind. The loading went on for an hour after the cabin had become a 20th-century steerage.

What I was seeing began to make sense when the man in the next seat said stolidly: "I hate this flight; it's always jammed full of kids who cry and it's always late."

"What do you mean?" I asked.

"The weekend flight to Colombia in January," he replied. "On the school holidays everyone, including me, endures this five hours of bedlam to go home to see the family. And today is the worst of all, the Feast of the Three Kings."

Where to Stay

We all emitted pig-like sounds of satisfaction, which indicated that our son was not 100 percent committed to

Customs in an instant — but our there. We were plunged

His Spanish was rapid, firm and assertive and our obligatory tourist anxieties about pickpockets and bad water were brushed aside. "On the bus, clutch your handbag as if you to get to the coast, I've been dying to go to the coast." When we got to our hotel in Cartagena, it was 81 degrees outside and the old folk opened the

enough to hold a folded Super-Bowl year of study in Colombia, and we were on our way to Bogotá to see him.

When the airborne bedlam had gone on for five hours and we were still in the air, I stood in the aisle for the rest of the flight — about an hour — to salvage myself from permanent folding, spindling and mutilation. When we landed at Eldorado Airport, we got through Customs in an instant — but our son was not there. We were plunged into an anarchy

Where to Eat

The tone of the aerograms from Bogotá had left some doubt that our son would be eager to have us stay at the Hilton; he was ever more concerned about poverty and imperialism. On the other hand, it had been easy to reserve a room at the Hilton while still in New York, and memories of the days when the student was a constant author of steamy bathrooms and soggy towels indicated that a hot

Kennedy International Airport, two passengers for every seat bec adults were draped with

shower might be a drawing card after four months.

Soon after we got settled at the hotel, our son arrived, explaining in five rows of combers sliding up it. A band was playing on the street below and we had a refrigerator already stocked with beer — both local and imported. It was the stuff of a high-school fantasy.

What flight? The 11 A.M. to Bogotá? Any Avianca flight? A Saturhad imagined. We sat on the balcony and drank cerveza while our son, a musician, gave informed comments on the rhythms of the music of Boca Grande.

Shopping

My husband and I realized that, despite our belief that we had chosen this day at random and despite the tourist cards tucked into our passports, we were just two more lemmings on the seasonal tide that draws families together in Colombia.

In September our son had forsaken the land of ski lifts and longies for a year of study in Colombia, and we were on our way to Bogotá to see him.

When the airborne bedlam had gone

of the flight — about an hour — to salvage myself from permanent folding, spindling and mutilation. When we landed at Eldorado Airport, we got through Customs in an instant — but our son was not there. We were plunged into an anarchy of cabbies. We managed to make some sort of deal and climbed into a car, grappling for our phrase books while speaking a word that required no translation: "Hilton."

Night Life

While I attempted to adjust to the altitude (8,700 feet), I had time to study the palaces that the Hilton rents for rooms in Bogotá: The faucets on the washbowls are labeled, left to right, "C" and "F." Left to right, they emit hot and cold water, as one expects.

The faucets in the shower, however, are labeled, left to right, "C" and "H," and despite this likewise emit, left to right, hot and cold.

I pondered this riddle while gazing out of the hotel window at a huge Christmas decoration on the Cerveza Bavaria building. The problem finally yielded and I prepared a little lecture saying that the dual-control washbowl plumbing must be domestic, and the shower plumbing from the United States. The plumbers, I thought, put the United States handles on backwards because the "C" they recognize as "caliente" for "hot."

For the Kids

That evening, as the Feast of the Three Kings was ending, we took a walk to the centro of Bogotá. The student plunged forward into jammed streets — which looked and smelled like Mulberry Street at San Gennaro — buying us pastries, bread, juices. His Spanish was rapid, firm and assertive and our obligatory tourist anxieties about pickpockets and bad water were brushed aside. "On the bus, clutch your handbag as if you love it," he said. "I've been drinking the water since September and I haven't had any trouble." We did as he said and suffered no ill effects. He introduced us to nispero, a fruit, to cheese wrapped in banana leaves, to kumis, a yogurt sort of thing, to the local liquor aguardiente, to foods unrecognizable but delicious, and we Mother Hilton, and, following a plan that our son had made, took a short flight to Cartagena, on Colombia's Caribbean coast. We had brought from a library a heavy Spanish-lansuffered no ill results save for the breath-taking effect of the altitude.

Here and There

The next day we packed up and left guage book on the architecture of Cartagena, and something in our brains had failed to register the words our son kept using: "I can hardly wait to get to the coast, I've been dying to go to the coast." When we got to our hotel in Cartagena, it was 81 degrees outside and the old folk opened the curtains to find that we were overlooking the beach of Boca Grande with five rows of combers sliding up it. A band was playing on the street below and we had a refrigerator already stocked with beer — both local and imported. It was the stuff of a high-school fantasy.

We all emitted pig-like sounds of satisfaction, which indicated that our son was not 100 percent committed to austerity and that his parents were

Feature stories

With big headlines

At least four feature stories were projected for each Travel section issue, and they were given an expansive treatment signaled by centered 60-point Bookman heads—the largest headline introduced so far in *The Times* in any section. The Travel section, with its bulk, its large, newly carved-out editorial spaces, and large photos, would carry headlines which were about two sizes larger than anything else in use in the paper at that time. To use headline type this big, the element of *scale*, discussed earlier in relation to pictures, becomes significant. It would be important to have this large type size play against other type elements of different sizes in a way that it would fit naturally into the page and not appear overbearing. To help accomplish this and to enable the editors to say more than the designated 60-point type would allow, subheads were provided as a *must*, not as an option, centered between two rules in a style unique to this section.

Bookman headlines and subheads on main features were centered, as were the department headings. But the smaller Bookman headings throughout the section were made to run flush

left, to provide a crisper, neater look and to contrast with the more important centered heads. In this instance, variety in these treatments does not to my mind become "inconsistency." Any newspaper benefits from consistency in general character, journalistic approach, and in a recognizable typographical style, but strict consistency in every detail can be a self-imposed handicap.

At the time of the design start-up, the 60-point type came off the Metroset typesetters with obviously poor letter spacing. The machines couldn't get the letter spacing tight enough and also exaggerated the inequalities of space between different combinations of letters. Set properly, the headline type could make a handsome graphic unit. But with unequal gaps between the letters, the type would appear oversize and gross and would dissipate the centered, focused look. Here, proper execution makes significant differences in whether a design works or fails. Bob Pel-

letier's extra effort helped make the design work. (Later, more sophisticated typesetting equipment was able to do the job.) Bob manually spaced the 60-point type instead of using the formatted keys, or sometimes he got the composing room staff to improve spacing in the paste-up. It was necessary for the editors to cooperate in generating these few words early in the schedule to facilitate this extra effort.

Scale: hooray for broadsheets

The El Camino Real double spread (see illustration) tried to take full advantage of the broadsheet page size to give a wealth of information in an efficient poster-size presentation. A map on the spread, almost 21 inches high, provided the reader with easy-to-find details, rivaling in usefulness almost any map available.

In this section, we began to fully exploit the

Brazil's Other Exotic

NORMAL

Brazil's Other Exotic Ci

KERNED

Letterspace

Shown is 60-point Bookman, reproduced in the actual headline size in the Travel section. Proper letterspacing becomes even more critical than usual in the big sizes. Top spacing is normal; the bottom is kerned for tighter, more equal spacing.

Dummy layouts

Facing page: With the large Bookman head, the subhead treatment between rules, and the oversize Franklin Gothic initials, the pages suggest magazine treatment. Captions are a generous 12-point Bookman, a departure from the previously used 8¾-point bold text face, Imperial. The large headings were to be written succinctly, so as not to overwhelm everything below.

155

horizontal half page, particularly two horizontal half pages running across the top of a spread. Since travel advertising seems to lend itself to these horizontals, the flexibility of the advertising makes this kind of arrangement frequently possible.

Big, black Franklin Gothic initials set into the main texts break up the gray masses of text type and help establish a sense of scale. Their exceptional size relates to the size of the Bookman heads, while their weight provides a sans serif blackness which sets off and plays against the delicacy in the design of the Bookman characters.

Service elements

The dummy projected a service box of some kind for each of the main features. Often, the box includes a map with other basic information (see dummy page illustrated). Sometimes this box includes so much information that it is treated more importantly as a sidebar or as a second story in its own right with a Bookman headline.

Service information, particularly appropriate in a Travel section, provides material for design variety. The broadsheet size allows the designer to make dramatic graphic presentations out of material that otherwise might be humdrum or even forbidding.

Long listings, sometimes going on for pages, are not uncommon. Schussboomer's Sampler, designed by art director Tom Bodkin, shows how a listing can be treated attractively with appropriate typography and only small graphic accents while being arresting and lively (see accompanying illustration).

Below, in a doublespread with only routine kinds of photos to work with, the service maps are used as the unifying design device to give the pages an organized look.

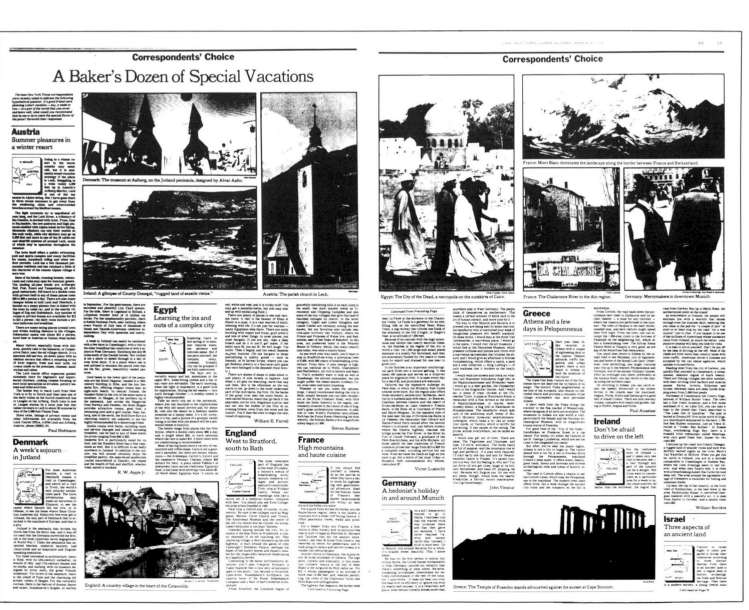

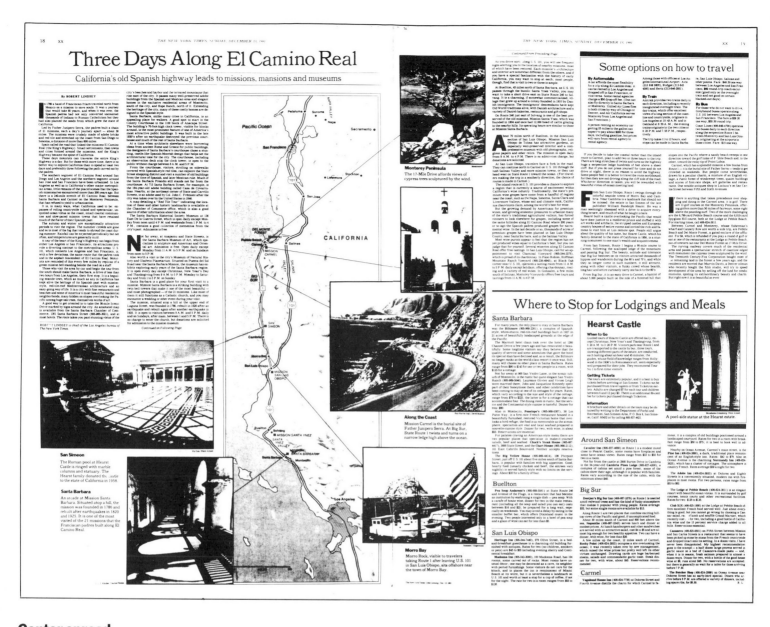

Center spread

A center spread permits the design to go across the gutter, tying the left and right pages into a single unit. The large map is intended to be used by a driver on an actual trip, with the mountains drawn in and photos whetting the browser's appetite. At bottom right is a box within a sidebar. The rules around the photos and map are weighted in favor of the photos because they are on a visual plane in *front* of the map. On the other hand, the double light rules around the map emphasize it as the centerpiece of the spread.

Scale

Facing page: The small delicate maps, acting as initials, give the photographs a sense of large-scale importance that they might not otherwise project.

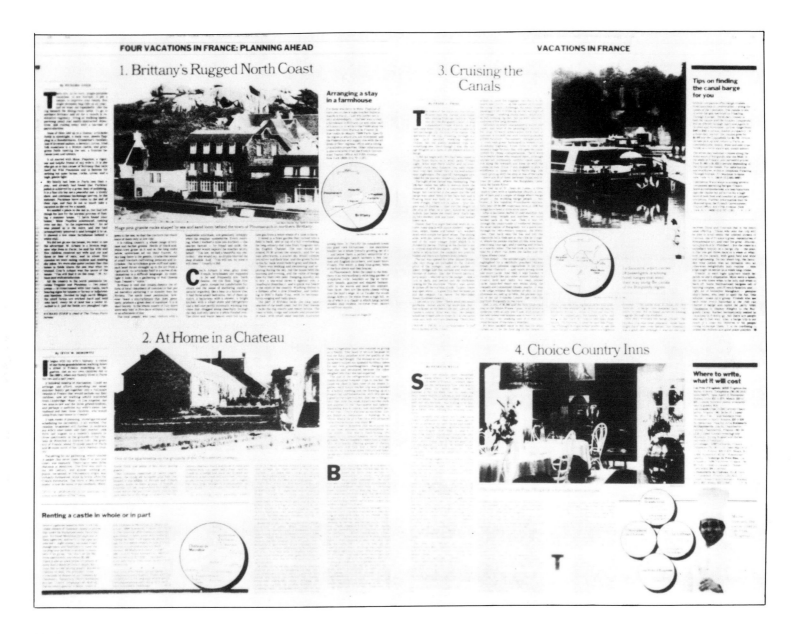

Circles

A spread, full of information, is given some design cohesion by the use of the maps in circles, providing airy relief in the rectangular grid of two pages of newspaper columns. The four little circles create a graphic punctuation mark, and enhance the scale of the first three circles.

Off-beat finale

Above: The inside back cover of the first issue shows how this final editorial space is used for an off-beat kind of article, a "surprise" ending.

Service plus

Facing page: A great deal of information about 42 resorts is handled simply and eloquently for easy reading. The little black silhouettes act almost like typographical dingbats, at home with the static rules but conveying interest and energy.

A Schussboomer's Sampler

Terrain descriptions, après-ski tips and more for 42 American and European resorts

The following selective listing was compiled to indicate the variety of resorts available to a ski vacationer in the coming season. It includes well-known destinations and those less renowned, but with features of interest to skiers.

The information on lodging, restaurant and après-ski activities is a sampling, intended to give a sense of the available options in each resort.

Lodging prices in the United States are given per night for two people sharing a room, unless otherwise indicated. Modified American Plan (MAP) includes breakfast and usually dinner. Prices are quoted where possible on a day rate as they are calculated by the individual resort lodging bureaus; sometimes nightly rates are available, and at other times they are obtained by dividing multiday package rates by the number of nights. Price range is for low and high season; Christmas/New Year peak prices are frequently higher. Multiday packages are usually considerably less, especially in the East during non-holiday weeks.

European prices are given for one-week packages which usually are sold in conjunction with air transportation. Unless otherwise noted, prices include breakfast and frequently dinner. Transfers from gateway airport to resort are also included. Prices quoted are per person, based on two sharing.

Claire Walter

MAINE

State Travel Bureau, 207-289-2423

Sugarloaf (Kingfield)

SKIING CHARACTERISTICS
Skiers make the long trek to west-central Maine for the only above-the-treeline skiing in the East, generally uncrowded conditions and a season that runs from mid-November to late April. The mountain is configured like a layer cake — easiest skiing on the bottom, intermediate in the middle and challenging on the top. Nearby touring center with 40 miles of trails.

LODGING
New slopeside condos ($68-90) around village mall. Sugarloaf Inn, Victorian lounge and access to upper lifts ($69-106 per person MAP, two nights). Widow's Walk, guest house ($16-22). Lumberjack Lodge, chalet-style apartment units ($40). Cathy's Place, motel ($20-30).

RESTAURANTS
Gladstone, rather elegant. Down East Ice Cream, old-fashioned parlor. Truffle Hound, full dinners. The Bag, light snacks.

APRES-SKI
Maxwell's and Jake Cassidy's for drinks and food. Gepetto's, after-ski drinks and live music. Maxwell's, evening disco and movies.

OTHER ACTIVITIES
Ice skating. Snowmobile rental.

INFO. PHONE
Snow 207-237-2000
Lodging 207-237-2861; 207-237-2000 for Mountainside Condominiums

VERMONT

Snow reports, 802-229-0531
State of Vermont Travel Division, 802-828-3236.

Bolton Valley (Bolton)

CHARACTERISTICS
Mostly beginning and intermediate skiing on this compact 1,100-vertical foot mountain, which is especially good for families. Some genuinely steep, though short, pitches are at the top. Thirty miles of cross-country trails. Night skiing 7-10, except Sunday.

LODGING
Bolton Valley Lodge, comfortable hotel adjacent to slopes ($84 per person for two days including lifts, plus optional $18 meal plan). Black Bear Lodge, rustic and small ($75 for two nights, with lifts). Trailside condo one bedroom units ($126) and larger available.

RESTAURANTS
Fireside Restaurant for country breakfasts and full dinners. Papa D's, Italian. Last Run Cafe, light meals.

APRES-SKI
Entertainment, after-ski drinks at James Moore Tavern, Last Run Cafe open till midnight.

OTHER ACTIVITIES
Teen center. Day nursery for younger children. Game rooms, saunas. In-room movies on TV. Exercise program.

INFO. PHONES
Snow 800-451-3220; 802-434-2131
Lodging 802-434-2131

Mount Mansfield (Stowe)

CHARACTERISTICS
The reputation of Stowe, thanks to a fistful of renowned precipices on mighty Mount Mansfield, is of super-expert terrain. In reality, 70 percent is for good intermediates, including nearly all the gondola-served runs and everything on Big and Little Spruce. Still, Stowe has bred, and attracts, some of the best skiers in the East. Four notable cross-country centers are are nearby.

LODGING
The Inn at the Mountain, luxurious and convenient inn ($120 MAP) and nearby townhouses. Topnotch, elegant atmosphere ($70-125). Stowehof, gracious ($66). Andersen's, small Austrian-accented motel ($48-66). Ski Inn, traditional ski lodge ($36-60). Siebeness, rustic ($40-56). Round Hearth, dorm ($18 per person).

RESTAURANTS
Lots of highly praised dining. Topnotch Stowehof and Inn at the Mountains are notable. Trapp Family Lodge, coffee shop service only this year. Foxfire, good Italian fare. Swisspot, quiche and fondue. Greenery, health food. Steen's, reasonable. Hearty skiers' breakfast at Scandinavia.

APRES-SKI
Drinks and piano at Mount Mansfield base lodge till dinner. Other spots: Three Green Doors, Whiskers, Matterhorn, Rusty Nail. Baggy Knees, live rock. Sister Kate's, live music, comedy, singalong.

OTHER ACTIVITIES
Forty-first annual Stowe Winter Carnival, Jan. 16-23. Horseback riding at Ryderbrook Stables. Snowmobile rentals. Shopping. Movie theater.

INFO. PHONES
Snow 802-253-8521
Lodging 802-253-7321

Sugarbush (Warren)

CHARACTERISTICS
Two for the price of one big-mountain skiing at the original Sugarbush and Sugarbush North (formerly Glen Ellen). Sugarbush has long beginners' chair, Gate House and Spring Fling for intermediates, and many runs off Valley House chair and gondola for experts. North has primarily novice and intermediate terrain. Free skiing first half hour each morning. Touring nearby.

LODGING
Ski-to condo village has scores of units in a variety of styles and sizes (from $70). Golden Horse, recently renovated ($30 per person, including breakfast). White Horse Inn at foot of Sugarbush North ($35 with breakfast). Sugarbush Inn, resort's most elegant ($29-100) and Sugartree Inn ($24-30 with breakfast), both modern country-style inns. Sgt. Pepper's Camp, bargain lodging for groups.

RESTAURANTS
Chez Henri, bistro. Las Cuevas, Spanish. Sam Rupert's, imaginative menu and atmosphere. Odyssey, reasonably priced family fare.

APRES-SKI
Chez Henri has disco as well as bistro. Disco too at the Valley Hideaway. Blue Tooth has been drawing action crowd for years. Downstreet, music and dancing.

OTHER ACTIVITIES
Indoor tennis, racquetball, squash, swimming, gym, saunas, whirlpool, jacuzzi and even food and drink at the sleek new Sugarbush Sports Center. Private hot tubs at Waterworks. Edison's Studio for movies, drinks and snacks.

INFO. PHONES
Snow 802-583-2381
Lodging 800-451-5030

Killington (Sherburne)

CHARACTERISTICS
An Eastern giant, Killington has over 500 acres on five peaks, a 3,060-foot vertical, snowmaking on more than half of its 75 runs and traditionally the longest season in the Northeast. Notable learn-to-ski program, special classes for good skiers who want to ski better. Snowshed, one of best learning hills around. Ramshead and Snowdon, mostly for intermediates. Great Eastern, three-and-a-half-mile gentle trail. Bear Mountain, wide, steep and mogully. Two nearby touring centers.

LODGING
Access road is flanked by lodges. Whiffletree and Edgemont, condos closest to mountain ($102-118 per person, two nights). Nearby, the new and luxurious Mountain Inn ($59-69). Chalet Killington Red Rob and Basin Lodge are casual ($30-50 MAP) Alpenhof and Pikes Lodge have rooms and dorms ($35-45 MAP). Summit Lodge, Panoramic views and many amenities ($50-60 MAP).

RESTAURANTS
Charity's 1887, popular and reasonable. Alpine Inn, Continental menu. Pasta Pot, informal Italian. Lauren's, prix fixe mostly French. Countrymen's Pleasure, Austrian and German.

APRES-SKI
Wobbly Barn and Pickle Barrel, lively at happy hour and again after dinner. Live entertainment at The Mountain Inn, Chalet Killington, Red Rob, Bilbo's and King's Four. Disco at Cortina Inn. Jazz and soft rock at Annabelle's.

OTHER ACTIVITIES
Indoor tennis. Four lodges with pools, several with saunas and whirlpools. Sleigh rides. Shopping and sightseeing in quintessential New England town of Woodstock, 15 miles.

INFO. PHONES
Snow 800-451-4301
Lodging 802-422-3711

NEW HAMPSHIRE

Snow conditions recording, 603-224-2525.

Gunstock (Laconia)

SKIING CHARACTERISTICS
Family mountain, long popular with Bostonians. Most terrain falls in intermediate range. Newly expanded top-to-bottom snowmaking on 1,400-foot vertical area has cross-country too.

LODGING
Margate, full resort motel ($50). Sheraton Inn, luxurious ($34, single). More than a thousand condo units are available for rent.

RESTAURANTS
B. Mae Denny's, New England specialties and beef. Christmas Island Steakhouse, popular and generous portions. Time Out, hometown eatery good for families.

APRES-SKI
Powderkeg Lounge at mountain draws early crowd. Later Margate for live entertainment and B. Mae Denny's for music and dancing.

OTHER ACTIVITIES
A page from Currier & Ives. Skating free on pond behind main lodge. Sliding hill for young children. Horse-drawn sleigh on weekends and holidays. Ski jumping competitions (National Nordic combined championship, Jan. 23-24). Winter carnival, Jan. 29-31, and Maple sugar festival, March 13-14.

INFO. PHONES
Snow 603-293-4341
Lodging 603-524-5531

NEW YORK

State Travel Bureau recorded ski conditions 518-474-5677 and 212-755-8100

Greek Peak (Cortland)

CHARACTERISTICS
Small mountain, just 880 vertical feet, but interesting and attractive beginners' and intermediate runs on two peaks. Night skiing till 10:30 except Sunday. Reasonable, good for families. Ski-touring center has 20 miles of trails.

LODGING
Most convenient is townhouse development at the base of the mountain. Studio units ($40-47, higher during holiday weeks). One-bedroom condos (start at $64-88). Holiday Inn, Quality Inn and other lodging in Cortland, 8 miles.

RESTAURANTS
Corinthian Trapazeria in base lodge, sit-down dinners and brunch. In Cortland, Golden Garter for seafood, Four Flags for steak and Little Italian kitchen for moderately priced dinners.

APRES-SKI
Dancing to live entertainment on weekends, recorded music on weekdays at the Taverna in the base lodge. Live entertainment in lounge of Cortland Holiday Inn. Many bars, especially near Cortland college.

OTHER ACTIVITIES
Ice skating, hockey, other sports and non-sports activities, mostly in Cortland. Second annual winter carnival, Feb. 5-7.

INFO. PHONES
Snow 607-835-3615, 800-252-9927 in New York State 800-847-6727, out of state
Lodging 607-835-6111

Hunter Mountain (Hunter)

CHARACTERISTICS
Hunter packs a lot onto a 1,600-foot vertical: 37 runs ranging from super-gentle to one of the steepest in the East, 15 lifts to handle weekend mobs and one of the biggest snowmaking systems anywhere. A midweek bargain that provides a lot of skiing less than two and a half hours' drive from New York.

LODGING
Since Hunter is mainly a weekend area, two-night per-person packages are quoted here; midweek lower. Modern Scribner Hollow ($130 MAP). The Forester and Sun View motels ($54). Villagio Resort Hotel ($112 MAP). Antonio's, old inn ($75). Clover Lodger, guesthouse ($84 MAP including lifts) Hunter Mountain Resort Ranch ($75 MAP, with bus from New York). Hunter Highlands Townhouses ($190 for one-bedroom unit, three nights).

RESTAURANTS
Many Italian restaurants, including La Griglia in Windham and Vesuvio in Hensonville. Werner's Swiss Chalet in Tannersville, highly regarded French-Swiss. Golden Rooster in Hunter, informal family place with big portions at moderate prices. Alfredo's in Hunter, steak.

APRES-SKI
Starts early with drinks at two bars in the base lodge. Crazy Richie's new and promising. The Club, piano player. Hunter House, loud live entertainment. Villagio disco and nightclub.

OTHER ACTIVITIES
Indoor tennis, indoor swimming, ice skating, snowmobile rentals and horseback riding in Hunter or nearby. Dinner theater at Sugar Maples in Maplecrest. Calendar full of special events and races at mountain, including women's pro skiing meet, Feb. 5-7.

INFO. PHONES
Snow 212-683-4933, 518-263-433
Lodging 518-263-4723, 800-631-7811 except in N.J. 201-371-4075

Whiteface (Wilmington near Lake Placid)

CHARACTERISTICS
The 3,216-foot giant on which the 1980 Olympic ski races were run is a classic Eastern mountain. Nearly half of the steep, twisting trails are rated for advanced skiers. Top-to-bottom snowmaking installed for the Games. Good, long intermediate runs and some novice terrain near the base. New day lodge. More than 100 miles of cross-country trails in region.

LODGING
Lake Placid Club Resort, newly refurbished grande dame on Mirror Lake ($36-48); own ski hill, Mount Whitney, good for beginners. Hilton ($38-48) and Holiday Inn ($36-76) modern, luxurious. Mon Amour, chalet lodge plus cottages ($22-36). Schulte's, rustic-style motel and cottages ($28-45).

RESTAURANTS
Continental cuisine at Interlaken. American and European dishes at Frederick's, Jeremiah's, Alpine Cellar and others. Cask & Cleaver, pleasant dining room of Ramada Inn.

APRES-SKI
Live entertainment at the Lake Placid Club Resort, Cristy's at the Holiday Inn, Hilton Inn lounge, and Sassafrass.

OTHER ACTIVITIES
Excellent skating, outdoors on Mirror Lake and Lake Placid Resort rink, indoors in Olympic Arena. Hockey games, ski jumping and speed skating events. Olympic bobsled rides. Dog sledding and horse-drawn sleighrides. Indoor tennis and swimming. Snowmobile rentals. Movie theater.

INFO. PHONES
Snow 518-946-7171
Lodging 518-946-2255

WYOMING

Recorded snow report, 307-777-7642
Other snow, weather and road information, 307-777-7777

Jackson Hole (Teton Village)

SKIING CHARACTERISTICS
With 3,200 skiable acres on a 4,200-foot vertical, the Hole is by many measures America's biggest. The 65-passenger tram to the summit of Rendezvous Peak opens steep bowls, ridges and perpendicular chutes that comprise challenging terrain. The Thunder, Casper and Apres-Vous sectors have genuine intermediate skiing. Also, guided out-of-bounds skiing and tremendous cross-country and mountain touring possibilities.

LODGING
Handful of lodges close to lifts. Elegant Alpenhof ($58-84, MAP), plus Sojourner ($49-59) and Inn at Jackson Hole ($55-85). Hostel-X is bargain ($24 per person). La Choumine, Tensleep and Sleeping Indian condos for up to four ($67-132). Other complexes have units accommodating up to 10 (to $275). Ramada Snow King, luxury lodge in town of Jackson, where accommodations are also available.

RESTAURANTS
Two respected restaurants are at the Inn, one is in the Alpenhof. Stockman's for beef. Mangy Moose for casual fare. Many restaurants in all price ranges in Jackson, 12 miles.

APRES-SKI
Live music at the Mangy Moose and the Taverne in the Sojourner. Dietrich's Disco for dancing. Authentic Western bars in Jackson are Million Dollar Cowboy Bar, Rancher, Silver Dollar and Shady Lady.

OTHER ACTIVITIES
Not to be missed, the day-long snowcat excursion into the winter wonderland of nearby Yellowstone Park, including Old Faithful, and the shorter ride to the 10,000-head National Elk Refuge. Swim at 8,000 feet in 105-degree water at granite Hot Springs. Indoor tennis.

COLORADO

Colorado Ski Country/USA snow, special events, weather and road conditions reports, 303-837-9907

Aspen Mountain, Buttermilk/ Tiehack and Aspen Highlands (Aspen)

CHARACTERISTICS
Aspen Mountain, a challenging 3,300-foot outcropping, is virtually synonymous with Aspen skiing. Relentlessly demanding, always interesting and one of America's skiing classics. New this year: $2.8-million snowmaking system concentrating on Spar Gulch and Little Nell. Management runs novice area at nearby Buttermilk/Tiehack. Under different ownership is Highlands, a 3,800-vertical-foot mountain with a good mixture of terrain for all ability levels. Several ski-touring centers nearby, including Ashcroft.

LODGING
Something for every taste but mostly pricey in this glamorous ex-mining town. Brass Bed, small and charming ($65-115). Aspen Meadows within-premises health club ($60-85). Boomerang, base of mountain ($64-90). Copper Horse and Endeavor, bargain dorms ($13.50-27 per person). Thousands of condo beds all over the valley. Aspen Square, Alpenblick, North of Nell among those close to town and lifts.

RESTAURANTS
Both quantity and quality abound. Copper Kettle, expensive and excellent with different cuisine nightly. Parlour Car, French. Paddy Bugatti's, "Irish-Italian." Golden Horn, Swiss. Ataat's, English. Toro's and Pablo's, Mexican. Souper Place and Firehouse Tavern, light meals. Happy Carrot, healthy.

APRES-SKI
Crystal Palace, dinner and cabaret. Hotel Jerome bar, top meeting place. Rock 'n Horse, rock disco. Sgt. Peppers, nightly entertainment. Aspen Meadows, jazz. Aviemore Arms, Scottish pub with entertainment.

OTHER ACTIVITIES
One needn't ski to enjoy Aspen's shops, galleries. Dogsled rides at Ashcroft. Swimming at many lodges. Tennis, squash and racquetball. Four movie theaters. Aspen Winterskol, Pro ski races, Dec. 3-4.

INFO. NUMBERS
Snow 303-925-1220
Aspen and Buttermilk 303-925-5300
Highlands Lodging 303-925-9000

Steamboat (Steamboat Springs)

CHARACTERISTICS
The long suit at this four-peak mountain is grand intermediate skiing, the best of which is on the upper slopes. Burgess Creek and Priest Creek sectors have a nice mix of intermediate and advanced terrain. Storm Peak's runs tend to be wide and gladed. A $3.7-million, state-of-the-art snowmaking system went in last summer. Six major touring centers are in the Steamboat region.

LODGING
Hotel accommodations at the newly expanded Sheraton (base of lifts), Holiday Inn, Ptarmigan and Ramada ($38-78). Condos at mountain include Lodge, Storm Meadows and Thunderhead ($32-52). Lower prices in town. Bristol, Harbor, Nite's Rest and Super 8, budget motels ($20-35). Within a half hour's drive, Elk River, Vista Verde and Lichen guest ranches.

RESTAURANTS
Cipriani's, elegant Italian at the mountain. Butcher Shop, Clock Tower and Cameo, Western atmosphere and beef-plus. Dos Amigos, Mexican. Gergey's, Hungarian. Bearpole Ranch, nightly buffet.

APRES-SKI
Afterglo Pub gets busy after lifts close. Tugboat, favored local hangout. Robber's Roost for live entertainment and dancing. Steamboat Landing with country-and-western music and Short Branch Saloon are top cowboy bars.

OTHER ACTIVITIES
Indoor tennis, ice skating and watching ski jumpers, all at Howelson Hill. Handball and racquet ball at athletic club. Hot springs pool in town. National Women's Ski Week, Jan. 17-23. Cowboy downhill, Jan. 20. Ranch town at its liveliest during Winter Carnival, Feb. 11-14; parade, special events.

INFO. PHONES
Snow 800-525-2501
Lodging 303-879-0740

Continued on Page 22

The section goes "live"

An advertising/configuration problem

In its seventh year, the redesigned Travel section continues to be a vehicle for lively layouts. After the initial issues, the first editor/art director team for the new section was Michael Leahy and Tom Bodkin. They, and a succession of art directors after Bodkin, demonstrated how varied the design could be within the format guidelines.

The illustration on the facing page shows one of the first issues, which was printed in 1981. With the simple bold impact of a poster, it is obvious that there is actually quite a lot going on in the page. The listing of port cities was put in as an afterthought to make the illustration more communicative and not merely decorative. Examples on this page show a few more widely varied treatments of the front page.

Format and implementation
Above: Three of the many different styles of layout and art treatment characteristic of the Travel section are shown. From left to right, a cartoon strip by Lou Myers, designed by Louis Silverstein, a collage treatment designed by Diane LaGuardia, and a poster treatment designed by Tom Bodkin.

A poster, not an illustration
Facing page: In this cover page published in the first weeks of the new design, the illustrator had difficulty visualizing the kind of poster design that was wanted. Four separate drawings were made, severely cropped, and positioned to complement each other. The listing in small type ties the four panels together and lends the weight of content to what otherwise would be a rather overblown use of an iconic image.

162

Ports of Call
Special Cruise Issue

Acapulco
Ajaccio
Alicante
Bali
Barcelona
Bermuda
Cannes
Capri
Cozumel
Djibouti
Dubrovnik
Elba
Ensenada
Funchal
Gibraltar
Haifa
Havana
Hong Kong
Honolulu
Ibiza
Istanbul
Izm

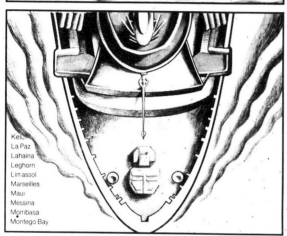

Ketc
La Paz
Lahaina
Leghorn
Limassol
Marseilles
Maui
Messina
Mombasa
Montego Bay

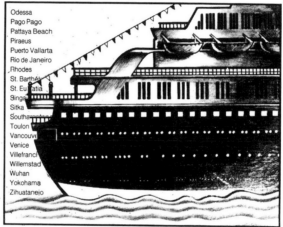

Odessa
Pago Pago
Pattaya Beach
Piraeus
Puerto Vallarta
Rio de Janeiro
Rhodes
St. Barthé
St. Eustatia
Singa
Sitka
Southa
Toulon
Vancouve
Venice
Villefranc
Willemstad
Wuhan
Yokohama
Zihuatanejo

Leslie Cabarga

A guide to 4,484 voyages on 48 lines in all parts of the world. Plus: Advice on avoiding bores on deck, by Enid Nemy / How to choose shore excursions, by Paul Grimes / And what to expect from a 'voyage to nowhere,' by Fred Ferretti. Pages 14 to 27.

The Ultimate Movable Feast

Craig Claiborne's three-state picnic adventure — Winterthur, Longwood Gardens and a crab banquet in Baltimore. Page 13.

Jean Gaumy / Magnum

Fletcher Knebel's Berlin; 'the most compelling of cities.' Page 39.

And Baby Makes Three...

on a Caribbean island. An ideal off-season vacation for one young family: renting a small house. By Frank Rich, Page 7.

Nathaniel's backyard boasted a beach

Frank Rich

163

Three-part section

The new Travel format was only a week old when an interesting variation was forced on it. The Advertising Department had committed itself earlier in the year to a special three-part section covering International, American West, and Caribbean travel. A real blockbuster, it would require each part to be separate from the others; in fact, advertising contracts had been written that way. This wreaked havoc, of course, with our carefully planned configuration and created production nightmares. More than ever, the solution demanded cooperation between the editor, Mike Leahy, the advertising make-up manager, Teddy Zaner, and myself if we wanted to give each separate part suitable bulk and display without going far beyond the editorial space allotment.

Instead of dividing the section into three parts behind the single Travel front, we settled on three distinct section fronts. There were, in effect, three Travel sections that day. Two sections were free-standing, while the third was folded into the second. Numbered consecutively, the three sections totaled 56 pages. The Sunday *Times* was even bulkier than usual that day.

Three-part section
Three separate fronts were designed to give each part maximum exposure and to honor advertising commitments, but it took a great deal of cooperative juggling to reconcile news, advertising, and production priorities.

Secret
Facing page: If there is any secret to success in the week-by-week production of the Travel section, it is in this schedule devised to help implement the new design. The Travel desk works three weeks ahead with specific page-by-page line-ups and six weeks ahead in lining up major stories. In the first months, key editors and designers met every week at a lunch meeting led by deputy managing editor Arthur Gelb, with a schedule from which design approaches could be kicked off.

	April 18	April 25	May 2
Cover graphs	Singapore & Jerusalem II Guidebooks Pentagon	Academies Jerusalem III Philadelphia Rancho	San Francisco Music chart Aggie's
Page 3 (top)	Advisory vg sc	Advisory vg ba	Advisory vg rjd
Page 3 (bottom)	Prac Fares	Prac Charters	Prac Passes
Page 4	Q&A	Q&A	Q&A
Page 6	FC Yogurt howe map	SW Parco trucco	FC Brunswick
Page 9 (top)	Guidebooks eder	Nabes bennetts WD Philly robbins Calendar	Aggie's trumbull map
Page 9 (bottom)			
Page 10	Pearl- Thompson WD Singapore hollie map	jump	SW Wedgwood rattn
Page 12	jump	FC Hungary apple	jump
Page 15	Jerusalem II wiesel Holy brilliant	Jerusalem III nusebeh + Shrines map	14-15 San Francis Harris Walks - goldberge WD - King
Page 16	jmp Holy	jump	jump
Page 19	SW Filene's	Rancho knebel map	Concerts Music chart
Pages 20, 21	jmp Guidebooks	Point feron map Middies clines map Air schmidt map	Music chart
Page 22	jump	jump	jump
Last	Pentagon halloran map	Baths treaster	Rocket stewart map
Extras	Sturbridge Rhodes Toothtrain		
Special			
	May 9 Oxford-Cambridge/ Knoxville/Italia	May 16 (Summer) Wyoming/Alps/Guard Ryokan/Summer cruise	May 23 Fleamarket/Raj- Kaye/Tuscany/ Bostoneats
	May 30 Nantucket/Vineyard Britwalks	June 6 Paris - August	June 13 (NE) Berkshires Monasteries

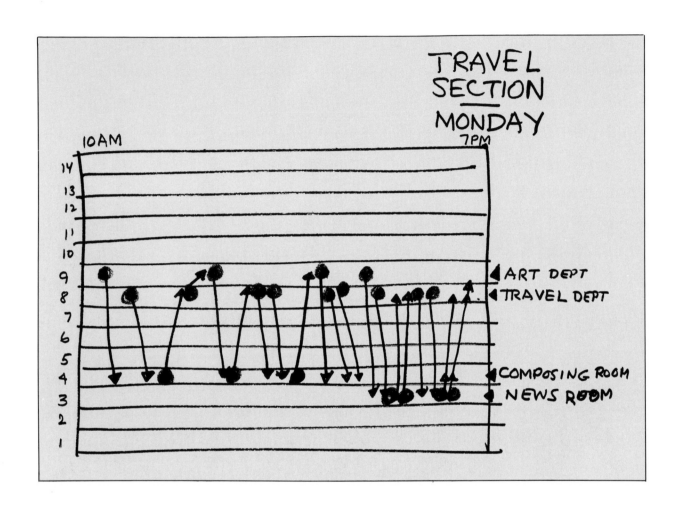

Interaction

I asked the art director of the Travel section, Diane LaGuardia, to keep track of the times in the course of one day's work when she made contact with the editors, or when the editors visited her in the Art Department, or when she went down to the composing room to supervise the paste-up of the Travel section (Monday was paste-up day). This diagram documents both her travels and the editor's travels in their cooperative effort. What does it prove? It proves: 1) The departments should be physically closer, and 2) it takes healthy cooperation between editor and designer to put out the section.

Second time around

But still not easy

The Times Metropolitan section went through two redesigns during my years in the newsroom. The first was in 1978 after The Times had expanded from two to four sections Monday through Friday. The first section was the main news section, including national and world news. Third was the newly created splashy C section, and fourth was the new Business Day. Only the second section, featuring local news but lacking a name or section heading of its own, was without its own identity.

Executive editor A. M. Rosenthal wanted to fill the gap. There were many meetings, including breakfast meetings in Rosenthal's apartment overlooking Central Park, the picture-perfect setting for talk about metropolitan news. Out of these discussions evolved the "Metropolitan Report" which ran for eight years until 1986.

The second redesign, in 1986, was a bolder, more interesting effort. But its path from meetings to realization was rocky compared to the other projects described in this book. This was because editorial considerations, predictably in this hard news section, were more demanding than in other sections; and because only a couple of months into the new design, newsroom management changed as A. M. Rosenthal retired and Max Frankel took over, bringing to the newsroom new points of view. While the broad outline and many of the features of the new design pre-

vailed, other aspects were dropped or changed. The illustrations in this chapter reflect prevailing ideas as well as some of the dead ends in the design process.

Background—the "Second Front"

When The Times was a smaller, simpler, two-part paper, broken into two parts mostly for production reasons, the first page of the second part of the paper carried only a smaller Old English logo, no other title, and a general adherence to the typestyle and make-up of Page One. The front page of the second section was referred to as the "Second Front."

When Rosenthal was assistant managing ed-

The "Second Front" before redesign
The content of the page and the horizontal look signaled a feature treatment contrasting with the basically vertical look of other news pages of The Times. Although surveys showed the News Summary and Index to be one of the most popular features in the paper in this easily accessible spot, it was moved to Page 2A for the offsetting gain of a full Metropolitan front page.

168

itor and Arthur Gelb was Metropolitan editor, around 1960, under executive editor Turner Catledge, they gave the page a new dimension, building it around a news feature centerpiece, pushing for more creative coverage. Both Rosenthal and Gelb had been distinguished Metropolitan editors themselves in their careers at *The Times*, and for this reason, their interest may have been even sharper than might be expected. They were responsible for getting an art person to move his desk from the Art Department (then on the eighth floor) to the News Department on the third, primarily so that Gelb could personally supervise the shaping of the page and help give it the visual interest he desired. The art person was Bill Scott, and he became in effect the art director for the page, working with the editors in the newsroom—often a swarm of them. It was a tough assignment. With perhaps one hour to design the first three pages and get the pictures off to engraving, buzzing around Bill's shoulders at 6 P.M. one would ordinarily find the photo editor, the make-up editor for the Metropolitan desk, the assistant managing editor, and the Metropolitan editor, not to mention various deputies. It was, and still is, a job that combines frustration with some power. After all, Scott was the only one involved who could actually produce the layout.

The Index and Summary ran in the bottom third of the page. Even with this mortgaged space, the page became the Second Front, a page with a character. In the whole daily news report, this was the place where the reader could expect to see a feature kind of picture, sometimes a silhouette, larger than anywhere else in the paper. Although I was asked to modernize the Index and Summary in the late 1960s, the top two-thirds of the page retained the basic character of the Second Front created by Gelb and Rosenthal.

Let's shift now to the middle of 1985. A new Metropolitan editor, John Vinocur, has recently been installed, with a new assistant editor, Sam Roberts. Rosenthal is executive editor, Seymour Topping is managing editor, Gelb is deputy managing editor. Everyone wants the Metropolitan Report to have a harder news edge. By now the original art director has been spread thin in the newsroom with other duties, and the new editors want an art director of their own, to do for the Metropolitan section on a daily basis what art directors have done in all the other sections of *The Times*. The editors want more space as well as a new philosophic approach and a new format design that will rescue the front page from the uneasy daily efforts to be newsy like Section A while maintaining some news feature aspect in the tradition of the Second Front.

In what proves to be the last major change in the daily paper made before his retirement, executive editor Rosenthal enlists Gelb's and my help in shaping a new Metropolitan section. I had just retired as assistant managing editor but was continuing to work for *The Times* as a consultant to The New York Times Company. There was a round of meetings with Vinocur and Roberts. At first the framework of the discussion was "The content is okay; make the section look better." But our mandate was widened around the principle that a major change in a major section could hardly be done effectively without modifying or adding to the content. Specifically, it seemed to me that as hard-hitting as the news report was becoming, areas of insights, information, and service material about the tri-state area needed to be tapped or presented better.

Newsroom

One wing of *The New York Times* newsroom shows the news desk and copy editors looking toward the photo desk in the rear.

First roughs

A harder-working summary

At the time we started work on the redesign, it was considered that the News Summary and Index would remain in the bottom third of the page, where it had been a popular fixture for many years. For a long time we in the News Department had weighed the option of moving the Summary elsewhere in order to gain a full front page for the Metropolitan section. But we knew that the Summary in that position was one of the most read features in the paper and were reluctant to move it.

The first layouts (see illustrations) attempted to make a more vital page, while retaining the Summary. However, the Summary needed to be redesigned to give it a more active part on the page.

Titles

The title was made bigger, to give it a strength equal to the daily themed sections. Rather than going to another face, it remained in Bookman in order to tie it into the hard news sections—A and D (Business Day). I proposed the name change from "Metropolitan Report" to "Metropolitan News" for two reasons: First, it read faster and sounded snappier and less oblique, going along with our desire to make it a harder-hitting news section. The second reason was visual: The shorter title gave the heading more impact; even one syllable less made it graphically more succinct.

"Metro Highlights"

The Metropolitan items were pulled out of the regular listing and emphasized under the strong heading "Metro Highlights"—one of several experimental efforts to manipulate the elements in the News Summary to make it possible to keep the Summary on the page and at the same time strengthen the "Metro" presence on the page.

Alternate treatments

In an alternate layout, Metropolitan items were removed from the News Summary and placed down the side with emphasis on the tri-state scope of the section, providing a double benefit. The Highlights become an active part of the Metropolitan news report instead of being part of a Summary that refers to the paper as a whole. Without the Metropolitan items, the remaining Summary takes up less space, providing more space in the top part of the page for stories and pictures.

In another layout, the Summary and the Metropolitan Highlights were reversed, with Metropolitan Highlights fitting at the bottom of the page as part of the Metropolitan coverage under the overall Metropolitan News page heading. A particularly logical solution, it consolidated Metro material in one major block on the page from top to bottom.

The World and National Summary and Index went down the side of the page. Since a significant part of the national report appeared in the B section as well as in A, the World and National Summary can be thought to refer back to A and forward to the inside of B. The Summary was made a little wider to roughly accommodate the required number of words.

First rough

Facing page: The initial approach tried to keep the Summary and Index material on the page, with the typography vitalized and with Metro Highlights pulled out of the Index and given extra display, echoing the theme of the section. The section heading at the top, though more emphatic than in the past, goes across the full width of the page as before.

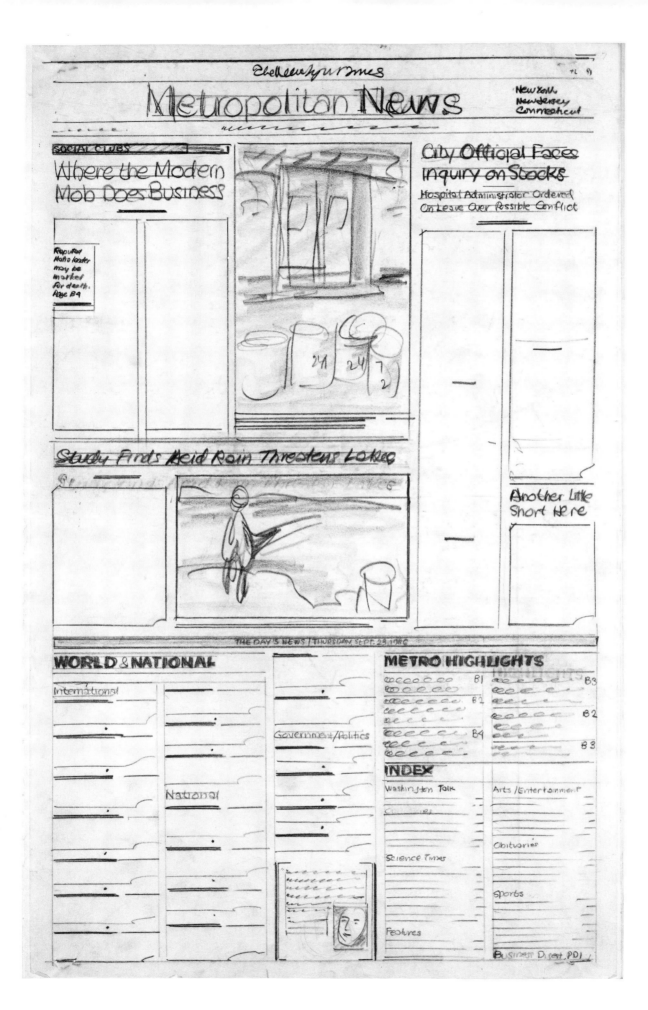

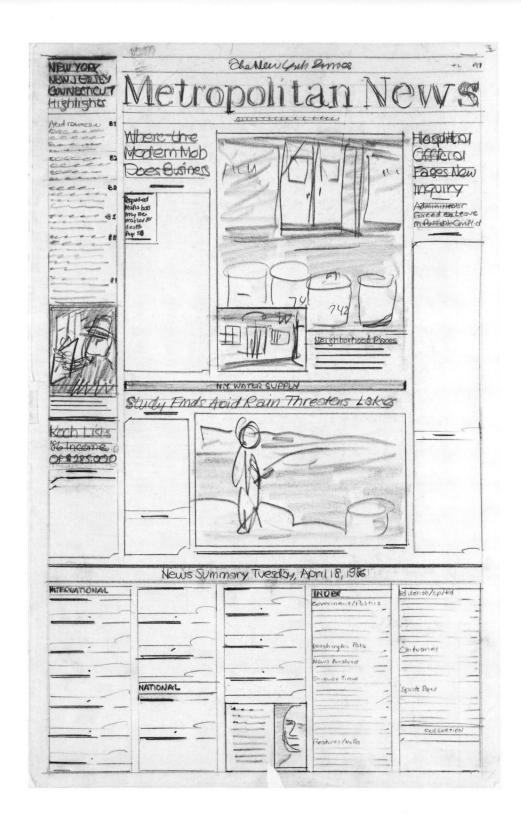

Summary variation

Above: Metropolitan Highlights are pulled out of the Summary and Index and are given a prominent place in the upper left corner, where the words "New York," "New Jersey," and "Connecticut" do double duty in referring both to the highlights and to the scope of the section. The highlights act also as reefers to inside stories.

Reversal

Facing page: Here Metropolitan Highlights fills out the bottom of the page, with a World and National Summary running down the left and the Index filling out the left column at the bottom. The column is made wider to accommodate the approximate number of words previously used. A new bracket treatment is suggested for the quotation.

172

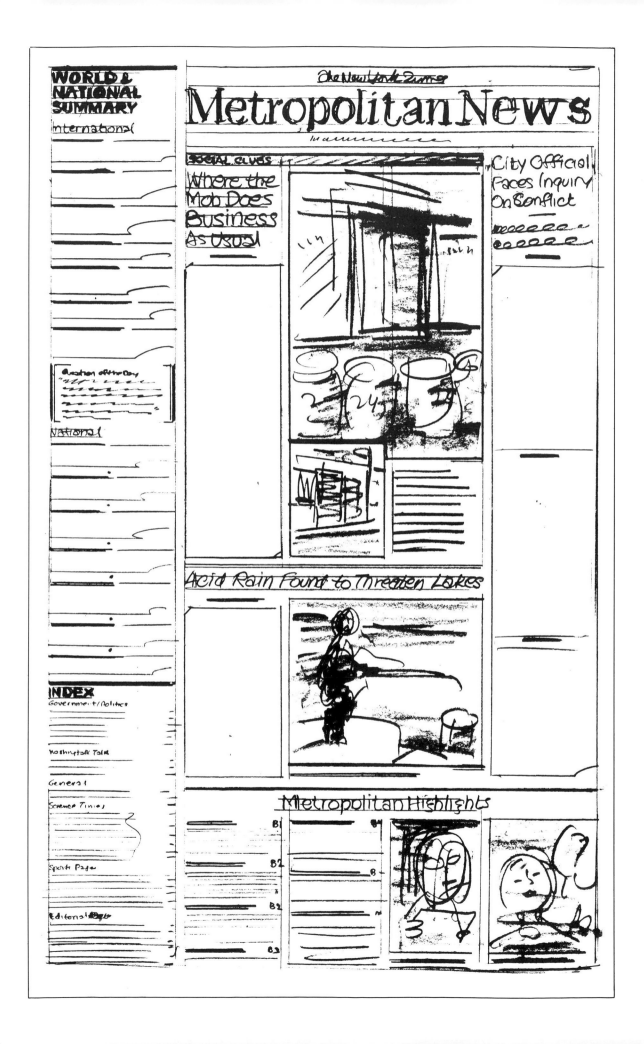

Interest in a new Metropolitan section seemed to increase as the project developed. From the Business people came an agreement to invest in a larger newshole for the section. Part of the additional space would be gained by moving the Summary and Index off the page and onto Page 2 of Section A, one of several options bandied about for years, now, suddenly, agreed upon. With the whole front page of Section B now open for Metro material, a new design approach was needed.

By this time, the idea of adding to the mix of the content was beginning to take hold. Vinocur and Roberts produced samples of six different columns or departments, each to run on a different day. These columns, capped with appropriate headings, were designed into the extreme left-hand column of the page. When the new design went live, the columns appeared under the label "Column One." Ultimately the column heading was changed with a small reefer box running at the top of the column.

Nameplate

As seen in the roughs, an initial dummy page kept the idea of a very big section title fitting flush left and right in the available space. This page was strongly visual; the large heading seemed consistent with the concept of a strong graphic impact.

Metropolitan
Metropolitan

Graphic spacing
Top: For a nameplate, even more than in such headlines as described in the Travel section (Chapter 6), a graphic look is important. Type in normal spacing, from the Metroset typesetter, has too much letterspacing. Bottom: Taking some of the space out (kerning) makes the head more cohesive and graphic.

Dummy page No. 1
Facing page: The decision to move the Summary and Index off the page led to new designs. This layout shows a strongly graphic approach, in keeping with the C sections. Running a column up the side gives the section its own structural character. Thus, each section of the four-section paper would have a different structure, united by a general typographical style. The pictures at the bottom could be reefers or stand-alones. Cheltenham Bold Condensed is introduced in the extreme right news story to emphasize the news character (echoing the condensed feeling of Latin Condensed on Page 1A).

Metropolitan News

NEW YORK, THURSDAY, JUNE 19, 1986

Ambitious

Washington strongly incess-to-be, is a fun-loving commoner with blue blood who proudly insists she will hold two jobs after marriage — one in graphic arts, the other as a royal.

Syrian officials were year-old, nick-named "Fergie," captured Prince Andrew less than nine months after they were paired up for the Royal Ascot races — reportedly by Miss Ferguson's close friend, Princess Diana.

On June 20, 1985, when they were first photographed together at Ascot, Miss Ferguson was involved in a three-year romance with Paddy McNally, a 48-year-old widower with two teen-age sons.

Running

A Details exploded in Colombo, scot races, Miss Ferguson stopped seeing McNally. Within days, she was dating Andrew, the 26-year-old second son of Queen Elizabeth II and Prince Philip.

Japanese were denialified w spent part of the Christmas holidays together but it wasn't until February that the British media first predicted that Andrew was serious about Miss Ferguson.

Those reports followed her ap-

Peter T. King, the Nassau

A Senate panel's appro week at the side of 24-year-old Princess Diana, wife of Prince Charles, the heir to the British throne. The princess and Miss Ferguson were seen first on a visit to Andrew's ship in London and then on the ski slopes at Klosters in Switzerland.

ment was announced, the couple said both intend to continue working after marriage — Andrew as an officer in the Royal Navy, Miss Ferguson as a sales executive for

Hot Issues

The military hierarchy wow...
Asked if she thought she would be able to combine a job and royal duties, she replied, "Absolutely. My job is a printing and publishing job, and since I work for myself, I have the freedom to sort of arrange things around what I do."

Six Job Corps centers in the s-to-be, is a fun-loving commoner with blue blood who proudly insists she will hold two jobs after marriage — one in graphic arts, the other as a royal.

The red-haired 26-year-old, nick-named "Fergie," captured Prince Andrew less than nine months after they were paired up for the Royal

Robert Abrams in the Novemb Nassau County Republican

Old Guard

West Virginia's economy the Ascot races, Miss Ferguson stopped seeing McNally. Within days, she was ond son of Queen Elizabeth II and Prince Philip.

An second on a computer frew spent part of the Christmas holidays together but it wasn't until February that the British media first predicted that Andrew was serious about Miss Ferguson.

Those reports followed her appearance twice in one week at the

And...

Three temblors rocked the ss Diana, wife of Prince Charles, the heir to the British throne. The Princess and Miss Ferguson were seen first on a visit to Andrew's ship in London and then on the ski slopes at Klosters in Switzerland.

interview with British television networks after the engagement, a fun-loving commoner with blue blood who proudly insists she will hold two jobs after marriage — one in graphic arts, the other as a royal.

The red-haired 26-year-old, nick-named "Fergie", captured

FINBACKS

Where the Mob Does Business As Usual

By FRANK LYNN

Investigators say that John Gotti, reputed Mafia leader, may be marked for death. B4 Page B4.

paternal grandmother, now tagu-Douglas-Scott from the f euch, Scotland's largest lando he can trace her descent to s II.

so related by marriage both Her paternal grandmother is lice, Duchess of Gloucester, uncle. Her father's first c married to Lady Jane Sp Diana's older sister.

Born in London on Oct. 15, 1959, Miss Fergus an older sister, Jane, who is married to Aust farmer and polo player Alex Makin.

She went to Daneshill boarding school nea father's 18th century farmhouse set in a 1,20(rolling Hampshire countryside at Dummer, th Hurst Lodge in Sunningdale where she excell sports rather than studies.

After school, she did a stint at St. James' secre college in London. She worked at an apartment i agency, then at a Covent Garden art gallery, a i public relations agency and most recently as a executive with B.C.K Graphic Arts in fashio Mayfair.

Miss Ferguson shares an apartment in Claphai up-and-coming neighborhood in south London, Carolyn Beckwith-Smith, whose cousin Anne lady-in-waiting to Princess Di'La.

She is an excellent cook, loves driving fast rench food and dancing. She is said to enjoy horse intend to continue working after marriage — Ar as an officer in the Royal Navy, Miss Ferguson sales executive for her graphic arts company.

Asked if she thought she would be able to coml job and royal duties, she replied, "Absolutely. My a printing and publishing job, and since I wor myself, I have the freedom to sort of arrange around what I do."

Andrew interjected, "Sarah is her own boss, s can make her own work schedules to suit herself. Miss Ferguson continued: "So when Andrew is a will work harder than when Andrew is here."

While not born a royal, Miss Ferguson is linked royal family by birth and friendship and has kno the queen's children since childhood.

Her father, Maj. Ronald Ferguson, became a friend of Prince Philip through polo and is now F Charles' polo manager.

"She is a very sweet girl. She is a very kind

Continued on Page B4

Neighbors

oppose State Attorney Gener didacy at a news confer flanked by the Nassau and Blake, respectively. Mr. Kin two children, Sean, 15, and ptroller, said yesterday that he Robert Abrams in the Nove Nassau County Republican ffolk County Republican chai

Hospital Official Faces New Inquiry

Forced on Leave Over Stock Conflict

By FRANK LYNN

Borough President Stanley Simon of the Bronx said yesterday that he had been asked to testify before a grand jury investigating leading Bronx Democrats.

"I'll testify; I'm not going to ask for immunity," Mr. Simon said. "I'm anxious to get this over with."

He said that he knew only by "rumor and innuendo" the targets of the investigation by Bronx District Attorney Mario Merola, but that he assumed he would be questioned about the Bronx Overall Economic Development Corporation, fund-raising for the borough presidential campaign last year and his ties to Stanley M. Friedman, the Bronx Democratic chairman.

"Anything Friedman has touched, they're looking into," Mr. Simon said.

Staff members of the Bronx development agency have been subpoenaed to testify before the grand jury today, said lawyers familiar with the inquiry. Mr. Friedman is chairman of the board of the agency, which under law has close ties with the Borough President's office.

Simon Appointee Testifies

Mr. Simon appointed Mr. Friedman as chairman and Kathleen L. Zamechansky as executive director of the agency which is located several floors above Mr. Simon's office in Bronx Borough Hall.

Last Friday, Mrs. Zamechansky completed about four and a half hours of testimony over four days, said her lawyer, Murray Richman, said. Mr. Richman said she had testified under immunity about the development agency and her acknowledged fund raising for Mr. Simon.

The Merola investigation, which has been described as "a fishing expedition" by several lawyers for prospective witnesses, has been under way for two months. There have been no indictments so far. Mr. Merola said last night, "I only investigate cases where we have complainants."

Marvin Raskin, the lawyer for Theodore E. Teah, secretary of the Bronx Democratic organization and a member of the City Planning Commission, said he knew of at least 20 Bronx politicians who had declined to testify before the grand jury unless granted immunity from prosecution. He said Mr. Teah was one of them.

Aide's Wife Is Questioned

Mr. Raskin said Mr. Teah's wife, Ann, a special assistant to the Board of Education, had testified with immunity in April. He said she had been questioned about her job and possible kickbacks.

Mr. Merola, who would neither confirm nor deny that many officials had refused to testify, said he was shocked at Mr. Raskin's statements about grand jury matters.

Mr. Merola's office said public officials were not required to testify, but that the Mayor could take disciplinary action. A spokesman for the Mayor, Larry Simonberg, said the Corporation Counsel

Brooklyn Activist Found of Larceny Act

Force to Leave In Stock Conflict

By JESUS RANGEL

the engagement was announced, the couple said intend to continue working after marriage — An as an officer in the Royal Navy, Miss Ferguson sales executive for her graphic arts company. sales executive for her graphic arts company.

Asked if she thought she would be able to comb job and royal duties, she replied, "Absolutely. My j a printing and publishing job, and since I worl myself, I have the freedom to sort of arrange tl

can make her own work schedules to suit her Miss Ferguson continued: "So when Andrew will work harder than when Andrew is her

While not born a royal, Miss Ferguson is lin royal family by birth and friendship and has the queen's children since childhood.

Her father, Maj. Ronald Ferguson, becam friend of Prince Philip through polo and is n Charles' polo manager.

"She is a very sweet girl. She is a very k Ferguson said in interviews after the engage announced. "She's got a great deal of comm She enjoys life to the full."

Miss Ferguson's mother, Susan, a niece aristocrat Viscount Powerscourt, divorced Fe 1974 to marry Argentine polo player Hector B

Miss Ferguson's paternal grandmother, n

Elmhirst, was a Montagu-Douglas-Scott from the f of the Duke of Buccleuch, Scotland's largest lando and through him she can trace her descent to century King Charles II.

Miss Ferguson is also related by marriage both queen and to Diana. Her paternal grandmother is cousin of Princess Alice, Duchess of Gloucester, of the queen's late uncle. Her father's first c Robert Fellowes, is married to Lady Jane Sp Diana's older sister.

Born in London on Oct. 15, 1959, Miss Fergusc an older sister, Jane, who is married to Aust farmer and polo player Alex Makin.

She went to Daneshill boarding school nea father's 18th century farmhouse set in a 1,20 rolling Hampshire countryside at Dummer, th Hurst Lodge in Sunningdale

FINBACKS

o|Blake, respectively. Mr. Kin d|two children, Sean, 15, and f|ptroller, said yesterday that he B|Robert Abrams in the Novemb Blake, respectively. Mr. Kin two children, Sean, 15, and ptroller, said yesterday that he Robert Abrams in the No (P.3)

TEMPEST'

Peter T. King, the folk County oppose State Att 2 years old, who didacy at a newsn, 12, is the first flanked by the N (P.4)

DISCOVERY

Peter T. King, the Nassau oppose State Attorney Genera didacy at a news conference flanked by the Nassau and Su

Inside
Politics

Cuomo's Petitioners henic. I am isolated and I am alone. I am never real. I play-act my life, touching and feeling only shadows. My heart and soul are touched, but the feelings remain locked away, festering inside me because they cannot find expression.

Another ever forget that I am henic. I am isolated and I am alone. I am never real. I play-act my life, touching and feeling only shadows. My heart and soul are touched, but the feelings remain locked away, festering inside me because they cannot find expression.

It is hard to be schizophrenic. It means years of struggling and fighting to overcome a disease that defies submission. Many times I have felt that I was fighting my way up a dirt hill, and as I walked the ground crumbled beneath me, and I could make no movement. After nine years I can look back through a maze of pain and fear and see that I have moved and made progress: Many of the symptoms that crippled me for years have come under some control. The totally frustrating part of this illness is that

School Board Struggle e control.
The totally frustrating part of this illness is that it is always growing, always changing. There are always new symptoms, new fears to conquer. Sometimes I get tired, and it is the weariness more than the pain that brings tears to my eyes the fierce battle that which conflicts becor

pect of schizophrenia is es on inside my head in irresolvable. I am so nd can divide on a subts subdivide over and ls like it is in pieces, and ed. At other times, I feel e my head, banging g desperately to escape only nonsense.

Problems in Production e now are different than when the illness first began but they are just as painful and just as powerful. At times my thinking about things around me becomes confused as is revealed by this entry in my journal:

Life for most schizophrenics is a nightmare full of fears and doubts about oneself and about reality; they have a distorted view of that most the fierce battle that goes on inside my head in which conflicts become irresolvable. I am so ambivalent that my mind can divide on a subject, and those two parts subdivide over and over until my mind feels like it is in pieces, and I am totally disorganized. At other times, I feel like I am trapped inside my head, banging against its walls, trying desperately to escape

Some of the symptoms I experience now are different than when the illness first began but they are just as painful and just as powerful. At times my thinking about things around me becomes confused as is revealed by this entry

Not A Winning Record s powerful. At times my thinking about things around me becomes confused as is revealed by this entry in my journal of natural.

Life for most schizophrenics is a nightmare full of fears and doubts about oneself and about reality; they have a distorted view of that most profound question of how they relate to the world around them. Boundaries become unclear and other people are frightening and not to be trusted. Thus, the very thing which could bring relief - closeness to other people - is shunned as something horrible and dangerous. For this reason it is absolutely essential to have someone to depend on, to draw the schizophrenic out of his jungle of terrors and eventually more into the less frightening world of reality.

Some of the symptoms I experience now are different than when the illness first began but

Trade Union Delighted ntial to have someone to depend on, to draw the schizophrenic out of his jungle of terrors and eventually more into the less frightening world of reality.

One of the hardest issues for me to deal with has been trust. My mind has created so many reasons to fear the real world and the people in it that trusting a new person or moving to a new level of trust with a familiar person presents a terrifying conflict that must be hammered out over and over until I can find a way to overcome my fears or in a few cases give up the battle, even if just for the time being.

Rescuing a Preserve rience now are different than when the illness first began but they are just as painful and just as powerful. At times my thinking about things around me becomes confused as is revealed by this entry in my journal of natural.

Life for most schizophrenics is a nightmare full of fears and doubts about oneself and about reality; they have a distorted view of that most profound question of how they relate to the world around them. Boundaries become unclear and other people are frightening and not to be trusted. Thus, the very thing which could it is always growing, always changing. There are always new symptoms, new fears to conquer. Sometimes I get tired, and it is the weariness more than the pain that brings tears to my

• • •

ADDED NOTES

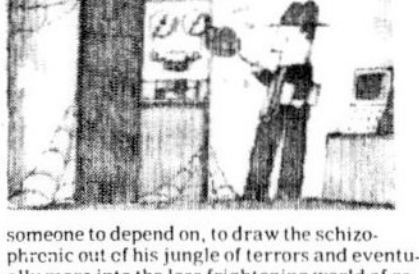

someone to depend on, to draw the schizophrenic out of his jungle of terrors and eventually more into the less frightening world of reality.

One of the hardest issues for me to deal with has been trust. My mind has created so many reasons to fear the real world and the people in it that trusting a new person or moving to a new level of trust with a familiar person presents terrifying conflict that must be hammered o clear and other people are frightening and not to be trusted. Thus, the very thing which could bring relief - closeness to other people - is shunned as something horrible and dangerous. For this reason it is absolutely essential to have someone to depend on, to draw the schizophrenic out of his jungle of terrors and eventually more into the less frightening world of reality.

One of the hardest issues for me to deal with has been trust. My mind has created so many reasons to fear the real world and the people in it that trusting a new person or moving to a new level of trust with a fa

The New York Times
NEW YORK NEW JERSEY CONNECTICUT
Metropolitan News

MONDAY, AUGUST 18, 1986

Edging Toward Power

Vallone Shows New Role for Party Leader

By JOYCE PURNICK

For this reason it is absolutely essential to have someone to depend on, to draw the schizophrenic out of his jungle of terrors and eventually more into the less frightening world of reality.

One of the hardest issues for me to deal with After nine years I can look back through a maze of pain and fear and see that I have moved and made progress: Many of the symptoms that crippled me for years have come under some control. The totally frustrating part of this illness is that it is always growing, always changing. There are always new symptoms, new fears to conquer. Sometimes I get tired, and is the weariness more than the pain that brings tears to my eyes.

The most wearing aspect of schizophrenia the fierce battle that goes on inside my head which conflicts become irresolvable. I am s ambivalent that my mind can divide on a subject, and those two parts subdivide over an over until my mind feels like it is in pieces, an I am totally disorganized. At other times, I feel like I am trapped inside my head, banging against its walls, trying desperately to escape while my lips can utter only nonsense.

Some of the symptoms I experience now ar different than when the illness first began be they are just as painful and just as powerful. / times my thinking about things around me becomes confused as is revealed by this entry

Life for most schizophrenics is a nightmare full of fears and doubts about oneself and about reality; they have a distorted view of that most profound question of how they relate to the world around them. Boundaries become unclear and other people are frightening and not to be trusted. Thus, the very thing which could bring relief - closeness to other people - is shunned as something horrible and dangerous For this reason it is absolutely essential to have someone to depend on, to draw the schizophrenic out of his jungle of terrors and eventually more into the less frightening world of reality.

One of the hardest issues for me to deal wit has been trust. My mind has created so man reasons to fear the real world and the people

The New York Times / A.J. Sundstrom

8:00 For e only. The copy you are reading is for style only, it is only to give color tyle for captions in the regular news section of the paper. No dummy copy ake editorial sense. For place only. The copy you are reading is for style out and not to. This is the style for captions in the regular news section of the

phrenic out of his jungle of terrors and event ally more into the less frightening world of r ality.

One of the hardest issues for me to deal wi has been trust. My mind has created so mar reasons to fear the real world and the people it that trusting a new person or moving to a ne level of trust with a fa

Some of the symptoms I experience now ar different than when the illness first began b they are just as painful and just as powerful. times my thinking about things around me t comes confused as is revealed by this entry my journal:

Life for most schizophrenics is a nightma full of fears and doubts about oneself and abo

8:45 The copy you are reading is for style ons in the regular news section of the sense. For place only. The copy you

12:00 ly, it is only to give aper. No dummy copy e reading is for style

4:00 the layout and not to. This is ded to look correct but not to is only to give color to the la

MY OLD TOWN

By PETER MAAS

Secaucus, Where is Thy Smell?

THERE another ever forget that I ar henic. I am isolated and I am alone. am never real. I play-act my life, touc ing and feeling only shadows. My hea and soul are touched, but the feelings rema locked away, festering inside me because the cannot find expression.

Life for most schizophrenics is a nightmar full of fears and doubts about oneself and abo reality; they have a distorted view of that mo profound question of how they relate to th world around them. Boundaries become u clear and other people are frightening and n to be trusted. Thus, the very thing which cou bring relief - closeness to other people - shunned as something horrible and dangerou For this reason it is absolutely essential to hav someone to depend on, to draw the schiz phrenic out of his jungle of terrors and event ally more into the less frightening world of r ality.

One of the hardest issues for me to deal wi has been trust. My mind has created so mar reasons to fear the real world and the people it that trusting a new person or moving to a ne level of trust with a familiar person presents terrifying conflict that must be hammered o over and over until I can find a way to overcom my fears or in a few cases give up the battl even if just for the time being.

Some of the symptoms I experience now a different than when the illness first began b they are just as painful and just as powerful. times my thinking about things around me t comes confused as is revealed by this entry my journal of natural.

Life for most schizophrenics is a nightma full of fears and doubts about oneself and abo reality; they have a distorted view of that mo profound question of how they relate to th world around them. Boundaries become u clear and other people are frightening and n to be trusted. Thus, the very thing which cou bring relief - closeness to other people - shunned as something horrible and dangerou For this reason it is absolutely essential to hav someone to depend on, to draw the schiz phrenic out of his jungle of terrors and event ally more into the less frightening world of r ality.

Life for most schizophrenics is a nightma full of fears and doubts about oneself and abo

world around them. Boundaries become u clear and other people are frightening and n to be trusted. Thus, the very thing which cou bring relief - closeness to other people - shunned as something horrible and dangerou For this reason it is absolutely essential to hav someone to depend on, to draw the schiz phrenic out of his jungle of terrors and event ally more into the less frightening world of r ality.

One of the hardest issues for me to deal wi has been trust. My mind has created so mar reasons to fear the real world and the people it that trusting a new person or moving to a ne level of trust with a familiar person presents terrifying conflict that must be hammered o over and over until I can find a way to overcom my fears or in a few cases give up the battl even if just for the time being.

Some of the symptoms I experience now a different than when the illness first began b they are just as painful and just as powerful. times my thinking about things around me t comes confused as is revealed by this entry my journal:

Life for most schizophrenics is a nightma full of fears and doubts about oneself and abo

EVERYONE it is hard to be schi: phrenic. It means years of struggli and fighting to overcome a disea that defies submission. Many time have felt that I was fighting my way up a d hill, and as I walked the ground crumbled l neath me, and I could make no movemer After nine years I can look back through a ma of pain and fear and see that I have moved a made progress: Many of the symptoms tł crippled me for years have come under so control. The totally frustrating part of this ness is that it is always growing, always char ing. There are always new symptoms, r fears to conquer. Sometimes I get tired, an is the weariness more than the pain that brir tears to my eyes.

New Report Warns of Revenue Problems

State Official Cites 1986 Tax Shortfall

By JANE GROSS

One of the hardest issues for mind has created so many reasons to fear the real world and the people in it that trusting a new person or moving to a new level of trust with a familiar person presents a terrifying conflict that must be hammered out over and over until I can find a way to overcome my fears or in a few cases give up the battle, even if just for the time being.

This is a test for the newspaper can ever forget that I am schizophrenic? I am isolated and I am alone. I am never real. I play-act my life, touching and feeling only shadows. My heart and soul are touched, but the feelings remain locked away, festering inside me because they cannot find expression.

It is hard to be schizophrenic. It means years of struggling and fighting to overcome a disease that defies submission. Many times I have felt that I was fighting my way up a dirt hill, and as I walked the ground crumbled beneath me, and I could make no movement. After nine years I can look back through a maze of pain and fear and see that I have moved and made progress: Many of the symptoms that crippled me for years have come under some control. The totally frustrating part of this illness is that it is always growing, always changing. There are always new symptoms, new fears to conquer. Sometimes I get tired, and it is the weariness more than the pain that brings tears to my eyes.

One of the hardest issues for me to deal with has been trust. My mind has created so many reasons to fear the real world and the people in it that trusting a new person or moving

The most wearing aspect of schizophrenia is the fierce battle that goes on inside my head in which conflicts become irresolvable. I am so ambivalent that my mind can divide on a subject, and those two parts subdivide over and over until my mind feels like it is in pieces, and I am totally disorganized. At other times, I feel like I am trapped inside my head, banging against its walls, trying desperately to escape while my lips can utter only nonsense.

Some of the symptoms I experience now are different than when the illness first began but they are just as painful and just as powerful. At times my thinking about things around me becomes confused as is revealed by this entry in my journal:

Life for most schizophrenics is a nightmare full of fears and doubts about oneself and about reality; they have a distorted view of that most profound question of how they relate to the world around them. Boundaries become unclear and other people are frightening and not to be trusted. Thus, the very thing

Indictment On Minority Contracts

By JANE GROSS

One of the hardest issues for me to deal with has been trust. My mind has created so many reasons to fear the real world and the people in it that trusting a new person or moving to a new level of trust with a familiar person presents a terrifying

One of the hardest issues for me to deal with has been trust. My mind has created so many reasons to fear the real world and the people in it that trusting a new person or moving to a new level of trust with a familiar person presents a terrifying conflict that must be hammered out over and over until I can find a way to overcome my fears or in a few cases give up the battle, even if just for the time being.

This is a test for the newspaper can ever forget that I am schizophrenic? I am isolated and I am alone. I am never real. I play-act my life, touching and feeling only shadows. My heart and soul are touched, but the feelings remain locked away, festering inside me because they cannot find expression.

It is hard to be schizophrenic. It means years of struggling and fighting to overcome a disease that defies submission. Many times I have felt that I was fighting my way up a dirt hill, and as I walked the ground crumbled beneath me, and I could make no movement. After nine years I can look back through a maze of pain and fear and see that I have moved and made progress: Many of the symptoms that crippled me for years have come under some control. The totally frustrating part of this illness is that it is always growing, always changing. There are always new symptoms, new fears to conquer. Some-

Main part of the page

More basic than any other question was what typography to use for the headlines in the section. It was necessary to keep some relationship to the hard news treatment in the preceding Section A, but at the same time it was clear that a modernized Section B would have to reflect some of the more contemporary-looking changes we had successfully introduced in the C sections, Business Day, the Sports report, and in the Sunday sections. In particular, one had to consider Business Day, where I felt we had achieved a graceful transfer from old to new in the headline style (see illustration). All headlines were Bookman, flush left, a departure from Section A. But the design of headings, banks, and subheads retained what I thought was the most essential journalistic characteristic of the headlines on the front page and allowed space for as many words as necessary to write a reasonably communicative headline.

Since Business Day typography worked so well, why not simply use the same typography for the Metropolitan section? Unfortunately the all-Bookman approach seemed too bland for the contemplated hard-hitting Metropolitan News. All-Bookman seemed to work for business news, but for the miscellaneous nature of city news, particularly following on the heels of Section A with its wide assortment of type faces, we needed a broader typographical palette.

The headline in the lead column on the right (see page 175) reflects one of many experiments to achieve the broader palette. The typeface is Cheltenham Bold, the italic of which is traditionally used on Page One and on hard news pages of *The Times*. Here the type is condensed about 10 percent to fit in more characters and also to suggest the squeezed feeling of Latin Condensed, the headline style that remains the chief visual trademark of *The Times* front page. In addition, the condensed type seems to suggest a newsy urgency.

The news feature in the center has the quieter Bookman treatment. In several places, Franklin Gothic is introduced in small sizes as a black accent, continuing a trend started with Business Day and carried on in the Sports pages and other parts of the paper.

A strong bottom of the page

Somewhere on the page, usually at the bottom, the dummy visualizes some kind of treatment other than just straight news. In one dummy, this consists of three photos, which could with their captions be reefers to stories on the inside of the section (illustration on page 175). Reverse panels (white letters on black background strips) for label heads would signal the special character of this element. Everyone from the executive editor down saw an exciting vitality in this proposed design, but the reverse strips struck some editors as being "too much" for the daily paper, too much blackness or perhaps simply too much of a resemblance to other papers. In addition, concern arose about the very big nameplate; therefore, in subsequent proposals, the size of the section title was reduced.

Dummy page No. 2

Facing page: The title heading is reduced to fit more quietly into the paper as a whole. Cheltenham Bold italic, one of our existing typefaces, has been adapted to a new one-column news treatment. Because it lacks vertical thrust, four lines are used in the headline to provide the *mass* required for the top of the page. Headlines are always flush left, abandoning the ladder sidestep of the 1A style. An essay, commissioned from an outside writer, is suggested for the bottom of the page. Franklin Gothic accents are used. The "Edging Toward Power" spread attempts to show how a "take" of pictures could be exploited to make a *picture story* with added sequential interest that, in addition, advances the idea of the story.

CUOMO AND LILCO SIGN A NEW ACCORD TO SHUT SHOREHAM

A SHIFT BY THE GOVERNOR

Agreement Does Not Require Legislative Approval — P.S.C. Will Set Rates

By PHILIP S. GUTIS
Special to The New York Times

ALBANY, Feb. 28 — In a major reversal, Gov. Mario M. Cuomo signed a new agreement today with the Long Island Lighting Company to close the $5.5 billion Shoreham nuclear power plant without the approval of the State Legislature.

The settlement is virtually identical to Mr. Cuomo's original plan to close the plant, which died after the Legislature refused to approve it, calling its guaranteed rate increases too expen-

A

A.T.&T. And Zenith In TV Deal

First Major Effort By U.S. Concerns in High-Definition Area

By CALVIN SIMS

The American Telephone and Telegraph Company and the Zenith Electronics Corporation yesterday announced a joint agreement to develop a system for high-definition television, which provides pictures twice as sharp as existing television.

The A.T.&T.-Zenith partnership is the first major effort among United States companies to compete with the Japanese and the Europeans in the emerging high-definition television business, which is expected to generate $50 billion in annual revenues by the year 2000.

B

Hospital Official Faces New Inquiry

Forced on Leave Over Stock Conflict

By FRANK LYNN

Borough President Stanley Simon of the Bronx said yesterday that he had been asked to testify before a grand jury investigating leading Bronx Democrats.

"I'll testify; I'm not going to ask for immunity," Mr. Simon said. "I'm anxious to get this over with."

He said that he knew only by "rumor and innuendo" the targets of the investigation by Bronx District Attorney Mario Merola, but that he assumed he would be questioned about the Bronx Overall Economic Development Corporation, fund-rais

C

New Report Warns of Revenue Problems

State Official Cites 1986 Tax Shortfall

By JANE GROSS

One of the hardest issues for nind has created so many reasons to fear the real world and the people in it that trusting a new person or moving to a new level of trust with a familiar person presents a terrifying conflict that must be hammered out over and over until I can find a way to overcome my fears or in a few cases give up the battle, even if just for the time being. This is a test for the newspaper can

D

One-column heads

(**A**) is the traditional *New York Times* one-column headline that runs on Page 1A, featuring *The Times* trademark Latin Condensed. (**B**) is the contemporary one-column treatment for Business Day, featuring all Bookman. (**C**) is one of the proposed headlines for the new Metropolitan section. The Cheltenham Bold Condensed picks up the condensed appearance of Latin Condensed, yet has a somewhat modern appearance in upper and lower case and in the high x-height, (height of lower-case x, a, o, n, and similar characters in relation to the capitals and letters with descenders and ascenders). Four lines provide more weight and allow more space for words. (**D**) is the one-column head finally used in the Metropolitan News section, the same Cheltenham Bold italic commonly used in hard news but used here flush left with the new strength of the four-line treatment, plus a two-line bank in the same face.

Dummy page No. 3

Facing page: The main effort here is to demonstrate the kind of graphic treatment that could be used at the bottom of the page. In addition, a harder-working picture caption treatment in Bookman is suggested for the regular run of pictures, with a Franklin Gothic lead-in.

Inside Politics

The New York Times
NEW YORK
NEW JERSEY
CONNECTICUT
Metropolitan News
MONDAY, AUGUST 18, 1986

Cuomo's Petitioners henic. I am isolated and I am alone. I am never real. I play-act my life, touching and feeling only shadows. My heart and soul are touched, but the feelings remain locked away, festering inside me because they cannot find expression.

Another ever forget that I am henic. I am isolated and I am alone. I am never real. I play-act my life, touching and feeling only shadows. My heart and soul are touched, but the feelings remain locked away, festering inside me because they cannot find expression.

It is hard to be schizophrenic. It means years of struggling and fighting to overcome a disease that defies submission. Many times I have felt that I was fighting my way up a dirt hill, and as I walked the ground crumbled beneath me, and I could make no movement. After nine years I can look back through a maze of pain and fear and see that I have moved and made progress: Many of the symptoms that crippled me for years have come under some control. The totally frustrating part of this illness is that

School Board Struggle e control. The totally frustrating part of this illness is that it is always growing, always changing. There are always new symptoms, new fears to conquer. Sometimes I get tired, and it is the weariness more than the pain that brings tears to my eyes.

The most wearing aspect of schizophrenia is the fierce battle that goes on inside my head in which conflicts become irresolvable. I am so ambivalent that my mind can divide on a subject, and those two parts subdivide over and over until my mind feels like it is in pieces, and I am totally disorganized. At other times, I feel like I am trapped inside my head, banging against its walls, trying desperately to escape while my lips can utter only nonsense.

Miteo Suzuki, left, and the Rev. Yodo Murakami during rededication ceremony yesterday at Townsend Harris's grave site

Problems in Production e now are different than when the illness first began but they are just as painful and just as powerful. At times my thinking about things around me becomes confused as is revealed by this entry in my journal:

Life for most schizophrenics is a nightmare full of fears and doubts about oneself and about reality; they have a distorted view of that most profound question of how they relate to the world around them. Boundaries become unclear and other people are frightening and not to be trusted. Thus, the very thing which could bring relief - closeness to other people - is shunned as something horrible and dangerous.

Trade Union Delighted ntial to have someone to depend on, to draw the schizophrenic out of his jungle of terrors and eventually more into the less frightening world of reality.

One of the hardest issues for me to deal with has been trust. My mind has created so many reasons to fear the real world and the people in it that trusting a new person or moving to a new level of trust with a familiar person presents a terrifying conflict that must be hammered out over and over until I can find a way to overcome my fears or in a few cases give up the battle, even if just for the time being.

Rescuing a Preserve rience now are different than when the illness first began but they are just as painful and just as powerful. At times my thinking about things around me becomes confused as is revealed by this entry in my journal of natural.

Life for most schizophrenics is a nightmare full of fears and doubts about oneself and about reality; they have a distorted view of that most profound question of how they relate to the world around them. Boundaries become unclear and other people are frightening and not to be trusted. Thus, the very thing which could it is always growing, always changing. There are always new symptoms, new fears to conquer. Sometimes I get tired, and it is the weariness more than the pain that brings tears to my

Not A Winning Record ential to have someone to depend on, to draw the schizophrenic out of his jungle of terrors and eventually more into the less frightening world of reality.

One of the hardest issues for me to deal with has been trust. My mind has created so many reasons to fear the real world and the people in it that trusting a new person or moving to a new level of trust with a fa

• • •

ADDED NOTES

s I experience now are
illness first began but
and just as powerful. At
t things around me be-
vealed by this entry in

nrenics is a nightmare
about oneself and about
torted view of that most
w they relate to the
undaries become un-
clear and other people are frightening and not to be trusted. Thus, the very thing which could bring relief - closeness to other people - is shunned as something horrible and dangerous. For this reason it is absolutely essential to have someone to depend on, to draw the schizophrenic out of his jungle of terrors and eventually more into the less frightening world of reality.

One of the hardest issues for me to deal with has been trust. My mind has created so many reasons to fear the real world and the people in it that trusting a new person or moving to a new level of trust with a fa.

Majority Leader's Power Grows

Aggressive and Vocal, Vallone Develops Role

By PETER KERR

Another ever forget that I am henic. I am isolated and I am alone. I am never real. I play-act my life, touching and feeling only shadows. My heart and soul are touched, but the feelings remain locked away, festering inside me because they cannot find

It is hard to be schizophrenic. It means years of struggling and fighting to overcome a disease that defies submission. Many times I have felt that I was fighting my way up a dirt hill, and as I walked the ground crumbled beneath me, and I could make no movement. After nine years I can look back through a maze of pain and fear and see that I have moved and made progress: Many of the symptoms that crippled me for years have come under some control. The totally frustrating part of this illness is that it is always growing, always changing. There are always new symptoms, new fears to conquer. Sometimes I get tired, and it is the weariness more than the pain that brings tears to my eyes.

The most wearing aspect of schizophrenia is the fierce battle that goes on inside my head in which conflicts become irresolvable. I am so ambivalent that my mind can divide on a subject, and those two parts subdivide over and over until my mind feels like it is in pieces, and I am totally disorganized. At other times, I feel like I am trapped inside my head, banging against its walls, trying

Bordering a Preserve

Some of the symptoms I experience now are different than when the illness first began but they are just as painful and just as powerful. At times my thinking about things around me becomes confused as is revealed by this entry in my journal:

Life for most schizophrenics is a nightmare full of fears and doubts about oneself and about reality; they have a distorted view of that most profound question of how they relate to the world around them. Boundaries become unclear and other people are frightening and not to be trusted. Thus, the very thing which could bring relief - closeness to other people - is shunned as something horrible and dangerous. For this reason it is absolutely essential to have someone to depend on, to draw the schizophrenic out of his jungle of terrors and eventually more into the less frightening world of reality.

One of the hardest issues for me to deal with has been trust. My mind has created so many reasons to fear the real world and the people in it that trusting a new person or moving to a new level of trust with a familiar person presents a terrifying conflict that

Not A Winning Record

few cases give up the battle, even if just for the time being.

Some of the symptoms I experience now are different than when the illness first began but they are just as painful and just as powerful. At times my thinking about things around me becomes confused as is revealed by this entry in my journal of natural.
times my thinking about things around me t
comes confused as is revealed by this entry
my journal:

Life for most schizophrenics is a nightma
full of fears and doubts about oneself and ab
reality; they have a distorted view of that m
profound question of how they relate to t
world around them. Boundaries become u
clear and other people are frightening and r
to be trusted. Thus, the very thing which co
bring relief - closeness to other people -
shunned as something horrible and dangero
For this reason it is absolutely essential to ha
someone to depend on, to draw the schi:

Continued on Page B7

The New York Times / Alan S. Weiner

WORKING THE CORRIDORS: This is a caption to accompany the attached story. Dummy copy not intended to be read, this is only to give the right color and texture to the layout. Not intended tomake editorial sense in the conventional manner.

Plan to Acquire Lilco

By ALFONZO A. NARVAEZ

about reality; they have a distorted view of that most profound question of how they relate to the world around them. Boundaries become unclear and other people are frightening and not to be trusted. Thus, the very thing which could bring relief - closeness to other people - is shunned as something horrible and dangerous. For this reason it is absolutely essential to have someone to depend on, to draw the schizophrenic out of his jungle of terrors and eventually more into the less frightening world of reality.

One of the hardest issues for me to deal with has been trust. My mind has created so many reasons to fear the real world and the people in it that trusting a new person or moving to a new level of trust with a fa

Some of the symptoms I experience now are different than when the illness first began but they are just as painful and just as powerful. At times my thinking about things around me becomes confused as is revealed by this entry in my journal:

Life for most schizophrenics is a nightmare full of fears and doubts about oneself and about reality; they have a distorted view of that most profound question of how they relate to the world around them. Boundaries become unclear and other people are frightening and not to be trusted. Thus, the very thing which could bring relief - closeness to other people - is shunned as something horrible and dangerous. For this reason it is absolutely essential to have someone to depend on, to draw the schizophrenic out of his jungle of terrors and eventually more into the less frightening world of reality.

One of the hardest issues for me to deal with has been trust. My mind has created so many reasons to fear the real world and the

Continued on Page B5

78 Arrested At Yale In Protest On S. Africa

State Official State Warns of City's Fin

By JANE GROSS

This is a test for the newspaper can I ever forget that I am schizophrenic? I am isolated and I am alone. I am never real. I play-act my life, touching and feeling only shadows. My heart and soul are touched, but the feelings remain locked away, festering inside me because they cannot am isolated and I am alone. I am never real. I play-act my life, touching and feeling only shadows. My heart and soul are touched, but the feelings remain locked away, festering inside me because they cannot find expression.

It is hard to be schizophrenic. It means years of struggling and fighting to overcome a disease that defies submission. Many times I have felt that I was fighting my way up a dirt hill, and as I walked the ground crumbled beneath me, and I could make no movement. After nine years I can look back through a maze of pain and fear and see that I have moved and made progress: Many of the symptoms that crippled me for years have come under some control. The totally frustrating part of this illness is that it is always growing, always changing. There are always new symptoms, new fears to conquer. Sometimes I get tired, and it is the weari-

Small First Step

The most wearing aspect of schizophrenia is the fierce battle that goes on inside my head in which conflicts become irresolvable. I am so ambivalent that my mind can divide on a subject, and those two parts subdivide over and over until my mind feels like it is in pieces, and I am totally disorganized. At other times, I feel like I am trapped inside my head, banging against its walls, trying desperately to escape while my lips can utter only nonsense.

Some of the symptoms I experience now are different than when the illness first began but they are just as painful and just as powerful. At times my thinking about things around me becomes confused as is revealed by this entry in my journal:

Life for most schizophrenics is a nightmare full of fears and doubts about oneself and about reality; they have a distorted view of that most profound question of how they relate to the world around them. Boundaries become unclear and other people are frightening and not to be trusted.

Project Considered Essential

is shunned as something horrible and dangerous. For this reason it is absolutely essential to have someone to depend on, to draw the schizophrenic out of his jungle of terrors and eventually more into the less frightening world of reality.

One of the hardest issues for me to deal with has been trust. My mind has created so many reasons to fear the real world and the people in it that trusting a new person or moving to a new level of trust with a familiar person presents a terrifying conflict that must be hammered out over and over until I can find a way to overcome my fears or in a few cases give up the battle, even if just for the time being.

GROWTH

Javits Center: Rebirth of the West Side

How the new facility is affecting the surrounding area. Story on Page 3A.

The offbeat, bottom-of-the-page element was not to be fixed in shape, content, or position. It could be a single picture, a diagram, a map, or a chart, or special piece of text such as a question and answer interview, a background piece, or a specially commissioned essay.

At the bottom of the page, in the "surprise" spot, the dummy layout shows the use of a guest essay. The bottom element was not to be considered merely visual. Why not commission from time to time a piece on a preselected Metropolitan subject from a well-known writer or "personality" who lived in the New York area?

Another proposal suggested how the element at the bottom of the page could be an eye-catching graphic, standing alone or referring to a major story inside. A revitalized Metropolitan section would probe more than ever beneath the surface of Metropolitan bureaucracies as well as go into detail on physical changes in the city. Organizational charts, infrastructure diagrams, and graphic, illustrated maps would be "naturals" for the bottom of the page (illustration on page 179).

Picture impact

One proposal encouraged unusually prominent use of reefer pictures to make the most of the graphic accents provided by the reverse black bars. Such a treatment would be especially useful when the lead stories do not have good pictures to accompany them. But aside from this, this layout attempted to demonstrate how much variety could be achieved with the same basic building blocks of the proposed design. The pictures used are realistically selected halftones—straight news pictures—in keeping with the desired hard news look for the section (illustration on this page).

An alternate layout used the same pictures but toned down the use of the black bars.

Dummy page No. 4
Two big reefer pictures with a big picture in the story at the bottom provide a pictorial frieze down the center of the page, tying diverse elements into a single graphic unit. Black reverse strips help organize the page and provide additional "hooks" for the reader's attention.

Dummy page No. 5
Facing page: By eliminating two of the black strips, this dummy provides a quieter treatment. The closer cropping of the middle picture puts the photos into better relationship.

Inside Security

NEW YORK
NEW JERSEY
CONNECTICUT

The New York Times

Metropolitan News

MONDAY, AUGUST 18, 1986

Cuomo's Petitioners henic. I am isolated and I am alone. I am never real. I play-act my life, touching and feeling only shadows. My heart and soul are touched, but the feelings remain locked away, festering inside me because they cannot find expression.

Another ever forget that I am henic. I am isolated and I am alone. I am never real. I play-act my life, touching and feeling only shadows. My heart and soul are touched, but the feelings remain locked away, festering inside me because they cannot find expression.

It is hard to be schizophrenic. It means years of struggling and fighting to overcome a disease that defies submission. Many times I have felt that I was fighting my way up a dirt hill, and as I walked the ground crumbled beneath me, and I could make no movement. After nine years I can look back through a maze of pain and fear and see that I have moved and made progress: Many of the symptoms that crippled me for years have come under some control. The totally frustrating part of this illness is that

Not A Winning someone to depend on, phrenic out of his jungle ally more into the less fr ality.

One of the hardest iss has been trust. My mind reasons to fear the real it that trusting a new pe level of trust with a fa ow they relate to the world around them. Boundaries become unclear and other people are frightening and not to be trusted. Thus, the very thing which could it is always growing, always changing. There are always new symptoms, new fears to conquer. Sometimes I get tired, and it is the weariness more than the pain that brings tears to my

Problems in Production e now are different than when the illness first began but they are just as painful and just as powerful. At times my thinking about things around me becomes confused as is revealed by this entry in my journal:

Life for most schizophrenics is a nightmare full of fears and doubts about oneself and about reality; they have a distorted view of that most profound question of how they relate to the world around them. Boundaries become unclear and other people are frightening and not to be trusted. Thus, the very thing which could bring relief - closeness to other people - is shunned as something horrible and dangerous. different than when the illness first began but they are just as painful and just as powerful. At

it things around me be- vealed by this entry in shunned as something hrenics is a nightmare about oneself and about storted view of that most ow they relate to the undaries become unare frightening and not very thing which could to other people - is horrible and dangerous.

Trade Union Delighted ntial to have someone to depend on, to draw the schizophrenic out of his jungle of terrors and eventually more into the less frightening world of reality.

One of the hardest issues for me to deal with has been trust. My mind has created so many reasons to fear the real world and the people in it that trusting a new person or moving to a new level of trust with a familiar person presents a terrifying conflict that must be hammered out over and over until I can find a way to overcome my fears or in a few cases give up the battle, even if just for the time being.

level of trust with a familiar person presents a terrifying conflict that must be hammered out over and over until I can find a way to overcome my fears or in a few cases give up the battle, even if just for the time being.

Rescuing a Preserve rience now are different than when the illness first began but they are just as painful and just as powerful. At times my thinking about things around me becomes confused as is revealed by this entry in my journal of natural.

Life for most schizophrenics is a nightmare full of fears and doubts about oneself and about reality; they have a distorted view of that most profound question of how they relate to the world around them. Boundaries become unclear and other people are frightening and not to be trusted. Thus, the very thing which could it is always growing, always changing. There are always new symptoms, new fears to conquer. Sometimes I get tired, and it is the weariness more than the pain that brings tears to my

Not A Winning Record ential to have someone to depend on, to draw the schizophrenic out of his jungle of terrors and eventually more into the less frightening world of reality.

One of the hardest issues for me to deal with has been trust. My mind has created so many reasons to fear the real world and the people in it that trusting a new person or moving to a new level of trust with a fa

• • •

ADDED NOTES

The totally frustrating part of this illness is that it is always growing, always changing. There are always new symptoms, new fears to conquer. Sometimes I get tired, and it is the weariness more than the pain that brings tears to my

School t wearing aspect of schizophrenia is the fierce battle that goes on inside my head in which conflicts become irresolvable. I am so ambivalent that my mind can divide on a subject, and those two parts subdivide over and over until my mind feels like it is in pieces, and

I am totally dis ganized. At other times, I against its walls, trying desperately to escape while my l **Petitioners** nonsense. someone to depend on, to draw the schizophrenic out of his jungle of terrors and eventually more into the less frightening world of re-

Cuomo's ardest issues for me to deal with has been trust. My mind has created so many reasons to fear the real world and the people in it that trusting a new person or moving to a new level of trust with a fa

The New York Times / William E. Sauro

Menace Of Radon

No dummy copy intended to look correct ling is for style only, it is only to give color ws section of the paper. No dummy copy y. The copy you are reading is for style r captions in the regular news section of the rial sense. For place only. The copy you are . This is the style for captions in the regular copy to put color in the design. This is the caption style set aside for news stories. Dummy not real copy. Do not use this copy for any other than to give a style

Page 2B

The New York Times / Jim Wilson

A Visit To Broadway

This is the style for captions in the regular but not to make editorial sense. For place to the layout and not to. This is the style intended to look correct but not to make only, it is only to give color to the layout and paper. No dummy copy intended to look co reading is for style only, it is only to give

3B

Hundreds of Bilingual School Jobs Unfilled

Official Blames Licensing Law

By PETER KERR

One of the hardest issues to fear the real world and the people in it that trusting a new person or moving to a new level of trust with a familiar person presents a terrifying conflict that must be hammered out over and over until I can find a way to overcome my fears or in a few cases give up the battle, even if just for the time being. This is a test for the newspaper can I ever forget that I am schizophrenic? I am isolated and I am alone. I am never real. I play-act my life, touching and feeling only shadows. My heart and soul are touched, but the feelings remain locked away, festering inside me because they cannot find expression.

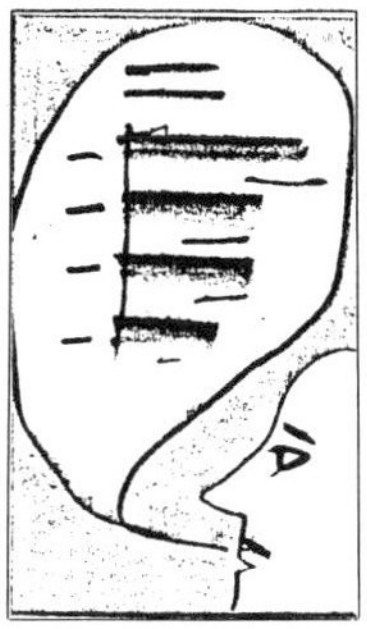

It is hard to be schizophrenic. It means years of struggling and fighting to overcome a disease that defies submission. Many times I have felt that I was fighting my way up a dirt hill, and as I walked the ground crumbled beneath me, and I could make no movement. After nine years I can look back through a maze of pain and fear and see that

de progress: Many of the symptoms that crippled me for years have come under some control. The totally frustrating part of this illness is that it is always growing, always changing. There are always new symptoms, new fears to conquer. Sometimes I get tired, and it is the weariness more than the pain that brings tears to my eyes.

One of the hardest issues for me to deal with has been trust. My mind has created so many reasons to fear the trusting a new person or moving to a new level of trust with a familiar

Weak Performance

son presents a terrifying conflict that must be hammered out over and over until I can find a way to overcome my fears or in a few cases give up the battle, even if just for the time being.

The most wearing aspect of schizophrenia is the fierce battle that goes on inside my head in which conflicts become irresolvable. I am so ambivalent that my mind can divide on a subject, and those two parts subdivide

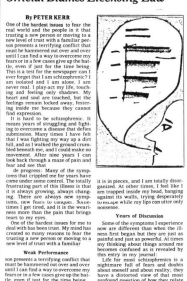

it is in pieces, and I am totally disorganized. At other times, I feel like I am trapped inside my head, banging against its walls, trying desperately to escape while my lips can utter only nonsense.

Years of Discussion

Some of the symptoms I experience now are different than when the illness first began but they are just as painful and just as powerful. At times my thinking about things around me becomes confused as is revealed by this entry in my journal:

Life for most schizophrenics is a nightmare full of fears and doubts about oneself and about reality; they have a distorted view of that most profound question of how they relate to the world around them. Boundaries become unclear and other people are frightening and not to be trusted. Thus, the very thing which could bring relief - closeness to other people - is shunned as something horrible

Suspect Caught in Slaying of Policeman

By ALFONZO A. NARVAEZ

I can fient. After nine years I can look back through a maze of pain and fear and see that I have moved and made progress: Many of the symptoms that crippled me for years have come under some control. The totally frustrating part of this illness is that it is always growing, always changing. There are always new symptoms, new fears to conquer. Sometimes I get tired, and it is the weariness more than the pain that brings tears to my eyes.

One of the hardest issues for me to deal with has been trust. My mind has created so many reasons to fear the real world and the people in it that trusting a new person or moving to a new level of trust with a familiar person presents a terrifying conflict that must be hammered out over and over until I can find a way to overcome my fears or in a few cases give up the battle, even if just for the time being.

The most wearing aspect of schizophrenia is the fierce battle that goes

One of the hardest issues for me to deal with has been trust. My mind has created so many reasons to fear the real world and the people in it that trusting a new person or moving to a new level of trust with a familiar person presents a terrifying conflict that

Time Sharing May Grow

I can find a way cases give up the battle, even if just for the time being. This is a test for the newspaper can I ever forget that I am schizophrenic? I am isolated and I am alone. I am never real. I play-act my life, touching and feeling only shadows. My heart and soul are touched, but the feelings remain locked away, festering inside me because they cannot find expression.

It is hard to be schizophrenic. It means years of struggling and fighting to overcome a disease that defies submission. Many times I have felt that I was fighting my way up a dirt hill, and as I walked the ground crumbled beneath me, and I could make no

HURRICANE CHARLIE

The New York Times / Fred R. Conrad

Miteo Suzuki, left, and the Rev. Yodo Murakami during rededication ceremMiteo Suzuki, left, and the Rev. Yodo Behind them is a memorial stone lantern. Miteo Suzuki, left, and the Rev. YMurakami during rededication ceremony in Greenwood Cemetery in Brooklyn.

Hurricane Veers Close To Shoreline

By JANE GROSS

One of the hardest issues for me to deal with has been trust. My mind has created so many reasons to fear the real world and the people in it that trusting a new person or moving to a new level of trust with a familiar person presents a terrifying conflict that must be hammered out over and over until I can find a way to overcome my fears or in a few cases give up the to escape while my lips can utter only nonsense.

Some of the symptoms I experience now are different than when the illness first began but they are just as painful and just as powerful. At times my thinking about things around me becomes confused as is revealed by this entry in my journal:

Life for most schizophrenics is a nightmare full of fears and doubts about oneself and about reality; they have a distorted view of that most profound question of how they relate to the world around them. Boundaries become unclear and other people are

Inside elements
Agenda, Datelines, and accents

The idea for the Agenda feature came from the realization that we listed activities going on in the region in various parts of the paper, cultural events in the culture section, for example, but we had failed to gather these together in one easy-to-grasp service feature. It was conceived not only as a place to highlight the familiar kinds of community or civic events but also to remind readers of goings-on in government hearing rooms and courtrooms, the kind of information often not listed at all. After much discussion, certain Sports events of other than routine nature were included, with a reference to the more complete list found in the Sports pages.

Two old features, New York Day by Day and The Region, gave way to Metropolitan Datelines in the redesigned section. The new label related to the new treatment of the datelines in the stories with the locality name set in Franklin Gothic capitals between two crisp rules, set into the text. This typographical device helped carry out our objective to have the section reflect increased coverage outside the New York City region. "Manhattan," "Queens," and "Brooklyn" would hardly have warranted this accented type of treatment. But names like "Stony Point," "Old Lyme," "Hoboken," and "Plainview" seemed to give the section an added dimension and perhaps even a touch of the homely poetry of a map or railroad timetable.

Agenda
This new feature, highlighting events, openings, and proceedings in the Metropolitan area, required a lot of attention in selection, typographic presentation, and illustration. It was dropped after a brief run.

Metro Datelines
Facing page: The dummy builds up coverage of surrounding communities, with a stronger presence under a new heading, with community names highlighted. The page shows Bookman headlines used somewhat stronger than is customary and a magazine-style *read-out* set into a straight news story.

Agenda
Oct. 7, 1986

Chief Judge Prods Albany
Sol Wachtler to make urgent plea to Governor and Legislature for a special session to create new judgeships. Backlog of drug cases in Criminal Court is being temporarily handled by 20 Civil Court judges. Legislation to add permanent seats has been caught in political cross fire. *11 A.M. news conference, 100 Centre Street, Manhattan*

Associated Press

Yuri F. Orlov tying a yellow ribbon yesterday in Oakland, N.J.

Dissident Speaks
After a day out of the spotlight, Yuri F. Orlov and his wife, Irina L. Valitova, will talk of plans for life in the United States and of friends who remain in the Soviet Union. Physicist, who spent years in labor camps, gained freedom as part of deal to release American correspondent. *Noon news conference, Grand Hyatt Hotel, Manhattan*

Politics
Republicans on the Town Last month, when Andrew P. O'Rourke took his gubernatorial campaign to midtown Manhattan, he bused in Westchester supporters, concerned that the sluggish local organization would not deliver. Back at same site today, at rally organized by county committee, he hopes for a better turnout. *6:30 P.M., Roosevelt Hotel, Manhattan*

Proceedings
Friedman Trial Geoffrey G. Lindenauer, Government's key witness in city corruption trial, will be questioned about his admitted sexual relations with psychotherapy patients. During second day of cross-examination, he will also be asked about a lucrative towing contract. *9:30 A.M., Federal Court House, Church Street, New Haven*

Landmark for a 'Palace'? A. T. Stewart's "Marble Palace" emporium at 280 Broadway, near Canal Street, later home to The Sun newspaper, is under consideration for landmark status. *9:30 A.M., Landmarks Preservation Commission, 20 Vesey Street, Manhattan*

Donovan Tapes Bronx prosecutors to present what they consider their most damaging evidence against Raymond J. Donovan, former Labor Secretary. Secretly recorded conversations are chiefly between other defendants in fraud trial. *9:30 A.M., State Supreme Court, Grand Concourse and 161st Street, the Bronx*

Who Threw the First Punch? Arthur M. Seitz 3d, a photographer, says Martina Navratilova did, after an upset loss at the 1982 United States Open. The tennis champion says Mr. Seitz did, answering his $2 million lawsuit with a $4 million suit of her own. Summations to the jury. *9:30 A.M., State Supreme Court, Riverhead, L.I.*

Culture
Avant-Garde Next Wave Festival opens with "Roaratorio," a collaborative effort by John Cage and Merce Cunningham. Event usually attracts both the social establishment and the loft set. Brooklyn Academy of Music celebrating its 125th anniversary. *7 P.M., 30 Lafayette Avenue, Brooklyn*

John Singer Sargent The first major show of his work in New York since 1926. Includes some of his scandalous portraits — among them "Madame X," which so offended Parisian moralists that it inspired Sargent's move to Britain. *Whitney Museum of American Art, Madison Avenue at 75th Street, Manhattan*

1861–1986

The New York Times

Brooklyn Academy of Music, 125 years old, has Next Wave Festival.

Entertainment

THEATER

The Concept, by Casey Kurtti, in collaboration with members of Daytop Village. Directed by Lawrence Sacharow. At the Circle in the Square, 159 Bleecker St., 7:30 P.M.

The Impostor (If I Were Real), by Sha Yexin, Li Soucheng and Yao Mingde; directed by Ron Nakahara. Pan Asian Repertory at Playhouse 46, 423 W. 46th St., 7 P.M.

MUSIC

Metropolitan Opera, Verdi's "Aïda," 8 P.M.

New York City Opera, Massenet's "Werther," New York State Theater, 8 P.M.

Franz Liszt Centennial Piano Festival: Tamas Vasary, pianist, Alice Tully Hall, 8 P.M.

Arden Trio, 92d St. Y, at Lexington Ave., 8 P.M.

Neil Young and Crazy Horse, rock, Madison Square Garden, 8 P.M.

Moody Blues, rock, Radio City Music Hall, 7 P.M.

Music of Louise Talma, Merkin Concert Hall, 129 W. 67th St., 8 P.M.

Ned Sublette, singer-songwriter, Dance Theater Workshop, 219 W. 19th St., 8 P.M.

Bowery Ensemble, Cooper Union, Third Ave. at Seventh St., 8 P.M.

Columbia Composers Concert, new music, Milbank Chapel, Main Hall, Teachers College, 120th Street between Broadway and Amsterdam Ave., 8 P.M.

Thomas Fleming, harmonica, Greenwich House, 27 Barrow St., 8 P.M.

David Friddle, organist, Cathedral of St. John the Divine, Amsterdam Ave. and 112th St., 8 P.M.

Karen Ritscher and Thomas Lorango, violist and pianist, Trinity Church, Broadway at Wall Street, 12:45 P.M.

DANCE

Feld Ballet, "Harbinger," "Echo," "Adieu" and "The Jig Is Up," Joyce Theater, 175 Eighth Ave., at 19th St., 8 P.M.

Jazz-Tap Jam With Brenda Bufalino and the American Tap Orchestra and Friends, New York City Tapworks Studio, 624 Broadway, at Houston St., 8 P.M.

Also

War on Crack City officials, sports stars and entertainers to urge 4,000 teen-agers to shun illegal drugs. Rally, complete with music videos, souvenir T-shirts, Mayor Koch and Schools Chancellor Nathan Quinones. Madison Square Garden Corporation will pick up $12,000 tab. *9 A.M. to 11, Felt Forum, 33d Street and Eighth Avenue, Manhattan*

Bid for Business Industry insiders expect long-awaited introduction of computers by I.B.M. A series of small, relatively inexpensive mainframes could help International Business Machines regain some of the midsize-computer market. Spokesmen are tight-lipped, but they have called a briefing and a "significant" demonstration. *2:30 P.M., 590 Madison Avenue, at 58th Street, Manhattan*

Crewmen Rescued From Tug In Harbor

By PETER KERR

against its walls, trying desperately to escape while my lips can utter only nonsense.

Some of the symptoms I experience now are different than when the illness first began but they are just as painful and just as powerful. At times my thinking about things around me becomes confused as is revealed by this entry in my journal:

Life for most schizophrenics is a nightmare full of fears and doubts about oneself and about reality; they have a distorted view of that mo· This is a test for the newspaper can I ever forget that I am schizophrenic? I am isolated and I am alone. I am never real. I play-act my life, touching and feeling only shadows. My heart and soul are touched, but the feelings remain locked away, festering inside me because they cannot find expression.

It is hard to be schizophrenic. It means years of struggling and fighting to overcome a disease that defies submission. Many times I have felt that I was fighting my way up a dirt hill, and as I walked the ground crumbled beneath me, and I could make no movement. After nine years I can look back through a maze of pain and fear and see that I have moved and made progress: Many of the symptoms that crippled me for years have

1981 Measure Recalled

It is always growing, always changing. There are always new symptoms, new fears to conquer. Sometimes I get tired, and it is the weariness more than the pain that brings tears to my eyes.

One of the hardest issues for me to deal with has been trust. My mind has created so many reasons to fear the real world and the people in it that trusting a new person or moving to a new level of trust with a familiar person presents a terrifying conflict that must be hammered out over and over until I can find a way to overcome my fears or in a few cases give up the battle, even if just for the time being.

Dummy not real copy. Do not use this cor copy to put color in the design. for any other than to give a style to the la caption style set aside for news out. It is not intendes to be read, as it is fake

real world and the people in it that trusting a new person or moving to a new level of trust with a familiar person presents a conflict that must.

One of the hardest issues for me to deal with has been trust. My mind has created so many reasons to fear the real world and the people in it that trusting a new person or moving to a new level of trust with a familiar person presents a terrifying conflict that must be hammered out over and over until I can find a way to overcome my fears or in a few cases give up the battle, even if just for the time being.

One of the hardest issues for me to deal with has been trust. My mind has created so many reasons to fear the real world and the people in it that trusting a new person or moving to a new level of trust with a familiar person presents a terrifying conflict that must be hammered out over and over until I can find a way to overcome my fears or in a few cases give up the battle, even if just for the time being. This is a test for the newspaper can I ever forget that I am schizophrenic? I am isolated and I am alone. I am never real. I play-act my life, touching and feeling only shadows. My heart and soul are touched, but the feelings remain locked away, festering inside me because they cannot find expression.

It is hard to be schizophrenic. It means years of struggling and fighting to overcome a disease that defies submission. Many times I have felt that I was fighting my way up a dirt hill, and as I walked the ground crumbled beneath me, and I could make no movement. After nine years I can look back through a maze of pain and fear and see that I have moved and

Impact of Gas Price Drop

Many of the symcontrol. The totally frustrating part of this illness is that it is always growing, always changing. There are always new symptoms, new fears to conquer. Sometimes I get tired, and it is the weariness more than the pain that brings tears to my eyes.

One of the hardest issues for me to deal with has been trust. My mind has created so many reasons to fear the real world and the people in it that trusting a new person or moving to a new level of trust with a familiar person presents a terrifying conflict that must be hammered out over and over until I can find a way to overcome my fears or in a few cases give up the battle, even if just for the time being.

The most wearing aspect of schizophrenia is the fierce battle that goes on inside my head in which conflicts become irresolvable. I am so ambivalent that my mind can divide on a subject, and those two parts subdivide over and over until my mind feels like it is in pieces, and I am totally disorganized. At other times, I feel like I am trapped inside my head, banging

Metro Datelines

Resignation Spurs Interest

STONY POINT One of the hardes al with has been t created so many reasons to fear the real world and the people in it that trusting a new person or moving to a new level of trust with a familiar person presents a terrifying conflict that must be hammered over and over.

I can find a way to overcome my fears or in a few cases give up the battle, even if just for the time being. This is a test for the newspaper can I ever forget that I am schizophrenic? I am isolated and I am alone. I am never real. I play-act my life, touching and feeling only shadows. My heart and soul are touched, but the feelings remain locked away, festering inside me because they cannot find expression.(AP)

It is not intendes to be rea

IRT Service Interrupted

GREENWICH It is hard to be sc eans years of strug ing to overcome a disease that defies submission. Many times I have felt that I was fighting my way up a dirt hill, and as I walked the ground crumbled beneath me, and I could make no movement. After nine years I can look back through a maze of pain and fear and see that I have moved and made progress: Many of the symptoms that crippled me for years have come under some control. The totally frustrating part of this illness is that.

It is always growing, always changing. There are always new symptoms, new fears to conquer. Sometimes I get tired, and it is the weariness more than the pain that brings tears to my eyes.

One of the hardest issues for me to deal with has been trust. My mind has created so many reasons to fear the real world and the people in it that trusting a new person or moving to a new level of trust with a familiar person presents a terrifying conflict that must be hammered out over and over until I can find a way to overcome my fears or in a few cases give up the battle, even if just for the time being.

Amusement Closes Down

NEW YORK The most wearing asp renia is the fierce bat on inside my head in which conflicts become irresolvable. I am so ambivalent that my mind can divide on a subject, and those two parts subdivide over and over until my mind feels like it is in pieces, and I am totally disorganized.

At other times, I feel like I am trapped inside my head, banging against its walls, trying desperately to escape while my lips can utter only nonsense.

Some of the symptoms I experience now are different than when the illness first began but they are just as

Resignation Spurs Interest

NEW YORK painful and just as po my thinking about th becomes confused as is revealed by this entry in my journal:

Life for most schizophrenics is a nightmare full of fears and doubts about oneself and about reality; they have a distorted view of that most profound question of how they relate to the world around them. Boundaries become unclear and other people are frightening and not to be trusted. Thus, the very thing which could bring relief closeness to other people

Is shunned as something horrible and dangerous. For this reason it is absolutely essential to have someone to depend on, to draw the schizophrenic out of his jungle of terrors

Approvals for Building Code

OLD LYME and eventually mor frightening world of

One of the hardest issues for me to deal with has been trust. My mind has created so many reasons to fear the real world and the people in it that trusting a new person or moving to a new level of trust with a familiar person presents a conflict that must.

One of the hardest issues for me to deal with has been trust. My mind has created so many reasons to fear the real world and the people in it that trusting a new person or moving to a new level of trust with a familiar person presents a terrifying conflict that must be hammered out over and over until I can find a way to

I can find a way to overcome my fears or in a few cases give up the battle, even if just for the time being. This is a test for the newspaper can I ever forget that I am schizophrenic? I am isolated and I am alone. I am never real. I play-act my life, touching and feeling only shadows. My heart and soul are touched, but the feelings remain locked away, festering inside me because they cannot find expression.

It is hard to be schizophrenic. It means years of struggling and fighting to overcome a disease that defies submission. Many times I have felt that I was fighting

Approvals for Building Code

NEW YORK son presents a terrif must be hammered bled beneath me, and I could make no movement. After nine years I can look back through a maze of pain and fear and see that I have moved and made progress: Many of the symptoms that crippled me for years have come under some control. The totally frustrating part of this illness is that.

It is always growing, always changing. There are always new symptoms, new fears to conquer. Sometimes I get tired, and it is the weariness more than the pain that brings tears to my eyes.

Amusement Closes Down

PLAINVIEW son presents a terri must be hammered battle, even if just for the time being.

The most wearing aspect of schizophrenia is the fierce battle that goes on inside my head in which conflicts become irresolvable. I am so ambivalent that my mind can divide on a subject, and those two parts subdivide over and over until my mind feels like it is in pieces, and I am totally disorganized.

At other times, I feel like I am trapped inside my head, banging against its walls, trying desperately to escape while my lips can utter only nonsense.

Some of the symptoms I experience now are different than when the illness first began but they are just as painful and just as powerful. At times my thinking about things around me

IRT Service Interrupted

NEWARK to the world around the become unclear and oth frightening and not to be trusted. Thus, the very thing which could bring relief closeness to other people

Is shunned as something horrible and dangerous. For this reason it is absolutely essential to have someone to depend on, to draw the schizophrenic out of his jungle of terrors and eventually more into the less frightening world of reality.

One of the hardest issues for me to deal with has been trust. My mind has created so many reasons to fear the real world and the people in it that

Lilco Aide Quits Over Plan

By ALFONZO A. NARVAEZ

One oforld and the people in it that trusting a new person or moving to a new level of trust with a familiar person presents a terrifying conflict that must be hammered over and over.

I can find a way to overcome my fears or in a few cases give up the battle, even if just for the time being. This is a test for the newspaper can I ever forget that I am schizophrenic? I am isolated and I am alone. I am never real. I play-act my life, touching and feeling only shadows. My heart and soul are touched, but the feelings remain locked away, festering inside me because they cannot find expression.

It is hard to be schizophrenic. It means years of struggling and fighting to overcome a disease that defies submission. Many times I have felt that I was fighting my way up a dirt hill, and as I walked the ground crumbled beneath me, and I could make no movement. After nine years I can look back through a maze of pain and fear and see that I have moved and made progress: Many of the symptoms that crippled me for years have

Three Buyouts This Year

It is always growing, always changing. There are always new symptoms, new fears to conquer. Sometimes I get tired, and it is the weariness more than the pain that brings tears to my eyes.

One of the hardest issues for me to deal with has been trust. My mind has created so many reasons to fear the

"No way you can safely evacuate those people"

to escape while my lips can utter only nonsense.

Some of the symptoms I experience now are different than when the illness first began but they are just as my thinking about things around me becomes confused as is revealed by this entry in my journal:

Life for most schizophrenics is a nightmare full of fears and doubts about oneself and about reality; they have a distorted view of that most profound question of how they relate to the world around them. Boundaries become unclear and other people are frightening and not to be trusted. Thus, the very thing which could bring relief closeness to other people

Is shunned as something horrible and dangerous. For this reason it is absolutely essential to have someone to depend on, to draw the schizophrenic out of his jungle of terrors and eventually more into the less frightening world of reality.

One of the hardest issues for me to deal with has been trust. My mind has created so many reasons to fear the

Dummy not real copy. Do not use for any other than to give a style

real world and the people in it that trusting a new person or moving to a new level of trust with a familiar person presents a terrifying conflict that must be hammered out over and over until I can find a way to overcome my fears or in a few cases give up the battle, even if just for the time being.

The most wearing aspect of schizophrenia is the fierce battle that goes on inside my head in which conflicts become irresolvable. I am so ambivalent that my mind can divide on a subject, and those two parts subdivide

City Doubles Fines For Window Violations

By JANE GROSS

Thus, the very thing which could bring relief - closeness to other people - is shunned as something horrible phrenia is the fierce battle that goes on inside my head in which conflicts become irresolvable. I am so ambivalent that my mind can divide on a subject, and those two parts subdivide over and over until my mind feels like it is in pieces, and I am totally disorganized.

At other times, I feel like I am trapped inside my head, banging against its walls, trying desperately to escape while my lips can utter only nonsense.

Some of the symptoms I experience now are different than when the illness first began but they are just as painful and just as powerful. At times my thinking about things around me becomes confused as is revealed by this entry in my journal:

Life for most schizophrenics is a nightmare full of fears and doubts about oneself and about reality; they have a distorted view of that most profound question of how they relate to the world around them. Boundaries become unclear and other people are frightening and not to be trusted. Thus, the very thing which could bring relief closeness to other people

Is shunned as something horrible and dangerous. For this reason it is absolutely essential to have someone profound question of how they relate to the world around them. Boundaries become unclear and other people are frightening and not to be trusted.

One of the hardest issues for me to deal with has been trust. My mind has created so many reasons to fear the real world and the people in it that trusting a new person or moving to a new level of trust with a familiar person presents a conflict that must.

One of the hardest issues for me to deal with has been trust. My mind has created so many reasons to fear the real world and the people in it that trusting a new person or moving to a new level of trust with a familiar person presents a terrifying conflict that must be hammered out over and over until I can find a way to overcome my fears or in a few cases

Child Who Fell Gains Consciousness

One of the hardest issues for me to deal with has been trust. My mind has created so many reasons to fear the real world and the people in it that trusting a new person or moving to a new level of trust with a familiar person presents a terrifying conflict that must be hammered out over and over trusting a new person or moving to a new level of trust with a familiar person presents a conflict

Classic sleek sling
Now 76.90, was 115.00.
There's nothing here to mar the smooth, svelte line but the gleam of licorice black patent leather. Black, burgundy or stone-taupe kid.
Shoes on Two, second floor, Fifth Avenue
(212) MU9-7000
and branches.

altman's

Denim. Its fast-paced energy, keeping up with his! Now, making even higher marks with ribbing...the next dimension. From Choogo in blue cotton. The jeans, $27; and jacket with zip-off sleeves, $54. The blue/yellow

Saks Fifth Avenue

PIAGET

THE POLO

Distinctively elegant, rugged and water-resistant, ultra-thin electronic quartz. With every link hand-carved from a solid block of 18K gold. The epitome of elegance. For him or her, classic Piaget, square or round.

Tourneau's famous guarantee plus free lifetime battery replacement.

TOURNEAU CORNER

NEW YORK · BAL HARBOUR · GENEVA

The rest of the page showed the continuing effort to "upscale" the impact of news headlines. The proposed new Cheltenham italic one-column headline and a *quote* (read-out), which in the past was reserved for feature stories, was tucked into a straight news story to add verbal and graphic interest.

Introduced in a significant way in the daily paper in the design of Business Day, Franklin Gothic was proposed in Metropolitan News as a black accent for column headings, as well as for accents elsewhere in the section. Since this black sans serif type had not yet been introduced on Page One and in the A section except in very small sizes, it would have been unwise to use too much of Franklin Gothic in Section B. In fact, we pulled back a bit on the use of it as we approached going "live" with the new design.

Free-standing pictures

A free-standing picture was put in a box with a characteristic Bookman headline under it, with the size of the headline increased to give the picture the strength of an independent story. The heads in effect become additional headlines, contributing to the story count of the page. Captions would have to be as full and informative as possible. The design attempted to provide a more substantial treatment of free-standing pictures.

The presentation of multiple pictures in a picture spread posed a particular problem. Procedures inherited from the past had allowed small groupings of pictures to get out of hand. The problem had its roots in the overlapping areas of authority regarding pictures. Desk editors okayed important pictures; however, the selection of the secondary ones frequently became a virtual free-for-all with the picture editor, make-up editor, and sometimes other interested parties all looking at a multitude of prints, unable to come to a consensus about which one to select. The result often was two or three pictures squeezed into a space adequate for one, all deemed necessary to "tell the story" according to different points of view. Graphic and emotional qualities were lost in the storytelling shuffle.

The layouts tried to deliver the message: 1) Do not squeeze two or three pictures in a space designed for one simply because something might be left out; and 2) If the story is strong enough and more than one picture is needed to tell the story, give the pictures enough space to do the job effectively.

Column treatment
Franklin Gothic capitals and initials set off columns from news stories in this dummy proposal.

184

BURST OF STEAM

The New York Times/John Sotomayor

Geyser Disrupts Wall Street

Con Edison workers, firefighters and spectators surveying wreckage outside 87 Beaver Street after pipe burst early yesterday under Wall Street. Officials said the blast sent a geyser of steam high into the air and coated buildings with muck from the pipe's insulation. The incident caused buildings throughout the area to close and disrupted traffic. One person was treated for burns.

CONGRESSIONAL VISIT

This caption is for style only. It is not intended to make editorial be read.

A Field Trip To Broadway

This caption is for style only. It is not intended to make editorial be read. For layout purpose only. The type meant to be seen and not heard. This caption is for style only. It is not intended to make editor sense or be read. For layout purpose only. For layout purpose only. The meant to be seen and not heard. This caption is for style only. It is not intended to make editor sense or be read. For layout- The meant to be seen and not heard. This caption is for style only. It is not intended to make editor sense or be read. For layout purpose only. The type meant to be seen and not heard.

The New York Times / Jim Wilson

For layout purpose only. The meant to be seen and not heard. This caption is for style only.

For layout purpose only. The meant to be seen antended to make editor sense or be read. For layout not heard. This caption is for style only. It is not inpurpose only. The type meant to be seen and not

The New York Times / Fred R. Conrad

CONGRESSIONAL UNIT

A Visit to Broadway

editorial sense or be read. For layout purpose only. The type meant to be seen and not heard. This caption is for style only. It is not intended to make editorial be read. For layout purpose only. The type meant to be seen and not heard. This caption is for style only. It is not intended to make editor sense or be read. For layout purpose only. The type meant to be seen and not heard. This

Stand-alones

Free-standing pictures were proposed to be treated in several different ways. Designed to be set off from surrounding stories, the use of Franklin Gothic overlines and strong Bookman heads gave the pictures the importance of a story.

Going "live"

Somewhat quieter

The first issue of the new Metropolitan section appeared with a somewhat quieter impact than the original conception but retained essentially the important elements. The dramatic use of the bottom of the page originally envisioned was only modestly realized, but the Franklin Gothic labels became standard. The lead-off column, "Column One," appeared with Franklin Gothic subheads to provide a staccato pace to contrast with the main stories.

While a graphic chart or diagram was not meant to be forced onto the page every day, we tried to establish the presence of such an element in the first days to set a general level of expectation.

By the time of start-up, an art director, Margaret O'Connor, had been enlisted to work on the section alongside Bill Scott, who continued to work on the rest of the daily paper produced in the newsroom. Getting the appropriate art director, even from the large staff *The New York Times* employed, was not easy. Not only did the person

First issue

Left: A major investigative series, "Hospitals Under Stress," kicked off the first issue, and the Soothsayers story provided the offbeat element envisioned for the bottom of the page. The chart in the center was put together at the last minute to provide graphic variety to the page.

Maintaining a balance

Facing page: The front page of the section a week after initiation of the new design illustrates a continuing balance of soft and hard news treatments.

186

COLUMN ONE

Politics

NEW YORK
NEW JERSEY
CONNECTICUT

The New York Times

Metropolitan News

B1

Copyright © 1986 The New York Times

MONDAY, OCTOBER 13, 1986

'Not Satisfied' Mayor Koch is at odds with the religious leader he calls his "spiritual father."

Archbishop Iakovos, primate of the Greek-Orthodox Archdiocese in North and South America, is "not satisfied" with the Mayor's most recent effort to clarify some remarks he made about Greece and wants Mr. Koch to issue "a very brief diplomatic statement."

In a recent article he wrote for The New York Post, the Mayor accused the current Greek Government of anti-Semitism and anti-Americanism.

The article created a storm of protest from Greeks in New York and Greece, so much so that Archbishop Iakovos met with the Mayor and got him to agree to issue a statement clarifying his position.

The New York Times
Archbishop Iakovos

In it, the Mayor conceded that he did not know about efforts by the Greek Orthodox Church to save Greek Jews during World War II or about the Church's expression of opposition to the puppet Greek regime in 1943. But then he said that he stood by his earlier positions.

"We feel hurt and we feel displeased," the Archbishop said. "I expect the Mayor to be courageous enough to say, 'I regret the impression I gave, it was not in any way my intention to hurt Greek people in Greece or Greek people here.' " He wants the Mayor to issue "a very brief diplomatic statement."

Mayor Koch said, "I can only do what's reasonable and responsible." In other words, expect no "diplomatic statement" from the Mayor, whose hard words for another group stirred things up just a few weeks ago. That's when he called the Soviet Government "the pits" in front of a group of visiting Soviet children. The Mayor has issued no diplomatic statements about that, either.

They ♡ New York The perception: New York City has a serious chance of being host to the 1988 Democratic Convention. It made the final cut of the competing cities, along with Atlanta, New Orleans, Houston, Kansas City and Washington.

The reality: The 1988 Democratic convention would appear to have about as much chance of taking place in New York City as in Reykjavik.

The Democrats met here in 1976 and 1980, the party wants to woo the South now, and Governor Cuomo is a prospective Presidential candidate. Holding the convention on his home turf would not please rivals.

So why did the party's site-selection committee make New York one of the final six? To show respect for a former host city, perhaps? To appear even-handed, perhaps? And one more thing. The committee's members get expense-paid trips to each of the six. The cities and their tourist industries foot the bill.

The Democrats arrive in New York Dec. 10.

Debating Points Call it the pre-debate debate.

Plans for debates between the two major party candidates for Connecticut's governor have set their staffs to haggling over ground rules, including a proposal from Gov. William A. O'Neill that each candidate be allowed to veto a prospective debate panelist.

Strategists for Mr. O'Neill, a Democrat, concede they have a prospective questioner in mind — former United States Representative Toby Moffett. The same Toby Moffett who challenged Mr. O'Neill for the Democratic nomination last month and lost. Mr. Moffett, a former member of Congress, has joined WVIT/TV-30 in West Hartford — the NBC affiliate in Connecticut — and will soon go on the air as an anchorman.

Mr. O'Neill's Republican opponent, Julie D. Belaga, does not want any veto power over the debate panels at all.

Political Exposure Campaign debates often serve as political tools — particularly, it seems, to front-runners who feel they don't need them.

Governor Cuomo has been avoiding debates with his Republican opponent, Andrew P. O'Rourke, and Senator Alfonse M. D'Amato is limiting himself to only two encounters. And Mr. D'Amato has arranged to have them scheduled in the same 24 hours — 8 P.M. Oct. 21 and 10:30 A.M. the next morning.

That means the two debates will get the publicity of one, which is not particularly helpful to candidates who need the free exposure. Candidates like Mark Green, Mr. D'Amato's Democratic opponent, who has said he wants to spend $2 million but has only $100,000 available right now.

He's got a lot of fund-raising events to come, starring such celebrity draws as Paul Newman and Warren Beatty.

But so far, even John S. Dyson, the wealthy Liberal Party candidate who lost to Mr. Green in the Democratic primary and is given little chance of winning, is outspending him in the general election, thanks mostly to Mr. Dyson's own money.

Space Per Inmate The female condition, in the view of Police Commissioner Benjamin Ward:

It was revealed at a news conference last week that women in city jails have more space per inmate than male prisoners do. The reason is that under court rules, only 50 prisoners may occupy a single room, and the women's dorms are simply larger than the men's.

A reporter asked why women get a better deal. Mr. Ward explained about the larger dorms. The reporter persisted. The Commissioner, sounding a bit exasperated, pared down his answer: "Because," he said, "women are women."

More Koch Nots Here are some further examples, taken from his own remarks, of what Mayor Koch has said he is not:

¶A yenta	¶A diplomat
¶A demagogue	¶A dupe
¶A magician	¶A showboat

Joyce Purnick

L.I. Baymen Face Toughest Winter

Loss of Scallops And Bass Puts Culture at Risk

By THOMAS J. KNUDSON
Special to The New York Times

EAST HAMPTON, L.I., Oct. 11 — After several years of hardship and turmoil, the baymen of eastern Long Island are facing their toughest season in decades — a season that could signal the end of a 300-year-old fishing culture.

"This simply is the bleakest season anyone can remember," said the secretary of the East Hampton Baymen's Association, Arnold Leo. "It's going to be a very hard winter — there's no question some people are going to be hurt."

Traditionally autumn has been the best of times for the baymen, a season when they have gone to the sea for rich harvests of striped bass and bay scallops — the two species that provide the bulk of their income.

But this fall, for the first time in recent memory, there will be no harvest. The state earlier this year banned striped bass fishing because of PCB contamination. And bay scallops have been virtually wiped out by mysterious algae.

Crowded by Development

Many baymen feel that the loss of the two species at such a crucial time, as well as the continuing loss of wetlands and waterfront property to housing development, may foreshadow the end of a fishing tradition.

"Their world is going to pieces," Mr. Leo said. "But it's not just fishing that's changing — it's the whole social structure. Once the baymen were a central part of the community. But today they find they are outsiders, living on the fringe of a well-to-do resort town. Their sense of standing tall has been destroyed."

The world of the bayman exists in a corner of East Hampton seldom seen by summer tourists — the scraggly pine forests around Springs and Amagansett, where the fishermen live in modest homes near the bays and ponds where they fish in plywood skiffs and wooden dories.

It is a world of wind and wing and wave, a world of immeasurable beauty.

"Every day you go down to the ocean, and you see things nobody ever sees," said Donnie Eames Jr. of Amagansett. "Every day the waves are different. Every day the sun rises different. I've seen three or four whales swimming right along the beach. I've caught different kinds of sharks."

"You know who you can count on," Mr. Eames said. "If you're in a jam, if your net's

The New York Times/Gary Gunsinger
Billy Havens, a 12th-generation fisherman on eastern Long Island, with his boat and equipment. He has given up fishing for a living and now works in a restaurant.

stuck or your boat's sinking, you know there'll be 5 or 6 or 10 guys to help you out."

But today the close-knit community of baymen is beginning to unravel. Fishermen like Mr. Eames, who is 30 years old, have left the sea for jobs in town. Others are talking about moving out of the region. And fishermen whose fathers were fishermen are telling their sons to stay off the water.

"Now I know how the Indians feel," said Billy Havens, a 12th-generation fisherman

and descendant of the first William Havens to fish these waters, in the 1600's. "The Indians were driven out, weren't they? The same thing is happening to us."

In July, after two decades of fishing with his father, brothers and uncles, Mr. Havens took a job at Harry's Hideaway, a restaurant and bar in Springs. "My father thought it was the best thing I've ever done," he said. "He

Continued on Page B2

Testimony Portraying Darker Side Of Manes

From Lindenauer, Memories of Greed

By RICHARD J. MEISLIN

The Federal corruption trial in New Haven is shedding a new and harsher light on the life and death of Donald R. Manes, the Queens Borough President who committed suicide by thrusting a knife into his heart last March.

Throughout the testimony of the Government's first two witnesses, Mr. Manes has been portrayed as a man conscious of and delighted by his public position and its attendant power, living a secret life of intense greed and enormous fear of losing it all by having his corrupt activities discovered.

It is a portrait in stark contrast to the affable image that Mr. Manes enjoyed for two decades in city politics, until the shock of his first, unsuccessful suicide attempt last Jan. 10.

"I've looked out my window and seen him going down the street with the President of the United States, arm in arm," said Michael G. Dowd, an executive of a debt-collection agency who was the Government's first witness, recalling the Manes most people knew. "He was the most powerful political public figure, certainly in Queens. The Mayor called him his best friend and said he didn't make a move without him."

'Another Way to Pay'

It was Mr. Dowd, too, who described how even while Mr. Manes was gasping for breath on a Queens racquetball court in April 1985, the Borough President sought to "work something out about another way to pay" the bribes Mr. Dowd had suspended some months before.

But it has been Geoffrey G. Lindenauer, the former deputy director of the city's Parking Violations Bureau, who has given the most startling accounts of Mr. Manes's activities in the course of describing his own. With Mr. Lindenauer's testimony, the Federal prosecutors have tried to establish that a bribery ring existed in the bureau, that Mr. Manes and Mr. Lindenauer were at the center of it, and that the five defendants participated in it.

Mr. Lindenauer, who said he "considered Donald to be my best friend," has also admitted to collecting bribes

Continued on Page B3

Levin Case Worrying O'Connor

By ROBERT O. BOORSTIN

John Cardinal O'Connor has publicly expressed concern that the support given by Catholic clergymen to the young man accused of killing Jennifer Dawn Levin could aggravate relations between Catholics and Jews.

In an article in the weekly newspaper Catholic New York, in which no names were mentioned, Cardinal O'Connor wrote, "I am worried that mercy toward a Catholic boy could be *perceived* as callousness toward a Jewish girl."

At least two Catholic clergymen, including Archbishop Theodore E. McCarrick of Newark, have become involved in the case in which the suspect, Robert E. Chambers Jr., was released earlier this month on $150,000 bail despite a plea by the Levin family.

Archbishop McCarrick, who has said he has known Mr. Chambers for years through his mother, wrote a letter in support of Mr. Chambers' character when bail was being considered.

'They've Seen It As a Tragedy'

Another clergyman, Msgr. Thomas P. Leonard of the Church of the Incarnation in Manhattan, agreed to supervise Mr. Chambers while he awaits trial.

Monsignor Leonard and a spokesman for Archbishop McCarrick said yesterday they have received no negative reaction from Jews about their roles in the case. "Nobody has seen it as a Jewish-Catholic question," Monsignor Leonard said. "They've seen it as a tragedy."

In an interview yesterday, Cardinal O'Connor said he raised the issue of Catholic-Jewish relations in the article in order to head off any potential bad feelings over the clergymen's actions on behalf of Mr. Chambers.

Predicting "enormous publicity" when the case goes to trial later this year, Cardinal O'Connor said, "I wanted it known in advance that my personal sympathies are with both families and that I would not be party to any injustice or perceived injustice toward either family."

"If perchance there was a sense of

Continued on Page B3

RISE OF THE REFINED RIDE

Limos Bring Luxury to the Masses

Stretch limousines and their drivers at Dav-El Livery at Pier 62 on the Hudson River.

The New York Times/Chester Higgins Jr.

Fancy and Fancier

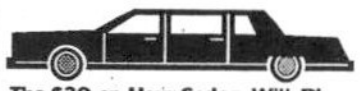

The $30-an-Hour Sedan, With Phone

The $45-to-$50-an-Hour Stretch, With Liquor, Velvet Seats and Quadraphonic Sound

By ELEANOR BLAU

Limousines, once the preserve of the ultra-rich, are everywhere these days, it seems, double-parked on crowded streets or inching forward in traffic. And they are carrying a varied breed.

Behind their discreet dark windows sit men with attaché cases, young people in jeans and high school seniors in formal attire, en route to airports, discotheques and proms.

"It's very convenient, and it's a heck of a lot of fun," said a public-relations man, Thomas Hartocollis, who uses them for a night on the town in New York and elsewhere, and who reports from Boston that limos are growing more popular there.

Indeed, extra-long limousines have been appearing in cities like Kansas City and St. Louis, where few were

seen in the past. But New York remains the largest limousine town.

Whether it is because of convenience, a lack of taxis, rising affluence or just plain chic, about 2,500 "stretch" limos are in use these days in the city and perhaps four times that number in the metropolitan area, according to industry estimates.

It is the stretch limousines that are mostly in evidence — that is, sedans extended by coach builders, who slice the cars in two to insert midsections. They charge about $50,000 for the more luxurious results.

These can include everything from a bar and television to a bed. And they have been known in extreme cases to span 60 feet — the height of a six-story tenement — although 22 feet or so is a more usual length. A sedan

Continued on Page B2

need to be a good designer but he or she had to be able to step into the demanding environment of the newsroom, working with editors who were in tune with daily deadlines and not so much with how designers worked. O'Connor's background included work on some of our weekly sections and earlier experience on daily news pages at *The San Francisco Examiner*. With some trepidation she took the job—a good decision for her and for the news operation. What had once been a notoriously frantic operation settled down with a philosophical approach and an art director of its own.

Newsroom art outpost
A satellite Art Department alongside the photo desk meets the newsroom's need for ready access and coordination of editorial, photo, graphic, and design efforts.

Graphics: A Side of Beef

THE NEW YORK TIMES

Toward journalistic graphics
Three levels

Graphics in a newspaper can be visualized in three levels of conceptual complexity. First is the **straight presentation** of material, relatively unadorned. Before the advent of computer-aided graphics and typesetting in newsrooms, it was no small accomplishment for most newspapers to produce tables and charts that were reasonably well executed and consistent. Computers made possible a degree of professionalism and accuracy that previously at this first level was achieved only with great difficulty.

Unadorned does not necessarily mean a flat presentation. If executed with a good eye for abstract design values such as scale; relationship of positive elements such as lines, bars, and shapes to the negative space around them; sophisticated use of different weights of type; and the controlled application of color and tints, the graphic result is likely to be clear and easy to look at. Archetypical of this level is what is generally called the Swiss style, the key to which is sophisticated economy of execution.

A second level encompasses **artistically embellished graphics,** including everything from a three-dimensional shadowbox to an enormously complex piece of art where the chart may be all but obliterated by cartoon drawings or other kinds of pictures. With the computer's ability to perform graphic complexities, it is increasingly rare that a graphic goes unembellished.

The third level in this analysis is what can be called **journalistic graphics,** graphic treatments so intertwined with some aspect of the story that they affect how the total presentation is made. At

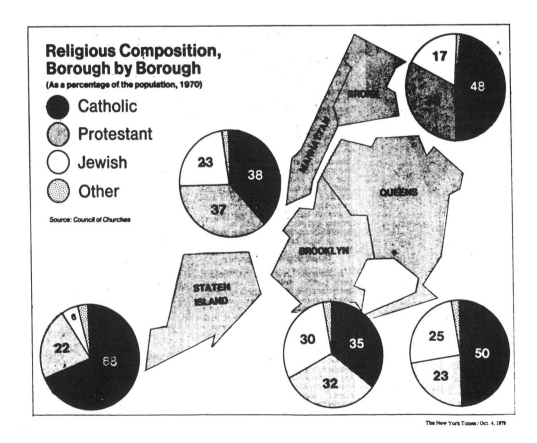

Religious Composition, Borough by Borough
(As a percentage of the population, 1970)

● Catholic
◐ Protestant
○ Jewish
⦿ Other

Source: Council of Churches

The New York Times / Oct. 4, 1979

Straight, direct, clean, and simple
A simple statistical map, such as can be produced in minutes by computer in most of today's newsrooms. Devoid of any obvious artistic embellishment, it nevertheless shows understated but strong use of the pure graphic elements—type, tones, and shapes. Note the shift from the bolder to the lighter but same size Helvetica in the upper left corner.

190

ON ABORTION

"I don't favor abortion. I don't think it's a good thing. I don't think most people do. The question is, who makes the decision. And I think it has to be the woman, in the exercise of her own conscience and religious beliefs, that makes that decision." **MICHAEL S. DUKAKIS**

"Yes my position has evolved, and it's continuing to evolve in favor of life. And I had a couple of exceptions that I support: rape, incest, and the life of the mother."

GEORGE BUSH

ON GUN CONTROL

"We already have some Federal restrictions on handgun ownership. I think there has to be some control over concealable handguns. I have no problem with hunters and weapons for sport or target practice, but Saturday-night specials, in my judgment, require regulation." **MICHAEL S. DUKAKIS**

"I have always opposed Federal gun registration or licensing of gun owners [but] we must balance the legitimate interests of gun owners with the rights of society. . . . We must do all we can to keep guns out of the hands of convicted criminals."

GEORGE BUSH

ON THE SUPREME COURT

"What I would do is appoint people to the federal bench that will not legislate from the bench, who will interpret the Constitution. I do not want to see us go to again — and I'm using this word advisedly — a liberal majority that is going to legislate from the bench."

GEORGE BUSH

"I've appointed prosecutors, I've appointed defenders. I don't appoint people I think are liberal, or people who I think are conservative; I appoint people of independence and integrity and intelligence, people who will be a credit to the bench." **MICHAEL S. DUKAKIS**

ON AIDS

"We must commit the resources and the will to find a cure. . . . I believe that continued research on the virus, combined with public education and testing, is the best path to curing the spread of AIDS. . . . We need testing, but only accompanied by guarantees that everyone is treated fairly." **GEORGE BUSH**

"I strongly support the efforts to increase funding for AIDS research and education to over $1 billion a year. An increasing commitment to research, treatment and education will be necessary in future years."

MICHAEL S. DUKAKIS

United Nations peacekeeping assignments

1948-present: Middle East
force set up to watch borders between Israel and neighboring Arab countries.

1949-present: India and Pakistan
troops in Indian state of Jammu and Kashmir to monitor cease-fire between India and Pakistan

1956-1967: Egypt
force sent to secure cease-fire between Egyptian forces and Israeli, French and British troops in Sinai.

1958: Lebanon
observation group sent to halt arms smuggling.

1960-1964: the Congo
operation to insure withdrawal of Belgian and other foreign troops and to prevent civil war.

1962-1963: West New Guinea
security force sent to keep peace after accord between Indonesia and the Netherlands.

1963-1964: Yemen
mission to certify disengagement of Arab forces in Yemen's civil war.

1964-present: Cyprus
force set up to prevent fighting between Turkish and Greek Cypriots; since 1974 partition, has maintained buffer zone.

1965-1966: India and Pakistan
mission to supervise cease-fire along border.

1973-1979: Sinai
force sent to oversee cease-fire between Egypt and Israel.

1974-present: Golan Heights
contingent supervises cease-fire between Israel and Syria.

1978-present: southern Lebanon
troops sent to confirm withdrawal of Israelis from area and to restore security.

April 1988-present: Afghanistan and Pakistan
small contingent set up to monitor Soviet pullout from Afghanistan and Pakistani and Soviet compliance with accords.

August 1988: Iran and Iraq
group formed to monitor provisions of cease-fire.

Magnum/Stele-Perkins

Simple, direct, but bland
Above: Simplicity and clarity are not adequate if type, tone, and space are not handled eloquently. This three-column box failed to add any graphic interest to the text page.

Small effort, big dividends
Left: A silhouetted picture, easily available, adds enormously to an otherwise quiet box. Even with this modest graphic addition, the box better justifies the space it occupies.

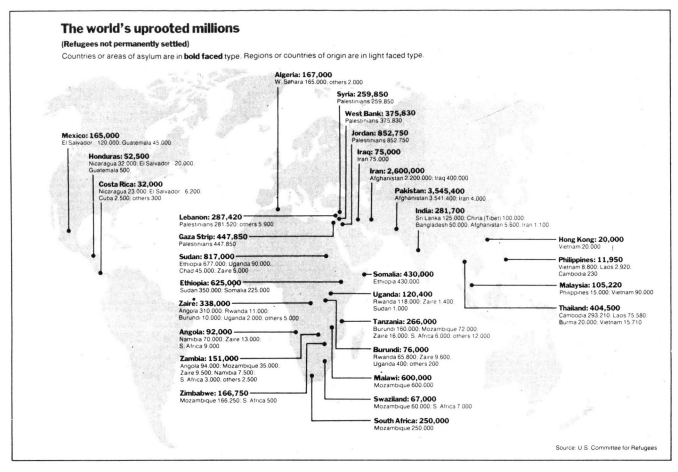

The world's uprooted millions

(Refugees not permanently settled)

Countries or areas of asylum are in **bold faced** type. Regions or countries of origin are in light faced type.

Algeria: 167,000
W. Sahara 165.000; others 2.000

Syria: 259,850
Palestinians 259.850

West Bank: 375,830
Palestinians 375.830

Jordan: 852,750
Palestinians 852.750

Iraq: 75,000
Iran 75.000

Iran: 2,600,000
Afghanistan 2.200.000; Iraq 400.000

Pakistan: 3,545,400
Afghanistan 3.541.400; Iran 4.000

India: 281,700
Sri Lanka 125.000; China (Tibet) 100.000;
Bangladesh 50.000; Afghanistan 5.600; Iran 1.100

Mexico: 165,000
El Salvador 120.000; Guatemala 45.000

Honduras: 52,500
Nicaragua 32.000; El Salvador 20.000;
Guatemala 500

Costa Rica: 32,000
Nicaragua 23.000; El Salvador 6.200;
Cuba 2.500; others 300

Lebanon: 287,420
Palestinians 281.520; others 5.900

Gaza Strip: 447,850
Palestinians 447.850

Sudan: 817,000
Ethiopia 677.000; Uganda 90.000;
Chad 45.000; Zaire 5.000

Ethiopia: 625,000
Sudan 350.000; Somalia 225.000

Zaire: 338,000
Angola 310.000; Rwanda 11.000;
Burundi 10.000; Uganda 2.000; others 5.000

Angola: 92,000
Namibia 70.000; Zaire 13.000;
S. Africa 9.000

Zambia: 151,000
Angola 94.000; Mozambique 35.000;
Zaire 9.500; Namibia 7.500;
S. Africa 3.000; others 2.500

Zimbabwe: 166,750
Mozambique 166.250; S. Africa 500

Somalia: 430,000
Ethiopia 430.000

Uganda: 120,400
Rwanda 118.000; Zaire 1.400;
Sudan 1.000

Tanzania: 266,000
Burundi 160.000; Mozambique 72.000;
Zaire 16.000; S. Africa 6.000; others 12.000

Burundi: 76,000
Rwanda 65.800; Zaire 9.600;
Uganda 400; others 200

Malawi: 600,000
Mozambique 600.000

Swaziland: 67,000
Mozambique 60.000; S. Africa 7.000

South Africa: 250,000
Mozambique 250.000

Hong Kong: 20,000
Vietnam 20.000

Philippines: 11,950
Vietnam 8.800; Laos 2.920;
Cambodia 230

Malaysia: 105,220
Philippines 15.000; Vietnam 90.000

Thailand: 404,500
Cambodia 293.210; Laos 75.580;
Burma 20.000; Vietnam 15.710

Source: U.S. Committee for Refugees

Playing it straight

Three graphics illustrate how straight can be beautiful or at least graphically eloquent. Even the simplest bar chart ought to be presented with the type in good scale and the proportions of the elements in good relation to the negative spaces. Swiss designers have made this kind of elegant simplicity their trademark. Above and bottom left: From *The New York Times;* Bottom right: By Tom Coleman, *Times Daily* (Florence).

Running Out of Space

Number of operating landfills in New York State.

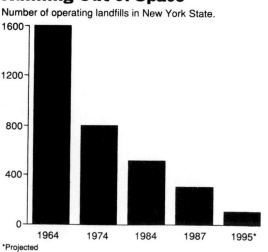

*Projected

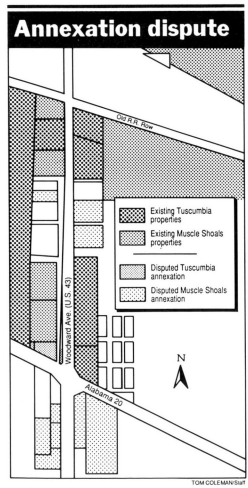

TOM COLEMAN/Staff

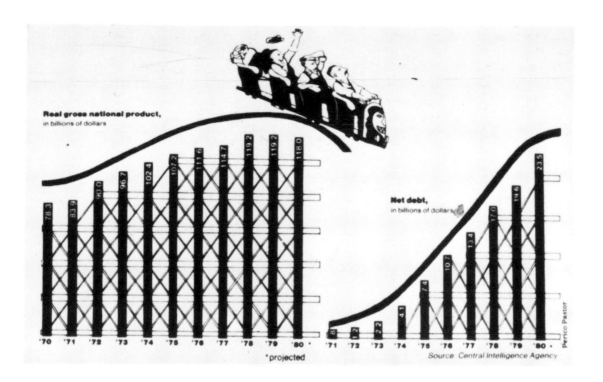

Real gross national product, in billions of dollars

Net debt, in billions of dollars

Source: Central Intelligence Agency

Perico Pastor

Embellishment

To the already infinite number of ways a chart or map can be embellished, the inexpensive computer in the newsroom has added significantly. On this page four examples hint at the range, from witty illustrative chart, to a map as a humorous graphic, to two provocative photographic embellishments. The trick in embellishing is to stop before the information is obscured or trivialized. Above: By Mike Todd for *The New York Times;* Bottom left: International Herald-Tribune; Center: Bob Eisner; Right: Nancy Kent.

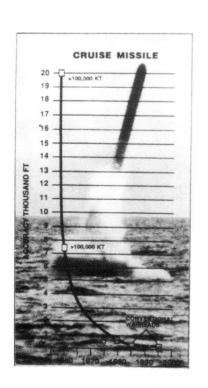

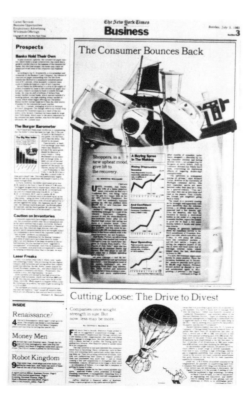

its simplest this can amount to, for example, no more than a time chart that takes the place of background text. More impressively, a journalistic graphic can provide the framework on which an entire presentation is hung, as illustrated in some of the following pages.

The three levels are obviously not clearly separate, clean-cut divisions. A cartoon-embellished panel can include a straight, Swiss-style chart, for example. In a broad sense every graphic that helps a story be understood is a journalistic graphic. Nevertheless, I think the analysis helps to assess the difference between merely decorative and more profound treatments that reflect the editor's mastery of a wide range of communication techniques.

Here's one way to analyze what graphic level is being used. If at the initiation of the graphic the editor says, "We need a graphic for this story showing the flight pattern of the plane that crashed," estimates the size of the space, and turns it over to a graphic artist to draw or execute on his computer to be fitted into the story presentation later, it can hardly be described as a journalistic graphic. Executed with artistic skill it would probably fit into the second category, artistically embellished graphics.

However, if the editor says, "We are going to lead the front page with a graphic presentation combining a diagram and a time chart under a dramatic headline showing, minute by minute, how the accident happened" and asks the designer or art director to design the page around this idea, this is truly a journalistic idea, where the editor uses graphic techniques as eloquently as he deals in words. If the designer sits at the editor's elbow and participates in the initial discussion, their combined, rather than separate, orientations are more likely to produce this kind of result.

Graphic headlines

Left: The front of an inside section of *The Times* dealing with the peace treaty signed by Egypt and Israel, stemming from talks at Camp David. The headline in three languages is part of the graphic treatment, and the dominant map with photos tells much of the story. The page was designed the day before, but details came in late in the afternoon, requiring frantic effort by many on deadline (in 1969, unaided by computers). Designed by Louis Silverstein and executed by *The Times* Map Department.

Drama of words

The Apollo 13 mission to circle the moon had been on television and the front pages all week. After near disaster, the astronauts were safely home. In The Week in Review we had the problem of presenting a fresh visualization that readers hadn't already seen. The solution was the diagram that works as a headline with day-by-day quotations from the astronauts themselves selected to reflect the euphoria, anxiety, and relief of the drama.

The drama of the words is the heart of the graphic idea. Designed by Louis Silverstein, executed by *The Times* Map Department.

Science, Law,
Education, Editorials, Letters.

© 1970 The New York Times Company

The New York Times

THE WEEK IN REVIEW

Sunday: "Looking in good shape."

Monday: "Hey, we've got a problem here!"

Tuesday: "That was a good burn."

Wednesday: "If I can get on that carrier I don't care how long it takes."

Thursday: "Aquarius is coming in."

Friday: "Aboard! Condition excellent."

5. Command module enters earth's atmosphere. 12:41 PM, Apr. 17

6. Splashdown. 1:07 PM, Apr. 17

1. Launching. 2:15 PM, Apr. 11

2. Translunar Injection. 4:48 PM, Apr. 11

TRANSEARTH COAST

TRANSLUNAR COAST

3. Oxygen tank ruptures. 10:08 PM, Apr. 13

4. LM engine fires to bring craft back to earth. 9:41 PM, Apr. 14

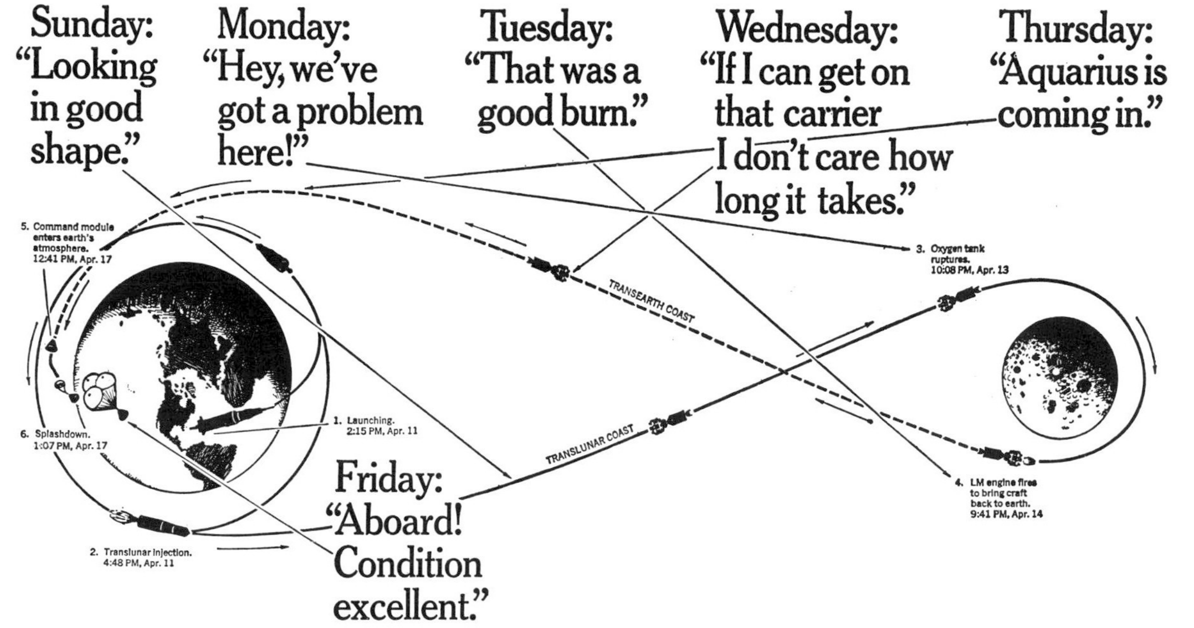

Space

Three Came Back as The World Held Its Breath

HOUSTON — There have been epic voyages of survival in the past, such as the 3,618-mile lifeboat voyage of Captain Bligh, of mutiny on the Bounty fame, in 1789, or the incredible journey of Sir Ernest Shackleton across the storm-torn Antarctic Ocean in 1916. But the world did not learn of these feats until years after the event. Last week's saga of Apollo 13 was fought out with most of mankind hanging on each move.

It began with a leisurely television show in which the trio of astronauts, en route for what was to be the third landing of men on the moon, demonstrated how they enter the lunar module, or LM, designed to lower two of them to the lunar surface. It ended with another television show, in which the three men, haggard but safe and smiling, stepped from a helicopter onto the deck of the carrier Iwo Jima in the South Pacific.

Between the two spectaculars stretched four anguished days of struggle for survival — a struggle in which human courage, endurance and ingenuity were pitted not against wave and wind and hunger but the perils of suffocating, burning up or freezing to death in space, or crashing onto the moon, or having the spacecraft miss the earth to become an eternal wanderer in the solar system.

The drama erupted last Monday, as the spacecraft neared the moon. The first indication of trouble was a loud bang that startled the astronauts in the otherwise serene environment of space flight. Although they did not know it until the mission was almost over, an explosion had blown out virtually one entire side of the cylindrical service module, or "engine room," that rode behind the cone-shaped command module carrying the astronauts.

The service module contained tanks of liquid hydrogen and liquid oxygen, as well as fuel cells in which oxygen and hydrogen are combined — in effect burned — to generate electric power

and manufacture water. Apparently one of the oxygen tanks exploded. Almost immediately an alarm light in front of the astronauts showed a drop in voltage on half their main electrical system.

"Hey, we've got a problem here!" was the call from space to the Mission Control Center on earth. Then the astronauts, James A. Lovell Jr., Fred W. Haise Jr., and John L. Swigert Jr., noticed that pressure in one of the main oxygen tanks was plunging.

At that point Fred Haise was emerging from the tunnel leading into the LM and pulled his weightless body into his command-module seat. As he did so his eye caught the instrument panel which showed that by now the voltage on half the electrical system had gone to zero and two of the spacecraft's three fuel cells were dead.

Something catastrophic had obviously happened. At first a meteorite impact was suspected, but a rise in oxygen pressure just before the rupture made an internal origin seem more likely.

Looking back toward the service module though one of the spacecraft's windows, the astronauts could see a blizzard of particles flying out, presumably from one or more ruptured tanks. The spacecraft kept trying to dip its nose and roll, apparently because this venting of gas was pushing it. Worst of all, despite desperate measure improvised on board and urged from the ground, nothing would halt the drop in oxygen pressure. One tank was empty and the other was losing pressure fast — evidently it had been ruptured by the explosion in the first tank. With all pressure gone, the last power generating fuel cell would also go dead.

All thought of a lunar landing was, of course, immediately abandoned. The problem now was to get the men safely back to earth. This could not be done by turning Apollo 13 around in mid-course. At that point in the trip the spaceship was, in effect, falling toward the moon, and it would have required far more rocket power than was available to defy the moon's gravity and head homeward. Instead, it was decided, the astronauts would ride around the moon, allowing lunar gravity, in a crack-the-whip manner, to throw the crippled vehicle back in the general direction of the earth.

Two things had to be done in a hurry. Enough oxygen had to be salvaged to supply the command module during re-entry into the earth's atmosphere — assuming they could get back to

James A. Lovell Jr.

Fred W. Haise Jr.

John L. Swigert Jr.

earth — and the gyros on the navigation system had to be kept going until the navigation equipment of the LM could be powered up.

With only minutes remaining, the astronauts fed oxygen into a reserve tank and hooked up emergency batteries to the navigation gyros. This kept them alive until they were able to warm up the LM navigation system and transfer their "sense of direction" there. That done, they promptly switched off the battery power, which was vital for their re-entry into the earth's atmosphere. From then on until just before re-entry the command module was dead.

Essential to survival of the astronauts was the presence of the LM riding on the nose of the command module. Early in the Apollo program it had been recognized that the LM could serve as a "lifeboat" in such emergencies. Designed to carry two men down to the moon, it was cramped quarters for three. So during sleep periods one man kept watch in the LM while the other two slept in the command module — until the latter became so cold that all three crowded into the LM.

The cold in the command module remained a critical problem, however. Without electric power for the command module heaters, it was feared that some of the instruments needed for re-entry would freeze beyond recovery. When possible, the spacecraft was put into a "barbecue mode" of rotation, so that the sun would uniformly heat all sides. But gas tanks ruptured by the explosion kept squirting their contents out into space, converting the barbecue motion into an unpredictable wobble.

In the LM, meanwhile, the chief concern was heat — the heating of the electronics, particularly of the navigation system and computer. The electronics were water-cooled, but the LM system was designed only for short flights, and water was scarce. The astronauts floated about in the spacecraft filling every plastic bag they could find with water.

The countless improvisations that nursed the crippled spacecraft along were in large measure the product of an extraordinarily elaborate assembly of simulators at the Manned Spacecraft Center in Houston and elsewhere. Every makeshift procedure carried out in space was first tried out on earth, and rejected if the simulators showed it to be dangerous or impractical.

The simulation crews, for example, had to figure out how to navigate from the LM when it was docked to the command module, whose bulk cut off much of the sky from the small, triangular LM windows. They had to devise ways in which the LM's little jet thrusters could be used to control the massive combina-

tion of LM, command module and service module. It was like trying to row a large yacht with oars. Furthermore, gas spurting from ruptured tanks pushed the craft in unpredictable ways. Yet it was essential to hold its orientation, or "attitude," steady for the rocket firings needed to bring it home.

"Why the hell are we maneuvering at all now? Are we still venting?" came a frustrated cry. Then a moment later: "Any time I try to—I can't take that doggone roll out." And finally in desperation: "What's the frappin' attitude?"

The first step proposed by the ground crew was to fire the LM engine briefly — the engine designed to lower the LM onto the moon—so as to push the combined spacecraft into a trajectory that, after circling the moon, would return it to earth. The maneuver was a tricky one. The trajectory being followed by the astronauts at the time of the explosion would have brought them to within an estimated 60 miles of the moon. A thrust in the wrong direction would result in a lunar impact.

It was essential to make sure the gyro-stabilized platform used aboard the LM as the reference base for guidance was properly aligned. The normal way to do this — to take star sights, but the spacecraft was enveloped in a cloud of frothy flakes generated by venting of gas after the accident. Every particle jettisoned or ejected from a ship in space tends to fly along with it.

'Foam Stars'

Debris kept shaking loose from the wrecked service module throughout the flight. "Hey, look out of that window!" one astronaut cried. And later: "Look at that big thing out there . . . It looks like a piece of wrapping for line." At one point what looked like a metal sheet drifted past.

On one side, sunlight reflected from various parts of the spacecraft was too bright for the stars to be visible. As to the opposite window: "It's pretty dark out that one," said the voice from the spacecraft, "But there are about a thousand or so foam stars out here — left over from some of the debris — it's hard to discern what's real and what's not real."

Since they could not see stars, men on the simulators back on earth found that if the craft's guidance were properly aligned a certain maneuver should bring the sun squarely into one of the spacecraft windows. It did. And so, with confidence, the LM rocket was fired, changing the path to clear the moon by 136 miles. Ground control told the astronauts the good news. Their sigh of relief could almost be heard across 200,000 miles.

"That's very nice!" one of them said.

The astronauts continued their plunge toward the moon. Then, suddenly, they were in the moon's shadow. Those on earth could eavesdrop on them. "Man, look at those stars!" "That view out there is fantastic!" For Lovell this was his second visit to the vicinity of the moon. He called out familiar landmarks. They made their closest approach and began drawing away, circling back toward earth. "You can see where we're zooming off." "Yes . . . We're leaving."

Another rocket thrust soon after rounding the moon, plus two slight corrective burns later on, put them squarely on a course for a South Pacific splashdown.

Ground control told the astronauts that the booster rocket that had originally pushed them toward the moon had crashed on the moon, as planned, to generate tremors for monitoring instruments left on the lunar surface by Apollo 12.

A major challenge on the journey home was to keep the air breathable. American astronauts breathe an atmosphere of pure oxygen, mixed with carbon dioxide they exhale. The air is circulated through lithium hydroxide canisters to purge it of this carbon dioxide. However, despite the numerous contingency provisions characteristic of Apollo the canisters for the command module were not made to be interchangeable with those for the LM. The LM canisters could not purge the air for the entire trip and the command module system was closed down.

The result was an intense effort at Houston to improvise ways to use canisters from the command module in the LM system. With sheets of plastic wrapping from equipment for the lunar landing, cardboard covers from the flight records — sticky tape, the astronauts, on instructions from earth, built contraptions that enabled them to connect the command module canisters to the LM air purification system.

The last great worry was getting rid of the service module and the LM before plunging into the atmosphere. Normally, the LM is dumped near the moon and the service module blasts itself free of the command module. But now the LM was still with them, and the service module was without the power needed for detaching itself. Improvisation led to a scheme whereby the LM was used to pull the command module clear of the service module and the LM was then shot away by release of its own internal air pressure — much like a deflating toy balloon shoots across the room.

The normal re-entry that followed on Friday was the most hair-raising mission in the short history of space flight.

Even before the splashdown a

"That's very nice!" one of them said.

top-level inquiry was being organized. The reason for the explosion was still not known.

"Farewell, Aquarius" — code name for the LM — "and we thank you," said Mission Control as space flight's first lifeboat sped off to burn up in the atmosphere. Before another manned launching, measures will surely be taken to make the LM more effective in that role.

—WALTER SULLIVAN

To Go Forward Or Not After Near Disaster?

Two flights to the moon, two landings, two returns to earth were carried through without a hitch. They were the grandest shows in the world, for all the machinery worked almost perfectly and everything that was supposed to happen did indeed happen. Yet now, despite this, a voice on the ill-fated Apollo 13 could perhaps justly say, "I'm afraid this is going to be the last moon mission for a long time."

As a matter of fact, despite the euphoria of the earlier successes, and the glory of footsteps on the moon, discontent with the space program had been gathering for some time.

For one thing, it was fearfully expensive — $24-billion to reach the moon — and this at a time when the cities are decaying, the environment is deteriorating and the social structure is crumbling.

More and more people had to ask whether the nation was merely engaged in a grandstand competition with the Soviet Union at the cost of its own wellbeing. Was the race for the moon a sign of social cancer, was it a kind of diseased overgrowth like the pyramids that bankrupted ancient Egypt or the Versailles Palace that bankrupted 17th-century France? Were we impelled to ever greater feats of empty show out of competitive vainglory? Was indeed the space program primarily intended to distract attention both inside the country and outside from the ever more serious decline of our social and economic fabric?

Reservations about the space program are even to be found

Continued on Page 2

The Great Dill Pickle

See Mimi Sheraton, Page C8

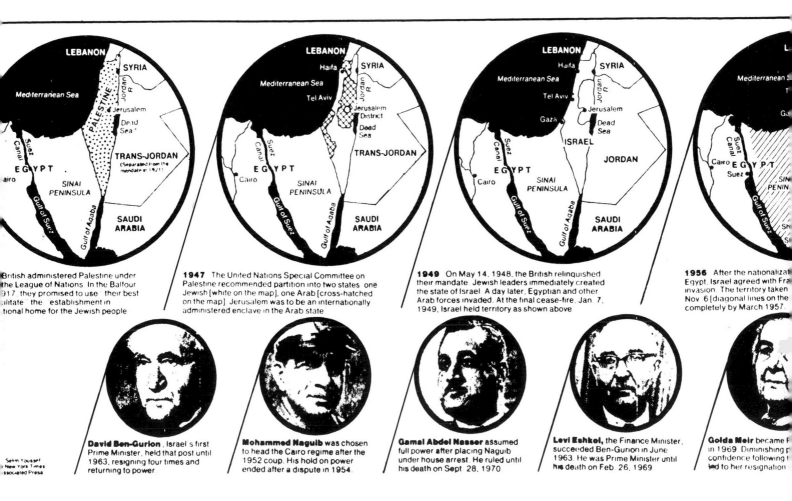

British administered Palestine under the League of Nations. In the Balfour 917. they promised to use "their best ilitate" the establishment in tional home for the Jewish people

1947 The United Nations Special Committee on Palestine recommended partition into two states one Jewish [white on the map]. one Arab [cross-hatched on the map] Jerusalem was to be an internationally administered enclave in the Arab state

1949 On May 14, 1948, the British relinquished their mandate. Jewish leaders immediately created the state of Israel. A day later, Egyptian and other Arab forces invaded. At the final cease-fire, Jan. 7, 1949, Israel held territory as shown above

1956 After the nationaliza Egypt, Israel agreed with Fra invasion. The territory taken Nov. 6 [diagonal lines on th completely by March 1957.

Sekm Youssef New York Times ssociated Press

David Ben-Gurion, Israel's first Prime Minister, held that post until 1963, resigning four times and returning to power.

Mohammed Naguib was chosen to head the Cairo regime after the 1952 coup. His hold on power ended after a dispute in 1954.

Gamal Abdel Nasser assumed full power after placing Naguib under house arrest. He ruled until his death on Sept. 28, 1970

Levi Eshkol, the Finance Minister, succeeded Ben-Gurion in June 1963. He was Prime Minister until his death on Feb. 26, 1969

Golda Meir became P in 1969. Diminishing p confidence following t led to her resignation

Time chart
Above: One of the best graphic devices for placing a breaking news event in the context of historical flow, the time chart combines geographical, political, and historical information. Designed by Louis Silverstein, executed by *The Times* Map Department.

A big idea
Facing page: When a rebus-like treatment culminates in a six-column-wide pickle, it is safe to say that the graphic idea has assumed more-than-routine journalistic substance. Is it overplay? (After all, how many people make pickles?) Or is it wholesome wit (a pickle across six columns!). Designed by Nancy Kent.

A side of beef

Graphics with something extra

At *The Times* we were planning our coverage of the first shuttle flight by the spaceship Columbia. The standard approach for such an important event, which would run to multipage coverage, was that the appropriate desk editor would parcel out assignments, covering every relevant aspect of the story. Top editors would participate in the planning. As the stories came in, a decision would be made to pin down the number of pages, allotting to headlines, pictures, and other graphic elements a percentage of space, usually one and a half columns per six-column page, or one quarter of the space. The desk editor or a deputy would begin to organize the stories on a page-to-page basis. So organized, the material would go to a make-up editor who, working with the photo editor or a deputy, would design the pages, subject to review by the news editor and the desk editor.

The reader would see essentially page after page of text broken up by pictures. Each page would have been laid out following traditional make-up patterns, more or less as a separate unit, with photos, charts, and other graphic materials spotted throughout to accompany the relevant stories.

Preplanned, multipage presentations executed in this way suffer from the entrenched procedures that dominate the run-of-the-mill daily news operation, adequately serving run-of-the-mill page make-up, but not going far enough to deal with a major story of any complexity. Missing in this approach is a truly comprehensive design of the multipage presentation as a whole. It is assembled but not designed. And of course it is built around a single axis, the story assignment list. While *The Times* could be expected to cover

the story of a first space flight from every conceivable angle, to a greater degree than most other publications, the page-by-page planning inevitably led to a predictable kind of presentation, dictated by the assignment-length stories laid out on a per-page basis. In this comprehensive but exhaustive coverage I felt we often blanketed a subject until it all but stopped breathing.

To work toward the goal of more effective design, the designer has to be involved in the planning right from the start. In the shuttle flight story, being involved in the initial planning, I did not propose the usual allotment of spaces spread out horizontally through the pages as rectangles breaking up text, but rather the designation of a doublespread, two full pages, that would bring together the technical and factual material in a concentrated, easy-to-grasp, visual manner. An

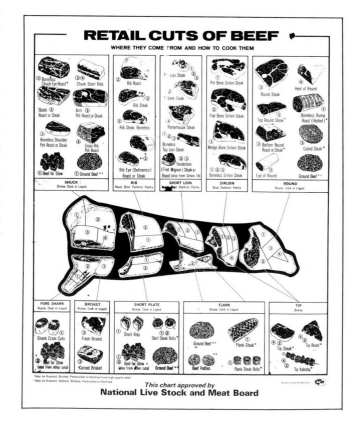

Cuts of beef

Right: A vintage poster from Catena's Meat Market in Southampton, New York, is an example of a useful informational graphic.

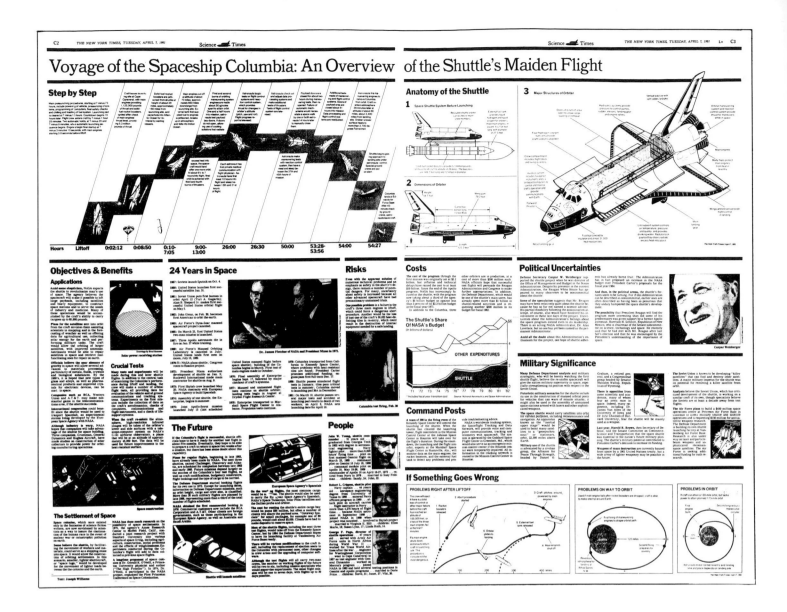

additional axis was provided on which we could hang our presentation—a graphic axis to complement the editor's story list.

I described the proposed spread to Abe Rosenthal as a large graphic unit that in effect would be an informational poster, much like the poster seen in a butcher shop showing the cuts of beef derived from a steer. Later, when the technique had become a familiar tool, Rosenthal and other people in the newsroom began to refer to it in shorthand speech as "a side of beef." (A few years later, speaking at one of Mario Garcia's seminars at the Poynter Institute in Florida, I heard participants in the seminar, from around the country, use the expression familiarly.)

A side of beef should not be thought of as merely a bunch of statistics brought together into a large single unit but as a creatively designed "collage" of words and graphics, assembled with

Graphic overview

This double spread on the first flight of the Columbia Shuttle shows the first crystallization of a *side of beef* as distinguished from a collection of statistics. Its interest stems primarily from its *journalistic* scope and treatment, ranging from narration, to lists, to analysis, to conjecture ("If something went wrong . . ."), all brought together as different facets of the same complex subject. The common denominator is graphic succinctness and harmony in the way the elements work together, abetted by the fact that the writing *followed* rather than preceded the layout. Designed by Louis Silverstein, executed by *The Times* Map Department.

199

Step by Step

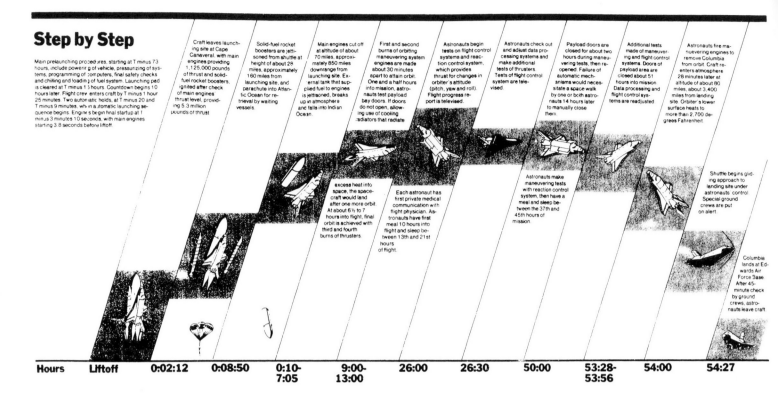

Main prelaunching procedures, starting at T minus 73 hours, include powering of vehicle, pressurizing of systems, programming of computers, final safety checks and chilling and loading of fuel system. Launching pad is cleared at T minus 15 hours. Countdown begins 10 hours later. Flight crew enters craft by T minus 1 hour 25 minutes. Two automatic holds, at T minus 20 and T minus 9 minutes, when automatic launching sequence begins. Engines begin final startup at T minus 3 minutes 10 seconds, with main engines starting 3.8 seconds before liftoff.

Craft leaves launching site at Cape Canaveral, with main engines providing 1,125,000 pounds of thrust and solid-fuel rocket boosters, ignited after check of main engines thrust level, providing 5.3 million pounds of thrust.

Solid-fuel rocket boosters are jettisoned from shuttle at height of about 28 miles, approximately 160 miles from launching site, and parachute into Atlantic Ocean for retrieval by waiting vessels.

Main engines cut off at altitude of about 70 miles, approximately 850 miles downrange from launching site. External tank that supplied fuel to engines is jettisoned, breaks up in atmosphere and falls into Indian Ocean.

First and second burns of orbiting maneuvering system engines are made about 30 minutes into flight. One and a half hours into mission, astronauts test payload bay doors. If doors do not open, allowing use of cooling radiators that radiate excess heat into space, the spacecraft would land after one more orbit. At about 6½ to 7 hours into flight, final orbit is achieved with third and fourth burns of thrusters.

Astronauts begin tests on flight control systems and reaction control system, which provides thrust for changes in orbiter's attitude (pitch, yaw and roll). Flight progress report is televised. Each astronaut has first private medical communication with flight physician. Astronauts have first meal 10 hours into flight and sleep between 13th and 21st hours of flight.

Astronauts check out and adjust data processing systems and make additional tests of thrusters.

Astronauts make maneuvering tests with reaction control system, then have a meal and sleep between the 37th and 45th hours of mission.

Payload doors are closed for about two hours during maneuvering tests, then reopened. Failure of automatic mechanisms would necessitate a space walk by one or both astronauts 14 hours later to manually close them.

Additional tests made of maneuvering and flight control systems. Doors of payload area are closed about 51 hours into mission. Data processing and flight control systems are readjusted.

Astronauts fire maneuvering engines to remove Columbia from orbit. Craft reenters atmosphere 28 minutes later at altitude of about 80 miles, about 3,400 miles from landing site. Orbiter's lower surface heats to more than 2,700 degrees Fahrenheit.

Shuttle begins gliding approach to landing site under astronauts' control. Special ground crews are put on alert.

Columbia lands at Edwards Air Force Base. After 45-minute check by ground crews, astronauts leave craft.

| Hours | Liftoff | 0:02:12 | 0:08:50 | 0:10-7:05 | 9:00-13:00 | 26:00 | 26:30 | 50:00 | 53:28-53:56 | 54:00 | 54:27 |

Close-ups

Some of the elements from the Shuttle double spread in the previous figure. Above: The diagonals in the time chart lend visual vitality to the whole spread. Below: Complex information assembled for easy accessibility is shown.

Objectives & Benefits

Applications

Amid some skepticism, NASA expects the shuttle to revolutionize man's use of space. The agency believes the spacecraft will make it possible to loft large payloads, including satellites and heavy equipment, to construct space stations and to serve the needs of industry and medicine. Many of these operations would be accomplished by the craft's ability to carry cargoes up to 65,000 pounds.

Plans for the satellites sent into orbit from the craft envision them assisting scientists in mapping and in the forecasting of weather as well as offering data for agricultural use, collecting solar energy for the earth and performing military tasks. The craft would allow the orbiting of larger satellites, with improved antennas. Astronauts would be able to repair satellites in space and retrieve malfunctioning ones for repair on earth.

Officials believe the near absence of gravity in space will allow several advances in materials processing, particularly of metals, fluids, crystals and biological substances. By the 1980's, it is hoped that new types of glass and alloys, as well as pharmaceutical products and improved crystals for electronic devices, can be made in space.

Companies such as RCA, Western Union and A.T.&T. may make substantial gains in the telecommunica-

Drawings by Brad Hamann
Solar power receiving station

Crucial Tests

Many tests and experiments will be made during this and later shuttle flights. In addition to the central task of examining the Columbia's performance during liftoff and landing, the crew will make a number of orbital flight tests, all providing data for evaluation of the vehicle and of ground communications and tracking systems. Experiments on the first mis-

---

24 Years in Space

1957: Soviets launch Sputnik on Oct. 4.

1958: United States launches first successful satellite Jan. 31.

1961: Soviet Union puts first human in orbit April 12 (Yuri A. Gagarin); Alan B. Shepard Jr. makes first successful United States orbital flight on May 5.

1962: John Glenn, on Feb. 20, becomes first American to orbit the earth.

1963: Air Force's Dyna-Soar manned spacecraft project canceled.

1965: On March 23, first United States two-man mission is launched.

1967: Three Apollo astronauts die in fire on Jan. 27 while training.

1969: Air Force's Manned Orbiting Laboratory is canceled in July; United States lands first men on moon, July 16, 1969.

1970-71: NASA plans shuttle; Congress votes to finance project.

1972: President Nixon authorizes development of shuttle on Jan. 5; Rockwell International made main contractor for shuttle on Aug. 9.

1973: First Skylab crew launched May 25; NASA contracts with European Space Agency to build Spacelab.

1974: Assembly of test shuttle, the Enterprise, begins in summer.

Dr. James Fl...

United States manned flight befo... space shuttle); building of the C... lumbia begins in March. First test main engines made in October.

1976: Final assembly of Enterpri... begins Sept. 17, followed by maj... checkout of craft's systems.

1977: Manned and unmanned flig... tests continue on shuttle orbite... landing tests begin in August... Dryden Flight Research Center.

imagination and a touch of wit in the selection and handling of the text as well as the graphic material. It focuses on a complex subject from different angles, giving the reader one highlight after another in succinct fashion. If successful, the visual result can be said to add up to more than the sum of its parts.

Smaller elements on the page show how different content materials suggest different treatments. The positioning of elements in relation to each other also inspires design variety, a sense of cinematic narrative developed through counterpoints and changes of pace in both visual treatment and subject matter. The subject matter in the Columbia spread goes from the technical, to the historic, to the anecdotal.

Dateline

To cap off the spread, the datelines on these pages feature a little shuttle trademark set between the name of the paper and the date. The dateline can be used to display small accenting labels when larger section heads are not called for. *The Times* uses this kind of label for subsections or pages such as "International News," "National News," "Sports Pages," "Education," and many other designations.

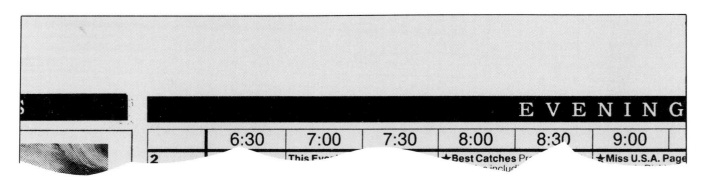

Glyph

A small glyph representing the shuttle accents the dateline and labels the spread. The symbol acts in the same way that words act as labels in datelines in various parts of *The Times*.

CONVENTION IN DALLAS

The Republicans

Who the Republicans Are

Percentage of Republicans in each category, from New York Times/CBS News polls.

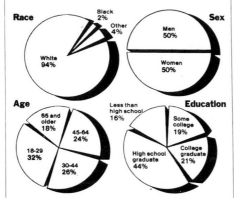

Race
White 94%
Black 2%
Other 4%

Sex
Men 50%
Women 50%

Age
65 and older 18%
45-64 24%
18-29 32%
30-44 26%

Education
Less than high school 16%
Some college 19%
College graduate 21%
High school graduate 44%

Regional Strengths and Weaknesses

The party's share of total electoral votes for President from 1968 through 1980, and seats in state legislatures in 1984, by region.

Electoral votes: 84%
Legislators: 57%

Electoral votes: 85%
Legislators: 42%

Electoral votes: 54%
Legislators: 39%

NORTHEAST

PLAINS AND MOUNTAINS

MIDWEST

FAR WEST

SOUTHWEST

SOUTH

Electoral votes: 93%
Legislators: 43%

Electoral votes: 65%
Legislators: 17%

Electoral votes: 71%
Legislators: 34%

If the electoral votes in the last four Presidential elections are totaled, Republicans have won a majority in every region of the United States and have taken less than 65 percent in only one region. Nationally, Republicans have won 72 percent of the electoral vote since 1968.

Another measure of strength, important in the long run, is a party's state legislative seats. By this measure, the Republicans are much weaker than the electoral vote indicates, with a majority of state legislative seats in only one regions and only 37 percent nationwide.

Republicans Point With Pride To the Reagan Record So Far

The New York Times
U.S. Army tanks on parade.

Republicans arrive in Dallas proud of the record compiled in what they hope will be only the first Reagan Administration. These are some sources of that pride:

National Defense
Defense is the government responsibility into which they have put the most new money, and they have advanced a range of new weapons systems. They argue that only when the nation has reversed a decline will it be safe to proceed on disarmament.

Inflation
Inflation is down sharply under the Reagan Administration, from 12.4 percent in 1980 to an annual rate of 4.8 percent in ing the first six months of this year, as measured by the Consumer Price Index.

Traditional Values
Support for school prayer, opposition to abortion, and an identification with the family and patriotism have been key elements of the Reagan Presidency.

Deregulation
The Republicans have been dedicated to reducing the scope of Federal authority, seeking to abolish agencies, to sharply reduce their regulatory power or to appoint officials who will hold a lighter rein.

Respect Abroad
Increased respect for the United States around the world has been another major goal of the Reagan Administration, exemplified in its willingness to commit American troops in Lebanon, to support the government in El Salvador and the rebels in Nicaragua, and to invade Grenada.

Associated Press
President Reagan at Utah Beach in Normandy, France, with Queen Elizabeth II and President François Mitterrand.

Standard-Bearer

After a campaign swing through the Midwest earlier in the week, President Reagan is scheduled to arrive in Dallas Wednesday. That evening, the convention will vote on his nomination. On Thursday, after a filmed introduction, Mr. Reagan is scheduled to deliver his acceptance speech.

The Party Is Not Without Some Long-Term Concerns

Despite an overall optimism, some Republicans worry about the party's future, with these major sources of concern:

Women
Women are increasingly negative about the party, and their weight in the electorate is increasing. Only 23 percent of American women consider themselves Republicans, according to a recent New York Times/CBS News Poll, as against 40 percent who call themselves Democrats. While much of this disaffection appears to have been stimulated by reactions to President Reagan himself, some strategists fear that the problem will remain with the party in the long run.

Blacks
Blacks have not been very sympathetic to Republicans since the election of Franklin D. Roosevelt; today only 3 percent call themselves Republicans. And blacks are voting in increasing numbers, holding the balance of power in a number of key states. Moreover, some Republican

moderates worry that the Administration's image as, at best, uninterested in blacks, will cost it support with some whites as well.

Image
A "country-club" image is another long-term worry. In the 1982 campaign, the President was persuaded to stop appearing in a dinner jacket, but the lavish style of some Republican events and Administration officials worries those who think the party must develop its appeal to blue-collar and middle-income voters.

The Deficit
The deficit is the one government problem that by traditional Republican standards has plainly worsened in the Reagan Administration. From $59.6 billion in the last year of the Carter Administration, it has risen to what is expected to be $174 billion in this fiscal year. Many Republicans see the long-term impact on interest rates as a key economic concern.

Sygma/Owen Franken
The 1977 National Women's Convention in Houston.

Some Gatherings Difficult to Match

The first Republican convention was held in Philadelphia in 1856, when the nominees were John C. Fremont of California for the Presidency and Wilburn L. Dayton of New Jersey for the Vice Presidency. Fremont attracted 520 votes, to 37 for John McLean of Ohio and 1 for William H. Seward of New York.

The longest Republican convention — it lasted 41 hours over six days — was that in Chicago in 1880, when the party finally nominated James A. Garfield after 36 ballots. Chester A. Arthur was nominated for the Vice Presidency on the first ballot.

In 1920, again in Chicago, it took 10 ballots to nominate Warren G. Harding for the Presidency. He placed sixth on the first ballot, but supporters had predicted that when none of the front-runners could command a majority, party leaders would repair to a "smoke-filled room" to settle on a candidate. Harding indeed turned out to be the compromise choice. Calvin Coolidge won the Vice-Presidential nomination that year on the first ballot.

The shortest convention was the one renominating Richard Nixon in Miami Beach in 1972, which lasted just over 17 hours.

President Warren G. Harding

Grand Old Party: A Variety of Views

The Republicans have a habit of having three bad years and one good one, and the good one always happens to be election years.

WILL ROGERS

• • •

Republicans are for both the man and the dollar, but in case of conflict the man before the dollar.

ABRAHAM LINCOLN

• • •

The Republican Party stands for a wise and regulated individualism. Socialism would destroy wealth; Republicanism would prevent its abuse."

REPUBLICAN PLATFORM, 1908

From "Crown's Book of Political Quotations," by Michael Jackman, Crown Publishers, New York, 1982

An Elephantine History

In the spring of 1874, as President Grant was at the height of his popularity, The New York Herald charged Grant with "Caesarism," planning to run for a third term and make himself a dictator. That summer, The Herald published a hoax — a report that the animals in the Central Park Zoo had broken out.

Thomas Nast, the caricaturist, combined elements from the two items in a cartoon that appeared in Harper's Weekly on Nov. 7, 1874. It depicted The Herald as an ass wearing a lion's skin that suggested the fearful aspects of "Caesarism" and terrifying other animals in the park, among them an elephant representing the Republican vote being frightened away from its normal allegiance.

A cartoon two weeks later, after Republicans fared badly at the polls, showed the elephant in a trap. Nast used the device repeatedly thereafter, and other cartoonists picked up the elephant as symbol of the party.

More on the Republicans, Page 14.

Side of beef saves the day

A graphic cover

The Republican National Convention was due to start in Dallas in May 1984. It had been an all too predictable, cut-and-dried campaign so far, with the renomination of Ronald Reagan a virtual certainty.

The issues were obscured by the incumbent's personal popularity and the Democrats' failure to dramatize successfully any distinctive program of their own. Yet journalistic priorities dictated that we give the convention special coverage with a special section, each day of its four days. For the first day in particular, when nothing much would be happening, there was the problem of designing an arresting first page for this presentation. The line-up of the article was thorough, including the campaign to date; the key players to watch; physical arrangements; the issues before the convention; a reporter's notebook (unexpectedly assigned to John Russell, *The Times'* chief art critic); and all the other expected angles. But none of these seemed strong enough to kick off the section's front page.

Unusual section cover

Facing page: A special section on the 1984 Republican Convention features this side of beef, ranging from statistical nitty-gritty to the peripheral and amusing. The design is perhaps deceptively simple, but the nature of the centerpiece is no less important here than in any other cover design. Here, the space around the drawing by Hirschfeld, the variety in scale of the elements, and the variety of graphic treatments—ink drawing, three-dimensional charts, news photos, a close-up of a campaign button—all contribute with the informative texts to a liveliness hardly generated by the Convention itself.

A two-page cover design

Right: The front page treatment spills over onto Page 2. Less effective than the front page, primarily because of the overstress on Faces at the Convention, it results in a lack of visual focal point, a good example of the often uneasy consequence when the writer and the designer are simply not talking the same language.

A side of beef entitled simply "The Republicans" was the answer. Featured was an Al Hirschfeld cartoon as the centerpiece as well as such offbeat items as the origin of the elephant as the Republican Party symbol.

Since more material existed than could comfortably be put on one page, rather than cram it in, we spilled it over onto the next page, making a two-page introduction to the regular text articles that followed. The second side of beef page featured a drawing of the likely second man on the ticket, George Bush. Together, both pages made an active introductory package to the special section.

203

The Future of Arms Control

Highlights in Arms Control History

Overview: Where The Candidates Stand

Reagan's View

The Nuclear Freeze Issue

Strategic Long Range Missile

Medium Range: Deployment in Europe

How could it work?

Leslie Gelb

The Walk In the Woods

Space Weapons: Five Possible Systems

Story of two projects

Advance planning and breaking news

Sides of beef offer a good technique to complement stories on important ongoing complex issues in the country's political and social life. Since issues such as arms control, foreign policy, problems of the old and young, the decline of the inner cities, and others are always with us, with news breaks certain to erupt from time to time, it would be a good idea to plan ahead on some of these subjects and prepare sides of beef ahead of time and keep them ready to run when the proper news story occurred. Rosenthal and managing editor Seymour Topping enthusiastically agreed.

The first one we worked on was a page on social security, the fate of which was then a high budgetary priority, given the Reagan Administration's determination to cut costs of running the federal government. A page of statistical information was put together, but unfortunately the more interesting possibilities were not realized and the page became a mere collection of charts. To make matters worse, the news desk ran it by itself without a news story to peg it to. The idea misfired.

Fortunately, Rosenthal and Topping realized that it was the execution, not the idea, that

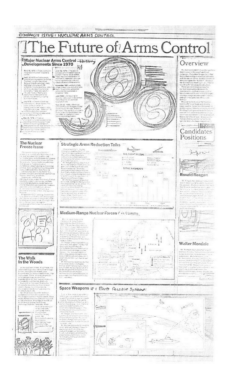

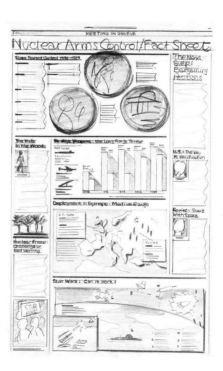

Step one, the rough layout
Facing page: At the time of the ongoing SALT talks, this rough layout was prepared and held ready for the next appropriate news "handle."

Step two, "Where's the graphic?"
Above left: With the text elements filled in a few days later, the graphic elements are getting squeezed to death. The complexity of the subject is clearly getting the better of the design concept.

Step three, a redrawing of the design
Above: An attempt is made to reestablish the essentially graphic and accessible character of the page. Note the scale and strength of treatment of the critical chart and map in the center of the page.

had failed, and not long after that unfortunate incident I was given the go-ahead for another side of beef—on arms control. The rough sketch that I proposed is illustrated here. An expert on the subject came up from the Washington Bureau to solidify the content and write the copy.

A walk in the woods

One of the more interesting details of the page was the account of the incident known as "the walk in the woods," which had occurred a few months earlier in the summer of 1982. The incident incited much discussion and seemed to reduce all the mind-numbing arms figures to a dramatic interchange between two human beings. (Inspired by this incident, a play by Lee Blessing, *A Walk in the Woods*, opened on Broadway in 1988.) At a meeting in Geneva, the American negotiator, Paul Nitze, and his Soviet counterpart, Yuli Kvitsinsky, had taken a stroll by themselves in a wooded area near the site of the formal negotiations. Here in this informal setting, "the walk in the woods," some significant conversation took place that pointed to areas of possible agreement.

This provided the kind of offbeat item that can make a side of beef so much more effective than a mere collection of statistics, lending a refreshing sidelight to otherwise formidable and difficult-to-grasp material.

Interim step

The page went into production in the map department with the copy as written, but it was too long. Written tightly but in regular discursive style, the page began to look more as if the graphic material was intruding on good stories, rather than a page of graphic presentation with copy attached. Clearly needing tightening and redefining, a new layout was made and was ready to go when the world of breaking news interrupted our speculative project. When news of Indira Gandhi's assassination reached newsrooms in the United States around midnight on October 31, 1984, our arms control project was shelved, not to be revived until months later in completely different form.

Assassination of Indira Gandhi

The news of the assassination broke late at night. In a side-of-beef mode, I shifted from arms control to India, got into the office early the next day, and roughed out a page of statistical information on India. As the day progressed and details on the assassination remained too vague to allow us to do a major diagram on the assassination itself, a background side of beef on India began to assume more importance.

Breaking news

Left: Concern about an arms control layout in the works (see preceding page) is wiped out by the news of Indira Gandhi's assassination, breaking late in the day with little hard information yet available.

Quick production

Facing page: In a side-of-beef mode, we produced this page as part of the first day's full coverage of the assassination. There was no time to develop offbeat items. We settled here for little more than an "India at a Glance" fact sheet, leavened only by the complexity of graphic shapes and the "World Relations" item at the bottom, which, significantly, was the most difficult element to get written quickly and is the only element that gives the page some immediate relevancy.

Assassination in India: Profile of a Vast Land

India

The People

Population in 1981: 685,184,692
Percent rural: 76.6%
Percent urban: 23.4%

Life expectancy: 54 years in 1983

Birth rate per thousand: 33.3 in 1981

Death rate per thousand: 12.5 in 1981

Literacy rate: 36.5% in 1983

Official languages: Hindi and English. The country has over 1,600 languages or dialects.

Sources: The Europa Yearbook, 1984; and World Christian Encyclopedia, 1983; Government of India

Religions
Percentage of population

Christian 3.9%
Sikh 2.0%
Other 3.7%
Hindu 78.8%
Moslem 11.6%

Faces of India: In 1981, almost 40 percent of the population was under 14 years old.

Associated Press; United Nations Population Division

The Land

A third the land area of the United States with climates that range from tropical heat to near arctic cold. The desert regions of west central India contrast sharply with the heavily forested east. The Himalayan mountains stretch across the northern border, and the country has a 3,500-mile coastline.

Largest cities: Greater Bombay and New Delhi.

Agricultural land: 54.3%

Major crops: Rice and wheat.

Punjab, one of India's 22 states, has been the site of major Sikh disturbances.

Sources: The Europa Yearbook, 1984, and World Christian Encyclopedia, 1983

The New York Times/William K. Stevens

Farmers in Punjab. In 1981, the population was 76.6 percent rural.

Recent History

1980: National Security Act authorized detention without trial for up to a year if disruptions threatened national security, domestic order or essential supplies and services.

Oct. 11, 1982: Some 3,000 to 5,000 Sikh militants storm Parliament house in New Delhi to protest deaths of 34 Sikhs in police custody.

Oct. 31, 1982: Indira Gandhi and Pakistan's President, Mohammad Zia ul-Haq, meet for first substantive talks in 10 years.

Jan. 5, 1983: In local elections the Congress Party, for the first time, loses control of the two southern states.

February 1983: Continuing violence in Assam brings the cumulative death toll to over 1,000, including 600 Moslems killed in attack by Hindus on Feb. 18.

Oct. 6, 1983: Punjab state government is dissolved by India's President after weeks of violence between Hindus and Sikhs.

March 29, 1984: Indira Gandhi's Congress Party wins majority of seats in indirect election.

June 5, 1984: Battle at Sikh temple in Amritsar.

June 6, 1984: Indian Army attacks and occupies Sikhs' Golden Temple at Amritsar.

June 14, 1984: Indira Gandhi declares four-day-old rebellion of Sikh soldiers "fully under control."

The Economy

A largely agrarian society with a relatively small but growing large-scale manufacturing and trading sector.

Gross National Product Per Person
In U.S. dollars

Source: World Bank

1976	1977	1978	1979	1980	1981	1982
$150	$150	$180	$190	$240	$260	$260

Food Grain Production
In thousands of tons

Legumes
Coarse grain
Wheat
Rice

150 — 125 — 100 — 75 — 50 — 25 — 0

76-77 78-79 80-81 82-83 83-84

Source: The Economist

The Work Force
Percentage of population in each occupation in 1983

Transportation and communication 3%
Industry, mining and construction 13%
Services, including Government 8%
Commerce 6%
Agriculture 70%

Source: Indian Government

The Government

Secular, democratic, federal republic consisting of upper and lower chambers of Parliament and a President. Actual power is held by the Council of Ministers, headed by the Prime Minister, that is chosen from among the Members of Parliament.

The upper chamber of Parliament, called the Council of State, consists of no more than 250 members and is indirectly elected by members of the constituent state legislatures. Members of this chamber serve for six years. The lower chamber, or House of the People, is directly elected and consists of no more than 544 members, who serve five-year terms.

India has three political parties:

● **Indian National Congress (I) Party** formed in 1978 as an opposition party under Mrs. Gandhi.

● **Indian National Congress (S) Party** formed in 1885 and later adopted a socialist label.

● **Janata Party** was established in 1977 to provide an alternative to Congress rule.

The seat of Parliament in New Delhi.

Luis Villota/The Stock Market of New York

The New York Times

CONFLICT: Villager in Chamaria, Assam, weeping after his home was destroyed in February 1983.

DISCUSSION: President Mohammad Zia ul-Haq of Pakistan at a meeting with Mrs. Gandhi.

Associated Press

PROTEST: Sikhs demonstrating in June against occupation of Golden Temple.

Associated Press

The Military

Total armed forces: 1,120,000
Army: 960,000
Navy: 47,000
Air Force: 113,000
Reserves: 200,000

Paramilitary forces (including border security and Coast Guard): 262,000

Air Force equipment includes 727 combat aircraft.

Naval fleet includes 8 Soviet F-class submarines, 1 British aircraft carrier, 2 Soviet-built destroyers and 21 frigates.

Total military spending: $5.5 billion in 1982-83, or 17.87 percent of total Government spending.

India manufactures its own artillery, tanks and infantry weapons, but buys its aircraft mainly from France and the Soviet Union.

Source: International Institute for Strategic Studies

Associated Press

Soldiers, including a Sikh, on duty in New Delhi in March 1983.

World Relations
United States

India's independence in 1947 was strongly supported by the United States and, although India has staunchly professed a policy of nonalignment, the United States has been India's greatest supplier of foreign aid. There have been strains in the relationship, most severely over the 1971 conflict with Pakistan and over India's explosion of an underground nuclear device in May 1974. India has refused to let the United States inspect its use of nuclear fuel, and as a result the United States has not supplied India with nuclear fuel.

Soviet Union

A 20-year peace and cooperation treaty between India and the Soviet Union was signed in 1971. The two countries have shared similar viewpoints on a range of foreign issues, reflecting the importance of Soviet aid and their mutual wariness of China. The Soviet Union has supported India in its dispute with

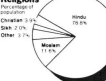

The New York Times

Mrs. Gandhi with President Reagan at the White House in 1982.

Pakistan over Kashmir. The Government of Indira Gandhi described the Soviet invasion of Afghanistan in 1979 as "an internal affair" of the Afghans and has recognized the pro-Soviet Government of Cambodia.

China

By the end of the 1950's, tension developed along the border between India and China and broke into military conflict in 1962. At issue are territory in eastern Kashmir — through which an important Chinese highway runs — and another piece of territory in the northeast. In 1976, however, ambassadors were exchanged for the first time in 14 years.

Pakistan

Old tensions between Moslems and Hindus resulted in the partition of the Indian subcontinent in 1947 into India and Pakistan, but frictions have not ceased. There have been periodic conflicts over Kashmir. In December 1971, a political crisis in East Pakistan and the flight of millions of Bengalis into India led to full-scale war. The independent nation of Bangladesh was created in the aftermath, and it has generally experienced warm relations with India. Since 1972, India and Pakistan have made efforts to share normal relations, though important differences have not been resolved despite continuing talks.

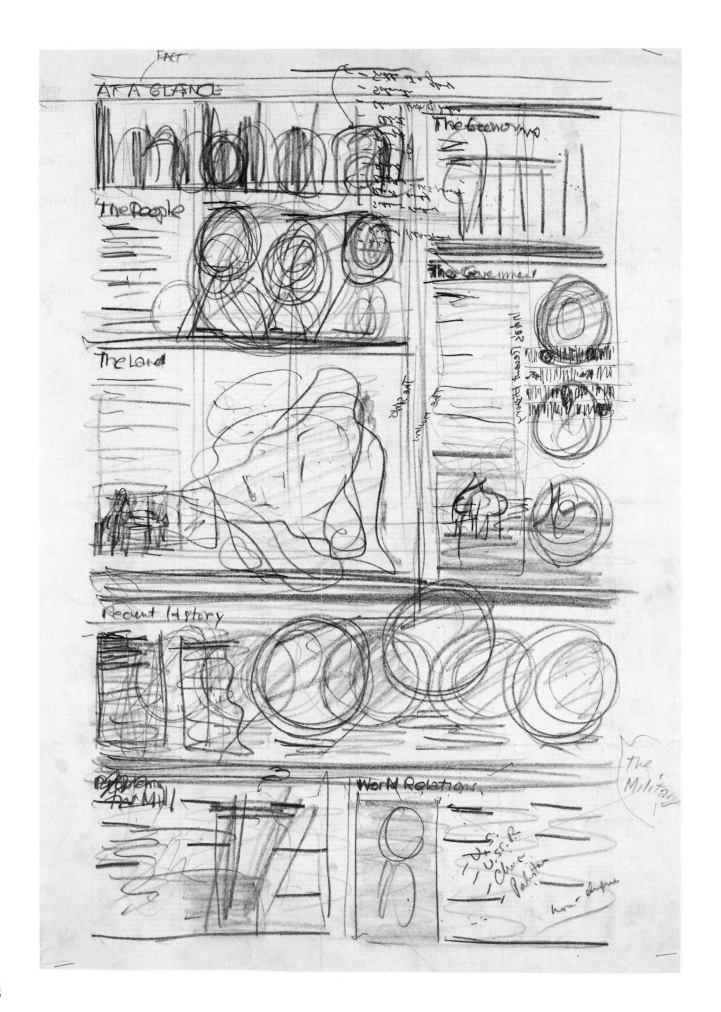

The illustrations on this and the following pages show the rough layout, how the page appeared the next morning and the way it fit into the general presentation.

The page clearly added a dimension to our overall coverage. It by no means fulfills all the possibilities that might have been executed if there had been more time. Essentially it is a "Facts about . . ." box, blown up with graphics and pictures, and even at that represents a great deal of compressed, dedicated effort by the graphics editor in the news room and by the map department. The element that puts it into the side-of-beef category is "World Relations" at the bottom.

It helps clarify the idea of a side of beef to realize that this was the only part of the whole page that posed a problem in execution. The rest of the page, boiled down statistical material, is what the regular channels in the newsroom are accustomed to handling. But "World Relations" was out of those channels. An expert on the foreign desk was required to express subtle and complicated relationships in succinct form for this essentially graphic presentation. With the foreign desk concentrating on the many stories in the works on the assassination that were normal for *its* operation, the situation required the managing editor to divert a desk editor's attention to supply copy for this part of the page. Had we enjoyed 24 hours more time, it would have been possible to produce a much more provocative page, with less dependence on almanac statistics and more expression of ideas, analysis, and offbeat approaches.

A quick rough

Facing page: The page as it went to press at 9:15 P.M. follows closely the rough illustrated here, produced in a few minutes early the same day.

When a story needs a lift

Above: Four consecutive pages in *The Times* presentation of the Indira Gandhi assassination story. Even with the somewhat bland subject matter of the graphic page, it is clear that the graphic treatment lends a hard, factual dimension to the report and a focal point that in the early hours was missing from correspondents' reports. The same graphic material scattered in small units would hardly have had the same enlivening effect.

Sarasota Herald-Tribune

SARASOTA, FLORIDA

Don't go messing with my newspaper

Voice of some of the people

In any newspaper redesign project, at least some degree of ambivalence is bound to occur —not merely the resentment staffers might feel toward an outside consultant but deeply rooted concerns that even sympathetic staffers might feel about potential changes subverting aspects of the paper's traditional character.

In Sarasota this ambivalence was especially apparent. Elven Grubbs, the *Herald-Tribune's* publisher, and Jack Harrison, president of The New York Times Regional Newspaper Group, emphasized, on the one hand, that the paper faced an increasingly competitive situation demanding modernization in every aspect from content and color to equipment and marketing. On the other hand, here was a paper with over 70 percent penetration in its home market with all the devoted following that such penetration implied. It considered itself one of the sound, somewhat conservative pillars of a solid, conservative, affluent community. It was not a coincidence that the *Herald-Tribune's* nameplate bore a resemblance to the nameplate of the respected *New York Herald-Tribune* or the *International Herald-Tribune.* Even the headline type was in the same Bodoni family as these two newspapers.

Elven Grubbs was new as publisher of the *Herald-Tribune.* He had been publisher at Lakeland, where he had overseen widespread changes in *The Ledger* (see Chapter 3) including conversion from afternoon to morning publication. He was fond of telling how, as the new publisher in Sarasota, he met at a welcoming party all the bigwigs for the first time. As he shook hands, almost each one looked him in the eye and muttered, "Now don't you go messing with my newspaper."

Hearing stories like this, my own zeal for change began to develop a nervous edge. I asked the publisher why he wanted the paper redesigned at all, why not do all the other things a publisher does to make a paper successful and leave the design alone? He said, "It's just not a good enough paper. I want to make it a good newspaper."

In a pattern that began at *The Ledger* a few years earlier, the redesign accompanied across-the-board changes in every phase of the newspaper operation. Seymour Topping, former managing editor of *The Times* and newly appointed director of editorial development for *The Times'* regional newspapers, made recommendations concerning the newsroom, working with a committee headed by Diane McFarlin, assistant managing editor and chairman of the paper's committee on conversion from afternoon to morning. A major step was to get Bill McIlwain, a widely respected editor with strong credentials earned at *The Bergen Record, Long Island Newsday,* and other papers, to serve as new executive editor. Other appointments were made to support the paper's developing ambitions. The New York Times Company's business, marketing, and production experts also stepped in to help with plans for a new printing plant with new emphasis on color, new personnel policies, and all the other aspects of the major changes contemplated.

On my first visit to Sarasota in 1984, I saw in the hallways downstairs a collection of linotype machines being prepared for shipment out of the building. They had been in use up to a few days before, making the *Sarasota Herald-Tribune* one of the last papers in its size range to enter the new era of cold type. The presses and allied equipment were equally outdated. Because of limited press capacity, for example, the Sports front page started on a back page and jumped forward, an ancient device most broadsheets had left behind a long time ago. As for the content, one had the feeling that while basic coverage was adequate, the content seemed to need focus, sharper editing, restructuring into sections on a regular basis, and more discipline in the use of elements both visually and journalistically. For example, one couldn't tell if a sports columnist was writing a column or reporting the news. The treatments, words and design, tended to be the same. In short, the paper badly needed a redesign.

The new design

Above right: Included were the same headline type as before, but adjusted for better spacing; a more legible, cleaner text; a new nameplate; and, perhaps most importantly, a new sense of structure. With new presses, the gradually increased use of color began. Story count is about the same as it was but *variety* of stories is emphasized. A reefer runs at the top right. The single hairline under the logo and the centered dateline maintain a formal appearance consistent with the logo, but the dateline is cleaner and less cluttered than before. The old page (above left) attempts to straddle a quiet classic type style and disposition and a contemporary horizontal feeling. The new design emphasizes a vertical *and* horizontal look, in the same proportion as the page itself.

Front page
Starting with the logo

Because it was thought that faithful readers might resent a newly designed logo on "their" newspaper, the existing logo was redrawn to be graphically more assertive, while keeping the essential Old English character. With the help of Ed Benguiat, a New York type designer, the thicks were made a little thicker, the thins thinner, and the word spaces were adjusted. Some letter forms were redrawn, particularly the three capital letters, to provide more graphic accents. The old "H" especially seemed weak, suggesting a lower case letter. (Both the new and the old "H" derive from classic forms.)

In redesigning, some newspapers are so bound to tradition that they rule out any redrawing of the logo. Or a paper may simply be unwilling to incur the expense of a first-class lettering job. Such inhibitions can place a heavy burden on any effort to modernize the front page. Logo redesign does not have to be all or nothing. A logo can be totally redesigned for a completely new image or be redrawn to be better-looking and more assertive without losing its traditional form. In this case the stronger logo, combined with the dateline to make a formal unit, achieved a crisper, cleaner appearance without loss of a "traditional" look. After the redesign, complaints were made about various aspects of the modernized paper, but none referred to the new nameplate. The chief complaint the first day had to do with our removal of "Today's Chuckle" from the paper (previously on Page 1A). We immediately restored it, on page 1B, in a prominent spot below the local columnist.

Top of the page

Since marketing strategy called for strengthened effort in outlying communities, designation of the various zoned editions became a prominent aspect of the front page flag display. A black sans serif type, Franklin Gothic Extra Condensed, contrasting with the Bodoni headlines, accents the zoned edition and plays against the blue rules and cursive lines of the logo. The five blue rules in turn play against the 4-point black

Sarasota Herald-Tribune

Sarasota Herald-Tribune

Thinner thins and thicker thicks
The letters of the new logo (bottom) are stronger but also more delicately drawn than the old logo (top), with authoritative-looking initials helping to make a decided improvement without making waves among readers.

New Page 1A
Facing page: Though structured, the page shows plenty of movement and variety. Boxed reefers, for example, Cooking Today, are used when warranted. A gray tint—sometimes used indiscriminately in newspaper boxes—gives, here in the box, a dominant focus to the page. Page layout, news desk.

Sarasota Herald-Tribune

61ST YEAR. No. 205 / SUNDAY, APRIL 27, 1986 / 75 CENTS

City Crime Reports Up 24%

By PETER DOBENS
Staff Writer

Police Blame Drug Abusers For Increase in Burglaries

There were 1,419 serious crimes reported in the city of Sarasota during the first three months of 1986 – or 273 more than the number of serious crimes committed during the same period in 1985.

In unincorporated areas of the county, reports of serious crime jumped by 686, from 2,131 during the first quarter of 1985 to 2,817 so far this year.

No figures were available for Venice.

Police and sheriff's deputies said their crime report figures add up to a 24 percent increase in the city and

a 32 percent increase in the unincorporated sections of the county.

Why the surge?

Police pointed to cases such as this: a man arrested last week told officers that he broke into a north county home in mid-March, took electronic equipment worth $400, and sold the stolen goods for $50. He said he needed the money to buy drugs.

"We would still have our burgla-

ries, robberies and larcenies, but they wouldn't be this high without the drugs," police Maj. Gordon Jolly said.

There was no uniform trend among the major crimes – murder, rape, robbery, aggravated assault and aggravated battery, burglary, larceny and motor vehicle theft.

There were twice as many rapes reported in the city of Sarasota, but almost an equal drop in rapes in the

county's unincorporated areas. Reports of robberies and aggravated assaults also went up in the city, but decreased in the county areas.

Burglaries and larcenies, however, showed major increases in both sets of statistics.

"It runs in cycles," said Sheriff Geoff Monge. "Last year's statistics showed us there was an increase in crime across the board in the county."

For several years during the early 1980s, crime in the county was on the decline, including an almost 10 percent drop in reports in 1983. Since then, however, crime has made a formidable comeback.

Continued on 14A

21st Annual
Cookbook
Today

Recipe

Schaub Itches To Be Back In Courtroom

By JUD MAGRIN
Staff Writer

Times change.

Frank Schaub doesn't.

Twenty years ago, he was wearing out a car a year riding through the huge 12th Judicial Circuit, prosecuting and winning some of the most infamous murder cases in state history.

He's tried to write about the time he calls the "Decade of Frontier Justice." But he's too busy living what may be the final chapter.

For Schaub, 64, is back where he really wants to be - almost.

He is once more the state attorney for the 12th Judicial Circuit, now made up of Sarasota, Manatee and DeSoto counties. He returned in 1985, winning election to a four-year term after a frustrating stint as a circuit court judge.

But administrative duties are keeping him from his second love: the courtroom and the prosecution of criminal cases. His first love is his family – wife Evelyn, five children and one grandchild.

Schaub doesn't know when he'll be able to return to the courtroom.

"I've got some problems right now," he said. "I'm keeping the staff pretty good and haven't had a resignation in quite a while. But you get one where you least expect it.

"I'll be happy when I can get these details off my neck and start trying cases."

Those "details" include recruiting experienced prosecutors, organizing the state attorney's office divisions, training - and getting reporters off his back.

Numerous newspaper stories have detailed how Schaub, Sarasota County Sheriff Geoff Monge and Manatee County Sheriff Charlie Wells spent a good chunk of time last year investigating each other.

Sarasota County detectives looked into allegations that two of Schaub's assistants were using drugs. The claims proved to be unfounded.

But Schaub was miffed because Monge had not informed him of the allegations or the investigation, so he ordered two Manatee County sheriff's detectives to investigate Sarasota County vice squad Capt. Wayne Bird.

Finally, the two Manatee detectives accused Schaub of sending them out on a smear campaign against

Continued on 9A

STAFF PHOTO/THOMAS BENDER
Frank Schaub goes home from work.

Reagan Denounces Terrorists, Vietnam

Urges End Of Siege In Cambodia

By TOM RAUM
Associated Press Writer

HONOLULU (AP) – President Reagan, wending his way across the Pacific on the longest trip of his presidency, declared Saturday that "cowardly acts against Americans" by terrorists and dictators would not go unanswered.

He said that the terrorists and dictators who commit such acts "had best be prepared for the consequences."

Earlier in the day, he had made use of his weekly radio address to emphasize the U.S. status as a "Pacific power" and to denounce the continued occupation of Cambodia by the communist government of Vietnam.

Reagan said efforts to resolve the Cambodian issue will be a principal item on the agenda when he meets with Southeast Asian allies in Indonesia.

After the president addressed a welcoming crowd at Hickam Air Force Base here, his motorcade made an unscheduled stop at a hospital on the Honolulu outskirts, where he and first lady Nancy Reagan visited a boy ill with leukemia.

Presidential aides said 13-year-old Randy Raquion thanked Reagan for White House intervention in helping his Filipino grandmother come to Hawaii. Aides said the grandmother previously had been unable to get a visa to be with her sick grandchild.

In the second stop of his 13-day trip, which will culminate with an economic summit meeting in Tokyo, Reagan was presented with a bright orange lei as he stepped from Air Force One. He arrived after a 5½-

Continued on 10A

AP LASERPHOTO
Employees at a British bank in Beirut, Lebanon, remove a steel door wrecked by a bomb blast Saturday. See Page 11A.

U.S. Officials Ponder Response to Terrorism

By BERNARD GWERTZMAN
N.Y. Times News Service

WASHINGTON - Senior Reagan administration officials say that 12 days after the American bombing of Libya, no consensus has developed within the government on how far to go in repeating such attacks to counter an expected rise in anti-American terrorism around the world.

Since the raid nearly two weeks ago, President Reagan has warned that the United States is ready to use its military power again if there are new terrorist attacks.

But in interviews in recent days, White House and State Department officials expressed concern that the public support that developed for the bombing of Libya would not necessarily be repeated if Washing-

ton became engaged in a regular pattern of tit-for-tat retaliatory raids.

Such raids might be mounted not only against Libya but also against such nations as Syria and Iran, which are believed by the administration to support terrorist groups.

"Libya was a relatively easy target, and we lost one F-111," a State Department official said. "Syria and Iran are more dangerous. We probably won't get away with such minimal losses. I wonder how long the polls will show a high approval rating in this country if the losses begin to mount without any evidence that terrorism has been ended."

There is also concern here that what one counterterrorism expert described as a "fear psychology" is

Continued on 11A

Gator running back seen as 1st-round pick. 1D

Neal Anderson

Van Wezel's summer concert series will feature popular groups and solo artists from the '50s and '60s. **1F**

Media coverage of terrorism involves complex challenges and life-and-death decisions. **1G**

Experts: Marcos Art Collection Is Full of Fakes

By JANE PERLEZ
N.Y. Times News Service

NEW YORK - The vast majority of works in the multimillion-dollar master-painting collection of Imelda R. Marcos, including one that she believed to be by Michelangelo, are inconsequential works by unimportant artists, according to the director of the Frick Collection and other art experts.

The wife of the ousted president of the Philippines paid $3.5 million to an Italian art dealer in 1983 for the purported Michelangelo, records found by the new Manila government of Corazon C. Aquino show.

But Everett Fahy, the director of the Frick, said the painting could not possibly be by Michelangelo. Fahy said only one Michelangelo painting was known to exist: the "Tondo Doni," which hangs in the Uffizi Gallery in Florence, Italy.

Fahy said the 75 paintings acquired by Marcos from the same Italian dealer, Mario Bellini, now hanging in a Manila museum, were not the works of Tintoretto, Canaletto and others of that rank, as many of them are purported to be.

Interviewed by telephone at a house he owns in Monte Carlo, Bellini said he had sold "some paintings"

Continued on 14A

STAFF PHOTO/SALLY PETTIBON

Crafty Look

Robert Elkins gives his 6-year-old son, Lane, a boost Saturday as they check out a jewelry display during the Siesta Fiesta, a juried arts and crafts fair on Siesta Key. Lane apparently got into the spirit with some facial expressionism. The fair will continue today from 10 a.m. to 5 p.m. on Ocean Boulevard. See Page 3B.

rule and provide a slightly decorative look to the whole nameplate. The parallel rules provide a graphic "trademark," becoming an identifying graphic device running through the whole paper in section headings. (Eventually these rules were also incorporated into the design of the paper's delivery trucks.)

The rules also provide space for a reefer at the extreme right. It was agreed that this reefer would not necessarily run every day, but only when there was something special to promote. After a time, it was expedient to use this space mostly for a weather item; important reefers were worked into boxes near the top of the page under the dateline. The design incorporated several different ways of working these onto the page in addition to standard "Inside" treatments at the bottom.

Open box

For stories and free-standing photos, the box consists of thin vertical rules to the full depth of the area, with bolder rules, usually 4-point, set inside the verticals but not touching the corners. The horizontal rules are cut off to line up with the text, an indent of about 12 points. This seems to be less static than a true, closed-in box. The lines create a sense of direction and tension. Space literally flows in and out at the corners. To this degree the elements in this box retain a more active relationship with other elements on the page than they would in a conventional box.

In addition to creating boxes, the rules can be used in a larger way to tie together two or more related major elements on the page, giving the whole page a basic structure.

Dream Finals Set Up in French Open

PARIS (AP) – John McEnroe is within one match of ending a 29-year American drought at the French Open tennis championships. His opponent in the men's singles final on Sunday will be Czechoslovakia's Ivan Lendl, who is in his fifth Grand Slam tournament championship match and still looking for his first victory.

The slow red clay at Roland Garros Stadium has stymied U.S. players in the

TV, 1 p.m., Ch. 8

men's singles ever since Tony Trabert successfully defended his title in 1955.

"Maybe it's a little overdue," McEnroe told reporters after crushing Connors on a sun-drenched center court.

In Sunday's final, McEnroe will face the No. 2 seed, Lendl, who scored a convincing 6-3, 6-3, 7-5 victory over Sweden's Mats Wilander, the 1982 champion and runner-up last year.

Another piece of history was certain to be made today when Martina Navratilova faces defending champion Chris Evert Lloyd in the women's singles final.

Navratilova is bidding to become only the fifth player and the third woman to win the elusive Grand Slam - successive victories at the world's four major tournaments.

Lloyd, who already holds a record 51 singles victories here, is aiming to become the first woman to win the title six times. Lloyd destroyed American Camille Benjamin 6-0, 6-0 Thursday.

"There'll be pressure on both of us – both of us will be making history in one way or another," Navratilova said after her 3-6, 6-2, 6-2 semifinal victory over Hana Mandlikova.

McEnroe's 7-5, 6-1, 6-2 victory over fellow American Jimmy Connors was his 42nd straight match without defeat and his first victory on the slow European clay over his great rival.

So closely have the two Americans been matched that McEnroe has now won 13 of their 25 matches. Connors had won their previous three encounters on clay.

But McEnroe, who had never gotten past the quarterfinals here previously, was totally in command on Friday, slamming 12 aces and a succession of first-service winners past the game's premier returner in a two-hour, 11-minute contest.

And while it was perfect McEnroe when it came to playing, his behavior was vintage McEnroe. The fiesty New York left-hander was fined $2,000 dollars *Continued on 4C*

Martina Navratilova reached today's final against Chris Evert Lloyd by stopping Hana Mandlikova 3-6, 6-2, 6-2 in Friday's semifinals.

AP WIREPHOTO

The open box

Letting air in at the corners, it relates what's in the box to the rest of the page. The little spaces provide a bit of tension; the eye has to make a jump to complete the box. With variations, this is used for a separate picture, story, or large unit with diverse elements (facing page).

STAFF PHOTO/GEORGE WILSON

The Gentry Eagle entry in the Superboat division throws up a rooster tail as it roars through the Gulf waters.

Race Spectators Master Art of Idling

By DAVID MARTIN
Staff Writer

Thousands of area residents and tourists, gathered along the Gulf and Bay shores Saturday, got a big lesson in powerboat racing – and in waiting – during the inaugural Suncoast Offshore Grand Prix, one of the biggest sporting events ever to hit local waters.

The raw horsepower displayed during a swift and thunderous if somewhat sporadic procession of 36 powerboats racing offshore found its counterpoint onshore in relative inertia as the crowds quickly mastered the art of becoming idle spectators during the long waits between boats while trying to follow a sport unprecedented in the vicinity.

"The nice thing about sitting on

More on the Suncoast Offshore Grand Prix.   **2C, 1D, 10D**

the sidelines here is that you know when you take time out for a beer or just to take a walk along the water, the race will still be waiting for you," summed up Pat Nichols of Sarasota.

The winner in the Superboat field of the Grand Prix competition, which carried a total purse of $26,000, was Al Copeland's Popeyes.

And when all was said and done, many participants, organizers and spectators agreed that that Popeyes had not been the only

winner. The consensus was that the grueling races had climaxed Sarasota's Summerfest 1985 in grand style, raising an early estimate of $225,000 for the Sarasota Foundation for Handicapped Children, which had held its groundbreaking ceremonies July Fourth.

The day had gotten off to an early start. Even as the racing teams were spending Friday night and the early hours of Saturday plotting strategy, early-rising local residents had glanced over the course maps to chart the optimal

vantage points for watching what promises to become a welcome annual event.

Then, after a cloudy morning sky and scattered thundershowers that apparently dampened some enthusiasm for the preliminary 9 a.m. sportsman's race, the spectators flocked to the shore. Widely varying estimates put crowds at between 200,000 and 300,000 for the noon superboat competition.

Police said they were "pleasantly surprised," however, that no major morning traffic jams had developed on roads leading to the numerous vantage points along the racecourse. Authorities said many spectators reached their destinations early, easing the burden on the otherwise often-choked beach roads.

Continued on 11A

STAFF PHOTO/SALLY PETTIBON

Spectators are packed on boats, bridges and the beach at Lighthouse Point to catch a glimpse of the racers.

Headlines and text

The same but different

In keeping with the mandate to produce a modernized version of the existing paper, it was agreed from the start that the existing headline style, an early Compugraphic cut of Bodoni, would be retained.

However, the basic appearance of the existing headline type was not technically good. Even classic Bodoni has an x-height that is relatively small, with long ascenders and descenders. The modern eye, increasingly conditioned to newer typefaces (spurred on in large degree by the designs of ITF, International Typefounders Inc.) expects larger x-heights, which project more aggressively than the older designs in the same point size.

The main problems lay in erratic spacing, which left big holes between letters and words, and in poor reproduction.

A plus about the existing Bodoni in Sarasota, however, was that it was cut a little bolder than the classic Bodoni.

Inquiries to the new manufacturer determined that a newer version of this Bodoni was available. However, the sample presented a version of the commonplace Bodoni Bold. Bodoni Bold was rejected because it would give the paper an unacceptably different character and was at that time an overly popular face used in many newspapers, rarely with handsome results. To move from the Bodoni in hand to Bodoni Bold would be a step in the wrong direction. Insisting on the procurement of the original typeface design, we concentrated on efforts to improve the spacing.

Samples were set with different increments of letter and word space, in standard sizes from 12 to 72 points. We made considerable adjustments, eventually settling on spacing that seemed optimum. These sizes and spaces were formatted into the system, no longer subject to day-by-day alteration.

As with *The Ledger* in Lakeland and other papers, we produced a style "book" laying down strict guidelines for space between lines, between headlines and text, and for all other spaces. Guidelines were kept as simple, consistent, and easy to use as possible. Banks, blurbs, read-outs, and other typographical "building-blocks" were also rationalized and formatted to make their way into the style book.

abcdefghij abcdefghi

60 POINT 60 POINT

X-height

X-height helps determine forcefulness of type. X-height is the typographer's term for the height of a lower-case letter that does not have ascenders or descenders, such as n, o, e, and x, contrasted to the full height of letters that include ascenders and descenders, such as b, d, and p. X-heights can vary significantly in typefaces that are nominally the same size, but there is no statutory measurement for x-height. If the user is not aware of it, comparative sizes may be confusing.

20 In Minibus Burned To Death

OSLO, Norway (AP) - A Norwegian tourist says she saw a Sinhalese mob pour gasoline on a minibus full of Tamils in Sri Lanka and burn them to death.

"A minibus full of Tamils was forced to stop just in front of us in Colombo," Eli Skarstein of Stavanger was quoted Thursday as saying in the Oslo newspaper Verdens Gang.

"A Sinhalese mob poured gasoline over the bus ~ ~t it on fire. They blocked th-

riots and violence," the newspaper said.

Verdens Gang quoted Mrs. Skarstein as saying:

"We can't believe the official casualty figures as reported here with only 60 or 70 people killed. Hundreds, maybe thousands, must have been killed already. The houses, shops and factories owned by tamiles were burned by mobs when the ethnic riots started last Mon-

OLD   ~~~ ~ted the Tamils ~

Language Group Nears Petition Goal

TALLAHASSEE (AP) - The chairman of a petition drive to make English Florida's official language said Thursday his organization needs just 70,000 more validated signatures to get the issue on the fall ballot.

"The government must run in English," said Dr. Mark LaPorta, a Miami Beach internist who serves

NEW

population speaks English as their primary language," he said. "Even in small areas, where there is a linguistic ghetto of predominately non-English-speaking persons, they are isolating themselves if they don't have an opportunity to master our language."

LaPorta said his campaign has 280,000 signatures validated by the Secretary of State'

respondents said their children should master English, LaPorta said.

"It's often been said that people who come to this country often have a greater appreciation (of) what it's all about than those of us who are born here," LaPorta said.

"It is our opinion ... that the ~~t way to teach students English

A cleaner look

Above top: Bodoni headlines and Bedford text used in the old format. Above bottom: The re-spaced Bodoni with Century Expanded text. The lighter, crisper text made the paper as a whole look cleaner and the headlines seem more forceful in contrast.

Evelyn Gobbie Deals With 'Baddy Daddies'

Soviet Central Committee OKs Bid to Limit

A tightened space

Bodoni headlines, old, as they ran (top) and new, with tightened spacing (bottom). Both the letterspace and the space between words affect how headlines read and look. The word space particularly is tightened here to a degree that allows each line to be grasped as a unit.

219

Text

A new text face, Century Expanded, was used in the new design, supplanting the old Bedford that looked too tight, squeezed, overly black, and blobby. New printing presses could have improved the reproduction, but the basically dark look of the Bedford type was a built-in handicap, playing against the comparatively light headline style. The lighter Century would be more compatible with the Bodoni headlines and easier to read and more pleasant to look at than the existing Bedford.

Word count was particularly important since the redesign took place at the same time the page size was made more narrow for the new presses. The effect this might have on the newshole and the consequent number of words in the news report was one of the critical issues in the redesign project. The new Century left the word count about the same, while obviously enhancing legibility.

Accent

Bodoni seems to encourage use of only the one type family, since it is difficult to employ a contrasting typeface to go with the Bodoni headlines. One reason for this may be that early on Bodoni was designed in so many weights, from Bodoni Light to the very black display face, Ultra Bodoni. The contrasts are so completely built in that it seems perverse to look elsewhere. Perhaps a more profound reason is the crisp, modern assertive feeling of the design. Most of all, the thick strokes in Bodoni are so black and assertive that only the blackest typefaces, serif or sans serif, provide adequate contrast for the accents needed in a newspaper.

Despite all this, it was imperative to get a different feeling into the paper in the blacker registers, to break the rhythm of the Bodoni design with a dark type that would be more unexpected and contemporary. This was Garamond Extra Bold italic, a relatively new member of the classic Garamond family, developed in the cold-type era. This was purchased on special order and programmed into the system with a slight condensation, for better word count and better harmony with the Bodoni headlines.

The style book decreed that the Garamond Extra Bold italic, in capitals or in upper and lower case, should be used *only as accents*—for standing heads, department designations, bold subheads in tabular material, and so on—but never as a headline and almost always in the smaller sizes: 12 to 24 points. The only exception is designer-produced treatments for special titles or headings.

To sum up, the type line-up shows the three basic ingredients usually needed: a clean, crisp text that is strong enough to be authoritative, yet not overly dark; a headline schedule that contrasts with the text but does not get monotonous and is not so black that it can't be used in large sizes; and finally a still darker type that can be used for graphic and journalistic accent.

art Exits Senate Race o Focus on Presidency

By PHIL GAILEY
N.Y. Times News Service

ERGREEN, Colo. - Sen. Gary announced Saturday that he not run for re-election this and all but announced plans to the Democratic presidential ation in 1988.

work has yet to be done," old a group of supporters at a rant in the mountains outside near his log cabin in a place hlesome Gul^

making some announcement about '88? Nope. Does it mean I still have an interest in being president? Yep."

Hart said he was confident that he could have won re-election, but had decided that the time had come for him to find new ways to focus attention "on our unmet agenda for the future."

Now that Hart has laid aside the burden of another Senate campaign, he is expected to devote him-

Some Others Have Presidential Potential

WASHINGTON (AP) – Sen. Gary Hart's announcement Saturday that he will not seek another Senate term positioned him to pursue the 1988 Democratic presidential nomination. Here is what other potential candidates in both parties are doing:

Democrats

■ Sen. Joseph Biden of Delaware ^n his speaking schedule d-raisers and con-

from a gubernatorial campaign in a run for the White House. But adds, "I'm not going to close a doors."

■ Gov. Charles Robb of Virgin enters private life, but is remainin active in party affairs through th Democratic Leadership Council, organization of elected officia determined to rid the Democrats their liberal image.

■ Gov. Br Arizor

Display line-up

Above: A typical line-up of the three basic typefaces, Bodoni headlines that register as medium weight, a clean Century text that registers light against the headlines, and Garamond Extra Bold italic providing

a black accent. The Garamond in roman would also have provided contrast, but the italic packs nicely, the letters seem to *roll* into each other, and the movement provides another kind of contrast with the formal cadence of the Bodoni.

A county board Monday refused to grant a zoning variance that would allow a New Jersey couple to move into a misplaced house that has swallowed $102,000 of their savings, spawned a lawsuit and cost a contractor his privilege to draw building permits in Manatee County.

Richard and Louise Malcomson now must rely on their lawsuit against contractor Gregg Glasser to get their money's worth out of their house, which was built beyond county-imposed setback lines in the Country Oaks subdivision off Lockwood Ridge Road.

"I feel that they listened to our point of view, but it was a negative," Louise Malcomson said of Monday's decision by the Board of Zoning Appeals.

The board voted 3-2 not to reconsider a decision they made in October to deny the variance request. Glasser and the Malcomson's attorney, Geoffrey Pflugner, had hoped to convince the board members that new information about mistakes made during con-

---

A county board Monday refused to grant a zoning variance that would allow a New Jersey couple to move into a misplaced house that has swallowed $102,000 of their savings, spawned a lawsuit and cost a contractor his privilege to draw building permits in Manatee County.

Richard and Louise Malcomson now must rely on their lawsuit against contractor Gregg Glasser to get their money's worth out of their house, which was built beyond county-imposed setback lines in the Country Oaks subdivision off Lockwood Ridge Road.

"I feel that they listened to our point of view, but it was a negative," Louise Malcomson said of Monday's decision by the Board of Zoning Appeals.

The board voted 3-2 not to reconsider a decision they made in October to deny the variance request. Glasser and the Malcomson's attorney, Geoffrey Pflugner, had hoped to convince the board members that new information about mistakes made

---

Squeezing text

Technology now allows fine adjustments in typesetting that can make a big difference in legibility and word count, even in type technically the same size. Above are two of the many text settings

produced in Sarasota: on the left, 9.2 on 9.5 (9.2-point type with 0.3-point leading) Century Expanded set normally; on the right, 9.2-point type condensed about 3%, with an additional 0.5-point leading to compensate for the squeezed feeling.

Opening spread
A bright beginning

The old Page 2 featured Weather at the bottom of the page and jumps from Page One at the top. Weather reports have probably always been considered important in Florida, but at the time of this redesign in 1984, weather reports were becoming more important all over the country. (*USA Today* had not yet emerged with its full-color, full-page report that pushed this trend into a gallop.) But even in modest terms, the Sarasota weather report demanded rethinking and redesigning.

The redesign organized the report into three clearly defined main parts—"Local Forecast," "Florida Zone Forecast" and "National Forecast." A state map dominated the design with zones defined by circled areas. To produce these circles every day under deadline with limited resources in the art department was considered a production problem at first. The device was nearly abandoned in the generally nervous atmosphere of the prechangeover week when editors and composing room staff were strained and tired. (This was just before the emergence of labor-saving Macintosh computers in the country's newsrooms.) A newspaper is made up of thousands of little details. It is all too easy to drop one as not being worth the production effort. This detail, however, I felt was worth fighting for. Eventually Bob Pelletier came up with a workable system of circles on acetate that solved production concerns. Other improvements included a heading that was more than a label and better presentation of tide and other water-related information for this Gulf Coast community. An innovation was the illustrated fish-of-the-day item, a happy combination of good information and a touch of visual appeal.

Perhaps the most interesting innovation was a short, by-lined, highly personal commentary in the local forecast. In order to get some personality and wit into the report, it was written by different members of the staff. This turned out to be a highly popular and distinctive part of the weather report. It inspired comments from readers and even outside contributions around the "Ms. Weather" persona.

People

The first idea was that "Weather," "People," and some sort of summary would make a varied, chockfull Page 2, with advertising on Page 3 leav-

1. Proposal
The first dummy proposal for Page 2 tried to pack People, Highlights, and a bigger Weather package together, but forced an awkward leakage of Weather information under the Highlights column. The larger-than-expected state map accented the new design and, in a page made up of small elements, gave the whole page focus and scale.

2. Issue

Highlights moved across the gutter when the paper went "live" with the new design, allowing adequate space for a beefed-up Weather report. The profile on Page 2 is designed to break up the large People presence and keep elements on the spread in a related scale. The silhouette treatment of the pictures in the top center also helps tie the top of the page together with the bottom, which features a silhouette shape of the map. The page contrasts with the newsy use of pictures on Page 3.

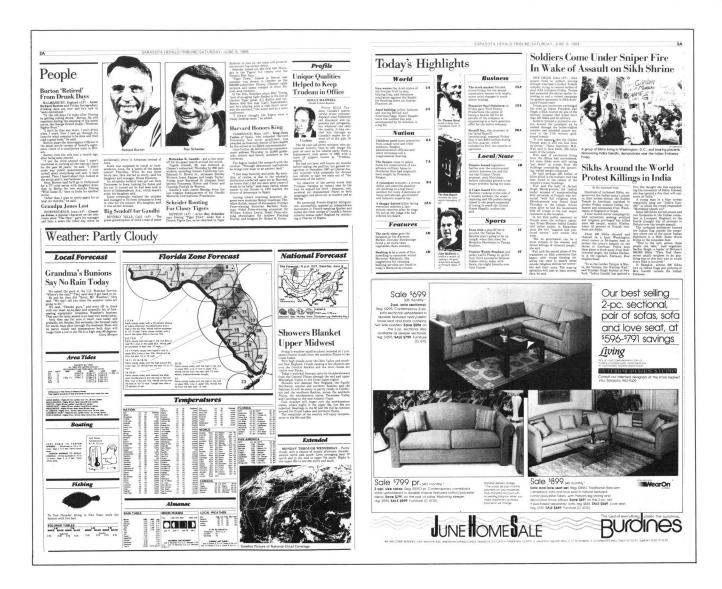

3. Accommodation

Above: When advertisers expressed interest in a half-page horizontal ad on Page 3, they were accommodated. An alternate design was made for Highlights in a quarter-page box treatment. A half-page was the maximum size agreed upon for the ad, allowing at least a quarter of a page for news.

Breezy weather

Right: The local weather forecast is built around the breezy, conversational-style message of a newly created personality, Ms. Weather, in an attempt to inject humor and personality into the report.

Local Forecast

The Cold, Hard Facts of Winter

There is no easy way to break this weather news to you, so here are the cold, hard facts.

An arctic air mass expected to equal the 1983 Christmas freeze will be moving into our area today, dropping nighttime temperatures tonight and Tuesday into the upper teens to the mid-20s.

What else can Ms. Weather say except to keep yourselves bundled up and warm, cover the plants and shrubs, and don't forget to see to the safety and comfort of those fur-bearing, four-legged members of your family by bringing them indoors with you for the next several days. No, not Uncle Joe – the dog and cat!

Today and Tuesday will be sunny, windy and cold, with highs in the mid- to upper 40s. Winds will be from the northwest at 20 mph, diminishing at night.

Lee Silverman

ing enough of a newshole to accommodate at least one good news story with a picture. However, the weather report needed more space; therefore, the summary, called "Today's Highlights," was moved to Page 3.

People, at the top of Page 2, started things off with gossipy interest. Day-by-day variation in the treatment of pictures was urged; the short "Profile" was added to vary the texture and provide some focus. The subheads were originally made as large as possible (22 points) consistent with the short items, in order to push for more bounce and vitality. When the page actually ran, these subheads were in fact made smaller (18 points) with a somewhat blander result.

Highlights

The *Herald-Tribune*, the oldest paper in Western Florida, sees itself as a full-spectrum newspaper. Serving 110,000 readers daily and 140,000 on Sunday, it is more like a small, big-city paper than a big, small-city paper, on which readers depend for a full range of national, international, local, and specialized news.

To reflect this, as well as the improved coverage of sports and business and the creation of new Style sections, a summary in some form would be effective somewhere on Page 2 or 3. A complete summary, however, would be too lengthy and tightly packed for the opening spread. Instead of speeding the reader into the newspaper with a feeling of anticipation, it might be formidable enough to have the opposite effect. Therefore, the summary became "Today's Highlights," encouraging a feeling of abundance without being too forbidding. Small pictures were used in a magazine contents page style.

The design of the Highlights feature attempted to deal with what at the time was a relatively new problem resulting from the adoption of Standard Advertising Units (SAU) guidelines then being strongly advocated by the American Newspaper Publishers' Association. One of the factors that had precipitated *The Tribune*'s redesign was conversion to the smaller, 13" x 21", page size and the standard six-column news page prescribed by SAU guidelines. The resulting column measure of 12 picas discourages going across two columns with a wide measure of type as we could readily do on the narrower columns of the old eight-column page. Beyond a 21- or 22-pica width in most text sizes, a column of type gets discouraging to read. In addition, a column of type set two full columns wide occupies one-third the width of the whole page, often giving distorted importance to the wide column. From these concerns came the Highlights design, a wide column set across 17 picas, with the remaining space set off with vertical hairline rules to allow for the accompanying pictures.

The format decreed specific sizes for these little pictures, two or three variables making production easy but still allowing some day-by-day variety. An efficient procedure was set up to ensure that pictures went to the news editor responsible for Highlights and to formalize liaison with the paper's three artists for easy access to the day's art work.

Within a week after the new design went into effect, advertisers expressed interest in appearing on Page 3, if a horizontal half-page could be accommodated. To satisfy this advertising interest, an alternative treatment of the Highlights was worked out and implemented. Some of the editors were unhappy about this tampering with the original design. But the problem illustrates how design can reconcile news and advertising requirements in a rational way and thus reduce the necessity for day-by-day ad hoc battles over space.

Fishing

Sheepshead are thick around area bridges and hitting shrimp, crabs, sand fleas and tube worms.

Fishing

Whiting are hitting shrimp at Turtle Beach.

Fish of the day
The best bet for gulf fishing is the handle for a service item that does double-duty as a graphic shape.

Inside news

Starting with the folio overlines

Two parallel hairline rules set off the dateline and folio with a special little flourish without being too intrusive. The dateline type had to fit snugly between the lines to make it work as a single visual unit. The bold folio type provided an accent at the top of the page and played against the very light type of the dateline, giving a "designed" look to the top of each page.

News in Brief

Parallel, vertical, half-point rules also set off the "News in Brief" elements. Designed to be used across a two-column measure, these elements could be adapted, if necessary, for other measures.

The light vertical rules give a structured appearance to the inside news pages, which could frequently look helter-skelter due to late deadlines of news items. The vertical rules also eat up some of the horizontal space, creating a line measure that is not too forbiddingly wide. The dummy page (see illustration) shows a maximum of 23 picas, a little more than is ideal for a flush left and right column in this type size. The ragged right treatment, however, makes the measure acceptable.

The format encourages the Briefs to be *brief*, to be edited in a succinct and snappy fashion. Briefs should *feel* different from the regular news stories on the page. The ideal number of briefs varies, of course, with different designs and different newspapers. (One newspaper designed recently—the Gannett Daily News—featured Briefs units that allowed for up to 20 or more items.) Small pictures were to be used at least every other day. A column of Briefs going down the full length of the page was discouraged, unless a larger picture was used to break up the "list"

appearance, which would be more like a newsletter than a newspaper.

Free-standing picture

Basic treatment for a free-standing (or stand-alone) picture depends on horizontal 3-point rules to separate it from the rest of the page. Vertical rules were optional since these pictures frequently run on the same pages as the Briefs columns, which already feature vertical rules.

AP WIREPHOTO

Tall Order
Rep. Fred Lippman, D-Hollywood, debates on the House floor Monday. Lippman was later referred to by a colleague as the "George Washington of Broward County." House Speaker Lee Moffitt then quipped: In light of a recent TV special, "it seems to me Washington was a lot taller."

Free-standing picture
Above: It fits between horizontal 3-point rules, set off from news stories, with optional use of vertical rules in an open box treatment. The vertical rules are optional because the picture sometimes runs alongside Briefs, which already includes a vertical rule.

Inside news page
Facing page: A typical inside news page is shown with ads stacked to the outside and news in the center around the gutter. Briefs sometimes carry pictures but are encouraged to be really brief. The Garamond Extra Bold italic provides accent.

NEWS IN BRIEF
World

Envoy Begins Peking Talks

Kirkpatrick

PEKING (AP) - Jeane J. Kirkpatrick, U.S. ambassador to the United Nations, told Foreign Minister Wu Xueqian on Monday that she came to China to discuss areas in which Peking and Washington have differences.

"You know, and I know, that we won't always agree," Mrs. Kirkpatrick said in a toast at a banquet hosted by Wu. "But I look forward to exploring with you those areas in which our two countries have differences."

Without mentioning the Soviet Union by name, Mrs. Kirkpatrick denounced the Soviet intervention in Afghanistan and Vietnam's Soviet-supported occupation of Cambodia, also known as Kampuchea.

Glemp in France for Visit

Glemp

PARIS (AP) - Cardinal Jozef Glemp, the primate of Poland, arrived in France Monday for the start of what he said was an eight-day pastoral visit to Paris and Rome.

The leader of Poland's Roman Catholic Church said he planned to give no interviews while in Paris and would not be meeting with any French officials.

"I am going to Paris and Rome in the framework of a trip that is going to last eight days," Glemp told reporters at Orly airport. "The purpose of my trip is pastoral."

He was met at the airport by several members of the French Episcopate and the Polish ambassador to France.

"I will pay a courtesy visit to Cardinal (Jean-Marie) Lustiger (the archbishop of Paris) and to the other bishops of France," Glemp said.

Nicaragua Says Force Routed

MANAGUA, Nicaragua (AP) - Government troops have routed most of the CIA-backed rebel fighting force in northern Jinotega province, but fighting continues in the area, a regional military commander said Monday.

"At these very moments our counterinsurgency units are fighting counterrevolutionaries near Santa Elena and Chamastro, in northern Jinotega province, and we have them surrounded," Cmdr. Javier Carrion, head of the 3rd Military Region, told a news conference in Managua.

The towns are about 90 miles north of the capital. He said the rebels were among 8,000 insurgents from the Nicaraguan Democratic Force who penetrated Nicaraguan territory in early March from bases in Honduras.

Governor General Installed

Sauve

OTTAWA (AP) - Jeanne Sauve was installed Monday as Canada's 23rd governor general, the first woman to hold the post.

The governor general is appointed by the British monarch on the advice of the Canadian prime minister.

"Peace should be our rallying cry, our foremost cause and the most compelling objective of our common action," the 62-year-old Mrs. Sauve said after taking the oath of office in the Senate chamber.

She then was honored at an outdoor ceremony on Parliament Hill with a 21-gun salute, a flyby of Canadian Forces aircraft, red-coated mounties and about 1,000 spectators.

Mrs. Sauve succeeds Edward Schreyer, whose five-year term expired last January and who was named ambassador to Australia.

15 Burned to Death in Bus

SANTA RITA DO PASSA QUATRO, Brazil (AP) - Fire started in the engine of a bus and swept through the vehicle, killing 15 people to death and injuring 13, police said Monday. Five of the victims were in serious condition.

The fire late Sunday night was caused by a short circuit in the engine, according to police in this town 160 miles northwest of Sao Paulo.

Child Killed, 21 Wounded in Beirut

BEIRUT, Lebanon (AP) - A mortar shell slammed into a school playground Monday, killing one child and wounding 21 others in the third straight day of artillery exchanges in Beirut.

Three other civilians were injured by shelling in an east Beirut neighborhood.

Prime Minister Rashid Karami vowed his two-week-old Cabinet would work to restore peace. He met with a committee of Christian and Moslem Cabinet members which drafted a policy statement on steps for ending the nine-year-old civil war.

Details of the statement were kept secret, but Karami said it would be submitted to the full Cabinet on Wednesday. Once approved by the Cabinet, the statement will be sent to Parliament for a vote.

Shortly before the committee met, mortar barrages broke out along the "green line" separating east and west Beirut and one shell crashed into the playground of the Annunciation Greek Orthodox school in east Beirut's Ashrafiyeh neighborhood.

A student identified as Gamal Nimeh, 12, was killed instantly and 21 of his schoolmates were wounded, according to both hospital officials and the Voice of Lebanon radio station of the rightist Christian Phalange party.

Officials at the St. Georges Hospital, where the wounded were taken, broadcast appeals for blood donations. The radio said many of the victims were in critical condition.

Witnesses at the blood-spattered playground said some students had been playing only two or three yards from where the shell hit.

All other schools in the Ashrafiyeh and other Christian neighborhoods near the green line were closed and students were bused home in case of more shelling at schools.

A mortar salvo hit the Furn el-Shubbak neighborhood of east Beirut, wounding three civilians.

Lebanese army troops and Moslem militiamen exchanged sniper fire and occasional blasts from rocket-propelled grenades along the green line throughout the afternoon.

The Lebanese army command issued a communique claiming its troops were not firing, pending the outcome of contacts by a security committee in charge of supervising the civil war truce.

Militant Jewish Settlers Stunned by Rabbi's Arrest

HEBRON, Occupied West Bank (AP) - Militant Jewish settlers near this West Bank town, stunned by the arrest of prominent Jewish settlement leader Moshe Levinger, said Monday that attacks on Palestinians would continue unless the government cracked down on Arab violence.

Rabbi Levinger was arrested Sunday night, reportedly under suspicion of having knowledge of terrorist attacks by Jewish settlers against Palestinians. Some news reports said Levinger may have been involved in planning some of the attacks.

Police were under court orders not to discuss the case but Israeli television quoted a senior police officer as saying the evidence against Levinger was flimsy and police would have to decide Tuesday whether to release him or request a court order for further detention.

Because of Levinger's stature, Prime Minister Yitzhak Shamir was reported by Israeli newspapers to have sought to delay his arrest until police had proof of his involvement with the Jewish terrorist underground.

Levinger, 48, is the most prominent of more than two dozen Israelis under arrest for a string of terrorist assaults starting with a 1980 car bombing that maimed two Palestinian mayors.

He openly advocated vengeance for Arab violence against Jews and believed that the Bible gave Jews an indisputable right to the West Bank of the Jordan River that left no room for Arabs to live there.

Section fronts
Headings and graphic trademarks

The trademark parallel rules on Page 1A also distinguish the section headings, with Garamond Extra Bold Condensed capitals making a strong punctuation against the rules and the headline display below. The small Old English logo is centered for formality's sake. The section title however is off-center, to help create a sense of movement left to right through the parallel rules, and to allow for a quote or reefer item on the extreme right. The large letter designation of the section on the left is set in Helvetica regular instead of the Garamond Extra Bold Condensed to avoid overweighting the top of the page and to provide a touch of graphic variety. The general graphic idea of the headings is to lock together the three different pieces of information in the running strip provided by the rules.

The parallel horizontal rules echo the theme at the top of Page 1A. I don't think such a visual echo is essential in a format design, but it can be a nice touch. In this case, the Page 1A motif was designed *after*, not before, the inside headings. Designing a Page One or cover of any publication, including books and promotion pieces, from the inside out is not a bad idea, and very often it's the best way. It seems to me that having a good grip on the organization, character, and typographical approach of the inside of a publication or promotion piece often provides the key to the cover design. Sometimes an actual physical element (in this case, the parallel rules) used inside can be picked up to use on the cover. In working with the intricacies of the actual material for the inside of a publication, the designer develops a deeper understanding of the material and is then better able to arrive at some visual or verbal synthesis that makes a good cover.

Hands-on collaboration
Executive editor Bill McIlwain (right) works with (left to right) news editor Dick Estrin, executive news editor Kyle Booth and chief artist Lew Agrell on a last-minute visual problem for a section page.

More than Briefs

We changed Briefs to "Dateline: Gulf Coast" and finally to "Along the Gulf." In describing the coverage area, the new design also signaled to readers the promoted increased coverage of neighboring communities. The datelines were given special design emphasis. (A few years later, a similar dateline device for Metro Briefs in the redesigned Metropolitan News section of *The New York Times* added the same kind of accent.)

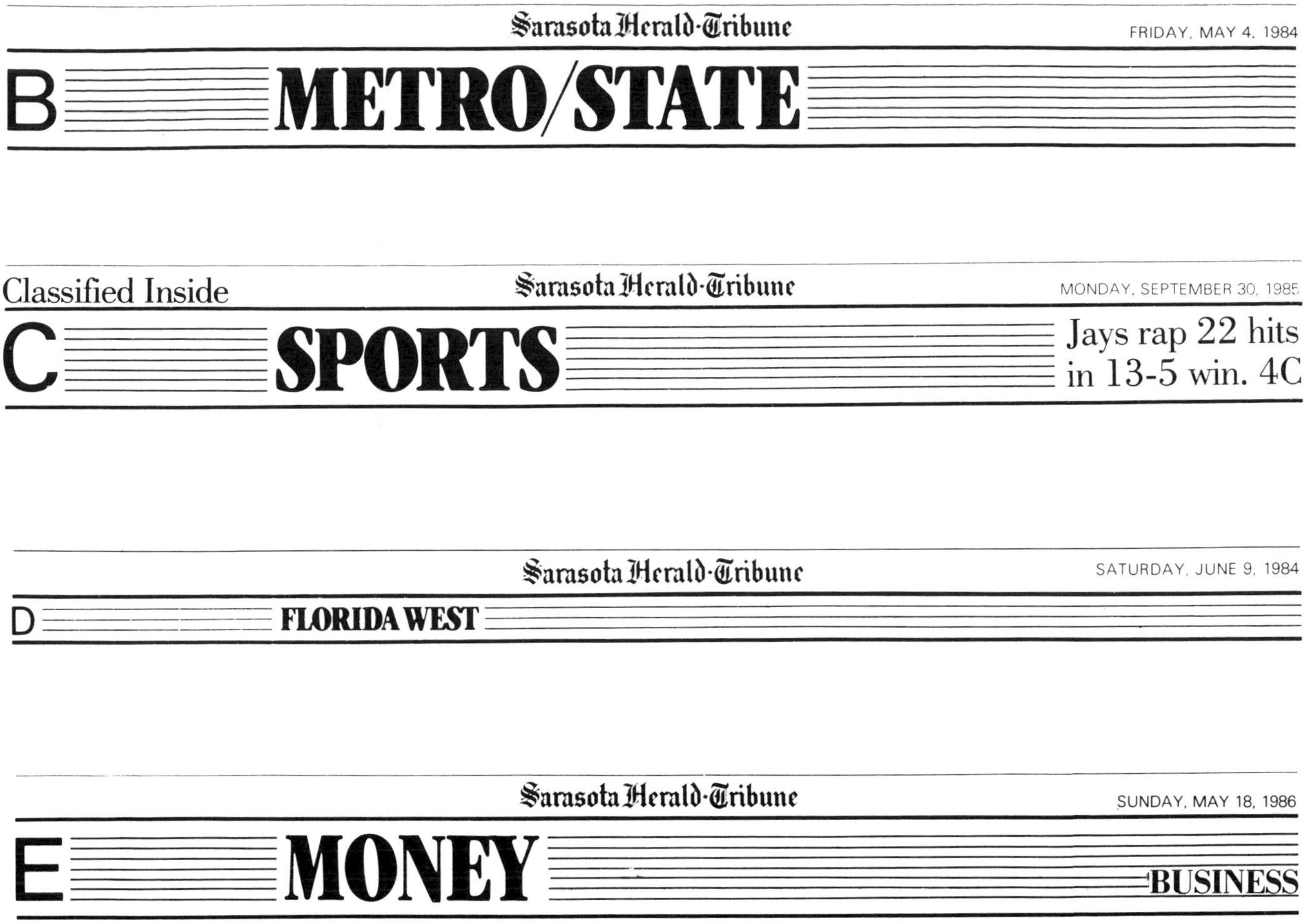

B METRO/STATE

Classified Inside

C SPORTS

Jays rap 22 hits
in 13-5 win. 4C

D FLORIDA WEST

E MONEY

BUSINESS

Section headings

Some of the section headings in the daily and Sunday *Tribune.* At the right, the characteristic rules could stop short to make way for a reefer, a subsidiary label, or quote. The touch of sans serif in the section letter designation makes the heading more graphically interesting and gives a little more prominence to the name. The Florida West heading is smaller because it runs each day with a different theme, the title of which is given especially large and graphic treatment.

SPORTS C

Music Academy in the Keys P. 4

C

SPORTS

Music Academy in the Keys P. 4

Variations on a theme

Two of the discarded earlier versions of the section headings.

In zoned editions to different communities, dateline items could easily be changed. Zoning became increasingly important in the paper's marketing plans. Regional bureaus were beefed up, and new titles were created for the page flags.

At the bottom

Any adequate format design must recognize that not all stories in the hard news parts of newspapers are equally "hard." A fire in the building across the street is hard news. An alarming increase in the number of fires in the neighborhood is a trend the newspaper may wish to explore and call to the attention of its readers. To signal an ongoing investigative series, a news analysis, a close-up, or any other kind of news feature, the Garamond Extra Bold italic, centered between two rules, has an important part to play.

This device was not necessarily a fixture for every day, but like every other device, was a "building block" to be used in a creative and varied fashion in the layout of the page, across different column measures, with or without pictures. The device was especially important in Sarasota because it paralleled the kind of in-depth, aggressive journalism that the new executive editor proposed to emphasize.

Home and zoned editions

Left: The home edition of the local section carries news of other communities "Along the Gulf." Other zoned editions carried different briefs geared to the communities in each zone. The special dateline treatment in the briefs column accents local area coverage.

Down the center

Facing page: As an optional layout, the Along the Gulf column is placed down the center of the page in unusual fashion. If wider display of the lead story is desired on the right, the column slides to its more customary position on the extreme left.

Sarasota Herald-Tribune MANATEE/AM FRIDAY, AUGUST 24, 1984

B BRADENTON/MANATEE

Local
Region
State

Too Much To Drink? Call CARE CAB

By DAVID GRIMES
Herald-Tribune Reporter

If you drink, you don't have to drive, thanks to a new program sponsored by Blake Memorial Hospital.

Called CARE CAB, the program is intended to provide free rides home for those who fird themselves too intoxicated to drive. The rides will be provided by local taxicab companies and the fare paid by the hospital. CARE CAB begins Aug. 31, the start of Labor Day weekend, and will be in operation 24 hours a day thereafter.

Blake's CARE CAB program is the first of its kind in Manatee County though some other cities offer a similar service under a different name. The idea is the same, however to try to reduce the number of accidents and deaths caused by drunken drivers.

"If we save just one life, than the program is worth it," said hospital spokesman Mary Louise Gerard.

Since it is a new program, Ms. Gerard said she was unsure how many people will use CAIE CAB, but thought 10 a night might be a good guess.

Here's how CARE CAB will work:

- A person who feels in no condition o drive, or a bartender or friend who feels a person shouldn't be driving, calls the Blake Hospital switchboard.
- The switchbo ard operator will call one of six local taxicab companies participating in the program and request a CARE CAB. The operator will provide the name of the rider, the location of the pickup and the destination.
- The CARE CAB is dispatched.
- The rider will be given a free ride home anywhere in Manatee County as long as the rider is not comatose or violent. Cab drivers have been instricted to turn those riders over to the police.
- Once home, the rider will be askd to sign a voucher stating the CARE CAB performd its service. The voucher is for hospital records only ard will not be used to obtain reimbursement or othewise harass users of the service, Ms. Gerard said.
- The hospital reimburses the cab comany later.

Bernard Sian, owner of Reliable Taxiat 1103 13th Ave. W., has joined the CARE CAB program and believes it's a good thing.

"I hope a lot of people use it," he said. 'I think it will stop a lot of people who have been dinking from wrapping their cars around trees or oher cars or killing pedestrians. It's what this town hs needed for a long time."

Sian said he estimated the average oneway fare for driving someone home from a bar at beween $3 and $6.50. If 10 people a night use the servce at $6.50 a ride, Blake will spend almost $24,000 : year on the CARE CAB program.

Virginia Drops Charge Against Ex-Candidate

By SYLVIA REED
Herald-Tribune Reporter

Sarasota while

The state of Viginia Thursday dropped a felay charge of obtaining money b false pretenses that had been filed against former Ma atee County Commission candlate Fulton Lewis III.

In a brief proeeding in a Fairfax County, Va., courtroom, assistant commowealth attorney Bill Minor sad he would not prosecute the harge against Lewis, who was present.

"I just don't feel at this time thatthere is enough evidence to go forward on it," Minc said in a telephone interview Thursday afternoon.

Lewis, the 48-year-old owner of a Bradenton advertising and public relations agency ad active in local Republican politics, earlier cited "hadball politics" as one of the reasons for his arrest in Ma on the Virginia charge.

Virginia law officers said in reports hat the charges against Lewis stemmed from a busines he co-founded in June 1981. Lewis and Jack Massarlli formed the National Automobile Buyers Associatin, a "shopping service" designed to locate choice cars br consumers.

Between the Lines

Simpson noticed another vehicle ii the parking lot, a Dodge, which was driven by Sharkey the report said.

Simpson flashed the emergency lihts on his patrol car as the three arrived at Wag's, thereport said.

After identifying Evers and Kenya as deputies, he radioed for a sheriff's office superisor, the report said.

Because the men were stopped outside the city limits, the investigation was turned over to the sherto the Sheriff's Department.

Although the report did not mentin alcohol, Pearson said Evers was tested with a beathalyzer and registered a blood alcohol content between .05 and .10 percent.

Lewis told the Herald-Tribunein an earlier interview that the corporation "neverjelled" and "died a natural death" after Massarelli rportedly cashed deposit checks and left town. Lewissaid he hasn't seen Massarelli since.

"I don't think Fulton ever felt tat he was guilty on D.C., said Thursday.

■ ■ ■

Later in 1981, the Fairfax Conty Department of Consumer Affairs received complints from three customers who made deposits from $70 to $1,080 with the business.

Along the Gulf

HERALD-TRIBUNE MIKE DIEMER
Part of crowd listens during debate.

Agreement to Prov Shelters Reached

CHARLOTTE After two years in the making, a six-county mutual aid agreement has been approved to provide inland evacuation shelters for the tens of would have to be evacuated in the face of a hurricane or other disaster.

County commissioners approved the mutual aid agreement this week with Sarasota, Collier, Lee, Glades and Hendry counties which establishes a system in which one county can help another county with evacuation and shelter needs.

The mutual aid agreement has already been approved by the other counties, and a final meeting on the document will be held Aug. 30 in Fort Myers, said John Derr, county disaster preparedness coordinator.

Broker Charged With Misdemeanor

PORT CHARLOTTE A Port Charlotte real estate broker has been charged with acting as a contractor without a license after he reportedly signed construction contracts for several homes according to local building officials and the 20th Judicial Circuit State Attorney's office.

According to state law, a per, who operates blood alcohol content between therokerage at whether the driver was intoxicatons recently his normal faculties were impaireof the mis-

A .10 percent blood alcohol levelge against drunk. Shirley, as-

Pearson said the investigation torney. less new information is presentwas issued to

Duke pleaded innocent to the charge and asked for a trial by jury, according to county court records.

A trial date should be set soon, Shirley said. up to one year in jail and/or a $1,000 fine, Shirley explained.

Red Tide Tests Turn Up Negative

CHARLOTTE Recent water samples taken from the Gulf of Mexico off Lee and Charlotte counties turned shellfish harvesting ban in the two counties wil remain in effect at least until next week, Department of Natural Resources officials said Wednesday.

Water samples obtained from inshore Gulf waters off the two counties Saturday were sent to the agency's St. Petersburg laboratory, where the results were read.

A shellfish harvesting ban was instituted in Charlotte and Lee counties Aug. 10, after it was imposed a few days earlier in Sarasota County.

Red tide produces an aerosol gas byproduct which kills fish and causes respiratory problems and watery eyes in humans. When shellfish become contaminated with red tide, they should not be eaten.

Pirate's Cove Nixed On Go-Cart Track

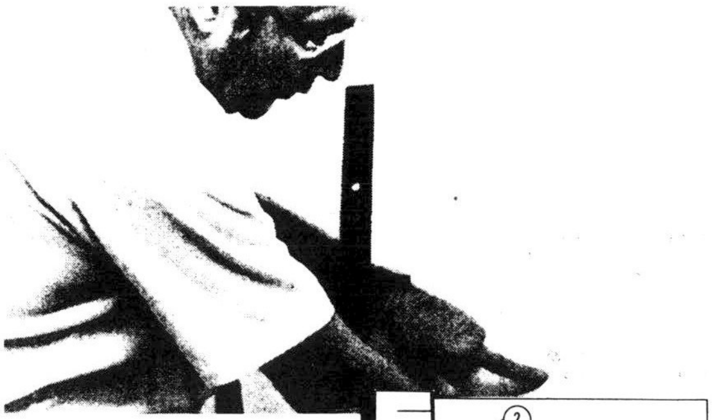

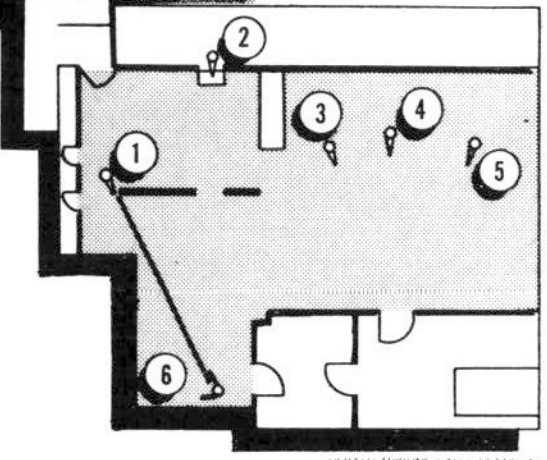

HERALD-TRIBUNE SALLY PETTIBON
Jason and Rececca Collier and Brad and Stacey Scheckner play on a sculpture at on the College That their teaching licenses.

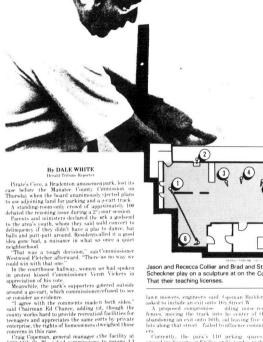

By DALE WHITE
Herald-Tribune Reporter

Pirate's Cove, a Bradenton amusemen park, lost its case before the Manatee County Cmmission on Thursday when the board unanimously ejected plans to use adjoining land for parking and a go-cart track.

A standing-room-only crowd of apprximately 100 debated the rezoning issue during a 2½ hour session.

Parents and ministers declared the ark a godsend to the area's youth, whom they said wuld convert to delinquency if they didn't have a plac to dance, bat balls and putt-putt around. Residents alled it a good idea gone bad, a nuisance in what ws once a quiet neighborhood.

"That was a tough decision," saiCommissioner Westwood Fletcher afterward. "There as no way we could win with that one."

In the courthouse hallway, women wo had spoken in protest kissed Commissioner Vern Vickers in appreciation of his vote.

Meanwhile, the park's supporters gahered outside around a go-cart, which commissioners efused to see or consider as evidence.

"I agree with the comments made n both sides," said Chairman Ed Chance, adding tt, though the county works hard to provide recreatical facilities for teenagers and appreciates the same eorts by private enterprise, the rights of homeowners otweighed those concerns in this case.

Craig Copeman, general manager the facility at 5410 14th St. W., asked commissione to rezone 4.4 vacant acres directly behind the park om residential to planned commercial development.

The plan was to place a go-cart track5 feet south of Aloha Estates, a neighboring tailer park, and a 311 space parking lot in the remining space. The lot would only be used for overflowparking during week end nights, and the go-carts wuld run quieter than lawn mowers, engineers said. Opeman Builders also asked to include an exit onto 16h Street W.

A proposed compromise dding noise reducing fences, moving the track into he center of the lot, abandoning an exit onto 16th, ad leaving five vacant lots along that street failed to nfluence commissioners.

Currently, the park's 110 prking spaces have proved inadequate on Friday and Saturday nights and the facility is using its west preerty for overflow parking. Doing so violates the zonng conditions outlined when the park was approved.The park is being fined $20 a day.

"We feel that any promise the make will not necessarily be kept," protested Aloh Estates resident Shirley Rumberger. "What's a violaton?

Law Officers Not Charged

By DAN DUFFEY
Herald-Tribune Reporter

Two Manatee County deputies and a Lngboat Key policeman were stopped for driving reklessly and speeding Wednesday morning, but were nt charged or disciplined for the incident.

The three, one of whom is the son f Bradenton Mayor Bill Evers, were stopped by a Braenton police police report said.

But an investigation by the sheriff's offie produced no proof of the charges, and no disciplinar action was taken, a sheriff's office spokesman said.

Deputies William Evers Jr., 23, SteverKenyan, 24, and Longboat Key policeman Martin Sarkey were detained in the incident, the report said.

But despite observations in the report hat the three were driving recklessly and speeding, tere were no "bona fide observations" onvhich to base charges, said Lt. Ken Pearson of the shriff's office.

"The officer is not alleging nuch," he said.

Their positions as police offers and Evers' status as the mayor's son had no infience in the investigation, Pearson said.

Bradenton policeman Melvi Simpson was headed north on 14th Street when e saw two cars, a 1977 Chevrolet, driven by Kenyn, and a 1974 Datsun, said.

The two cars "appeare to be racing" the report said. But Simpson never nntioned the speed the two cars were traveling.

Simpson turned south ad followed the two cars through the intersection of Cortez Road, the report said. The two cars turned into parking lot near Wag's Restaurant, and continued to cive at high speeds until they reached the restaurant.

Step Right Up, Take a Swig

Gulping the Blame for Water Fountain Project

HERALD-TRIBUNE SALLY PETTIBON
Jason and Rececca Collier and Brad and Stacey Scheckner play on a sculpture

By SYLVIA REED
Herald-Tribune Reporter

The state o quickly,ginia Thursday dropped a to quibny charge of obtaining morlscapingy false pretenses that ost of tl been filed against formenk abouiatee County Commission cermit ulate Fulton Lewis III.

In a brief when reeding in a Fairfax Countyble abu., courtroom, assistant comi requirrealth attorney Bill Minor ie watr he would not prosecute thet gettiarge against Lewis, who wantil it sent.

"I just don't feel at this tinough evidence to go forward on it, telephone interview Thursday afte

Lewis, the 48-year-old ownedvertising and public relations ag local Republican politics, earlier cites" as one of the reasons for his arrerginia charge.

Virginia law officers said inarges against Lewis stemmed from unded in June 1981. Lewis and Jacd the National Automobile Buyers pping service" designed to locate choers.

Later in 1981, the Fairfax nt of any more, what wial substitutes available. Water coret and it is not likely to put you in make things go better, add life, or ou attractive to girls in tight swim s

Although water h a long time, it seems to have rece favor. A good advertising agency this around, of course, especially ifater agreed to expand their productater would be a big hit among dieteror L.A. Water might syphon off s market. Low-cholesterol and lowld be popular among people with h and you could always produce orhe health food freaks.

Unfortunately, thoners made no mention of providincialty waters at the new courthousy citizens can expect to drink nothan chilled city water, pumped frombonated Evers Reservoir.

Perhaps worst of alis planning to offer the water freeis an unwise decision by the comt it not only deprives the county ofs people from showing off their weaneys, derelicts and columnists can jo the fountain and get a drink of ving a fee or flashing a membershiply runs coun-

Sports on TV

7 AM	Bill Dance Outdoors, Ch. 40
8 AM	Sportscenter, ESPN
Noon	Sportscenter Plus, ESPN
Noon	Wrestling, USA
12:30 PM	NBA Playoffs: Celtics vs. Knicks, Ch. 11, 13
1:05 PM	Baseball: Braves vs. Expos, WTBS
1:30 PM	Baseball: Astros vs. Mets, WOR
2:15 PM	Baseball: Padres vs. Cubs, WGN
2:30 PM	Golf: Tournament of Champions, Ch. 8, 20
2:30 PM	USFL Football: Stars vs. Stallions, Ch. 10, 40
3 PM	Top Rank Boxing, ESPN
3:30 PM	NBA Playoffs: Lakers vs. Mavericks, Ch. 11, 13
4:30 PM	Sportsworld, Ch. 8, 20
7 PM	Sportscenter, ESPN
8 PM	College Baseball: Miss. St. vs. Alabama, ESPN
11 PM	Sportscenter, ESPN

Sports on Radio

12:45 PM	Padres vs. Braves, WPLP (570)
1:20 PM	Baseball: Dodgers vs. Pirates, WOFN (1490)
2:05 PM	White sox vs. Red Sox, WQSA (1220)

Tom Watson scratched out a two-stroke lead entering today's final round of the $400,000 MONY-Tournament of Champions golf tournament. Today's final round will be shown on NBC, Channels 8 and 20 beginning at 2:30 p.m.

Sports Trivia

Jackson   Strawberry   Kittle

Major Leaguers with highest strikeout ratios

1. Reggie Jackson, Angels, 1 SO every 2.83 at bats.
2. Darryl Strawberry, Mets, 1 SO every 3.28 AB.
3. Ron Kittle, White Sox, 1 SO every 3.46 AB
4. Mike Schmidt, Phillies, 1 SO every 3.60 AB
5. Gorman Thomas, Mariners, 1 SO every 3.61 AB.

SOURCE: Baseball Digest

Uplifting the agate

Above and left: The Sports Scoreboard page features at the top a TV and Radio box that stands out prominently from the surrounding agate. At the bottom, boxes were planned on a daily basis, like the Sports Trivia box. Both boxes provide convenient vehicles for live and relevant photos.

Using the building blocks

Facing page: A typical front page of the Sports section shows a well-executed page design with many of the typographical building blocks at work, particularly the reefer in the heading and the Garamond Extra Bold italic, effective in setting off the "Tennis Classic" story at the bottom. An extension of the original design is the use of sans serif Helvetica in the tint box, upper right. Picking up the sans serif from the C in the heading, it effectively contrasts with the headlines. Page layout: Peter Gentile.

Classified Inside

Sarasota Herald-Tribune

MONDAY, NOVEMBER 16, 1987

C SPORTS

Mayotte wins 5th tourney of year. 3C

Officials Help Vikings Beat Buccaneers 23-17

By NATHAN HUANG
Staff Writer

MINNEAPOLIS – It was a game that began in controversy and ended in controversy. And there was still more controversy in between.

But the fact that there were several questionable officiating calls doesn't alter the only circumstance that matters to the Tampa Bay Buccaneers – a 23-17 loss Sunday to the Minnesota Vikings at the Metrodome before 48,605 fans.

The Bucs could have strengthened significantly their chances for a wild-card playoff berth with a victory. But it is the Vikings who are 5-4 and in second place in the NFC Central Division. The Bucs are 4-5 and in danger of fading to oblivion.

These Vikings – not the laughable strike replacements who were 0-3 – are now 5-1 and are clearly more talented than the real Bucs, now 2-4. But that can't mask the fact that Tampa Bay appeared to have made several key plays – plays that could have influenced the outcome – only to have them vanish at the discretion of the officials.

"I don't like to belittle any kind of calls," Bucs head coach Ray Perkins said. "I think, overall, that evens out. But I did question several calls. I didn't think they (officials) had a real good day. That's just my personal opinion. I think overall they didn't do a good job."

Someone asked quarterback Steve DeBerg if he had the feeling that something – like a victory – was taken from him and the Bucs.

"Yes," DeBerg said. "Definitely."

Few people will remember the notable performances in this game. DeBerg completing 22 of 37 passes for 284 yards, two touchdowns and one interception. Phil Freeman's catch of a deflected pass that became a 64-yard TD and put the Bucs in position to win the game.

James Wilder's unbelievable output – zero rushing attempts. The Bucs' running attack – nine carries (a team-record low) for 15 yards. Minnesota's Chris Doleman, the linebacker turned lineman, who had two sacks and caused DeBerg to fumble twice.

The Vikings' Darrin Nelson, who darted and twisted to 103 yards on 17 carries, leading Minnesota to 224 rushing yards, its best output since 1976.

The scoring plays seemed almost incidental. DeBerg also had a 20-yard TD pass to tight end Calvin Magee and Donald Igwebuike kicked a 26-yard field goal.

The Vikings' Chuck Nelson made three field goals – 29, 27 and 26 yards – but also missed from 21 and 41 yards. Fullback Rick Fenney had a 1-yard TD run and quarterback Tommy Kramer threw a 2-yard scoring pass to tight end Steve Jordan.

Forget statistics. What the Bucs will recall from this game is the frustration of

Continued on 7C

The Bowl Picture

AP LASERPHOTO

Michigan State's Lorenzo White gains a few of his school-record 292 yards against Indiana Saturday in East Lansing. Michigan State won 27-3, clinching the Big Ten title and thus earning a trip to the Rose Bowl.

Who's Going Where?

- **Here are the probable participants in many of the college bowl games. All pairings are unofficial until invitations go out Saturday.**
- **ORANGE (Jan. 1, 8 p.m.):** Miami vs. Oklahoma-Nebraska winner
- **FIESTA (Jan. 1, TBA):** Florida State vs. Oklahoma-Nebraska loser.
- **ALOHA (Dec. 25, 3:45 p.m.):** Florida vs. opponent to be determined.
- **SUGAR (Jan. 1, 8 p.m.):** Syracuse vs. Southeastern Conference winner.
- **COTTON (Jan. 1, 1:30 p.m.):** Notre Dame vs. Southwest Conference winner.
- **ROSE (Jan. 1, 5 p.m.):** Michigan State vs. Southern Cal-UCLA winner.
- **CITRUS (Jan. 1, noon):** Clemson vs. Penn State.
- **GATOR (Dec. 31, 2:30 p.m.):** South Carolina vs. SEC team to be determined.
- **HALL OF FAME (Jan. 2, TBA):** Michigan vs. SEC team to be determined.
- **LIBERTY (Dec. 29, 8 p.m.):** Georgia vs. SWC team to be determined.
- **PEACH (Jan. 2, 2 p.m.):** Tennessee vs. Indiana.
- **FREEDOM (Dec. 30, 8 p.m.):** Air Force vs. Arizona State.
- **HOLIDAY (Dec. 30, 8 p.m.):** Iowa vs. Western Athletic Conference champion.
- **SUN (Dec. 25, 2:30 p.m.):** Oklahoma State vs. opponent to be determined.
- **BLUEBONNET (Dec. 31, 9 p.m.):** Pittsburgh vs. SWC team to be determined.
- Story, 4C. Complete bowl list, 2C.

NFL Week 9

Vikings 23, Bucs 17	1C
Colts 40, Dolphins 21	1C
Browns 27, Bills 21	6C
Cowboys 23, Patriots 17, OT	7C
Redskins 20, Lions 13	6C
Oilers 23, Steelers 3	6C
Rams 27, Cardinals 24	6C
Jets 16, Chiefs 9	6C
Bengals 16, Falcons 10	7C
Seahawks 24, Packers 13	7C
Saints 26, 49ers 24	6C
Giants 20, Eagles 17	6C
Chargers 16, Raiders 14	6C

Tonight: Bears at Broncos, 9 p.m.

Convincing Colts Sock Miami 40-21

By TIM LEONE
Staff Writer

MIAMI – Maybe these guys are for real.

Remember the bumbling Indianapolis Colts, Irsay's idiots, the team that entering this season had gone a collective 12-36 since skipping out on Baltimore in 1984? They've changed, enough to register an impressive 40-21 win over the Miami Dolphins on Sunday at Joe Robbie Stadium and lay claim to half of first place in the jumbled AFC East.

The Colts, who raised their record to 5-4 and moved into a first-place tie with the New York Jets, overcame deficits of 14-0 and 21-17 to end a 14-game losing streak against the error-prone Dolphins before a crowd of 65,433. Miami, shut out in the second half, was hurt by five turnovers as it dropped to 4-5 and joined Buffalo and New England in the cellar of a division in which all five teams began play Sunday tied at 4-4.

"I said at the beginning of the week that if we could beat Miami, it would mark the resurgence of the Colts," Indianapolis coach Ron Meyer said. "Well, we beat Miami and we're in first place, so I guess the resurgence is here."

Indianapolis was 0-13 when Meyer replaced Rod Dowhower last year. Under Meyer, the Colts won their final three games of 1986 and suddenly are in the playoff hunt in 1987.

What's new?

Mix together a blockbuster trade that brought Pro Bowl running back Eric Dickerson from the Los Angeles Rams, the maturation of a number of top draft picks and an infusion of enthusiasm generated by Meyer, and you've got a contender. A team that has suffered from the idiosyncrasies of Owner Robert Irsay, a team that was the laughing stock of the NFL just last year, may have arrived. Quickly.

"They're an excellent football team and

Continued on 7C

Win or Lose, Trickle Draws Flood of Fans

Martin Fennelly

Butch Miller was holding his trophy with one arm on Sunday. The other arm cheesecaked with beauty queen. He'd won.

In Desoto Speedway's infield, Dick Trickle was lighting up his first post-race Marlboro. He'd lost.

A kid, part of his racing team, came running over.

"Here ya go Dick, here's a beer," says the kid.

Dick Trickle pops the top. The kid foams.

"Woulda run over sooner with it, Dick, but you know how they hate drinkin' before the checkered flag, 'specially in the infield."

Trickle shrugs, kicking a cowboy boot toward a spot of oil. A long sip and a shaking of dirty brown hair.

"Busted valve or something," he says. A tanned and weathered face grimaces. It's an effort; Trickle doesn't put up with grimaces much. But he'd run his race, just like he's run thousands in the last 29 years or so. Run it damned near perfect. Was running second, right behind Miller.

"I had him all set up," Trickle says. "Just like last year. His tires were wearing out. I woulda caught him last 20 laps. I think I would of. Either way, it woulda been a hell of a battle."

STAFF PHOTO/MIKE DIEMER

Dick Trickle checks out his car prior to Sunday's race at DeSoto.

The kid again: "Dick, you going to the pits now?"

Trickle nods. He throws his Marlboro away and pats his racing suit for a rumpled pack. Soon, another is ignited.

A crew member comes over. Trickle doesn't wait for questions.

"Valve, or engine. Damn. That's racing."

Maybe not. Maybe, on the short tracks of this country, Dick Trickle is racing.

Walk through the pits with him. Win or lose, expect a long walk. Caesar with a side order of grease, his legions doing everything short of crossing wrenches for him to parade under. This emperor has more short-track victories than anybody. Ever. "1,100, maybe 1,200," Trickle says. He's not sure. Perfect. "They all kind of run together." Just like the pit groupies do when they see him. To any little kid hanging onto hot-rodding pop, this is granpap. To any teen who's ever charged a battery, he's a father figure. And to any fella who's ever rat-raced somewhere between hell and bent, Trickle is a 5-foot-7 big daddy. What Chuck Yeager was to fighter jocks, Dick Trickle is to short tracks.

"I never expected this," Trickle says. "All this attention. People think what they do. I just run the race and have my laughs."

Trickle hits the pits, beer in hand, cigarette pursed between lips. He's not laughing yet. A track car has just pushed past his ungrateful beached whale – his No. 99 – that went belly up 162 laps into Sunday's Coca-Cola 200. Trickle stares angrily, as if it were an empty beer glass or something.

"I'm 46, but you learn to accept this," he says. "Days like this. I've been at this 29 years. You have to accept it. Of course, I've won a few."

Heavy woman, too-tight stretch shirt, approaches.

"Dick, darling, you're still my favorite."

Trickle hugs her. "That's enough for me, then."

Continued on 5C

Sarasota Tennis Classic

STAFF PHOTO/THE N. PHAM

Jaime Fillol goes for a winner with his overhead smash en route to a 7-5, 6-2 victory over Ross Case in the final of the Sarasota Tennis Classic.

Fillol Is Too Fast For Case

By MIC HUBER
Staff Writer

Jaime Fillol likes people, and people like him. That mutual admiration might have something to do with Fillol winning the $40,000 Sunshine Buick Dealers Sarasota Tennis Classic over the weekend at the Sarasota Bath and Racquet Club.

Fillol, using all the help he could get from his friends, passed by Ross Case 7-5, 6-2 on Sunday to win the event, part of the Grand Champions tour sponsored by Prudential-Bache Securities. Maybe he should think about passing around some of the $8,000 he won.

"We wore him down and you got him," Colin Dibley cracked as he and Fillol's brother, Alvaro, greeted the winner shortly after the match's end.

The Fillols and Dibley stayed together at the same house this week. Case had to struggle through long matches against Alvaro Fillol on Friday and Dibley on Saturday to reach Sunday's final against Jaime Fillol.

"I was tired going in (to the match)," Case said after being mercilessly run around the court by Jaime Fillol. "Normally I'm the one who runs players around and gets them tired. This time, Jaime did that to me."

Case then had to return to play doubles, but Sherwood Stewart and Kim Warwick stopped Case and Dick Stockton 6-3, 3-6, 6-3.

In the singles final, Fillol jumped to a 4-1 lead before Case could get untracked. Case couldn't find an answer for Fillol's shots, as the former Chilean Davis Cup captain threaded the needle whenever Case gave the slightest opening.

"It feels good when you start out like that," Fillol said about his play at the beginning. "That's what makes tennis fun."

Fillol is big on having fun on the court. He believes you have to be in good balance to have fun and play good tennis. He

Continued on 5C

Themed lifestyle sections

A highly visible improvement

The size of the paper, over 100,000 circulation, the nature of the community, and the paper's new marketing ambitions in competitive Florida all pointed to the need to do much more with lifestyle sections than had been done in the past. In a smaller paper, with a smaller staff, a decision might be made to downplay the themed aspect of the titles since limited resources could not adequately implement a different section each day. But here, a different magazinelike section each day offered an opportunity to make a highly visible improvement. Consequently, the umbrella title "Florida West," which was chosen for the section, was played down, while the new daily theme titles were dramatically played up.

Keeping the horizontal rules of the "Local/ State," "Sports," and other section headings as a motif provided a consistent look, even though the Florida West title was made smaller. Unusually large scale and variety characterize the treatment of theme section titles and derive from two concerns: first, the desire to emphasize the uniqueness of each section—to give the reader a sense of a different "magazine" each day; second, the observation that in many papers, attempts at creative variety in lifestyle and other feature sections frequently result in headline treatments, hand-lettered or otherwise arrived at, that are poorly conceived, executed, or both. In many newspapers, creative efforts that miss the mark are looked upon tolerantly by the top editors, if indeed they are noticed at all.

The format design attempted to give the editors of the lifestyle sections an exceptionally strong logo element for each theme that would change every day and would run under the section flags, becoming part of the "live" part of the page each day.

Admittedly, an additional layout problem was created because live elements had to fit *around* the title logo. To make this situation workable, various devices were perfected in a series of practice pages and built into the designs, including use of quotes and reefers as well as suggestions for handling column headings and items around the titles.

Veloxes of the headings were supplied to *The Tribune* in the correct size and with placement

Themed sections

Left: A dummy layout shows the theme name of the section *under* the section heading, becoming an active part of the "live" part of the page. Initials and bullets break up the wide column on the left. Useful information is packaged at the bottom. A news story in the center adds to the "mix."

The variation

Facing page: Innovative implementation of the basic format includes addition of special display type in the Edgar Voss story, and effective use of a large tint box. This layout is recognized as a desirable variation only when the material justifies the display. On days with less impressive leads, another story, preferably a service item, would be expected at the bottom. Page design: Juli Cragg.

Style

New York critics aren't bully on the Broadway production of 'Teddy and Alice.' See Page 8E.

Marjorie Marsh
Let's Talk

Brave Bidding Raises $20,000

Bravissimo '87, the brave, new fund-raiser for the Florida West Coast Symphony that worked, to the sweet tune of $20,000, welcomed several hundred Manatee and Sarasota supporters to taste the wine, enjoy a buffet catered by Beasley's and do madcap bidding on a variety of items.

The most spirited was for the beautiful originals by local artists and for a wine vault that holds 700 bottles in controlled temp and humidity (the latter finally went for $1,400).

Least favored was chairman **Sally Fine** and **Marie Woolley**'s practical joke item, a multi-colored plastic plant and mushroom light-fixture floor accessory. Several guests rolled their eyes (discreetly, of course) at the unbelievable minimum bid, $1,005. Sally 'fessed up later that the item is one that has made the rounds of all the board members and still keeps landing in the trash.

• • •

Two in One: It's rare when an author of international renown is an equally good speaker, but **Ruth Gruber** merits the recognition. Ruth, the speaker at the **Golda Meir** 90th anniversary luncheon in the Summerhouse on Siesta Key, enthralled about 100 guests (many, long-time friends) with her stories as an author and foreign correspondent.

Ruth talked about her latest book, "Rescue" – the exodus of the Ethiopian Jews, being the only correspondent allowed to cover "Operation Moses," as it was called. Her "Raquela: A Woman of Israel," won the National Jewish Book Award and she's been recommended for the Nobel Prize in Literature this year.

The luncheon was sponsored by the Sarasota-Manatee Women's Division State of Israel Bonds, whose members have contributed $465,000 toward Israeli bonds this year. **Adeline Silverman** was chairman.

The affair also served to honor former investment adviser **Marion Benjamin** for her philanthropic contributions. Among other distinctions, she and her husband, **Lou**, were the first couple ever awarded Honorary Fellowships at Technion.

• • •

On A Roll: **Edgar Vos** and **Alyce Kalin** toasted each other with cups of coffee in Alexander's the other day celebrating Alyce's most recent fashion coup. It's a tribute to Alyce's tenacity and fashion savvy that her Gilded Lily will show Italian designer's new **Max Mara**'s new ready-to-wear line exclusively in the Sarasota area.

"Mara is fantastic," Edgar said, "the best in Europe."

Alyce has seen his work in Italy and waited patiently until she heard he was ready to come stateside. A few chits were pulled in from European fashion friends, and voila, Mara will be on the racks here in December.

• • •

People Watching: Former British pub, nightclub and French restaurant owner from London, **Tom Richardson**, has just bought Express Pizza on Osprey Avenue, saying it was time to go into an All-American food venture.

Farrah Fawcett Plays 'Poor Little Rich Girl'

By JERRY BUCK
AP Television Writer

LOS ANGELES – In a new NBC miniseries, Farrah Fawcett, coiffed, costumed and wearing million-dollar bangles, portrays a famed dime store heiress whose extravagant and eccentric lifestyle shocked the world.

Fawcett

She stars as Barbara Hutton, who inherited $50 million and became prey for a platoon of notorious playboys with royal titles as questionable as their ethics in separating her from her money.

"Poor Little Rich Girl: The Barbara Hutton Story," which will be televised Monday and Tuesday, follows a familiar television premise: that money always buys unhappiness, but only real money brings true misery.

Fawcett's performance takes her from Hutton's elaborate coming-out ball at the height of the Depression to her final days in 1979 when drugs, alcohol and an obsessive desire to be loved and admired alienated her from her true friends.

"That part of life is not completely foreign to me," says Fawcett. "I've been to the South of
Continued on 4E

By MARJORIE MARSH
Columnist

The Japanese look – layers upon layers and boxy styles with exaggerated shoulders – is over, declared Sarasota's fashion guru, Dutch designer Edgar Vos. "This generation of women is discovering fun with femininity for the first time and love it," he said, a sparkle of approval in his eyes.

Not for Vos are the unformed, rough-cut diamonds of recent fashion seasons, but rather pearls of fashion wisdom – the result of 30 years sketching and designing for beautiful people, trekking to Paris and Italy, window shopping in New York, being inspired by clouds and trees, and imagining color combinations. And Vos showered those pearls like soft petals on many of the area's best-dressed women during a private showing at Alyce Kalin's Gilded Lily Saturday.

Vos will be at the Gilded Lily with his fashions today through Friday from 9:30 until 5.

Vos' fashions show not what is today – "It's already been done" – but what will be next season.

The vibrant colors of the rainbow were used sparingly, often to accessorize. But mostly, Vos swathed his models in black, brown, mocha, taupe and rust in form-hugging little numbers. "They said that hemlines were down; we said hemlines were up. . . . and *we* got the publicity."

So what appeared to be confusion on the fashion pages was really a high-stakes insider's game of push me-pull me, with women, striving to keep up, caught in the middle between the couturiers and the ready-to-wear houses.

"It is difficult because of the emancipation of ladies," Vos said. "They are making a little bit their own fashion. But they must look carefully in the mirror. Age is not the criteria for hem length; it is the body."

Hem lengths, however, may be the only choice that liberated women get. Vos is very definite about what to pack away and what is *au courant.*

No more long, long straight skirts. "Cut them off," he said, "or add pleats.

"Keep the shoulder pads, but only to define and enhance, not for exaggeration."

The cinched-to-the-body haute couture will bring out a plethora of belts: wide, glittery, tied, even the tightly laced corset wraparounds.

"It's all feminine," Vos said. "Young girls never saw this style before and they like the way the boys react.

"When a woman is young, she dresses for the boys," he said. "When she is older, she dresses for the girls, but she is not oblivious to the fact that the men like it, too.

"If a man could choose, he would dress attractive women in very short black satin, black stockings and high heels. Even for his wife, he finds this combination very sexy."

For fashion-conscious women who have tracked styles for several decades and want to peg this year's collection to a previous era: Be warned that Vos will take offense.

"Fashion never repeats," he said. "It's the media that will say collections are from the '30s, '40s or '50s. This is just not so. What doesn't change is the body, but clothes do."

While cocktail dresses are strapless ("as low as a woman will risk"), short and sexy, they were made to make a woman feel beautiful, Vos said.

Suits, on the other hand, are always considered "high fashion." Again, though, Vos says the exaggerated shoulders and loose, boxy jackets are passe. Clean, classic lines will be emphasized, accented with color, especially turquoise, and big collars that lie mid-shoulder, drawing the eye to the defined waist.

STAFF PHOTOS/RICO MILLINGTON

Dutch designer Edgar Vos displays his fashion collection on elegant models Yuette Dessauzagie and Elke Osthus. Vos and his fashions will be at the Gilded Lily through Friday.

Vos' ruched red and blue cocktail dresses create intriguing patterns for nighttime wear. Neutral-colored dresses, accented with a wide belt and large brooch, look sexy and elegant.

indicated for each. The Lifestyle staff, numbering five people at the time of the redesign under the leadership of assistant managing editor Diane McFarlin, seized the opportunity to make this part of the paper the daily showcase. At that time the paper employed two artists, Lew Agrell and Ian Lee, who produced illustrations as well as graphics.

During the months of working on the redesign, we were concerned that our ambitious format design would need a professional designer on hand when we went "live." However, the paper was fortunate to have in place people who had a feeling for layout and were able to successfully implement the new design on a day-to-day basis, including, among others, McFarlin; the news editor, Kyle Rote; and the senior artist, Lew Agrell. The question of a staff art director was deferred. Pelletier helped out for a couple of weeks, and Mary Holdt, regional senior designer for *The Times* group, also came to help, particularly in the advance design of style pages.

Variation

Above right: Another style page features two main stories, the theme name in color, and the column illustration sliding up around the title. Bolstered by the built-in script lettering, the page is quite simply and easily put together.

Science and Health

Right: Wednesday's theme, constructed like the Style page above, squeezes a studio photo, a health-related story, and a provocative "Stress Quiz" under the department heading Feeling Good. The page is effective in tying up an ambitious staff-produced diagram with an arresting local story.

Different every day

Facing page: The five basic theme sections that run Monday to Friday. Color is used as page design dictates. Various layout devices were developed to fit live material around the theme names, which then became active parts of the page.

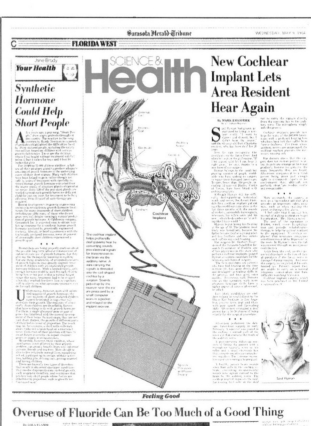

C | **Sarasota Herald-Tribune**
| **FLORIDA WEST**

WEEKEND

C | **Sarasota Herald-Tribune**
| **FLORIDA WEST**

SCIENCE &
Health

C | **Sarasota Herald-Tribune**
| **FLORIDA WEST**

Home

C | **Sarasota Herald-Tribune**
| **FLORIDA WEST**

LIVING

C | **Sarasota Herald-Tribune**
| **FLORIDA WEST**

Business Monday

Tabloid in two steps

Sarasota had been publishing a special tabloid section called "Business Monday." The section had good content and was in the hands of an able editor, Mike Vizarey. It was decided to hold off total redesign of this one part of the paper for a later date, relieving some of the pressure on the start-up deadline. However, as a first step, a new heading for the front page and translation of the inside to the new typography made the section conform to the new format.

About a year after the start-up of the new format, we attacked the section more comprehensively, giving it a contents page to reflect its increased substance, and a letter from the editor titled "Signals" for Page 3. Headings on the inside were strengthened, emphasizing the strong regional and service nature of the material.

Business tabloid

Above right: *Business Monday*, an existing tabloid, was given at first only a minor face-lift with a new section head. The new design echoed the trademark parallel rules and the Garamond Extra Bold capitals of the other sections. A restrained, uncluttered photo makes an ideal background for the controlled handling of the text. Design: Mike Vizarey.

Second time around

Right and facing page: A more complete redesign was executed a year after the redesign of the rest of the paper. The heading was made stronger with a look more of a magazine, and features a reefer handled like a handwritten memo as part of the regular design. On the facing page are some of the many regionally directed departments that, added to the news stories, give the section a local service cast.

Q & A For Success

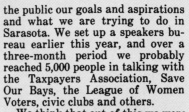

NAME: Robert O. Smedley Jr.
POSITION: President, Sun Bank/
 Sarasota County; President,
 Sarasota County Committee of
 100.
EDUCATION: 1964 graduate of
 Sarasota High School; bachelor's
 degree from Georgia State Uni-
 versity.

positions with First Georgia Bank and
joined Flagship Bank in Tampa

the public our goals and aspirations
and what we are trying to do in
Sarasota. We set up a speakers bureau earlier this year, and over a
three-month period we probably
reached 5,000 people in talking with
the Taxpayers Association, Save
Our Bays, the League of Women
Voters, civic clubs and others.

We think that out of this we were
able to show these people that when
we talk about bringing industry
here, we are really talking about
bringing business to Sarasota.
When we talked about indu-

Area Interest Rates

Financial Institution	Money Mkt. Acct.	6 mo CDs Rate/Yield	1 yr CDs Rate/Yield	5 yr CDs Rate/Yield
Amerifirst Federal S&L	8.75	12.00 12.00	12.25 12.25	12.00 12.00
California Federal	10.00	11.75 11.75	12.10 12.86	12.40
Coast Federal Savings & Loan	10.00	11.25	12.0	

Stocks of Area Interest

Company and Market	Price						Volume		Earnings and Dividends				P/E Ratio	
	Last Wk's Close	Pct. Change		Year to Date	5-Year		Last Week's		Earnings per Share		5-Yr. Ann. Grwth Rate	Indi-cated Divi-dend Yield	5-Year Aver-age	Cur-rent
		Last					Shares Traded	Pct. of Shares Out-stndng	Last 12 Months					
		Week	4 Wks		High	Low			Amnt.	Chnge				
	$		%	%	$	$	(000)	%	$	%	%	%	—	—

Barometer

Gross Sales

Source: Florida Dept. of Revenue

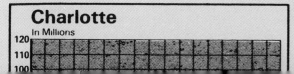

Sunday

Arts and Travel

In the Sunday paper, variations are designed into the front pages to give the large package elements of special interest.

The Arts/Travel section's bulletinlike treatment, under the heading, "Top Billing," allows for accents in Garamond Bold italic of labels such as "Drama," "Film," and "Gallery." Vertical rules add to the bulletin or calendar feeling. The format forces a different kind of layout from the other sections, smaller pictures, silhouettes, and shorter blocks of type.

A little more than a third of the bottom part of the page is given to a single travel item, with one main photograph and a rather large mass of type, contrasting with the busier bulletin treatment in the top part of the page.

The paper before redesign had run travel articles inside a Sunday feature section, where they failed to make their presence felt sufficiently. The new design recognized the fact that Sarasota's affluent citizens did a lot of traveling.

Text dominated

Top left: The Sunday Comment section provides a vehicle for major year-end presentation. The page design offers a text-dominated mass that stands out from the other Sunday sections. Design: Joan Cullers.

New "books" page

Bottom left: Book reviews are given a strong presentation on an open page in the Arts/Travel section. The bold rules (3-point) surrounding the book titles and the five-line initials make moderate accents. The easy-to-read and simple-to-produce Best Seller List, adapted from *The New York Times*, adds a designed element to the page and some welcome white space.

Dual-subject layout

Facing page: An early tissue layout shows the conception of a dual-subject section that repeats the heading design for the bottom two-fifths of the page. The proportion is important because if the lower heading was moved up too high the feeling of a front page might dissipate and the top part might weaken excessively, so that the page would lack focus.

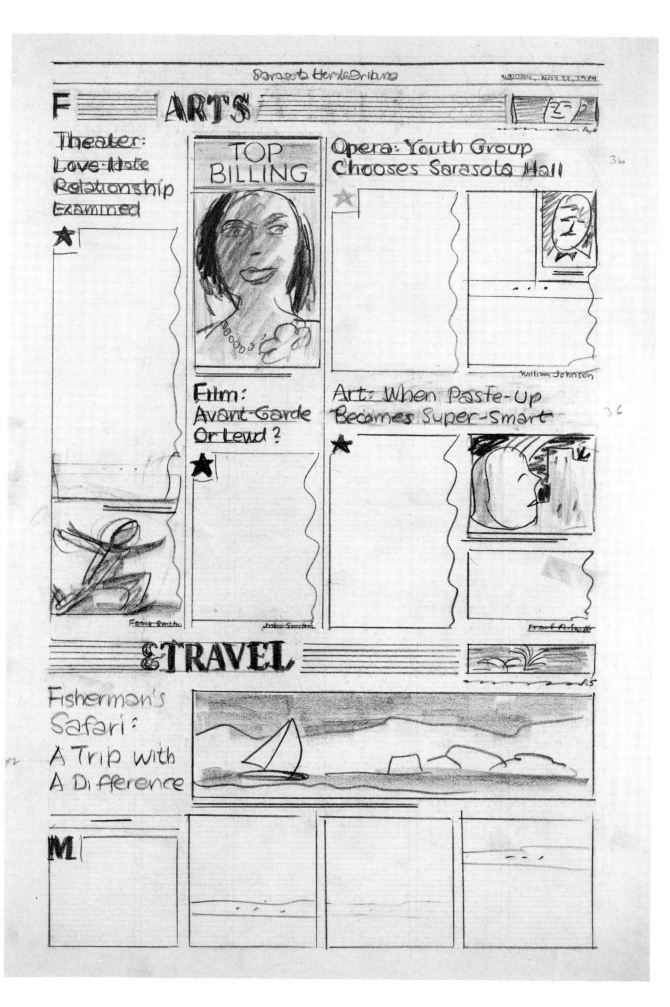

F   ARTS

Theater:
Love-Hate
Relationship
Examined

TOP BILLING

Opera: Youth Group
Chooses Sarasota Hall

William Johnson

Film:
Avant-Garde
Or Lewd?

Art: When Paste-Up
Becomes Super-Smart

Frank Smith   John Smith   Frank Arbott

&TRAVEL

Fisherman's
Safari:
A Trip with
A Difference

M

Bulletin idea

Arts/Travel section fronts on Sunday show the ways in which the bulletin idea offers possibilities for interesting variety. The bulletin approach is a logical way to suggest the richness of cultural offerings that Sarasota residents are proud of, but it also provides a different *texture* from the rest of the sections, which regularly build around a more traditionally conceived centerpiece story. The heading "Top Billing," dropped after a while (top right), gave the top part of the page more meaning and focus. Top right: Joan Cullers.

Sunday splash

Right: On Sunday, the Florida West section featured People, with a big feature treatment that departed somewhat from the more service-oriented daily sections.

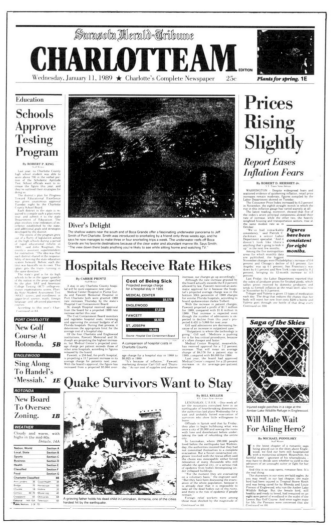

Local identity

Zoned editions are given expanded emphasis with
newly designed front page nameplates. While
preserving the *Sarasota Herald-Tribune*'s identity with
the logo and the trademark multiple parallel rules,
the zoned nameplates seek to identify with the zoned
regions as much as possible. The design signaled
increased coverage and bureau representation in
each area.

Increased emphasis

Right: Shown is a later effort, in 1989, to make the
Charlotte/AM paper even more competitive.
Redesigning paralleled an enlarged staff, more
newshole, and increased marketing efforts. The
design built in local reefers at the top and bottom of
the page, with easy replating for local stories.

Hitting home

Above: the *Charlotte/AM* local section emphasizes home coverage. The *Charlotte/AM* logo is designed in outline to pick up the outline design of the *Sarasota Herald-Tribune* logo on Page 1A. Briefs features community datelines in reverse panels. At the bottom, a group of special features were designed—features that could be produced easily on a pre-planned basis and run on a rotating basis to provide variety every day and hit home on matters of local interest. In addition to Sidewalk Talk, there are profiles, picture essays, and others.

Charlotte Today

Above: Page 2B, the second page of the Local/State section of the Charlotte paper, brings together on an open page diverse elements of special local interest that nevertheless can be produced with minimum strain of deadline pressure. While a Calendar of things to do in this retirement community is an important centerpiece, other interchangeable elements are designed to fit into the basic design in building-block fashion. A masthead list runs on the page to emphasize the special local identity of the papers.

Sunday

Facing page: This is a typical Sunday issue of the Metro Edition news sections of the *Sarasota Herald-Tribune* several years after the initial redesign.

Sarasota: new format, new truck
Design for a new fleet of trucks accompanied the new
format for the paper and the new printing plant. In
orange, blue, and black, the design emphasized that
the *Sarasota Herald-Tribune* was a morning paper.

Big-time competition: state-of-the-art response

Front page: integration

Implementation: with the help of a graphics editor

Opening spread: starting with a columnist

Inside news pages: Briefs are not a dumping ground

Local section: headings—more than a label

Style sections: format, people, procedure

Big-time competition

State-of-the-art response

When *The Press Democrat* was redesigned in 1986, some of the background aspects of the situation included:

1. A new, state-of-the-art $31 million printing plant was going to be built.

2. Color was going to be very important.

3. The community was eager for a new, modernized paper.

4. Medium-sized, circulation 75,000 daily and about 100,000 Sunday at time of redesign, *The Press Democrat* faced big-league competition in its peripheral market regions from *The San Francisco Chronicle*. Santa Rosa is about 55 miles north of San Francisco at the opening to the north of the vineyards of Sonoma County, known in the region as the Redwood Empire. To the north, the competition consisted of scattered smaller papers in small communi-

A nice place to live
In rapidly growing and forward-looking Sonoma Valley, just north of San Francisco, the climate was considered inviting for a thoroughly redesigned newspaper.

ties. To the south, however, in Marin County, where a growing population spilled over from San Francisco, *The Chronicle* presented a marketing challenge with some 18 percent penetration. A number of West Coast papers pay great attention to design, color, and graphics. Overall improvement was obviously needed, but a strong graphic approach that would carry *The Press Democrat* into the competitive future would be particularly important.

5. Where competition was most severe, single copy sales, in "honor" boxes, were critical. The front page would need a bold, colorful top to trigger purchase.

Memo to the file

The following are some notes from the first meeting with the editors and the publisher in Santa Rosa:

A new design should have the feeling of giving the reader a great deal, more than we do now. Since we can't use as much newsprint and don't have as many people as *The Chronicle*, we should get as much as possible onto each page. This suggests the following:

1. *Text size:* In a redesign some years ago, *The Press Democrat* went from an earlier size that was considered too small to a larger text size than the average paper employs. The new design should probably go back to a somewhat smaller text size, allowing us to get more items and variety on a page, providing more of a big-city feeling.

2. *Sections: The Chronicle* that I looked at had six sections, the smallest numbering eight pages. *The Press Democrat* should try for a standard four-section paper, with additional strong inside section fronts. (A six-section paper had been suggested, but at the cost of some only four-page sections.)

3. *Editing:* Stories in *The Press Democrat* seem longer than necessary in a great many cases, raising editing questions in relation to the design—a tighter approach to actual word editing and a review of content priorities.

4. *Graphics:* For visual effectiveness on most pages, the paper currently depends on a single, very large photograph. This photo, the rather large text size, and the light headline face, which forces the use of large-size headlines, all contribute to an overly simple appearance and emphasize what needs to be done to create the impression of more material and variety on each page. The newshole-to-advertising ratio seems reasonable and even generous in places. We should be able to get a lot more in the paper than we do now.

5. *Local coverage:* A San Francisco paper cannot compete with us effectively in local coverage. We should give local coverage special display emphasis with plenty of service material, well representing outlying communities.

First rough

The page is built around a three-part division: The top third is promotional display, the center is news, and the bottom is a news feature. This layout was roughed out with a slab-serif typeface such as Stymie for headlines, which was dropped later in favor of the easier-to-read Times family.

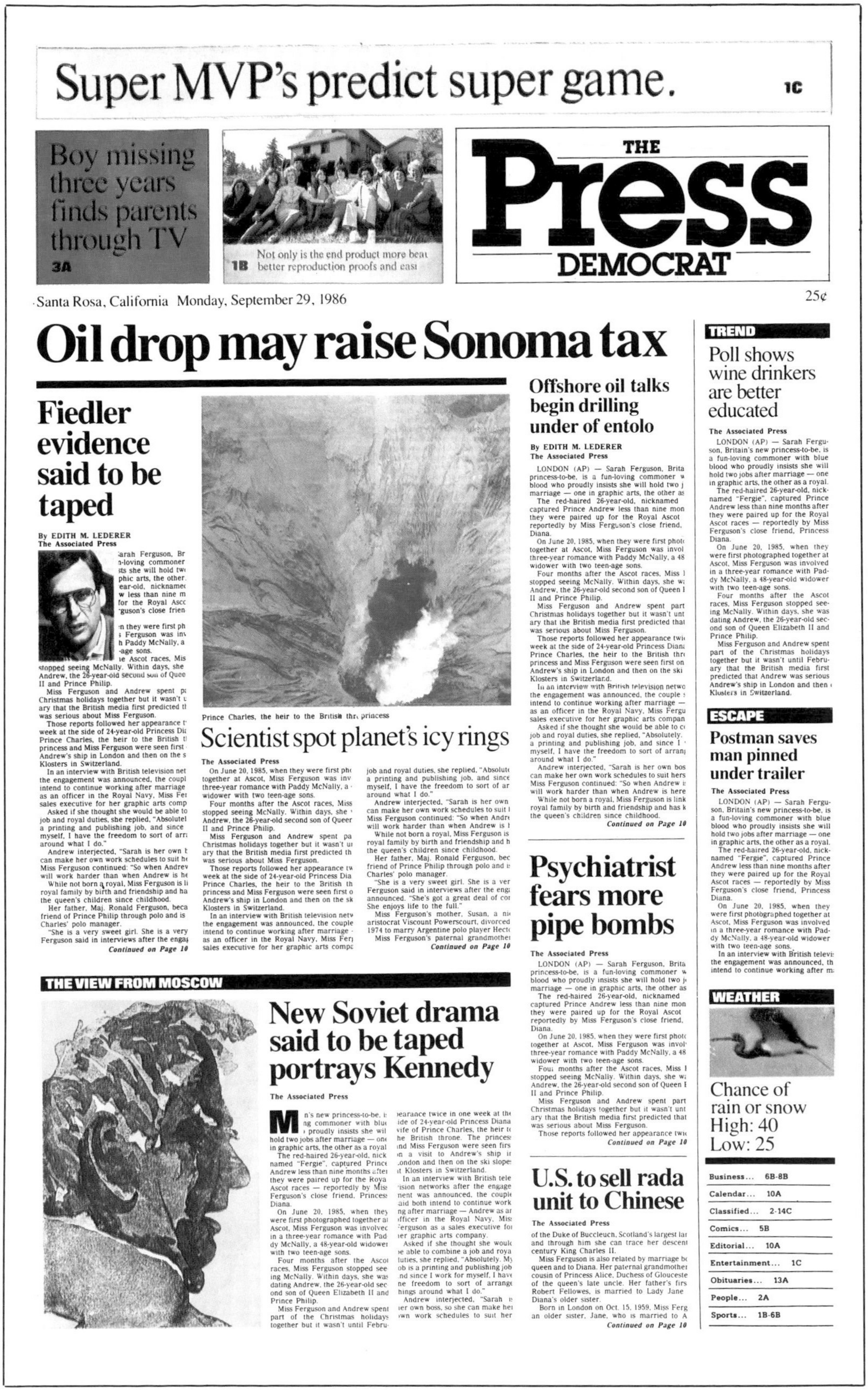

Super MVP's predict super game.

1C

Boy missing three years finds parents through TV

3A

Not only is the end product more beau better reproduction proofs and easy

1B

THE Press
DEMOCRAT

Santa Rosa, California Monday, September 29, 1986   25¢

Oil drop may raise Sonoma tax

Fiedler evidence said to be taped

By EDITH M. LEDERER
The Associated Press

arah Ferguson, Br n-loving commoner sts she will hold tw phic arts, the other ear-old, nicknamed w less than nine m for the Royal Asco 'guson's close frien

n they were first ph Ferguson was inv h Paddy McNally, a age sons. e Ascot races, Mis stopped seeing McNally. Within days, she Andrew, the 26-year-old second son of Quee II and Prince Philip.

Miss Ferguson and Andrew spent Christmas holidays together but it wasn't ary that the British media first predicted th was serious about Miss Ferguson.

Those reports followed her appearance t week at the side of 24-year-old Princess Di Prince Charles, the heir to the British t princess and Miss Ferguson were seen first Andrew's ship in London and then on the s Klosters in Switzerland.

In an interview with British television net the engagement was announced, the coupl intend to continue working after marriage as an officer in the Royal Navy, Miss Fer sales executive for her graphic arts comp

Asked if she thought she would be able to job and royal duties, she replied, "Absolutel a printing and publishing job, and since myself, I have the freedom to sort of arr around what I do."

Andrew interjected, "Sarah is her own t can make her own work schedules to suit he Miss Ferguson continued: "So when Andrew will work harder than when Andrew is h royal family by birth and friendship and ha the queen's children since childhood.

Her father, Maj. Ronald Ferguson, beca friend of Prince Philip through polo and is Charles' polo manager.

"She is a very sweet girl. She is a very Ferguson said in interviews after the enga

Continued on Page 10

Prince Charles, the heir to the British thr: princess

Scientist spot planet's icy rings

The Associated Press

On June 20, 1985, when they were first pho together at Ascot, Miss Ferguson was inv three-year romance with Paddy McNally, a widower with two teen-age sons.

Four months after the Ascot races, Miss stopped seeing McNally. Within days, she Andrew, the 26-year-old second son of Quer II and Prince Philip.

Miss Ferguson and Andrew spent pa Christmas holidays together but it wasn't u ary that the British media first predicted th was serious about Miss Ferguson.

Those reports followed her appearance tv week at the side of 24-year-old Princess Dia Prince Charles, the heir to the British th princess and Miss Ferguson were seen first o Andrew's ship in London and then on the sk Klosters in Switzerland.

In an interview with British television netv the engagement was announced, the couple intend to continue working after marriage as an officer in the Royal Navy, Miss Fer sales executive for her graphic arts compa

job and royal duties, she replied, "Absolute myself, I have the freedom to sort of ar around what I do."

Andrew interjected, "Sarah is her own can make her own work schedules to suit I Miss Ferguson continued: "So when Andre will work harder than when Andrew is h

While not born a royal, Miss Ferguson is royal family by birth and friendship and h the queen's children since childhood.

Her father, Maj. Ronald Ferguson, is friend of Prince Philip through polo and is Charles' polo manager.

"She is a very sweet girl. She is a ver Ferguson said in interviews after the eng: She enjoys life to the full."

Miss Ferguson's mother, Susan, a no aristocrat Viscount Powerscourt, divorced 1974 to marry Argentine polo player Hecto Miss Ferguson's paternal grandmother

Continued on Page 10

THE VIEW FROM MOSCOW

New Soviet drama said to be taped portrays Kennedy

The Associated Press

Mn's new princess-to-be, i ng commoner with blu proudly insists she wil hold two jobs after marriage — on in graphic arts, the other as a roya The red-haired 26-year-old, nick named "Fergie", captured Princ Andrew less than nine months after they were paired up for the Roya Ascot races — reportedly by Mis Ferguson's close friend, Princess Diana.

On June 20, 1985, when they were first photographed together at Ascot, Miss Ferguson was involved in a three-year romance with Pad dy McNally, a 48-year-old widower with two teen-age sons.

Four months after the Ascot races, Miss Ferguson stopped see ing McNally. Within days, she was dating Andrew, the 26-year-old sec ond son of Queen Elizabeth II and Prince Philip.

Miss Ferguson and Andrew spent part of the Christmas holidays together but it wasn't until Febru-

>earance twice in one week at the ide of 24-year-old Princess Diana vife of Prince Charles, the princess he British throne. The princess and Miss Ferguson were seen firs n a visit to Andrew's ship i London and then on the ski slope it Klosters in Switzerland.

In an interview with British tele ision networks after the engage nent was announced, the couple aid both intend to continue work ng after marriage — Andrew as ar fficer in the Royal Navy, Miss Ferguson as a sales executive fo ier graphic arts company.

Asked if she thought she would ie able to combine a job and roya luties, she replied, "Absolutely. My ob is a printing and publishing job nd since I work for myself, I have ne freedom to sort of arrange hings around what I do."

Andrew interjected, "Sarah i ier own boss, so she can make her ›wn work schedules to suit her

Offshore oil talks begin drilling under of entolo

By EDITH M. LEDERER
The Associated Press

LONDON (AP) — Sarah Ferguson, Brita princess-to-be, is a fun-loving commoner w blood who proudly insists she will hold two j marriage — one in graphic arts, the other as

The red-haired 26-year-old, nicknamed captured Prince Andrew less than nine mon they were paired up for the Royal Ascot reportedly by Miss Ferguson's close friend, Diana.

On June 20, 1985, when they were first phot together at Ascot, Miss Ferguson was invol three-year romance with Paddy McNally, a 48 widower with two teen-age sons.

Four months after the Ascot races, Miss stopped seeing McNally. Within days, she w Andrew, the 26-year-old second son of Queen II and Prince Philip.

Miss Ferguson and Andrew spent part Christmas holidays together but it wasn't unt ary that the British media first predicted that was serious about Miss Ferguson.

Those reports followed her appearance twi week at the side of 24-year-old Princess Diana Prince Charles, the heir to the British thr princess and Miss Ferguson were seen first on Andrew's ship in London and then on the ski Klosters in Switzerland.

In an interview with British television netwo the engagement was announced, the couple intend to continue working after marriage — as an officer in the Royal Navy, Miss Fergu sales executive for her graphic arts compan

Asked if she thought she would be able to c job and royal duties, she replied, "Absolutely. a printing and publishing job, and since I myself, I have the freedom to sort of arrang around what I do."

Andrew interjected, "Sarah is her own bos can make her own work schedules to suit hers Miss Ferguson continued: "So when Andrew i will work harder than when Andrew is here

While not born a royal, Miss Ferguson is link royal family by birth and friendship and has k the queen's children since childhood.

Continued on Page 10

Psychiatrist fears more pipe bombs

The Associated Press

LONDON (AP) — Sarah Ferguson, Brita princess-to-be, is a fun-loving commoner w blood who proudly insists she will hold two j marriage — one in graphic arts, the other as

The red-haired 26-year-old, nicknamed captured Prince Andrew less than nine mon they were paired up for the Royal Ascot reportedly by Miss Ferguson's close friend, Diana.

On June 20, 1985, when they were first phot together at Ascot, Miss Ferguson was invol three-year romance with Paddy McNally, a 48 widower with two teen-age sons.

Four months after the Ascot races, Miss stopped seeing McNally. Within days, she w Andrew, the 26-year-old second son of Queen II and Prince Philip.

Miss Ferguson and Andrew spent part Christmas holidays together but it wasn't unt ary that the British media first predicted that was serious about Miss Ferguson.

Those reports followed her appearance her

Continued on Page 10

U.S. to sell rada unit to Chinese

The Associated Press

of the Duke of Buccleuch, Scotland's largest lai and through him she can trace her descen century King Charles II.

Miss Ferguson is also related by marriage b queen and to Diana. Her paternal grandmother cousin of Princess Alice, Duchess of Glouceste of the queen's late uncle. Her father's firs Robert Fellowes, is married to Lady Jane Diana's older sister.

Born in London on Oct. 15, 1959, Miss Ferg an older sister, Jane, who is married to A

Continued on Page 10

TREND

Poll shows wine drinkers are better educated

The Associated Press

LONDON (AP) — Sarah Fergu- son, Britain's new princess-to-be, is a fun-loving commoner with blue blood who proudly insists she will hold two jobs after marriage — one in graphic arts, the other as a royal.

The red-haired 26-year-old, nick- named "Fergie", captured Prince Andrew less than nine months after they were paired up for the Royal Ascot races — reportedly by Miss Ferguson's close friend, Princess Diana.

On June 20, 1985, when they were first photographed together at Ascot, Miss Ferguson was involved in a three-year romance with Pad- dy McNally, a 48-year-old widower with two teen-age sons.

Four months after the Ascot races, Miss Ferguson stopped see- ing McNally. Within days, she was dating Andrew, the 26-year-old sec- ond son of Queen Elizabeth II and Prince Philip.

Miss Ferguson and Andrew spent part of the Christmas holidays together but it wasn't until Febru- ary that the British media first predicted that Andrew was serious Andrew's ship in London and then Klosters in Switzerland.

ESCAPE

Postman saves man pinned under trailer

The Associated Press

LONDON (AP) — Sarah Fergu- son, Britain's new princess-to-be, is a fun-loving commoner with blue blood who proudly insists she will hold two jobs after marriage — one in graphic arts, the other as a royal.

The red-haired 26-year-old, nick- named "Fergie", captured Prince Andrew less than nine months after they were paired up for the Royal Ascot races — reportedly by Miss Ferguson's close friend, Princess Diana.

On June 20, 1985, when they were first photographed together at Ascot, Miss Ferguson was involved in a three-year romance with Pad- dy McNally, a 48-year-old widower with two teen-age sons.

In an interview with British televi the engagement was announced, th intend to continue working after m

WEATHER

Chance of rain or snow
High: 40
Low: 25

Business...	6B-8B
Calendar...	10A
Classified...	2-14C
Comics...	5B
Editorial...	10A
Entertainment...	1C
Obituaries...	13A
People...	2A
Sports...	1B-6B

Dummy paste-up

In anticipation of resistance to giving the heading a full third of the page, this paste-up showed the minimum depth it could be. We ultimately wound up with two alternate depths for flexibility. Here the extreme right column incorporates a place for brief offbeat stories.

251

Front page

Integration

As it was

The old design had featured a rather weak Century, but had just recently been changed to Helvetica as a stop-gap measure. The change to Times Roman was decided on because Times provided a richer variety in letter forms and texture than the evenly-weighted Helvetica. The new logo would obviously have to better integrate the word "Democrat" into the design.

In the proposed new design of *The Press Democrat,* reefer boxes were given an unusually dominant role on the page, becoming integrated and compelling parts of the whole page with far more journalistic presence and visual impact than reefers usually have. When the paper was folded, the reefer boxes together with the main headline, always visible above the fold, could be seen almost as a magazine cover in a Mondrianlike design. Such an approach obviously required a lot of special attention to produce, but the increased display value of the elements and the variation of color and type seemed more than worth the effort, particularly since single-copy sales were important in the marketing scheme.

Written notes accompanied the layout proposal, to spell out the content ideas. Here is the memorandum that accompanied the original layout:

SANTA ROSA FRONT PAGE LAYOUT

- The page should be considered in three parts. The top part, probably but not necessarily a fixed depth, is a bold colorful poster, including the logo, reefers, color picture, or other kind of excellent "cover" visual material that need not be confined to deadline material, but by no means need exclude deadline material. This is the "top" of the page in the traditional sense, but when the page is folded, together with the headlines below, it constitutes a "cover," a newsy magazine cover.

  This cover should vary, sometimes widely, from day to day according to the play of events, adapted to preplanned possibilities, such as the variations on a modular break-up illustrated here.

  With preplanned variations in type, color blocks, grays (or just outlined boxes), black and white pictures, color pictures and art work, the possibilities for visual variations are infinite. For example, variations are possible, too, in forceful and witty use of words in the panels, relating them to each other.

The picture and word reefers can relate to, or be part of, the front page lead stories below.

- The lead stories go on the second part of the page, with one significant variation possible from other newspapers. It is not necessary to "force" big pictures into this part. Text would be just as welcome visually in this format design. It's acceptable to use a big picture, but the front page stories can be considered independently from it. As previously noted, this part of the page can tie up directly, or indirectly, with pictures or text in the top part of the page.

- The bottom part of the page is less graphically fixed than the first two parts. Nevertheless, it should be considered a third "area," with special possibilities, from large pictures to news feature stories.

At *Times* headquarters, this proposed design was greeted with enthusiasm by some and with apprehension by others.

Fortunately, however, the publisher of the paper, Jim Weeks, his executive editor, Mike Parman, and Randy Wright, the graphics editor, were enthusiastic, and the project went ahead from the very first layout without a single change in the logo or the concept.

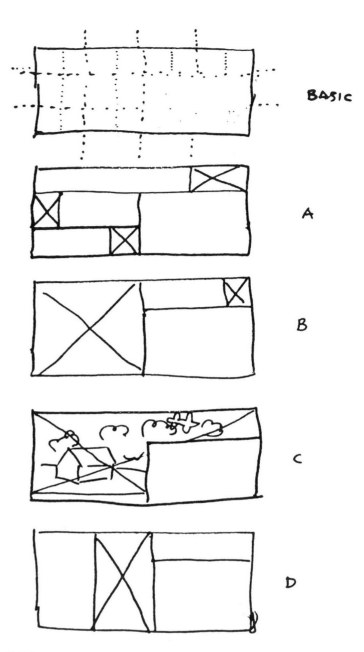

Grid
Sketches illustrated possibilities for variation in top-of-the-page reefers.

Super MVP's predict suedict 1C

State officials gran subpoenaed in 3A

State insurance officials ju subpoenaed by grand 1C

State insurance officials subpoenaed by grand jury 1C

We hold these truths to be d equal, that they alienable rights. **3A**

Top of the page
Above: Veloxes like these were made in about six different combinations, and type treatments were spelled out for foreseeable needs.

An actual issue
Facing page: One of the early papers shows strict adherence to the format. Bold initials help identify a feature treatment at the bottom, and a reefer "bug" is used in the central "Peggy Sue" story. A modified "brace" make-up gets a lot of action above the mid-page fold.

Santa Rosa, California, Friday, October 10, 1986   129th Year, No. 395   25¢

Captive: CIA directed flights

Senate convicts federal judge

Claiborne

Los Angeles Times
WASHINGTON — The Senate, exercising its impeachment powers for only the fifth time, found U.S. District Judge Harry E. Claiborne guilty of "high crimes and misdemeanors" Thursday and removed him from his $78,700-a-year lifetime post.

By a margin that far exceeded the two-thirds majority necessary for conviction, senators adopted three of the four articles of impeachment to oust the Las Vegas, Nev., judge, who is serving a prison term for federal income tax evasion.

The only article rejected, by a 46-17 vote, was Article III, which *Continued on Page A16*

Job losses feared with Measure B

By PAUL INGALLS
Staff Writer

Several businessmen charged Thursday that the Nuclear Free Zone initiative could cost 24,000 jobs in Sonoma County while a prominent Santa Rosa lawyer said the measure is so vague and poorly written it would result in a barrage of lawsuits.

They spoke in Santa Rosa's Courthouse Square with other opponents of Measure B on Sonoma County's November ballot. The initiative, proposed by a coalition of peace and anti-nuclear activists, would ban virtually all activities in Sonoma County related to nuclear weapons and their components, enriched radioactive material and radioactive wastes.

Continued on Page A16

Toxic price tag in the millions

By WALTER NEARY
Correspondent

CLOVERDALE — Cleanup of the toxic industrial contamination from MGM Brake Company could cost anywhere from $6 million to $14 million, according to federal estimates.

A study released this week by the Environmental Protection Agency warns children to stay away from the 2.5-acre MGM site, but says the health risk from PCBs there is "minimal."

About 700 people live within one mile of the MGM casting plant, which was contaminated between 1966 to 1972 by polychloric biphe-

A carload of Santa Rosa High School cheerleaders arrive at Coddingtown Cinemas for the 'Peggy Sue' premiere in Jim Showalter's 1957 Ford Fairlane

'Peggy Sue' gets premiered

MOVIE REVIEW, PAGE D3

By DAN TAYLOR
Staff Writer

In a scene right out of the golden age of Hollywood, search lights swept the sky and crowds applauded as limousines drew up outside the theater for the Sonoma County premiere of "Peggy Sue Got Married."

Star Kathleen Turner couldn't make it Thursday night, but hundreds of happy movie-goers, including some who worked as extras on the film, carried on without her in high style. People formed long lines to see the screening, a benefit for the Santa Rosa High School Foundation and Petaluma's Main Street Project.

Director Francis Coppola shot the film entirely on *Continued on Page A16*

Edith Lovato removes snail meat from the shells at Enfant Riate, a Petaluma firm specializing in escargot

American reveals contra supply system

New York Times

MANAGUA, Nicaragua — An American captured when a plane delivering supplies to rebels was shot down here said Thursday that the supply flights were directly supervised by members of the CIA in El Salvador.

Two Cuban naturalized Americans that work for the CIA did most of the coordination for the flights and oversaw all of our housing, transportation, also refueling and some flight plans," the prisoner, Eugene Hasenfus, said at a news conference here with Nicaraguan officials seated beside him.

Hasenfus then named the two reported CIA officials and gave the most detailed account so far of rebel supply operations out of El Salvador and Honduras. His statements are being treated as a major political victory by the Nicaraguan government.

"I was told we were working out of the El Salvador air force base at Ilopango," Hasenfus said. "We would be flying into Honduras to an air base called Aguacate and there we would load up small arms and ammunition and fly into Nicaragua. There it would be dropped to the contra."

The American prisoner looked healthy and Nicaraguan officials said he had been well treated. But reporters could not verify the conditions under which he has been held and questioned, and Hasenfus' future treatment could depend on the statements he is willing to make here.

The Drug Enforcement Administration said the plane that was shot down was earlier involved in a *Continued on Page A16*

Vegetables star

Ethnic specialties booming as tastes for produce change

By BRUCE KEPPEL
Los Angeles Times

In a Los Angeles supermarket, a middle-aged shopper squinted intently at a recipe for "Polynesian french fries" pasted to a homely brown tuber. It was a taro root, which Polynesians don't make into french fries but traditionally boil and mash into poi, hardly a fast-food specialty.

Other shoppers examined more than a dozen varieties of squash. One who tried her hand at spaghetti squash, based on a recipe attached to the melon-size vegetable whose cooked flesh resembles pasta, said she also consulted "my corner ethnics" and came up with "a Japanese-Jewish-Italian spaghetti squash — it was wonderful!"

No doubt about it, people's tastes are changing. And the changes, on display in the nation's supermarkets, are making their mark all along the nation's food chain.

• Growers are turning to exotic, and profitable, crops.

• Enterprising wholesalers are seeking high-value agricultural novelties.

• Astonished retailers have seen long-neglected produce departments develop star quality as a draw for customers.

All this spells new and profitable sales opportunities for those who can develop and satisfy consumer tastes for full-grown but miniature vegetables, golden-spiny "jelly melons," fresh herbs, red pears, white tomatoes, elephant-heart plums, pepino (a lemon-sized melon) and habaro (a melon masquerading as a cucumber).

A major factor behind the proliferation of such specialty items in supermarket produce departments is pioneering Los Angeles-based wholesaler Frieda Caplan, who said she got into the wholesale business because the odd hours allowed her to nurse her daughter, Karen, now president and chief operating officer.

Her company, Frieda's Finest/Specialty Produce Inc., in its quarter of a century of existence has opened up market after market for new items in an era when overall demand for food is leveling off as this country as family size shrinks.

Over the years, Caplan has been credited with elevating the fuzzy and dusky Chinese gooseberry into the now-familiar kiwifruit and with finding farmers willing to invest in growing such formerly imported items as cherimoya, a custard-like fruit from South America.

In a similar way, Mike Beynes and a partner formed Enfant Riant Escargot, which he describes as the *Continued on Page A16*

Implementation

With the help of a graphics editor

The logo, the type, the boxes, and the color on the front page of *The Press Democrat* are in dynamic relationship to one another and to the rest of the front page below. The dateline is a good deal larger than usual, unconfined by the usual horizontal rules going across the width of the page. The type elements seek to push to the limit a typographical tension where each element is strong: The dateline, for example, is about as big as it can be, providing a typographical bridge between the top and the middle parts of the page.

In the first weeks after the new format went "live," layouts seemed to fall too predictably into the basic pattern of the original design, a usual occurrence when a new format is first implemented. Soon, however, a healthy variety of layouts began to be developed.

An important factor in the implementation of the front page design was editor Mike Parman's decision to put it primarily in the hands of Randy Wright, the graphics editor. In particular, the graphic top of the page became Wright's responsibility. Wright was formerly features editor at *The Modesto Bee.* In school he had studied typography and design. In short, he was an art-oriented person who became an editor. It's not every graphics editor who can be put in charge of the top of the front page.

Sidelights

Along the right side of the page ran a journalistic and typographical sidelight, one or more stories of definite front-page interest, which in a traditional format might never make it to the front page. Offbeat sidelights, light or serious, or something of ongoing local interest, these would run under little black reverse labels, signalling a difference from the other front page news stories.

Make-up variation

The design opens the possibility for a modest use of "brace" make-up, where one headline tucks in under another. Most newspaper people seek to avoid this, probably because it can be confusing. However, this make-up sometimes holds great possibilities, if properly planned as part of the format and not arrived at through ad hoc innovation on deadline. As one of its advantages, this make-up packs more headlines in less space high on the page. Another strictly graphic advantage is the grouping of the display types to provide greater typographic concentration, a powerful focal point.

Stories and treatment at the bottom of the

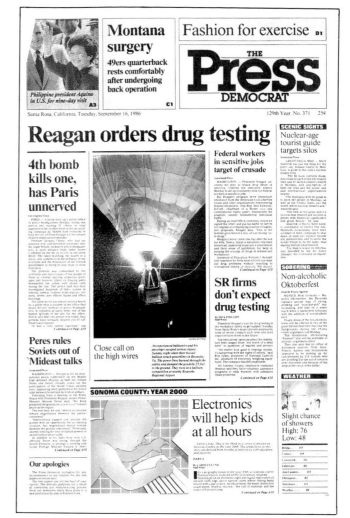

Variety

Three front pages, from 1986 and 1987, show healthy variety below the dateline and in the top reefer part of the page. Top left shows special feature treatment; top right shows a stand-alone photo; and left, shows extra pictorial emphasis at the top of the page.

Golden anniversary for the gorgeous Gate   Pull-out section inside

THE Press DEMOCRAT

Santa Rosa, California, Friday, May 22, 1987   130th Year. No. 213   ○25¢

Iraqis agree to compensate U.S.

By DON OBERDORFER
and EDWARD WALSH
The Washington Post

**U.S. SHIPS
IN GULF
AT RISK, A3**

WASHINGTON — Iraq has agreed to pay compensation for the deaths, injuries and damages arising from last Sunday's attack on the USS Stark in which 37 U.S. seamen were killed, U.S. and Iraqi officials said Thursday night.

The Iraqi move came as the Senate voted overwhelmingly to require the Reagan administration to inform Congress of the security situation in the Persian Gulf before the United States becomes more deeply involved in protecting Kuwaiti oil tankers in the volatile region.

Iraqi Ambassador to the United States Nizar Hamdoon said a diplomatic note delivered to the State Department late Thursday accepts in principle the payment of damages in accordance with international law and practices. No specific figure was mentioned by the United States in its demand for compensation, which was presented to Iraq Wednesday, nor was any figure given in the Iraqi reply.

U.S. members of a joint U.S.-Iraqi investigating team will leave today for Baghdad to begin looking into why the attack took place and how such incidents can be prevented in the future. U.S. officials said they understand the team will be permitted to interview the pilot of the Iraqi warplane that attacked the U.S. ship.

A U.S. Navy team is already in the Persian Gulf to conduct a separate investigation.

President Reagan, Secretary of Defense Caspar W. Weinberger and other senior officials will attend a memorial service for the 37 dead seamen at 11:30 a.m. today at
See Iraqis, Page A18

Senate wants briefing on U.S. in gulf

Hong Kong man slain in Petaluma

By RANDI ROSSMAN
Press Democrat Bureau

PETALUMA — A Hong Kong businessman was gunned down Thursday morning as he arrived at an eastside business park to visit a friend.

The dead man is Johnny Fong, 31. Police said he was a director of John Henry Holdings LTD, apparently a real estate investment company.

Police said he may have been shot twice with an automatic pistol as he stepped from his brown BMW. His body was found next to the car, the driver's door open.

Police have not found a weapon or witnesses to the slaying.

There was no identification on the corpse, nor a watch or other valuables.

"At this point, robbery appears to be the motive," said Detective Sgt. Mike Kerns. He added, however, that other possibilities will be investigated.

An autopsy is to be done today, Kerns said.

"Anytime there is a homicide in Petaluma it's unusual. But there are a lot of unusual aspects to the case," said Police Chief Dennis DeWitt.

"We don't want to jump to certain conclusions but it's really unusual where it happened and how it happened and who this person (the victim) is.

"I hate these kind, they're really tough to solve," DeWitt said.

Police Capt. Patrick Parks said there is no reason to believe drugs were involved.

The car was registered to Fong at an address in the exclusive community of Hillsborough south of San Francisco. The address is apparently that of Fong's mother.

Fong was found at 10:30 a.m. by a passer-by who asked employees of nearby Mobile Fidelity Sound Lab to call for help.

Fong was arriving to visit a friend an
See Killing, Page A20

Petaluma officers, from left, ID technician Margaret Paulson, Sgt. Jim Wesson, ID technician Tony Travers and Detective John Dunn check the area where Johnny Fong was killed as he left his BMW

Donors describe North's influence

By DAVID E. ROSENBAUM
New York Times

**ISRAELI
SUBPOENA
PROTEST,
PAGE A3.**

WASHINGTON — Three wealthy supporters of conservative causes testified on Thursday that Lt. Col. Oliver L. North, as a member of the White House staff, had influenced them to make large contributions to the Nicaraguan rebels after Congress cut off official United States aid.

In one case, William J. Casey, then the director of central intelligence, put a donor, the beer magnate Joseph Coors, in touch with North.

In two other cases, according to the testimony before the congressional committees investigating the Iran-contra affair, North worked as a team with Carl R. Channell. Channell pleaded guilty last month to a conspiracy in connection with his fund-raising and named North as a co-conspirator.

This was the first direct testimony showing how Reagan administration officials helped raise private donations for the contras.

North, who was on President Reagan's White House staff until his dismissal last November, was the central figure in the arms sales to Iran and the administration's efforts on behalf of the contras. He is not scheduled to testify before next month.

In testimony on Thursday afternoon, Maj. Gen. John K. Singlaub said that Elliott Abrams, an assistant secretary of state, had agreed to provide assurances to two Asian
See Hearings, Page A18

Robbin' hoods, wearin' auto parts

By CLARK MASON
Staff Writer

Blame it on the Beastie Boys.

Maybe they didn't start it, but the popular "rap" music group's penchant for wearing automobile hood ornaments is spurring a similar trend among youth.

Auto parts dealers are reporting a big jump in the sale of emblems and hood ornaments. But the sales are not to teenyboppers. They're to people whose emblems have been stolen from their cars, typically expensive foreign sedans like Mercedes and BMW, though Volkswagen and Cadillacs are prime targets, too.

"It's kids pretty much, who just break them off," said Bryan Scotchler, assistant parts manager at Torvick Mercedes, referring to the hood stars that are stolen from the luxury sedans. "A lot of kids you see walking around with them hanging off their neck."

Though the Beastie Boys are partial to Volkswagen emblems in their MTV videos and publicity photographs, the trend extends to other car models.

Scotchler said that last year Torvick sold 130 Mercedes hood stars. In the first five months of this year the dealership has already sold 180.

The prestigious Mercedes symbols go for $15 to $25 a pop, he said, and some motorists have had to replace more than one.
See Ornaments, Page A20

LICENTIOUS PLATES

FUNATCALDMV

Staff weeds out multilingual smut

By DAVID LARSEN
Los Angeles Times

SACRAMENTO — Late last month an **I** letter was sent from here to a California motorist.

"The records of the Department of Motor Vehicles ... show that Environmental License Plates IV NIK 8 were issued to you.

"The Department has determined that said plates carry connotations offensive to good taste and decency in that IV NIK 8 phonetically states 'fornicate.'

"Therefore, the letter continued, the plates were being canceled. The owner was ordered to return them.

Such recalls amount to only about 1 percent of the 909,597 environmental, personalized or "vanity" plates currently registered in California (out of a total of about 23 million), according to Marlys Whiteside, program manager with the department.

But that is enough to be a pain in the trunk.

Little did anyone anticipate problems 17 years ago when the Legislature enacted and then-Gov. Ronald Reagan signed into law an innocent-enough measure that sought to raise funds for environmental projects by charging a fee to vehicle owners who wished to create their own license plate letters and numbers.

In fact, in that first year, only about 11,000 requests were made. They've women, who became known as "the dirty dozen," sifted out the questionable
See Plates, Page A16

Reagan leaning toward required testing for AIDS

By LEO RENNERT
McClatchy News Service

WASHINGTON — President Reagan, tilting against Surgeon General C. Everett Koop, generally supports proposals for mandatory AIDS testing of applicants for marriage licenses and prospective immigrants, the White House said Thursday.

A few hours later, in an initial congressional test, the Senate rejected the idea, 63-32, defeating an amendment by Sen. Jesse Helms, R-N.C., which would have required states to impose such tests for marriage licenses under threat of losing federal funds.

California's two senators, Democrat Alan Cranston and Republican Pete Wilson, voted against the proposed amendment to an emergency spending bill.

A formal White House position on the controversial issue — which has divided public health authorities and conservatives — is expected to be hammered
See AIDS, Page A16

UPSCALE POLL

Rich aren't so different, just a lot wealthier

Associated Press

NEW YORK — The rich really aren't so different from the rest of us, a survey concludes. Assuming, of course, that the rest of us are middle-aged Republicans with $140,000 incomes and $200,000 homes.

"Upper affluent Americans are not, by and large, what have come to be represented in the media as a group of underage, overpaid and arrogant recent graduates of the nation's top business and law schools," said the poll, conducted by Louis Harris and Associates.

Take that, yuppies. Most of the really rich are about 48, married, have grown children.

There were very few surprises. Humphrey Taylor, president of the Harris organization, said he was "struck by how totally unremarkable you rich Americans are."

TOURIST TRAP

Golden Gate roller coaster

Bay City News Service

California's state archives contain records that show that an engineer once proposed that the Golden Gate Bridge's suspension towers be the base for a roller coaster called the Bolt.

The proposal was made almost 50 years ago by Joseph Bazzeghin, who told the California Public Works Commission that a Golden Gate Bridge Bolt might be just the tourist attraction needed to attract visitors to the 1939 Golden Gate Exposition.

Blueprints for the Bolt circulated earlier this month by the office of Secretary of State March Fong Eu show a 300-foot extension atop the tower. The cars of the roller coaster were to climb north then drop about 700 feet.

Then, climbing to the top of the second tower, the Bolt would have plunged 1,000 feet, reaching speeds of 220 mph before stopping somewhere in Marin County.

WEATHER

Morning clouds, clearing High: 67 Low: 43

front page adhered to the idea outlined in the original proposal. It was simple to find stories that could be set off in this semifeature style. Placement under the color bar provided a natural way to set off preplanned features.

Weather

Instead of the usual sun and rain glyphs or cartoon figure, we ran a different small photo each day, showing some aspect of Santa Rosa's environs, which would complement the words of the forecast in a general way. Santa Rosa is a pleasant small city in a beautiful and photogenic natural environment of hills, low mountains in the distance, vineyards, redwood trees, forests, and rocky coast. At first the photo would be in black and white, and then in color as soon as production pressures eased. A built-in graphic building block on the page, the photo acts as a booster to suggest a reader constituency in a widening arc from Santa Rosa, one of the marketing goals. The paper would invite readers to send in pictures and acknowledge them with names and hometown credits. Separated for platemaking in advance and kept on file for quick and easy use, the pictures provided the use of color, reader participation, a bit of boosterism, and a warm, homey touch!

WEATHER

KARY WIND/GEYSERVILLE

Sunny and warm
High: 75
Low: 41

Reader participation

The weather box on the front page features a different photo every day, with most of the pictures supplied by readers, who are appropriately credited together with their communities.

A blockbuster top

Facing page: The original concept of top-of-the-page extraordinary graphic emphasis outlined dramatic use of the whole top quarter of the page for a single picture on a selected special occasion. This option is used here on an important anniversary. At Christmas a colorful Currier and Ives scene was similarly employed.

Opening spread

Starting with a columnist

Verified by a readership survey and to no one's surprise, the most popular feature in the paper was a long-running daily column by Gaye LeBaron. LeBaron had been writing the column for many years. A historian of the region and a prominent citizen in the community, she combines authoritative knowledge of everything going on with a lively personal style. Previously not anchored anywhere in the paper, it seemed a good idea in the new design to build an effective opening around her column. This would force the weather package off Page 2, to the back page of the section, where it could benefit from half a page of space and color.

LeBaron's column was set to a bastard-size wide measure. The rest of the space, except for a horizontal publisher's box, was sold to a large advertiser, a group of shopping malls. *The Press's* advertising director was, of course, enthusiastic about this advertising space. Running with Gaye LeBaron's column, it was an easy sale at a premium price.

Highlights

A contents feature was created, not to be a complex index summary but to give the reader the highlights of the day. Subdivided to spotlight new features and sections, it was to be illustrated daily. Good selection and cropping of pictures would be necessary to make the most of the small scale. The Highlights column was set to the same wide measure as LeBaron's column. Together, they defined a large and effective space bridging the gutter of the opening spread.

The Highlights column seemed a good idea because:

- We were adding a lot of new things to the paper, and this was a way of promoting them.

- A Highlights feature would communicate a sense of "muchness" in the paper, a big-city feeling that would help it compete with *The Chronicle.*

- It made an anchor for a second front page. Between Gaye's column and Highlights and

dominating the spread, the strongest stories appeared that had not made it to Page One. The large, importantly placed ad on Page 2 was the trade-off for an open Page 3, making virtually a second front. Obviously, this would demand strong stories and treatment. One variation shows a logo in reduced size, placed in the upper part of the page, to give the page the literal connotation of a second Page One. However, this idea caused some concern about overkill and "busyness" and was dropped.

260

Opening spread

Above: Pages A2 and A3 are designed for strong news presence, with the mix of news constituting a continuation of the front page mix. The newly created Highlights on the right leads the reader into the paper. LeBaron's column is given an important spot, in balance with the wide column Highlights. The large ad, especially sized and premium priced, is the result of a trade-off in return for the open Page 3. It was arranged for a spot drawing to be done for LeBaron's column every day, with a specific time allotment made for it.

A second front proposal

Facing page: Page A3, supposed to be a second front page in news content, is in this dummy page treated as a junior front with a miniature flag at the top of the page. The idea was dropped for make-up flexibility.

Inside news pages

Briefs are not a dumping ground

It was emphasized that "Briefs" should not be just a dumping ground for a few short stories that otherwise would go into a layout. Also, they should be edited to be truly brief, to run no longer than a few inches, though the first item could be longer than the others, with a minimum of five stories per grouping. The black heads, in Folio typeface, provide extra punch and contrast with the regular Times Roman Bold headlines, though we had to be careful with the size. The Folio pushes typographical "presence" about as far as it can go without becoming overbearing or distracting from more important elements on the page. It would be simpler and more harmonious, for example, to keep the heads in Times Roman Bold, the same as the headlines. Instead, the Folio typeface is used as big as possible to create a tension with the Times Roman headlines, giving the Briefs items as much importance as possible. Briefs columns generally are often bland and look so much like listings that the eye slides over them. Also, a column of Briefs that is too long loses some of its newsy quality. The column begins to resemble a newsletter rather than part of a newspaper.

Keeping Briefs active

A 1988 design of the Gwinnett Daily News, a Times Company paper in a competitive situation in the Atlanta, Georgia, suburbs, demonstrates four ways to make Briefs more active: a graphically strong heading; variety in display treatment—particularly a stronger headline at the top; use of pictures—even in constricted space; and typographical emphasis on datelines.

GWINNETT

From staff reports

Bond experts rate county's schools

LAWRENCEVILLE Agents from a bond rating service came to Gwinnett County on Tuesday to evaluate the school system's financial status as a preliminary step before the issuance of $70 million in school bonds.

The agents got on-site looks at two schools, toured the county and met with school administrators and county business leaders as part of a school system effort to convince the agents to improve the system's bond rating.

Standard and Poor's has ranked Gwinnett school bonds AA-, and school officials are hoping to raise that rating to AA, which could save hundreds of thousands in interest costs on the new bond issue, School Superintendent Alton Crews said Tuesday.

That bond issue would fund a $90 million, three-year building program that would add more than 500

Crews

classrooms, some at three new schools; renovate facilities; and buy land for new school sites and expansions of existing schools. Voters overwhelming approved the bond issue in a Feb. 9 referendum.

Children's play scheduled

STONE MOUNTAIN Three male adults and three female adults are needed to perform in the children's play, "Wiley and the Hairy Man" to be presented during "Old South Days" at Stone Mountain Park in April.

The A.R.T. Station Inc., producers of the play, will hold auditions for the parts from 7 until 9 p.m. on both Monday, March 7, and Tuesday, March 8. Adults of any age may try out for the play, staff member Betty Hirt said. The center is located at 985 Third Street in Stone Mountain Village.

Grayson faces sewer woes

GRAYSON Just after the Grayson City Council had granted its approval of a business license for Crafty Corenrs, a shop which will open on

Main Street and specialize in ceramics, city officials warned the shop's owner to be aware of the septic system that serves the old buildings along that portion of the street.

"We have a screwy septic system along here," Mayor Jim Hinkle told owner Eva Conn.

"What do we look for?" Ms. Conn

Hinkle

asked.

THE PRESS DEMOCRAT, TUESDAY, SEPTEMBER 9, 1986

WORLD
IN BRIEF

Japanese remarks on Korea cause furor

TOKYO — Education Minister Masayuki Fujio was fired on Monday over his published remarks defending Japan's annexation of Korea in 1910 and other events in this country's military past.

The governments of South Korea, North Korea and China assailed Fujio's comments, which were published in the widely circulated monthly Bungei Shunju.

South Korea said it would postpone the visit of Foreign Minister Choi Kwang-soo to Tokyo, scheduled for Wednesday.

China's official news agency Xinhua said Fujio was trying to "defend Japan's war of aggression launched by the Japanese militarists and denied the crimes they had committed." North Korea's Korean Central News Agency broadcast similar criticism.

Fujio said he made the remarks as a matter of principle. He told a news conference he could not hand his resignation to Prime Minister Yasuhiro Nakasone "because that would mean admitting that I am at fault."

In the magazine, he said Korea was partly responsible for what is regarded as Japan's forcible annexation of the peninsula in 1910, because Korean leaders were "consulted." The 35 years of Japan's harsh, sometimes brutal colonial rule are considered the most humiliating period in Korean history.

Fujio also said the 1937 "Rape of Nanking," in which Japanese troops massacred an estimated 200,000 Chinese civilians, was an "unredressed event" to break down enemy resistance.

Fujio cast doubts on the Tokyo war crimes trials, in which Prime Minister Gen. Hideki Tojo and other Japanese war criminals were hanged.

China remembers Mao with mixed emotions

PEKING — China marks the 10th anniversary of the death of Mao Tse-tung today with little pomp and words of praise tempered by reminders of his mistakes.

Government officials said they were not aware of any plans to commemorate the anniversary beyond publication of several new editions of Mao's works concentrating on his earlier, less controversial years as communist China's founder and leader.

Mao is revered as the man who led communist forces to power in 1949 and laid the socialist foundation that bettered the lives of millions of impoverished Chinese.

But he also is blamed by the current pragmatists led by Deng Xiaoping with causing considerable hardship. Deng and his followers are particularly critical of Mao's 1958 Great Leap Forward, which overnight tried to turn China into an industrial power and the 1966-76 Cultural Revolution, the leftist convulsion that led China to the brink of civil war.

Pyramid drilling halted

GIZA, Egypt — A team hoping to drill into hidden cavities inside the largest of the Great Pyramids announced Monday a temporary halt to their effort only a few feet from their goal.

Jacques Montlucon, an engineer with France's national electric company and spokesman for the French members of the Franco-Egyptian team, said Egyptian authorities will decide the next step.

The project was scheduled to drill only three bores in an attempt to poke a camera-like device into the hidden chamber.

Using a system related to sonar, two French architects discovered the previously undetected chambers last winter in the Pyramid of Cheops.

Wedding bloodbath

CAGAYAN DE ORO, Philippines — A grenade thrown by Moslem rebels exploded in a Roman Catholic church in the midst of a wedding, killing nine people and injuring more than 100, including the bride, officials reported Monday.

Militiamen killed two of the rebels in a gunbattle after the attack Sunday in Salvador, 500 miles southeast of Manila, according to Army Col. Raul Aquino.

Polish bishops urge political freedom

WARSAW, Poland — Poland's Roman Catholic bishops Monday issued a strong call for the expansion of political freedom and the release of all prisoners in an indication of the church's condition for cooperating with a new government political program.

A communique of the Catholic episcopate, made up of the nation's bishops, called for the respect of the right of free assembly and said public activity should be permitted that was independent of the communist party, the Polish United Workers Party.

"The lack of that possibility," the statement said, "causes the impoverishment of public life."
Press Democrat news services

Crews douse the last of the flames following a riot between Hindus and Moslems in New Delhi, India, which resulted in the burning of 17 shops

---

Bhutto released from jail
Protest rallies vowed

Los Angeles Times

KARACHI, Pakistan — The government here Monday released Pakistan People's Party leader Benazir Bhutto from jail, where she had spent 26 days for leading an anti-government rally in defiance of a ban on demonstrations, but warned that it would not tolerate further unrest.

Bhutto, 33, immediately vowed to hold more rallies in her attempt to force elections to remove Pakistan's President Mohammed Zia ul-Haq and Prime Minister Mohammed Khan Junejo. But Bhutto, the daughter of former Pakistan Prime Minister Zulfikar Ali Bhutto, admitted that anti-government efforts had been set back by her arrest and subsequent violent clashes between police and demonstrators that claimed at least 29 lives.

She said that she would consult with other opposition leaders before making any new moves. "Unfortunately, our opponents believe in using violence; they believe in opening fire on peaceful citizens and we have to review the entire situation and adopt our strategy according ly," she told crowds of chanting supporters gathered on the lawn of her sprawling family home in a wealthy area of Karachi.

Bhutto said that she and other opposition leaders in Pakistan had not expected the government to react so severely to their plans for rallies on Aug. 14, the day she was arrested. Hundreds of Peoples' Party and other opposition leaders were arrested on the eve of the rallies. Bhutto was arrested after she led a small procession of supporters here in Karachi.

The Sind provincial government released Bhutto and several hundred of her supporters the day before she was to appear in court and challenge the constitutionality of her arrest and her incarceration at a jail for boys in Landhi, 20 miles from Karachi.

"This magnanimous gesture of the government should not be misunderstood as the government is prepared to deal firmly with any future interference with the law," a government spokesman said.

After her release Monday, she said that she had not been "physically mistreated" at the jail, but she was kept in a cell littered with insects and rats. "I had no worries of these mosquitoes, flies and rats because several thousands of my colleagues have been in similar conditions all over Pakistan," she said.

Obviously elated to be free, Bhutto laughed with friends and ate lotus fruit as she sat under a large painting of her father, who was removed in a 1977 coup d'etat led by Zia.

Two years after the coup, Zulfikar Ali Bhutto was executed by hanging after a Pakistan court found him guilty of murder on charges brought by the Zia martial law government.

Benazir Bhutto, who was educated at Harvard and Oxford University, has been the main challenger to Zia since her father's death.

Zia, meanwhile, has emerged as a skillful politician who claims to be gradually steering Pakistan's 90 million people toward democracy. A year and a half ago, he supervised national parliamentary elections in which political parties such as the Pakistan People's Party were not permitted to participate. He has repeatedly rejected demands for new elections, saying that democracy was restored when he lifted martial power in December and appointed Junejo to head a civilian government. Zia holds the title of army chief of staff in addition to the presidency.

Bhutto would not discuss specific plans for future demonstrations or actions against the Zia government. She admitted that opposition leaders had been "preempted" by the August arrests and claimed 40 supporters were killed by government forces while she was in jail.

Benazir Bhutto talks to reporters at her Karachi home after being released from Borstal jail

---

Bombings in Germany, Netherlands

Associated Press

A bomb damaged West Germany's counterespionage agency in Cologne on Monday, slightly injuring a passerby and blowing out windows in nearby buildings.

In Gouda, the Netherlands, a bomb exploded Monday at an office of the Netherlands' largest construction company, which anti-nuclear activists have said is working at a cruise missile deployment site. Police said no one was injured in the blast.

The explosion started a fire and shattered windows on the ground floor of a building housing a branch office of the Hollandse Beton Groep.

In Germany, officials said the leftist Red Army Faction terror gang was suspected in the agency attack. West Germany will step up security around government buildings following the pre-dawn blast, the third bomb attack on government offices in a month, officials said in Bonn.

The 3:45 a.m. explosion went off outside the Constitutional Protection Office in Cologne. It blew a gaping hole in the facade, destroyed a conference room and scattered glass, dirt and debris around the surrounding residential area.

The bomb caused hundreds of thousands of dollars in damage, said Alexander Prechtel, spokesman for the federal prosecutor's office.

The bomb was hidden in a red Volkswagen Golf and was detonated by cable from about 30 yards away, Prechtel told The Associated Press.

Career criminals detected
Study focuses on drug users

WASHINGTON (AP) — The criminal justice system should rely more heavily on evidence of drug use and juvenile crime to pinpoint career criminals, a report conducted for the federal government concluded Monday.

The study by a panel of the National Research Council found that criminals who are drug abusers commit crimes at least twice as often as other offenders and may commit as many as six times more crimes during periods of heavy drug use.

The council panel also said that offenders who had criminal records as juveniles are much more likely to become chronic offenders as adults.

Information on drug use and juvenile offenses should be given greater weight in pre-trial release, plea bargaining, sentencing and parole, said the panel chaired by Alfred Blumstein, dean of the school of urban and public affairs at Carnegie-Mellon University in Pittsburgh.

"The younger an offender starts committing crimes and the more serious are his or her drug habits, the greater is the likelihood of a serious and long-continuing criminal career," said James K. Stewart, director of the National Institute of Justice, the agency that commissioned the study.

The study also said that giving longer prison sentences for convicted chronic offenders might result in a 5 percent to 10 percent reduction in crime, with a corresponding 10 percent to 20 percent increase in prison populations.

Achieving a 10 percent reduction in crime through tougher prison terms for all offenders would require doubling the number of prisoners, the study said.

The findings of the study were presented at a conference that opened Mo...

Inmate populations top half-million mark in state eral prisons last year, up n percent since 1977, accor recent federal survey. L 12.4 million major crime reported to authorities, a to the FBI.

Attorney General Edwin Meese, right, joins James K. Stewart, director of National Institute of Justice, in releasing report on crime

---

NATION
IN BRIEF

Mayors ask for help on narcotics fight

WASHINGTON — A group of mayors politely told President Reagan's chief adviser on drug abuse Monday that the federal government must give local police more help to fight narcotics on city streets.

"We're getting cutbacks on a lot or programs for cities," Boston Mayor Raymond Flynn told Carlton Turner, who is in charge of developing administration drug policy. "We're taking real scarce dollars for critically needed services, putting it into our narcotics units.

"Why isn't the money there to match the slogans?" Flynn, a Democrat, asked Turner at a meeting of the U.S. Conference of Mayors' task force on drugs.

"Sending Marines into Bolivia is one thing, but we also need the dollars in the streets of American cities as well as in the jungles of Bolivia," Flynn said.

Cop kills himself after tragic crash

EAST MEADOW, N.Y. — An off-duty New York City policeman, arrested for alleged drunken driving in a car crash that killed his female companion driving in a car crash that killed his female companion Monday, snatched a county officer's revolver and killed himself, police said.

The shooting occurred as Michael McNamara, 28, of Bellmore, was emerging from an ambulance at the Nassau County Medical Center in East Meadow, where he was to be treated for injuries and given a breath test.

McNamara, a five-year veteran of a mounted police unit, was driving when his car struck a pole at 3:34 a.m., killing the unidentified woman in his car.

Girl with tube in her neck goes to school

VENUS, Texas — A 7-year-old girl who must use a plastic tube to breathe is attending second grade this year after a year-long fight with school officials who didn't want to help her clear the tube each day.

Shelley Clower's windpipe wasn't fully developed at birth. Doctors inserted a tube in her neck, enabling her to breathe.

But the tube must be cleared by suction up to three times a day, and school officials declined to do it, fearing liability if something went wrong.

The district relented after a group representing handicapped Texans filed a complaint with the U.S. Department of Education. The school district, with 30 miles southwest of Dallas, agreed in May to provide a machine to perform the procedure and train staff members to use it.

Movie features boy amputated at waist

WEST ALIQUIPPA, Pa. — Kenny Easterday, a 13-year-old boy whose birth defect cost him the lower half of his body, has inspired a movie about his and his family's struggle to cope with his handicap.

"Instead of talking about the problems the handicapped have, we talk about the problem the family can have when there is a handicapped person in the family," said Claude Gagnon, director of "The Kid Brother."

"I think it's a movie that does say a few things about society," Gagnon said during filming here in Kenny's blue-collar hometown, 20 miles northwest of Pittsburgh.

Kenny was born with sacral agenesis, a deformation which left a gap between his chest and pelvis. Surgeons removed his legs and reconstructed his torso, leaving him only 24 inches tall at age 13.
Associated Press

First black sorority at Alabama University

TUSCALOOSA, Ala. — University of Alabama President Joab Thomas officially welcomed the school's first black sorority to Sorority Row.

More than 100 students and faculty members joined Thomas on Sunday outside the new home of Alpha Kappa Alpha, a site where two students burned a cross last spring.

John Merrill, president of the Student Government Association, said AKA's move onto the previously all-white Sorority Row "helps bring the University of Alabama into the 20th century."

Acid spill injures 61

ROME, Ga. — Sulfuric acid spilled at a paper mill Monday, injuring 61 people.

The gas at the Georgia Kraft Co. plant was created in the 1 p.m. accident when the acid leaked into a drainage ditch carrying other chemicals used in paper-making, officials said.

Caribbean storm keeps weather watchers wary

MIAMI (AP) — Tropical Storm Danielle made a slight turn northward Monday into the Caribbean Sea, bringing its 50 mph winds over warm water that will provide energy for its development, forecasters said.

"Anytime you have a storm in the Caribbean at the peak of the hurricane season, we encourage anybody who's got any interest to pay close attention," said forecaster Mark Zimmer.

At 3 p.m. PDT, the season's fourth named storm was centered near latitude 13.3 north, longitude 64.0 west or about 380 miles south southeast of San Juan, Puerto Rico, in the southeastern Caribbean, the National Hurricane Center in Coral Gables reported.

With maximum sustained wind of 50 mph and higher gusts in squalls, Danielle moved through the Windward Islands earlier Monday and continued heading west-northwest over the Caribbean at about 20 mph.

"It's moving on through the islands on a track that would bring it into open waters of the Caribbean," Zimmer said. "There is a likelihood of some strengthening."

Our primary marketing tool is the Press Democrat.

Jean McVicar and her son Jim co-own and manage the four Toy & Model stores in the Coddingtown Mall, Rohnert Park, Montgomery Village and Ukiah.

"We run a 13½ inch ad every Saturday. I believe in frequency so the public can watch for our ad. One recent Saturday we advertised a $190 toy and sold out by Monday afternoon."

Let the Press Democrat show you how you can increase your sales. Call today!

Retail: 526-5870   Classified: 546-7355

The Press Democrat

Coretta King ires black leaders
Botha meeting controversial

By WILLIAM CLAIBORNE
The Washington Post

CAPE TOWN, South Africa — Archbishop Desmond Tutu, in his first day as head of the Anglican Province of Southern Africa, Monday waded through the ankle-deep mud and sewage of the squatter shantytown of Crossroads and found himself embroiled in a controversy between U.S. civil rights activist Coretta Scott King and militant South African black nationalists.

Wearing sunglasses and a peasant watchman's cap, Tutu, accompanied by the Most Rev. Robert A.K. Runcie, archbishop of Canterbury, made a whirlwind tour of Crossroads, where last May and June upwards of 70,000 black squatters were driven out of their makeshift shacks in a government-backed campaign of mass population resettlement.

Shadowed almost constantly by security forces in armored trucks, Tutu and Runcie spent about an hour in Crossroads, trailed by carloads of journalists in one of the most elaborately organized media events in the Western Cape Province in recent years.

Tutu, Cape Town's first black archbishop, used the occasion to make a plea for President Pieter W. Botha to commute the death sentences of three black nationalists scheduled to be hanged Tuesday in a Pretoria prison for their involvement in terrorist activities.

Later, Tutu repeated his tour of Crossroads for King, showing her coils of razor wire surrounding the squatter area and telling her that "South Africa's Berlin Wall."

King said the squalid resettlement camp "really defies the imagination," adding, "Evil and injustice cannot reign forever ... It will have to give way."

Runcie said he was appalled by the squalor of Crossroads, and called on the white-minority government of South Africa to make more effort to solve the country's "clear social problems."

Bishop Tutu, center, leads the Archbishop of Canterbury, Robert Runcie, left, and a local bishop on a tour of Crossroads

---

here who've never had jobs. The barbed wire, all the security vehicles, seem to me to say that the government is not directly interested in solving the problems," said Runcie, the spiritual leader of 65 million Anglicans worldwide.

However, the Crossroads tour by the two archbishops was overshadowed, in part, by a growing controversy over King's plans to meet with Botha, who to many blacks is a symbol of the government's attachment to the policy of racial separation and continued white rule.

King also has planned a controversial meeting with Gatsha Buthelezi, the Zulu tribal chieftan who has sought to reach an accommodation with Botha's government and who is viewed as a government collaborator by many militant blacks.

Because of King's planned meeting with Botha, two prominent black nationalist leaders, Winnie Mandela and the Rev. Allan Boesak, reportedly have balked at meeting with the widow of the United States' best-known civil rights activist, Martin Luther King Jr.

Mandela is the wife of the imprisoned African National Congress leader, Nelson Mandela, and King said.

Boesak is the president of the World Alliance of Churches and was Cape Town's best-known antiapartheid activist until the arrival here of Tutu.

Mandela's confidants said that a meeting with King would be impossible as long as she insisted upon seeing Botha, and Boesak told reporters Sunday that if King met with the president, he would not meet with her, because, he said, Botha's "hands are literally dripping with the blood of our children."

Tutu, who angered many militant black nationalists because he met twice with Botha, said, "I've not been involved in that. ... Who she sees is up to her. I'm not involved in her private agenda."

King, in a brief interview at the posh Mount Nelson Hotel, where she is staying with an entourage of security guards and public relations advisers, said her plans were unchanged.

"It's important to dialogue with all sides. We'll have to see how things work out, but it's really important to have dialogue with people who hold opposing views," King said.

Contras say training in U.S. probable

TEGUCIGALPA, Honduras (AP) — The military commander of the largest Contra fighting force says Nicaraguan rebels probably will be trained in the United States.

Enrique Bermudez told The Associated Press in a weekend interview that he would like to have the training conducted inside Nicaragua, where he said Contra leaders already were conducting some training.

But he said, "For the training, the United States is the most likely possibility. Any military installation could be used if it is permitted by the appropriations bill. The training will be by U.S. military instructors."

The rebels are supported by the United States and are trying to overthrow Nicaragua's leftist Sandinista government.

The U.S. Congress has approved a $100 million aid package for the Contras that calls for U.S. military personnel to work with the rebels. Details are still being worked out in Washington.

The Reagan administration says that Nicaragua is trying to export revolution to other Central American nations and is too closely tied to Cuba and the Soviet Union.

A U.S. diplomat, speaking on condition of anonymity for political reasons, said last week one possibility would be to have U.S. experts give specialized training to rebel leaders who then could provide basic training for recruits.

Bermudez, military chief and one of the seven directors of the Nicaraguan Democratic Force, or FDN, said, "Every regional commander has the responsibility for training their people in the field."

He said recruits receive 45 days of training in guerrilla warfare, use of weapons and human rights.

The FDN claims to have 18,000 fighters although military analysts say the figure much lower, some estimating as few as 10,000. It has been waging a hit-and-miss guerrilla warfare in Nicaragua since 1982, and maintains bases in southern Honduras along the Nicaraguan border.

Wage freeze in dock pact

Associated Press

NEW YORK — The International Longshoremen's Association and four management groups, including the New York and Boston shipping associations and all container-terminal shipping from Maine to Texas, have reached tentative agreement on terms of a new three-year master contract.

The proposal calls for a two-year wage freeze at $17 an hour, with a $1 raise in the final year.

Longshoremen's President Teddy Gleason and Anthony Tozzoli, president of the New York Shipping Association, said in a joint statement released Monday: "The accord will allow the ILA to maintain its wage scale while helping to meet management's need to reduce overall labor costs."

The new contract also institutes a shift system designed to put idle longshoremen to work by limiting overtime. Specifics were not revealed.

In most ports, longshoremen are guaranteed an annual income, whether they work or not. The union won this benefit in 1966 to cushion workers displaced by automation. But it has been a sticking point for management ever since.

Beyond the wage package, exact terms of the settlement, accepted late Friday by about 200 union delegates meeting in Washington, were not revealed.

Sincerely yours

DISTINCTIVE GIFT IDEA...
"THE BIRTHDATE NEWSPAPER"

Give your family and friends the actual historic newspaper issued on the day they were born. Surprise them with a carefully preserved, rare, original newspaper and a certificate of authenticity—a personal time capsule enclosed in a hand-finished presentation case, gold-embossed with their name. Give them a unique gift and a fine collectible.

Available Exclusively at Sincerely Yours
with case $65*
plus a small UPS charge   newspaper only $29⁵⁰

Montgomery Village • 2410 Magowan Drive
Santa Rosa, CA 95405 • 707-579-4008 • Mon.-Sat. 10-6, Thurs. 'til 9

NEED A HOME LOAN?
JUST LOOK AT OUR RATES!

TYPE	FIXED	FIXED
TERM	**15 Years**	**30 Years**
RATE	**9.50%**	**9.75%**
APR	**10.03%**	**10.22%**
FEES	2%+$200	2%+$200

RATES SUBJECT TO CHANGE WITHOUT NOTICE. 30-YEAR ADJUSTABLE AND SECOND TRUST DEEDS ALSO AVAILABLE

Independence Savings
and loan association

339 South E Street, Suite 3, Santa Rosa, CA 95404
(707) 579-1911

TOP PRICES PAID for GOLD!

Gold Scrap
Dental Gold
Gold Jewelry

or other types of 10, 14, 18K gold

We also buy Diamonds & Diamond Jewelry

EARTHWORKS

Santa Rosa Speech & Language Services, I

John M. Samples, Ph
Dianne L. Samples, M
Licensed Speech-Language Patholo

ANNOUNCE
the addition of therapists:
Ann Mattern, M.S., and
Ingrid Schwab, M.S.
Specializing in
Swallowing Therapy and Servi
to the Head Injured

Services provided at Santa Rosa,
Petaluma and Healdsburg locations

Referrals, further information or brochure

542-1154 or 765-905

1154 Montgomery Dr., Suite 7
Santa Rosa, CA. 95405

We Get You Ready For A Real Job. Then We Help You Find One.

EMPIRE COLLEGE SPECIALIZES IN HIGH-QUALITY CAREER TRAINING IN FIELDS WHERE THERE ARE PLENTY OF GOOD JO

• Bookkeeping/Data Entry   • Court Reporting
• Accounting/CPA Preparation   • Medical Transcriptionist
• Word processing   • Medical Administrative Medical
• Legal Clerical   • Medical Secretary
• Computerized Accounting   • Executive Secretary
• Accelerated Business Essentials • General Secretary
                                  • Travel and Tourism

Register Now! Classes begin September 29, 1986
Financial Aid Available to Those Who Qualify

CALL 546-4000

A Quarter of a Century of Commitment to Business Educatio

OUR GRADUATES GET GOOD JOB

EMPIRE COLLEG

The Business College That Specializes in Career Training

3033 Cleveland Ave., Santa Rosa, CA 95401

Hard news

Pages A4 and A5 from the start-up issue shows Briefs treatments as flags labeling the pages, and items running under forceful contrasting headings.

263

Weddings

SHARON TAUSSIG

DWIGHT VALLELY

PETE SMITH

COC

ollester-Wessa

Jennifer Luise Wessa and
ewart Pace Collester were
d in a garden ceremony at the
me of her parents, Dr. and
s. Fredrick J. Wessa of Santa
sa. The bride attended Santa
sa High School and Santa
rbara City College. Her
sband, the son of Mr. and Mrs.
ewart Monroe Collester of
rk City, Utah, attended
wport High School and is a
dscape contractor in Santa
rbara. They are living in
nta Barbara.

Pfeil-Bodle

Carol E. Bodle and James
Allan Pfeil were wed in the Mt.
Soledad Presbyterian Church in
La Jolla. Daughter of Dr. and
Mrs. John Bodle of Santa Rosa,
the bride attended Piner High
School, Point Loma College, and
San Diego State University. She
is a teacher in San Diego. Her
husband is the son of Mrs. and
Mrs. Shirley Pfeil of Los
Angeles. He attended
Westchester High School, Los
Angeles, and SDSU. He works
for Bluebird Systems, Carlsbad,
producing computer software.
They are living in Encinitas.

Shaw-Holz

Julie J. Holz and John W. Shaw
exchanged marriage vows in the
Burbank Center for the Arts in
Santa Rosa. The bride is the
daughter of Vonna and Carl Holz
of Santa Rosa. She attended
Piner High School, California
State University at Chico, where
she earned a bachelor's degree,
and Humboldt State University,
where she earned a master's
degree in speech pathology. She
is a speech pathologist for
Lassen County School in
Susanville. Her husband is the
son of JoAnn Shaw of Fremont
and Carl Shaw of Reno, Nev.
They are making their home in
Susanville.

Wallace-Blank

The Santa Rosa Golf and
Country Club was the setting
the marriage of Lori Blank an
Brian Wallace. She is the
daughter of Barbara Parks o
San Diego and Milton Blank c
Los Angeles; his parents are
Marie and Everett Wallace o
Los Angeles. The bride atten
Union High School in Los
Angeles and Santa Rosa Juni
College. She is a teller for
Imperial Savings. Her husba
attended Concord High Scho
Los Angeles and SRJC. He is
electronics technician. They
making their home in Santa
Rosa.

Engagements

awrence
ella-Maggiora

December wedding at St. Fran-
Solano Church in Sonoma is
nned by Kathleen Maria Della-
ggiora and Stephen L. Law-
ce.
aughter of Rose Della-Mag-
ra of Sonoma, she is a graduate
Montgomery High School, Santa
a Junior College and California
te University, Chico. She
ches elementary school in Santa
z County.
er fiance is the son of Mr. and
. George Lawrence of Santa

Strach III will be married in Janu-
ary at Berean Baptist Church in
Rohnert Park.
She is the daughter of Claude and
Judy Spivey of Rohnert Park; her
fiance's parents are Betty Strach of
Rohnert Park and Jerome Strach II
of Mill Valley.
The bride-elect is a graduate of
Rancho Cotate High School and is a
student at Santa Rosa Junior Col-
lege, majoring in business adminis-
tration. She is a bookkeeper-clerk
at TG&Y in Rohnert Park.
He was graduated from Cardinal
Newman high School and majors in
computer science and physics at
Sonoma State University. He works

She is the daughter of Charles W.
and Nancy Jo Wagoner of Fair
Oaks. His parents are Robert W.
and Carolyn Gaul of San Mateo.
The bride-elect is a computer
programmer for Unocal Geother-
mal in Santa Rosa. Both are graduates of California State Polytechnic
Institute in San Luis Obispo and her
fiance is a computer programmer
for Commerce Clearing House in
San Rafael.

McKean-Memeo

Montgomery High School and Sa
ta Rosa Junior College and is
utility clerk-stenographer for I
cific Gas and Electric Co.
Her fiance attended the sa
schools and is a telecommuni
tions technician for PG&E.

Richards-Wulff

Marla Wulff and Ronald Al
Richards plan a late October w
ding at the Church of the Incar
tion in Santa Rosa.
The daughter of Mr. and M
Frank Wulff, Santa Rosa, she i
Montgomery High School gradu

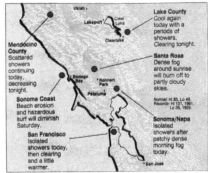

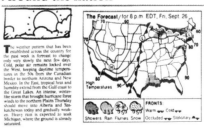

Weather

Above: Reflecting most Americans' interest in weather reports, this one, formerly on an inside page in black and white and illustrated only with a national map, now occupies a half-page on the back cover of Section B where it can run in generous size, with color. Emphasis is put on local reports placed on a large topographical map. Care had to be taken to put enough information on the map to justify its size, but not so much that the type gets too small or the map too busy. A conversational tone is given the heading, and the area forecast gets a by-line.

Bride and groom

Facing page: Configuration requirements place Weddings and Engagements toward the back of the local section, not in their more customary Lifestyle place. Given a thoughtful, organized treatment, these warm, informal bride and groom pictures contrast effectively with the usual presentation of stiff studio bride shots.

Sports

Echo of 1A

Like the other section headings, the "Sports" heading allows the placement of information right up to the top of the page. A reefer, a quote, or a picture and caption appear in any of several predesigned ways. Type and box treatments echo the design of Page 1A.

Column right

The most unusual part of the page is the anchored placement of two sports columns, one above the other, in a wide measure down the right-hand side. This came from the sports editor's desire to feature not one but two columnists in an important way. How better to signal to readers that the new *Press Democrat* was giving them something new and different, and *more*, than by this unusual and highly visible placement? Of course, this would require a daily line-up of good columnists. The top columnist every day was a local writer and the bottom a selected syndicated columnist. Formerly, such columns had bounced around the sports pages to such a degree that they lacked a feeling of place and familiarity, both important attributes for that special association readers are said to develop with sports columnists.

The actual design of the column headings could hardly be simpler. A larger version of the black accent Folio type used throughout the paper emphasized the writer's name. The original dummy layout displayed these names in blue,

in an attempt to build color functionally into the page.

Bottom lines

To ensure interest from top to bottom, a reefer feature was suggested to give the reader some variety at the bottom of the page and to provide the editor with an opportunity for an interesting picture.

This was a variation of the more common use of the space for a news feature that could be visually highlighted with a label overline. Here was an opportunity to do something graphically special on the page with little extra effort.

Sports front

Right: A dummy paste-up. Facing page: A fairly typical, actual front page. The most unusual feature is the placement of the two columns on the right, reflecting the editor's great interest in having a good local columnist and a good syndicated columnist associated with the section. The dummy treatment of the boxes in the heading seemed disjointed, leading to the more discreet use of color when the paper went live. The box at the bottom ranged from reefer, to stand-alone photo, to news feature. Layout, facing page: Don Shelton.

276

SPORTS

Santa Rosa, California, Monday, September 22, 1986 ..

49ers find a new hero

Kemp riddles Saints as Niners earn 26-17 win

By RALPH LEEF
Sports Editor

SAN FRANCISCO — He may not be the second coming of Dan Marino, but Jeff Kemp's performance on a day when the special teams seemed intent on passing out gifts was enough to unwrap a San Francisco 49ers victory over the New Orleans Saints.

Kemp completed 29 of 44 passes for 332 yards and one touchdown, and Ray Wersching booted four field goals to lead the 49ers to a 26-17 victory before 58,297 fans at Candlestick Park.

The 49ers will take a 2-1 record into next Sunday's showdown with the Marino-led Miami Dolphins, who scored 45 points against the New York Jets on Sunday, but gave up 51 and fell to 1-2.

The 49ers were hoping to come up with a strong running attack and solid special teams play to help take the pressure off Kemp, who was making only his second start filling in for injured Joe Montana. Instead, it was Kemp who came through to relieve the pressure when the game was on the line.

The 49ers' running game netted only 136 yards on 42 carries (a 3.2-yard average) and the special teams' kickoff coverage unit gave up returns of 101, 63 and 34 yards.

"The pressure was really on him (Kemp) and look what he did today," said 49ers' receiver Jerry Rice, who caught seven passes for 120 yards. "This erased any doubt in my mind. Jeff can take us to the Super Bowl."

Kemp seemed at his best in third-down situations when the pressure was the greatest.

With the 49ers trailing 17-13 late in the third quarter, Kemp hooked up with Rice (17 yards) and Roger Craig (7 yards) on two third-down plays leading to running back Derrick Harmon's 5-yard touchdown run.

Continued on Page C2

Jeff Kemp scrambled away from the New Orleans rush enough times to pass for 332 yards, the 49ers' best passing performance this season

OTTO GREULE

Kemp no longer the man Saints forgot

By LARRY STONE
Staff Writer

SAN FRANCISCO — In his post-game press conference, New Orleans Saints' coach Jim Mora inadvertently referred to San Francisco 49ers' quarterback Jeff Kemp as "Jack."

He had obviously confused Kemp momentarily with his father, the U.S. congressman and former Buffalo Bills' quarterback who just happened to be Mora's college roommate and teammate at Occidental College.

It figured. After all, Kemp had confused New Orleans all day, turning in a performance that will ensure the Saints will remember his name in the future.

"Joe Montana couldn't have done any better than Kemp did," said defensive back Johnny Poe after Kemp had riddled the Saints secondary for 332 yards in San Francisco's 26-17 win. "I felt Jeff did just as good a job audiblizing at the

line as Joe, and Joe is the greatest in football at that. That's probably the ultimate compliment I can give him."

"Kemp was far better than we expected," added free safety Frank Wattelet. "I think we might have subconsciously let down without Montana in there, but Kemp made us pay for it. We'll give him a lot more respect next time."

Sunday's game will also go a long way toward making a household name of Mel Gray. In Santa Rosa, of course, it already is, but this Mel Gray is no relation to the former Montgomery High School and St. Louis Cardinal standout. Except in talent.

Gray, a USFL refugee from the Los Angeles Express, nearly snatched the game away from the 49ers with 186 yards in kickoff returns, including a team-record 101-yard scamper for a touchdown to start the second half and give New Orleans its only lead, 17-13.

Continued on Page C3

Rookie Charles Haley, who was rough on Saints' quarterbacks all day, decks Dave Wilson

OTTO GREULE

NFL THRILLER

Wesley Walker beats Don McNeal and awaits the touchdown pass that won it for the Jets

ASSOCIATED PRESS

Jets claim miracle win over Miami

Associated Press

Call it the Miracle of the Meadowlands.

They're already casting this one for Hollywood, with Wesley Walker, Ken O'Brien and Dan Marino in the starring roles.

Walker plays the conquering hero after catching a 21-yard touchdown pass from O'Brien to tie the game as regulation time expired, then hauling in a 43-yard throw in overtime to give the New York Jets a 51-45 NFL victory over the Miami Dolphins Sunday afternoon in East Rutherford, N.J.

Until Walker, who caught four touchdown passes from O'Brien, staged his sensational heroics on Sunday, the spotlight belonged to Marino, who threw for six touchdowns.

"I was down on myself because I fumbled the ball. I thought I lost the game for the team," said Walker, whose bobble led to Miami's go-ahead touchdown at 45-38.

"I was just grateful I was given the opportunity to make it up.

"I have confidence in myself in situations like this. You just hope you have the chance to come back and make up for your mistakes."

O'Brien, the eternal optimist, couldn't afford to have his key receiver moping around with a game on the line.

"He said, 'I just lost it for us,' " O'Brien said of Walker. "I told him, 'No, Wes, believe we'll come back.'

"You just have to keep it positive and keep trying. Nobody on this team will quit. We proved that today."

On the tying touchdown, Walker split two defensive backs.

"When I came down, I knew I had to lean," Walker said. "I couldn't believe I wasn't hit immediately. When I realized I was in the end zone, it was instant shock. I didn't even realize there was no time left on the clock."

On the game-winner, he sailed past free safety Bud Brown down the right sideline.

"Any time Wes gets a step on a defender, he's gone," O'Brien said. "I just threw it and the next thing I knew, people were jumping all over me.

"This should end any talk about Wesley being over the hill," O'Brien said. "This should answer all the questions. And he's not even 100 percent."

Continued on Page C4

RICH MELLOTT

Niners' defense turned the tide

SAN FRANCISCO — With the game hanging in the balance and momentum hanging out on the New Orleans Saints' sidelines, the 49er defense got together and decided enough was enough.

Actually, what was decided was that 17 points were enough.

"We huddled up and reminded ourselves that we had to shut them down the rest of the way," said nose tackle Michael Carter. "We knew we couldn't give up anything else and expect to win."

A guy named Mel Gray had just returned the second half's opening kickoff 101 yards to give the Saints a 17-13 lead, and the situation didn't look particularly promising for the home team.

Their quarterback, Jeff Kemp, hadn't yet perfected his Joe Montana impersonation. And the way the 49er kickoff team was performing, it appeared that every touchdown the Niners would score probably would be answered immediately by another 101-yard kickoff return by the Saints.

So what's a team to do?

"We knew what we had to do," said safety Ronnie Lott. "We had to shut them out. No more touchdowns. No more field goals. No more mistakes."

And that's exactly what the 49er defense did. It rallied to stop the Saints and insure a 26-17 victory. It rallied to make life easy — well, relatively easy — for Kemp and the 49er offense, which did some rallying of its own to help pull this one out.

Bill Walsh, the 49ers' head coach, gave the game ball to Kemp, who, if you insist on giving footballs away, obviously deserved it. Receivers Jerry Rice and Dwight Clark were worthy recipients, too, combining as they did for 14 catches for 120 yards.

But rookie defensive end Larry Roberts had another player in mind.

"They ought to give another ball to Charles Haley," he said. "He was all over the place."

Ah yes, Charles Haley.

"Charles Haley," said Walsh, "is going to be a great football player one day."

Considering how he played against the Saints, that day isn't far off.

Haley, who played his college ball at James Madison, was the fifth player chosen by the 49ers in the draft this year. But his play in his first three pro games has been worthy of a No. 1 choice.

Continued on Page C2

GEORGE VECSEY

Mets erred by following rituals

Having escaped the good, the bad and the ugly out there in public, the New York Mets observed the champagne ritual in their clubhouse after clinching their division title Wednesday night.

Just asking, but given the national drug scandal, and given the number of athletes with alcohol problems, do drunken clubhouse celebrations fit in with Peter Ueberroth's squeaky-clean plans for baseball? Or is booze looped on champagne somehow better than zonked on dope?

Some of the Mets looked and sounded pretty shaky Wednesday night, unless they were acting for the omnipresent hand-held cameras. ("Look, Ma, I'm on Channel 9, wearing a garbage bag and shaving cream.")

When word came the next day that some of the Mets had celebrated in a suburban hangout half an hour from Shea Stadium, the teen-ager in our household asked, "How did they get there — by train or bus?" Not by their own vehicles, one would like to think.

One New York Islander player was arrested following a Stanley Cup celebration a few years back. There could have been others; he just happened to be nabbed.

• • •

Like most other people 45 or younger, the Met players have grown up watching television and learning how to act from strangers. They have seen grown men squirting champagne and cavorting in crowded locker rooms, so that is what they do.

It is such a specific ritual that Margaret Mead could have saved some air fare and written about the rites of passage of championship baseball teams. These days, the ritual has been expanded to include the modern shamans of the electronic tom-toms, the television broadcasters.

The celebrations used to be mostly by and for the players, with assembled journalists and radio and television broadcasters allowed to watch. But today's players have grown up watching benign people with good hair, good teeth and microphones in one hand; they talk familiarly with them, as they would talk with members of their own families.

The players sneak up behind visitors from the 11 o'clock news and douse them with champagne or shaving cream, the modern urban family at play, an MTV video in the making.

From all appearances, the broadcasters welcome their splattering. The shaving cream on their tie, the champagne on their hair, are what dueling scars were to centuries of Heidelberg students.

Being mobbed by loutish fans can be dangerous as proven Sunday when Rick Aguilera had to miss a turn because his shoulder had been damaged by a fan in Wednesday's melee.

Sometimes the celebration inside can be dangerous, too. Tim McCarver, the former catcher now an announcer with the Mets, recalls the scene in 1967 when the St. Louis Cardinals clinched in Boston and broke out the bottled stuff.

Continued on Page C7

SIDE LINES

Navratilova not guilty in injury suit

A jury in Riverhead, N.Y., found Thursday that tennis star Martina Navratilova did not injure a 44-year-old photographer when she took his camera and exposed his film at the U.S. Open Tennis Championships in 1982.

The six-member jury, however, did award Arthur Seitz $50 for the roll of film that Navratilova exposed during a skirmish following her quarterfinal loss to Pam Shriver on Sept. 7, 1982.

Seitz had claimed in a $2 million suit that Navratilova injured his elbow and shoulder during a battle for his camera.

Floyd, Warriors agree on pact

SANTA BARBARA — Veteran guard Eric "Sleepy" Floyd has agreed to sign a new four-year contract with the Golden State Warriors of the National Basketball Association.

Veteran Eric 'Sleepy' Floyd will return to the Warriors' backcourt

The Warriors also announced on Wednesday that veteran free agent Gary Plummer had agreed to a one-year contract. Plummer, a forward, had serious knee surgery last year.

Details of the two contracts weren't released. Floyd and Plummer were scheduled to sign the contracts on Thursday in Oakland and to join the team at its Santa Barbara training camp today, said Cheri White, a spokesman for the Warriors.

McMahon decides against surgery

TV SPORTS

10 AM	CFL Football: ESPN Stampeders at Tiger-Cats
4:35 PM	Baseball:Astros at Braves, TBS Matt Keough (4-3) vs. Doyle Alexander (5-6)
5:30 PM	Harness Racing: ESPN 1986 Breeders Crown.
6 PM	Boxing: HBO WBC Champ Hector Camacho (30-0, 16 KO's) vs. Cornelius Boza-Edwards (44-5-1, 34 KO's) WBA Champ Livingstone Bramble (24-1-1, 15 KO's) vs. Edwin Rosario (23-2, 19 KO's).

RADIO

8:05 PM	Giants vs. Dodgers, at San Francisco, KNBR 68
5:35 PM	A's vs. Royals, at Kansas City, KSFO 560

Charlie Leibrandt will pitch for the Royals today against Oakland

Details

Above: A TV and Radio box enlivens the top of the Scoreboard page. Left: A column of short items runs down the side of the page. Little pictures can do a big job in enriching a page and making other, large pictures on the page look even bigger.

Black and white Sports

Facing page: Another page shows an unusual arrangement of elements that gets away from a "blocky" feeling in favor of a dynamic step-down from the horizontal black bar in the center to the black bar at the bottom. Color might have added interest in a specific photo, but unquestionably the dynamic design carries a great deal of interest without any color. In fact, color might have lessened the cohesiveness and unity of the page. Layout: Don Shelton.

Fernando finally wins his 20th C3

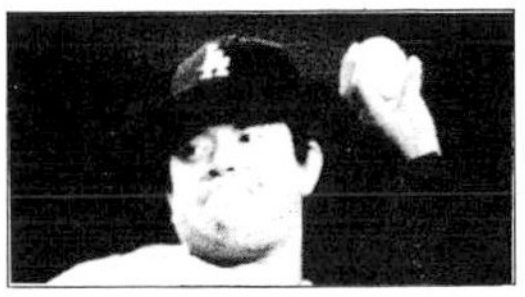

The Press Democrat **C**

SPORTS

Santa Rosa, California, Tuesday, September, 23, 1986••

Montana may play this year

By RALPH LEEF
Sports Editor

But 49ers take more conservative view on quarterback's return

REDWOOD CITY — Joe Montana could play the final five or six games this season for the San Francisco 49ers if his rehabilitation from back surgery goes without a hitch.

That was the best-case scenario on Monday from Dr. Arthur White, who performed the spinal surgery on the San Francisco quarterback eight days ago.

But team physician Dr. Michael Dillingham Monday took a more conservative view, saying Montana is not likely to play for at least three months, which means he would miss the remainder of the regular season but conceivably might be available if the team makes the playoffs.

"Things are optimistic, but no one can make a promise (when) Joe will return to play," said Dillingham. "One thing we can say is that he decreased his risk of getting hurt again by having the surgery."

White, who was the principal surgeon for the operation, said Montana was released from St. Mary's Hospital at 11 a.m. Monday after already beginning his rehabilitation program.

Montana's early progress led White to believe he may play later this year.

"Joe was on his feet the day after surgery, he's been off medication for three days, he walked almost a mile yesterday (Sunday), and even did some light workouts on a Nautilus machine," said the doctor. "The absolute soonest he'd be able to play is two months, but that would be a phenomenal effort. Most individuals who have this surgery start doing athletics in three months and reach a peak in athletics in six months. But Joe isn't most individuals. He's strong and in excellent shape."

Coach Bill Walsh said the 49ers are in no great hurry to rush Montana back to work.

"He'd have to work out extensively over a period of time before we'd activate him," said Walsh.

There are 10 weeks before the 49ers face the toughest part of their schedule — consecutive games with the New York Giants and Jets at home and New England Patriots on the road before the final game, at Candlestick Park, against the Los Angeles Rams.

White and Dillingham met members of the media Monday to explain in detail Montana's history of back problems and the reason it was decided to operate.

"Montana was having progressive neurological loss," said White. "It is very rare that we feel surgery is indicated in this kind of injury, but we couldn't sit by and watch anybody lose the feeling and strength before our eyes. It became a surgical emergency."

White said Montana's severe back pain and numbness in a portion of his left foot, did not respond to medication and caused alarm among the five attending physicians.

"I think we got to Joe before it got too extensive and I think any neurological loss that he has now will go on to recover," said White.

Montana has no feeling in an area six inches wide by two to three inches wide on the edge of his left foot.

White said that some nerve loss could be permanent, but, because the affected nerves grow out slowly, there is no way to know yet if Montana will regain full feeling

Continued on Page C7

RICH MELLOTT

Hunting season endangers QBs

It was late August, the Raiders' summer camp in Oxnard was winding down and head coach Tom Flores was growing tired of answering questions about his quarterback problem — the one he never admitted having in the first place.

You remember — the one involving Marc Wilson and Jim Plunkett, and the question of who should start and who should come in as soon as the other gets wiped out.

"I guess some people think it's a problem," Flores said. "I don't. It's a long season and these days you need two quarterbacks. It's hard to expect one man going through a full season."

Flores went on to point out that of the 28 NFL teams last year, no fewer than 20 had to start their backups in at least one game. Flores also pointed out that he had to start his backup in 15 games, including one playoff contest.

The way Flores made it sound, Wilson was his starting pitcher and Plunkett his ace reliever. You half-expected the Raider coach to say, "I'm just hoping to get eight to 10 strong games out of Marc, and then we can bring in Jim, our veteran reliever, to finish up. He'll be fresh and he'll just blow the ball by all those defensive backs."

You still have to wonder about the Raiders' quarterback problem. They are 0-3, Wilson is out, Plunkett is in, and the offense appears determined never to score a touchdown again.

But it's hard arguing with Flores' philosophy about having two good quarterbacks around.

It's just too bad he can't find a couple.

Good quarterbacks are hard to find. Their numbers also tend to dwindle during hunting season, which, you may have noticed, is upon us. More than ever, defenses go after quarterbacks with everything, including some well-known kitchen appliances.

All this blitzing, stunting and red-dogging sends quarterbacks running for their lives — or at least for their limbs. And sometimes, as Joe Montana proved two weeks ago, a quarterback doesn't even have to be clobbered by a defensive lineman to be seriously injured. All Montana was doing was running from them and throwing at the same time.

Sunday, the Saints' Bobby Hebert went down in the first quarter with a broken foot, thanks in part to 49er rookie Charles Haley, who, considering his talents and determination, has a bright future in the business of injuring quarterbacks. Hebert will be out four to six weeks. There's a chance the Saints won't miss him because backup Dave Wilson might be just as good.

Continued on Page C4

PRIDE AND POISE?

Bad times

Raiders, Dolphins proof the mighty have fallen

Associated Press

The Pride and Poise boys are bruised and battered — and 0-3. The Killer Bees defense is feeling the sting of two losses in which it surrendered at least 500 yards and 50 points.

The Los Angeles Raiders and the Miami Dolphins, two of the NFL's winningest franchises, are sharing the bottom of the standings with teams like Buffalo. The defenseless Dolphins are 1-2. That's one more win than the punchless Raiders have.

Something strange is going on.

"It's frustrating. Frustrating and maddening," All-Pro cornerback Mike Haynes said after the Raiders' 14-9 loss to the New York Giants Sunday.

Lyle Blackwood of the Miami Dolphins describes a different emotion. "It's an embarrassment to go into the fourth game of the season with 111 points against us. Some teams don't give up that much in a season," said Blackwood after the Dolphins lost to the New York Jets 51-45 in overtime.

What's happening? In Miami's case, it appears to be a slow erosion of talent caused by age and injury, a decline masked by the genius of coach Don Shula and the brilliance of Dan Marino and his receivers.

The Dolphins, who play the San Francisco 49ers this Sunday in Miami, opened with a 50-28 loss in San Diego. Although they bounced back with a 31-10 win over Indianapolis, they are reeling from Sunday's defensive debacle.

Since assistant coach Bill Arnsparger left to become head coach at LSU, the defense, under the direction of former 49er assistant Chuck Studley, has been awful. Key positions are manned by rookies and aging veterans — such as the 36-year-old Blackwood, who was cut, then re-signed three weeks ago. Its most talented player, linebacker Hugh Green, broke a kneecap against the Jets and is gone for at least two months.

> "I'm not a clairvoyant, but 0-3 definitely wasn't in my wildest imagination."
>
> HOWIE LONG

"That's devastating now, especially in the situation we're in," said Shula. "We're losing one of our best defensive players, if not our best. It just compounds our problems."

Even the usually unflappable Marino sounds panicky. "As a team, we're going to have to start doing better real soon or else we're going to lose a lot of games," said Marino, whose 448 yards and six touchdowns weren't enough on Sunday. "I don't know what it is, but we'd better do something."

The Raiders, off to one of their worst starts ever, also have their share of problems. Foremost are desperate situations at quarterback and wide receiver.

The offense that hasn't scored a touchdown in two games got more bad news on Monday when Tom Flores announced that star running back Marcus Allen may miss a game because of a sprained ankle suffered Sunday.

"There's not much you can do for an ankle," said Flores of the condition of the league's Most Valuable

Continued on Page C4

The Raiders might be without their most potent weapon, MVP Marcus Allen, for their game with San Diego because of a sprained ankle

TOM JACKSON

Are 49ers running out of excuses?

Randy Cross, the 49ers' resident pitchman/television host/philosopher, had a headache about the size of New Orleans' nose tackle Tony Elliott, who goes a trim 295 pounds. "I'm really not thinking too clearly," he mumbled.

So the duty of explaining how it happened that the San Francisco 49ers' runners barely dented the Saints' defense — despite the 49ers' 26-17 triumph Sunday — fell to Bubba Paris, the deep-freeze tackle.

"We've got everything that is essential to having not just a good running game, but a dominant running game," Paris said. "Today was the genesis of a new focus."

Huh? Howzat again, Bubba?

"I'm excited," he said.

You've got to admire Paris' optimism, which plainly is every bit as robust as his imposing girth. Anyone who can get juiced over a 3.2 yards-per-rush average, who sees the birth of greatness when two starting running backs manage a meager 85 yards on 32 carries, whose eyes glisten at one — count it, ONE rushing touchdown — that is a four-star optimist.

Commanded an exultant Paris: "You can go ask Wilks and you can go ask Geathers, and you can go ask anybody who lined up how they liked our running game. Ask them did they get moved off the ball."

The gentlemen in question, right side defensive tackles Jim Wilks and James Geathers, had fled the Saints' clubhouse by the time emissaries brought this shocking news from Paris. But Elliott, a sturdy fifth-year nose man, still was about the place.

"We shut down their offense enough," sniffed Elliot. Furthermore, he said he couldn't recall being driven off the line with any genuine frequency.

• • •

And then there was outside linebacker Rickey Jackson, a two-time Pro Bowl starter, away from whom the 49ers scrupulously pointed their offense. "I chased the ball all day," he shrugged. "Maybe they thought I'd get tired. I just wish they had come my way a few times."

"Their personnel was best to be attacked on (the other) side," said Bill Walsh, the 49ers' head coach. He, too, seemed to have a slightly better grasp than Paris on the real world.

Jeff Kemp's encouraging proficiency at quarterback, and a typically iron-fisted workday by San Francisco's defense aside: Without more convincing signs of life from the guys Eddie DeBartolo pays to run the football, there's bound to be trouble in Ninerland.

"I can't explain . . . what is happening, but we are not running the ball like we expected going into this game, going into the season," Walsh said.

Indeed, His Geniusness had previously suggested that a 200-yard rushing day didn't seem out of the question, that in fact, 200 yards would represent a resounding measure of success.

Continued on Page C4

Giants rap Reds, take over second

CINCINNATI — San Francisco manager Roger Craig says the Giants' wild 10-7 victory over Cincinnati Monday night was meaningful, all appearances aside.

The Giants committed three errors that led to four unearned runs, but overcame the sloppy play on the strength of Dan Gladden's first career grand slam to take sole possession of second place in the National League West.

Craig said finishing second wouldn't be a hollow honor.

"It means a lot," he said. "This club lost 100 games last year. To come back and finish second, it means a lot for next year. No matter what happens from here on out, the attitude is going to carry over to next year."

Giants' first baseman Joel Youngblood dropped a popup and booted a grounder to let the first two Cincinnati batters

Continued on Page C3

BLACK AND BLUE

ASSOCIATED PRESS

Tim Lewis of the Packers lands a good right cross on Keith Ortego of the Bears during Monday's rough-and-tumble action

Bears pull away from fired-up Pack

Associated Press

GREEN BAY, Wis. — For the second consecutive game, the defending Super Bowl champion Chicago Bears won ugly. But coach Mike Ditka didn't complain.

"It was not pretty. Still we won," Ditka said shortly after his Bears beat the winless Green Bay Packers 25-12 in a Monday night NFL game. "Our execution wasn't very good."

But this time it didn't have to be, because a big effort by the Chicago defense turned the game around in the fourth quarter.

The Bears trailed the Packers 12-10 entering the final quarter but scored 15 points in the last 15 minutes to overtake the Packers. A blocked field goal by Dan Hampton and a safety by Steve McMichael were the crucial plays.

Continued on Page C4

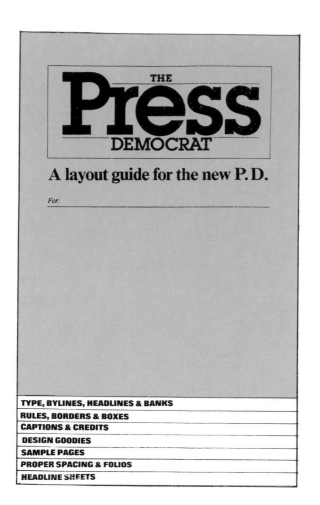

A layout guide for the new P. D.

TYPE, BYLINES, HEADLINES & BANKS
RULES, BORDERS & BOXES
CAPTIONS & CREDITS
DESIGN GOODIES
SAMPLE PAGES
PROPER SPACING & FOLIOS
HEADLINE SHEETS

Watch that spacing!
(What to look for in a proof)

The most common, classic difficulties in spacing are:
1. **Jamitosis:** Not enough space between headlines and text, especially when the headline has no descenders. Or too much space. Also between heads and reverses, or heads and photos, or stories and other stories ...
EDITORS: Don't jam in that one extra line!

Charlotte bids for NBA team
Los Angeles Times

This is the tailor, dealing in porn, who dressed the man all tattered and torn, that kissed the maiden all forlorn that milked the cow with the crumpled horn that tossed the dog that worried the cat that killed the rat that lived in the house that Jack built.

And if that wasn't enough already, here it is again: This is the tailor, dealing in porn, who dressed the man all tattered and torn, that kissed the maiden all forlorn that milked the cow with the crumpled

WRONG

Charlotte bids for NBA team
Los Angeles Times

This is the tailor, dealing in porn, who dressed the man all tattered and torn, that kissed the maiden all forlorn that milked the cow with the crumpled horn that tossed the dog that worried the cat that killed the rat that lived in the house that Jack built.

And if that wasn't enough already, here it is again: This is the tailor, dealing in porn, who dressed the man all tattered and torn, that kissed the maiden all forlorn that milked the cow with the crumpled

WRONG

Charlotte bids for NBA team
Los Angeles Times

This is the tailor, dealing in porn, who dressed the man all tattered and torn, that kissed the maiden all forlorn that milked the cow with the crumpled horn that tossed the dog that worried the cat that killed the rat that lived in the house that Jack built.

And if that wasn't enough already, here it is again: This is the tailor, dealing in porn, who dressed the maiden all forlorn that milked the cow with the crumpled

PERFECT

2. **Rulitis:** Throwing in an extra rule just to fill up space. There are certain specific uses for rules as outlined herein. Do not stray.
3. **Creditectomy:** Trying to save — or consume — space by knifing the photo credit away from its mooring. Space between credit and cutline is precise. Don't change it.
4. **Jamitosis Advertimoso:** You can figure this one out. Leave 18 points (1½ picas). No more, no less.
5. **Quote Bloat:** Don't add extra space between the lines of a pull-out quote. Don't put a knife to these poor, defenseless, pre-spaced elements!
6. **Lateral Constipation:** The paper will have a variety of column widths, but in ALL CASES there will be 1 pica of space between columns. If you find it necessary to calculate a bastard measure, be accurate.
7. **The Bends:** There was a crooked headline... Use the *baseline of the type* to judge straightness, not the edge of the film.
8. **Malignment:** Line up legs of type in a story *precisely* with the with the top edge of the byline.

By ELAINE ITUP
Los Angeles Times

This is the tailor, dealing in porn, who dressed the man all tattered and torn, that kissed the maiden all forlorn that milked the cow with | the crumpled horn that tossed the dog that worried the cat that killed the rat that lived in the house that Jack built.

WRONG

By ELAINE ITUP
Los Angeles Times

This is the tailor, dealing in porn, who dressed the man all tattered and torn, that kissed the maiden all forlorn that milked the cow with | the crumpled horn that tossed the dog that worried the cat that killed the rat that lived in the house that Jack built.

And if that wasn't enough already, here it is again: This is the

PERFECT

PROPER SPACING & FOLIOS

Style book, etc.

Randy Wright worked all night to get a style book assembled in this useful way in time for the day of conversion. In addition to distributing the style pages, meetings were held to familiarize everyone with the contents, and marked-up sample pages were placed around the composing room. Prototype pages had been printed in a sample dodger, which was also made readily available in the composing room and in the newsroom.

Sting officials subpoenaed in grand jury probe
10 point

Sting officials subpoenaed in grand jury probe
10 point

Sting officials subpoenaed in grand jury probe
12 point

Sting officials subpoenaed in grand jury probe
12 point

Sting officials subpoenaed in grand jury probe
14 point

Sting officials subpoenaed in grand jury probe
14 point

Sting officials subpoenaed in grand jury probe
16 point

Sting officials subpoenaed in grand jury probe
16 point

Sting officials subpoenaed in grand jury probe
18 point

Sting officials subpoenaed in grand jury probe
18 point

Sting officials subpoenaed in grand jury probe
22 point

Sting officials subpoenaed in grand jury probe
22 point

Sting officials subpoenaed in grand jury probe
24 point

Sting officials subpoenaed in grand jury probe
24 point

Sting officials subpoenaed in grand jury probe
30 point

Sting officials subpoenaed in grand jury probe
30 point

HEADLINE SHEETS

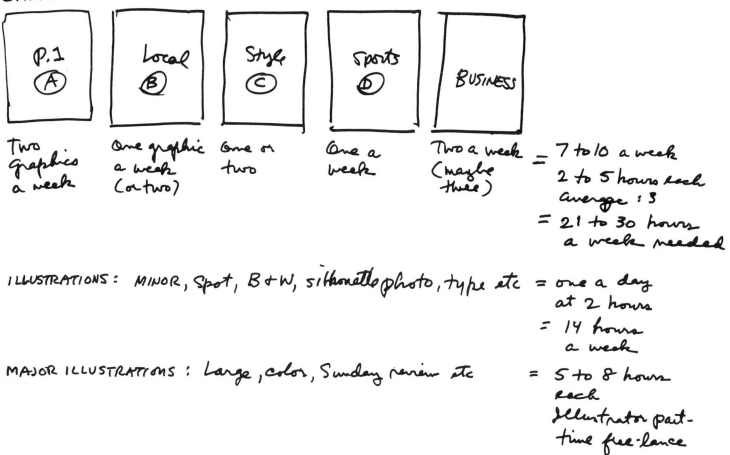

GRAPHICS WANTED

P.1 (A)	Local (B)	Style (C)	Sports (D)	BUSINESS
Two graphics a week	One graphic a week (or two)	One or two	One a week	Two a week (maybe three)

= 7 to 10 a week
2 to 5 hours each
average : 3
= 21 to 30 hours
a week needed

ILLUSTRATIONS: MINOR, Spot, B+W, silhouette photo, type etc = one a day
at 2 hours
= 14 hours
a week

MAJOR ILLUSTRATIONS: Large, color, Sunday review etc = 5 to 8 hours
each
Illustrator part-
time free-lance

Graphics reckoning and productivity, pre-Mac and post-Mac

At a lunch table in Santa Rosa with executive editor Mike Parman, I worked out the chart above. At that point the art staff included graphics editor Randy Wright and one hands-on person, Sharon Henry, an excellent young illustrator who was hired to do graphics as well as drawings. As we approached start-up time for the new design, it seemed clear that this one person would not be able to fulfill our ambitions in both graphics and illustrations. The chart was worked out to accomplish two things. First, to build into the format an informal agreement on how many graphics, on average, were to run in the paper, particularly in the first days after the start-up date, when it was important to make an initial favorable impression. To guarantee their desired use, graphics, like news stories, could be part of a budget planning process. Second, to make a case for getting additional free-lance illustrators lined up to supplement staff capability. Our chart showed realistically what we wanted and could expect to get from available man-hours. The shortfall made it clear that we would need extra illustration help.

Shortly after the redesign, the paper acquired its first Macintosh computer, which changed productivity estimates. I checked revised estimates with the executive editor of the *Ocala Star-Banner* in Florida, Mark Mathes, who is one of the most prolific and creative advocates of graphics I know. We agreed on the following estimates: Short of slave labor conditions, a computer operator can be expected to average between one and two hours per graphic, for a total of about four to five graphics a day. In addition, the operator can be expected to spend an average of 30 minutes to an hour on each graphic received on the computer from other sources, which may have to be adjusted in some way. Roughly, seven or eight graphics might be processed in a day. Thus, one computer artist, working a five-day week, in reasonable working conditions, could be expected to create from 20 to 25 graphics a week, perhaps 18 black and white, and the balance in color; or perhaps 10 in color and 6 in black and white. In addition, a few graphics received from services and networks might be used daily.

An important note is that reasonable working conditions include ready cooperation from editors and writers in supplying information.

critical changeover period. In addition, I was prepared to devote a considerable part of my own efforts to this part of the paper during the week of conversion. Indulging in this many staff may seem like overkill; however, it must be remembered that Miss Leathers joined only in the last 10 days, and Randy Wright's responsibilities included steering the entire project, much of the formatting, and specific design for Pages 1A and 1B.

With the addition of the assistant editor, it was clear that now the fractured procedure had to change to make the Lifestyle desk responsible for the pages right through the composing room. In fact, in the immediate days before the live conversion, the problems of fractured responsibility became more painful, as the greater demands of the new style for accuracy, proper spacing, and attention to detail in the composing room stretched the news desk beyond their ability to follow through in the paste-up process. They had their hands full with the hard news sections. Consequently, within a few weeks, procedures and responsibilities were changed to allow the Lifestyle desk to take over complete responsibility for its own sections.

Sideways

The Lifestyle sections featured headings that were variations on the boxed treatment. Here, as in Sarasota, each section heading was given its own typographical treatment, though the title was kept in the heading itself and, unlike Sarasota, did not spill over into the news part of the page.

Headings of their own

Above: Three of the daily themed sections show a variety of treatments, including the heading run sideways in Science and Health, an unorthodox treatment I had earlier used for The Guide in *The New York Times*. The key word "Health" appears quite plainly above the fold. The idea was to let the big graphic impact of the illustration and the big type of the lead story strike the reader directly. Layout left and center: Susan Leathers. Right: Randy Wright.

Home & Garden

Facing page: A Home and Garden section continues the combination of big impact and detailed information. The page illustrates a happy incorporation of color into the design. The rectangles carrying pink at the top, blue and yellow in the middle, and yellow and orange at the bottom hold the page in strict intrarelated structure, and the color seems natural and integral. One is aware of a *design*, not a flood of color. Layout: Susan Leathers.

The Press Democrat D

Romantic friendships 2
Kids and fitness 6
Vollenweider in concert 7

HOME & GARDEN

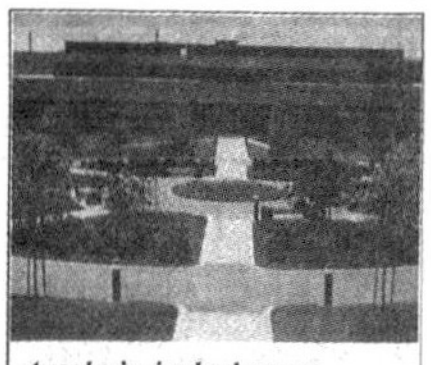

Award-winning landscape at Optical Coating Laboratory, Santa Rosa. See below.

Santa Rosa, California, Thursday, September 25, 1986

Perfect turf

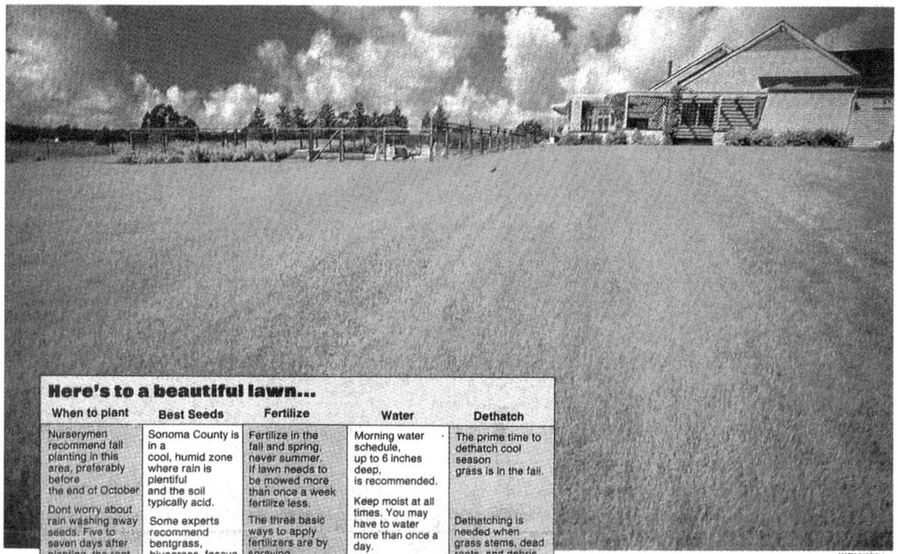

MARY CARROLL

Henry and Marilyn Hansel's one-acre grass lawn is a mixture of bluegrass and rye.

Here's to a beautiful lawn...

When to plant	Best Seeds	Fertilize	Water	Dethatch
Nurserymen recommend fall planting in this area, preferably before the end of October	Sonoma County is in a cool, humid zone where rain is plentiful and the soil typically acid.	Fertilize in the fall and spring, never summer. If lawn needs to be mowed more than once a week fertilize less.	Morning water schedule, up to 6 inches deep, is recommended.	The prime time to dethatch cool season grass is in the fall.
Dont worry about rain washing away seeds. Five to seven days after planting, the root system is established enough to hold.	Some experts recommend bentgrass, bluegrass, fescue and ryegrass, which tend to stay green all year.	The three basic ways to apply fertilizers are by spraying, broadcast spreading or drop spreading.	Keep moist at all times. You may have to water more than once a day. New lawns should be watered with a fine spray.	Dethatching is needed when grass stems, dead roots, and debris build up, stopping water and fertilizer from reaching soil.

Landscape firms victorious in war against weeds

By GEORGE HOWER
Staff Writer

Two Santa Rosa landscape contracting firms did okay — one did super — in the eyes of their peers.

And their wheelbarrows still runneth over.

The two firms filled their wheelbarrows with awards at the seventh annual Landscape Achievement Awards presentation, the California Lanscape Contractors' Association announced in its September bulletin.

Redwood Landscaping won first place in five categories and won the Judges Award for a total of six awards, and Leiser Lanscaping won a first in the seventh category.

> It's a constant battle to keep it from looking like a field.

The awards:

• Small residential installation — Leiser Landscaping, Hansel residence, Santa Rosa.

• Residential maintenance — Redwood Landscaping, Hansel residence, Santa Rosa.

• Judges award — Redwood Landscaping, Hansel residence, Santa Rosa.

• Large commercial installation — Redwood Landscaping, Hanna Boys Center, Sonoma.

• Small commercial maintenance — Redwood Landscaping, West Berry Condominiums. Santa Rosa.

• Large commercial maintenance — Redwood Landscaping, Stony Point Business Park, Santa Rosa.

• Sweepstakes maintenance — Redwood Landscaping, Optical Coating Laboratory, Santa Rosa.

Bill Davidson and Lebo Newman own Redwood Landscaping and Newman said "It was gratifying to have qualified peers inspect the work and have it come out on top. We were thrilled. There is a lot of competition in these awards programs. Firms enter their best projects and it's judged by our peers — landscape architects and contractors from the City and Bay Area" come up and judge work done at various locations.

"We usually win a few awards every year," Newman said, "but never that many.

"It was the first time a contractor won that many in the same category," Newman said.

The Judges Award and Sweepstakes Maintenance award were the two plums.

Probably the two most challenging

Continued on Page D3

TIME FOR DREAMING

Today's labor, spring's beauty

HENRY MITCHELL
The Washington Post

WASHINGTON — Apparently winter is settling in. Winter is that long season in which you have to put a sheet or even a blanket over you in bed.

But it is not altogether a season of gloom. It begins (now) with thinking about spring bulbs that are planted from September to Thanksgiving, with preference given to October except for tulips, which go in on Nov. 12. I like to give a specific date, otherwise you may dawdle.

Garden shops are or soon will be full of bulbs, a far greater assortment than gardeners were used to in the old days. The color pictures attached to the bins of bulbs are quite accurate; the blooms will indeed look like that, only more beautiful.

The first dollar should always be spent on daffodils, I think, as they give a greater show early in the year and last longer than most other things. If you give them reasonable care they will go on indefinitely, barring a siege of basal rot, nematodes or — but let's not start on all that.

Daffodils fall into three categories. Those used for bold clumps in front of hollies, azaleas and other shrubs; those planted in rows back among the turnips, just for cutting for the house; and those that are grown for their incredible beauty as individual flowers.

There is no law about the way to use daffodils. Where there is space, they look best to me in clumps of one variety, then another variety. But in a small garden they are quite wonderful in a bed of varieties all mixed up, one bulb of each kind.

The city gardener should not miss the early daffodils that start blooming with me about March 10 to March 16. This is a few days before the other early-midseason kinds come out. Fortunately the stores always have 'February Gold,' which will usually provide color for at least three weeks, sometimes five weeks.

Equally useful and pretty is 'Peeping Tom,' both of these on 12-inch stems, and with them 'Tete a Tete,' a small yellow, is pretty though it does not last in the sometimes cruel spring weather as long as the other two.

Three widely available daffodils for late in the season — kinds I think anybody would like — are the lovely poet variety, "Actaea," which in a great year can produce show-winning blooms but is usually too irregular for a show flower, but very lovely all the same with its red eye and nice scent; the two-or three-flowered (on one stem) white nodding "Thalia," also fragrant, and very lovely once the clump has thickened up and it is rather starved, otherwise it lacks grace; and "Cheerfulness," a scented variety with white (touched with yellow) pompons of flower, several to the stem. All three are virtually indestructible.

In between are the hundreds of midseason kinds. Take your choice. You should

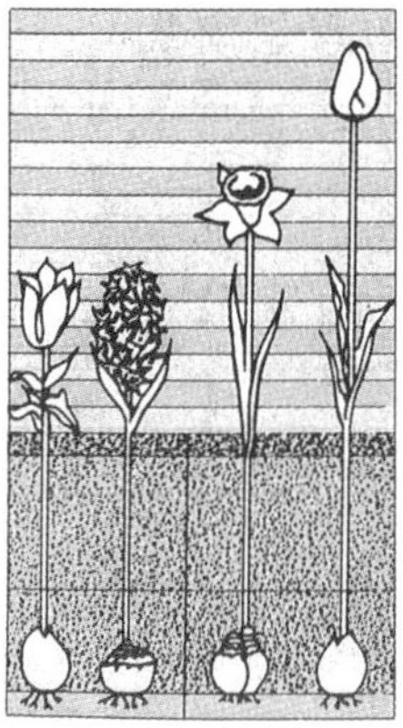

know, however, that the most beautiful daffodils are grown by specialists and there is neither the supply nor the demand to get them in the average garden center, the bulbs of which usually come from the great wholesale growers of Holland.

But if the gardener has mental energy enough to want to take up daffodils as a passionate hobby he should join a daffodil society, write for specialists' catalogues and order his bulbs in spring for the following fall. Still, I have noticed at our daffodil shows in the spring that some of the loveliest daffodils do not rate well with many visitors, the preference often being for gross size and gaudy color (red against yellow) no matter how heavy and overbalanced the trumpet is, and no matter how coarse the texture is. For general display in the garden, however, the cheapest and toughest kinds do as well as any others, since at a few feet's distance they all look much alike.

I would certainly want some snowdrops, the common Galanthus nivalis. These do not bloom as early with me as I think they should. I growl at them every year. But they come along in late February, and considering their little nodding white blooms almost hug the ground it is surprising how exciting they are to see.

There should also be some crocuses, preferably by the tens of thousand, but even a clump of six will seem rewarding enough on a late winter day. Especially

Continued on Page D3

SUSAN SWARTZ

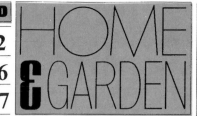

Car wash extravaganza

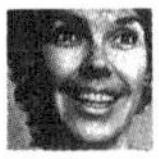

You who swore you'd never own a food processor or carry a personal color chart are being tempted again. Can you resist taking the family Wo-Wo in to be done?

For the price of a Sunday brunch you can make that car preen like a limo, with a full wash and dry, including a scrubbing behind the mud flaps and a sheepskin fluffing. This frees you for other things, like shopping.

The evolution of the car wash has occurred over only a few short years. Even people who have just earned their car keys will recall the Saturday morning curbside ritual.

This called for hands and a sponge, a bucket of suds and a garden hose. It was fun the first few times, on your first car, in the summer and until you realized you had to dry the thing.

The best part was the cool water puddling on the hot asphalt and bare feet. The worst part was your father or some other expert, usually male, fussing over invisible water spots.

From this, we progressed to those little washing barns with the water wands that refused to squirt where pointed. The little gusher would always go limp half way through, demanding more quarters. It was an entertaining show for the drivers awaiting their turn as the washer attempted to maintain grace while flooding his shoes.

Next came the drive-through car wash, always fun for the gigglers in the back seat and a thrill for the driver sliding down in hers as the giant rubber wheel, capable of sucking up wipers as easily as hairballs on a rug, advanced menacingly.

It's a wonderful mystery of engineering that it lifts off right before smashing through the windshield and the car is burped out into the street, wet and blinking in the sunshine.

There have always been high school pep squad car washes, known for their enthusiasm and good cause. The technique is quick and questionable by little squirts who have

Continued on Page D3

ANNA QUINDLEN

Helpless feeling

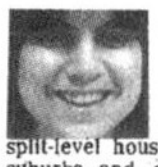

New York Times Service

NEW YORK — When I was 19 years old, the temporary female caretaker of four younger siblings and a split-level house on a corner plot in the suburbs and desperate to get back to college, I put an advertisement in the local paper. It read:

HOUSEKEEPER
to cook and clean for five children. Own room. References required.

At the time I was surprised that only one person called. (Now, I am amazed that anyone did.) I arranged an interview with the sole applicant and read the letters from past employers that she carried in her purse. Then I hired her. Her name was Ida. She moved in with a collection of wigs, a half-dozen housecoats with snaps up the front and a Bible with a black leatherette cover. She was my salvation.

Ida is blind now and lives in Florida. "Girl," she said at the christening of my second child, her sinewy hand curled around that of the woman who was caring for my children, "if the Lord had not taken my eyes you'd be out of a job." And she was right. Ida was perfect. She was a passable cook, a marvelous raconteur and a good sport. Most important, she believed she was on a mission from God.

One day in her second week of work, a strong wind blew through the open windows of our house and Ida took it to be the meteorological incarnation of my deceased mother. It did no good to mention that my mother was not the strong-wind type; Ida felt that she had been called and that God had charged her with looking after us.

I have been thinking of Ida lately because the person who most recently helped with my children left us in the lurch. I like to think that I would not be so angry if she had handled it better, but that is a delusion. When Kay, who after two years with my children had become my friend as well as theirs, gave me plenty of time to plan for her departure, I was irrationally enraged. How dare she leave, I thought, not

Continued on Page D3

Sea Center to reopen, below.

Santa Rosa, California, Monday,

Floral

Pleasures abound at Mendocino gardens

By YVONNE SAVIO
Special to The Press Democrat

In the lush gardeners' fantasyland of the Northern California coast is a 17-acre garden where fuchsias are left to fend for themselves. The Mendocino Coast Botanical Gardens just south of Fort Bragg has established, instead, a living museum of other perennials and California coast natives.

In the 1960s, the property was privately-owned and presented as an exhibition garden of dahlias, gladiolus, irises, with some fuchsias and rhododendrons. In the early 1970s, a portion of the original acreage was transferred to the non-profit Mendocino Coast Recreation and Park District through a grant from the California Coastal Conservancy. Since 1983, the Garden has been transformed into a complex of gardens highlighting annuals, perennials, and herbaceous and woody plants. Three acres of neatly-tended perennial beds and

Business

Above: Space for business news and financial tables was increased by half a page to three full pages. Ads may run on the front, up to a maximum of 9″ x 3 columns, in a trade-off for space inside, a little more than a quarter of a page running across the top of Page 2 over the stock tables. It's important to get news stories, and perhaps a small feature, on the inside to make the section feel like one, and not come off as a single page backed by tables.

Jazz

Right: On the Go runs on Monday and includes more than entertainment. It helps the paper's active California readers plan various outings and trips. Biking, Water Fun, Jogging, and other lively activities inspired the jazzy heading, which here shows no fewer than five reefers to activities in the section, all enjoying good display. A subtle purple-gray in the top bar adds richness without detracting from the dramatic black and white of the silhouetted figure in the "O."

286

ON THE GO

...otember 29, 1986

fantasyland

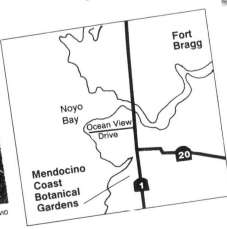

Garden visitors enjoy wine, conversation in beautiful setting.

YVONNE SAVIO

grass pathways near the entrance evolve into less-defined trails through mature plantings and natural areas to the coast. From plants typical in Mediterranean climes, the trails wind by a lily pond and through eight acres of 20-year-old rhododendrons and fuchsias, native forest, and fern canyon, finally opening onto the coastal headland bluffs.

A map provided at the entrance illustrates the three miles of hard-surface and gravel trails, dirt paths, and planted and natural areas. The transitions between these areas are gradual, inviting relaxed wandering. Many of the Garden's plantings are identified, and more comprehensive informational signs along the way include history and growing needs of specific plants.

Continued on Page D8

Fort Bragg

Noyo Bay

Ocean View Drive

20

Mendocino Coast Botanical Gardens

1

PLANNING AHEAD

FESTIVAL

ITALIAN DAYS. The Italian America... tage Foundation and the City of S... will sponsor the 10th annual Italian... Festival Saturday and Sunday at th... Clara County Fairgrounds, 344 Tul... between Monterey Highway an... Road, San Jose. There will be c... entertainment, Italian food, arts a... strolling musicians and street da... village atmosphere. Admission... adults, 50 cents for children unde...

WATER FUN

Petaluma's D Street bridge raises for boaters

DELTA CRUISES. The f... California Delta cruise... to Stockton will contin... on the m/v Glacier Bay... visit Sausalito, cruise... uon and Angel Island... Bay, entering Suisun B... arriving at Stockton... There will be a morn... tasting at a local wir... for Old Sacramento,... tour of the Sacram... tain's Farewell D... proaches San Fran... ing of Day Four. R... through travel ager...

REDWOOD PADD...
...539-8202

Silent train turns 'talkie'

there'll be "authentic Bavarian music, dancing and food; a rollicking beer garden;
...log-sawing and nail-driving con-
...opportunities

Unusual at the time of redesign was the Science and Health heading in which the title panel runs sideways up the left side of the page. This was accepted with bold enthusiasm by the publisher, with great reservation by the graphics editor and with, I believe, pure benevolence by *The Times'* corporate executives. The rationale for it was that by getting the heading off to the side, a magazine kind of story with a big type display could run right up to the top of the page with enormously increased impact. The story would have to be good, of course, and the whole design was predicated on the graphics editor's ability to produce excellent visual presentations.

More Jazz
Right: On Friday, the theme is Entertainment. Here again, some graphic fun is had with the heading. The design of the page itself departs from the normal centerpiece concept to act more as a bulletin board labeling the various lively and creative arts. Layout: Susan Leathers.

Sunday
Above: Profiles is the people-plus theme section for Sunday, allowing latitude for a variety of stories. The heading is given the same individualistic treatment as the other themed sections. Layout: George Delmerico and news staff.

...ptember 26, 1986

" is part of Gump's 125th celebration, "Ports of Call."

ART

Gump's turns 125 celebrates in style

By DAN TAYLOR
Staff Writer

SAN FRANCISCO — Sally Stanford, the San Francisco madam who became mayor of Sausalito, called Gump's "the Metropolitan Museum with cash registers."

And when Jack Benny visited Northern California's oldest art gallery, he wrote in the guest book: "Spent an entertaining afternoon at Gump's — that's all I spent."

It would take a legendary skinflint to get out of Gump's without spending a cent.

"The only thing that's not for sale is one Buddha," said William Goulet, Gump's Vice President.

Gump's, 250 Post St., San Francisco, will celebrate its 125th anniversary with a store-wide celebration titled 'Ports of Call,' opening Oct. 6. The show includes three special exhibits:

• "Recollections: 125 Years of California Artists at Gump's, 1861-1986" a collection of more than 70 paintings, watercolors and graphics by California artists.

• "Robes of the Emperor, His Imperial and Princely Families," 18th- and 19th-century silk robes, including the ceremonial court costumes and informal wear of a Ch'ing Dynasty emperor and empress and their relatives.

• "Eleanor Forbes," a tribute to

Imperial black ... *gown, circa 170...*

Gump's interi...
furniture desi...

The imperi...
just as approp...
retrospective...
anniversary...
major claim...
gallery o...
source of a...

Goulet li...
about the g...
has one ab...
A.L. Gum...
buy art. A...
servants...
wooden...
small ve...
asked $...

FESTIVAL

Valley of the Moon festival underway

By DAN TAYLOR
Staff Writer

SONOMA — The Valley of the Moon Vintage Festival, a celebration of Sonoma ... and the wine

Also, the Sonoma Valley Art Center will present this year's Vintage Festival Art Show in Sonoma Plaza from 10 a.m. to 5 p.m. Sept. 27 and Sunday.

At least 50 artist members of the art center are expected to display oil, acrylic, watercolor and pastel ...

MUSIC

A graphic statement
As in Lakeland, new truck designs became part of the
redesign project.

Chronology of Change

TWO DECADES AT THE NEW YORK TIMES

1967
Text type changed
from 8-pt. Ideal to 8½-pt.
Imperial

1967
Proposal for an
afternoon paper

Prototype

1967
Book Review
redesigned

1969
News of the Week in Review
redesigned

1969
Proposal for tabloid-size
Asian Weekly

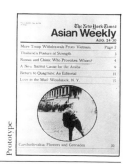

Prototype

1970
Sunday Business and Finance
redesigned

1970
Op-Ed page
introduced

1973
Week in Review
redesigned

1973
First of the contemporary
Part IIs of the Magazine

1974
Sunday Arts and Leisure
redesigned

1974
The New York
Times Magazine
redesigned

1976
New Jersey Weekly and
Long Island Weekly
introduced

1976
Weekend introduced
on Fridays, the first of the
four-part daily papers

1976
6 x 9 format introduced;
8 columns changed
to 6 news, 9 advertising

1976
The Living Section
introduced

1977
Westchester Weekly
and Connecticut Weekly
introduced

1977
The Home Section
introduced

1977
Book Review
redesigned

1978
SportsMonday
introduced

1978
Business Day
introduced

1978
Science Times
introduced

1978
Economic Survey introduced:
first of contemporary series
of editorial tabloid sections

Prototype

1979
Home Entertaining section
introduced as Part II
of the Magazine

1980
National Edition
introduced

Prototype

1980
Sunday Business
redesigned

1980
The Guide introduced

1980
Daily style pages
redesigned

1981
Washington Talk
page introduced in
daily paper

1981
Travel section
redesigned

1982
Real Estate section
redesigned

1982
Personal Investing
introduced

1983
Large Type Weekly
re-introduced

1983
The Sophisticated
Traveler introduced

1984
Book Review
redesigned as
newsprint tabloid

1986
Redesigned
Metropolitan News
introduced

Index